WITHDRAWN
UTSA LIBRARIES

Translation of Addictions Science into Practice

Translation of Addictions Science into Practice

Edited by

Peter M. Miller, Ph.D.
Center for Drug and Alcohol Programs
Department of Psychiatry and Behavioural Sciences
Medical University of South Carolina
Charleston, SC 29425, USA

and

David J. Kavanagh, Ph.D.
School of Medicine
University of Queensland
Herston 4029
Australia

Amsterdam • Boston • Heidelberg • London • New York
• Oxford • Paris • San Diego • San Francisco
• Singapore • Sydney • Tokyo
Pergamon is an imprint of Elsevier

Pergamon is an imprint of Elsevier
525 B Street, Suit 1900, San Diego, CA 92101-4495, USA
Linacre House, Jordan Hill, Oxford OX2 8DP, UK
Radarweg 29, PO Box 211, 1000 AE Amsterdam, The Netherlands

First edition 2007

British Library Cataloguing in Publication Data
Translation of addictions science into practice
  1. Substance abuse 2. Substance abuse - Treatment
  3. Substance abuse - Treatment - Psychological aspects
  I. Miller, Peter M. (Peter Michael), 1942- II. Kavanagh,
  David John
  616.8'6

Library of Congress Cataloging-in-Publication Data
A catalog record for this book is available from the Library of Congress

ISBN: 978-0-08-044927-2

For information on all Pergamon publications
visit our website at books.elsevier.com

Printed and bound in Great Britain

07 08 09 10 11   10 9 8 7 6 5 4 3 2 1

TABLE OF CONTENTS

SECTION III: PSYCHOLOGY AND SOCIOLOGY

LIST OF CONTRIBUTORS

Numbers in parentheses indicate the pages on which the authors' contributions begins

Raymond F. Anton (123), Center for Drug and Alcohol Programs, Department of Psychiatry and Behavioral Sciences, Medical University of South Carolina, 67 President Street, Charleston, SC 29425, USA

Alicia M. Baros (123), Center for Drug and Alcohol Programs, Department of Psychiatry and Behavioral Sciences, Medical University of South Carolina, 67 President Street, Charleston, SC 29425, USA

Mary F. Brunette (275), New Hampshire-Dartmouth Psychiatric Research Center, Concord, NH 03301, USA

Adrian Carter (437), Queensland Brain Institute, University of Queensland, St. Lucia, Queensland 4072, Australia

David Castle (81), Mental Health Research Institute of Victoria, Parkville, Victoria 3052, Australia

L. Judson Chandler (103), Department of Neurosciences and Center for Drug and Alcohol Programs, Medical University of South Carolina, Charleston, SC 29425, USA

TeChieh Chen (361), University of California at San Francisco, San Francisco, CA 94110, USA

Duncan B. Clark (339), Department of Psychiatry and Pharmaceutical Sciences, Western Psychiatric Institute and Clinic, University of Pittsburgh, School of Medicine, Pittsburgh, PA 15213, USA

Jack R. Cornelius (339), Department of Psychiatry and Pharmaceutical Sciences, Western Psychiatric Institute and Clinic, University of Pittsburgh, School of Medicine, Pittsburgh, PA 15213, USA

Christopher J. Correia (415), Department of Psychology, Auburn University, Auburn, AL 36849-5214, USA

John A. Cunningham (397), Centre for Addiction and Mental Health, Toronto, Ontario, Canada M5S 2S1

Sharon Dawe (319), Griffith University, School of Psychology, Brisbane, Queensland 4111, Australia

Lynne Dawkins (237), School of Psychology, University of East London, London E15 4LZ, UK

Philippe De Witte (57), UCL – Biologie du Comportement, B-1348 Louvain-la-Neuve, Belgium

Peter R. Dodd (3), School of Molecular and Microbial Sciences, Molecular Biosciences Building, University of Queensland, Brisbane Queensland 4072, Australia

John Grabowski (143), Substance Abuse Research Center, Department of Psychiatry and Behavioral Sciences, University of Texas Health Science Center, 1300 Moursund St., Houston, TX 77030, USA

Matthew J. Gullo (319), Griffith University, School of Psychology, Brisbane, Queensland 4111, Australia

Wayne Hall (437), School of Population Health, University of Queensland, St. Lucia, Queensland 4072, Australia

Justin L. Hay (39), Discipline of Pharmacology, School of Medical Sciences, University of Adelaide, Adelaide, SA 5005, Australia

Amber M. Henslee (415), Department of Psychology, Auburn University, Auburn, AL 36849-5214, USA

David Herin (143), Substance Abuse Research Center, Department of Psychiatry and Behavioral Sciences, University of Texas Health Science Center, 1300 Moursund St., Houston, TX 77030, USA

Jennifer E. Hettema (361), University of California at San Francisco, San Francisco, CA 94143-0852, USA

Jessica G. Irons (415), Department of Psychology, Auburn University, Auburn, AL 36849-5214, USA

Bankole A. Johnson (167), Department of Psychiatry and Neurobehavioral Sciences, University of Virginia, Charlottesville, VA 22908-0623, USA

Nicolas Kambouropoulos (319), Deakin University, School of Psychology, Burwood, Victoria 3125, Australia

David J. Kavanagh (275), University of Queensland, K Floor, Mental Health Centre, Royal Brisbane and Womens Hospital, Herston, Queensland 4029, Australia

Serena M. King (23), Department of Psychology, Hamline University, Saint Paul, MN 55104-1284, USA

Natalie J. Loxton (319), Griffith University, School of Psychology, Brisbane, Queensland 4111, Australia

James MacKillop (187 & 209), Center for Alcohol and Addiction Studies, Brown University, Providence, RI 02909, USA

Peter M. Miller (377), Center for Drug and Alcohol Programs, Department of Psychiatry and Behavioral Sciences, Medical University of South Carolina, Charleston, SC 29425, USA

Peter M. Monti (187 & 209), Center for Alcohol and Addiction Studies, Brown University, Providence, RI 02909, USA

Kim T. Mueser (275), New Hampshire-Dartmouth Psychiatric Research Center, Concord, NH 03301, USA

Patrick J. Mulholland (103), Center for Drug and Alcohol Programs, Medical University of South Carolina, Charleston, SC 29425, USA

Laura Perdon (319), Griffith University, School of Psychology, Brisbane, Queensland 4111, Australia

Jane Powell (237), Department of Psychology, Goldsmiths, University of London, New Cross, London SE14 6NW, UK

James L. Sorensen (361), University of California at San Francisco, General Hospital, San Francisco, CA 94110, USA

Petra K. Staiger (319), Deakin University, School of Psychology, Burwood, Victoria 3125, Australia

Scott H. Stewart (377), Center for Drug and Alcohol Programs, Department of Psychiatry and Behavioral Sciences, and Division of General Internal Medicine, Department of Medicine, Medical University of South Carolina, Charleston, SC, USA

Suresh Sundram (81), Mental Health Research Institute of Victoria, University of Melbourne, Parkville, Victoria 3052, Australia

Ken Weingardt (257), Center for Healthcare Evaluation, Menlo Park, CA 94025, USA

Jason M. White (39), Discipline of Pharmacology, School of Medical Sciences, University of Adelaide, Adelaide, SA 5005, Australia

Paula Wilbourne (257), Center for Healthcare Evaluation, VA Palo Alto, Menlo Park, CA 94025, USA

Andrew Wood (319), Griffith University, Brisbane, Queensland 4111, Australia

Tara M. Wright (123), Center for Drug and Alcohol Programs, Department of Psychiatry and Behavioral Sciences, Medical University of South Carolina, 67 Persident Street, Charleston, SC 29425, USA

PREFACE

From Bench to Bedside: Diffusing Addictions Science into the Real World

Peter M. Miller[1] and David J. Kavanagh[2]
[1]Medical University of South Carolina, Charleston, SC, USA
[2]University of Queensland, Brisbane, Australia

Abstract: Translation of basic to clinical sciences and from clinical sciences to the applied arena is an essential step toward our understanding and successful treatment of substance abuse disorder. Unfortunately, the movement of addictions research along this continuum has been a sluggish one, and the gap between what we know about addictions and what we practice is wide. We know much more than we apply. The ultimate aim of this volume is to provide a forum to close that gap, and speed the process of technology transfer.

Recent research on the genetic, neurochemical, behavioral and cultural underpinnings of addiction has lead to rapid advances in our understanding of addiction as a disease. Scientific progress in basic science and the resulting development of new pharmacological and behavioral therapies are occurring at a faster pace than can be assimilated, not only by clinical researchers, but also by policy makers and practitioners. Translation of science-based addictions knowledge into prevention and treatment is increasingly important.

Currently, there is a wide gap between the development of science-based knowledge of the nature (e.g., as a brain disease) and/or treatment (i.e., pharmacotherapies) of addictions and the application of these ideas and treatments in the real world. This is due to many factors, all of which are outlined and discussed in our final chapter on "Pathways to Innovation in Addiction Practice."

An illustrative example of this research/treatment disparity is the limited uptake of adjunctive pharmacotherapy in the treatment of alcohol dependence. Most alcoholism practitioners have little knowledge of FDA-approved medications for alcohol dependence (e.g., naltrexone, acamprosate) and, despite evidence of efficacy, many practitioners question their utility in clinical practice (Meza et al., 2001). Evidence-based pharmacotherapy is not in widespread use among alcoholism practitioners (Anton & Swift, 2003; McLellan, 2002) and, even physicians who specialize in addiction medicine prescribe alcoholism medications for less than 15% of their alcoholic patients (Mark et al., 2003).

This gap between addictions research and clinical practice has been the subject of an influential Institute of Medicine (IOM) report (Lamb, Greenlick & McCarty, 1998) that prompted substantial responses from several federal agencies in the USA. Such programs as the Center for Substance Abuse Treatment's (CSAT) Addiction Technology Transfer Centers and its Practice Research Collaboratives, the National Institute on Alcohol Abuse and Alcoholism's (NIAAA) Research-to-Practice Forums and its Researcher-in-Residence Program, and the National Institute on Drug Abuse's (NIDA) Clinical Trials Network have been established to address this problem.

The primary aim of this book is to provide a needed link between advances in addiction science and innovations in clinical practice. Our goal is to stimulate ideas designed to close the gap between bench and bedside, and to do so as rapidly as possible. While the pace of scientific advances in the addictions field is ever-increasing, the process of moving from basic to clinical to applied research is a slow and tedious one. Unless this transfer process is expedited, as Brown (1995, 2000) has aptly noted, clinical innovations may be created only to be interred on the shelves of academia or in the files of remote federal agencies.

While this book is focused primarily on translation, it also encompasses scientific advances that are relevant to dissemination and implementation, and will provide a useful tool for encouraging innovative thinking. In fact, we see the term "translation" as an all-encompassing one that runs the gamut from single-cell neurochemical research with animals (e.g., as in the later chapter by Mulholland and Chandler) to dissemination and implementation of evidence-based treatments into real-world clinical practice (as in the chapter by Sorensen, Hettema, & Chen). Translation is an attempt to move research progress more rapidly along this continuum, so that neurochemical research is smoothly translated into drug development, drug development into initial laboratory testing, laboratory testing into clinical trials, clinical trials into effectiveness studies in real world settings, and finally, studies into implementation research with treatment providers.

Translational efforts to increase the impact of basic or clinical research on the next stage of research development can take many forms. Examples are collaboration among basic and applied scientists, speculation on the future implications of current research work, and research that specifically focuses on a better understanding of ways to progress research more efficiently along the translational continuum. For example, the goal of animal research into single brain cells or neurotransmitters is to not simply to increase our understanding of addictions for its own sake. The ultimate goal is that this knowledge will lead to more effective prevention and treatment strategies, and to public policies that can address the tragic and worldwide impact of addiction on individuals, their social networks, and their societies.

Accordingly, this book is intended to generate interest in application opportunities emanating from both research and theoretical advances. We invited distinguished and experienced addictions researchers to prepare chapters that summarized recent scientific advances and their immediate or short-term applications. We also asked them to speculate creatively on applied possibilities of the research in the longer term. Speculation by experts in the field is rarely encouraged or even allowed in traditional scientific journals or even in formal presentations at most scientific conferences. While focusing on empirical data and avoiding speculation that goes beyond that data is a basic characteristic of good science, we argue that conjecture, supposition, and educated guesswork certainly have an important place in generating novel ideas that may lead to future breakthroughs. At the very least, these activities may grease the wheels of translation, and speed the bench-to-bedside movement of research. So, while we intend that this book should provide a concise summary of existing research and thinking on key areas of the science and practice of addictions, our ultimate aim is to generate new and exciting ideas for the application of basic research to improve clinical practice and social policy.

The concept for this volume grew out of Addictions, 2004, an international conference on "Crossing Boundaries: Implications of Advances in Basic Sciences for the Management of Addiction." The conference, sponsored by Elsevier, was held in Queensland, Australia, and included noted addictions researchers from around the world. Conference proceedings were published in *Addictive Behaviors* as a Special Issue (Volume 29, Number 7, 2004) as part of the journal's *Annual Review of Addictions Research and Treatment* series. So much enthusiasm and cross-fertilization of ideas transpired at this interdisciplinary conference that the idea of this more comprehensive edited book was born.

Many of the same researchers contributed to *Addictions 2004* and the current book. This volume includes chapters from addictions researchers at various stages on the translational continuum, and with very different research interests. The combination of these disparate sub-specialities and interest areas is intended to provide a cross-fertilization of ideas that goes far beyond the contribution of the individual chapters.

Our hope is that this volume will help to speed the "bench-to-bedside" translational process and to encourage cross-collaborations and cross-fertilization of ideas among basic scientists, clinical researchers, and practitioners. If just one new idea or new application is derived from reading this book, the effort will have been worthwhile.

REFERENCES

Anton, R. F., & Swift, R. M. (2003). Current pharmacotherapies: A U.S. perspective. *American Journal on Addictions, 12*, S53–S68.

Brown, B. S. (1995). Reducing impediments to technology transfer in drug abuse programming. In G. Soucy (Ed.), *Reviewing the Behavioral Science Knowledge Base on Technology Transfer* (pp. 169–185). Rockville, MD: National Institute on Drug Abuse.

Brown, B. S. (2000). From research to practice: The bridge is out and the water's rising. In A. Levy, R. C. Stephens, & D. C. McBride (Eds.), *Advances in Medical Sociology* (pp. 345–365). Greenwich, CT: JAI Press.

Lamb, S., Greenlick, M., & McCarty, D. (Eds.). (1998). *Bridging the Gap: Forging New Partnerships in Community-based Drug Abuse Treatment*. Washington, DC: National Academy Press.

Mark, T. L., Kranzler, H. R., Song, X., Bransberger, P., Poole, V. H., & Crosse, S. (2003). Physicians' opinions about medications to treat alcoholism. *Addiction, 98*, 617–626.

McLellan, A. T. (2002). Technology transfer and the treatment of addiction: What can research offer practice? *Journal of Substance Abuse Treatment, 22*, 169–170.

Meza, E. F., Cunningham, J. A., el-Guebaly, N., & Couper, L. (2001). Alcoholism: Beliefs and attitudes among Canadian alcoholism treatment practitioners. *Canadian Journal of Psychiatry, 46*, 167–172.

SECTION I
GENETICS AND NEUROSCIENCE

CHAPTER 1

The Interplay between Genotype and Gene Expression in Human Brain: What Can it Teach Us about Alcohol Dependence?

Peter R. Dodd

School of Molecular and Microbial Sciences, University of Queensland, Brisbane, Australia

Abstract: Molecular expression studies of the pharmacological profiles of receptors in key brain regions and cell types delineate alterations in neurotransmission in alcoholic brain. Individual variations in propensity for brain damage and comorbidity modulate these changes. Receptor subunit composition and switching that play central roles in cell killing will define likely paths to neuroprotection. This will guide the development of new precisely targeted ameliorative and preventive drugs.

Abbreviations: AMP, adenosine monophosphate; ATP, adenosine triphosphate; DNA, deoxyribonucleic acid; GABA, γ-aminobutyric acid; NMDA, N-methyl-D-aspartate; mRNA, messenger ribonucleic acid; SFC, superior prefrontal cortex; SNP, single nucleotide polymorphism; WHO, World Health Organization; 5HT, 5-hydroxytryptamine (serotonin)

DRUG AND ALCOHOL ABUSE

The current era has seen a tremendous upsurge in the abuse of psychoactive substances around the world. Despite the public attention lavished on illicit drugs (psychostimulants, heroin, marijuana) and the "war" to contain them, by far the greatest impact on human health and societal well-being is exerted by two licit drugs, tobacco and alcohol, which are highly comorbid in usage. Alcohol consumption has declined slowly in recent years in developed countries, although this may not continue because transnational corporations "aggressively … target young people in advertising and promotion campaigns (WHO, 2004)". Consumption has grown steadily in developing countries, particularly in WHO's Western Pacific region (WHO, 2004). Subjects in the region show patterns of hazardous drinking that exacerbate the harmful effects of alcohol on the brain (WHO, 2004). Understanding the mechanisms that constitute this harm is a major research priority.

On a standardized estimate of disease load, disability-adjusted life years, tobacco gives a value of 4.1%, alcohol 4.0%. In contrast, all illicit drugs combined contribute an average of 0.8% to global disease burden (WHO, 2004). Figures are higher for men and markedly higher in special populations. A comprehensive transnational survey found that although the prevalence of hazardous/harmful drinking varies from country to country, drinking behavior and alcohol-related problems show many common features (Saunders et al., 1993). Harmful drinking in Australia was estimated at ~12% in a recent survey (Simpson et al., 2000).

ALCOHOLIC BRAIN DAMAGE

Harper and colleagues used quantitative stereometric analyses to establish that alcohol misuse leads to selective brain pathology (Harper & Kril, 1993). Global effects such as generalized brain shrinkage, reduced white-matter volume, and dendritic pruning, may be reversible with abstinence. Superior prefrontal cortex (SFC) is particularly vulnerable, while most cortical regions are much less affected (Kril et al., 1997; Kril & Harper, 1989). Alcoholics differ markedly in their neuropathological presentation, ranging from little or no damage to severe frontal lobe and/or cerebellar atrophy. Common comorbidities of alcohol abuse, including cirrhosis of the liver and the Wernicke–Korsakoff syndrome, are associated with greater brain atrophy (Harper & Kril, 1993). These diseases are more prevalent with high rates of alcohol consumption (Saunders & Latt, 1993), so it appears that the pathology worsens with increasing disease severity.

Discrete Subsets of Neurones may be Selectively Vulnerable

Neurones in specific regions of the brain (cerebellar Purkinje cells and SFC neurones) are selectively damaged (Harper & Kril, 1990, 1993; Kril & Harper, 1989); the alterations in SFC are in line with known changes in cognitive function. Subsets of neurones may be particularly susceptible to ethanol toxicity as a consequence of possessing a specific protein profile (Dodd & Lewohl, 1998; Kril et al., 1997; Kril & Harper, 1989). While neuronal losses are apparent in alcoholics without comorbidity, the severity of damage is greater in alcoholics with concomitant cirrhosis of the liver (Kril & Halliday, 1999). Hence, liver damage may have additive effects on alcohol neurotoxicity. One possibility is that alcoholics with varying degrees of pathology represent stages on a dosage continuum, with more-severe damage correlating with greater lifetime consumption. Alternatively, alcoholics with liver damage may be more susceptible to alcohol neurotoxicity as a result of a genetic predisposition.

Mechanisms Influencing Brain Function

Alcohol abuse leads to cognitive, physiological, and structural changes in several cortical and sub-cortical structures. The cellular and molecular mechanisms that bring this about are poorly understood. Ligand-gated ion channels mediate acute drug intoxication (Weight et al., 1992). In experimental animals, channels for anions (negatively charged ions) that are gated by γ-aminobutyric acid (GABA) and glycine, and channels for cations (positively charged ions) that are gated by glutamate, acetylcholine, 5HT, and ATP, are affected by physiologically relevant concentrations of alcohol. Of these, $GABA_A$ and N-methyl-D-aspartate (NMDA) receptors are major cell-membrane targets (Toropainen et al., 1997). Glutamate operates 67–73% of cortical synapses in human brain and is the major excitatory transmitter: the influx of cations it mediates depolarises post-synaptic cells, which have a negative internal polarity in the resting state. In contrast, the influx of anions mediated by GABA (and glycine) hyperpolarizes the post-synaptic cell; GABA is used at 16–25% of cortical synapses, where it is the major inhibitor (Hornung & de Tribolet, 1995). Excitation-inhibition balance is a key determinant of neuronal viability: when tilted toward excessive excitation it is termed *excitotoxicity* (Olney, 1994).

In experimental studies, such a shift may be elicited in several ways. What is not clear is whether such mechanisms occur in human brain *in vivo*, and how the localization of pathology comes about. Plausible options include locally overactive NMDA or underactive $GABA_A$ receptors, and a diminished clearance of glutamate from the synaptic cleft (Dodd, 2002). Receptor and transporter pharmacology are determined by the expression of many genes; if some are switched off, and others switched on, profound changes in receptor function or transport capacity are brought about. It is thus of interest that alcoholism risk is differentially associated with alleles of several transmission-related genes. The products of these genes (receptors, transporters) are targets for several drugs used to treat alcoholism.

ALCOHOLISM CAUSES CHANGES IN TRANSCRIPT mRNA AND PROTEIN EXPRESSION

Sustained ethanol exposure in animals changes the expression of many genes, including those for mediators of the actions of transmitters, signalling molecules, molecular chaperones, transcription factors, and cytokines (Miles, 1995). Differential display and microarray studies have revealed altered expression of mitochondria- and genome-encoded genes in the brains of alcohol-treated rats and human alcoholics (Chen, Hardy, & Wilce, 1997; Fan et al., 1999; Lewohl et al., 2000). It is not possible to predict which genes are involved from *a priori* neurobiological or pharmacological considerations. Recent advances in microarray technology have enabled the simultaneous analysis of more than 50,000 messenger-RNA (mRNA) transcripts in SFC in chronic alcoholics and controls (Lewohl et al., 2000; Liu et al., 2004; Mayfield et al., 2002). Differentially expressed transcripts fall into functional groups that include metabolism, immune response, cell survival, cell communication, signal transduction, and energy production. Transcripts coding for several synaptic proteins differ in abundance by 40% (1.4 fold) or more between alcoholics and controls, suggesting that synaptic transmission is affected by chronic alcohol use. Pathologically vulnerable and resistant cortical regions show distinctive patterns, such that alcoholics and controls partition completely (Liu et al., 2004).

It is not known whether alcohol has a direct effect on alcohol-responsive genes, or an indirect effect involving many systems. Activation or repression of alcohol-responsive transcription factors could alter the expression of genes that possess the corresponding control elements (Miles, 1995). In contrast, alcohol misuse is known to alter the translation of some proteins without changing mRNA levels. We found marked differences in $GABA_A$ receptor α_3 isoform protein expression between alcoholic and control SFC, but little difference in α_3 mRNA – whereas α_1 isoform protein and mRNA varied in concert (Dodd & Lewohl, 1998). On a gene-by-gene, protein-by-protein basis, it is difficult to discern general patterns. Small changes in low-abundance transcripts can lead to profound changes in cell function. This is often reflected in large variations in protein abundance through altered mRNA half-life brought about by modified activity of post-translational processing enzymes. These proteins are targets for therapeutic intervention.

Neuroadaptive models posit long-lasting changes at the molecular and cellular level to explain compulsive drug use. Differing adaptive responses may account for individual differences in susceptibility to alcohol. Alcohol can be metabolised by mitochondrial oxidation, especially in brain, giving rise to high levels of free radicals, particularly peroxides. Free radicals are highly reactive with protein. While the cell has effective mechanisms for repairing DNA that is damaged by free-radical action, there are no repair mechanisms for damaged proteins. These accumulate within cells and become increasingly defective with time. Adaptive changes that lead to chronicity (such as receptor adaptation) underpin short-term withdrawal, but other factors such as morphological or biochemical remodelling in sensitive cells are important mediators of alcohol-related behaviors in the longer term (Koob, Sanna, & Bloom, 1998). In support of this concept are observations of changes in second messengers and inducible transcription factors, and thence in the expression of downstream genes, in animals following repeated exposure (Koob, Sanna, & Bloom, 1998).

Preliminary Proteomic Studies

We performed a study on samples that had been used for microarray analysis to assess mRNA expression by Lewohl et al. (2000). Samples were SFC pieces taken at autopsy from well-characterized chronic alcoholics and controls matched for age, sex, and cause of death. Poly-drug abusers and cases with comorbid liver cirrhosis or Wernicke encephalopathy were excluded. Tissue pieces were homogenized in water and frozen, and 2-dimensional proteomics was performed on the soluble fraction (Lewohl et al., 2004).

Overall, 182 proteins differed by more than 2-fold between case and control samples. Of these, 144 were less abundant in alcoholics, 33 more abundant, and 8 were new or absent. To date, 63 of these proteins have been identified using MALDI-MS and MS–MS. Four 14-3-3 isoforms (ϵ, γ, η, ζ) and two members of the synuclein family of proteins (α- and β-synuclein) were identified to be at least 2-fold lower in SFC of alcoholics (see Table 1). A varied group of proteins were up-regulated in alcoholic SFC (Table 2). Comparison of the protein and mRNA data sets revealed several patterns, although both sets had members that did not appear in the other. Some proteins and transcripts had comparable differential expression between alcoholics and controls. However, in several instances the trends were not the same. A number of proteins that showed differential expression in this pilot study of pathologically "simple" alcoholic brain damage also occur in published lists from the proteomic analysis of pathologically "complex" Alzheimer disease (Schonberger et al., 2001; Tsuji et al., 2002). This may provide insights into common pathways of neurodegeneration.

Table 1
Some Examples of Proteins Down-regulated in Alcoholics

Fold change[*]	Database entry[†]	Protein name
−14.90	SYUB_HUMAN	β-synuclein
−5.80	L36674	α-synuclein
−3.40	143F_HUMAN	14-3-3 protein η
−2.40	143E_HUMAN	14-3-3 protein ε
−2.40	NM_003406	14-3-3 protein ζ
−2.30	gi12655023	14-3-3 activation protein
−2.10	143Z_HUMAN	14-3-3 protein ζ/δ
−2.10	gi481360	14-3-3 protein γ

[*]Expression abundance, Alcoholics/Controls.
[†]Annotation in the SwissProt database. Triplicate protein profiles of control and alcoholic SFC tissue extracts were analyzed for differential display using PDQUEST v7.0 image analysis software (Bio-Rad, Hercules, CA, USA). Images were obtained in triplicate for each sample, for two pH gradients, pH 4–7 and 6–11.

Table 2
Some Examples of Proteins Up-regulated in Alcoholics

Fold change[*]	Database entry[†]	Protein name
+5.20	PDX2_HUMAN	Peroxiredoxin 2 (Thioredoxin peroxidase I)
+2.20	FABB_HUMAN	Fatty acid-binding protein, brain
+3.10	AOP2_HUMAN	Antioxidant protein 2
+2.00	KRCB_HUMAN	Creatine kinase, B chain
+6.50	HS7C_HUMAN	Heat shock cognate 71 kDa protein
+1.90	HNT1_HUMAN	Histidine triad nucleotide-binding protein
+2.10	POR1_HUMAN	Voltage-dependent anion-selective channel #1
+3.90	KPY1/2_HUMAN	Pyruvate kinase, M1 or M2 isozyme

[*]Expression abundance, Alcoholics/Controls.
[†]Annotation in the SwissProt database.
See Table 1 legend for details.

GENETICS OF ALCOHOL MISUSE

Individuals vary in their propensity for alcohol misuse through a complex interaction among societal, environmental, and genetic factors. Subjects may be susceptible to drug misuse problems for a variety of reasons, including genetic predisposition, inherent personality traits, and so on. Alcoholics also vary in their likelihood of developing comorbidities such as cirrhosis of the liver. There are gender differences in alcoholism, and the number of female alcoholics is increasing in most countries (Walter et al., 2003). Women are more sensitive to alcohol than men because they have less body water, and hence higher blood alcohol levels after equal alcohol intake (Baraona et al., 2001; Brienza & Stein, 2002; Ely et al., 1999; Hommer et al., 2001; Tapert et al., 2001; Walter et al., 2003).

Linkage and twin–adoption studies are generally not feasible with severe alcohol abusers. Such subjects are often itinerant, and it is rarely possible to obtain clinical histories or DNA from next of kin, so extensive pedigrees often cannot be constructed. Genetic effects can be small, and epistasis and other interactions can confound analysis. A large linkage study of alcoholics under way in the USA (COGA) has produced low LOD scores with broad peaks, in part through difficulties in diagnosis and ascertainment. It has been estimated that these approaches have identified less than half the chromosomal regions containing genes for dependence. Nevertheless, they have suggested number of gene candidates for further study and fine mapping, and they underpin genome–wide scans of informative single nucleotide polymorphisms (SNPs).

Case–control studies of candidate genes are used to search for genetic associations. An adjunct approach is to ask whether genotype partitions the extent of brain damage in alcoholic subjects, and the molecular mechanisms that underpin it. The drawbacks to this approach are that plausible markers must first be found; that the marker often has to be very close to the disease locus for a significant association to be detected; and that population stratification can compromise analyses where cases and controls potentially contain subjects of differing ethnicities (some populations may be over–represented among drug abusers). Differences in allele frequencies between cases and controls can be confounded with differences in population allele frequencies.

Candidate Genes for Alcohol Misuse (for references see Foley et al., 2004)

Drug dependence is linked to mesolimbic/cortical dopamine reward and reinforcement mechanisms. Alcohol activates dopaminergic transmission in experimental animals, and some dopaminergic drugs reduce alcohol intake. Bromocriptine, a D2 agonist, is most effective for treating alcoholics who possess *DRD2* A1 alleles. *DRD2 Taq* I A and B polymorphisms have been associated with alcoholism. The dopamine transporter DAT1 gene (*SLC6A3*) contains a 3′ UTR variable tandem repeat; associations have been found between 9-repeat alleles and alcohol withdrawal symptoms. 5HT reuptake inhibitors have some value in the treatment of alcoholism, but genotyping studies on the 5HT transporter gene (*SLC6A4*) 5HTTLPR polymorphism have been inconsistent. A glutamate transporter EAAT2 gene (*SLC1A2*) polymorphism is associated with risk-taking behavior in alcoholics. Alcohol dependence has been rather unstably associated with variants of the NMDA receptor NR2 subunit gene *GRIN2B* (Schumann et al., 1995, 2003). The NMDA receptor enhancer and GABA$_B$ receptor antagonist acamprosate reduces relapse rates in recovering alcoholics. Ethanol interacts with GABA$_A$ receptors; benzodiazepines, which are GABA$_A$ modulators, are used to treat alcohol withdrawal. The GABA$_A$ subunit gene cluster at 5q33-34 is implicated in alcoholism by studies of gene knockouts, mRNA expression, comparisons of subunit amino acid differences that alter alcohol responses, and human genetic associations. Genetic polymorphism at the *ADH1C* locus results in ADH1C isoenzymes of varying activity; individuals with two *ADH1C*1* alleles have the most active enzyme, *ADH1C*2/*2* homozygotes the least. Meta-analysis suggests that a lower risk of alcoholism and cirrhosis is associated with the genotype encoding the most active enzyme.

Our results for combined genotypes are consistent with previous studies that support the idea of a concerted genetic influence in susceptibility to alcoholism. In individuals with no *DRD2 Taq* I B1, *GABRB2* T1412, or *SLC1A2* A603 alleles, we found an association between *ADH1C* genotype and alcoholism. The association of *DRD2 Taq* I alleles with alcoholism was most apparent in cases with the major *GABRB2* and *SLC1A2* genotypes.

SYNTHESIS

Developments in neuroscience and molecular biology have converged to provide new approaches to the study of pathogenesis in human autopsy brain. These explore gene-expression differences in local populations of cortical neurones. A range of neurotransmission–related parameters can be accurately determined in human brain obtained at autopsy (Hynd et al., 2003). The form and function of these key mediators of neural excitation and inhibition can then be related to pathogenesis and dependence.

Drug abuse can continue for 20 years and more in human cases, which makes it difficult to model in animals. Over the last two decades techniques have been developed and validated that use human brain tissue obtained at autopsy (Dodd et al., 1988). The key processes of transmission are depolarization-induced transmitter release; ligand-receptor binding and activation; and transmitter disposal by re-uptake, can be quantified in preparations obtained from well-characterized cases. A series of studies showed that the $GABA_A$ site is highly variable at the molecular level. RNA is quite stable in human brain post mortem (Barton et al., 1993; Hynd et al., 2003) and mRNA transcripts may be assayed to determine whether altered expression underlies the observed variations in receptor pharmacology. mRNA and protein expression may be quantified in human cortical extracts, and the parameters obtained are insensitive to post-mortem interval, age at death, agonal state, and time in storage, when tissue collection, freezing, and storage are optimal (Lewohl, Crane, & Dodd, 1997b; Lewohl et al., 2001). Localization of pathology is both an object of study and a servant of experimental design, in that samples from affected and spared areas are compared. Alcoholics without comorbidity may be differentiated from cases with comorbid Wernicke encephalopathy or liver cirrhosis to delineate disease- and area-specific effects. These techniques are useful where animal models are either unavailable or questionable (Dodd et al., 1988; Hynd et al., 2003). Findings in human brain differ in key respects from those in animal models; the same systems can be affected, but the nature of the change may be different.

The actions of GABA are mainly mediated by the $GABA_A$ receptor, which is a pentameric complex comprised of different subunit isoforms classified α_{1-6}, β_{1-3}, γ_{1-3}, δ, ε, π, and θ. The most common complex in the brains of laboratory animals is the $\alpha_1\beta_2\gamma_2$ combination (Davies et al., 1997; Hedblom & Kirkness, 1997; Jechlinger et al., 1998; Neelands et al., 1999; Whiting, 1999).

Subunit switching alters the efficacy of receptors. Cl^- currents are much stronger for a given GABA application in $\alpha_1\beta_3$ combinations of $GABA_A$ subunits than in $\alpha_1\beta_1$ or $\alpha_1\beta_2$ sets (Wisden & Seeburg, 1992). Responses are further modified if the GABARAP anchoring protein is co-expressed with the subunits (Kittler et al., 2002). Switching also modifies pharmacology. GABA activation of diazepam binding is weak in $\alpha_1\beta_1\gamma_2$ and $\alpha_2\beta_1\gamma_2$ combinations of $GABA_A$ subunits, and much greater in $\alpha_3\beta_1\gamma_2$ combinations (Pritchett et al., 1989). More than 20 $GABA_A$ subunit isoforms exist, including splice variants: not all subunit switches change every parameter. It is not feasible to test all combinations (over 4 billion permutations are possible), nor predict the properties of all combinations (Wisden & Seeburg, 1992), so it is necessary to define the local properties of the receptors that actually occur in human brain.

A proportion of $GABA_A$ receptor protein occurs in a cytoplasmic reserve that may be mobilized to the cell surface by (metabolic) stress (Akinci & Johnston, 1993). Receptor complexes labelled in membrane-binding assays may differ in composition from those inside cells. Isoform-specific antibodies are useful for assaying subunit proteins in brain extracts, and immunocytochemistry can be used to study their distribution in tissue sections. Receptors are subject to phosphorylation and glycosylation, which affect pharmacology (Brandon et al., 1999). These modifications may not persist post-mortem sufficient to allow their detection, but if they do, selective antibodies are available (Pandey, 1996).

Receptor Studies in Human Alcoholic Brain

Pharmacological diversity is characterized using a range of ligands and allosteric modulators, and is best explained by altered subunit composition. The affinity of different benzodiazepine ligands, and the extent to which diazepam binding can be activated by GABA, varies in (a) different, closely circumscribed, cortical areas and (b) the same area in cases with different diseases and comorbidities (Dodd et al., 1996, 1992; Lewohl, Crane, & Dodd, 1997c). These indices of GABAergic transmission conform to pathology. We have some evidence that $GABA_A$ receptors differ more between female alcoholics and controls than between male subjects (Dodd, 1995).

The low amounts of receptor mRNA in human brain make Northern blots unsatisfactory (Thomas, Harper, & Dodd, 1998), so quantitative RT-PCR methods based on co-amplified synthetic internal complementary RNA standards have been developed (Buckley & Dodd, 2003; Lewohl, Crane, & Dodd, 1997a). These and similar techniques have been used to show that $GABA_A$ α_{1-3} and β_{1-3} mRNA and protein expression vary locally and disease-selectively (Buckley & Dodd, 2004; Lewohl, Crane, & Dodd, 1997b; Lewohl et al., 2001; Mitsuyama et al., 1998); and that α_1 and α_3 subunit expression conform to the GABA activation of diazepam binding we had previously observed (Dodd & Lewohl, 1998). The altered expression of $GABA_A$ receptors in alcoholic SFC is consistent with reduced protection against excitotoxicity (Dodd et al., 1992; Freund & Ballinger, 1988; Lewohl, Crane, & Dodd, 1996; Thomas & Dodd, 1993).

Glutamate binding site density is reportedly up-regulated in the superior frontal cortex of alcoholics (Freund & Anderson, 1996; Lavoie et al., 1987; Michaelis, Mulvaney, & Freed, 1978), although we have detected no difference in [^{3}H]MK-801 binding to NMDA sites other than altered glutamate-activation profiles in cirrhotic alcoholics. The latter is evidence for subunit switching. KA and AMPA receptors did not differ between cases and controls. Up-regulation of glutamate binding sites might follow excessive glutamate release through positive feedback. The increased glutamate release would overstimulate glutamate receptors, in the presence of locally compromised GABA-mediated inhibition (above), to over-excite prefrontal neurones and promote their susceptibility over the long duration of human alcohol abuse (Dodd, 2002).

The differential effects on $GABA_A$ and glutamate-NMDA receptor expression that are seen when cirrhotic alcoholics are compared with alcoholics without comorbid disease highlight the differing vulnerabilities of various organs. There is evidence that modes of drinking – steady heavy consumption or binge drinking – have different consequences for liver and brain damage, for example (Hunt, 1993, 1996; Kim & Shukla, 2006). Drinking patterns can be culturally conditioned, but the organ preferentially targeted for damage may also be influenced by the subject's genetic make-up (Whitfield, 1997) – there is a sense that, "to save your brain, destroy your liver" (and perhaps vice-versa). Binge drinking may be particularly deleterious for the brain because the repeated cycles of intoxication and withdrawal lead to sustained alterations in glutamate-NMDA receptors (Hardy, Chen, & Wilce, 1999). This would suggest that NMDA antagonist therapy (Acamprosate or its congeners currently under development) might be a fruitful therapeutic path (Ansoms et al., 2000).

Genotype and Gene Expression

An emerging literature shows that knocking out single genes in mice alters the expression of hundreds of transcripts, many with no association with the target gene. Knockout strains that differ in their alcohol responsiveness have been compared to search for transcripts that show concerted changes (Ponomarev et al., 2004). Genes so identified reside on a range of chromosomes, not only that of the knocked-out gene. Effect sizes in these studies are generally small, in the 1.2–1.5-fold range typical of studies of human subjects (Lewohl et al., 2000). There is a multiplier effect in that proteins show larger effect sizes than mRNA transcripts (Ghaemmaghami et al., 2003). Expressed proteins are more readily linked to function than transcripts are, but it is more difficult to quantify protein than mRNA in brain tissue samples (Lewohl et al., 2004; see above). A human analog of a gene knockout is the *ALDH2* gene in alcoholism (*ALDH2*2/*2* homozygotes have no ALDH activity). Allelic variants of misuse-associated genes might affect the expression of a range of genes; the effect sizes might be smaller, or the ranges lesser in extent, than in knockout studies.

Alcohol is known to influence a range of dependence networks in the brain (Koob et al., 1998). One potential consequence of this is that highly focused drugs aimed at only one receptor are likely to be less effective than broadspectrum agents, or combinations of agents, that target several, possibly interacting, systems (Kiefer et al., 2003).

A limited subset of genes may influence $GABA_A$ receptor subunit expression and NMDA-site binding in alcoholics (Dodd et al., 2004). Animal studies suggest that the observed differences probably arise as a consequence of alcohol misuse, rather than occurring intrinsically in subjects predisposed to alcohol misuse (Grobin, Papadeas, & Morrow, 2000). We found that $\beta_3:\beta_2$ subunit ratio tended to be lower in alcoholic SFC, but only in subjects with certain alcoholism-related genotypes. There were significant, regionally selective interactions of *DRD2B*, *ADH1C*, *SLC1A2*, and *APOE* genotypes with β protein expression when alcoholics were compared with controls. In each instance possession of the alcoholism-associated allele altered β isoform expression toward a less-efficacious form of the $GABA_A$ receptor in SFC, by two distinct mechanisms: some alleles conferred a lower level of β_3-subunit expression; others led to higher β_2-subunit expression. Whatever their origin, lower $\beta_3:\beta_2$ ratios are likely to have profound functional consequences. In recombinant experiments, $GABA_A$ receptors that include the β_3 isoform show enhanced inhibitory function (relative to β_1- or β_2-containing receptors) when activated by GABA (*v.i.*). Mice in which the β_2 isoform has been knocked out show shorter sleep times when given alcohol (Blednov et al., 2003; Ymer et al., 1989). Alcohol potentiation of muscimol-stimulated $^{36}Cl^-$ influx is reduced in β_2 knockout mice, possibly because they express fewer functional $GABA_A$ receptors (Blednov et al., 2003). Locally altered $GABA_A$ pharmacology could contribute to selective neuronal vulnerability in SFC (Dodd et al., 2004).

The distinction between whether a subject's genetic predisposition is manifest prior to the onset of alcohol misuse, or whether gene expression is modulated by heavy drinking, is an aspect that requires further exploration as it can have major consequences for therapy and counselling. It is intrinsically difficult to explore by autopsy studies, due to the unitary nature of individual mortality (with all due respect to James Bond). However, as we have argued previously, if sufficient numbers of subjects that exhibit varying severity and duration of alcoholism at death can be collected, it is feasible to apply regression techniques to estimate, on the balance of probabilities, which of the options is more likely (Hynd et al., 2003). While most alcoholism-associated genes make only small contributions to predisposition risk (Crabbe et al., 1999), there are indications that the children of some alcoholics, especially those with comorbid Wernicke–Korsakoff syndrome, may exhibit metabolic and other abnormalities prior to any alcohol (mis-)use (Mukherjee et al., 1987). If at-risk offspring from vulnerable families can be identified by simple genetic tests, as the report of a probable associated gene suggests (Guerrini et al., 2005), it may be appropriate to counsel them to avoid alcohol use altogether. As noted above, animal studies show that gene expression can be modified by alcohol use; moreover, in some paradigms expression changes are reversible with abstinence (Devaud et al., 1997; Grobin, Papadeas, & Morrow, 2000; Mitsuyama et al., 1998). If this scenario applies to identifiable genotype–phenotype interactions – which will require much more work – the scope for counselling and therapy with active alcohol misusers may be significantly broadened, and a risk-minimization strategy might be justified.

Is Transmitter Reaching the Receptors?

The level of glutamate is markedly elevated in the brains of rats treated chronically with alcohol (Keller, Cummins, & von Hungen, 1983; Ledig, M'Paria, & Mandel, 1982). Chronic ethanol administration causes a significant decrease in stimulus-coupled glutamate release from rat brain terminals (Keller, Cummins, & von Hungen, 1983; Sabria et al., 2003). These studies were carried out on whole-brain or brain-slice extracts, which include both the synaptic-vesicle (transmitter) and metabolic compartments: the influence of chronic alcohol intake on glutamate levels within the nerve terminals was not determined.

We developed and optimized an electrical stimulation paradigm to investigate the dynamics of synaptosomal amino acid transmitter release in tissue obtained at autopsy. This mode of stimulation was used because extensive preliminary studies showing that the K^+ dependence of amino acid transport precluded K^+ or 4-aminopyridine as depolarising agents. We found that synaptosomal glutamate release was selectively increased in alcoholics, whereas GABA release did not differ between alcoholics and controls (Kuo & Dodd, 2005 and submitted: Figure 1). The disparities between the human and animal studies (above) could be due to differences in tissue preparation, the stimulation paradigm, or the species utilized (Muzzolini et al., 1997). Chronic alcohol administration reportedly does not affect GABA concentrations in synaptosomes isolated from the frontal cortex of rats

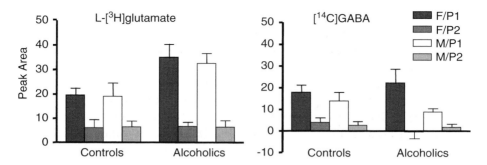

Figure 1 Ca^{2+}-dependent stimulus-coupled release. Tissue was obtained at autopsy from 11 alcoholics without comorbid disease (average daily consumption >10 standard drinks/d throughout adulthood) and 10 controls (light social drinkers and teetotallers). Cortical areas were dissected from fresh tissue, and frozen and stored optimally to preserve physiological function (Dodd et al., 1986). Synaptosomes were prepared by differential and sucrose–density–gradient centrifugation (Dodd et al., 1981), labelled with L-[^{3}H]glutamate and [^{14}C]GABA, washed, loaded into a superfusion apparatus, and perfused with Krebs-HEPES buffer at 37 °C. The chambers were stimulated twice with trains of electrical pulses (10 V bipolar contiguous square waves, 0.4 ms pulse width, 100 pulses/sec) for 1.5 min epochs in the presence and absence of Ca^{2+} ions. Stimulus-evoked fractional release rate peaks were corrected for baseline; bars show net Ca^{2+}-dependent release. F, Superior frontal; M, primary motor; P1, 1st stimulus; P2, 2nd stimulus. L-[^{3}H]glutamate P1 release differed significantly between controls and alcoholics ($P < 0.05$). There was no significant difference in [^{14}C]GABA release between groups. Unpublished data from the author's laboratory.

(Frye & Fincher, 1988). Rats treated acutely with ethanol exhibit no increase in cerebral GABA (Gordon, 1967).

FUTURE DIRECTIONS

Characterization of all aspects of the transmission triad (release, receptor activation, and disposal) is essential for determining how functional neurotransmission is altered in disease. The relationship between candidate genes and receptor parameters needs to be further explored. The allelic status of test subjects on a range of genes should be determined, and the interactions between alcoholism-associated genes and potential pathogenic processes in susceptible brain regions delineated.

Assays for NMDA receptor NR1, NR2A, and NR2B transcripts have already been developed and validated (Figure 2). Internally standardized RT-PCR methods for quantifying NMDA receptor subunit mRNA expression in human brain have been developed (Hynd, Scott, & Dodd, 2003a, 2003b). Tissue mRNA levels may not correspond to the equivalent isoform protein. Identification of such apparent anomalies may pinpoint where alcohol abuse might act in the transcription/translation process, and guide the formulation of hypotheses for further testing.

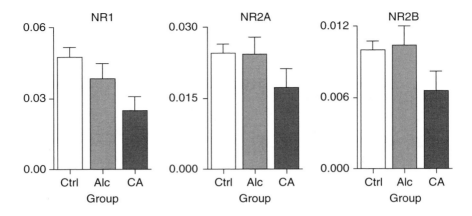

Figure 2 Expression of NMDA receptor subunit mRNA. The abundances of the subunit mRNA transcripts in Superior Frontal Cortex relative to that of GAPDH were measured by Real Time PCR methods from cases and controls collected as described in Figure 1. For NR1 ($P = 0.005$) and NR2B ($P = 0.03$) transcripts, controls (Ctrl) differed significantly from cirrhotic alcoholics (CA), and there was a trend ($P = 0.07$) for NR2A transcripts when alcoholic cirrhotics were compared with controls. Unpublished data from the author's laboratory.

Will studies such as these be useful in guiding future therapeutic strategies? Drugs such as naltrexone and Acamprosate are more effective than placebo, but give relatively modest effects that can diminish further with time, leading to relapse (Kiefer et al., 2003). It is likely that alcoholics (and other substance mis-users) fall into different categories, in part defined by their genetic make-up (Howard, Kivlahan, & Walker, 1997). It is thus to be expected that they will also respond differentially to different medications and other therapeutic modalities. Analyses of the ways that genotype influences receptor expression are likely to be informative in this context, given (for example) Acamprosate's known interaction with the glutamate-NMDA receptor, and naltrexone's interaction with the μ-opiate receptor. Similarly, benzodiazepines are widely used in the treatment of substance-use disorders; the interactions between genotype and the expression of subtypes of $GABA_A$-benzodiazepine receptors are likely to have profound effects on treatment outcomes. Autopsy studies such as those outlined above will under-pin the burgeoning field of PET studies of living alcoholics as better PET ligands become available, further helping to define and target appropriate therapies.

CONCLUDING REMARKS

Integration of the findings outlined above suggests that the homeostasis between excitation and inhibition seems to be disrupted in chronic alcoholics. Increased glutamate release may enhance excitotoxicity by the over-stimulation of neurones. A reduction in GABA-mediated inhibition may permissively allow increased efficacy of glutamatergic inputs that could exacerbate this localized excitotoxicity. Development of this approach will provide a complete picture of the parameters of amino acid transmission in alcohol abusers. The molecular biology studies will delineate mechanisms underlying changes in transmission-mediating processes, and yield information on the detailed pharmacological profiles of receptors that are either lost or retained. Knowledge of how individuals vary in their propensity for brain damage, and in their likelihood of developing a comorbid disease such as cirrhosis of the liver, will be a useful aid to counselling and treatment. This would be further assisted by the availability of simple genetic tests of appropriate markers, which these studies will help to delineate. As well, the growing evidence that amino acid receptor subunit composition and switching play a central role in the mechanism underlying cell killing will be important for specifying the subunit targets that are most likely to be appropriate for neuroprotective drugs. This is particularly salient with amino acid transmitters, because they are used so widely in the nervous system that general agonists and antagonists are of limited value in a therapeutic context. The more precisely we can define the subunit complexes expressed in particular brain regions and cell types, the more precisely we can target drug development. This process is already under way: agents that interact with $GABA_A$ receptors comprised of different combinations of subunits, which are confined to discrete brain regions, show promise for development as alcohol–misuse therapeutics (McKay et al., 2004; Platt et al., 2005).

ACKNOWLEDGMENTS

We are grateful to Neuropathologists in the Brisbane Area Health Authority and the Queensland and NSW nodes of the National Neural Tissue Resource Consortium for providing tissue samples, and to the next of kin for providing informed written consent for the studies. Financial support was provided by the National Institutes of Alcoholism and Alcohol Abuse (USA) under grant NIH AA12404 and the National Health and Medical Research Council (Australia) under grant #401551.

REFERENCES

Akinci, M. K., & Johnston, G. A. R. (1993). Sex differences in the effects of acute swim stress on binding to $GABA_A$ receptors in mouse brain. *Journal of Neurochemistry*, 60, 2212–2216.

Ansoms, C., Deckers, F., Lehert, P., Pelc, I., & Potgieter, A. (2000). An open study with acamprosate in Belgium and Luxemburg: Results on sociodemographics, supportive treatment and outcome. *European Addiction Research*, 6, 132–140.

Baraona, E., Abittan, C. S., Dohmen, K., Moretti, M., Pozzato, G., Chayes, Z. W., et al. (2001). Gender differences in pharmacokinetics of alcohol. *Alcoholism: Clinical and Experimental Research*, 25, 502–507.

Barton, A. J. L., Pearson, R. C. A., Najlerahim, A., & Harrison, P. J. (1993). Pre- and postmortem influences on brain RNA. *Journal of Neurochemistry, 61*, 1–11.

Blednov, Y. A., Jung, S., Alva, H., Wallace, D., Rosahl, T., Whiting, P. J., et al. (2003). Deletion of the α_1 or β_1 subunit of $GABA_A$ receptors reduces actions of alcohol or other drugs. *Journal of Pharmacology and Experimental Therapeutics, 304*, 30–36.

Brandon, N. J., Uren, J. M., Kittler, J. T., Wang, H., Olsen, R., Parker, P. J., et al. (1999). Subunit-specific association of protein kinase C and the receptor for activated C kinase with GABA type A receptors. *Journal of Neuroscience, 19*, 9228–9234.

Brienza, R. S., & Stein, M. D. (2002). Alcohol use disorders in primary care: Do gender-specific differences exist? *Journal of General Internal Medicine, 17*, 387–397.

Buckley, S. T., & Dodd, P. R. (2003). Quantitation of human brain $GABA_A$ receptor β isoforms by competitive RT-PCR. *Brain Research Protocols, 11*, 19–26.

Buckley, S. T., & Dodd, P. R. (2004). $GABA_A$ receptor β subunit mRNA expression in the human alcoholic brain. *Neurochemistry International, 45*, 1011–1020.

Chen, W., Hardy, P., & Wilce, P. A. (1997). Differential expression of mitochondrial NADH dehydrogenase in ethanol-treated rat brain: Revealed by differential display. *Alcoholism: Clinical and Experimental Research, 21*, 1053–1056.

Crabbe, J. C., Phillips, T. J., Buck, K. J., Cunningham, C. L., & Belknap, J. K. (1999). Identifying genes for alcohol and drug sensitivity: Recent progress and future directions. *Trends in Neurosciences, 22*, 173–179.

Davies, P. A., Hanna, M. C., Hales, T. G., & Kirkness, E. F. (1997). Insensitivity to anæsthetic agents conferred by a class of $GABA_A$ receptor subunit. *Nature, 385*, 820–823.

Devaud, L. L., Fritschy, J. M., Sieghart, W., & Morrow, A. L. (1997). Bidirectional alterations of $GABA_A$ receptor subunit peptide levels in rat cortex during chronic ethanol consumption and withdrawal. *Journal of Neurochemistry, 69*, 126–130.

Dodd, P. R. (1995). Benzodiazepine binding sites in alcoholic cirrhotics: Evidence for gender differences. *Metabolic Brain Disease, 10*, 93–104.

Dodd, P. R. (2002). Excited to death: Different ways to lose your neurones. *Biogerontology, 3*, 51–56.

Dodd, P. R., Foley, P. F., Buckley, S. T., Eckert, A. L., & Innes, D. J. (2004). Genes and gene expression in the brain of the alcoholic. *Addictive Behaviors, 29*, 1295–1309.

Dodd, P. R., Hambley, J. W., Cowburn, R. F., & Hardy, J. A. (1988). A comparison of methodologies for the study of functional transmitter neurochemistry in human brain. *Journal of Neurochemistry, 50*, 1333–1345.

Dodd, P. R., Hardy, J. A., Baig, E. B., Kidd, A. M., Bird, E. D., Watson, W. E. J., et al. (1986). Optimization of freezing, storage, and thawing conditions for the preparation of metabolically active synaptosomes from frozen rat and human brain. *Neurochemical Pathology, 4*, 177–198.

Dodd, P. R., Hardy, J. A., Oakley, A. E., Edwardson, J. A., Perry, E. K., & Delaunoy, J.-P. (1981). A rapid method for preparing synaptosomes: Comparison, with alternative procedures. *Brain Research, 226*, 107–118.

Dodd, P. R., Kril, J. J., Thomas, G. J., Watson, W. E. J., Johnston, G. A. R., & Harper, C. G. (1996). Receptor binding sites and uptake activities mediating GABA neurotransmission in chronic alcoholics with Wernicke encephalopathy. *Brain Research, 710*, 215–228.

Dodd, P. R., & Lewohl, J. M. (1998). Cell death mediated by amino acid transmitter receptors in human alcoholic brain damage: Conflicts in the evidence. *Annals of the New York Academy of Sciences, 844*, 50–58.

Dodd, P. R., Thomas, G. J., Harper, C. G., & Kril, J. J. (1992). Amino acid neurotransmitter receptor changes in cerebral cortex in alcoholism: Effect of cirrhosis of the liver. *Journal of Neurochemistry, 59*, 1506–1515.

Ely, M., Hardy, R., Longford, N. T., & Wadsworth, M. E. (1999). Gender differences in the relationship between alcohol consumption and drink problems are largely accounted for by body water. *Alcohol and Alcoholism, 34*, 894–902.

Fan, L., van der Brug, M., Chen, W., Dodd, P. R., Matsumoto, I., Niwa, S., et al. (1999). Increased expression of mitochondrial genes in human alcoholic brain revealed by differential display. *Alcoholism: Clinical and Experimental Research, 23*, 408–413.

Foley. P. F., Loh, E.-W., Innes, D. J., Williams, S. M., Tannenberg, A. F. G., Herper, C. G., & Dodd, P. R. (2004). Association studies of neurotransmitter gene polymorphisms in alcoholic Caucasians. *Annals of the New York Academy of Sciences, 1025*, 39–46.

Freund, G., & Anderson, K. J. (1996). Glutamate receptors in the frontal cortex of alcoholics. *Alcoholism: Clinical and Experimental Research, 20*, 1165–1172.

Freund, G., & Ballinger, W. E., Jr. (1988). Decrease of benzodiazepine receptors in frontal cortex of alcoholics. *Alcohol, 5*, 275–282.

Frye, G. D., & Fincher, A. S. (1988). Effect of ethanol on γ-vinyl GABA-induced GABA accumulation in the substantia nigra and on synaptosomal GABA content in six rat brain regions. *Brain Research, 449*, 71–79.

Ghaemmaghami, S., Huh, W. K., Bower, K., Howson, R. W., Belle, A., Dephoure, N., et al. (2003). Global analysis of protein expression in yeast. *Nature, 425*, 737–741.

Gordon, E. R. (1967). The effect of ethanol on the concentration of γ-aminobutyric acid in the rat brain. *Canadian Journal of Physiology and Pharmacology, 45*, 915–918.

Grobin, A. C., Papadeas, S. T., & Morrow, A. L. (2000). Regional variations in the effects of chronic ethanol administration on $GABA_A$ receptor expression: Potential mechanisms. *Neurochemistry International, 37*, 453–461.

Guerrini, I., Thomson, A. D., Cook, C. C., McQuillin, A., Sharma, V., Kopelman, M., et al. (2005). Direct genomic PCR sequencing of the high affinity thiamine transporter (SLC19A2) gene identifies three genetic variants in Wernicke Korsakoff syndrome (WKS). *American Journal of Medical Genetics B Neuropsychiatric Genetics, 137*, 17–19.

Hardy, P., Chen, W., & Wilce, P. A. (1999). Chronic ethanol exposure and withdrawal influence NMDA receptor subunit composition and splice variant expression in the rat cerebral cortex. *Brain Research, 819*, 33–39.

Harper, C. G., & Kril, J. J. (1990). Neuropathology of alcoholism. *Alcohol and Alcoholism, 25*, 207–216.

Harper, C. G., & Kril, J. J. (1993). Neuropathological changes in alcoholics. In W. A. Hunt, & S. J. Nixon (Eds.). *Alcohol-Induced Brain Damage* (1st ed., pp. 39–69). Rockville, MD: NIH Publications.

Hedblom, E., & Kirkness, E. F. (1997). A novel class of $GABA_A$ receptor subunit in tissues of the reproductive system. *Journal of Biological Chemistry, 272*, 15346–15350.

Hommer, D., Momenan, R., Kaiser, E., & Rawlings, R. (2001). Evidence for a gender-related effect of alcoholism on brain volumes. *American Journal of Psychiatry, 158*, 198–204.

Hornung, J.-P., & de Tribolet, N. (1995). Chemical organization of the human cerebral cortex. In D. Tracey, G. Paxinos, & J. Stone (Eds.), *Neurotransmitters in the human brain. Advances in Behavioural Biology*, Vol. 43 (pp. 41–99). New York, NY: Plenum Press.

Howard, M. O., Kivlahan, D., & Walker, R. D. (1997). Cloninger's Tridimensional theory of personality and psychopathology: Applications to substance use disorders. *Journal of Studies on Alcohol, 58*, 48–66.

Hunt, W. A. (1993). Are binge drinkers more at risk of developing brain damage? *Alcohol, 10*, 559–561.

Hunt, W. A. (1996). Role of acetaldehyde in the actions of ethanol on the brain – a review. *Alcohol, 13*, 147–151.

Hynd, M. R., Lewohl, J. M., Scott, H. L., & Dodd, P. R. (2003). Biochemical and molecular studies using human autopsy brain tissue. *Journal of Neurochemistry, 85*, 543–562.

Hynd, M. R., Scott, H. L., & Dodd, P. R. (2003a). Quantitation of alternatively spliced NMDA receptor NR1 isoform mRNA transcripts in human brain by competitive RT-PCR. *Brain Research Protocols, 11*, 52–66.

Hynd, M. R., Scott, H. L., & Dodd, P. R. (2003b). Quantitation of NMDA receptor NR2 mRNA transcripts in human brain by competitive RT-PCR. *Brain Research Protocols, 11*, 67–79.

Jechlinger, M., Pelz, R., Tretter, V., Klausberger, T., & Sieghart, W. (1998). Subunit composition and quantitative importance of hetero-oligomeric receptors: GABA$_A$ receptors containing α_6 subunits. *Journal of Neuroscience, 18,* 2449–2457.

Keller, E., Cummins, J. T., & von Hungen, K. (1983). Regional effects of ethanol on glutamate levels, uptake and release in slice and synaptosome preparations from rat brain. *Substance and Alcohol Actions and Misuse, 4,* 383–392.

Kiefer, F., Jahn, H., Tarnaske, T., Helwig, H., Briken, P., Holzbach, R., et al. (2003). Comparing and combining naltrexone and acamprosate in relapse prevention of alcoholism. *Archives of General Psychiatry, 60,* 92–99.

Kim, J. S., & Shukla, S. D. (2006). Acute in vivo effect of ethanol (binge drinking) on histone H3 modifications in rat tissues. *Alcohol and Alcoholism, 41,* 126–132.

Kittler, J. P., Rostaing, P., Schiavo, G., Fritschy, J. M., Olsen, R., Triller, A., et al. (2002). The subcellular distribution of GABARAP and its ability to interact with NSF suggest a role for this protein in the intracellular transport of GABA$_A$ receptors. *Molecular and Cellular Neuroscience, 18,* 13–25.

Koob, G. F., Roberts, A. J., Schulteis, G., Parsons, L. H., Heyser, C. J., Hyytia, P., et al. (1998). Neurocircuitry targets in ethanol reward and dependence. *Alcoholism: Clinical and Experimental Research, 22,* 3–9.

Koob, G. F., Sanna, P. P., & Bloom, F. E. (1998). Neuroscience of addiction. *Neuron, 21,* 467–476.

Kril, J. J., & Halliday, G. M. (1999). Brain shrinkage in alcoholics: A decade on and what have we learned? *Progress in Neurobiology, 58,* 381–387.

Kril, J. J., Halliday, G. M., Svoboda, M. D., & Cartwright, H. (1997). The cerebral cortex is damaged in chronic alcoholics. *Neuroscience, 79,* 983–998.

Kril, J. J., & Harper, C. G. (1989). Neuronal counts from four cortical regions of alcoholic brains. *Acta Neuropathologica (Berlin), 79,* 200–204.

Kuo, S.-W., & Dodd, P. R. (2005). Stimulus-coupled amino acid transmitter release in human alcoholics. *Proceedings of the Australian Neuroscience Society, 16,* 33.

Lavoie, J., Giguère, J. F., Pomier-Layrargues, G., & Butterworth, R. F. (1987). Amino acid changes in autopsied brain tissue from cirrhotic patients with hepatic encephalopathy. *Journal of Neurochemistry, 49,* 692–697.

Ledig, M., M'Paria, J. R., & Mandel, P. (1982). Free amino acids in the brain of ethanol treated rats. *Substance and Alcohol Actions and Misuse, 3,* 25–30.

Lewohl, J. M., Crane, D. I., & Dodd, P. R. (1996). Alcohol, alcoholic brain damage, and GABA$_A$ receptor isoform gene expression. *Neurochemistry International, 29,* 677–684.

Lewohl, J. M., Crane, D. I., & Dodd, P. R. (1997a). A method for the quantitation of the α_1, α_2 and α_3 isoforms of the GABA$_A$ receptor in human brain. *Brain Research Protocols, 1,* 347–356.

Lewohl, J. M., Crane, D. I., & Dodd, P. R. (1997b). Expression of the α_1, α_2 and α_3 isoforms of the GABA$_A$ receptor in human alcoholic brain. *Brain Research, 751,* 102–112.

Lewohl, J. M., Crane, D. I., & Dodd, P. R. (1997c). Zolpidem binding sites on the GABA$_A$ receptor in brain from human cirrhotic and non-cirrhotic alcoholics. *European Journal of Pharmacology, 326,* 265–272.

Lewohl, J. M., Huygens, F., Crane, D. I., & Dodd, P. R. (2001). GABA$_A$ receptor α subunit proteins in human chronic alcoholics. *Journal of Neurochemistry, 78,* 424–434.

Lewohl, J. M., Van Dyk, D. D., Craft, G. E., Innes, D. J., Mayfield, R. D., Cobon, G., et al. (2004). The application of proteomics to the human alcoholic brain. *Annals of the New York Academy of Sciences, 1025,* 14–26.

Lewohl, J. M., Wang, L., Miles, M. F., Zhang, L., Dodd, P. R., & Harris, R. A. (2000). Gene expression in human alcoholism: Microarray analysis of frontal cortex. *Alcoholism: Clinical and Experimental Research, 24,* 1873–1882.

Liu, J., Lewohl, J. M., Dodd, P. R., Randall, P. K., Harris, R. A., & Mayfield, R. D. (2004). Gene expression profiling of individual cases reveals consistent transcriptional changes in alcoholic human brain. *Journal of Neurochemistry, 90,* 1050–1058.

Mayfield, R. D., Lewohl, J. M., Dodd, P. R., Herlihy, A., Liu, J., & Harris, R. A. (2002). Patterns of gene expression are altered in the frontal and motor cortices of human alcoholics. *Journal of Neurochemistry, 81*, 802–813.

McKay, P. F., Foster, K. L., Mason, D., Cummings, R., Garcia, M., Williams, L. S., et al. (2004). A high affinity ligand for GABA$_A$-receptor containing α_5 subunit antagonizes ethanol's neurobehavioral effects in Long-Evans rats. *Psychopharmacology (Berlin), 172*, 455–462.

Michaelis, E. K., Mulvaney, M. J., & Freed, W. J. (1978). Effects of acute and chronic ethanol intake on synaptosomal glutamate binding activity. *Biochemical Pharmacology, 27*, 1685–1691.

Miles, M. F. (1995). Alcohol's effects on gene expression. *Alcohol Health and Research World, 19*, 237–243.

Mitsuyama, H., Little, K. Y., Sieghart, W., Devaud, L. L., & Morrow, A. L. (1998). GABA$_A$ receptor α_1, α_4, and β_3 subunit mRNA and protein expression in the frontal cortex of human alcoholics. *Alcoholism: Clinical and Experimental Research, 22*, 815–822.

Mukherjee, A. B., Svoronos, S., Ghazanfari, A., Martin, P. R., Fisher, A., Roecklein, B., et al. (1987). Transketolase abnormality in cultured fibroblasts from familial chronic alcoholic men and their male offspring. *Journal of Clinical Investigation, 79*, 1039–1043.

Muzzolini, A., Bregola, G., Bianchi, C., Beani, L., & Simonato, M. (1997). Characterization of glutamate and [^{3}H]D-aspartate outflow from various *in vitro* preparations of the rat hippocampus. *Neurochemistry International, 31*, 113–124.

Neelands, T. R., Fisher, J. L., Bianchi, M., & Macdonald, R. L. (1999). Spontaneous and γ-aminobutyric acid (GABA)-activated GABA$_A$ receptor channels formed by ε subunit-containing isoforms. *Molecular Pharmacology, 55*, 168–178.

Olney, J. W. (1994). New mechanisms of excitatory transmitter neurotoxicity. *Journal of Neural Transmission Supplementum, 43*, 47–51.

Pandey, S. (1996). Protein kinase C: Molecular and cellular targets for the action of ethanol. *Alcoholism: Clinical and Experimental Research, 20*, A67–A71.

Platt, D. M., Duggan, A., Spealman, R. D., Cook, J. M., Li, X., Yin, W., et al. (2005). Contribution of α_1GABA$_A$ and α_5GABA$_A$ receptor subtypes to the discriminative stimulus effects of ethanol in squirrel monkeys. *Journal of Pharmacology and Experimental Therapeutics, 313*, 658–667.

Ponomarev, I., Schafer, G. L., Blednov, Y. A., Williams, R. W., Iyer, V. R., & Harris, R. A. (2004). Convergent analysis of cDNA and short oligomer microarrays, mouse null mutants and bioinformatics resources to study complex traits. *Genes, Brain and Behavior, 3*, 360–368.

Pritchett, D. B., Sontheimer, H., Shivers, B. D., Ymer, S., Kettenmann, H., Schofield, P. R., et al. (1989). Importance of a novel GABA$_A$ receptor subunit for benzodiazepine pharmacology. *Nature, 338*, 582–585.

Sabria, J., Torres, D., Pasto, M., Peralba, J. M., Allali-Hassani, A., & Pares, X. (2003). Release of neurotransmitters from rat brain nerve terminals after chronic ethanol ingestion: Differential effects in cortex and hippocampus. *Addiction Biology, 8*, 287–294.

Saunders, J. B., Aasland, O. G., Amundsen, A., & Grant, M. (1993). Alcohol consumption and related problems among primary health care patients: WHO collaborative project on early detection of persons with harmful alcohol consumption – I. *Addiction, 88*, 349–362.

Saunders, J. B., & Latt, N. (1993). Epidemiology of alcoholic liver disease. In P. C. Hayes (Ed.), *Clinical Gastroenterology* (pp. 555–579). Sydney: Ballière Tindall.

Schonberger, S. J., Edgar, P. F., Kydd, R., Faull, R. L., & Cooper, G. J. (2001). Proteomic analysis of the brain in Alzheimer's disease: Molecular phenotype of a complex disease process. *Proteomics, 1*, 1519–1528.

Schumann, G., Rujescu, D., Singer, P., Szegedi, A., Wiemann, S., Wellek, S., et al. (1995). Alcohol dependence is associated with an NMDA-receptor 2B gene variant. *Psychiatric Genetics, 5*, 171–176.

Schumann, G., Rujescu, D., Szegedi, A., Singer, P., Wiemann, S., Wellek, S., et al. (2003). No association of alcohol dependence with a NMDA-receptor 2B gene variant. *Molecular Psychiatry, 8*, 11–12.

Simpson, J. M., Oldenburg, B., Owen, N., Harris, D., Dobbins, T., Salmon, A., et al. (2000). The Australian National Workplace Health Project: Design and baseline findings. *Preventive Medicine, 31*, 249–260.

Tapert, S. F., Brown, G. G., Kindermann, S. S., Cheung, E. H., Frank, L. R., & Brown, S. A. (2001). fMRI measurement of brain dysfunction in alcohol-dependent young women. *Alcoholism: Clinical and Experimental Research, 25*, 236–245.

Thomas, G. J., & Dodd, P. R. (1993). Transmitter amino acid neurochemistry in chronic alcoholism with and without cirrhosis of the liver. *Drug and Alcohol Reviews, 12*, 91–98.

Thomas, G. J., Harper, C. G., & Dodd, P. R. (1998). Expression of GABA$_A$ receptor isoform genes in the cerebral cortex of cirrhotic and alcoholic cases assessed by S1 nuclease protection assays. *Neurochemistry International, 32*, 375–385.

Toropainen, M., Näkki, R., Honkanen, A., Rosenberg, P. H., Laurie, D. J., Pelto-Huikko, M., et al. (1997). Behavioral sensitivity and ethanol potentiation of the N-methyl-D-aspartate receptor antagonist MK-801 in a rat line selected for high ethanol sensitivity. *Alcoholism: Clinical and Experimental Research, 21*, 666–671.

Tsuji, T., Shiozaki, A., Kohno, R., Yoshizato, K., & Shimohama, S. (2002). Proteomic profiling and neurodegeneration in Alzheimer's disease. *Neurochemical Research, 27*, 1245–1253.

Walter, H., Gutierrez, K., Ramskogler, K., Hertling, I., Dvorak, A., & Lesch, O. M. (2003). Gender-specific differences in alcoholism: Implications for treatment. *Archives of Women's Mental Health, 6*, 253–258.

Weight, F. F., Aguayo, L. G., White, G., Lovinger, D. M., & Peoples, R. W. (1992). GABA- and glutamate-gated ion channels as molecular sites of alcohol and anesthetic action. *Advances in Biochemical Psychopharmacology, 47*, 335–347.

Whitfield, J. B. (1997). Meta-analysis of the effects of alcohol dehydrogenase genotype on alcohol dependence and alcoholic liver disease. *Alcohol and Alcoholism, 32*, 613–619.

Whiting, P. J. (1999). The GABA$_A$ receptor gene family: New targets for therapeutic intervention. *Neurochemistry International, 34*, 387–390.

WHO. (2004). *Neuroscience of psychoactive substance use and dependence.* Geneva: WHO.

Wisden, W., & Seeburg, P. H. (1992). GABA$_A$ receptor channels: From subunits to functional entities. *Current Opinion in Neurobiology, 2*, 263–269.

Ymer, S., Schofield, P. R., Draguhn, A., Werner, P., Köhler, M., & Seeburg, P. H. (1989). GABA$_A$ receptor β subunit heterogeneity: Functional expression of cloned cDNAs. *European Molecular Biology Organization Journal, 8*, 1665–1670.

CHAPTER 2

Common Genetic Influences on Antisociality and Addictions: Implications for Clinical Science and Practice

Serena M. King

Department of Psychology, Hamline University, Saint Paul, MN, USA

Comorbidity of Addictions and Antisociality:
    An Introduction
Shared Genetic Vulnerabilities to Antisociality
    and Addictions
Molecular Genetics of Antisociality and Addictions:
    Examples from the Study of Alcoholism
Implications of Common Genetic Influences of
    Antisocial Personality and Addictions for
    Conceptualizing and Classifying Psychopathology
From Genes to Clinical Practice: Implications of
    Genetic Research for Advancing Clinical Care
Summary and Conclusions
References

Abstract: Behavioral genetic, molecular genetic, and epidemiological studies suggest that addictions and antisocial behaviors commonly co-occur and share genes. In this chapter, research is critically reviewed and a research agenda for advancing theory and applications is proposed. Evidence for overlapping genetic etiologies among these disorders has resulted in proposals to reframe diagnostic categories and has implications for the delivery of treatments. Molecular genetic work suggests complex mechanisms of gene action and a polygenetic etiology of these disorders. Translational research on the addiction–antisociality overlap has the possibility to reshape diagnostic practices, advance treatment discoveries, and merge traditionally disparate areas of inquiry.

COMORBIDITY OF ADDICTIONS AND
ANTISOCIALITY: AN INTRODUCTION

One of the most commonly reported findings in the scientific literature on addictions is the co-occurrence of addictions with antisocial personality traits (or "comorbidity").[1] Antisocial traits are characterized by disinhibited behaviors, impulsivity, and norm and rule-breaking. The current diagnostic system describes this constellation of behaviors under the category of Antisocial Personality Disorder (ASPD; Diagnostic and Statistical Manual of Mental Disorders, Fourth Edition or DSM-IV, American Psychiatric Association, 1994). Understanding the nature of common and specific etiological contributions to antisocial personality and addictions has significant potential to inform and change the way addictions are diagnosed, treated, and prevented. In this chapter, recent advances in the state of science are presented alongside a synthesis of the existing research. Because much of the science is in its earliest stages, the related clinical implications are rarely described in literature. This chapter is an effort to elucidate the complex interrelationships between antisociality and addictions, propose implications for practice, and provide directions for translational research agendas.

The last 30 years of addictions research has undergone a paradigmatic shift from isolating specific origins of addictions and antisociality, to increasing numbers of studies focusing on common etiological factors. Unfortunately, this large domain of research has existed apart from efforts aimed to directly impact psychological services and research in this area and is often published in journals focusing on questions of basic science. Some theorists have suggested methods for conceptualizing comorbidity that have included sub-typing approaches (Bohman et al., 1987; Wiesbeck et al., 2005) and proposals to merge Diagnostic and Statistical Manual of Mental Disorders (DSM) diagnostic categories (Krueger et al., 2005). Recent advances in etiological research on addictions have suggested common and specific genetic and environmental factors responsible for the co-variation of addictions and ASPD.

Comorbidity of antisocial and addictive behaviors has been observed across the lifetime, leading many addiction scientists to explore whether these syndromes have similar etiological foundations. Researchers have found that antisocial, impulsive behaviors and traits are some of the strongest predictors of substance use disorders and pathological gambling behaviors (Slutske et al., 2001). In young adulthood, antisocial personality traits are robust predictors of heavy

---

[1]In this chapter, we refer to addictions broadly but focus mainly on all substance use disorders and antisociality refers to a constellation of personality traits that are indicative of impulsivity, disinhibition, or aggressivity.

drinking and drug use. Impulsive, disinhibited personality traits consistently show larger effects in predicting the onset and persistence of substance use disorders when compared with negative emotionality (negative affect, depression, and anxiety) (Elkins et al., 2006; Sher, Bartholow, & Wood, 2000). While the strength of the relationships between addiction and negative emotionality vary by substance (with nicotine and marijuana showing stronger relationships with negative emotionality), the links between antisociality and addictions are consistently strong across several substances (Elkins et al.). Antisocial traits predict early involvement with substance use and whether individuals progress to a substance use diagnosis. One of the strongest pieces of evidence in support of antisociality playing an etiological role in substance use problems is that children with impulsive, disinhibited personality traits tend to onset earlier in their substance use than those without such traits (McGue et al., 2001).

In adulthood, individuals with ASPD tend to have a comorbid substance use disorder. Those with ASPD tend to be cross-addicted to more than one substance. Childhood disorders (Oppositional Defiant Disorder, Attention Deficit Hyperactivity Disorder) have also been linked to addictive behaviors and there is co-morbidity between different childhood disinhibitory behavioral disorders (King, Iacono, & McGue, 2004; Burt et al., 2001). Given that childhood and adolescent disinhibitory psychopathology are strong predictors of later substance use disorders, researchers have sought to understand the underlying common contributions to these disorders.

Earlier research on co-morbidity of antisociality and substance use addictions has uncovered patterns of familial transmission of alcoholism, drug use disorders, and ASPD. Epidemiological family studies indicate that offspring of alcoholic parents tend to have higher rates of antisocial traits, conduct disorder, and addictive problem behaviors. In a similar vein, offspring of ASPD parents have higher rates of substance use problems, conduct disorder, and antisocial personality traits (Iacono et al., 1999). Childhood disorders indicative of behaviorally disinhibited traits have been consistently associated with the onset and progression of problematic substance use disorders (King, Iacono, & McGue, 2004; Iacono et al., 1999).

Research on the psychiatric epidemiology of co-occurring disorders has supported the idea that antisocial personality and substance use disorders commonly co-aggregate. Krueger et al. (1998) statistically modeled the structure of comorbidity among ten of the major psychiatric disorders in the DSM-Third Edition and found that two major dimensions of symptomatology clustered together: (1) a clustering of disorders including conduct disorder (at age 18) or ASPD (at age 21), alcohol dependence, and marijuana dependence (labeled "externalizing"), and (2) major depressive disorder, phobias, anxiety disorders, and dysthymia (labeled "internalizing"). Additional empirical support for high rates of psychiatric comorbidity of antisocial personality and substance use disorders has been demonstrated by Compton et al. (2005) using a nationally representative sample (NESARC). These results indicated that almost all of the statistical associations between ASPD, adult antisocial behaviors, and substance use disorders were significant and positive (Compton et al., 2005). In a major family study of the covariation of alcohol dependence and psychiatric disorders, Nurnberger et al. (2004) found that ASPD tended to co-occur in families with alcohol dependence and other forms of substance use disorders.

In a focused exploration of the nature of the association between ASPD and alcoholism, Bucholz et al. (2000) performed a latent class analysis to determine if certain sub-groupings were found for ASPD, and in turn, whether these potential subgroups were differentially associated with alcoholism. Their results suggested that severity of antisociality was systematically related to alcoholism, with the highest prevalence of ASPD being found in the most severely affected alcoholics. The findings thus suggest that antisociality is found at higher rates among those more severely affected cases of alcoholism, and therefore may suggest that the two disorders may be arrayed together along a spectrum of severity. Results from epidemiological samples consistently find that ASPD is one of the most commonly comorbid psychiatric conditions with substance use disorders (Helzer & Prybeck, 1988; Kessler et al., 1997; Nurnberger et al., 2002). In sum, results from family studies of the co-aggregation of antisocial personality and addictions support common co-occurrence and suggest further exploration of common mechanisms of effect.

SHARED GENETIC VULNERABILITIES TO ANTISOCIALITY AND ADDICTIONS

Twin study methods have provided important insights into the causes of comorbidity of antisociality and addictions. In a classic twin study design, the co-twin resemblance of monozygotic (MZ) twins (who share 100% of their genetic material) and dizygotic (DZ) twins (who share 50% of their genetic material) are compared to infer the genetic and environmental contributions to the measured behavior or diagnosis (phenotype). This design is well suited to examine the common genetic and environmental causes of two or more different diagnoses or behaviors (i.e., ASPD, substance use disorders, or anxiety and mood disorders). In a twin study of the causes of comorbidity, these relationships are statistically modeled and a proportion or percentage of common variation is estimated.

Twin research designs and family studies that have examined common and specific contributions to antisocial personality and substance use disorders have found that a large portion of the co-variation between ASPD and substance use disorder can be accounted for by common genetic factors (Waldman & Slutske, 2000).

In a sample of twins followed between the ages of 17 and 24, Malone et al. (2004) demonstrated that there was significant genetic influence on both ASPD and alcohol dependence through the developmental period, and that almost all of the covariation between alcohol dependence and ASPD symptoms can be accounted for by genetic, rather than environmental factors.

In a large-scale twin study, Slutske et al. (2002) demonstrated that genetic influences on personality factors indicative of behavioral undercontrol, accounted for a large proportion of the genetic factors responsible for alcohol dependence among men and women. Krueger et al. (2002) demonstrated that genetic factors accounted for a large proportion of the co-morbidity between these ASPD, personality and substance use disorders. Hicks et al. (2004) modeled the association within families and twin pairs of ASPD, all substance dependence diagnoses, and childhood conduct disorder. A largely heritable general factor (referred to as "externalizing") accounted for the covariation in these disorders and results were suggestive of a general, rather than disorder-specific form of familial transmission. While the findings of Hicks and colleagues are compelling, they suggested that their results are not incompatible with the idea that there are some disorder-specific factors that are transmitted within families. Extending this idea notion to other addictions, Slutske et al. (2001) demonstrated that a substantial proportion of the covariation between pathological gambling behaviors and ASPD was due to common genetic influences.

In a recent study, Krueger et al. (2005) argued for change to the current classification system in the DSM) and advocated for a continuous conceptualization of these disorders under the name "externalizing" (ASPD and substance use disorders). In their paper, they suggested that collapsing the categories and creating a continuous spectrum would more accurately represent their common etiological roots. They argued that because factor analytic work demonstrated that externalizing disorders formed a coherent spectrum that was separate from anxiety and depression (internalizing psychopathology), the new version of the DSM should consider lumping these disorders into a unified group. They also argued for a hierarchical model, which accommodates a "lumping and splitting" position to classifying psychopathology and conceptualizes and differentiates externalizing disorders within the spectrum by unique genetic and environmental effects. In their paper, they described a common factor impacting general risk for addictive behaviors and antisocial personality traits, with specific genes impacting which drug is abused and how it is metabolized (Krueger et al.).

Current initiatives are underway for a dimensional model of psychopathology where ASPD and addictions are grouped together and measured on a continuum. Krueger et al. (2005) suggest that research evidence supports the merging of Axis I and Axis II in the DSM-V because common personality traits are thought to unite the two axes. Moreover, Krueger et al. (2005) suggest that the shift to a dimensional approach that links the addictive disorders and antisociality in the diagnostic system would result in a more "generalized" approach to treating traits in common to the disorders (e.g., behavioral undercontrol) and for developing specific care approaches for the individual disorders expressed within the realm of "externalizing" (e.g., specific strategies to treat cannabis dependence compared to antisocial personality). Krueger et al. (2005) suggested his model could result in a "coordinated theory of several disorders can be formulated rather than separate theories for each disorder..." (p. 546). Proponents of this model (Krueger et al., 2005; Cuthbert, 2005) suggest that the rampant comorbidity of substance use disorders and antisocial personality suggests that they are better categorized under the same dimension. Moreover, proponents suggest that common genes impacting these disorders are further evidence for grouping them together along a dimension.

Psychophysiological evidence demonstrates that antisocial personality, behavioral undercontrol, and substance use disorders share common heritable physiological vulnerabilities. One example of a possible genetic risk indicator for alcoholism and other disinhibitory psychopathology is a reduced P300 amplitude. P300 amplitude is a psychophysiological measure of event-related brain potential, or electrical impulse generated in response to a novel auditory or visual stimulus. Many studies have demonstrated that children of alcoholics (particularly sons) have reduced P300 amplitude. In a sample of twin boys, Iacono et al. (2002) demonstrated that P300 amplitude reductions were not specific for risk for only alcoholism, but may reflect a generalized risk for disorders reflective of externalizing (or antisociality, acting out, and delinquency and substance use). In a twin study on the overlapping genetic influences on P300 amplitude and heavy drinking during adolescence and young adulthood, King et al. (2005) demonstrated that there were common genetic influences impacting P300 amplitude and heavy drinking in men, but not women. Overall, based on these and other emerging findings, P300 amplitude may index an inherited risk for a spectrum of disorders reflective of externalizing and substance use disorders, but this risk may be specific to males.

In sum, results from twin research on the comorbidity of antisocial traits and substance use disorders suggest common genetic influences. Moreover, evidence from psychophysiological research suggests that there is a heritable brain marker that may index risk for substance use disorders and externalizing psychopathology. As Krueger et al. (2002) theorize, adopting a hierarchical structure to understanding the common and specific factors impacting these disorders may be important to differentiating specific factors impacting addictions and antisociality. Twin research, in combination with molecular genetic technologies will allow for identification of the specific processes responsible for overlap between antisociality and addictions.

MOLECULAR GENETICS OF ANTISOCIALITY AND ADDICTIONS: EXAMPLES FROM THE STUDY OF ALCOHOLISM

The study of the molecular genetics of alcoholism provides an excellent illustration of how we can understand mechanisms explaining the relationship between antisociality and addictions. Although studies on the molecular genetics of alcoholism have been underway for more than a decade, recent research has resulted in major advances in our understanding of how genes affect alcoholism and how these genes link up with other psychological traits. As technologies available for molecular genetics became widely available, researchers are able to conduct basic association studies to determine which candidate genes were most likely to impact which phenotypes (or behaviors). As is the case with other complex behavioral disorders (such as schizophrenia or bipolar disorder), no single gene is likely responsible for individuals developing alcoholism or its comorbid conditions (Schuckit et al., 2003).

One of the most commonly cited polymorphisms (ALDH2*2) is thought to affect alcohol metabolism (Cook et al., 2005). This gene affects one's risk for alcoholism through its effect on the liver's ability to process alcohol and thus results in a negative physiological response to alcohol (flushing response and possible nausea). This polymorphism is seen more frequently in some Asian racial groups than in Caucasians, thus reducing the overall risk for alcoholism in some groups of Asians and Asian Americans (Cook et al., 2005).

Other genes have been associated with alcoholism that may affect neurotransmitter functioning in the brain. For example, genes responsible for dopamine action and other neurotransmitters are related to alcoholism risk (Hill et al., 1999). In their review, Hill and colleagues point out that different genes are responsible for different aspects of risk for alcoholism. For example, some are responsible for liver metabolism and some for traits that may lead a person to seek addictive substances. Thus, as genes combine to affect alcohol use behaviors, certain traits may be more or less likely to develop in affected groups. In their review, Hill et al. suggested that alcoholics with antisocial personality traits might share serotonin deficits in common. The serotonin system is responsible for behavioral impulsivity, and has been recently linked extensively to antisocial personality traits and alcoholism (Cadoret et al., 2003; Hill et al., 1999; LeMarquand, Pihl, & Benkelfat, 1994). In particular, lowered serotonergic activity is associated with impulsive, antisocial forms of alcoholism (Hill et al.). However, even within the realm of serotonin candidate genes, there are a large number of possible chromosomal locations that differentially impact activity in that system (Hill et al.). For example, some locations code for neurotransmitter reuptake processes, whereas others code for metabolism, synthesis, or are specifically geared toward other neurotransmitter activity.

that the costs of having to re-train clinicians in new systems of psychological diagnosis would set back years of study and treatment advances. He also discussed the possible implications for the re-training of other mental health professionals (including psychiatrists, counselors, nurses, and social workers) in a new diagnostic system. First (2005) criticized the proposed dimensional changes to the DSM by citing the years of meta-analytic research on different syndromes in the DSM-IV that would need re-appraisal if a dimensional system were enacted. Moreover, other critics suggest that it may be premature to develop a dimensional system based on comorbidity and the extant etiological research on common genetic and environmental factors that explain comorbidity. Finally, a very important practical concern raised by First (2005) is the idea that cutoff scores would need to be ultimately utilized to make treatment, insurance, and payment decisions.

FROM GENES TO CLINICAL PRACTICE: IMPLICATIONS OF GENETIC RESEARCH FOR ADVANCING CLINICAL CARE

Emerging research advances in molecular genetics raise important diagnostic and treatment implications. The development of molecular genetic technologies and a growing knowledge base on the effects of genes related to addictions and antisociality raise questions about how these methods might be used in clinical settings and how these technologies would be utilized to inform research on treatment. While studies merging molecular genetic technologies and treatment outcome are in their early development and are rarely found in literature, they raise promising possibilities that may shed light on intervention.

One possibility for future research is examining the differential effects of interventions on populations with specific "risky" configurations of genes (serotonergic functioning and alcohol metabolizing gene polymorphisms). That is, research could test the efficacy of interventions among those with and without genes related to antisocial personality. Molecular genetic techniques could potentially be combined with brain imaging techniques to map neurophysiological changes in the brain in response to treatment (Roffman et al., 2005). Given the fact that there are few known efficacious psychotherapeutic interventions for ASPD, brain-imaging studies in combination with molecular genetic methods may be a particularly fruitful area for future research. In developing strategies to target difficult behavioral problems, a window on brain functioning may be particularly helpful. While there has been increased interest in combining genetic methods with treatment research, most of the research to date has been on pharmacological interventions, rather than psychosocial interventions (Goldman et al., 2005).

Research on common vulnerabilities to substance use and addictions suggests important intervention and prevention implications. First, if common genetic influences are important to these two groups of behaviors, interventions that help to prevent the development of antisocial personality traits may also impact the progression of substance use. However, it may be premature to conclude that common genes and comorbidity *necessarily* suggest similar etiologies to these disorders. Despite the fact that common genes may impact the development of antisociality and addictions, it does not follow that they necessarily share the same etiological processes. Among those with the same genetic material, in utero environments, psychosocial environments, and neurobiological developmental processes may determine who develops antisociality, addictions, or both. These issues raise concerns about a "one-size-fits-all" approach to intervening with addictions and antisociality. Although substantially more complex to plan and enact, a research agenda that accommodates the heterogeneity of causal pathways to developing addictions and antisociality would likely result in the best prevention and intervention approaches.

With emerging twin and molecular genetic research suggesting some common etiological influences between these two disorders, there will be a growing emphasis on psychosocial intervention targeting both disorders. A multi-layered research approach that coordinates psychosocial and pharmacological interventions, molecular genetic technologies, and brain imaging would allow for the greatest potential advances. Goldman et al. (2005) used genetic methods to determine the pharmacological interventions that show the most promise in alcoholism treatment. In their paper, they examined how genetic information on reward centers in the brain can elucidate the mechanisms involved with efficacious pharmacological treatment (Goldman et al., 2005). If research groups such as these begin to integrate psychosocial interventions (e.g., cognitive behavioral treatment for addictions, or dialectical behavior therapy for personality disorders), innumerable treatment advances may be possible. Isolating the specific neurobiological effects of psychotherapy among those with antisocial alcoholism could spur major progress in the treatment of addictions. Combining these methods has significant potential for developing effective treatments targeted at reward pathways in the brain, pathways regulating disinhibition systems (as in antisociality), and specialized brain pathways that may be sensitized to the effects of one drug over another (opiates compared to alcohol).

The merger of antisocial personality and addictions in the DSM also raises implications for the treatment of the disorders. Currently, there are some specific empirically validated treatments that have demonstrated efficacy with different addictions. In contrast, at present, there are few, if any, psychological interventions for ASPD that have demonstrated a high degree of efficacy (Tyrer & Davidson, 2000). However, there is some evidence that individuals with comorbid drug addiction and antisociality respond to contingency management techniques paired with cognitive and behavioral interventions (Messina, Farabee, & Rawson, 2003). The potential merger of antisociality with addictions in the new DSM could change the way Health Maintenance Organizations view acceptable empirically validated treatments for this new "dimension" encompassing antisociality and addictions. This re-conceptualization could result in significant changes in the interventions currently viewed as acceptable for treating addictions.

Merging the categories of antisociality and addictions has considerable importance to the pharmacological treatment of these conditions. Traditionally, personality disorders have not been seen as highly amenable to pharmacological interventions. Aside from mood stabilizers being prescribed for Borderline Personality Disorder, there have been few examples of widespread acceptance of pharmacological treatments for these disorders. In contrast, pharmacological treatment of the addictions is one of the largest areas of scientific inquiry in the psychiatric treatment literature. This relative inconsistency will likely have implications for the way addictions and ASPD are treated and studied. For example, will insurance companies reimburse for empirically validated pharmacological interventions with opioid addiction if the drug does not simultaneously treat the symptoms of the antisocial personality? Given the vast amount of research that has focused on how drugs like naltrexone treat drug addiction, and now alcoholism, the practice of prescribing these drugs will not be likely to end as a result of a re-conceptualization of the diagnostic classification system. Will new drugs that address the mood, aggression, and disinhibition components (involved in personality disorder) along with the pleasure pathways in the brain (involved in the addictions) need to be developed? Perhaps what will occur is recognition among the psychiatric and psychological community of the inter-relatedness of addictions and their comorbid personality traits. This may result in a subsequent re-formulation of how such disorders are treated. In addition, combining Axis I and Axis II disorder (drug and alcohol disorders and personality disorders) may result in a resurgence of scientific interest on the efficacy of pharmacological and psychological interventions. Because genetic research has demonstrated common genes and neurobiological pathways to addictions and antisociality, the scientific community may need to re-design pharmacological interventions to address symptom reduction of both addictions and antisociality. A new research agenda that accommodates the diagnostic and etiological overlap of these areas will need to be undertaken. This agenda may include developing more effective pharmacological interventions for antisocial personality traits that deal with punishment and reward systems in the brain (an area of research that has already been demonstrated to be important to understanding some mechanisms of pharmacological action involved in drug and alcohol addictions).

As medicine, psychology, and molecular genetics make headway on research techniques for understanding the genetic bases for addiction and antisociality, important ethical and medical dilemmas may arise (see Dixon, 2005 for possible ramifications of genetic research for public policy). With advances such as the mapping of the human genome, it is increasingly important to combine expertise from bioethicists, medical doctors, geneticists, psychologists, genetic counselors, and legal experts. Interdisciplinary work will prove important to developing novel interventions that utilize information on the genetic underpinnings of antisociality and addictions (Meyer, 2001). Inevitably, the possibility of genetic testing raises concerns about public health care access and decisionmaking. Researchers and clinicians embarking on genotyping studies and interventions may need to address concerns about whether insurance companies will misuse information on genetic risk for psychiatric disorders. For example, which genetic risk groups might receive reimbursement for their treatment, and how many sessions of treatment will be offered to those groups with severe forms of alcoholism and antisociality? The advances in this area suggest many common genetic effects on antisociality and addictions, offering exciting possibilities for research directions.

SUMMARY AND CONCLUSIONS

Recent advances in molecular genetics, behavioral genetics, and treatment research have the potential to produce illuminating insights for clinical practice. Research evidence suggests a significant genetic overlap between antisocial personality traits and addictions. The accumulation of etiological and nosological research on their commonalities has resulted in proposals for reformation of the DSM. This reform could lead to a merger of the two categories and ultimately a dimensional approach to diagnosis with far-reaching implications for intervention and assessment. Behavioral genetics, molecular genetics, and treatment intervention research programs will eventually need to converge on common goals and mutual research agendas in order to advance translational research in this area.

A balanced approach that accommodates a clinical perspective on the implementation of new diagnostic and treatment practices has the greatest potential for success. Additionally, appreciation of the multifaceted nature of gene action influencing both addictions and antisociality is particularly important to developing treatment approaches. Current scientific evidence suggests that multiple genes impact these two behavioral phenotypes. Genes interact and express themselves differently on the basis of environmental influences (Heath et al., 2001), multiplicative genetic effects, changes in gene activation over the lifetime, treatment changes, and other influences. These facts must not be minimized as genetic information is used to develop novel treatment interventions. Perhaps most importantly, future research on the translation of genetic work on the antisociality-addiction overlap will need to consider using this information to develop novel and effective psychosocial and pharmacological treatment approaches. Moving these cutting edge findings into the clinic will rely heavily on the conversations and research collaborations between clinical practitioners, treatment scientists, and genetic researchers.

REFERENCES

American Psychiatric Association. (1994). *Diagnostic and Statistical Manual of Mental Disorders* (4th ed.). Washington, DC: American Psychiatric Association.

Bohman, M., Cloninger, R., Sigvardsson, S., & Von Knorring, A. L. (1987). The genetics of alcoholisms and related disorders. *Journal of Psychiatric Research, 21*(4), 447–452.

Bucholz, K., Hesselbrock, V. M., Heath, A. C., Kramer, J. R., & Schuckit, M. A. (2000). A latent class analysis of antisocial personality disorder symptom data from a multi-centre family study of alcoholism. *Addiction, 95*(4), 553–567.

Burt, S. A., Krueger, R. F., McGue, M., & Iacono, W. G. (2001). Sources of covariation among attention-deficit/hyperactivity disorder, oppositional defiant disorder, and conduct disorder: The importance of shared environment. *Journal of Abnormal Psychology, 110*(4), 516–525.

Cadoret, R. J., Langbehn, D., Caspers, K., Troughton, E. P., Yucuis, R., Sandhu, H. K., & Philibert, R. (2003). Associations of the serotonin transporter promoter polymorphism with aggressivity, attention deficit, and conduct disorder in an adoptee population. *Comprehensive Psychiatry, 44*(2), 88–101.

Compton, W. M., Conway, K. P., Stinson, F. S., Colliver, J. D., & Grant, B. F. (2005). Prevalence, correlates and comorbidity of antisocial personality syndromes and alcohol and specific drug use disorders in the United States: Results from the National Epidemiologic Survey on Alcohol and Related Conditions. *Journal of Clinical Psychiatry, 66*(6), 677–685.

Cook, T. A. R., Luczak, S. E., Shea, S. H., Ehlers, C. L., Carr, L. G., & Wall, T. L. (2005). Associations of ALDH2 and ADH1B genotypes with response to alcohol in Asian Americans. *Journal of Studies on Alcohol, 66,* 2005.

Cuthbert, B. N. (2005). Dimensional models of psychopathology: Research agenda and clinical utility. *Journal of Abnormal Psychology, 114*(4), 565–569.

Dixon, M. (2005). *Brave new choices? Behavioral genetics and public policy: A discussion Document.* London: Institute for Public Policy.

Elkins, I. J., King, S. M., McGue, M., & Iacono, W. G. (2006). Personality traits and the development of nicotine, alcohol, and illicit drug disorders: Prospective links from adolescence to young adulthood. *Journal of Abnormal Psychology, 115*(1), 26–39.

First, M. B. (2005). Clinical utility: A prerequisite for the adoption of a dimensional approach in DSM. *Journal of Abnormal Psychology. Special Issue: Toward a Dimensionally Based Taxonomy of Psychopathology, 114*(4), 560–564.

Goldman, D., Oroszi, G., O'Malley, S., & Anton, R. (2005). COMBINE genetics study: The pharmacogenetics of treatment response: Genes and mechanisms. *Journal of Studies on Alcohol, Suppl*(15), 56–64.

Heath, A. C., Whitfield, J. B., Madden, P. A. F., Bucholz, K. K., Dinwiddie, S. H., Slutske, W. S., Bierut, L. J., Statham, B., & Martin, N. G. (2001). Towards a molecular epidemiology of alcohol dependence: Analysing the interplay of genetic and environmental risk factors. *British Journal of Psychiatry, 178*(Suppl 40), s33–s40.

Helzer, J. E., & Prybeck, T. R. (1988). The co-occurrence of alcoholism with other psychiatric disorders in the general population and its impact on treatment. *Journal of Studies on Alcohol, 49*(3), 219–224.

Hicks, B. M., Krueger, R. F., Iacono, W.G., McGue, M., & Patrick, C. J. (2004). Family transmission and heritability of externalizing disorders. *Archives of General Psychiatry, 61*, 922–927.

Hill, E. M., Stoltenberg, S. F., Burmeister, M., Closser, M., & Zucker, R. A. (1999). Potential associations among genetic markers in the serotonergic system and the antisocial alcoholism subtype. *Experimental and Clinical Psychopharmacology, 7*(2), 103–121.

Iacono, W. G., Carlson, S. R., Malone, S. M., & McGue, M. (2002). P3 event-related potential amplitude and the risk for disinhibitory disorders in adolescent boys. *Archives of General Psychiatry, 59*, 750–757.

Iacono, W. G., Carlson, S. R., Taylor, J., Elkins, I. J., & McGue, M. (1999). Behavioral disinhibition and the development of substance use disorders: Findings from the Minnesota Twin Family Study. *Development & Psychopathology, 11*, 869–900.

Kessler, R. C., Crum, R. M., Warner, L. A., & Nelson, C. B. (1997). Lifetime co-occurrence of DSM-III-R alcohol abuse and dependence with other psychiatric disorders in the National Comorbidity Survey. *Archives of General Psychiatry, 54*(4), 313–321.

King, S. M., Burt, S. A., Malone, S. M., McGue, M., & Iacono, W. G. (2005). Etiological contributions to heavy drinking from late adolescence to young adulthood. *Journal of Abnormal Psychology. Special Issue: Toward a Dimensionally Based Taxonomy of Psychopathology, 114*(4), 587–598.

King, S. M., Iacono, W. G., & McGue, M. (2004). Childhood externalizing and internalizing psychopathology in the prediction of early substance use. *Addiction, 99*(12), 1548–1559.

Krueger, R. F., Caspi, A., Moffitt, T. E., & Silva, P. A. (1998). The structure and stability of common mental disorders (DSM-III-R): A longitudinal-epidemiological study. *Journal of Abnormal Psychology, 107*(2), 216–227.

Krueger, R. F., Hicks, B. M., Patrick, C. J., Carlson, S. R., Iacono, W. G., & McGue, M. (2002). Etiologic connections among substance dependence, antisocial behavior, and personality: Modeling the externalizing spectrum. *Journal of Abnormal Psychology, 111*(3), 411–424.

Krueger, R. F., Markon, K. E., Patrick, C. J., & Iacono, W. G. (2005). Externalizing psychopathology in adulthood: A dimensional-spectrum conceptualization and its implications for the DSM-V. *Journal of Abnormal Psychology, 114*(4), 537–550.

Kupfer, D. J., First, M. B., & Regier, D. A. (Eds.). (2002). *A Research Agenda for DSM-V.* Washington, DC, US: American Psychiatric Association, xxiii.

LeMarquand, D., Pihl, R. O., & Benkelfat, C. (1994). Serotonin and alcohol intake, abuse, and dependence: Clinical evidence. *Biological Psychiatry, 36*(5), 326–337.

Malone, S. M., Taylor, J., Marmorstein, N. R., McGue, M., & Iacono, W. G. (2004). Genetic and environmental influences on antisocial behavior and alcohol dependence from adolescence to early adulthood. *Development and Psychopathology, 16*, 943–966.

McGue, M., Iacono, W. G., Legrand, L. N., Malone, S., & Elkins, I. (2001). Origins and consequences of age at first drink: I. Associations with substance-use disorders, disinhibitory behavior and psychopathology, and P3 amplitude. *Alcoholism: Clinical and Experimental Research, 25*, 1156–1165.

Messina, N., Farabee, D., & Rawson, R. (2003). Treatment responsivity of cocaine-dependent patients with antisocial personality disorder to cognitive behavioral and contingency management interventions. *Journal of Consulting and Clinical Psychology, 71*(2), 320–329.

Meyer, R. E. (2001). Finding paradigms for the future of alcoholism research: An interdisciplinary perspective. *Alcoholism: Clinical and Experimental Research, 25*(9), 1393–1406.

Nurnberger, J. I., Wiegand, R., Bucholz, K., O'Connor, S. O., Meyer, E. T., Reich, T., Rice, J., Schuckit, M., King, L., Petti, T., Bierut, L., Hinrichs, A. L., Kuperman, S., Hesselbrock, V., & Porjesz, B. (2004). A family study of alcohol dependence. *Archives of General Psychiatry, 61*, 1246–1256.

Roffman, J. L., Marci, C. D., Glick, D. M., Dougherty, D. D., & Rauch, S. L. (2005). Neuroimaging and the functional neuroanatomy of psychotherapy. *Psychological Medicine, 35*(10), 1385–1398.

Schuckit, M., Kelsoe, J. R., Braff, D. L., & Wilhelmsen, K. C. (2003). Some possible genetic parallels across alcoholism, bipolar disorder, and schizophrenia. *Journal of Studies on Alcohol, 64*(2), 157–159.

Schuckit, M., Mazzanti, C., Smith, T. L., Ahmed, U., Radel, M., Iwata, N., Goldman, D. (1999). Selective genotyping for the role of 5-HT/2-sub(A), 5-HT/2-sub(C), and GABA-sub(α)/6 receptors and the *serotonin* transporter in the level of response to alcohol: A pilot study. *Biological Psychiatry, 45*(5), 647–651.

Sher, K. J., Bartholow, B. D., & Wood, M. D. (2000). Personality and substance use disorders: A prospective study. *Journal of Consulting and Clinical Psychology, 68*, 818–829.

Slutske, W. S., Eisen, S., Xian, H., True, W. R., Lyons, M. J., Goldberg, J., & Tsuang, M. (2001). A twin study of the association between pathological gambling and antisocial personality disorder. *Journal of Abnormal Psychology, 110*(2), 297–308.

Slutske, W. S., Heath, A. C., Madden, P. A. F., Bucholz, K. K., Statham, D. J., & Martin, N. G. (2002). Personality and the genetic risk for alcohol dependence. *Journal of Abnormal Psychology, 111*(1), 124–133.

Tyrer, P., & Davidson, K. (2000). Cognitive therapy for personality disorders. In J. G. Gunderson, & G. O. Gabbard (Eds.). *Psychotherapy for Personality Disorders. Review of Psychiatry*, Vol. 19(3) (pp. 131–149). Washington, DC: American Psychiatric Publishing.

Waldman, I. D., & Slutske, W. S. (2000). Antisocial behavior and alcoholism: A behavioral genetic perspective on comorbidity. *Clinical Psychology Review, 20*(2), 255–287.

Wiesbeck, G. A., Dursteler-MacFarland, K. M., Walter, M., Weijers, H., & Boening, J. (2005). A three-axes approach of subtyping the alcohol dependence syndrome. *Psychopathology, 38*, 91–96.

Zucker, R. A., Ellis, D. A., & Fitzgerald, H. E. (1994). Developmental evidence for at least two alcoholisms: I. Biopsychosocial variation among pathways into symptomatic difficulty. In T. F. Babor, V. M. Hesselbrock, R. E. Meyer, & W. Shoemaker (Eds.). *Types of Alcoholics: Evidence from Clinical, Experimental, and Genetic Research. Annals of the New York Academy of Sciences*, Vol. 708 (pp. 134–146). New York, NY, US: New York Academy of Sciences.

CHAPTER 3

Opioids, Pain and Addiction: Cause and Consequence

Jason M. White and Justin L. Hay
Discipline of Pharmacology, School of Medical Sciences, The University of
Adelaide, Adelaide, Australia

Abstract: Long-term opioid administration is associated with physiological dependence and tolerance. However, evidence is emerging that chronic opioid use is also associated with an increased sensitivity to certain types of pain. This raises questions about the impact that long-term opioid administration has on addiction, whether other systems demonstrate similar responses to opioids and the potential for acute pain management in opioid tolerant patients. This chapter reviews the pertinent literature, examines the implications that chronic opioid use has for pain and addiction treatments and proposes future directions for translational science related to addiction and pain.

Drugs age you after mental excitement. Lethargy then. Why? Reaction.
—James Joyce "Ulysses"

The isolation of morphine from opium occurred over 200 years ago. Prior to that time, opium was used for thousands of years, principally for its medicinal properties. Subsequent to the isolation of morphine, many new opioids have been developed and there has been a considerable research effort to try to understand how these powerful drugs produce their varied effects. In that time, great advances have been made, but despite these, we are still learning more about opioids.

This chapter describes some developments in our understanding of the effects of opioids on the pain response. Relief of pain and addiction are sometimes viewed as completely separate aspects of the actions of opioid drugs. However, the research described below shows that pain responses change considerably with long-term opioid administration. These changes in pain response may themselves contribute to the development of addiction, but may also provide a model for how other opioid effects are modified by repeated use, leading to the escalation in use that is characteristic of addiction.

OPIOID-INDUCED HYPERALGESIA

One of the notable characteristics of opioids is the pronounced tolerance that develops with repeated administration. Of all drug classes, administration of members of the opioid group seems to produce the greatest degree of tolerance. Doses of heroin that dependent people use would produce respiratory depression, sedation, vomiting, coma and even death in a non-tolerant person. When a heroin-dependent person enters an opioid maintenance program, their tolerance and physical dependence are maintained with a controlled, regular dosing regimen of opioids. Owing to the cross tolerance that occurs across the opioid class, it is possible to use a variety of drugs for such maintenance treatment. Methadone and buprenorphine are the most widely used, but morphine in slow-release formulations and heroin itself are also employed in some countries.

Opioid-maintained patients administering methadone show marked tolerance, as opioid effects are relatively small compared to what a similar methadone dose would produce in an opioid-naïve person. This opioid tolerance has been shown in studies that have investigated the physiological effects of methadone during the intra-dosing period of 24h in methadone maintained patients. Opioid effects such as respiratory depression and reduced pupil diameter continue to occur in methadone maintained patients, even when plasma methadone concentrations are at their lowest. However, the magnitude of opioid effect is relatively small in methadone maintained patients compared to control subjects (Dyer et al., 1999; Newcombe et al., 2004), indicating tolerance to the opioid effects of methadone.

To date we have a good understanding of tolerance, particularly opioid tolerance, which includes recognition of the variability in rates of tolerance development across responses, some understanding of the underlying mechanisms as well as its role in addiction. However, evidence presented below challenges this conventional understanding. The research on which it is based comes from studies of responses to pain and the effects of prolonged opioid exposure.

PAIN RESPONSES IN OPIOID MAINTENANCE PATIENTS

Experimental pain models can be used to measure different aspects of pain perception. Pain can be induced by electrical, thermal, ischemic, chemical or mechanical methods. These experimental models yield reproducible and reliable data useful for the assessment of pain sensitivity and tolerance. While experimental pain models may not precisely reflect clinical pain conditions, they can be used to investigate changes in pain sensitivity caused by analgesic drugs as well as factors affecting pain sensitivity. The main advantages of experimental pain models are the high degree of control over pain intensity (in contrast to clinical pain where there is no such control) and the ability to use it in any population, rather than just those people who are experiencing pain. These experimental pain models have been used for investigating the pain sensitivity of people maintained on methadone for the treatment of addiction.

Electrical stimulation as a pain stimulus has been used to investigate changes during the 24h dosing interval in methadone maintained patients. Methadone concentration in plasma is typically lowest around the time of dosing (trough), then rises to a peak about 3h later, before gradually declining to the trough over the remaining 24h. Results have indicated that methadone maintained patients, in comparison with controls, experience a similar degree of pain sensitivity at the time of trough plasma methadone concentration, but analgesia at the time of peak concentration. Thus, while methadone maintained patients show considerable tolerance to opioid effects such as respiratory depression and miosis, the pain response to electrical stimulation still continues to change with fluctuations in plasma methadone concentration (Dyer et al., 1999). This result is similar to other physiological measures, including respiration rate and pupil size. In a similar manner, it has been shown that when subjected to mechanical pressure, methadone maintained patients are just as pain sensitive as control subjects when the methadone concentration is at trough. Likewise, as plasma methadone concentration rises, pain sensitivity to mechanical pressure declines to a minimum at the time of peak methadone concentration (Schall et al., 1996).

The most widely used experimental pain stimulus is cold-pressor pain. While there are variations in the model used, the essential component involves the subject immersing their arm into a container of ice water. There is an initial strong sensation of cold that changes to a feeling of deep, penetrating pain after some seconds. Eventually the pain becomes intolerable and the subject removes their arm. The time at which pain is first experienced (pain threshold) and the time of removal of the arm (pain tolerance) are both recorded.

When used to evaluate the pain responses of opioid-dependent people, the cold-pressor model produces a different pattern of results from the electrical stimulation and mechanical pressure tests described above. The cold-pressor results also differ in a very fundamental way from the tolerance seen with physiological measures such as respiratory rate and pupillary constriction. In particular, the pattern of pain tolerance seen with pain models such as electrical stimulation is not seen with cold-pressor pain; instead of pain sensitivity similar to control values at trough methadone concentrations, methadone maintained patients demonstrate hypersensitivity to pain induced by the cold-pressor test. Based on our data (Doverty et al., 2001) methadone maintained patients have a pain tolerance duration approximately one-third that of controls. While cold-pressor tolerance increases 3 h following methadone administration (around the time of peak concentration), the analgesia observed is only moderate and nowhere close to the levels of the control subjects.

This observation of pain hypersensitivity is consistent with early studies investigating pain tolerance in drug using subjects. As early as 1965, Martin and Inglis (1965) found that female "known narcotic addicts" had a lower cold-pressor tolerance compared to matched non-addict controls. Subsequently, Ho and Dole (1979) found that drug-free ex-addicts and methadone maintained patients were more pain sensitive to the cold-pressor test than their drug-free siblings. Compton and colleagues (1994) compared the cold-pressor tolerance of current and abstinent cocaine users and opioid users and found that methadone maintained patients were pain intolerant when compared to current or abstinent cocaine abusers.

While the earlier research had pointed to the different responses to cold-pressor pain compared to mechanical pressure and electrical stimulation, differences in methodology meant that the role of pain stimulus type was not clearly recognised. Results from different studies simply seemed to be contradictory. Doverty et al. (2001) demonstrated that in the same methadone maintained subjects, it was possible to observe hypersensitivity to cold-pressor pain, but not to pain induced by electrical stimulation. Furthermore, the differences were more pronounced for pain tolerance than for pain threshold.

GENERALITY OF HYPERALGESIA

Hyperalgesia is not restricted to patients in methadone maintenance treatment. While not as extensively studied, buprenorphine maintained patients also show hyperalgesia when measured using the cold-pressor test (Compton,

Charuvastra, & Ling, 2001) and this observation has also been made with patients maintained on slow release oral morphine (Mitchell et al., in press). Similar pain intolerance has been reported in heroin addicts entering treatment (Ling et al., 2003). This is supported by recent research by Pud et al. (2006), who found that heroin and methadone opioid addicts entering a detoxification program, with no previous history of being in a methadone maintenance program, experience hyperalgesia.

This research using experimental pain models provides evidence that methadone and buprenorphine maintained patients, as well as heroin users, are hypersensitive to cold-pressor pain. While these results imply that long-term opioid exposure induces hyperalgesia, it does not exclude the possibility that increased pain sensitivity is a predisposing factor leading to opioid dependence or that there is a genetic or other influencing factor that may result in both opioid dependence and hyperalgesia. While the hypothesis that long-term opioid administration leads to hyperalgesia could be theoretically determined by administering opioids chronically to a cohort of healthy controls, this is restricted by the ethical issues attached to such an experimental paradigm. However, there is experimental evidence from other areas of research that support the notion that hyperalgesia can be induced by both acute and chronic opioid use.

Recent research investigating the pain sensitivity of chronic pain patients managed with long-term administration of methadone or morphine shows that people in this group exhibit a similar response to experimentally induced pain when evaluated against methadone maintained patients in treatment for opioid addiction. Using electrical stimulation, the pain sensitivity of opioid managed chronic pain patients is similar to that of methadone maintained patients, which in turn is similar to that of control subjects. However, the cold-pressor tolerance of both opioid managed chronic pain patients and pain free, methadone maintenance patients indicates that both groups are hyperalgesic to cold-pressor pain compared to a control group of drug-free controls (Hay et al., 2005b). Thus, similar results are obtained regardless of the aetiology of the chronic opioid use.

Only one prospective study has been reported in pain patients commencing chronic opioid administration. Chu, Clark, and Angst (2006) provided preliminary data from six subjects showing hyperalgesia in the first month of treatment. Unfortunately, not all subjects were opioid naïve and hence the results need further confirmation. Such studies can only be done in chronic pain patients: it is unlikely that a sample of potential illicit opioid users could be studied prior to and following their first period of illicit opioid use.

There is evidence that the hyperalgesia associated with opioid administration may begin following short-term opioid exposure. Studies that have investigated the administration of remifentanil and fentanyl given to patients undergoing surgery have investigated the effects these opioids have on pain sensitivity during the postoperative period. It has been reported that higher doses of these opioids administered during surgery exacerbate postoperative pain when compared to lower doses (Chia et al., 1999; Guignard et al., 2000). When the effects of acute opioid administration on experimental pain have been examined, similar findings have been obtained. Following a single dose of morphine or hydromorphone, withdrawal was precipitated with naltrexone 2–4h later and cold-pressor tolerance measured. Results indicated that physiological and subjective withdrawal effects were associated with greater pain sensitivity (Compton, Athanasos, & Elashoff, 2003). Infusion of the ultra-short acting opioid agonist remifentanil can expand an area of hyperalgesia on the body surface compared to baseline measurements (Koppert et al., 2003). In summary, studies involving acute opioid administration to human volunteers not being treated for opioid addiction have shown that opioids can induce hyperalgesia in humans.

Cross-sectional studies investigating former opioid users can shed some light on whether the discontinuation of opioids is associated with resolution of opioid-induced hyperalgesia. An early study by Andrews (1943) measured heat pain threshold in former opiate addicted men. This study found that baseline pain thresholds of former addicts "were quite comparable with those obtained with non–addicts." Compton (1994) found that abstinent drug abusers were able to tolerate cold-pressor pain to a greater degree than currently using subjects. In this study, cocaine users were included together with opioid users so the data can be regarded as suggestive only. The only prospective study that has investigated the pain sensitivity of former users measured pain responses when the subjects entered detoxification treatment after using illicit opioids and again 28 days later (Pud et al., 2006). Using the cold-pressor test, the study found that these subjects were just as hyperalgesic, 28 days following detoxification as they were when they entered treatment. Whether there is a permanent change in pain sensitivity following chronic opioid use and subsequent discontinuation is yet to be elucidated in longitudinal, prospective studies, but the evidence to date indicates that there is no rapid return to normal pain sensitivity.

Finally, the last lines of evidence to suggest that opioid use is associated with greater pain sensitivity come from animal studies. Early animal studies focused on measuring hypersensitivity to pain associated with the cessation of opioid administration or following the precipitation of withdrawal by an opioid antagonist. As a consequence, many of these studies measured the degree of opioid dependence expressed as opioid withdrawal induced hyperalgesia. However, Vanderah et al. (2001) demonstrated that hyperalgesia can occur in animals during prolonged morphine administration. In this study, rats were implanted with morphine pellets subcutaneously; given in this manner there was no opportunity for a drug-associated, conditioned response to develop. Initially, animals demonstrated analgesia to radiant heat pain; however, after 4 days of continuous opioid administration, clear hyperalgesia was seen when compared to control rats. In a similar manner to methadone maintained patients, ongoing opioid administration is associated with altered pain sensitivity in rats. Furthermore, this hyperalgesia developed very rapidly.

In summary, hyperalgesia occurs in populations chronically exposed to opioids because of pain or addiction, appears not to be readily reversible on cessation of administration, and in an animal model can be demonstrated as a consequence of opioid administration. This evidence suggests that the hyperalgesia exhibited by opioid maintained patients is opioid induced.

IMPLICATIONS FOR OPIOID DEPENDENCE TREATMENT

Traditional notions about the consequences of long-term drug use suggest that prolonged exposure to a drug leads to tolerance; that is, the response to the drug is still present, but is diminished in magnitude. It is evident that many responses to opioids show this kind of changed pattern. They include pupillary constriction, respiratory depression and analgesia to pain induced by electrical and mechanical stimulation. It is also clear that cold-pressor pain does not follow this model. Rather than simply developing tolerance to the opioid drug, the person appears to be 'hyperadapted,' responding in a manner opposite to the direct effects of the opioid drug even while using it. This difference is important in understanding how people develop opioid addiction and how their treatment needs can best be met.

HYPERALGESIA, CHRONIC PAIN AND THE AETIOLOGY OF ADDICTION

Increasing pain sensitivity caused by chronic opioid use may partially explain the observation that people with chronic pain are disproportionately represented in the methadone maintained population. Cross-sectional research has shown that chronic pain of moderate or greater intensity is present in 37% (Rosenblum et al., 2003) of methadone maintained patients, which corresponds to the upper range of chronic pain prevalence in the general population (Verhaak et al., 1998). This estimate is increased to over 60% when chronic pain of any intensity is considered (Jamison, Kauffman, & Katz, 2000).

There are several ways in which hyperalgesia may contribute to a pattern of addictive opioid use, ultimately resulting in maintenance treatment. Among people who use heroin it would be expected that those who have some form of chronic pain may be predisposed to develop opioid dependence. Administration of opioid drugs can produce two major reinforcing effects: a euphoric state and relief of emotional distress (Jasinski, 1991; Panksepp, 2003). These 'benefits' of opioid administration are important in maintaining patterns of continued and escalating use of opioid drugs following initial administration of the drug. Such effects may be particularly powerful in vulnerable individuals who have few other sources of pleasure in their lives and/or a considerable level of emotional distress due to present or past experiences.

In a similar manner, relief of pain may be a powerful reinforcer in those with some form of chronic pain. Brands et al. (2004) noted that, of the methadone maintenance patients who reported chronic pain, a high proportion of them reported the onset of this pain prior to commencing methadone maintenance treatment. Thus, the chronic pain was present during the pattern of addictive opioid use and potentially prior to the development of that pattern. Analgesia is recognised as the major therapeutic effect of opioids, but it is likely that it also plays an important role in the development of opioid addiction.

If pain relief is an additional reinforcing property of opioids in people who have chronic pain, hyperalgesia may provide the rationale for escalation of use. While the immediate effect of opioid administration is pain relief, the longer-term effect is the development of hypersensitivity to pain (or at least some forms of pain). This long-term change in basal pain sensitivity may be of little immediate importance in someone without significant pain. However, in someone with chronic pain, an increase in pain sensitivity increases their degree of suffering, and hence the potential for administration of an opioid drug to provide powerful reinforcing effects through pain relief. In these circumstances such relief will likely require greater doses of opioids than the person previously used in order to reduce pain intensity. If the opioid user increases his or her dose to compensate for the hyperalgesia, this can result in a pattern of escalating use characteristic of addiction.

There is increasing concern with problems of addiction arising from use of prescription opioids, particularly in the US (Compton & Volkow, 2006). This greater interest has arisen for two main reasons. Firstly, there has been a rapid rise in the number of prescriptions being written for opioid drugs. The data have been most clearly presented for the US (Compton & Volkow, 2006), but similar trends are likely in other Western countries. While there are debates about both the causes of this increase (which is not evident to as great an extent for most other prescription psychotropic drugs) and its appropriateness (is pain now being treated more appropriate or excessively?), the availability of opioid drugs in the community is increasing.

The second factor is the recognition that addiction occurs in a significant minority of people who use prescription opioids. Early estimates had suggested that this proportion was extremely low, but more recent surveys have revealed much higher figures. One review (Fishbain, Rosomoff, & Rosomoff, 1992) suggested that proportions ranging from 3% to 19% of people becoming addicted after long-term opioid use. In some populations the figure may be considerably higher: among some at risk populations, it may be closer to 30% (Chabal et al., 1997).

These findings, together with evidence of increasing abuse of prescription opioids that is separate from the heroin using sub-culture, suggest that there is considerable overlap in chronic pain and addiction treatment. People who experience chronic pain may use opioids, develop hyperalgesia and escalate their dose and/or frequency of administration of the opioid in order to compensate for this change in pain sensitivity. An escalating pattern of use coupled with a prioritising of opioid administration compared to other activities may be very similar to the type of addiction that is associated with illicit opioid use. If the number of people who develop a pain-related addiction continues to increase they are likely to become an increasing proportion of the opioid treatment population.

Hyperalgesia will also develop in opioid users without chronic pain, but as mentioned above, without having immediate impact. If, however, the opioid user develops some form of chronic pain after commencing opioid use this may also contribute to addiction in the manner already described. Such pain is more likely to occur in opioid users because of their high rate of injury due to falls, accidents, etc. (Cameron, 1964; Sapira, 1968). The major difference between the opioid user who has an accident or other pain-inducing event and the non-user suffering the same fate is that hyperalgesia in the opioid user will magnify the intensity of the pain experienced from the injuries incurred. What may be a minor nuisance in the non-opioid user can be magnified by hyperalgesia into a significant chronic pain experience in the long-term opioid user. The only way this person can relieve the pain and associated distress is by further opioid administration. Again, this has the potential to set up a cycle of escalating use and exacerbation of addiction.

TREATMENT OF ACUTE PAIN

Opioid cross-tolerance and hyperalgesia are significant barriers to the provision of effective analgesia in the opioid-dependent patient. Opioid-dependent patients would be expected to require significantly higher and more frequent doses of opioids for the provision of adequate pain management (Mitra & Sinatra, 2004). Research using experimental pain models confirms that methadone maintained patients are cross-tolerant to the use of high and ultra-high doses of morphine (Doverty et al., 2001; Athanasos et al., 2006). The use of the same experimental pain models has also indicated that the use of non-opioid medications, such as ketamine or ketorolac, either alone or in combination with morphine provides only limited analgesia in opioid-dependent patients (Athanasos et al., 2006).

The use of opioids with higher intrinsic opioid agonist activity may be an effective alternative strategy for the management of acute pain in opioid tolerant and opioid addicted patients (De Leon-Casasola & Lema, 1994). Preliminary reports have indicated that the use of the highly potent opioid drug remifentanil can significantly increase pain tolerance times for the cold-pressor test in opioid maintenance patients (Hay et al., 2005a). While these patients require higher doses of this drug than those shown to be effective in opioid-naïve subjects, confirming that these patients are cross-tolerant to other opioids, very marked reductions in pain sensitivity have been observed. While drugs such as remifentanil, with its ultra-short half-life, are useful as a research tool and in certain clinical situations, future research should investigate the utility of other high potency opioids.

Opioid-dependent patients represent a population with unique acute pain management needs. There is a common misconception that the presence of the opioid maintenance drug is enough to treat pain symptoms, in addition to preventing withdrawal, during painful procedures. However, the research described here indicates that opioid maintained patients are more sensitive to some kinds of pain despite the presence of the opioid maintenance medication. Effective acute pain management strategies for these patients remain limited due to the lack of evidence-based guidelines. The use of experimental acute pain models can provide valuable insights into the effectiveness of existing and emerging analgesic pharmacotherapies and may help in the development of precise dosing guidelines.

FUTURE DIRECTIONS

Assessment, Treatment and Prevention of Hyperalgesia

If hyperalgesia could be ameliorated or at least partially reversed in the opioid-dependent patient then problems such as chronic pain could be reduced. This would potentially reduce the need for long-term opioid treatment with a concomitant decrease in the problems associated with the presentation of chronic pain in opioid maintained patients. In addition, modulation of hyperalgesia such that pain sensitivity is closer to normal levels would make the treatment of acute pain in opioid maintained patients less complicated.

At present there are no treatment modalities available for either preventing or reversing the hyperalgesia seen in opioid maintained patients. However, this may be possible in the future as animal studies have shown the potential to modulate hyperalgesia associated with opioid use. Many recent studies have shown that it is possible to prevent or at least limit the withdrawal effects (including hyperalgesia) associated with the cessation of opioid medications. Potential pharmacotherapies that may be able to 'turn off' hyperalgesia are being revealed by studies that have investigated the mechanistic causes of increased pain sensitivity due to opioid use. These pharmacotherapies are based on an understanding of the mechanisms underlying hyperalgesia. In the spinal cord, excessive excitation, facilitation of pain pathways and a reduction of inhibition of these pathways are thought to mediate opioid-induced hyperalgesia (Porreca, Ossipov,

& Gebhart, 2002). The chemical mediators include dynorphin acting at NMDA receptors, nitric oxide and substance P (acting at NK1 receptors) (Vanderah et al., 2000; Li, Angst, & Clark, 2001).

One promising pharmacotherapy that may either prevent or reverse hyperalgesia seen in opioid maintained patients is the co-administration of an ultra-low dose of an opioid antagonist. Existing opioid antagonists such as naloxone and naltrexone are commonly used for the blockade of opioid effects caused by opioid agonists such as morphine. However, studies suggest that when ultra-low doses of naloxone or naltrexone are used in combination with morphine, they enhance the analgesic effects of the opioid agonist and prevent the development of tolerance. This combination approach has shown promise in pre-clinical studies in both enhancing the positive effects of opioids and attenuating their negative effects (Crain & Shen, 1995; Crain & Shen, 2001). This could have benefits for the general community, including all those who use opioids in an acute situation as well as patients who use opioids as part of a chronic regimen, whether it is for maintenance therapy, pain management or both.

ADAPTATION AND HYPERADAPTATION

The research on hyperalgesia has very important implications for understanding both the nature of dependence and the functional state of opioid-dependent people on admission to and during treatment. What is being proposed is that our conventional model of drug tolerance is an inadequate account of the changes that occur with repeated or prolonged exposure to a drug. Tolerance fits well with many drug effects. In the case of opioids, pupil constriction and respiratory depression follow this model. However, as argued above, it does not provide an adequate description of the changes underlying the response to cold-pressor pain. In this case the person is experiencing a drug-opposite response during the time they are exposed to the opioid. This change appears to be induced generally by opioids and is most likely a direct consequence of opioid exposure. Some mechanisms involving descending pain modulatory pathways in the spinal cord have been suggested to mediate these changes.

The suggestion that adaptation may be exaggerated for some responses, leading to a drug-opposite or withdrawal-like state during drug administration is similar, in some respects, to the notion of hedonic homeostatic dysregulation. Koob and Le Moal (1997) characterised addiction in terms of a cycle of spiralling distress. One of the major drivers of this cycle is the adaptive change that occurs in response to drug administration. They also indicated that this could result in a change in hedonic 'set point,' with baseline affect reset to some lower level, although they did not predict dysphoria during drug administration. The results described here suggest that the magnitude of adaptive change is greater than that suggested by Koob and Le Moal (1997) and that our account of such changes should extend beyond hedonic state to other drug-related changes. In addition, the example of cold-pressor pain shows that we can measure the extent of adaptation, determine its reversibility, and isolate the neuronal substrate(s) mediating the adaptational change. Further research on these neuronal substrates should help in understanding why the reaction to some drug effects is conventional adaptation leading to tolerance during administration and withdrawal on cessation, while for others it is hyperadaptation, leading to a withdrawal-like state during drug administration.

The evidence that cold-pressor pain fits a hyperadaptational model raises the question of whether there are other systems/responses that might behave in the same way. While there has been no formal examination of this hypothesis, some preliminary data suggest that at least one other important response may be affected by chronic opioid use in a similar manner to cold-pressor pain.

MOOD CHANGES

Changes in mood and subjective experience are understood to be one of the major reasons for use of opioid drugs (Jasinski, 1991). The most important changes in subjective experience produced by opioids are euphoria and diminished emotional distress. That is, there is both induction of a positive mood state and reduced negative mood states. Heroin users self-report that these changes are important reasons for continued use of the drug. However, with prolonged administration there is evidence of hyperadaptation for mood, consistent with the results from cold-pressor pain. At present, there is less supportive evidence and no clear neuropharmacological mechanism for this phenomenon, but the data are convincing in showing that during methadone administration patients experience drug-opposite responses as negative mood states.

An early study by Price et al. (1975) showed that the Profile of Mood States (POMS) scale is sensitive enough to detect changes in mood disturbance – either negative states (depression, tension, anger, fatigue and confusion) or positive mood states (vigour) – characteristic of methadone administration. When the POMS scale is used to measure mood during the inter-dosing period in methadone maintenance patients, the data show that these subjects have considerably greater mood disturbance, including both higher negative mood states scores and lower positive mood state scores, compared to drug-free controls (Dyer et al., 2001). Importantly, mood is responsive to methadone dosing, with the level of mood disturbance decreasing as methadone concentration increases. At the time of peak methadone concentration the level of mood disturbance is minimal and approaches that of control subjects not dependent on any drug. Therefore, despite the fact that opioid administration is associated with euphoria and diminished emotional distress, patients maintained on methadone show significantly more negative mood states than controls. This is evidence for a drug-opposite response during drug administration similar to that observed for cold-pressor pain.

An alternative explanation is that anxiety and other mood disorders are common co-morbidities in the methadone maintained population. Their level of mood disturbance at any given point in time will be worse than controls because of these co-occurring disorders. However, in the research described above people with diagnosed mental health disorders (other than addiction) were specifically excluded from the sample. In addition, there is earlier, more direct evidence to suggest that chronic opioid administration may be associated with negative mood states. Martin et al. (1973) administered methadone to six subjects over 15 weeks. While the initial effects of methadone administration included euphoria, consistent with Price et al. (1975), longer-term administration was associated with greater dysphoria. Similar effects have been found with repeated administration of heroin (McNamee et al., 1976; Mirin, Meyer, & McNamee, 1976a; Mirin et al., 1976b). While these studies are somewhat confounded by increases in dose of the opioid administered over the period in which the response changes from euphoria to dysphoria, they are consistent with a change towards negative mood states with chronic opioid administration.

It is clear from the results here that people dependent on opioids cannot be characterised as simply experiencing diminished opioid effects due to tolerance. Rather, they are best characterised as being, at least for some measures, in a constant state of withdrawal or hyperadaptation that is diminished partly by further opioid administration. This suggests that patients would be expected to be extremely dysfunctional simply based on the fact that they experience these drug-opposite responses on a constant basis. A state of pronounced negative mood and hypersensitivity to pain is likely to make normal functioning extremely difficult. This level of dysfunction will be coupled with fluctuations in the severity of disturbance according to the level of opioid present. When heroin is being used, the rate of fluctuation will be rapid, while methadone and buprenorphine will markedly reduce the rate of change.

This account further suggests that stabilising patients on a maintenance agent such as methadone or buprenorphine achieves only part of the process of reversing addiction. The hyperadaptational state will still be present, negatively influencing the person's ability to function normally. We still lack an effective approach in reducing this hyperadaptation through pharmacological or other means. Until this can be achieved, our focus should be on maximising the ability of opioid-dependent people to cope with the level of disturbance they experience.

FUTURE RESEARCH

There is still much to be learned about the hyperalgesia associated with opioid administration. A number of issues that need to be examined have been

mentioned already. While much progress has been made on identifying the neural substrates underlying opioid-induced hyperalgesia, these have yet to be clearly
defined. Progress on this front will guide the development of pharmacotherapies
that have the potential to prevent and/or reverse hyperalgesia. In the meantime,
we need to learn more about the management of people with co-occurring pain
and dependence problems. It is predicted that this group will become an increasing proportion of the people who present for opioid dependence treatment, but
as yet there is little information about the optimal treatment approaches and
whether these differ from approaches used in patients without significant pain.

At a practical level, strategies for managing acute pain in this population are
badly needed. The research using the opioid remifentanil, described above, shows
considerable promise. In contrast, most guidelines on pain management in this
population are based on little more than clinical impression and are contradictory
when placed alongside each other. More recently, the problem is being recognised and attempts are being made to devise reasonable guidelines (for example,
Alford, Compton, & Samet, 2006; Mehta & Langford, 2006), including the
recognition of hyperalgesia in this population. However, the evidence base for
analgesic strategies remains very thin. For patients in maintenance therapy this is
a very significant issue. Their perception of pain under-treatment in hospital settings can result in fewer hospital admissions and consequent under-treatment of
medical disorders.

With regard to the aetiology of opioid dependence, mood changes may
play a more significant role than pain. While increased sensitivity to pain may
affect a proportion of the opioid using population, mood changes will be universal. Based on the model discussed here, the effect of individual opioid administrations will be to elevate mood temporarily, but repeated administration will
result in the underlying mood becoming more dysphoric. This raises a number
of questions for future research as the data to date are suggestive only. Both the
nature of the mood changes during and following the development of
dependence and the role of such changes in patterns of addictive drug use need
to be characterised. Research described here focuses on opioid drugs, but the
same issues could be examined in studies of mood changes with other drug
classes. Are such mood changes common to all classes of abused drugs? Are they
critical to the development of addiction or incidental only? Can they be alleviated with medications or psychological therapies designed to treat mood disorders arising for other reasons?

GENERAL CONCLUSION

Chronic opioid administration is useful as a maintenance pharmacotherapy
for the treatment of opioid dependence. However, there is increasing evidence

that long-term exposure to opioid drugs markedly increases the sensitivity to some types of painful stimuli, a phenomenon known as opioid–induced hyperalgesia. The prolonged use of opioids may result in the expression of increased sensitivity to pain, including the aggravation of underlying pain. This may have a significant impact on addiction and dependence through the escalation of dose to alleviate the increased pain. This changing pain response is a challenge to conventional notions of drug tolerance. Rather than adaptation, for some responses the change following prolonged drug exposure may be better characterised as hyperadaptation. Preliminary evidence suggests that mood may be another such response.

REFERENCES

Alford, D. P., Compton, P., & Samet, J. H. (2006). Acute pain management for patients receiving maintenance methadone or buprenorphine therapy. *Annals of Internal Medicine*, *144*(2), 127–134.

Andrews, H. L. (1943). The effect of opiates on the pain threshold in post-addicts. *The Journal of Clinical Investigation*, *22*(41), 511–516.

Athanasos, P., Smith, C. S., White, J. M., Somogyi, A. A., Bochner, F., & Ling, W. (2006). Methadone maintenance patients are cross-tolerant to the antinociceptive effects of very high plasma morphine concentrations. *Pain*, *120*(3), 267–275.

Brands, B., Blake, J., Sproule, B., Gourlay, D., & Busto, U. (2004). Prescription opioid abuse in patients presenting for methadone maintenance treatment. *Drug Alcohol Depend*, *73*(2), 199–207.

Cameron, A. J. (1964). Heroin addicts in a casualty department. *British Medical Journal*, 1, 594.

Chabal, C., Erjavec, M. K., Jacobson, L., Mariano, A., & Chaney, E. (1997). Prescription opiate abuse in chronic pain patients: Clinical criteria, incidence, and predictors. *The Clinical Journal of Pain*, *13*(2), 150–155.

Chia, Y. Y., Liu, K., Wang, J. J., Kuo, M. C., & Ho, S. T. (1999). Intraoperative high dose fentanyl induces postoperative fentanyl tolerance. *Canadian Journal of Anaesthesia*, *46*(9), 872–877.

Chu, L. F., Clark, D. J., & Angst, M. S. (2006). Opioid tolerance and hyperalgesia in chronic pain patients after one month of oral morphine therapy: A preliminary prospective study. *Journal of Pain*, *7*(1), 43–48.

Compton, M. A. (1994). Cold-pressor pain tolerance in opiate and cocaine abusers: Correlates of drug type and use status. *Journal of Pain and Symptom Management*, *9*(7), 462–473.

Compton, P., Athanasos, P., & Elashoff, D. (2003). Withdrawal hyperalgesia after acute opioid physical dependence in nonaddicted humans: A preliminary study. *Journal of Pain*, *4*(9), 511–519.

Compton, P., Charuvastra, V. C., & Ling, W. (2001). Pain intolerance in opioid-maintained former opiate addicts: Effect of long-acting maintenance agent. *Drug and Alcohol Dependence*, *63*(2), 139–146.

Compton, W. M., & Volkow, N. D. (2006). Major increases in opioid analgesic abuse in the United States: Concerns and strategies. *Drug and Alcohol Dependence*, *81*(2), 103–107.

Crain, S. M., & Shen, K. F. (1995). Ultra-low concentrations of naloxone selectively antagonize excitatory effects of morphine on sensory neurons, thereby increasing its antinociceptive potency and attenuating tolerance/dependence during chronic cotreatment. *Proceedings of the National Academy of Science of United States of America*, *92*(23), 10540–10544.

Crain, S. M., & Shen, K. F. (2001). Acute thermal hyperalgesia elicited by low-dose morphine in normal mice is blocked by ultra-low-dose naltrexone, unmasking potent opioid analgesia. *Brain Research*, *888*(1), 75–82.

De Leon-Casasola, O. A., & Lema, M. J. (1994). Epidural bupivacaine/sufentanil therapy for post-operative pain control in patients tolerant to opioid and unresponsive to epidural bupivacaine/morphine. *Anesthesiology, 80*(2), 303–309.

Doverty, M., Somogyi, A. A., White, J. M., Bochner, F., Beare, C. H., Menelaou, A., & Ling, W. (2001). Methadone maintenance patients are cross-tolerant to the antinociceptive effects of morphine. *Pain, 93*(2), 155–163.

Doverty, M., White, J. M., Somogyi, A. A., Bochner, F., Ali, R., & Ling, W. (2001). Hyperalgesic responses in methadone maintenance patients. *Pain, 90*(1–2), 91–96.

Dyer, K. R., Foster, D. J., White, J. M., Somogyi, A. A., Menelaou, A., & Bochner, F. (1999). Steady-state pharmacokinetics and pharmacodynamics in methadone maintenance patients: Comparison of those who do and do not experience withdrawal and concentration-effect relationships. *Clinical Pharmacology and Therapeutics, 65*(6), 685–694.

Dyer, K. R., White, J. M., Foster, D. J., Bochner, F., Menelaou, A., & Somogyi, A. A. (2001). The relationship between mood state and plasma methadone concentration in maintenance patients. *Journal of Clinical Psychopharmacology, 21*(1), 78–84.

Fishbain, D. A., Rosomoff, H. L., & Rosomoff, R. S. (1992). Drug abuse, dependence, and addiction in chronic pain patients. *The Clinical Journal of Pain, 8*(2), 77–85.

Guignard, B., Bossard, A. E., Coste, C., Sessler, D. I., Lebrault, C., Alfonsi, P., Fletcher, D., & Chauvin, M. (2000). Acute opioid tolerance: Intraoperative remifentanil increases postoperative pain and morphine requirement. *Anesthesiology, 93*(2), 409–417.

Hay, J. L., White, J. M., Somogyi, A. A., Bochner, F. (2005a). *Analgesic Effects of Remifentanil In Methadone Maintained Patients*. Paper Presented at the 67th Annual Scientific Meeting of the College on Problems of Drug Dependence, Orlando.

Hay, J. L., White, J. M., Somogyi, A. A., Bochner, F., Semple, T., & Rounsefell, B. (2005b). *Opioid-Induced Hyperalgesia in Chronic Pain Patients*. Paper Presented at the 11th World Congress of Pain, Sydney.

Ho, A., & Dole, V. P. (1979). Pain perception in drug-free and in methadone-maintained human ex-addicts. *Proceedings of the Society of Experimental and Biological Medicine, 162*(3), 392–395.

Jamison, R. N., Kauffman, J., & Katz, N. P. (2000). Characteristics of methadone maintenance patients with chronic pain. *Journal of Pain and Symptom Management, 19*(1), 53–62.

Jasinski, D. R. (1991). History of abuse liability testing in humans. *British Journal of Addiction, 86*(12), 1559–1562.

Koob, G. F., & Le Moal, M. (1997). Drug abuse: Hedonic homeostatic dysregulation. *Science, 278*(5335), 52–58.

Koppert, W., Angst, M., Alsheimer, M., Sittl, R., Albrecht, S., Schuttler, J., & Schmelz, M. (2003). Naloxone provokes similar pain facilitation as observed after short-term infusion of remifentanil in humans. *Pain, 106*(1–2), 91–99.

Li, X., Angst, M. S., & Clark, J. D. (2001). A murine model of opioid-induced hyperalgesia. *Brain Research. Molecular Brain Research, 86*(1–2), 56–62.

Ling, W., Cunningham-Rathner, J., Fradis, J., Torrington, M., Keating, M., & White, J. (2003). *Opioid-induced Hyperalgesia: Effects of Buprenorphine Treatment*. Paper Presented at the Meeting of the College on Problems of Drug Dependence, Miami, FL.

Martin, J. E., & Inglis, J. (1965). Pain tolerance and narcotic addiction. *British Journal of Social and Clinical Psychology, 4*(3), 224–229.

Martin, W. R., Jasinski, D. R., Haertzen, C. A., Kay, D. C., Jones, B. E., Mansky, P. A., & Carpenter, R. W. (1973). Methadone – a reevaluation. *Archives of Genral Psychiatry, 28*(2), 286–295.

McNamee, H. B., Mirin, S. M., Kuehnle, J. C., & Meyer, R. E. (1976). Affective changes in chronic opiate use. *British Journal of Addiction to Alcohol and Other Drugs, 71*(3), 275–280.

Mehta, V., & Langford, R. M. (2006). Acute pain management for opioid dependent patients. *Anaesthesia, 61*(3), 269–276.

Mirin, S. M., Meyer, R. E., & McNamee, H. B. (1976a). Psychopathology and mood during heroin use: Acute vs chronic effects. *Archives of General Psychiatry, 33*(12), 1503–1508.

Mirin, S. M., Meyer, R. E., McNamee, H. B., & McDougle, M. (1976b). Psychopathology, craving, and mood during heroin acquisition: An experimental study. *The International Journal of the Addictions, 11*(3), 525–544.

Mitchell, T. B., White, J. M., Somogyi, A. A., & Bochner, F. (2006). Switching between methadone and morphine for maintenance treatment of opioid dependence: Impact on pain sensitivity and mood status. *American Journal on Addictions, 15*(4), 311–315.

Mitra, S., & Sinatra, R. S. (2004). Perioperative management of acute pain in the opioid-dependent patient. *Anesthesiology, 101*(1), 212–227.

Newcombe, D. A., Bochner, F., White, J. M., & Somogyi, A. A. (2004). Evaluation of levo-alpha-acetylmethdol (LAAM) as an alternative treatment for methadone maintenance patients who regularly experience withdrawal: A pharmacokinetic and pharmacodynamic analysis. *Drug and Alcohol Dependence, 76*(1), 63–72.

Panksepp, J. (2003). Neuroscience. Feeling the pain of social loss. *Science, 302*(5643), 237–239.

Porreca, F., Ossipov, M. H., & Gebhart, G. F. (2002). Chronic pain and medullary descending facilitation. *Trends in Neuroscience, 25*(6), 319–325.

Price, B. B., Moran, S., Crunican, M. A., Rothenberg, S., & Cutter, H. S. (1975). Mood, primary heroin withdrawal, and acute methadone administration. *The International Journal of the Addictions, 10*(4), 613–631.

Pud, D., Cohen, D., Lawental, E., & Eisenberg, E. (2006). Opioids and abnormal pain perception: New evidence from a study of chronic opioid addicts and healthy subjects. *Drug and Alcohol Dependence, 82*(3), 218–223.

Rosenblum, A., Joseph, H., Fong, C., Kipnis, S., Cleland, C., & Portenoy, R. K. (2003). Prevalence and characteristics of chronic pain among chemically dependent patients in methadone maintenance and residential treatment facilities. *The Journal of the American Medical Association, 289*(18), 2370–2308.

Sapira, J. D. (1968). The narcotic addict as a medical patient. *American Journal of Medicine, 45*(4), 555–588.

Schall, U., Katta, T., Pries, E., Klöppel, A., & Gastpar, M. (1996). Pain perception of intravenous heroin users on maintenance therapy with levomethadone. *Pharmacopsychiatry, 29*(5), 176–179.

Vanderah, T. W., Gardell, L. R., Burgess, S. E., Ibrahim, M., Dogrul, A., Zhong, C. M., Zhang, E. T., Malan, T. P., Jr., Ossipov, M. H., Lai, J., & Porreca, F. (2000). Dynorphin promotes abnormal pain and spinal opioid antinociceptive tolerance. *Journal of Neuroscience, 20*(18), 7074–7079.

Vanderah, T. W., Suenaga, N. M., Ossipov, M. H., Malan, T. P., Jr., Lai, J., & Porreca, F. (2001). Tonic descending facilitation from the rostral ventromedial medulla mediates opioid-induced abnormal pain and antinociceptive tolerance. *Journal of Neuroscience, 21*(1), 279–286.

Verhaak, P. F., Kerssens, J. J., Dekker, J., Sorbi, M. J., & Bensing, J. M. (1998). Prevalence of chronic benign pain disorder among adults: A review of the literature. *Pain, 77*(3), 231–239.

Imbalance between Neuroexcitatory and Neuroinhibitory Amino Acids causes Craving for Ethanol: From Animal to Human being Studies

Philippe De Witte

UCL – Biologie du Comportement, Place Croix du Sud,
1-bte 10, B-1348 Louvain-la-Neuve, Belgium. dewitte@uclouvain.be

Abstract: The hypofunction of $GABA_A$ receptors and enhanced function of NMDA receptors are suggested to be responsible for ethanol withdrawal symptoms. Because multiple and repeated periods of chronic ethanol consumption and withdrawal often occur in alcohol abusers, animal studies on the changes in glutamate following chronic ethanol treatment (CET) that is interrupted by repeated ethanol withdrawal episodes may be of clinical relevance for the development of treatment strategies. The elevated glutamate released in the hippocampus during the first cycle of ethanol withdrawal episode was exacerbated in subsequent withdrawal episodes. Acamprosate, a drug used during human alcohol detoxification, is able to completely block the glutamate increase observed during the first as well as the third withdrawal of ethanol.

When repeated ethanol injections were cued with a vinegar stimulus that had previously been associated with the same ethanol injection, a significant increase in glutamate microdialysate content was assayed. By comparison, a saline injection had no effect in rats naïve for ethanol as well as in rats receiving ethanol injections but not paired with the cue. It appears probable that these conditioned responses by extracellular glutamate concentrations may participate in the environmental cue–induced conditioned cravings for ethanol that are thought to be related to the high frequency of relapse in detoxified alcoholics.

INTRODUCTION

There is increasing evidence to suggest that ethanol may affect the central nervous system (CNS) by interfering with amino acid neurotransmitter systems. Among the amino acid neurotransmitter systems are excitatory amino acids (aspartate and glutamate) that activate postsynaptic cells and the inhibitory amino acids (GABA and taurine) that depress the activity of the postsynaptic cells. Glutamate is the major neuroexcitatory amino acid in the CNS. It activates receptors, which are gated to ion channels, or activates proteins mediating a second messenger. This neurotransmitter has been reported to play an important role in alcoholism (Tsai, Gastfriend, & Coyle, 1995; Tsai et al., 1998). Glutamate receptors in the mammalian CNS are divided into ionotropic (NMDA, kainate, and AMPA) and metabotropic receptors.

The NMDA receptor, which is coupled to a voltage–sensitive ion channel, is permeable to calcium and monovalent cations Na^+ and K^+, and has been implicated in many physiological and pathological processes, including synaptic plasticity, learning and memory, epileptiform seizures, and neurotoxicity.

EFFECTS OF ETHANOL ON GLUTAMATE

ACUTE EFFECT OF ETHANOL

A decrease in glutamate extracellular striatal concentration occurred in an in vivo microdialysis study after administration of 2 g/kg ethanol (Carboni et al., 1993), while another microdialysis study showed a biphasic response with either 0.5 (increase) or 2 g/kg (decrease) ethanol on the glutamate release in both hippocampus and nucleus accumbens regions (Moghaddam & Bolinao, 1994). Ethanol appears to be less potent in inhibiting the non–NMDA ionotropic glutamate receptors (Hoffman, Moses, & Tabakoff, 1989; Lovinger, White, & Weight, 1989). Alteration in NMDA receptor function during development can lead to severe and potentially permanent brain dysfunction (Weaver et al., 1993) as well as ethanol–presented long-term potentiation (LTP), which is a process that underlies learning (Maren & Baudry, 1995), particularly in the hippocampus (Morissett & Swartzwelder, 1993).

CHRONIC EFFECT OF ETHANOL

Chronic ethanol intoxication results in an up-regulation of NMDA receptor number and function caused by the physiological response to the depressant effects of ethanol (Chandler et al., 1993; Michaelis et al., 1990; Snell, Tabakoff, & Hoffman, 1993; Trujillo and Akil, 1995; Whittington, Lambert, & Little, 1995). Western blot analysis indicates that chronic ethanol treatment (CET) up-regulates NMDA receptor subunits NR1, NR2A, and NR2B in the rat cerebral cortex and hippocampus; these returned to almost control levels 48 h after the last dose of ethanol administration (Kalluri, Mehta, & Ticku, 1998). CET enhances NMDA-stimulated, but not kainate-stimulated, intracellular calcium levels. Seven days after treatment with 100 mM ethanol, the magnitude of cell death mediated by NMDA receptors, but not AMPA, increases (Smothers, Mrotek, & Lovinger, 1997). Up-regulation of the NMDA receptors is thus a consequence of a physiological response to the depressant effects of ethanol (Figure 1).

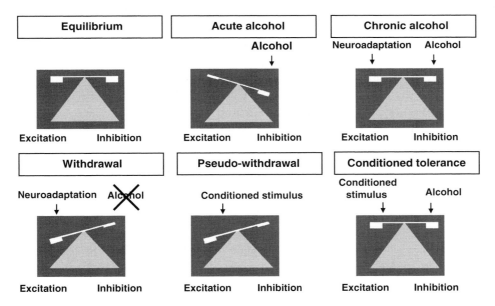

Figure 1   This figure represents the brain (triangle) submitted by different excitation and inhibition processes maintaining the brain in a regular equilibrium. Acute alcohol disrupts the equilibrium by exaggerating the inhibitory processes (mainly GABA and taurine). Chronic alcohol consumption induces neuroadaptation (up-regulation of glutamate) to counteract the inhibitory action of alcohol. The withdrawal of alcohol leads the brain in an overexcitation state due to the excess of neuroadaptative excitatory processes. Conditioned stimulus alone may lead the brain to a state similar to withdrawal state called as mini-withdrawal. Conditioned tolerance may also occur through the presence of alcohol together with conditioned stimulus.

ETHANOL WITHDRAWAL

Cessation of CET leads to seizures, hyperexcitability, and ethanol withdrawal. Animal studies have revealed that overactivation of glutamate receptors contribute to the generation of these symptoms (Grant et al., 1990; Gulya et al., 1991) and could lead to excitotoxicity death (Davidson, Shanley, & Wilce, 1995; Iorio, Tabakoff, & Hoffman, 1993). Human studies have indicated that excitatory neurotransmitters were elevated in the cerebrospinal fluid of alcohol-dependent patients and a positive correlation between excitatory neurotransmitters and oxidative markers has been observed (Tsai & Coyle, 1998).

Recent microdialysis studies show that ethanol withdrawal is associated with increases in glutamate in the striatum (Rossetti & Carboni, 1995), the nucleus accumbens (Dahchour, Quertemont, & De Witte, 1996), and hippo campus (Dahchour & De Witte, 1998) approximately 5–8h after cessation of ethanol inhalation, with a maximal value at 12h. In this last experiment, groups of rats were maintained in an isolated plastic chamber ($160 \times 60 \times 60$ cm^3) in an alcohol containing atmosphere with a mixture of alcohol and air pulsed into the chamber via a mixing system, allowing the quantity of alcohol to be increased every 2 days during the whole 4-week experimental procedure. A control group received only air for the same period, while in an isolated plastic chamber. Blood alcohol levels were measured three times per week and at the beginning of the ethanol withdrawal, 12 and 24h later (Table 1). Blood samples were taken from the tail and the blood ethanol levels were assayed by the alcohol dehydrogenase method (Boehringer Mannheim, Germany).

During the third week, rats were removed from the chamber for surgery. Chloral hydrate (400mg/kg i.p.) was used as an anesthetic, and a guide cannula was implanted 1mm above the targeted area (i.e., nucleus accumbens, hippocampus, or amygdale), using standard stereotaxic techniques. The rats were then allowed to recover for 1 day before returning back to the appropriate environment within the chambers for a further week. After 4 weeks of chronic

Table 1

Blood Alcohol Levels for the 12 and 24h Ethanol Withdrawal Following the Third Withdrawal of a Group of 10 Rats

Blood alcohol level (g/l) Time after withdrawal (h)	W1	W2	W3
0	2.19 ± 0.10	1.61 ± 0.26	1.86 ± 0.09
12	1.24 ± 0.11	0.96 ± 0.11	1.14 ± 0.12
24	0.01 ± 0.001	Non detectable	Non detectable
Weight (g)	350 ± 27		327 ± 16
Liquid intake (ml/day)	23 ± 2		7 ± 2

ethanol administration or air inhalation, the microdialysis experiments commenced by inserting the probe into the appropriate brain region. Samples were
collected every 20 min during the first 12 h after chronic ethanol cessation, and
were analyzed by HPLC with electrochemical detection and OPA/BME column
derivatization. These experiments were approved by the Belgian governmental
agency under the authorization LA1220028 as well as the European Communities
Council Directive concerning the use of laboratory animals. The amino acids
concentration in the outflow was assayed by HPLC and the relative concentration
calculated as "recovery in vitro $= C_{out}/C_{in}$". The mean in vitro recovery for the
microdialysis probe was 13.72F1 ± 42% for glutamate. Data were represented as
means ± SEM and analyzed by analysis of variance (ANOVA) with repeated
measures followed by the Fisher's Least Significance Difference Test to determine
statistical significance.

The basal concentration of glutamate following correction for in vitro
recovery detected no significant changes after 4 weeks of chronic alcohol intoxication (Figure 2). On the contrary, glutamate concentration increased significantly at 6 h after alcohol withdrawal to approximately fourfold by 12 h after
withdrawal (Figure 3). The increase of glutamate release during the initial ethanol
withdrawal period can be explained in terms of known adaptations that occur
during CET (Figure 1). During chronic ethanol intoxication, the brain shows a
multitude of cellular adaptations that include the activation of voltage-sensitive
Ca^{++} (Lynch & Littleton, 1983) as well as changes in the sensitivity of NMDA
receptors (Davidson, Wilce, & Shanley, 1993), which causes enhanced release of
glutamate from neuronal synapses and up-regulation in vivo of both NMDA
receptors (Gulya et al., 1991) and dihydropyridine binding sites (Greenberg,
Carpenter, & Messing, 1987; Messing et al., 1986).

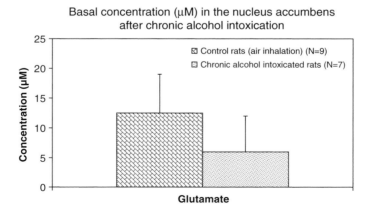

Figure 2 Basal concentration (μM) in the nucleus accumbens of control rats and of chronic alcohol
intoxicated rats.

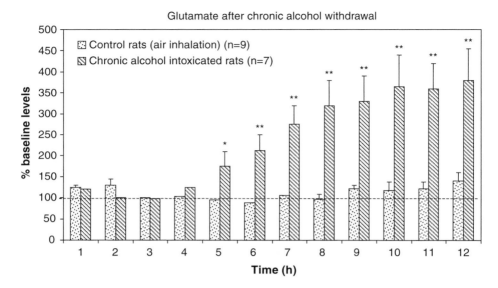

Figure 3 Percentage change in glutamate microdialysate over 12 h in control rats and in chronic alcohol intoxicated rats during the first withdrawal. Results are presented as percent of baseline level ± SEM. $^*p < 0.05$; $^{**}p < 0.01$.

When chronic ethanol intoxication ceases, the ethanol withdrawal syndrome commences with symptoms, such as hyperexcitability and sometimes even seizures and convulsions, which are present particularly during the initial stages of withdrawal, corresponding to the increased release of glutamate. The activation of glutamate release may be a consequence of processes related to increased calcium released in neurons, which in turn cause protein kinase C activation, free radical generation, and NO production. Such processes may activate glutamate release causing neurotoxicity during ethanol withdrawal.

The excitatory amino acid plasma levels are increased in alcohol-dependent patients (Tsai et al., 1998; Ward et al., 1999) and show positive correlations with hepatic damage (Ward et al., 1999) and oxidative stress (Tsai et al., 1998).

MULTIPLE ETHANOL WITHDRAWAL

Because multiple and repeated periods of chronic ethanol consumption and withdrawal often occur in alcohol abusers, the study in animal models of the glutamate changes following CET interrupted by repeated ethanol withdrawal episodes will be of clinical relevance for the development of treatment strategies. The hippocampus could be expected to play an important role during detoxification because this brain region has been implicated in anxiety and seizures (Gray, 1982), which are typically associated with detoxification. Microdialysis experiments were carried out during the 24h withdrawal periods. The first group (control group) was placed in the air chamber for 4 weeks and the microdialysis experiment was performed. The second group was also withdrawn from alcohol for 24h but without performing the microdialysis experiment. The same group was placed back into the chamber for a fifth week of CET before another 24h withdrawal with no microdialysis, then back into the chamber for a sixth week of CET before the third withdrawal period. During this last withdrawal period (W3), the microdialysis experiment was performed (Figure 4). The dramatic increase in glutamate levels in the microdialysate during the first ethanol withdrawal period (Dahchour et al., 1996) is now extended to repeated and alternate cycles of CET and withdrawal. There have been many previous behavioral investigations of the effects of repeated ethanol withdrawal on the severity of the withdrawal episodes and hypermotility in rats (Dahchour & De Witte, 1999; Poldrugo & Snead, 1984; Veatch & Gonzalez, 1996) and mice (Becker, Diaz-Granados, & Hale, 1997; Becker & Hale, 1993). These studies have reported an increase in seizure scores (Becker et al., 1997), seizure sensitivity (McCown & Breese, 1990), and electrographic activity (Veatch & Gonzalez, 1996). The increased glutamate levels during the first cycle of withdrawal, when compared to its baseline values, supports our previous studies using microdialysis of the nucleus accumbens (Dahchour et al., 1996, 1998). It is noteworthy that during the third cycle of ethanol withdrawal, the glutamate increase was much higher than during the first episode of withdrawal. The initial increased release of glutamate

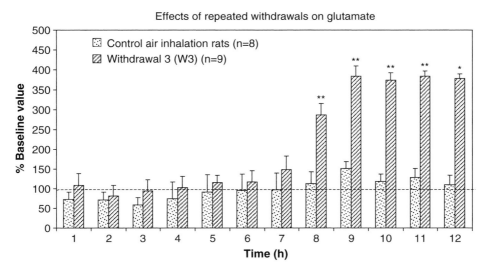

Figure 4   Percentage change in glutamate microdialysate over 12h in control rats and in chronic alcohol intoxicated rats during the third withdrawal. Results are presented as percent of baseline level ± SEM. $^*p < 0.05$; $^{**}p < 0.01$.

during the first cycle of withdrawal could thus have caused neuronal sensitization to glutamate receptor activation, probably by exacerbating Ca^{++} entry into neurons through glutamate-controlled voltage-sensitive channels.

ACAMPROSATE AND REPEATED ETHANOL WITHDRAWAL

Pharmacological agents for the treatment of alcoholism are an important part of the treatment plan for dependent chronic alcohol abusers that includes substantial education, psychological therapy, and social support. Many drugs have been developed during the last decade to combat the side effects induced by chronic alcohol abuse, such as alcohol withdrawal, craving, and relapse related to alcohol abuse, as well as drugs to decrease alcohol intake. Among the drugs currently used for the treatment of alcoholism, acamprosate, a homotaurine derivative, has been shown to be beneficial. Its passage through the blood–brain barrier is facilitated by the acetylation of amine function and calcium salification. Acamprosate (i.e., calcium–acetyl homotaurinate) has been shown to be effective in attenuating relapse in human alcoholics. Its efficacy has been proven in several basic (animal research) and clinical trials and registered in most European countries.

The purpose of the following study was to combine a chronic oral acamprosate treatment, as it was delivered to human beings, with a chronic ethanol exposure interrupted by repeated withdrawals, on extracellular glutamate within the hippocampus of freely moving rats by the microdialysis technique. The dosage of acamprosate, 400 mg/kg/day, as well as pulmonary alcohol exposure repeatedly interrupted by withdrawals, precisely followed the same experimental designs used in previous experiments (Dahchour & De Witte, 1999, 2003a, 2003b; Dahchour et al., 1998). The acamprosate treatment started the first day of the introduction of animals to the plastic chamber and ended just before starting the microdialysis. The dosage of acamprosate (400 mg/kg/day) was chosen because of the effectiveness of this dosage to decrease preference and dependence for alcohol intake in the rat laboratory (Dahchour et al., 1998; Spanagel et al., 1996). As Figure 5 shows, acamprosate is able to modulate the glutamatergic neurotransmission in the hippocampus. The ability of acamprosate to block the brain glutamate increase during ethanol withdrawal represents an important finding for the therapeutic treatment of alcoholism. Furthermore, by blocking the glutamate exacerbation after repeated withdrawal, excitotoxicity could also be reduced by acamprosate.

Acamprosate is extremely safe, well tolerated by patients and is not an antidepressant, nor a neuroleptic, nor a tranquilizer (Nalpas et al., 1990) and could thus be an interesting adjuvant for maintaining abstinence in detoxified alcoholics.

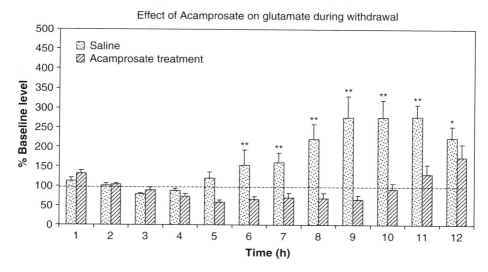

Figure 5 Percentage change in glutamate microdialysate over 12h in control rats and in chronic alcohol intoxicated rats treated with acamprosate during the third withdrawal. Results are presented as percent of baseline level ± SEM. $^*p < 0.05$; $^{**}p < 0.01$.

CONDITIONING ASSOCIATED WITH ETHANOL

Excitatory amino acids neurotransmission has been implicated in learning associations between external stimuli and intrinsic reward value, such that it may play a key role in conditioned drug effects. The amygdala is a key component of the limbic system, and is involved in emotion, motivation, learning, and memory (Figure 6). The amygdaloid complex receives sensory information from other brain regions, such as visually related areas, olfactory information, and taste. Much of the sensory information of the amygdala is directed to the lateral nucleus, which has intrinsic projections to the basal nucleus, periamygdaloid cortex, nucleus accumbens, and other regions (Amaral et al., 1992).

According to drug conditioning theory, a stimulus which is repeatedly associated with drugs of abuse may further elicit actions originally induced by the drug administration and is referred to as a conditional stimulus (CS; Stewart, 1992). Two types of drug–conditioned effects have been described (O'Brien et al., 1992): the drug–like conditioned responses and the drug–opposite conditioned responses.

In the drug–like conditioned responses, the CS, after repeated pairings, can produce by itself comparable effects previously induced by the drug. For example, the environmental cues associated with the pleasurable effects of certain drugs may further elicit positive affects by themselves. This is the principle of the place

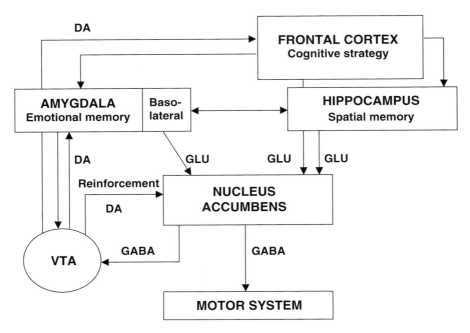

Figure 6 Diagram drawing the relationships existing between different brain structures, i.e., frontal cortex elaborating the cognitive strategy of behaviors, amygdala processing affective memory, hippocampus dealing with spatial memory, nucleus accumbens, and ventral tegmental area (VTA) reinforcing the reward loop of behaviors. It must be noted that the ascending pathways were mainly dopaminergic (DA) while the descending pathways were mainly glutamatergic (GLU) and gabaergic (GABA).

conditioning studies in which a particular environment is repeatedly paired with the effects of a drug. Subsequently, the experimental animals are tested for their place preference, that is, that they will spend more time in the environment paired with a drug that possesses rewarding effects (Reid et al., 1985).

On the other hand, repetitive association of a stimulus with a drug may also produce drug-opposite conditioned responses. In this case, it is the adaptation response of the organism that becomes conditioned to the CS, which therefore leads to drug-opposite responses. This type of drug-conditioned effect was most clearly demonstrated in the phenomenon of "environment-dependent tolerance" in which greatest tolerance to the drug effect was observed in an environment which was repeatedly associated with the drug administration (Littleton, al-Qatari, & Little, 1996; Siegel, 1987). In the absence of drug administration after the presentation of the CS, the conditioned adaptive response induced by the stimulus may contribute to the relapse observed in detoxified drug users by unbalancing the brain toward the opposite direction of the acute drug effects (Figure 1). Such conditioned drug effects have been demonstrated to a wide range of drugs, which include alcohol. In particular, the phenomenon of environment-dependent toler-ance has been shown in various ethanol effects, such as hypothermic, sedative, and antinociceptive effects (Le, Khanna, & Kalant, 1987; Mansfield & Cunningham, 1980; Siegel, 1987; Tiffany, Mc Cal, & Maude-Griffin, 1987).

Although the biochemical mechanisms underlying such ethanol-conditioned effects remain unknown, these must be very rapid to oppose ethanol effects almost immediately after administration. An increased release of the excitatory amino acid glutamate could be one of the biochemical mechanisms responsible for the environment-dependent tolerance to ethanol.

Indeed, such an increased release would compensate the ethanol depressant effect on brain cells and, more precisely, the inhibitory effect of acute ethanol on excitatory amino acid receptors, such as NMDA receptors (Lovinger, 1996).

We thus investigate by the in vivo microdialysis technique, the effects of a stimulus repeatedly associated with acute ethanol injections (2 g/kg i.p.) on the basolateral amygdale extracellular concentration of glutamate. During the 2-week period of the experiment, the animals were daily conditioned to associate vinegar odor, 5 ml vinegar impregnated into tissue paper contained within a jar placed in the cage immediately after the intraperitoneal injection of either 2 g/kg body weight ethanol (15% v/v, in 0.9% saline) or equivalent volume of saline (0.9%), and removed 20 min later. Following the injection, dialysate samples were collected every 20 min for 5 h.

Six groups of rats were utilized for the microdialysis experiment:

1. A control group which had been conditioned to associate vinegar odor with i.p. injections of saline and then injected with saline during microdialysis.
2. Another group was conditioned with saline and then injected with ethanol (2 g/kg, i.p.) during the microdialysis procedure (pseudo-conditioned group). This experimental group assessed the effects of acute ethanol on the microdialysate glutamate content of rats which had been daily conditioned with another substance, e.g., saline. For these animals, the vinegar cue was never associated with ethanol injection.
3. Another group which had been conditioned with ethanol (2 g/kg, i.p.) was also administered with ethanol (2 g/kg, i.p.) during the microdialysis experiment (ethanol-cued group). This group assessed the effects of ethanol on the microdialysate glutamate content of rat repeatedly ethanol-injected in a conditioning paradigm.
4. A fourth group was conditioned with ethanol (2 g/kg, i.p.) and was injected with saline during the microdialysis experiment (conditioned stimulus group). This ethanol-conditioned group was utilized to assess the effect of an ethanol-associated stimulus on the microdialysate glutamate content of conditioned rats free of ethanol.

5. A fifth group was daily conditioned to associate vinegar odor with saline injections but was also daily administered with ethanol (2 g/kg, i.p.) 8 h apart (unpaired group). During the microdialysis, these rats received a saline injection combined with the vinegar cue. This impaired control group was matched for prior exposure to ethanol with the ethanol-conditioned experimental groups such that non–associative effects of repeated ethanol exposures can be distinguished from learned conditioning effects.

   Each of the injections during these microdialysis experiments was combined with the presentation of the vinegar stimulus.

6. Finally, an ethanol non-cued group of rats was added to clarify the effects of repeated ethanol injection. This group was daily conditioned with ethanol (2 g/kg, i.p.) but in the absence of the vinegar cue. Omitting the explicit ethanol-conditioned stimulus, i.e. vinegar cue, might be expected to decrease the conditioned responses of the brain but to leave intact the direct effects of the ethanol administration on glutamate content which could be different after period exposure to ethanol (eight daily injections) by comparison to naïve rats.

In ethanol-naive rats (pseudo-conditioned group), there was no change in the glutamate microdialysate content of the basolateral amygdala after an acute 2 g/kg ethanol injection. However, when repeated ethanol injections were cued with a vinegar stimulus which had previously been associated with the same ethanol injection (ethanol-cued group), a significant increase in glutamate microdialysate content was assayed which lasted for 220 min after the injection (Figure 7). Furthermore, when the vinegar cue was omitted (ethanol non-cued group), the ethanol injection induced no changes in glutamate microdialysate content in rats which had been previously ethanol conditioned. By comparison, saline injection had no effect on extracellular glutamate concentration in rats naive for ethanol (control group) or in rats daily administered with repeated ethanol injections (conditioned stimulus group and impaired group).

The effects of conditioning with ethanol combined with a cue (vinegar odor) clearly identified that when the cue was presented together with an acute injection of ethanol to rats which had been conditioned with ethanol, a long-lasting, significant increase in glutamate was assayed. Previous studies have mainly focused on the release of dopamine after conditioning of the rats with various excitatory drugs, such as amphetamine, for 7 days (Dietze & Kuschinsky, 1994), but no other neurotransmitters were assayed.

Our results show that a significant glutamate increase was assayed when the ethanol-conditioned cue was combined with ethanol injection, but not when the ethanol-conditioned cue was given with saline injection or when ethanol was injected without the ethanol cue. This latter result excludes the

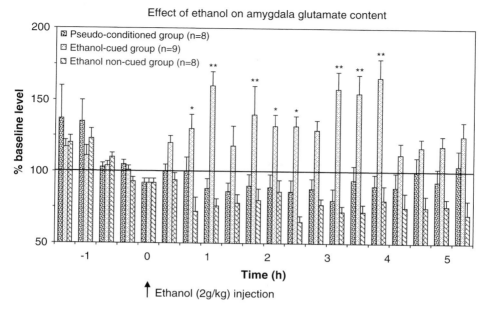

Figure 7   Time course for the percentage of change in glutamate content of the microdialysate from the basolateral amygdala before and after an IP ethanol (2 g/kg, body weight) injection combined with vinegar odor or not in three groups of rats, the pseudo-conditioned group, the ethanol-cued group, and the ethanol non-cued group. The vinegar odor had no particular significance for the saline-conditioned group (pseudo-conditioned group) in contrast to the ethanol-conditioned rats (ethanol-cued group) which had associated the vinegar odor with the ethanol effects. Data are expressed as mean ($\pm$ SEM) percentage of baseline level, which was calculated for each rat by averaging the concentration of the three sample values before injection. $^*p < 0.05$; $^{**}p < 0.01$ relative to respective baseline level.

possibility that the change in glutamate content was simply caused by alcohol sensitization after repeated exposures. This increase in glutamate would indicate a compensatory response by the amygdala to oppose the inhibitory effects of the acute ethanol dose of 2 g/kg, which stimulates gabaergic neurotransmission (Nevo & Hamon, 1995; Ollat, Parvez, & Parvez, 1988). However, the ethanol-conditioned stimulus alone without ethanol administration was insufficient to induce an increase in the glutamate microdialysate content from the amygdala. Indeed, drug effects are typically signaled by compound stimuli, which are constituted by multiple cues that accompany drug administration in addition to explicitly drugpaired stimulus, such as the vinegar cue in the present experiments. For example, handling the animal or injecting it with a hypodermic needle, also called the injection ritual, provides cues for the drug effects. Furthermore, the early interceptive affects of the drugs inevitably signal its later effects such that the drug alone can serve as a cue for itself. It has also been shown that the absence of a part of these multiple cues decreases the probability of observing the conditioned response (Siegel, 1989).

In the present experiment, there is no doubt that the early peripheral effects of ethanol signal its later central effects to a similar extent as the explicitly associated vinegar cue. This could explain why both the animals from the conditioned stimulus which were confronted by the ethanol-conditioned vinegar stimulus but without ethanol injection, and those of the ethanol non-cued group which were ethanol administered in the absence of the vinegar cue failed to show an increase in their glutamate microdialysate content, in contrast to the rats of the ethanol-cued group which received ethanol challenge together with the vinegar cue. It thus appears probable that the conditioned glutamate increase may participate in the environmental cue-induced conditioned cravings for ethanol which are thought to be related to the frequent relapse in detoxified alcoholics.

EXCITATORY AMINO ACIDS AND ETHANOL IN HUMANS

CEREBRAL EXCITATORY DURING WITHDRAWAL

From animal studies, the short and longer term effects of alcohol may be described as follows:

1. Acute ethanol exposure reduces the activity of the excitatory NMDA receptor and VOCC neurotransmitter system and increases the inhibitory action of the GABA receptor neurotransmitter system.
2. Chronic ethanol exposure results in multiple adaptive responses, up-regulation of the excitatory system, and down-regulation of the inhibitory system.
3. The adaptive responses can become conditioned to the behavior and environment associated with the ethanol exposure.
4. Acute ethanol withdrawal results in a hyperactivity state due to removal of inhibition of the up-regulated system.

During alcohol withdrawal, the increase in neuronal excitatory can be measured directly by EEG.

Among the various EEG parameters, the alpha slow wave index (ASI) is a well-validated, simple index of cerebral excitability (Matejcek, 1982). A recent study has compared the evolution of the ASI in alcohol-dependent subjects undergoing detoxifications (Boeijinga et al., 2004). ASI was measured in 12 subjects fulfilling DSM-IV criteria for alcohol dependence who were planning an acute detoxification for which benzodiazepine use was not anticipated to be necessary. ASI was estimated before and at 3 time points after the start of the detoxification. The ASI increased 2 days after detoxification compared to baseline and continued to increase over the following 14 days, indicating an increase in cerebral excitability. Interestingly, the same study, another group of 12 subjects fulfilling the same criteria were treated with acamprosate (2 g/day) for 8 days before and 15 days after stopping alcohol consumption. In the acamprosate treated group of subjects, the ASI decreased, indicating a more rapid return to normal levels of cerebral excitability in this latter group. The effect was most pronounced in the left parietotemporal regions and, to a lesser extent, in the contiguous anterior and posterior regions and the contralateral parietotemporal cortex (Figure 8).

This effect of reduced cerebral excitability induced by acamprosate was confirmed by a study using magnetic resonance imaging (MRI). In this study, the effect of acamprosate on central glutamatergic function addressed by MRI (Bolo et al., 1998) was performed on eight healthy male volunteers participating in a random seal, double-blind, crossover, placebo-controlled study. All subjects included in the study had a negative urine test result for the presence of opioids, cocaine,

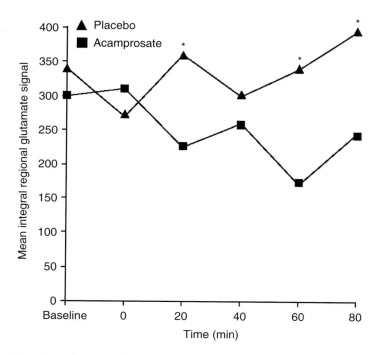

Figure 8   Mean integral regional glutamate signal determined by magnetic resonance spectroscopy in subjects receiving placebo or intravenous acamprosate (15 mg/kg) (reproduced with permission from Bolo et al., 1998). *Indicates a significant difference between the placebo and acamprosate groups ($p < 0.05$).

cannabis, and benzodiazepines; were HIV, HVC, and HbS negative, had clinically relevant blood test disturbance, and had a weight within 10% of the standard weight. Acamprosate was administered intravenously at a dose of 15 mg/kg
which had been shown previously to provide similar plasma concentrations to the
standard therapeutic oral dosage of 2 g/day.

Spectra were acquired using spin-echo volume-selective localized spectroscopy before drug administration and every 20 min thereafter. Compared
with placebo, the median integral values for the N-acetylaspartate and glutamate signal were decreased from 20 min after the infusion began. These data are
consistent with the preclinical data obtained using microdialysis in rats, which
showed that acamprosate reduced the extracellular concentrations of glutamate
in the brain.

ALCOHOL WITHDRAWAL AS A NEUROTOXIC EVENT

Acute effects of ethanol disrupt glutamatergic neurotransmission by reducing the sensitivity of the NMDA receptor (Lovinger, 1993). Prolonged inhibition
of NMDA receptors by ethanol induces their up-regulation. When chronic alcohol consumption ceased, the up-regulation combined with an increased release
of excitatory amino acids can result in acute excitatory (Tsai & Coyle, 1998).
Neurobiological effects of alcohol on the brain, such as intoxication, withdrawal
symptoms, and Wermicke–Korsakoff syndrome can be understood as consequences of effects of ethanol on the glutamatergic system. Specifically, our animal
studies demonstrated that ethanol withdrawal is associated with increased extracellular glutamate. Moderate to high levels of glutamate promote the production
of hydroxyl radicals (Ferger et al., 1998). It has been reported that reactive oxygen species were able to present astrocytic glutamate uptake mechanisms through
a direct action on the transporter protein (Berman & Hastings, 1997) and thereby
perpetuate oxidate damage. The excessive generation of reactive oxygen species
in the brain, an environment where there is comparatively low antioxidant and
cytoprotection protection, despite the high oxygen metabolism, may contribute
to the pathogenesis of alcoholic brain disease (Pratt et al., 1990). The in vivo
measurement of highly reactive oxygen species such as hydroxyl radicals particularly in brain is very difficult. However, the salicylate trap method, which is based
on the ability of $°OH$ to attack the benzene ring of the aromatic molecule, has
been proposed as a sensitive method for the identification and quantification of
hydroxyl radical formation in a variety of clinical diseases (Halliwell, Kaur, &
Ingelman-Sunberg, 1991). In vivo, the drug salicylate will react with hydroxyl
radicals to form 2,3-DHBA, which is not CYP2E1 dependent (Dupont et al.,
1999). An enhanced oxidative stress occurred during the ethanol withdrawal
stages that was exemplified by the elevated 2,3-DHBA in the hippocampus

microdialysate commencing approximately 3h after alcohol withdrawal and maintained for a further 5h (Figure 9) (Dahchour et al., 2005).

In our previous studies (Dahchour et al., 1998; Dahchour & De Witte, 2003a, 2003b), an increased glutamate release occurred during this time period in this brain region. This set of experiments clearly demonstrate that ethanol withdrawal causes excessive damage in the brain, primarily due to the increased fluxes of calcium, causing increased glutamate release and oxidative damage as exemplified by enhanced 2,3-DHBA in the hippocampus microdialysate.

The hippocampus, a neural structure rich in excitatory amino acids projections, appeared thus to be particularly sensitive to the neurotoxic effects after intermittent ethanol exposures (Lundqvist et al., 1994, 1995) resulting in memory impairments in rats (Franke et al., 1997). Hippocampus lesions seem to be due to both excitatory (Davidson et al., 1993; Sepulveda et al., 1995) and glucocorticoids (Elliot & Sapolsky, 1992; Yusim et al., 2000).

While alcohol-induced oxidative stress may cause global brain impairment, the frontal lobes can be specially injured by glutamate-mediated excitotoxicity because frontal lobes are particularly rich in excitatory amino acids pathways (Kril et al., 1997). Using neuropsychological and radioisotopical methods, it was

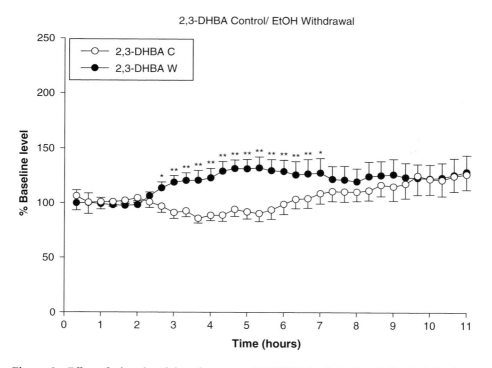

Figure 9 Effect of ethanol withdrawal on mean 2,3-DHBA levels in chronically alcoholized rats compared to non-alcoholized rats.

recently demonstrated that frontal lobe hypometabolism in detoxified alcoholics induced specifically a major impairment of executive functions (Noël et al., 2001a; Schweinburg et al., 2001). It was also demonstrated that the impairment of executive functions (decision-making, flexibility, double-task) was a major clinical issue because it dramatically contributed to the risk of short-term relapse after detoxification (Noël et al., 2001b).

CLINICAL IMPLICATIONS

(1) During ethanol withdrawal, a dramatic increase of glutamate was reported; glutamate is involved in learning, memory, and control of behavior, indicating that every stimulus occurring during withdrawal will be memorized and learned more efficiently. Thus, the withdrawal period seems appropriate for patients to learn new strategies to avoid relapse.

(2) Repeated withdrawals lead to exacerbation of the glutamate increase observed after one withdrawal. Too much glutamate may induce excitotoxicity and may thus induce neuronal swelling followed by neuronal degeneration (Peterson, Neal, & Cotman, 1989; Regan & Choi, 1991). This may be one of the mechanisms by which ethanol induces neuronal and behavioral terato-genecity as particularly observed during foetal development (Tsai et al., 1995).

(3) The withdrawal syndrome in alcohol-dependent patients appeared to be a major stressful event whose intensity increased with repetition of detoxifications according to a kindling process. These phenomena could be at least partly responsible for a progressive increase of the reinforcing power of addictive drugs including alcohol, and for brain damage through an excitotoxic mechanism due to an increasing release of excitatory amino acids during withdrawals. Progressive neurotoxic lesions due to excitotoxicity in the frontal lobe could be a major consequence of repeated alcohol withdrawal, with major neuropsychological deficits negatively influencing the outcome after detoxification.

(4) Conditioning with environmental cues can induce increase in gluta-mate after ethanol injection. This glutamate increase was never observed with ethanol injection alone, meaning that environmentally associated cues with ethanol can be learned and memorized through the glutamate increase and the mini-withdrawal it precipitates. The combination of these influences may induce ethanol relapse. Mini-withdrawal, because the amount of glutamate so released, is less important than the glutamate release during withdrawal follow-ing chronic ethanol exposure.

(5) Acamprosate decreased the elevated glutamate microdialysate levels during repeated withdrawal. This strongly suggests that acamprosate exerts its therapeutic action by acting on the glutamatergic system to restore the imbalance between excitatory and inhibitory amino acids, and may thus possess neuroprotective action.

(6) Alcoholism is a major health problem in which several neurotransmission systems are involved, including the glutamatergic, serotonergic, dopaminergic, and opioidergic systems. Several other neurochemical compounds, such as thyrotropin-releasing and adrenocorticotrophic hormones (Little et al., 1996; Roberts & Koob, 1997), have also been implicated. The most relevant question of such a multifunctional mechanism found in alcoholic disease is whether ethanol acts directly upon neurotransmitters and their receptors or whether it functions indirectly by altering the neurotransmission network equilibrium in the brain. We must also question the classical concept that one neurotransmitter alone could be responsible for one dysfunction. The brain is a network of systems and most neurotransmitters are linked to each other either by the metabolism route (e.g., GABA and glutamate) or by the neuronal connections (e.g., GABA–glutamate–dopamine) and those systems work in equilibrium, meaning that if one system is affected, the imbalance would appear in all systems.

REFERENCES

Amaral, D. G., Price, J. L., Pitkänen, A., & Carmichael, S. T. (1992). Anatomical organization of the primate amygdaloid complex. In J. P. Aggleton (Ed.), *The Amygdala: Neurobiological Aspects of Emotion, Memory, and Mental Dysfunction*, (pp. 1–66). New York: Wiley-Liss.

Becker, H. C., Diaz-Granados, J. L., & Hale, R. L. (1997). Repeated ethanol withdrawal increases the severity and duration of subsequent withdrawal seizures in mice. *Alcohol*, *14*, 319–326.

Becker, H. C., & Hale, R. L. (1993). Repeated episodes of ethanol withdrawal potentiate the severity of subsequent withdrawal seizures: An animal model of alcohol withdrawal "kindling". *Alcoholism: Clinical and Experimental Research*, *17*, 1994–1998.

Berman, S. B., & Hastings, T. G. (1997). Inhibition of glutamate transport in synaptosomes by dopamine oxidation and reactive oxygen species. *Journal of Neurochemistry*, *69*, 1185–1195.

Boeijinga, P. H., Parot, P., Soufflet, L., Landron, F., Danel, T., Gendre, I., Muzet, M., Demazières, A., & Luthringer, R. (2004). Pharmacodynamic effects of acamprosate on markers of cerebral function in alcohol dependent subjects administered as pre-treatment and during alcohol abstinence. *Neuropsychobiology*, *50*(1), 71–77.

Bolo, N., Nedelec, J. F., Muzet, M., De Witte, P., Dahchour, A., Durbin, P., & Macher, J.-P. (1998). Central effects of acamprosate – part 2: Acamprosate modifies the brain in-vivo proton magnetic resonance spectrum in healthy young male volunteers. *Psychiatry Research Neuroimaging*, *82*, 115–127.

Carboni, S., Isola, R., Gessa, G. L., & Rossetti, Z. L. (1993). Ethanol prevents the glutamate release induced by N-methyl-D-aspartate in the rat striatum. *Neuroscience Letters*, *152*, 133–136.

Chandler, L. G., Newson, H., Summer, C., & Crews, F. (1993). Chronic ethanol exposure potentiates NMDA excitotoxicity in cerebral cortical neurons. *Journal of Neurochemistry*, *60*, 1578–1581.

Dahchour, A., & De Witte, P. (1998). Effect of repeated ethanol withdrawal on microdialysate glutamate release in the hippocampus. *Alcoholism: Clinical and Experimental Research*, *22*(A109), 175.

Dahchour, A., & De Witte, P. (1999). Effect of repeated ethanol withdrawal on glutamate microdialysate in the hippocampus. *Alcoholism: Clinical and Experimental Research*, *10*, 1698–1703.

Dahchour, A., & De Witte, P. (2003a). Excitatory amino acid changes during repeated episodes of ethanol withdrawal: An in vivo microdialysis study. *European Journal of Pharmacology*, *459*, 171–178.

Dahchour, A., & De Witte, P. (2003b). Effects of acamprosate on excitatory amino acids during multiple ethanol withdrawal periods. *Alcoholism: Clinical and Experimental Research*, *27*, 465–470.

Dahchour, A., De Witte, P., Bolo, N., Nedelec, J. F., Durbin, P., & Macher, J. P. (1998). Central effect of acamprosate: Part 1. Acamprosate blocks the glutamate increase in the nucleus accumbens microdialysate during ethanol withdrawn rats. *Psychiatry Research Neuroimaging Section*, *82*, 107–114.

Dahchour, A., Lallemand, F., Ward, R. J., & De Witte P. (2005). Production of reactive oxygen species following acute ethanol or acetaldehyde and its reduction by acamprosate in chronically alcoholized rats. *European Journal of Pharmacology*, *520*, 51–58.

Dahchour, A., Quertemont, E., & De Witte, P. (1996). Taurine increases in the nucleus accumbens microdialysate after acute ethanol administration to naïve and chronically alcoholised rats. *Brain Research*, *735*, 9–19.

Davidson, M., Shanley, B., & Wilce, P. (1995). Increased NMDA-induced excitability during ethanol withdrawal: A behavioural and histological study. *Brain Research*, *674*, 91–96.

Davidson, M. D., Wilce, P., & Shanley, B. C. (1993). Increased sensitivity of the hippocampus in ethanol dependent rats to toxic effect of N-methyl-D-aspartic acid in vivo. *Brain Research*, *606*, 5–9.

Dietze, S., & Kuschinsky, K. (1994). Effects of conditioning with D-amphetamine on the extracellular concentration of dopamine and its metabolites in the striatum of behaving rats. *Naunyn-Schmiedeberg's Archive of Pharmacology*, *350*, 22–27.

Dupont, I., Berthou, F., Bedenez, P., Bardou, L., Guirriec, C., Stephan, N., Dreano, Y., & Lucas, D. (1999). Involvement of cytochroms P-450 2E1 and 3A4 in the 5-hydroxylation of salicylate in humans. *Drug Metabolism and Disposition*, *27*, 322–326.

Elliot, E. M., & Sapolsky, R. M. (1992). Corticosterone enhances kainic acid-induced calcium elevation in cultured hippocampal neurons. *Journal of Neurochemistry*, *59*, 1033–1040.

Ferger, B., van Amsterdam, C., Seyfried, C., & Kuschinsky, K. (1998). Effects of α-phenyl-*tert*-butylnitrone and selegiline on hydroxyl free radicals in rat striatum by local application of glutamate. *Journal of Neurochemistry*, *70*, 276–280.

Franke, H., Kittner, H., Berger, P., Wikner, K., & Schramek, J. (1997). The reaction of astrocytes and neurons in the hippocampus of adult rats during chronic ethanol treatment and correlations to behavioral impairments. *Alcohol*, *14*, 445–454.

Grant, K. A., Valverius, P., Hudspith, M., & Tabakoff, B. (1990). Ethanol-withdrawal seizures and the NMDA receptor complex. *European Journal of Pharmacology*, *176*, 289–296.

Gray, J. A. (1982). *The Neuropsychology of Anxiety*. Oxford, UK: Oxford University Press.

Greenberg, D. A., Carpenter, C. L., & Messing, R. O. (1987). Ethanol-induced components of $45Ca^{++}$ uptake in PC 12 cells is sensitive to Ca^{++} channel modulating drugs. *Brain Research*, *410*, 143–146.

Gulya, K., Grant, K. A., Valverius, P., Hoffman, P. L., & Tabakoff, B. (1991). Brain regional specificity and timecourse of changes in the NMDA receptor–ionophore complex during ethanol withdrawal. *Brain Research*, *547*, 129–134.

Halliwell, B., Kaur, H., & Ingelman-Sunberg, M. (1991). Hydroxylation of salicylate as an assay for hydroxyl radicals: A cautionary note. *Free Radical Biology and Medicine*, *10*, 439–441.

Hoffman, P. L., Moses, F., & Tabakoff, B. (1989). Selective inhibition by ethanol of glutamate-stimulated cyclics GMP production in primary cultures of cerebellar granule cells. *Neuropharmacology*, *28*, 1239–1243.

Iorio, K. R., Tabakoff, B., & Hoffman, P. L. (1993). Glutamate-induced neurotoxicity is increased in cerebellar granule cells exposed chronically to ethanol. *European Journal of Pharmacology*, *248*, 209–212.

Kalluri, H. S., Mehta, A. K., & Ticku, M. K. (1998). Up-regulation of NMDA receptor subunits in rat brain following chronic ethanol treatment. *Molecular Brain Research*, *58*, 221–224.

Kril, J. J., Halliday, G. M., Svoboda, M. D., & Cartwright, H. (1997). The cerebral cortex is damaged in chronic alcoholics. *Neuroscience*, *79*, 983–998.

Le, A. D., Khanna, J. M., & Kalant, H. (1987). Role of the Pavlovian conditioning in the development of tolerance and cross-tolerance to the hypothermic effect of ethanol and hydralazine. *Psychopharmacology*, *92*, 210–214.

Little, P. J., Price, R. R., Hinton, R. K., & Kuhn, C. M. (1996). Role of noradrenergic hyperactivity in neonatal opiate abstinence. *Drug and Alcohol Dependence*, *41*, 47–54.

Littleton, J., al-Qatari, M., & Little, H. (1996). The neurobiology of craving: Potential mechanisms for acamprosate. In M. Soyka (Ed.), *Acamprosate in Relapse Prevention of Alcoholism*, (pp. 27–76). Munich, Germany: Springer.

Lovinger, D. M. (1993). Excitotoxicity and alcohol-related brain damage. *Alcoholism: Clinical and Experimental Research*, *17*, 19–27.

Lovinger, D. M. (1996). Ethanol and the NMDA receptor: Implications for intoxication, tolerance, dependence, and alcoholic brain damage. In M. Soyka (Ed.), *Acamprosate in Relapse Prevention of Alcoholism*, (pp. 1–26). Munich, Germany: Springer.

Lovinger, D. M., White, G., & Weight, F. F. (1989). Ethanol inhibits NMDA-activated ion current in hippocampal neurons. *Science*, *243*, 1721–1724.

Lundqvist, C., Alling, C., Knoth, R., & Volk, B. (1995). Intermittent ethanol exposure of adults rats: Hippocampal cell loss after one month of treatment. *Alcohol and Alcoholism*, *30*, 737–748.

Lundqvist, C., Volk, B., Knoth, R., & Alling, C. (1994). Long-term effects of intermittent versus continuous ethanol exposure on hippocampal synapses of the rat. *Acta Neuropathologica*, *87*, 242–249.

Lynch, M. A., & Littleton, J. M. (1983). Possible association of alcohol tolerance with increased synaptic calcium sensitivity. *Nature*, *303*, 175–176.

Mansfield, J. G., & Cunningham, C. L. (1980). Conditioning and extinction of tolerance to the hypothermic effect of ethanol in rats. *Journal of Comparative and Physiological Psychology*, *94*, 962–969.

Maren, S., & Baudry, M. (1995). Properties and mechanisms of long-term synaptic plasticity in the mammalian brain: Relationships to learning and memory. *Neurobiology of Learning and Memory*, *63*, 1–18.

Matejcek, M. (1982). Vigilance and the EEG: Psychological and pharmacological aspects. In W. M. Herrmann (Ed.), *Electroencephalography in Drug Research*, (pp. 508). Stuttgart: Fischer.

McCown, T. J., & Breese, G. R. (1990). Multiple withdrawals from chronic ethanol "kindles" inferior collicular seizure activity: Evidence for kindling of seizures associated with alcoholism. *Alcoholism: Clinical and Experimental Research*, *14*, 394–399.

Messing, R. O., Carpenter, C. L., Diamond, I., & Greenberg, D. A. (1986). Ethanol regulates calcium channels in clonal neural cells. *Proceedings of the National Academy of Sciences of the United States of America*, *83*, 6213–6215.

Michaelis, E. K., Freed, W. J., Galton, N., Foye, J., Michaelis, M. L., Phillips, I., & Kleinmann, J. E. (1990). Glutamate receptor changes in brain synaptic membranes from human alcoholics. *Neurochemical Research*, *15*, 1055–1063.

Moghaddam, B., & Bolinao, M. L. (1994). Biphasic effect of ethanol on extracellular accumulation of glutamate in the hippocampus and the nucleus accumbens. *Neuroscience Letters*, *178*, 99–102.

Morissett, R. A., & Swartzwelder, H. S. (1993). Attenuation of hippocampal long-term potentiation by ethanol: A patch-clamp analysis of glutamatergic and GABAergic mechanisms. *Journal of Neuroscience*, *13*, 2264–2272.

Nalpas, B., Dabadie, H., Parot, P., & Paccalin, J. (1990). Acamprosate. From pharmacology to therapeutics. *Encephale*, *16*, 175–179.

Nevo, I., & Hamon, M. (1995). Neurotransmitter and neuromodulatory mechanisms involved in alcohol abuse and alcoholism. *Neurochemistry International*, *26*, 305–336.

Noël, X., Paternot, J., Van der Linden, M., Sferrazza, R., De Mol, J., Pelc, I., & Verbanck, P. (2001a). Correlation between inhibition, working memory and delimited frontal areas blood flow measured by ^{99m}Tc-bicisate SPECT in alcohol-dependent patients. *Alcohol and Alcoholism*, *36*, 556–563.

Noël, X., Van der Linden, M., Sferrazza, R., Schmidt, N., De Mol, J., Hanak, C., Pelc, I., & Verbanck, P. (2001b). Supervisory attentional system in recently detoxified alcoholic patients. *Archives of General Psychiatry*, *58*, 1152–1158.

O'Brien, C. P., Childress, A. R., Mc Lellan, A. T., & Ehrman, R. (1992). Classical conditioning in drug-dependent humans. *Annals of the New York Academy of Sciences, 654*, 400–415.

Ollat, H., Parvez, H., & Parvez, S. (1988). Alcohol and central neurotransmission. *Neurochemistry International, 13*, 275–300.

Peterson, C., Neal, J. H., & Cotman, C. W. (1989). Development of N-methyl-D-aspartate excito-toxicity in culturef hippocampal neurons. *Developmental Brain Research, 48*, 187S–195S.

Poldrugo, F., & Snead, O. C. (1984). Electroencephalographic and behavioral correlates in rats during repeated ethanol withdrawal syndromes. *Psychopharmacology, 83*, 140–146.

Pratt, O. E., Rooprai, H. K., Shaw, G. K., & Thomson, A. D. (1990). The genesis of alcoholic brain tissue injury. *Alcohol and Alcoholism, 25*, 217–230.

Regan, R. F., & Choi, D. W. (1991). Glutamate neurotoxicity in spinal cord cell culture. *Neurosciences, 43*, 585–591.

Reid, L. D., Hunter, G. A., Beaman, C. M., & Hubbell, C. L. (1985). Toward understanding ethanol's capacity to be reinforcing: A conditioned place preference following injections of ethanol. *Pharmacology, Biochemistry and Behavior, 22*, 483–487.

Roberts, A. J., & Koob, G. F. (1997). The neurobiology of addiction: An overview. *Alcohol Health and Research World, 14*, 10–11.

Rossetti, Z. L., & Carboni, S. (1995). Ethanol withdrawal is associated with increased extracellular glutamate in the rat striatum. *European Journal of Pharmacology, 283*, 177–183.

Schweinburg, B. C., Taylor, M. J., Alhassoon, O. M., Videen, J. S., Brown-Patterson, T. L., Berger, F., & Grant I. (2001). Chemical pathology in brain white matter of recently detoxified alcoholics: A 1 h magnetic resonance spectroscopy investigation of alcohol-associated frontal lobe injury. *Alcoholism: Clinical and Experimental Research, 25*, 924–934.

Sepulveda, C., Bustos, G., Gysling, K., Seguel, M., & Labarca, R. (1995). Effect of in vitro ethanol and chronic ethanol consumption on the release of excitatory amino acids in the rat hippocampus. *Brain Research, 674*, 104–106.

Siegel, S. (1987). Pavlovian conditioning and ethanol tolerance. *Alcohol and Alcoholism, 1*(Suppl), 25–36.

Siegel, S. (1989). Pharmacological conditioning and drugs effects. In A. J. Goudie & M. W. Emmett-Oglesby (Eds.), *Psychoactive Drugs: Tolerance and Sensitization*, (pp. 115–180). Clifton, NJ: Humana Press.

Smothers, C. T., Mrotek, J. J., & Lovinger, D. M. (1997). Chronic ethanol exposure leads to a selective enhancement of N-methyl-D-aspartate receptor function in cultured hippocampal neurons. *Journal of Pharmacological and Experimental Therapeutics, 283*, 1214–1222.

Snell, L. D., Tabakoff, B., & Hoffman, P. L. (1993). Radioligand binding to the N-methyl-D-aspartate receptor/ionophore complex: Alterations by ethanol in vitro and by chronic in vivo ethanol ingestion. *Brain Research, 602*, 91–98.

Spanagel, R., Holter, S. M., Allingham, K., Landgraf, Z., & Zieglgansberger, W. (1996). Acamprosate and alcohol: I. Effects of alcohol intake following alcohol deprivation in the rat. *European Journal of Pharmacology, 305*, 39–44.

Stewart, J. (1992). Neurobiology of conditioning to drugs of abuse. *Annals of the New York Academy of Sciences, 654*, 335–346.

Tiffany, S. T., Mc Cal, K. J., & Maude-Griffin, P. M. (1987). The contribution of classical conditioning to tolerance to the antinociceptive effects of ethanol. *Psychopharmacology, 92*, 524–528.

Trujillo, K. A., & Akil, H. (1995). Excitatory amino acids and drugs of abuse: A role of NMDA receptors in drug tolerance, sensitization and physical dependence. *Drug and Alcohol Dependence, 38*, 139–154.

Tsai, G. C., & Coyle, J. T. (1998). The role of glutamatergic neurotransmission in the pathophysiology of alcoholism. *Annual Review of Medicine, 49*, 173–184.

Tsai, G. C., Gastfriend, D. R., & Coyle, J. T. (1995). The glutamatergic basis of human alcoholism. *American Journal of Psychiatry, 152*, 332–340.

Tsai, G. E., Ragan, P., Chang, R., Chen, S., Linnoila, V. M., & Coyle, J. T. (1998). Increased glutamatergic neurotransmission and oxidative stress after alcohol withdrawal. *American Journal of Psychiatry, 155*, 726–732.

Veatch, L. M., & Gonzalez, P. (1996). Repeated ethanol withdrawal produces site-dependent increases in EEG spiking. *Alcoholism: Clinical and Experimental Research, 20*, 262–267.

Ward, R. J., Marshall, E. J., Ball, D., Martinez, J., & De Witte, P. (1999). Homeostasis of taurine and glutamate plasma levels after acute and chronic ethanol administration in man. *Neuroscience Research Communications, 24*, 41–49.

Weaver, M. S., Lee, Y. H., Morris, J. L., Randall, P. K., Schallert, T., & Leslie, S. W. (1993). Effects of in vitro ethanol and fetal ethanol exposure on glutathione stimulation of N-methyl-D-aspartate receptor function. *Alcoholism: Clinical and Experimental Research, 17*, 643–650.

Whittington, M. A., Lambert, J. D. C., & Little, H. J. (1995). Increased NMDA receptor and calcium channel activity underlying ethanol withdrawal hyperexcitability. *Alcohol and Alcoholism, 30*, 105–114.

Yusim, A., Franklin, L., Brooke, S., Ajilore, O., & Sapolsky, R. (2000). Glucocorticoids exacerbate the deleterious effects of gp120 in hippocampal and cortical explants. *Journal of Neurochemistry, 74*, 1000–1007.

CHAPTER 5

Cannabis and the Brain: Implications of Recent Research

Suresh Sundram and David Castle
Mental Health Research Institute of Victoria, and
University of Melbourne and St. Vincent's Health, Parkville, Australia

**Psychiatric Symptoms Associated
    with Cannabis**
Cannabis and Schizophrenia
    The Endocannabinoid System
    Psychotic Disorders
    Addictive Disorders
    Mood and Anxiety Disorders
Summary and Future Directions
References

Abstract: The psychiatric effects of *Cannabis sativa* ("cannabis") have been recognized for millennia. It is only in recent times that we have been able to examine in more detail the clinical consequences of cannabis consumption, and in particular its short- and longer-term effects on psychiatric symptom domains including mood, psychosis, and cognition. This endeavour has been fuelled by an increased understanding of the nature of the psychoactive component of cannabis, and of the endocannabinoid system itself. This chapter provides an overview of new developments in our understanding of the impact of cannabis on the human brain. We review epidemiological and clinical studies on the psychiatric effects of cannabis; describe current understandings of the endocannabinoid system; discuss how this system may be disturbed in neuropsychiatric disorders; and outline how modulating it may provide new therapeutic strategies.

81

PSYCHIATRIC SYMPTOMS ASSOCIATED WITH CANNABIS

There is a wealth of literature on the psychiatric/psychological symptomatology associated with cannabis exposure. The mid-19th century saw the publication of Ludlow's (1857) "The Hasheesh Eaters", with extensive descriptions of the euphoric and time-altering phenomena he experienced with regular heavy cannabis use. These experiences were echoed by Marshall (1897), who also described the 'horrors' after a very high dose of cannabis, where he saw appalling visions, including demons. Goode (1970), in his book "The Marijuana Smokers" and Berk and Hernton (1974) in "The Cannabis Experience" provided more contemporary accounts of cannabis intoxication, encompassing the phenomena detailed in Table 1.

More recent population-based surveys of cannabis users emphasize the relaxing and stress-relieving properties of the drug, but also the adverse consequences including panic attacks, paranoia, and apathy/laziness (see Thomas, 1996; Atha & Blanchard, 1997; Reilly et al., 1998).

Human experiments with cannabis have also been conducted. Ames (1958) fed medical volunteers cannabis plants, and they reported a fairly stereotyped response, including fatuous laughter, detachment from reality, 'restriction of the field of awareness', and a sense of the prolongation of the passage of time. Isbell et al. (1967) administered various doses of synthetic Δ^9-tetrahydrocannabinol (THC), the major psychoactive component of cannabis, to former opiate addicts, and found that most experienced symptoms that were dose-related; some, however, had a much more marked response even at low dose, experiencing depersonalization/derealization, paranoia, and auditory and visual hallucinations.

Table 1
Synopsis of Effects of Cannabis Intoxication as Recoded by Goode (The Marijuana Smokers, 1970) and Berke and Hernton (The Cannabis Experience, 1974)

- An initial 'buzz' with tingling and lightheadedness
- Euphoria and fatuous laughter
- An enhanced sensitivity of perception, for example, seeing colors very vividly
- An enhanced appreciation of art and music
- Synesthesia: 'seeing' music, for example
- Visual and auditory hallucinations, which are usually transient and ill-formed
- Fantasies, which border on delusions, usually of a grandiose nature
- A feeling of 'double consciousness'

Source: Data from Iversen (2000, pp. 79–87); from Castle, D. J., Solowij, N. from *Marijuana and Madness* (Eds. Castle & Murray). Cambridge University Press 2004, reproduced with permission.

In a general population cohort study, van Os et al. (2002), as part of the Netherlands Mental Health Survey and Incidence Study (NEMESIS), followed up over 4,000 individuals over a period of three years. There was an elevated risk of the manifestation of psychosis in individuals who used cannabis, but the effect was much more marked in those individuals with a psychosis diagnosis at baseline ($n = 59$). Thus, the risk of psychotic symptoms on the Brief Psychiatric Rating Scale (BPRS) was 1.8% in those cannabis users without baseline psychosis, compared with 46.7% in those with baseline psychotic illness. These clinical and epidemiological studies underline the crucial concept of psychosis–proneness in determining the likelihood of an individual experiencing a psychotic reaction to cannabis. This issue has been the subject of a number of further investigations.

In a prospective study of the effects of cannabis in relation to 'psychosis proneness' in a non-clinical sample, Verdoux et al. (2003) used the Experience Sampling Method (ESM), essentially a diary recording cannabis exposure and psychotic experiences. Subjects ($n = 79$) were assessed over a seven-day period with five diary entries per day, prompted by random bleeps on a wristwatch. There was a strong association between cannabis exposure and unusual perceptions in the ensuing three hours across the whole sample. However, the effect was much more marked for those subjects who had been previously assessed as having high 'psychosis proneness'.

Precisely what determines 'psychosis proneness' is not fully established, though a family history of schizophrenia or related disorders would be an obvious candidate. Exploration of the genetic underpinnings of this phenomenon has also gathered pace. Specifically, individuals with certain allelic variations of the catechol-o-methyl transferase (COMT) gene appear more likely to experience psychotic symptoms in the face of cannabis exposure. Thus, in a population-based birth cohort study, Caspi et al. (2005) found that individuals homozygous for the polymorphism, and who used cannabis, were 10.9 (95% CI 2.2–54.1) times more likely to develop a schizophreniform psychosis than those who did not use cannabis; those subjects heterozygous for the polymorphism were at no elevated risk of this diagnostic outcome even in the face of cannabis exposure (OR 1.1 (95% CI 0.2–5.4). Of course these findings require replication in other samples, and other researchers have cautioned against over-interpreting the results (Macleod et al., 2006). Irrespective, the findings suggest mechanisms for gene–environment interaction that have major potential in explaining why certain environmental stressors impact negatively on some individuals, while others appear to be 'protected'.

The effects of pre-medication with cannabinoid CB1 receptor or dopamine D2 receptor blockers on the experience of cannabis intoxication has also been the subject of scientific scrutiny. Huestis et al. (2001) pre-treated subjects with the CB1 blocker SR141716 (Rimonabant) and then gave them cannabis (2.46% THC) or placebo cigarettes to smoke. Rimonabant served to reduce the 'psychosis-like'

Table 2

Psychiatric Symptoms Associated with Cannabis Consumption, and Putative Brain Areas Involved (Based on Text by Iverson, 2004)

Putative brain area involved	Effect of THC
Basal ganglia, cerebellum	In rats, low dose THC → ↓ activity
	high dose THC → ↑ activity and catalepsy
	In humans, impairs balance and fine motor control
Hippocampus	Acute intoxication → impaired short-term memory
Neo cortex	Effects on sleep/wake cycle; sleep-like EEG pattern
Hypothalamus	↑ appetite ("munchies")
Brainstem	Acts synergistically with opiates in relief of
(interactive with opioid system)	acute and chronic pain

phenomena associated with THC, pointing to the central role of this pathway in the pathogenesis of such symptoms on exposure to THC. In contrast, D'Souza et al. (2002) reported that pre-treatment with the dopamine D2 blocker haloperidol ameliorated only some of the psychosis-like response to intravenous THC, and actually accentuated other symptoms, emphasizing the limitations of a purely dopaminergic expostulation of the mechanism whereby THC exerts its psychotomimetic effects.

Iversen (2004) has provided a useful overview of how cannabis works in the brain, linking effects of cannabinoids in particular brain regions to sets of symptoms. A synopsis is provided in Table 2.

CANNABIS AND SCHIZOPHRENIA

An association between cannabis consumption and schizophrenia has been widely acknowledged. Studies from across the globe have found that people with schizophrenia use cannabis (and other illicit substances) at much higher rates than in the general population. For example, the Australian Study of Low Prevalence (Psychotic) Disorders (Jablensky et al., 2000) found lifetime rates of alcohol abuse or dependence among people with schizophrenia and related disorders or bipolar disorder to be 38.7% for males and 17.0% for females (comparable 12-month general population estimates were 9.4% for males and 3.7% for females). For illicit drugs, rates were 36.3% for males and 15.7% for females (3.1% and 1.3% in the general population, respectively). Among the illicit drugs, cannabis was the most commonly used − 40.9% of the sample, followed by amphetamines − 17.8% (Kavanagh et al., 2004). In a clinical study of people with psychosis, Spencer, Castle, and Michie (2002) confirmed high rates of drug use, and also found that around half of the patients were polydrug users (i.e., using more than one drug of dependence). In a review of the world literature, Cantor-Graae, Nordstrom, and McNeil (2001) found that around 40–60% of people with schizophrenia used illicit drugs; again, cannabis is the most frequently used.

An important issue is to try to understand why so many people with schizophrenia use cannabis (and other illicit drugs). Oft-quoted is the 'self-medication' hypothesis, but clinically most people with schizophrenia acknowledge that cannabis makes their positive psychotic symptoms worse. They do, however, usually report a calming effect from cannabis, which is desirable. In a study specifically addressing this issue, Spencer et al. (2002) performed a factor analysis of potential motivations for use of alcohol and illicit substances (mostly cannabis) endorsed by individuals with a psychotic illness (mostly schizophrenia). The strongest factor (accounting for 37% of the variance) was 'to deal with negative affect', including items covering such motivations as dealing with boredom, depression, anxiety, and insomnia. A further robust but less powerful factor was 'enhancement', such as 'to get high' (10% of the variance). A social factor (e.g. 'because my friends do it') accounted for 8% of the variance. Only 4% of the variance was due to self-medication of symptoms such as voices, or medication side effects. Thus, the 'self medication' hypothesis does not stand when it comes to alleviation of positive symptoms, but is sustainable when consideration is given to negative symptoms. These findings have been largely supported by other investigators. For example, Schofield et al. (2006) explicitly considered self-medication of antipsychotic side effects, and found patients with psychosis were likely to use cannabis to deal with boredom, anxiety, sleep problems, and negative psychotic symptoms, but neither positive symptoms of psychosis nor medication side effects. It is not as though these motivations for use are different from those reported by cannabis users who do not have schizophrenia: it is just that people with schizophrenia have 'negative affect' to a greater degree than people without the illness, and they are also more likely to experience social isolation and social anxiety.

It is also generally agreed among clinicians that the continuing use of cannabis has a negative impact on the longitudinal course of schizophrenia. For example, Negrete et al. (1986) followed up 137 people with schizophrenia over a period of 6 months, and found the 25 cannabis users had a higher rate of relapse and more severe delusions and hallucinations. Linszen, Peters, and Haan (2004) have reviewed this literature and confirmed an association between cannabis consumption and worse outcomes in people with schizophrenia. In their own first episode sample, Linszen et al. (2004) found ongoing cannabis use to be one of the three main predictors of poor outcome (along with lack of insight and erratic medication adherence). In particular, cannabis use was associated with more disorganization symptoms, impacting on the ability to engage in meaningful activities such as work or study. A new study (Hides et al., 2006) also examined the effect of psychotic symptoms on cannabis use in people with schizophrenia over a six-month period. Here, the relationship between cannabis use and psychotic symptoms was bidirectional with cannabis use exacerbating psychotic symptoms and worsening psychotic symptoms increasing cannabis use. Importantly, medication adherence was associated with lower cannabis use.

A more contentious issue is whether cannabis actually *causes* schizophrenia. Early cross-sectional studies of this question were bedevilled by methodological problems including lack of establishment of primacy (i.e., whether cannabis use preceded or was promoted by the schizophrenic illness) and confounding by factors such as socioeconomic status and exposure to other illicit substances. What does seem to be the case, however, is that those people with schizophrenia who were particularly likely to relapse on exposure to cannabis are those with a family history of schizophrenia (Semple, McIntosh, & Lawrie, 2005), again emphasizing the importance of underlying vulnerability/predisposition. Clinicians will be more than aware of the propensity of certain of their schizophrenia patients to relapse fairly predictably when using cannabis.

A number of cohort studies have added considerably to the debate about whether cannabis is a causal factor for schizophrenia. Arseneault et al. (2004) have provided a useful review of the main cohort studies addressing this topic (see Table 3). These studies converge in the finding that cannabis consumption in adolescence or early adulthood is indeed associated with a higher probability of the later development of schizophrenia, even after controlling for obvious confounding factors. The authors of the review conclude that, while cannabis is neither a sufficient nor necessary cause for schizophrenia, it may be considered a 'component cause', in that in certain individuals it interacts with other vulnerabilities (perhaps, largely genetically mediated) to result in the manifestation of the illness. Of course, this needs to be counterpoised by the fact that the vast majority of people who use cannabis will not develop schizophrenia, and that the population attributable fraction for schizophrenia associated with cannabis is probably of the order of 5–8% (see Arsenault et al., 2004).

THE ENDOCANNABINOID SYSTEM

Understanding the clinical and epidemiological associations between cannabis and neuropsychiatric disorders provides insights as to nature and function of the endogenous system through which cannabis must act. Although Δ^9-THC is the major psychoactive component of cannabis, it is only one of at least 66 compounds in the *Cannabis sativa* plant with pharmacokinetic or pharmacodynamic properties (Mechoulam & Hanus, 2000). It is the combined effects of these compounds that give cannabis its acute and long-term CNS consequences, but this complexity also confounds drawing direct links between cannabis use and endogenous effects. Further, the lipophilicity of Δ^9-THC has created difficulties for research into its sites of CNS action, with many researchers originally believing it

Table 3

Findings from Epidemiological Studies on Cannabis use and Schizophrenia

	Risk (OR, 95% CI)	Adjusted risk (OR, 95% CI)	Confounding variables controlled for	Dose-response relationship	Specificity of risk factor	Specificity of outcome
Swedish conscript cohort	1. 6.0 (4.0–8.9) for those who used cannabis >50 times at 18	2.3 (1.0–5.3)	Psychiatric diagnosis at conscription; Parents divorced	Yes	No	N/A
	2. 6.7 (4.5–10.0) for those who used cannabis >50 times at age 18	3.1 (1.7–5.5)	Diagnosis at conscription; IQ score; Social integration; Disturbed behavior; Cigarette smoking; Place of upbringing	Yes	Yes	Yes
NEMESIS	1. 3.25 (1.5–7.2)	2.76 (1.2–6.5)	Age; Sex; Ethnic group; Single marital status; Education; Urbanicity; Discrimination	Yes	Yes	N/A
	2. 28.54 (7.3–110.9)	24.17 (5.44–107.5)				
	3. 16.15 (3.6–72.5) for cannabis use at baseline (age 16–17)	12.01 (2.4–64.3)				
Dunedin study	1. 6.91 (5.1–8.7) (B)*	6.56 (4.78–8.34)*	Sex; Social class; Psychotic symptoms prior to cannabis use	N/A	Yes	Yes
	2. 4.50 (1.1–18.2) Users by the age of 15 and continued at 18	3.12 (0.7–13.3)				

Notes: OR, odds ratio; CI, confidence interval; NEMESIS, Netherlands Mental Health Interview Survey and Incidence Study. *Beta of multiple linear regression. Arseneault et al. (2004, pp. 101–118) from *Marijuana and Madness* (Eds. Castle & Murray). Cambridge University Press, 2004, reproduced with permission.

acted through non-specific membrane perturbation (Mechoulam & Hanus, 2000). The synthesis of less lipophilic and behaviorally more potent agents (Johnson et al., 1981) facilitated the identification of a single specific membrane bound protein (Devane et al., 1988). In 1990 this was cloned and termed the cannabinoid 1 receptor (CB1R) (Matsuda et al., 1990). From this there emanated a rapid series of discoveries, including endogenous ligands for the CB1R (Devane et al., 1992; Sugiura et al., 1995), identification of an additional cannabinoid 2 receptor, CB2R (Munro, Thomas, & Abu-Shaar, 1993) and of synthetic and degradative enzymes for the ligands (Di Marzo et al., 1994; Stella, Schweitzer, & Piomelli, 1997) and insights on the endogenous function of this collective endocannabinoid system. As this work progresses, there is emerging information about how this system may be perturbed in psychiatric and other disorders, and how modulation of the endo-cannabinoid system by pharmacological agents may open new therapeutic avenues for these and other disorders.

The Cannabinoid Receptors

The CB1R is the primary cannabinoid receptor in the CNS, and mediates the central effects of cannabinoids (Ledent et al., 1999; Zimmer et al., 1999). In humans, the gene for CB1R is located in region q14–15 on chromosome 4 (Hoehe et al., 1991) and encodes a 472 amino acid protein (Matsuda, 1997). The brain expression and functional significance of a 411 amino acid post-transcriptional splice variant, CB1AR (Shire et al., 1995), is still being debated (Howlett et al., 2002). The CB1R has a heptahelical structure typical of the G-protein-coupled receptor (GPCR) superfamily and binds to an inhibitory guanine nucleotide-binding protein (Gi-protein) (Matsuda, 1997). Functionally this results in inhibition of adenylyl cyclase and decreased production of the second messenger protein, cyclic adenosine monophosphate (cAMP), resulting in decreased phosphorylation of protein kinase A and subsequent signalling steps. Although this is the canonical signalling pathway for the CB1R, there are other signalling pathways that are activated by agonist binding to the receptor (for review see Howlett et al., 2002).

The CB1R in the human brain appears at surprisingly high densities with levels approaching that of whole brain glutamate, cortical benzodiazepines and striatal dopamine receptor densities (Herkenham et al., 1990). The highest densities are in the basal ganglia – globus pallidus, substantia nigra pars reticulata, hippocampus – subiculum, Ammon's horn, molecular layer of the dentate gyrus and the cerebellum (see Figure 1). Lower levels are found in the neocortex, the rest of the hippocampus, striatum, entorhinal cortex, and amygdaloid complex. Variation in receptor density appears between neocortical regions and is lami-nated. Thalamic, hypothalamic, nucleus solitarius, and central gray substance

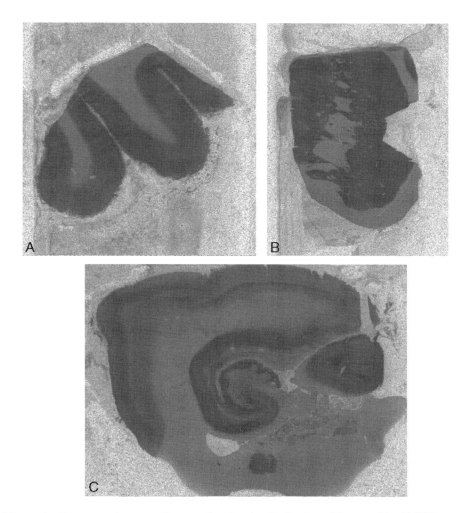

Figure 1 Representative autoradiograms showing the distribution of the cannabinoid CB1 receptor in (A) the dorsolateral prefrontal cortex, (B) caudate putamen and (C) hippocampus and surrounding entorhinal cortex from post-mortem human brain as demonstrated by the total binding of the tritiated cannabinoid CB1 receptor ligand, [^{3}H] CP 55940.

receptor levels are of moderate density while brainstem and area postrema levels are minimal (Glass, Dragunow, & Faull, 1997; Westlake et al., 1994). It is speculated that the low CB1R density in the brainstem accounts for its relative lack of lethality in overdose.

Neuronally, the distribution of the CB1R shows species variation. In rodents it is found predominantly on axons and presynaptic boutons, with little or no presence on dendrites, neuronal soma, and limited presence on post-synaptic terminals whereas greater dendritic spine and synaptic receptor densities are found in primates (Ong & Mackie, 1999; Tsou et al., 1998). It is primarily co-localized with glutamate and cholecystokinin positive GABA neurons (Tsou et al., 1998, 1999). However, CB1R is also found on other GABA interneurons, GABA medium spiny projection neurons from the striatum and corticostriatal glutamate projection neurons (Howlett et al., 2004). There is also co-localization with cholinergic neurons and with both serotonin and dopamine receptors (Hermann, Marsicano, & Lutz, 2002; Lu, Ong, & Mackie, 1999).

The CB2R is located mainly in the periphery especially within the immune system (Howlett et al., 2002). Within the CNS it is restricted to the vascular endothelium and microglia where it is unlikely to play a role in neurotransmission. A recent report of mRNA for the CB2R in neurons within the CNS, especially the brainstem, remains to be replicated and is of uncertain functional significance at this time (Van Sickle et al., 2005).

Endogenous Cannabinoid Receptor Ligands

Following the description of the CB1R explorations for the endogenous ligand uncovered the first endocannabinoid, a fatty acid ethanolamide, anandamide (AA), named from the Sanskrit word *ananda* meaning bringer of inner bliss and the presence of an amide bond in its structure (Devane et al., 1992). Subsequently, a second endocannabinoid, 2-arachidonoylglycerol, 2-AG, was discovered peripherally (Mechoulam et al., 1995) and then centrally (Sugiura et al., 1995). A number of other acylethanolamides with varying degrees of in vitro and in vivo activity have been postulated as endocannabinoids however, their functional significance, if any, in neurotransmission remains to be determined (Piomelli, 2003).

The synthesis of AA and 2-AG is unusual for neurotransmitters in that they are synthesised on demand from phospholipid precursors by N-acyltransferase and phospholipase D for AA and phospholipase C and diacylglycerol lipase for 2-AG following calcium influx into the cell (Elphick & Egertova, 2001). The exact process of exocytosis or release of endocannabinoids from the nerve terminal has not been fully clarified. Termination of action is known to involve enzymatic hydrolysis by fatty acid amide hydrolase (FAAH) (Cravatt et al., 1996; Goparaju et al., 1998) and monoglyceride lipase for 2-AG only (Dinh et al., 2002), and an incompletely characterized transport process (Di Marzo et al., 1994) that is yet to be identified in the human CNS.

Functions of the Endocannabinoid System

Our understanding of the physiological role of the endocannabinoid system is in its infancy. In contrast, there is much clinical and behavioral evidence for the effects of cannabis on a variety of centrally mediated processes and disorders (e.g., see, Castle & Murray, 2004). This discrepancy prevents causal or mechanistic inferences being drawn easily between cannabis use, behavioral functions or disorders and the endocannabinoid system but it is also the subject of much current inquiry. It is important to recognize when drawing these inferences the discordance between the gross indiscriminate synaptic effects of exogenously administered cannabinoids and the localized and highly regulated synaptic release of endocannabinoids.

At a synaptic level, the best characterized role for the endocannabinoid system is as a retrograde modulator of synaptic signalling. Post-synaptic signalling by the co-localized neurotransmitter triggers the release of an endocannabinoid that diffuses retrogradely to stimulate the pre-synaptically located CB1R. This Gi/o coupled receptor then inhibits calcium and permits potassium conductances that decrease neurotransmitter release from the pre-synaptic terminal. This process has been characterized in the dorsal striatum (Gerdeman, Ronesi, & Lovinger, 2002), cerebellum (Kreitzer & Regehr, 2001) and hippocampus (Ohno-Shosaku, Maejima, & Kano, 2001; Wilson & Nicoll, 2001), and mediates the electrophysiological phenomena known as depolarization-induced suppression of inhibition and excitation. These phenomena, in the hippocampus, are thought to underpin elements of learning, and in amygdaloid circuits the extinction of fear-based aversive conditioning (Marsicano et al., 2002).

Much human and animal work propose roles for the endocannabinoid system in short-term memory; motor control through extra pyramidal and cerebellar systems; hypothalamic control of appetite and thermoregulation (although thermoregulation does not apply in humans); and less well-established roles in cognition, anxiety and fear, reward, mood, traumatic central and peripheral nervous system injury, nociception, and neuroprotection. A central point in these roles of the endocannabinoid system is that blockade of the system through the use of pharmacological antagonists or by knocking out the CB1R gene does not result in the abolition of any function. Rather, the system through its activity-dependent inhibition of neurotransmitter release is able to modulate the intensity of synaptic signalling, making it a very intriguing therapeutic target.

The Endocannabinoid System and Psychiatric Disorders

As for the physiological role of this system, its implication with psychiatric disorders relies primarily on observational data from clinical and epidemiological studies, which are discussed above. The first wave of experimental studies directly examining the endocannabinoid system in these disorders is now providing testable paradigms of how this system may be perturbed, and is opening windows for future therapies.

PSYCHOTIC DISORDERS

The first experimental evidence directly linking the endocannabinoid system to schizophrenia was the observation that a perceptual phenomenon termed binocular depth inversion was seen in subjects with schizophrenia and also followed cannabis use in healthy controls (Schneider et al., 2002). The same group reported a marked elevation in endocannabinoid levels in the cerebrospinal fluid of people with schizophrenia (Leweke et al., 1999) which was subsequently replicated in a much larger cohort (Giuffrida et al., 2004). This study demonstrated an eight-fold increase in AA in antipsychotic-naïve first-episode psychosis patients and a smaller but significant elevation in atypical antipsychotic-treated subjects but no elevation in typical antipsychotic-treated schizophrenia, dementia, or affective disorder subjects. Weak negative correlations between AA levels and symptoms led these authors to conclude that the endocannabinoid system may be dysregulated as a compensatory or homeostatic response to the pathology of schizophrenia.

Evidence of the dysregulation of cannabinoid receptors in schizophrenia has also emerged. Increased densities of the CB1R in schizophrenia from post-mortem brain tissue have been described in the dorsolateral prefrontal (Dean et al., 2001) and anterior cingulate cortices (Zavitsanou, Garrick, & Huang, 2004), but not in the striatum or hippocampus (Dean et al., 2001). This suggests that the observations were not non-specific responses to chronic antipsychotic drug treatment. In support of this view, animal treatment studies examining for antipsychotic drug effects on CB1R density do not show changes in the frontal cortex with typical or atypical antipsychotics (Sundram, Copolov, & Dean, 2005). Changes in the dorsolateral prefrontal cortex were independent of cannabis use, whereas an increase in CB1R in the striatum was found in cannabis users, regardless of schizophrenia diagnosis. These observations demonstrate the specificity of the receptor changes for cannabis use and schizophrenia (Dean et al., 2001).

It is premature to draw mechanistic relationships from the early findings. However, the close relationship between the endocannabinoid and dopamine systems (Giuffrida et al., 1999) and the established role of the latter in psychosis make it plausible that the endocannabinoid system may also be involved. Supportive of this is a study demonstrating in post-mortem tissue that the dopamine transporter density in the striatum of non-cannabis exposed subjects with schizophrenia was decreased, compared with cannabis-using subjects with schizophrenia, other cannabis users and healthy controls (Dean, Bradbury, & Copolov, 2003). These authors concluded that cannabis use may be a "self-medication" attempt to restore the dopamine system to homeostasis.

These data raise the possibility that modulation of the endocannabinoid system may have therapeutic potential in psychosis. One single-blind-controlled trial examined effects of placebo,10mg haloperidol or 20mg of the CB1R antagonist, rimonabant per day over a 6-week period (Meltzer et al., 2004). The result was inconclusive. However, the dose of rimonabant may have been inadequate, and a partial agonist may have been a more relevant antipsychotic agent than an antagonist. A natural cannabinoid, cannabidiol, has also been trialled in schizophrenia, even though it has extremely low affinity for the CB1R (Mechoulam & Hanus, 2002). One small study was negative (Zuardi et al., 2006), but, an adequately powered placebo-controlled trial is currently being undertaken (F. M. Leweke personal communication, 2006).

ADDICTIVE DISORDERS

Despite much early controversy about the addictive potential of cannabis, it is now clear that it is both addictive and involves release of dopamine within the shell of nucleus accumbens (Tanda, Pontieri, & Di Chiara, 1997). This dopamine release is central to all reward processes including food, sex, nicotine, and all illicit substances (Koob, Sanna, & Bloom, 1998). Much animal experimental data demonstrates that modulation of the endocannabinoid system attenuates substance ingestion including illicit drugs (Maldonado, Valverde, & Berrendero, 2006). Studies in humans are limited. The most developed research target has been the use of rimonabant for obesity, where two large double-blind, randomized and placebo-controlled trials with fixed dosing have shown it to increase weight loss (Pi-Sunyer et al., 2006; Van Gaal et al., 2005). Initial support from a large-scale placebo-controlled trial of rimonabant for smoking cessation has also returned strongly favorable results, and investigations in alcohol use are currently being undertaken (Gelfand & Cannon, 2006). Markedly less alcohol intake has already been observed in CB1R knockout mice, but increased alcohol intake has been seen in female FAAH knockout mice, suggesting the presence of complex gender interactions (Basavarajappa et al., 2006).

MOOD AND ANXIETY DISORDERS

As already noted, acute ingestion of cannabis typically produces euphoria or relief of dysphoria (Ames, 1958). However, emerging epidemiological evidence argues that early prolonged cannabis use may increase the subsequent development of major depression, especially in females (Fergusson, Horwood, & Swain-Campbell, 2002; Patton et al., 2002; Rey et al., 2002), although these findings are not unchallenged (Arseneault et al., 2002). Animal studies do not provide simple interpretations for these conflicting human studies (Sundram, 2006), partly because potent CB1R agonists have been used, with a diversity of effects. The development of more moderate agents that enhance endocannabinoid levels has been more promising, with initial studies suggesting antidepressant activity in rodent models of depression (Gobbi et al., 2005). Arguments have also been proposed for the use of CB1R antagonists for depressive disorders (Witkin et al., 2005a, Witkin, Tzavara, & Nomikos, 2005b), and human clinical trials may be the only way to determine the effectiveness of each approach in mood disorders.

A primary subjective experience of cannabis use in humans is its anxiolytic property and hence the contribution of the endocannabinoid system to anxiety has been investigated. In contrast to its stimulation of appetitive behaviors, facilitation of the endocannabinoid system would be predicted to reduce anxiety. However, similar to mood, potent agonism of CB1R results in diverse and unwanted effects in addition to anxiolysis. The development of inhibitors of FAAH and the AA transporter have been proposed as more subtle amplifiers of the endocannabinoid system, and have been investigated in animal models of anxiety. In rodents, increasingly potent inhibitors of FAAH, which result in increased brain levels of AA, produce anxiolytic effects on various tests (Bortolato et al., 2006; Kathuria et al., 2003). Further, akin to human phobic states, the endocannabinoid system in rodents is central to the extinction of aversive memories and fear conditioning (Chhatwal et al., 2005, Kamprath et al., 2006; Marsicano et al., 2002). Modulation of endocannabinoid levels through the use of FAAH and transporter inhibitors has thus been proposed as a therapeutic strategy in phobic and post-traumatic stress disorders (Chhatwal et al., 2005).

SUMMARY AND FUTURE DIRECTIONS

Our recent and limited scientific understanding of the endocannabinoid system contrasts with the ancient and enduring use of cannabis. Nevertheless, this rich historical experience of the medicinal and psychoactive properties of cannabis underpins current investigations into the potential of modulating the endocannabinoid system for therapeutic purposes. Clinical and epidemiological data link cannabis use both beneficially and detrimentally to a variety of neuropsychiatric disorders including schizophrenia and psychosis, mood, anxiety, substance use, movement, pain, eating, and cognitive disorders (see Castle & Murray, 2004). The elucidation of the CB1R as the primary nervous system cannabinoid receptor, its endogenous ligands and their synthetic and degradative machinery has permitted investigation of the endocannabinoid system, and the modulation of this system for therapeutic gains. In neurons it appears to underpin an activity-dependent retrograde signalling system that dampens synaptic transmission. Central to this modulatory effect is the dispensability of the system, as evidenced by the survival and generally mild systemic disturbance of CB1R knockout mice (Ledent et al., 1999; Zimmer et al., 1999). It should therefore be possible to subtly regulate other neurotransmitter systems by altering endocannabinoid functioning.

The therapeutic use of cannabinoids including cannabis and dronabinol is widespread for disorders such as cancer and chronic pain, appetite stimulation in cachexia and muscle spasticity and has been usefully reviewed elsewhere (e.g., see Baker et al., 2003; Watson, Benson, & Joy, 2000). Pharmaceutical work examining alternative delivery systems, other CB1R agonists and partial agonists promise better tolerated cannabinoids for these and other disorders (Baker et al., 2003). Studies into the therapeutic role of CB1R antagonists are progressing rapidly, and rimonabant already shows efficacy in decreasing weight. Given animal data implicating the CB1R in other substance use disorders and rimonabant's effectiveness in reducing substance intake, it may be predicted that this drug would be useful in the treatment of substance use disorders in humans. Research on smoking already shows benefits, and work on other substance targets is currently in progress. Early inconclusive data in mood, anxiety, and psychotic disorders indicate that more rigorous and extensive studies are required to determine if this class of agents is useful for these disorders. Finally, agents that amplify the endogenous cannabinoid signal by decreasing hydrolysis of AA show promising effects in a range of disorders albeit at an animal model stage. This appears most exciting for anxiety and phobic disorders, but may also benefit mood and pain disorders.

The integral function of the endocannabinoid system remains mysterious, despite much work to uncover its functions in the CNS. Its dense and extensive presence in the brain and our prolonged fascination with consuming its ligands resulting in a multiplicity of behavioral and clinical outcomes hint at many possible roles and opportunities for therapeutic interventions that remain to be uncovered.

REFERENCES

Ames, F. R. (1958). A clinical and metabolic study of acute intoxication with *Cannabis sativa* and its role in the model psychoses. *Journal of Mental Science, 104*, 972–999.

Arseneault, L., Cannon, M., Witton, J., & Murray, R. (2004). Cannabis as a causal factor in schizophrenia. In D. J. Castle & R. M. Murray (Eds.). *Marijuana and Madness* (pp. 101–118). Cambridge: Cambridge University Press.

Arseneault, L., Cannon, M., Poulton, R., Murray, R., Caspi, A., & Moffitt, T. E. (2002). Cannabis use in adolescence and risk for adult psychosis: Longitudinal prospective study. *British Medical Journal, 325*, 1212–1213.

Atha, M. J., & Blanchard, S. (1997). *Regular Users. Self-Reported Consumption Patterns and Attitudes Towards Drugs Amongst 1333 Regular Cannabis Users.* London, UK: Independent Drug Monitoring Unit.

Baker, D., Pryce, G., Giovannoni, G., & Thompson, A. J. (2003). The therapeutic potential of cannabis. *Lancet Neurology, 2*, 291–298.

Basavarajappa, B. S., Yalamanchili, R., Cravatt, B. F., Cooper, T. B., & Hungund, B. L. (2006). Increased ethanol consumption and preference and decreased ethanol sensitivity in female FAAH knockout mice. *Neuropharmacology, 50*, 834–844.

Berk, J., & Hernton, C. (1974). *The Cannabis Experience.* London: Quartet Books.

Bortolato, M., Campolongo, P., Mangieri, R. A., Scattoni, M. L., Frau, R., Trezza, V., La Rana, G., Russo, R., Calignano, A., Gessa, G. L., Cuomo, V., & Piomelli, D. (2006). Anxiolytic-Like Properties of the anandamide transport inhibitor AM404. *Neuropsychopharmacology, 31*, 2652–2659.

Cantor-Graae, E., Nordstrom, L. G., & McNeil, T. F. (2001). Substance abuse in schizophrenia: A review of the literature and a study of correlates in Sweden. *Schizophrenia Research, 48*, 69–82.

Caspi, A., Moffitt, T. E., Cannon, M., McClay, J., Murray, R., Harrington, H., Taylor, L., Arseneault, B., Williams, A., Braithwaite, R., Poulton, & Craig, I. W. (2005). Moderation of the effect of adolescent-onset cannabis use on adult psychosis by a functional polymorphism in the catechol-O-methyltransferase gene: Longitudinal evidence of gene × environment interaction. *Biological Psychiatry, 57*, 1117–1127.

Castle, D., & Murray, R. (Eds.). (2004). *Marijuana and Madness*. Cambridge: Cambridge University Press.

Castle, D. J., & Solowij, N. (2004). Acute and subacute psychomimetic effects of cannabis in humans. In D. J. Castle, & R. M. Murray (Eds.). *Marijuana and Madness* (pp. 41–54). Cambridge: Cambridge University Press.

Chhatwal, J. P., Davis, M., Maguschak, K. A., & Ressler, K. J. (2005). Enhancing cannabinoid neurotransmission augments the extinction of conditioned fear. *Neuropsychopharmacology, 30*, 516–524.

Cravatt, B. F., Giang, D. K., Mayfield, S. P., Boger, D. L., Lerner, R. A., & Gilula, N. B. (1996). Molecular characterization of an enzyme that degrades neuromodulatory fatty-acid amides. *Nature, 384*, 83–87.

Dean, B., Bradbury, R., & Copolov, D. L. (2003). Cannabis-sensitive dopaminergic markers in post-mortem central nervous system: Changes in schizophrenia. *Biological Psychiatry, 53*, 585–592.

Dean, B., Sundram, S., Bradbury, R., Scarr, E., & Copolov, D. (2001). Studies on [3H]CP-55940 binding in the human central nervous system: Regional specific changes in density of cannabinoid-1 receptors associated with schizophrenia and cannabis use. *Neuroscience, 103*, 9–15.

Devane, W. A., Dysarz, F. A., 3rd, Johnson, M. R., Melvin, L. S., & Howlett, A. C. (1988). Determination and characterization of a cannabinoid receptor in rat brain. *Molecular Pharmacology, 34*, 605–613.

Devane, W. A., Hanus, L., Breuer, A., Pertwee, R. G., Stevenson, L. A., Griffin, G., Gibson, D., Mandelbaum, A., Etinger, A., & Mechoulam, R. (1992). Isolation and structure of a brain constituent that binds to the cannabinoid receptor. *Science, 258*, 1946–1949.

Di Marzo, V., Fontana, A., Cadas, H., Schinelli, S., Cimino, G., Schwartz, J. C., & Piomelli, D. (1994). Formation and inactivation of endogenous cannabinoid anandamide in central neurons. *Nature, 372*, 686–691.

Dinh, T. P., Carpenter, D., Leslie, F. M., Freund, T. F., Katona, I., Sensi, S. L., Kathuria, S., & Piomelli, D. (2002). Brain monoglyceride lipase participating in endocannabinoid inactivation. *Proceedings of the National Academy of Sciences U.S.A, 99*, 10819–10824.

D'Souza, D. C., Cho, H-S., Perry, E. S., & Krystal, J. H. (2004). Cannabinoid 'model' psychosis, dopamine-cannabinoid interactions and implications for schizophrenia. In B. J. Castle, & R. M. Murray (Eds). *Marijuana and Madness* (pp. 142–165). Cambridge: Cambridge University Press.

Elphick, M. R., & Egertova, M. (2001). The neurobiology and evolution of cannabinoid signalling. *PhilosophicalTransactions of the Royal Society of London B Biological Sciences, 356*, 381–408.

Fergusson, D. M., Horwood, L. J., & Swain-Campbell, N. (2002). Cannabis use and psychosocial adjustment in adolescence and young adulthood. *Addiction, 97*, 1123–1135.

Gelfand, E.V., & Cannon, C. P. (2006). Rimonabant: A cannabinoid receptor type 1 blocker for management of multiple cardiometabolic risk factors. *Journal of the American College of Cardiology, 47*, 1919–1926.

Gerdeman, G. L., Ronesi, J., & Lovinger, D. M. (2002). Postsynaptic endocannabinoid release is critical to long-term depression in the striatum. *Nature Neuroscience, 5*, 446–451.

Giuffrida, A., Leweke, F. M., Gerth, C. W., Schreiber, D., Koethe, D., Faulhaber, J., Klosterkotter, J., & Piomelli, D. (2004). Cerebrospinal anandamide levels are elevated in acute schizophrenia and are inversely correlated with psychotic symptoms. *Neuropsychopharmacology*, *29*, 2108–2114.

Giuffrida, A., Parsons, L. H., Kerr, T. M., Rodriguez de Fonseca, F., Navarro, M., & Piomelli, D. (1999). Dopamine activation of endogenous cannabinoid signaling in dorsal striatum. *Nature Neuroscience*, *2*, 358–363.

Glass, M., Dragunow, M., & Faull, R. L. (1997). Cannabinoid receptors in the human brain: A detailed anatomical and quantitative autoradiographic study in the foetal, neonatal and adult human brain. *Neuroscience*, *77*, 299–318.

Gobbi, G., Bambico, F. R., Mangieri, R., Bortolato, M., Campolongo, P., Solinas, M., Cassano, T., Morgese, M. G., Debonnel, G., Duranti, A., Tontini, A., Tarzia, G., Mor, M., Trezza, V., Goldberg, S. R., Cuomo, V., & Piomelli, D. (2005). Antidepressant-like activity and modulation of brain monoaminergic transmission by blockade of anandamide hydrolysis. *Proceedings of the National Academy of Sciences USA*, *102*, 18620–18625.

Goode, E. (1970). *The Marijuana Smokers*. New York: Basic Books.

Goparaju, S. K., Ueda, N., Yamaguchi, H., & Yamamoto, S. (1998). Anandamide amidohydrolase reacting with 2-arachidonoylglycerol, another cannabinoid receptor ligand. *FEBS Letters*, *422*, 69–73.

Herkenham, M., Lynn, A. B., Little, M. D., Johnson, M. R., Melvin, L. S., de Costa, B. R., Rice, K. C. (1990). Cannabinoid receptor localization in brain. *Proceedings of the National Academy of Sciences USA*, *87*, 1932–1936.

Hermann, H., Marsicano, G., & Lutz, B. (2002). Coexpression of the cannabinoid receptor type 1 with dopamine and serotonin receptors in distinct neuronal subpopulations of the adult mouse forebrain. *Neuroscience*, *109*, 451–460.

Hides, L., Dawe, S., Kavanagh, D. J., & Young, R. M. (2006). Psychotic symptom and cannabis relapse in recent-onset psychosis. Prospective study. *British Journal of Psychiatry*, *189*, 137–143.

Hoehe, M. R., Caenazzo, L., Martinez, M. M., Hsieh, W. T., Modi, W. S., Gershon, E. S., Bonner, T. I. (1991). Genetic and physical mapping of the human cannabinoid receptor gene to chromosome 6q14-q15. *New Biologist*, *3*, 880–885.

Howlett, A. C., Barth, F., Bonner, T. I., Cabral, G., Casellas, P., Devane, W. A., Felder, C. C., Herkenham, M., Mackie, K., Martin, B. R., Mechoulam, R., & Pertwee, R. G. (2002). International Union of Pharmacology. XXVII. Classification of Cannabinoid Receptors. *Pharmacology Review*, *54*, 161–202.

Howlett, A. C., Breivogel, C. S., Childers, S. R., Deadwyler, S. A., Hampson, R. E., & Porrino, L. J. (2004). Cannabinoid physiology and pharmacology: 30 years of progress. *Neuropharmacology*, *47*(Suppl. 1), 345–358.

Huestis, M. A., Gorelick, D. A., Heishman, S. J., Preston, K. L., Nelson, R. A., Moolchan, E. T., & Frank, R. A. (2001). Blockade of effects of smoked marijuana by the CB1-selective cannabinoid receptor antagonist SR 141716. *Archives of General Psychiatry*, *58*, 322–328.

Isbell, H., Gorodetzky, C. W., Jasinski, D., Clausser, U., van Spolak, F., & Korte, F. (1967). Effects of delta-9-trans-tetrahydrocannabinol in man. *Psychopharmacologia*, *11*, 184–188.

Iversen, L. (2004). How cannabis works in the brain. In D. J. Castle, & R. M. Murray (Eds.). *Marijuana and Madness* (pp. 19–40). Cambridge: Cambridge University Press.

Jablensky, A., McGrath, J. J., Herrman, H., Castle, D. J., Gureje, O., Morgan, V., & Korten, A. (2000). Psychotic disorders in urban areas: An overview of the Study on Low Prevalence Disorders. *Australian & New Zealand Journal of Psychiatry*, *34*, 221–236.

Johnson, M. R., Melvin, L. S., Althuis, T. H., Bindra, J. S., Harbert, C. A., Milne, G. M., & Weissman, A. (1981). Selective and potent analgetics derived from cannabinoids. *Journal of Clinical Pharmacology*, *21*, 271S–282S.

Kamprath, K., Marsicano, G., Tang, J., Monory, K., Bisogno, T., Di Marzo, V., Lutz, B., & Wotjak, C. T. (2006). Cannabinoid CB1 receptor mediates fear extinction via habituation-like processes. *Journal of Neuroscience, 26,* 6677–6686.

Kathuria, S., Gaetani, S., Fegley, D., Valino, F., Duranti, A., Tontini, A., Mor, M., Tarzia, G., La Rana, G., Calignano, A., Giustino, A., Tattoli, M., Palmery, M., Cuomo, V., & Piomelli, D. (2003). Modulation of anxiety through blockade of anandamide hydrolysis. *Nature Medicine, 9,* 76–81.

Kavanagh, D. J., Waghorn, G., Jenner, L., Chant, D. C., Carr, V., Evans, M., Herrman, H., Jablensky, A., & McGrath, J. J. (2004). Demographic and clinical correlates of comorbid substance use disorders in psychosis: Multivariate analyses from an epidemiological sample. *Schizophrenia Research, 66,* 115–124.

Koob, G. F., Sanna, P. P., & Bloom, F. E. (1998). Neuroscience of addiction. *Neuron, 21,* 467–476.

Kreitzer, A. C., & Regehr, W. G. (2001). Cerebellar depolarization-induced suppression of inhibition is mediated by endogenous cannabinoids. *Journal of Neuroscience, 21,* RC174.

Ledent, C., Valverde, O., Cossu, G., Petitet, F., Aubert, J. F., Beslot, F., Bohme, G. A., Imperato, A., Pedrazzini, T., Roques, B. P., Vassart, G., Fratta, W., & Parmentier, M. (1999). Unresponsiveness to cannabinoids and reduced addictive effects of opiates in CB1 receptor knockout mice. *Science, 283,* 401–404.

Leweke, F. M., Giuffrida, A., Wurster, U., Emrich, H. M., & Piomelli, D. (1999). Elevated endogenous cannabinoids in schizophrenia. *Neuroreport, 10,* 1665–1669.

Linszen, D., Peters, B., & de Haan, L. (2004). Cannabis abuse and the course of psychosis. In D. J. Castle, & R. M. Murray (Eds.). *Marijuana and Madness* (pp. 119–126). Cambridge: Cambridge University Press.

Ludlow, F. H. (1857). *The Hasheesh Eaters.* New York: Harper.

Lu, X. R., Ong, W. Y., & Mackie, K. (1999). A light and electron microscopic study of the CB1 cannabinoid receptor in monkey basal forebrain. *Journal of Neurocytology, 28,* 1045–1051.

Macleod, J., Davey Smith, G., & Hickman, M. (2006). Does cannabis cause schizophrenia? *Lancet, 367,* 1055 (letter).

Maldonado, R., Valverde, O., & Berrendero, F. (2006). Involvement of the endocannabinoid system in drug addiction. *Trends in Neuroscience, 29,* 225–232.

Marshall, C. R. (1997). The active principle of Indian hemp: A preliminary communication. *Lancet, I,* 235–238.

Marsicano, G., Wotjak, C. T., Azad, S. C., Bisogno, T., Rammes, G., Cascio, M. G., Hermann, H., Tang, J., Hofmann, C., Zieglgansberger, W., Di Marzo, V., & Lutz, B. (2002). The endogenous cannabinoid system controls extinction of aversive memories. *Nature, 418,* 530–534.

Matsuda, L. A. (1997). Molecular aspects of cannabinoid receptors. *Critical Reviews in Neurobiology, 11,* 143–166.

Matsuda, L. A., Lolait, S. J., Brownstein, M. J., Young, A. C., & Bonner, T. I. (1990). Structure of a cannabinoid receptor and functional expression of the cloned cDNA. *Nature, 346,* 561–564.

Mechoulam, R., Ben-Shabat, S., Hanus L., Ligumsky, M., Kaminski, N. E., Schatz, A. R., Compton, D. R., Pertwee, R. G., Giffin, G., Bayewitch, M., Brag, J., & Vogol, Z. (1995). Identification of an endogenous 2-monoglyceride, present in canine gut, that binds to cannabinoid receptors. *Biochemical Pharmacology, 50*(1), 83–90.

Mechoulam, R., & Hanus, L. (2000). A historical overview of chemical research on cannabinoids. *Chemistry and Physics of Lipids, 108,* 1–13.

Mechoulam, R., & Hanus, L. (2002). Cannabidiol: An overview of some chemical and pharmacological aspects. Part I: chemical aspects. *Chemistry and Physics of Lipids, 121,* 35–43.

Meltzer, H. Y., Arvanitis, L., Bauer, D., & Rein, W. (2004). Placebo-controlled evaluation of four novel compounds for the treatment of schizophrenia and schizoaffective disorder. *American Journal of Psychiatry, 161,* 975–984.

Munro, S., Thomas, K. L., & Abu-Shaar, M. (1993). Molecular characterization of a peripheral receptor for cannabinoids. *Nature*, *365*, 61–65.

Negrete, J. C., Knapp, W. P., Douglass, D. E., & Smith, B. (1986). Cannabis affects the severity of schizophrenic symptoms: Results of a clinical survey. *Psychological Medicine*, *16*, 515–520.

Ohno-Shosaku, T., Maejima, T., & Kano, M. (2001). Endogenous cannabinoids mediate retrograde signals from depolarized postsynaptic neurons to presynaptic terminals. *Neuron*, *29*, 729–738.

Ong, W. Y., & Mackie, K. (1999). A light and electron microscopic study of the CB1 cannabinoid receptor in primate brain. *Neuroscience*, *92*, 1177–1191.

Patton, G. C., Coffey, C., Carlin, J. B., Degenhardt, L., Lynskey, M., & Hall, W. (2002). Cannabis use and mental health in young people: Cohort study. *British Medical Journal*, *325*, 1195–1198.

Piomelli, D. (2003). The molecular logic of endocannabinoid signalling. *Nature Reviews in Neuroscience*, *4*, 873–884.

Pi-Sunyer, F. X., Aronne, L. J., Heshmati, H. M., Devin, J., & Rosenstock, J. (2006). Effect of rimonabant, a cannabinoid-1 receptor blocker, on weight and cardiometabolic risk factors in overweight or obese patients: RIO-North America: A randomized controlled trial. *Journal of the American Medical Association*, *295*, 761–775.

Reilly, D., Didcott, P., Swift, W., & Hall, W. (1998). Long-term cannabis use: Characteristics of users in an Australian rural area. *Addiction*, *93*, 837–846.

Rey, J. M., Sawyer, M. G., Raphael, B., Patton, G. C., & Lynskey, M. (2002). Mental health of teenagers who use cannabis. Results of an Australian survey. *British Journal of Psychiatry*, *180*, 216–221.

Schneider, U., Borsutzky, M., Seifert, J., Leweke, F. M., Huber, T. J., Rollnik, J. D., & Emrich, H. M. (2002). Reduced binocular depth inversion in schizophrenic patients. *Schizophrenia Research*, *53*, 101–108.

Schofield, D., Tennant, C., Nash, L., Degenhardt, L., Cornish, A., Hobbs, C., & Brennan, G. (2006). Reasons for cannabis use in psychosis. *Australian & New Zealand Journal of Psychiatry*, *40*, 570–574.

Semple, D. M., McIntosh, A. M., & Lawrie, S. M. (2005). Cannabis as a risk factor for psychosis: Systematic review. *Journal of Psychopharmacology*, *19*, 187–194.

Shire, D., Carillon, C., Kaghad, M., Calandra, B., Rinaldi-Carmona, M., Le Fur, G., Caput, D., & Ferrara, P. (1995). An amino-terminal variant of the central cannabinoid receptor resulting from alternative splicing. *Journal of Biological Chemistry*, *270*, 3726–3731.

Spencer, C. (2004). Motives that maintain cannabis use amongst individuals with psychotic disorders. In D. J. Castle, & R. M. Murray (Eds.). *Marijuana and Madness* (pp. 166–185). Cambridge: Cambridge University Press.

Spencer, C. R., Castle, D., & Michie, P. (2002). Motivations that maintain substance use amongst individuals with psychotic disorders. *Schizophrenia Bulletin*, *28*, 233–247.

Stella, N., Schweitzer, P., & Piomelli, D. (1997). A second endogenous cannabinoid that modulates long-term potentiation. *Nature*, *388*, 773–778.

Sugiura, T., Kondo, S., Sukagawa, A., Nakane, S., Shinoda, A., Itoh, K., Yamashita, A., & Waku, K. (1995). 2-Arachidonoylglycerol: A possible endogenous cannabinoid receptor ligand in brain. *Biochemical and Biophysical Research Communications*, *215*, 89–97.

Sundram, S. (2006). Cannabis and neurodevelopment: Implications for psychiatric disorders. *Human Psychopharmacology*, *21*, 245–254.

Sundram, S., Copolov, D., & Dean, B. (2005). Clozapine decreases [3H] CP 55940 binding to the cannabinoid 1 receptor in the rat nucleus accumbens. *Naunyn Schmiedebergs Archives of Pharmacology*, *371*, 428–433.

Tanda, G., Pontieri, F. E., & Di Chiara, G. (1997). Cannabinoid and heroin activation of mesolimbic dopamine transmission by a common mu1 opioid receptor mechanism. *Science*, *276*, 2048–2050.

Thomas, H. (1996). A community survey of adverse effects of hashish. *Drug and Alcohol Dependence*, *42*, 201–207.

Tsou, K., Brown, S., Sanudo-Pena, M. C., Mackie, K., Walker, J. M. (1998). Immunohistochemical distribution of cannabinoid CB1 receptors in the rat central nervous system. *Neuroscience, 83*, 393–411.

Tsou, K., Mackie, K., Sanudo-Pena, M. C., & Walker, J. M. (1999). Cannabinoid CB1 receptors are localized primarily on cholecystokinin-containing GABAergic interneurons in the rat hippocampal formation. *Neuroscience, 93*, 969–975.

Van Gaal, L. F., Rissanen, A. M., Scheen, A. J., Ziegler, O., & Rossner, S. (2005). Effects of the cannabinoid-1 receptor blocker rimonabant on weight reduction and cardiovascular risk factors in overweight patients: 1-year experience from the RIO-Europe study. *Lancet, 365*, 1389–1397.

van Os, J., Bak, M., Bijl, R. V., DeGraaf, R., & Verdoux, H. (2002). Cannabis use and psychosis: A longitudinal population-based study. *American Journal of Epidemiology, 156*, 319–327.

Van Sickle, M. D., Duncan, M., Kingsley, P. J., Mouihate, A., Urbani, P., Mackie, K., Stella, N., Makriyannis, A., Piomelli, D., Davison, J. S., Marnett, L. J., Di Marzo, V., Pittman, Q. J., Patel, K. D., & Sharkey, K. A. (2005). Identification and functional characterization of brainstem cannabinoid CB2 receptors. *Science, 310*, 329–332.

Verdoux, H., Gindre, C., Sorbara, F., Tournier, M., & Swendsen, J. (2003). Cannabis use and the expression of psychosis vulnerability in daily life. *Psychological Medicine, 33*, 23–32.

Watson, S. J., Benson, J. A., Jr., & Joy, J. E. (2000). Marijuana and medicine: Assessing the science base: A summary of the 1999 Institute of Medicine report. *Archives of General Psychiatry, 57*, 547–552.

Westlake, T. M., Howlett, A. C., Bonner, T. I., Matsuda, L. A., & Herkenham, M. (1994). Cannabinoid receptor binding and messenger RNA expression in human brain: An in vitro receptor autoradiography and in situ hybridization histochemistry study of normal aged and Alzheimer's brains. *Neuroscience, 63*, 637–652.

Wilson, R. I., & Nicoll, R. A. (2001). Endogenous cannabinoids mediate retrograde signalling at hippocampal synapses. *Nature, 410*, 588–592.

Witkin, J. M., Tzavara, E. T., Davis, R. J., Li, X., & Nomikos, G. G. (2005a). A therapeutic role for cannabinoid CB1 receptor antagonists in major depressive disorders. *Trends in Pharmacological Science, 26*, 609–617.

Witkin, J. M., Tzavara, E. T., & Nomikos, G. G. (2005b). A role for cannabinoid CB1 receptors in mood and anxiety disorders. *Behavioural Pharmacology, 16*, 315–331.

Zavitsanou, K., Garrick, T., & Huang, X. F. (2004). Selective antagonist [3H]SR141716A binding to cannabinoid CB1 receptors is increased in the anterior cingulate cortex in schizophrenia. *Progress in Neuropsychopharmacology and Biological Psychiatry, 28*, 355–360.

Zimmer, A., Zimmer, A. M., Hohmann, A. G., Herkenham, M., & Bonner, T. I. (1999). Increased mortality, hypoactivity, and hypoalgesia in cannabinoid CB1 receptor knockout mice. *Proceedings of the National Academy of Sciences USA, 96*, 5780–5785.

Zuardi, A. W., Hallak, J. E., Dursun, S. M., Morais, S. L., Faria Sanches, R., Musty, R. E., & Crippa, J. A. (2006). Cannabidiol monotherapy for treatment-resistant schizophrenia. *Journal of Psychopharmacology, 20*, 683–686.

SECTION II
PHARMACOTHERAPY

CHAPTER 6

The Plasticity of Alcohol Addiction Suggests Novel Approaches to Pharmacological Intervention

Patrick J. Mulholland and L. Judson Chandler
Department of Neurosciences and Center for Drug and Alcohol Programs,
Medical University of South Carolina, Charleston, SC, USA

Neurobiology of Alcohol Addiction
Glutamatergic System
Glutamate and Alcohol
Dendritic Spines and the Post–Synaptic Density
Ethanol and the Post–Synaptic Density
Metabotropic Glutamate Receptors
Cannabinoid Receptors
Implications for Treatment
References

Abstract: Recent observations from diverse studies suggest that plastic processes, which underlie experience-dependent brain plasticity, also play an important role in adaptations that underlie alcohol addiction. A critical mediator of experience-dependent plasticity is the excitatory neurotransmitter glutamate, and there is considerable evidence that acute and chronic alcohol affects glutamatergic neurotransmission. The primary focus of this article is the molecular and cellular alterations in the glutamatergic system that appear to underlie alcohol-associated plasticity. Greater understanding of these adaptations may point to novel approaches to more effective treatments for alcohol dependency, craving, and relapse that target these adaptive processes.

According to the World Health Organization (2001), alcohol abuse disorders are a prevalent mental disorder and are a leading cause of disability. In the US, the cost of alcohol-related health care alone in 1992 was estimated to be $18.8 billion and the total US economic costs of alcohol-related disorders were approximately $185 billion in 1998 (Harwood, Fountain, Livermore, 1998). In spite of increasing public awareness of the adverse consequences of alcohol abuse, the prevalence of alcohol abuse and dependence has increased from 7.41% in 1991–1992 to 8.46% in 2001–2002, affecting nearly 18 million adult Americans (Grant et al., 2004). Over half of American families have a family member who currently or previously suffered from alcohol dependence (Dawson & Grant, 1998).

The fact that alcohol is one of the most widely abused drugs with considerable adverse economic and social consequences underscores the need to develop more effective treatments. Currently, naltrexone, disulfiram, and acamprosate are the only medications approved by the US Food and Drug Administration for the treatment of alcohol dependency (Table 1). However, these medications have limited efficacy and small effect sizes. In addition, the preferred treatment to reduce potentially life-threatening withdrawal syndrome continues to be benzodiazepines. This is noteworthy when one considers that the pharmacological management of withdrawal has remained unchanged for over 40 years and that the severity of subsequent withdrawals increases and becomes refractory to benzodiazepine intervention. Moreover, treatment of alcohol withdrawal with benzodiazepines has been associated with increased relapse (Malcolm et al., 2002), further underscoring the fact that relapse is the most difficult clinical problem to address in addiction

Table 1

Medications for the treatment of alcohol dependency that are either approved by the Food and Drug Administration (FDA) or are under investigation in clinical trials and animal models for potential future use.

Medication	Mechanism of action	Availability
Disulfiram	Aldehyde dehydrogenase blocker	FDA approved
Naltrexone	m-Opioid receptor antagonist	FDA approved
Acamprosate	Glutamate modulator★	FDA approved
Topiramate	Anticonvulsant[†]	Clinical trials
Gabapentin	Anticonvulsant[‡]	Clinical trials
Ondasentron	5-HT3 antagonist	Clinical trials
Baclofen	GABA-B agonist	Clinical trials
Sertraline, fluvoxamine	5-HT3 reuptake lnhibitor	Clinical trials
Rimonabant	CB_1 antagonists	Clinical trials
Kudzu	Plant extract with multiple putative mechanisms	Clinical trials
Memantine	Use-dependent NMDAR channel blocker	Clinical trials
Potential development	MGluR5 antagonists	Animal models
Potential development	Phosphodiesterase inhibitor	Animal models
Potential development	CRF antagonists	Animal models
Potential development	Neuropeptide Y	Animal models

★Multiple proposed mechanisms including modulation of NMDA receptor activity, as well as increasing GABAergic tone.
[†]Multiple putative mechanisms including voltage-sensitive sodium channel blockade, calcium channel inhibition, increasing potassium and GABA-mediated chloride conductance, inhibiton of glutamate-mediated neurotransmission and carbonic anhydrase isoenzyme inhibition.
[‡]Unknown Mechanism of Action.

(O'Brien, 2005). These findings underscore the need to continue to examine the causes and consequences of alcohol abuse and to increase efforts to develop new strategies for the treatment of alcohol dependency.

NEUROBIOLOGY OF ALCOHOL ADDICTION

While most drugs of abuse are distinct in their molecular structure, they produce similar behavioral patterns of addiction. The acute euphoria associated with drug intake leads to subsequent episodes of consumption. In vulnerable individuals, this pattern of behavior ultimately ends in addiction. Addiction to alcohol and other drugs is characterized by tolerance, dependence, craving, compulsive drug-seeking, and relapse. These changes in behavior appear to have a cellular and molecular basis that is common across all drugs of abuse. Considerable evidence suggests that neuroadaptations mediating addiction occur within the brain's mesolimbic dopamine system (Nestler, 2005). It is this pathway that is activated during natural rewards (sex, food), natural addictions (gambling, over-eating), and by all drugs of abuse, including alcohol. The mesocorticolimbic reward pathway includes midbrain dopaminergic cell bodies in the ventral tegmental area (VTA) that send axonal projections to the nucleus accumbens and other structures including the prefrontal cortex, extended amygdala, and hippocampus. While it is clear that a relationship exists between dopamine and addiction to alcohol and other drugs, modulators of dopaminergic function have not shown efficacy for the treatment of addictive disorders. This suggests that additional critical factors underlie addiction to alcohol and other drugs.

GLUTAMATERGIC SYSTEM

Unlike the discrete distribution of dopaminergic-containing neurons, the vast majority of neurons across all brain regions possess glutamatergic inputs, with half of the synapses using glutamate as a neurotransmitter. Glutamate affects neuronal function by activating either postsynaptic ionotropic (iGluR) or metabotropic (mGluR) receptors (for detailed review, see Dingledine et al., 1999; Cull-Candy, Brickley, & Farrant, 2001). Glutamate, acting at iGluRs, elicits fast excitatory neurotransmission by allowing K^+, Na^+, or Ca^{2+} influx resulting in depolarization, whereas mGluRs mediate slower responses via coupling to secondary messenger systems. The iGluR family is divided into N-methyl-D-aspartate (NMDA), α-amino-3-hydroxy-5-methyl-4-isoxazole propionic acid (AMPA), and kainate receptors. AMPA and kainate receptors form homomeric or heteromeric receptors from a family of subunits that includes GluR1-4 and GluR5-7/KA1-2, respectively. NMDA receptors co-assemble from an obligatory NR1 subunit and one or more NR2A-D subunits that are thought to play a regulatory role in controlling functional properties, such as gating kinetics and trafficking. For example, NMDA receptors containing NR2B subunits demonstrate increased Ca^{2+} permeability and longer deactivation times in comparison with those containing NR2A subunits (Cull–Candy et al., 2001; Monyer et al., 1994). Interestingly, recent evidence describing a family of NR3A-B subunits indicates they may be involved in axo–myelinic signaling in oligodendrocytes (Karadottir et al., 2005; Micu et al., 2006; Salter & Fern, 2005).

While AMPA and kainate receptors mediate fast depolarization at most synapses, NMDA receptor activation is more associated with induction of various forms of synaptic plasticity, such as long-term potentiation (LTP), long-term depression (LTD), and homeostatic plasticity. It is thought that NMDA receptors act as coincidence detectors due to their voltage-dependent Mg^{2+} block at resting membrane potential. To activate NMDA receptors, glutamate must bind to the receptor and the membrane must also be depolarized to release the Mg^{2+} block. Ca^{2+} influx through NMDA receptors is a critical regulator of intracellular signaling processes and activity-dependent synaptic plasticity. In addition, recent evidence suggests that mGluRs may also shape and modify synaptic strength at glutamatergic synapses (for review, see Maiese, Chong, & Li, 2005).

GLUTAMATE AND ALCOHOL

The physiological effects of alcohol require the consumption of large amounts due to its simple structure and low potency. This is in striking contrast with other drugs of abuse, such as morphine that has high affinity for opioid receptors. Thus, it was originally thought that intoxication resulted from non-specific effects of alcohol on membrane lipids (Franks & Lieb, 1994; Peoples, Li, & Weight, 1996). However, even at elevated doses, pharmacologically relevant concentrations of alcohol selectively affect the function of certain membrane-bound proteins and signal transduction processes. For example, acute ethanol exposure attenuates NMDA receptor currents and potentiates $GABA_A$ receptor currents while not affecting AMPA receptor currents. It is well established that physiologically relevant concentrations of ethanol inhibit NMDA receptor activity (Woodward, 2000). It is thought that ethanol non–competitively inhibits NMDA receptors without altering glutamate or glycine binding (Fadda & Rossetti, 1998). Evidence suggests that NMDA receptors possibly contain multiple binding pockets for ethanol and that ethanol inhibits NMDA receptor activity by changing its phosphorylation state (for review, see Ron, 2004). Many of the behavioral manifestations of alcohol dependency involve the NMDA receptor system. Evidence from both humans and animal models suggest that alterations in NMDA receptors are major mediators of alcohol dependency, tolerance, craving, and relapse (for review, see Kumari & Ticku, 2000). Because the NMDA receptor is critically involved in alcohol dependency, understanding the cellular and molecular mechanisms that mediate ethanol–induced NMDA receptor alterations are of great interest.

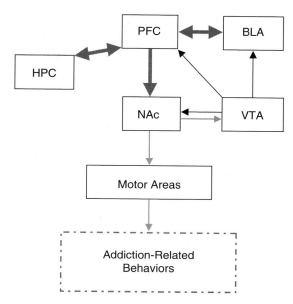

Figure 1 Hypothesized brain regions and afferents involved in neuroadaptations underlying alcohol addiction. It is posited that the cellular and molecular changes within the glutamatergic system play a substantial role in the development of tolerance and dependence to alcohol. Additionally, emerging evidence suggests that chronic ethanol consumptions affects glutamatergic neurotransmission in a manner similar to changes observed during learning, experience-dependent synaptic plasticity, and survival. These sub-cellular alterations may enhance glutamatergic "tone" during periods of withdrawal or abstinence, thereby leading to craving and relapse. Dark gray, light gray, and black arrows indicate glutamatergic, GABAergic, and dopaminergic afferents, respectively. Basolateral Amygdala, BLA; Hippocampus, HPC; Nucleus Accumbens, NAc; Prefrontal Cortex, PFC; and Ventral Tegmental Area, VTA.

As noted above, the molecular adaptations underlying addiction are thought to be similar to those described for learning and memory (Chandler, 2003). It is hypothesized that these changes likely play a role in addiction processes and may underlie the expression and development of drug seeking and consumption (Robinson & Kolb, 2004; Figure 1). Numerous studies have demonstrated that AMPA receptors move in and out of the synapse as a mechanism to control synaptic efficacy (Lissin et al., 1998; Lissin, Malenka, & Von Zastrow, 1999; O'Brien et al., 1998). Recently, it has also been shown that NMDA receptors are subject to synaptic targeting and activity-dependent trafficking (Carroll & Zukin, 2002; Wenthold et al., 2003). NMDA receptors can move laterally through the membrane between synaptic and extrasynaptic sites as well as removal from and insertion into the membrane. For example, pharmacological inhibition of NMDA receptors results in the movement of NMDA receptors from extrasynaptic to synaptic sites (Tovar & Westbrook, 2002). Changes in the phosphorylation state of NMDA receptors by activation of kinases or phosphatases likely regulate receptor function and likely play an important role in controlling their sub-cellular localization. Phosphorylation of the NR1 subunit of the NMDA receptor by protein kinases A and C increase for-warding trafficking to the plasma membrane (Scott, Blanpied, & Ehlers, 2003). Recent evidence also suggests that Src kinase inhibition attenuates NMDA receptor phosphorylation and membrane localization of NR2A subunits (Thornton et al., 2003), whereas dephosphorylation of NMDA receptor NR2A subunits via tyrosine results in subunit internalization (Vissel et al., 2001). Interestingly, dopamine D1 receptors are involved in post-synaptic targeting of NMDA receptors through a Fyn kinase-mediated tyrosine phosphorylation (Dunah et al., 2004). These findings are of interest in light of reports that Fyn kinase plays an important role in adaptive behavior responses to ethanol.

Neuroadaptive alterations during consumption of alcohol over long periods are thought to contribute to the physical dependence on alcohol and may play an important role in tolerance development and relapse (Lovinger & Crabbe, 2005). These neuronal adaptations likely occur at the molecular, cellular, and systems level resulting from cyclical periods of heavy consumption followed by abstinence. In an attempt to gain greater understanding of the adaptive processes involved in alcohol addiction, researchers have employed both in vivo and in vitro animal models. For example, in a mouse model of multiple withdrawals, the severity of withdrawal-induced seizures correlate with the number of withdrawal episodes (Becker, 1998), similar to what has been described in alcoholics. Freund and Anderson (1996) reported an increase in the number of NMDA receptors in post mortem brain of alcohol-dependent individuals. Similar increases in NMDA receptors have been observed by others using primary neuronal cultures and organotypic slice cultures (Fadda & Rossetti, 1988; Harris et al., 2003). On the other hand, while there is almost universal agreement that chronic ethanol leads to increases in NMDA recep-tor responses, a number of in vivo and in vitro studies have not observed increases in total NMDA receptor density (Chandler, 2003). Consistent with a recent study by Carpenter-Hyland, Woodward, and Chandler (2004) showing that chronic ethanol induces an increase in synaptic but not extrasynaptic receptors, the above mentioned studies on NMDA receptor density indicate that ethanol-induced changes are more complex than simple increases in the total receptor number.

Cellular models of synaptic plasticity have demonstrated changes in the sub-cellular localization of glutamate receptors that are accompanied by molecular re-organization of dendritic spines (Gomez et al., 2002; Ackermann & Matus, 2003; Hering & Sheng, 2003). Spines are tiny membrane protuberances that form the vast majority of post-synaptic contact sites at glutamatergic synapses and have long been considered to represent sites of experience-dependent structural plasticity. As experi-ence-dependent synaptic plasticity involves alterations in spine morphology, alcohol-induced modifications in synaptic efficacy may therefore contribute to alterations in dendritic spines and synapse formation. As discussed in further detail in the follow-ing sections, ethanol may regulate activity-dependent NMDA receptor trafficking at the post-synaptic density (PSD) of dendritic spines, which may explain ethanol-induced adaptive processes that underlie alcohol dependency. AMPA receptors may also play a role in neuroplastic changes associated with alcohol-seeking behavior. Indeed, mice given an AMPA receptor antagonist or mice deficient for the GluR-C AMPA subunit displayed a blunted ethanol deprivation effect and attenuated cue-induced reinstatement response (Sanchis-Segura et al., 2006).

DENDRITIC SPINES AND THE POST-SYNAPTIC DENSITY

As mention above, it has long been suggested that structural changes in dendritic spines are the basis of long-lasting experience-dependent modifications in brain (for review, see Lamprecht & LeDoux, 2004). Changes in dendritic spines are critically dependent upon dynamic regulation of their cytoskeleton, and it is now widely accepted that changes to the cytoskeleton occur during experience dependent plasticity such as learning and memory. For example, the induction of LTP leads to alterations in the shape and number of dendritic spines (Muller et al., 2002; Yuste & Bonhoeffer, 2001). Increasing evidence also suggests that structural changes may be associated with the development and maintenance of addiction to alcohol and other drugs.

Before addressing the role that structural modifications play in alcohol dependency, a description of the factors that regulate dendritic spines and associated cytoskeleton will be described. The PSD is an electron-dense region at the head of the spine that contains ionotropic and metabotropic receptors, secondary messengers and other signaling molecules, and scaffolding proteins. It is thought that scaffolding proteins form multiple complexes within the PSD, thus providing compartmentalization and specificity for both temporal and spatial organization of signaling pathways. Compartmentalization of signaling pathways in the PSD allows for efficient and effective responses to inputs by controlling the localization of kinases and phosphatases. In particular, PSD protein 95 (PSD-95) plays a critical role in organizing proteins at the PSD (Kim & Sheng, 2004). PSD-95 regulates NMDA receptor trafficking by promoting surface expression and concurrently attenuating receptor internalization (Lin et al., 2004). Upregulation of the expression of PSD-95 occurs during the late-phase of LTP when new and/or enlarged spines accumulate stable populations of glutamate receptors (Williams et al., 2003; Lamprecht & LeDoux, 2004). Choquet and Triller (2003) hypothesized that altering the balance between synaptic and extrasynaptic receptor pools involve changes in expression of scaffolding proteins in post-synaptic membrane. The cytoplasmic C-terminus of the NR2 subunit binds to PSD-95/disc large/ZO 1 (PDZ) domain of PSD-related proteins known as membrane-associated guanylate kinases (MAGUKs) (Ponting et al., 1997). In addition to MAGUKs, a large number of other cytoskeleton-associated proteins interact with NR subunits to serve as a macromolecular complex for signal transduction processes. Thus, understanding the effects of chronic ethanol on PSD-95 expression and other scaffolding proteins may contribute to homeostatic processes underlying alcohol dependency.

Previous studies have reported that chronic attenuation of synaptic activity leads to an increase in the number of spines (Kirov & Harris, 1999; Kirov, Goddard, & Harris, 2004) and in the size of the PSD (Murthy et al., 2001). In addition, the magnitude of glutamate-induced currents positively correlates with the shape of the spine (Matsuzaki et al., 2001; Smith, Ellis-Davies, & Magee, 2003). The capacity of spines to undergo changes in morphology appears to be related to dynamic changes in filamentous actin (F-actin) through activity-dependent processes (Ackermann & Matus, 2003; Fukazawa et al., 2003). Compounds that antagonize actin polymerization suppress LTP (Krucker, Siggins, & Halpain, 2000), whereas LTP induction increases the content of F-actin in rodent hippocampus that persisted 5 weeks following induction (Fukazawa et al., 2003). Interestingly, NMDA receptor activity regulates the balance between F-actin and monomeric actin (Okamoto et al., 2004). Thus, the rapid formation and persistence of F-actin following NMDA receptor stimulation indicates that it contributes to spine dynamics during plastic responses. It is now clear that the PSD is a dynamic sub-structure that plays a vital role in regulating NMDA-dependent synaptic plasticity, especially as it relates to changes within the cytoskeleton.

ETHANOL AND THE POST-SYNAPTIC DENSITY

It has been known for some time that chronic ethanol exposure results in the development of tolerance and dependence that are products of neuroadaptive changes, particularly within the glutamatergic system. For example, some studies demonstrated that treatment of primary neuronal or organotypic cultures increased NMDA receptor subunit expression (Fadda & Rossetti, 1988; Harris et al., 2003), whereas others demonstrated increases in the function of NMDA receptors without concurrent changes in receptor levels (Chandler et al., 1997; Winkler et al., 1999). However, as noted previously, there is increasing evidence that chronic ethanol exposure results in sub-cellular alterations that extend beyond simple increases in the number and function of glutamatergic receptors. Using cultured hippocampal neurons, Chandler and colleagues demonstrated that 4-day ethanol exposure increased NR1 and NR2B clusters located in the synapse, effects that were prevented by inhibition of protein kinase A or by co-exposure to a sub-toxic concentration of NMDA (Carpenter-Hyland, Woodward, & Chandler, 2004). It should be noted that no effects were observed in the localization of AMPA receptor or in NMDA receptors located extrasynaptically. These data would suggest that dynamic regulation of NMDA receptor trafficking to the synapse is a key mechanism underlying chronic ethanol-associated neuroadaptive plasticity. More recent evidence demonstrated an ethanol-induced enhancement of synaptic PSD-95 and F-actin clustering, suggesting an increase in spine size (Carpenter-Hyland & Chandler, 2006). Thus, synaptic targeting of NMDA receptors also involves expansion of the PSD, possibly allowing for homeostatic changes in response to chronic ethanol.

Recent studies using post-mortem tissue from alcoholics and rodent brain demonstrated differential expression of selective genes associated with alcohol abuse across various brain regions (for review, see Flatscher-Bader et al., 2006). For example, in the prefrontal cortex, changes have been demonstrated in alcohol-responsive genes that encoded transcription factors, DNA repair proteins, mito-chondrial proteins, and regulatory proteins for cAMP (Flatscher-Bader et al., 2005; Iwamoto et al., 2004). In addition, a downregulation of myelination-related genes has been reported in alcoholic prefrontal cortex (Lewohl et al., 2000; Flatscher-Bader et al., 2005). Given that neuronal loss is observed in the prefrontal cortex of some alcohol-dependent individuals, it is not surprising that alcohol-responsive gene expression changes are associated with neurodegeneration and apoptosis. Perhaps more important, changes in alcohol-responsive genes associated with plas-ticity were demonstrated in mesocorticolimbic system, specifically within the nucleus accumbens and VTA (Flatscher-Bader et al., 2005, 2006). In particular, the authors reported induction and downregulation of genes affecting cellular architecture, cell–cell adhesion, structural function, cellular signaling, and protein trafficking, specifically those that may affect the actin skeleton. These data point to changes in gene expression profiles that suggest neuroadaptation in the reward cir-cuitry in human alcoholics, lending evidence for alcohol-induced persistent changes in subcellular constituents controlling synaptic plasticity. It is also note-worthy that a recent study examining the genetic basis for alcohol preference in mice reported an over-representation of proteins involved in regulation of the actin cytoskeleton in the alcohol-preferring lines (Mulligan et al., 2006).

Understanding the sequelae of events by which ethanol affects sub-cellular micro-circuitry is of importance in understanding the mechanisms that lead to the development of ethanol tolerance and dependence. Although it is beyond the scope of this chapter, increasing numbers of studies on molecular, cellular and behavioral levels are now focused on examining the effect of ethanol on intracellular signaling cascades and scaf-folding/anchoring proteins (for reviews, see Ron, 2004; Newton & Messing, 2006). There is increasing interest in the effect of ethanol on signaling cascades involving cAMP, protein kinases A and C, tyrosine kinase Fyn, phospholipase D, and CREB. For exam-ple, Chandler and colleagues (2005) demonstrated that acute ethanol exposure inhibited ERK/protein kinase B/CREB signaling in rodents. Interestingly, phosphodiesterase (PDE) inhibitors, which prevent breakdown of cAMP, serve as putative cognitive enhancers (Vitolo et al., 2002) and have been shown to restore ocular dominance plas-ticity in an animal model of fetal alcohol exposure (Medina, Krahe, & Ramoa, 2006). Thus, PDE inhibitors serve as a potential therapeutic target for treatment of cognitive impairments associated with alcohol consumption.

Scaffolding proteins contribute to the specificity of signal transduction by providing temporal and spatial organization of intracellular constituents within the PSD. For example, the scaffolding protein RACK1 localizes Fyn in proximity to NMDA receptors containing the NR2B subunit and allows for

Fyn phosphorylation of the receptor following the appropriate signal (Yaka et al., 2002; Yaka, Phamluong, & Ron, 2003). Chronic ethanol exposure alters the compartmentalization and function of RACK1 resulting in differences in c-fos expression (Vagtset al., 2003). In addition to RACK1, DARPP-32 also regulates NMDA receptors, particularly within medium spiny neurons of the neo striatum (Greengard, Allen, & Nairn, 1999). It has been demonstrated that ethanol phos-phorylates DARPP-32, which enhances NMDA receptor function via an unknown mechanism (Maldve et al., 2002).

Homer proteins (Homer1-3) are an integral constituent of signaling com-plexes at the PSD (Shiraishi et al., 2003; Sala et al., 2003). These proteins inter-act with inositol triphosphate and ryanodine receptors, Group I metabotropic receptors, and NMDA receptors (Shiraishi et al., 2004; for review see, de Bartolomeis & Iasevoli, 2003). Recent evidence suggests an active role for nucleus accumbens Homer2 in alcohol-associated neuroplasticity. Szumlinski and colleagues demonstrated that Homer2 knock-out mice displayed increased sensi-tivity to ethanol-induced motor impairment and failed to exhibit tolerance fol-lowing repeated ethanol administration (Szumlinski et al., 2005). Consistent with the suggestion that Homer proteins modulate plasticity, repeated ethanol admin-istration in these mice did not demonstrate extracellular rises in glutamate or dopamine in the nucleus accumbens (Szumlinski et al., 2005). Moreover, over-expression of accumbens Homer2 facilitated the rewarding aspects of ethanol administration. Given the role that Homer proteins play in regulating glutamate-PSD signaling, Szumlinski hypothesized that the lack of plasticity observed in Homer2 knock-out mice exposed to repeated ethanol may be related to impaired NMDA receptor trafficking or reduced function of Group I mGluR.

METABOTROPIC GLUTAMATE RECEPTORS

While much of the work on glutamate and drug addiction over the last two decades has focused on ionotropic glutamate receptors, a clear role for metabotropic glutamate receptors (mGluRs) in alcohol addiction is beginning to emerge (for reviews, see Kenny & Markou, 2004; Olive, 2005). Eight different G-protein-coupled mGluRs have been described that are classified into three groups, each with distinct signaling properties and neuroanatomical distribution (Conn & Pin, 1997; Hermans & Challiss, 2001). Group I mGluRs (mGluR1 and mGluR5) couple to phosphoinositide hydrolysis and protein kinase C activation. In addition, evidence suggests that Group 1 mGluRs can stimulate adenylate cyclase and block voltage-dependent Ca^{2+} channels, as well as mobilize stores of cytosolic Ca^{2+}. In comparison, Group II (mGluR2 and mGluR3) and Group III (mGluR4 and mGluR6-8) are negatively coupled to adenylate cyclase and when activated lead to a reduction in the formation of cAMP. Interestingly, relatively high expression levels of mGluR5 protein and mRNA occur within the addiction circuitry (Sahara, Kubota, & Ichikawa, 2001; for review, see Olive, 2005). Consistent with the suggestion that addiction involves process associated with the plasticity of learning and memory, mGluR5 play a role in memory formation and certain forms of LTP and LTD (Lu et al., 1997; Balschun & Wetzel, 2002; Naie & Manahan-Vaughan, 2004).

Much of what is known concerning the role of mGluR5 in alcohol dependency stems from studies using mGluR5 agonists (R,S-2-chloro-5-hydroxyphenylglycine; CHPG) and antagonists (MPEP and MTEP) and mGluR5-deficient mice. CHPG exposure results in elevated glutamate release (Pintor et al., 2000) and augments NMDA-mediated membrane depolarization in striatal slices (Pisani et al., 2001). MPEP, a selective antagonist, decreased LTD at corticostriatal synapses suggesting that mGluR5 contributes to synaptic plasticity (Sung, Choi, & Lovinger, 2001). mGluR antagonists have beneficial effects against neurodegeneration and in animal models of pain and anxiety (Bordi & Ugolini, 1999; Spooren et al., 2001). Perhaps most interesting, pharmacological and genetic data suggest a role for mGluR5 in addictive processes. At high concentrations, ethanol has been shown to inhibit glutamate-stimulated chloride flux in *Xenopus* oocytes expressing mGluR5 (Minami et al., 1998), possibly through a protein kinase C-dependent mechanism (Olive et al., 2005). MPEP administration prevented cue-induced responding for alcohol, decreased alcohol consumption during operant self-administration in mice, and prevented the repeated alcohol deprivation effect in rats (Backstrom et al., 2004; Schroeder, Overstreet, & Hodge, 2005). Additionally, MPEP and MTEP significantly reduced operant responding for ethanol self-administration and attenuated consumption in a two-bottle preference test in rodents (Cowen, Djouma, & Lawrence, 2005; McMillen et al., 2005; Olive et al., 2005). Hodge and et al. (2006) recently demonstrated that MPEP regulated the onset and maintenance of ethanol self-administration in mice, suggesting that mGluR5 antagonism reduced the rewarding effects of ethanol. Taken together, these data implicate a role for mGluR5 in modulating the reinforcing properties of alcohol and other drugs of abuse and suggest that mGluR5 antagonists may be an effective, novel pharmacotherapeutic target in the treatment of alcohol abuse and dependency (Olive, 2005).

Recent data has demonstrated a physical link between mGluR5 and NMDA receptors by anchoring proteins at synaptic and perisynaptic sites (Awad et al., 2000; Bruno et al., 2001; Spooren et al., 2001). Specifically, the link between NMDA receptors and Group I mGluR via Shank–Homer–PSD95 complexes in the PSD likely plays an integral role in post-synaptic function, possibly by controlling cytosolic Ca^{2+} stores, ERK phosphorylation, and overall neuronal signaling (Sala et al., 2005). In hippocampal CA1, activation of mGluR5 potentiated NMDA receptor function (Mannaioni et al., 2001), possibly through phosphorylation of NMDA receptors by protein kinase C

(Aniksztejn, Bregestovski, & Ben-Ari, 1991). In turn, NMDA receptor activity may prevent desensitization of mGluR5 via calcineurin (Alagarsamy et al., 1999). It has been suggested that acamprosate possesses binding and functional characteristics similar to mGluR5 antagonists and the authors speculated that the ability of acamprosate to reduce alcohol relapse might result from altered mGluR5 activity through links with NMDA receptors (Harris et al., 2003). Thus, it is likely that the cross talk between NMDA receptors and mGluR5 may play a role in alcohol-associated homeostatic responses at the PSD that contribute to relapse and craving. However, further work is necessary to understand the relationship between NMDA, mGluR, and glutamatergic signaling associated with chronic ethanol consumption to fully elucidate the mechanisms underlying adaptations within the PSD that control ethanol-seeking and relapse behavior.

CANNABINOID RECEPTORS

The endocannabinoid (EC) system is thought to affect cognition and motivation, as well as regulate pain, sleep, and appetite (Breivogel & Childers, 1998), and a role for ECs in the pathophysiology of alcoholism is beginning to emerge (Vinod & Hungund, 2005). EC are known to bind to cannabinoid (CB) receptors and exert behavioral and pharmacological properties similar to Δ^9-tetrahydrocannabinol (THC), the psychoactive compound in marijuana. The CB receptor system consists of CB_1 and CB_2 G-protein-coupled receptors that are negatively coupled to adenylyl cyclase and positively coupled to mitogen-activated protein kinases via $G_{i/o}$ proteins. CB_1 receptors exhibit localized expression in neural tissue (i.e. cortex, limbic structures, basal ganglia), whereas CB_2 receptors are located in the periphery and are associated with immune function (Munro, Thomas, & Abu-Shaar, 1993).

To date, the findings that the EC system contributes to alcohol-seeking behavior are threefold. First, chronic ethanol exposure increases levels of the endogenous ECs N-arachidonyl ethanolamide (AEA) and 2-arachidonyl glycerol (2-AG) (Basavarajappa & Hungund, 1999a). In addition to increase in endogenous ECs, chronic ethanol decreased signaling associated with CB_1 receptors and CB_1 receptor density in cortex, hippocampus, striatum, and cerebellum (Basavarajappa et al., 1998; Basavarajappa & Hungund, 1999b; Vinod & Hungund, 2005). The sensitivity associated with these changes was evident during ethanol withdrawal (Vinod & Hungund, 2005), suggesting neuroadaptive alterations of the EC systems during prolonged ethanol consumption. Thus, desensitization of CB_1 receptors may be due to reduced inhibition of adenylyl cyclase activity, resulting in cAMP–PKA–CREB activation that may contribute to the development of ethanol tolerance and dependence (Vinod & Hungund, 2005).

The second line of evidence comes from pharmacological manipulations using CB_1 receptor antagonists and agonists that demonstrate involvement of EC on voluntary ethanol consumption. Administration of SR 141716A (Rimonabant) prior to a preference test markedly decreased ethanol intake, an effect that returned to normal on subsequent days without the CB_1 receptor antagonist (Hungund et al., 2003). SR 141716A has also been shown to reduce voluntary intake in rodents, while acute treatment with the CB_1 receptor agonist CP-55,940 increased ethanol consumption (Gallate & McGregor, 1999; Gallate et al., 1999; Rodriguez de Fonseca et al., 1999). Finally, in mice with altered CB_1 receptor function or in CB_1 receptor knock out mice, studies have demonstrated ethanol consumption and preference to significantly differ when compared with control animals (Hungund & Basavarajappa, 2000; Hungund et al., 2003; Poncelet et al., 2003). Taken together, these studies suggest that neuroadaptations within the EC system contribute to tolerance and dependence to ethanol and point to a novel therapeutic target for the treatment of alcoholism. Indeed, Phase II clinical trials are underway to examine the efficacy of Rimonabant against alcohol abuse and dependence.

IMPLICATIONS FOR TREATMENT

A major goal of studies aimed at elucidating the molecular changes associated with chronic ethanol exposure in cellular and animal models is to identify novel targets for more effective therapeutic interventions for the treatment of alcohol abuse and dependence. There is emerging evidence that chronic alcohol use affects the glutamatergic system, which is critically involved in learning, survival, and experience-dependent synaptic plasticity. Data presented in this review suggest that molecular and cellular alterations within the glutamatergic system appear to underlie alcohol-associated plasticity. The ultimate goal of future studies is to address these adaptations to develop more effective pharmacological treatments for alcohol dependency, craving, and relapse. Further understanding of the mechanisms that reverse the neuroadaptations associated with chronic ethanol exposure would likely lead to the development of more efficacious pharmacotherapies, especially if studies demonstrate concurrent changes in alcohol-seeking behaviors.

Based on the evidence discussed in this article, there are numerous potential targets for the further development of therapeutic agents for alcohol-related disorders. For example, data from molecular and animal models have implemented mGluR and EC systems in alcohol-associated behaviors. There are plans of future studies to address the efficacy of compounds that act on these targets to determine their role as potential pharmacotherapies in alcohol-dependent individuals. In addition, recent findings from sub-cellular models have suggested that ethanol affects signaling cascades that regulate glutamatergic synapses. Recent evidence also suggests that adaptations in ERK signaling cascades in the amygdala and in glutamatergic neurotransmission in the prefrontal cortex projections to the nucleus accumbens contribute to drug relapse (Kalivas et al., 2005; Lu et al., 2005; Robinson & Berridge, 2003). As a result of evidence implicating glutamatergic neuroadaptations in addiction, there is increasing interest in modulators of NMDA receptor function for the treatment of alcoholism (Nagy, 2004). Although neuroadaptations associated with continuous ethanol consumption may be unique in comparison with other drugs of abuse, there is evidence to suggest that there are common molecular pathways (i.e. cortical hypofrontality) that contribute to addiction across a variety of drugs (Nestler, 2005). Most alcohol-dependent individuals are poly-substance abusers (O'Brien, 2005), with estimates of the prevalence of alcohol and tobacco co-dependency ranging from 50% to nearly 95% (Marks et al., 1997; Walton et al., 1981). Experimental approaches that focus on reversing neuroadaptations that are common to other drugs of abuse would likely increase the efficacy of novel pharmacotherapies in poly-drug abusers.

REFERENCES

Ackermann, M., & Matus, A. (2003). Activity-induced targeting of profilin and stabilization of dendritic spine morphology. *Nature Neuroscience, 6*, 1194–1200.

Alagarsamy, S., Marino, M. J., Rouse, S. T., Gereau, R. W. 4th, Heinemann, S. F., & Conn, P. J. (1999). Activation of NMDA receptors reverses desensitization of mGluR5 in native and recombinant systems. *Nature Neuroscience, 2*(3), 234–240.

Aniksztejn, L., Bregestovski, P., & Ben-Ari, Y. (1991). Selective activation of quisqualate metabotropic receptor potentiates NMDA but not AMPA responses. *European Journal of Pharmacology, 205*(3), 327–328.

Awad, H., Hubert, G.W., Smith, Y., Levey, A.I., & Conn, P.J. (2000). Activation of metabotropic glutamate receptor 5 has direct excitatory effects and potentiates NMDA receptor currents in neurons of the subthalamic nucleus. *Journal of Neuroscience, 20*(21), 7871–7879.

Backstrom, P., Bachteler, D., Koch, S., Hyytia, P., & Spanagel, R. (2004). mGluR5 antagonist MPEP reduces ethanol-seeking and relapse behavior. *Neuropsychopharmacology, 29*(5), 921–928.

Balschun, D., & Wetzel, W. (2002). Inhibition of mGluR5 blocks hippocampal LTP in vivo and spatial learning in rats. *Pharmacology Biochemistry and Behavior, 73*(2), 375–380.

Basavarajappa, B. S., & Hungund, B. L. (1999a). Chronic ethanol increases the cannabinoid receptor agonist anandamide and its precursor *N*-arachidonoylphosphatidylethanolamine in SK-N-SH cells. *Journal of Neurochemistry, 72*(2), 522–528.

Basavarajappa, B. S., & Hungund, B. L. (1999b). Down-regulation of cannabinoid receptor agonist-stimulated [35S]GTP gamma S binding in synaptic plasma membrane from chronic ethanol exposed mouse. *Brain Research, 815*(1), 89–97.

Basavarajappa, B. S., Cooper, T. B., Hungund, B. L. (1998). Chronic ethanol administration down regulates cannabinoid receptors in mouse brain synaptic plasma membrane. *Brain Research, 793*(1–2), 212–218.

Becker, H. C. (1998). Kindling in alcohol withdrawal. *Alcohol Health and Research World, 22*, 25–33.

Bordi, F., & Ugolini, A. (1999). Group I metabotropic glutamate receptors: Implications for brain diseases. *Progress in Neurobiology, 59*(1), 55–79.

Breivogel, C. S., & Childers, S. R. (1998). The functional neuroanatomy of brain cannabinoid receptors. *Neurobiology of Disease, 5*(6), 417–431.

Bruno, V., Battaglia, G., Copani, A., Cespedes, V. M., Galindo, M. F., Cena, V., Sanchez-Prieto, J., Gasparini, F., Kuhn, R., Flor, P. J., & Nicoletti, F. (2001). An activity-dependent switch from facilitation to inhibition in the control of excitotoxicity by group I metabotropic glutamate receptors. *European Journal of Neuroscience, 13*(8), 1469–1478.

Carpenter-Hyland, E. P., Woodward, J. J., & Chandler, L. J. (2004). Chronic ethanol induces synaptic but not extrasynaptic targeting of NMDA receptors. *Journal of Neuroscience, 24*, 7859–7868.

Carpenter-Hyland, E. P., & Chandler, L. J. (2006). Homeostatic plasticity during alcohol exposure promotes enlargement of dendritic spines. *European Journal of Neuroscience, 24*(12), 3496–3506.

Carroll, R. C., & Zukin, R. S. (2002). NMDA-receptor trafficking and targeting: Implications for synaptic transmission and plasticity. *Trends in Neurosciences, 25*, 571–577.

Chandler, L. J., & Sutton, G. (2005). Acute ethanol inhibits extracellular signal-regulated kinase, protein kinase B, and adenosine 3′: 5′-cyclic monophosphate response element binding protein activity in an age- and brain region-specific manner. *Alcoholism-Clinical and Experimental Research, 29*, 672–682.

Chandler, L. J., Sutton, G., Norwood, D., Sumners, C., & Crews, F. T. (1997). Chronic ethanol increases N-methyl-D-aspartate-stimulated nitric oxide formation but not receptor density in cultured cortical neurons. *Molecular Pharmacology, 51*, 733–740.

Choquet, D., & Triller, A. (2003). The role of receptor diffusion in the organization of the postsynaptic membrane. *Nature Reviews Neuroscience, 4*, 251–265.

Conn, P. J., & Pin, J. P. (1997). Pharmacology and functions of metabotropic glutamate receptors. *Annual Review of Pharmacology and Toxicology, 37*, 205–237.

Cowen, M. S., Djouma, E., & Lawrence, A. J. (2005). The metabotropic glutamate 5 receptor antagonist 3-[(2-methyl-1,3-thiazol-4-yl)ethynyl]-pyridine reduces ethanol self-administration in multiple strains of alcohol-preferring rats and regulates olfactory glutamatergic systems. *Journal of Pharmacology and Experimental Therapeutics, 315*(2), 590–600.

Cull-Candy, S., Brickley, S., & Farrant, M. (2001). NMDA receptor subunits: Diversity, development and disease. *Current Opinion in Neurobiology, 11*, 327–335.

Dawson, D. A., & Grant, B. F. (1998). Family history of alcoholism and gender: Their combined effects on DSM-IV alcohol dependence and major depression. *Journal of Studies in Alcohol, 59*, 97–106.

de Bartolomeis, A., & Iasevoli, F. (2003). The Homer family and the signal transduction system at glutamatergic postsynaptic density: Potential role in behavior and pharmacotherapy. *Psychopharmacology Bulletin, 37*(3), 51–83.

Dingledine, R., Borges, K., Bowie, D., & Traynelis, S. F. (1999). The glutamate receptor ion channels. *Pharmacological Reviews, 51*, 7–61.

Dunah, A. W., Sirianni, A. C., Fienberg, A. A., Bastia, E., Schwarzschild, M. A., & Standaert, D. G. (2004). Dopamine D1-dependent trafficking of striatal N-methyl-D-aspartate glutamate receptors requires Fyn protein tyrosine kinase but not DARPP-32. *Molecular Pharmacology, 65*, 121–129.

Fadda, F., & Rossetti, Z. L. (1998). Chronic ethanol consumption: From neuroadaptation to neurodegeneration. *Progress in Neurobiology, 56*, 385–431.

Flatscher-Bader, T., van der Brug, M., Hwang, J. W., Gochee, P. A., Matsumoto, I., Niwa, S., & Wilce, P. A. (2005). Alcohol-responsive genes in the frontal cortex and nucleus accumbens of human alcoholics. *Journal of Neurochemistry, 93*, 359–370.

Flatscher-Bader, T., van der Brug, M. P., Landis, N., Hwang, J. W., Harrison, E., & Wilce, P. A. (2006). Comparative gene expression in brain regions of human alcoholics. *Genes and Brain Behavior, 5*, 78–84.

Franks, N. P., & Lieb, W. R. (1994). Molecular and cellular mechanisms of general anaesthesia. *Nature, 367*, 607–614.

Freund, G., & Anderson, K. J. (1996). Glutamate receptors in the frontal cortex of alcoholics. *Alcoholism-Clinical and Experimental Research, 20*, 1165–1172.

Fukazawa, Y., Saitoh, Y., Ozawa, F., Ohta, Y., Mizuno, K., & Inokuchi, K. (2003). Hippocampal LTP is accompanied by enhanced F-actin content within the dendritic spine that is essential for late LTP maintenance in vivo. *Neuron, 38*, 447–460.

Gallate, J. E., & McGregor, I. S. (1999). The motivation for beer in rats: Effects of ritanserin, naloxone and SR 141716. *Psychopharmacology, 142*(3), 302–308.

Gallate, J. E., Saharov, T., Mallet, P. E., & McGregor, I. S. (1999). Increased motivation for beer in rats following administration of a cannabinoid CB1 receptor agonist. *European Journal of Pharmacology, 370*(3), 233–240.

Gomez, L. L., Alam, S., Smith, K. E., Horne, E., & Dell'Acqua, M. L. (2002). Regulation of A-kinase anchoring protein 79/150-cAMP-dependent protein kinase postsynaptic targeting by NMDA receptor activation of calcineurin and remodeling of dendritic actin. *Journal of Neuroscience, 22*, 7027–7044.

Grant, B. F., Dawson, D. A., Stinson, F. S., Chou, S. P., Dufour, M. C., & Pickering, R. P. (2004). The 12-month prevalence and trends in DSM-IV alcohol abuse and dependence: United States, 1991–1992 and 2001–2002. *Drug and Alcohol Dependence, 74*, 223–234.

Greengard, P., Allen, P. B., & Nairn, A. C. (1999). Beyond the dopamine receptor: The DARPP-32/protein phosphatase-1 cascade. *Neuron, 23*, 435–447.

Harris, B. R., Gibson, D. A., Prendergast, M. A., Blanchard, J. A., Holley, R. C., Hart, S. R., Scotland, R. L., Foster, T. C., Pedigo, N. W., & Littleton, J. M. (2003). The neurotoxicity induced by ethanol withdrawal in mature organotypic hippocampal slices might involve cross-talk between metabotropic glutamate type 5 receptors and *N*-methyl-D-aspartate receptors. *Alcoholism-Clinical and Experimental Research, 27*, 1724–1735.

Harwood H. J., Fountain, D., & Livermore, G. (1998). In M. Galanter (Ed.). *Recent Developments in Alcoholism, Volume 14: The Consequences of Alcoholism.* New York: Plenum Press.

Hering, H., & Sheng, M. (2003). Activity-dependent redistribution and essential role of cortactin in dendritic spine morphogenesis. *Journal of Neuroscience, 23*, 11759–11769.

Hermans, E., & Challiss, R. A. (2001). Structural, signalling and regulatory properties of the group I metabotropic glutamate receptors: Prototypic family C G-protein-coupled receptors. *Biochemical Journal, 359*(3), 465–484.

Hodge, C. W., Miles, M. F., Sharko, A. C., Stevenson, R. A., Hillmann, J. R., Lepoutre, V., Besheer, J., & Schroeder, J. P. (2006). The mGluR5 antagonist MPEP selectively inhibits the onset and maintenance of ethanol self-administration in C57BL/6J mice. *Psychopharmacology, 183*(4), 429–438.

Hungund, B. L., & Basavarajappa, B. S. (2000). Distinct differences in the cannabinoid receptor binding in the brain of C57BL/6 and DBA/2 mice, selected for their differences in voluntary ethanol consumption. *Journal of Neuroscience Research, 60*(1), 122–128.

Hungund, B. L., Szakall, I., Adam, A., Basavarajappa, B. S., & Vadasz, C. (2003). Cannabinoid CB1 receptor knockout mice exhibit markedly reduced voluntary alcohol consumption and lack alcohol-induced dopamine release in the nucleus accumbens. *Journal of Neurochemistry, 84*(4), 698–704.

Iwamoto, K., Bundo, M., Yamamoto, M., Ozawa, H., Saito, T., & Kato, T. (2004). Decreased expression of NEFH and PCP4/PEP19 in the prefrontal cortex of alcoholics. *Neuroscience Research, 49*, 379–385.

Kalivas, P. W. (2005). How do we determine which drug-induced neuroplastic changes are important? *Nature of Neuroscience, 8*(11), 1440–1441.

Kalivas, P. W., Volkow, N., & Seamans, J. (2005). Unmanageable motivation in addiction: A pathology in prefrontal-accumbens glutamate transmission. *Neuron, 45*(5), 647–650.

Karadottir, R., Cavelier, P., Bergersen, L. H., & Attwell, D. (2005). NMDA receptors are expressed in oligodendrocytes and activated in ischaemia. *Nature, 438*, 1162–1166.

Kenny, P. J., & Markou, A. (2004). The ups and downs of addiction: Role of metabotropic glutamate receptors. *Trends in Pharmacological Sciences, 25*(5), 265–272.

Kim, E., & Sheng, M. (2004). PDZ domain proteins of synapses. *Nature Reviews Neuroscience, 5*, 771–781.

Kirov, S. A., Goddard, C. A., & Harris, K. M. (2004). Age-dependence in the homeostatic upregulation of hippocampal dendritic spine number during blocked synaptic transmission. *Neuropharmacology, 47*, 640–648.

Kirov, S. A., & Harris, K. M. (1999). Dendrites are more spiny on mature hippocampal neurons when synapses are inactivated. *Nature of Neuroscience, 2*, 878–883.

Krucker, T., Siggins, G. R., & Halpain, S. (2000). Dynamic actin filaments are required for stable long-term potentiation (LTP) in area CA1 of the hippocampus. *Proceedings of the National Academy of Sciences of USA, 97*, 6856–6861.

Kumari, M., & Ticku, M. K. (2000). Regulation of NMDA receptors by ethanol. *Progress in Drug Research, 54*, 152–189.

Lamprecht, R., & LeDoux, J. (2004). Structural plasticity and memory. *Nature Reviews of Neuroscience, 5*, 45–54.

Lewohl, J. M., Wang, L., Miles, M. F., Zhang, L., Dodd, P. R., & Harris, R. A. (2000). Gene expression in human alcoholism: Microarray analysis of frontal cortex. *Alcoholism-Clinical and Experimental Research, 24*, 1873–1882.

Lin, Y., Skeberdis, V. A., Francesconi, A., Bennett, M. V., & Zukin, R. S. (2004). Postsynaptic density protein-95 regulates NMDA channel gating and surface expression. *Journal of Neuroscience, 24*, 10138–10148.

Lissin, D. V., Gomperts, S. N., Carroll, R. C., Christine, C. W., Kalman, D., Kitamura, M., Hardy, S., Nicoll, R. A., Malenka, R. C., & von Zastrow, M. (1998). Activity differentially regulates the surface expression of synaptic AMPA and NMDA glutamate receptors. *Proceedings of the National Academy of Sciences of USA, 95*, 7097–7102.

Lissin, D. V., Malenka, R. C., & Von Zastrow, M. (1999). An immunocytochemical assay for activity-dependent redistribution of glutamate receptors from the postsynaptic plasma membrane. *Annals of New York Academy of Science, 868*, 550–553.

Lovinger, D. M., & Crabbe, J. C. (2005). Laboratory models of alcoholism: Treatment target identification and insight into mechanisms. *Nature of Neuroscience, 8*, 1471–1480.

Lu, L., Hope, B. T., Dempsey, J., Liu, S. Y., Bossert, J. M., & Shaham, Y. (2005). Central amygdala ERK signaling pathway is critical to incubation of cocaine craving. *Nature of Neuroscience, 8*(2), 212–219.

Lu, Y. M., Jia, Z., Janus, C., Henderson, J. T., Gerlai, R., Wojtowicz, J. M., & Roder, J. C. (1997). Mice lacking metabotropic glutamate receptor 5 show impaired learning and reduced CA1 long-term potentiation (LTP) but normal CA3 LTP. *Journal of Neuroscience, 17*(13), 5196–5205.

Maiese, K., Chong, Z. Z., & Li, F. (2005). Driving cellular plasticity and survival through the signal transduction pathways of metabotropic glutamate receptors. *Current Neurovascular Research, 2*, 425–446.

Malcolm, R., Myrick, H., Roberts, J., Wang, W., Anton, R. F., & Ballenger, J. C. (2002). The effects of carbamazepine and lorazepam on single versus multiple previous alcohol withdrawals in an outpatient randomized trial. *Journal of General Internal Medicine, 17*, 349–355.

Maldve, R. E., Zhang, T. A., Ferrani-Kile, K., Schreiber, S. S., Lippmann, M. J., Snyder, G. L., Fienberg, A. A., Leslie, S. W., Gonzales, R. A., & Morrisett, R. A. (2002). DARPP-32 and regulation of the ethanol sensitivity of NMDA receptors in the nucleus accumbens. *Nature of Neuroscience, 5*(7), 641–648.

Mannaioni, G., Marino, M. J., Valenti, O., Traynelis, S. F., & Conn, P. J. (2001). Metabotropic glutamate receptors 1 and 5 differentially regulate CA1 pyramidal cell function. *Journal of Neuroscience, 21*(16), 5925–5934.

Marks, J. L., Hill, E. M., Pomerleau, C. S., Mudd, S. A., & Blow, F. C. (1997). Nicotine dependence and withdrawal in alcoholic and nonalcoholic ever-smokers. *Journal of Substance Abuse Treatment, 14*, 521–527.

Matsuzaki, M., Ellis-Davies, G. C., Nemoto, T., Miyashita, Y., Iino, M., & Kasai, H. (2001). Dendritic spine geometry is critical for AMPA receptor expression in hippocampal CA1 pyramidal neurons. *Nature of Neuroscience, 4*, 1086–1092.

McMillen, B. A., Crawford, M. S., Kulers, C. M., & Williams, H. L. (2005). Effects of a metabotropic, mglu5, glutamate receptor antagonist on ethanol consumption by genetic drinking rats. *Alcohol and Alcoholism, 40*(6), 494–497.

Medina, A. E., Krahe, T. E., & Ramoa, A. S. (2006). Restoration of neuronal plasticity by a phosphodiesterase type 1 inhibitor in a model of fetal alcohol exposure. *Journal of Neuroscience, 26*, 1057–1060.

Micu, I., Jiang, Q., Coderre, E., Ridsdale, A., Zhang, L., Woulfe, J., Yin, X., Trapp, B. D., McRory, J. E., Rehak, R., Zamponi, G. W., Wang, W., & Stys, P. K. (2006). NMDA receptors mediate calcium accumulation in myelin during chemical ischaemia. *Nature, 439*, 988–992.

Minami, K., Gereau, R. W. 4th, Minami, M., Heinemann, S. F., & Harris, R. A. (1998). Effects of ethanol and anesthetics on type 1 and 5 metabotropic glutamate receptors expressed in *Xenopus laevis* oocytes. *Molecular Pharmacology, 53*(1), 148–156.

Monyer, H., Burnashev, N., Laurie, D. J., Sakmann, B., & Seeburg, P. H. (1994). Developmental and regional expression in the rat brain and functional properties of four NMDA receptors. *Neuron, 12*, 529–540.

Muller, D., Nikonenko, I., Jourdain, P., & Alberi, S. (2002). LTP, memory and structural plasticity. *Current Molecular Medicine, 2*, 605–611.

Mulligan, M. K., Ponomarev, I., Hitzemann, R. J., Belknap, J. K., Tabakoff, B., Harris, R. A., Crabbe, J. C., Blednov, Y. A., Grahame, N. J., Phillips, T. J., Finn, D. A., Hoffman, P. L., Iyer, V. R., Koob, G. F., & Bergeson, S. E. (2006). Toward understanding the genetics of alcohol drinking through transcriptome meta-analysis. *Proceedings of the National Academy of Sciences of USA, 103*, 6368–6373.

Munro, S., Thomas, K. L., & Abu-Shaar, M. (1993). Molecular characterization of a peripheral receptor for cannabinoids. *Nature, 365*(6441), 61–65.

Murthy, V. N., Schikorski, T., Stevens, C. F., & Zhu, Y. (2001). Inactivity produces increases in neurotransmitter release and synapse size. *Neuron, 32*, 673–682.

Nagy, J. (2004). The NR2B subtype of NMDA receptor: A potential target for the treatment of alcohol dependence. *Current Drug Targets. CNS Neurological Disorder, 3*(3), 169–179.

Naie, K., & Manahan-Vaughan, D. (2004). Regulation by metabotropic glutamate receptor 5 of LTP in the dentate gyrus of freely moving rats: Relevance for learning and memory formation. *Cerebral Cortex, 14*(2), 189–198.

Nestler, E. J. (2005). Is there a common molecular pathway for addiction? *Nature of Neuroscience, 8*, 1445–1449.

Newton, P. M., & Messing, R. O. (2006). Intracellular signaling pathways that regulate behavioral responses to ethanol. *Pharmacological Therapeutics, 109*, 227–237.

O'Brien, C. P. (2005). Anticraving medications for relapse prevention: A possible new class of psychoactive medications. *American Journal of Psychiatry, 162*, 1423–1431.

O'Brien, R. J., Kamboj, S., Ehlers, M. D., Rosen, K. R., Fischbach, G. D., & Huganir, R. L. (1998). Activity-dependent modulation of synaptic AMPA receptor accumulation. *Neuron, 21*, 1067–1078.

Okamoto, K., Nagai, T., Miyawaki, A., & Hayashi, Y. (2004). Rapid and persistent modulation of actin dynamics regulates postsynaptic reorganization underlying bidirectional plasticity. *Nature of Neuroscience, 7*, 1104–1112.

Olive, M. F. (2005). mGlu5 receptors: Neuroanatomy, pharmacology, and role in drug addiction. *Current Psychiatry Reviews, 1*, 197–214.

Olive, M. F., McGeehan, A. J., Kinder, J. R., McMahon, T., Hodge, C. W., Janak, P. H., & Messing, R. O. (2005). The mGluR5 antagonist 6-methyl-2-(phenylethynyl)pyridine decreases ethanol consumption via a protein kinase C epsilon-dependent mechanism. *Molecular Pharmacology, 67*(2), 349–355.

Peoples, R. W., Li, C., & Weight, F. F. (1996). Lipid vs protein theories of alcohol action in the nervous system. *Annual Review of Pharmacology and Toxicology, 36*, 185–201.

Pintor, A., Pezzola, A., Reggio, R., Quarta, D., & Popoli, P. (2000). The mGlu5 receptor agonist CHPG stimulates striatal glutamate release: Possible involvement of A2A receptors. *Neuroreport, 11*(16), 3611–3614.

Pisani, A., Gubellini, P., Bonsi, P., Conquet, F., Picconi, B., Centonze, D., Bernardi, G., & Calabresi, P. (2001). Metabotropic glutamate receptor 5 mediates the potentiation of *N*-methyl-D-aspartate responses in medium spiny striatal neurons. *Neuroscience, 106*(3), 579–587.

Poncelet, M., Maruani, J., Calassi, R., & Soubrie, P. (2003). Overeating, alcohol and sucrose consumption decrease in CB1 receptor deleted mice. *Neuroscience Letters, 343*(3), 216–218.

Ponting, C. P., Phillips, C., Davies, K. E., & Blake, D. J. (1997). PDZ domains: Targeting signalling molecules to sub-membranous sites. *Bioessays, 19*, 469–479.

Robinson, T. E., & Berridge, K. C. (2003). Addiction. *Annual Review of Psychology, 54*, 25–53.

Robinson, T. E., & Kolb, B. (2004). Structural plasticity associated with exposure to drugs of abuse. *Neuropharmacology, 47*, 33–46.

Rodriguez de Fonseca, F., Roberts, A. J., Bilbao, A., Koob, G. F., & Navarro, M. (1999). Cannabinoid receptor antagonist SR141716A decreases operant ethanol self administration in rats exposed to ethanol-vapor chambers. *Zhongguo Yao Li Xue Bao, 20*(12), 1109–1114.

Ron, D. (2004). Signaling cascades regulating NMDA receptor sensitivity to ethanol. *Neuroscientist, 10*, 325–336.

Sahara, Y., Kubota, T., & Ichikawa, M. (2001). Cellular localization of metabotropic glutamate receptors mGluR1, 2/3, 5 and 7 in the main and accessory olfactory bulb of the rat. *Neuroscience Letters, 312*(2), 59–62.

Sala, C., Futai, K., Yamamoto, K., Worley, P. F., Hayashi, Y., & Sheng, M. (2003). Inhibition of dendritic spine morphogenesis and synaptic transmission by activity-inducible protein Homer1a. *Journal of Neuroscience, 23*, 6327–6337.

Sala, C., Roussignol, G., Meldolesi, J., & Fagni, L. (2005). Key role of the postsynaptic density scaffold proteins Shank and Homer in the functional architecture of Ca^{2+} homeostasis at dendritic spines in hippocampal neurons. *Journal of Neuroscience, 25*(18), 4587–4592.

Salter, M. G., & Fern, R. (2005). NMDA receptors are expressed in developing oligodendrocyte processes and mediate injury. *Nature, 438*, 1167–1171.

Sanchis-Segura, C., Borchardt, T., Vengeliene, V., Zghoul, T., Bachteler, D., Gass, P., Sprengel, R., & Spanagel, R. (2006). Involvement of the AMPA receptor GluR-C subunit in alcohol-seeking behavior and relapse. *Journal of Neuroscience, 26*, 1231–1238.

Schroeder, J. P., Overstreet, D. H., & Hodge, C. W. (2005). The mGluR5 antagonist MPEP decreases operant ethanol self-administration during maintenance and after repeated alcohol deprivations in alcohol-preferring (P) rats. *Psychopharmacology, 179*(1), 262–270.

Scott, D. B., Blanpied, T. A., & Ehlers, M. D. (2003). Coordinated PKA and PKC phosphorylation suppresses RXR-mediated ER retention and regulates the surface delivery of NMDA receptors. *Neuropharmacology, 45*, 755–767.

Shiraishi, Y., Mizutani, A., Mikoshiba, K., & Furuichi, T. (2003). Coincidence in dendritic clustering and synaptic targeting of homer proteins and NMDA receptor complex proteins NR2B and PSD95 during development of cultured hippocampal neurons. *Molecular and Cellular Neuroscience, 22*, 188–201.

Shiraishi, Y., Mizutani, A., Yuasa, S., Mikoshiba, K., & Furuichi, T. (2004). Differential expression of Homer family proteins in the developing mouse brain. *Journal of Comparative Neurology, 473*(4), 582–599.

Smith, M. A., Ellis-Davies, G. C., & Magee, J. C. (2003). Mechanism of the distance-dependent scaling of Schaffer collateral synapses in rat CA1 pyramidal neurons. *Journal of Physiology, 548*, 245–258.

Spooren, W. P., Gasparini, F., Salt, T. E., & Kuhn, R. (2001). Novel allosteric antagonists shed light on mglu(5) receptors and CNS disorders. *Trends in Pharmacological Sciences, 22*(7), 331–337.

Sung, K. W., Choi, S., & Lovinger, D. M. (2001). Activation of group I mGluRs is necessary for induction of long-term depression at striatal synapses. *Journal of Neurophysiology, 86*(5), 2405–2412.

Szumlinski, K. K., Lominac, K. D., Oleson, E. B., Walker, J. K., Mason, A., Dehoff, M. H., Klugmann, M., Cagle, S., Welt, K., During, M., Worley, P. F., Middaugh, L. D., & Kalivas, P. W. (2005). Homer2 is necessary for EtOH-induced neuroplasticity. *Journal of Neuroscience, 25*(30), 7054–7061.

Thornton, C., Yaka, R., Dinh, S., & Ron, D. (2003). H-Ras modulates N-methyl-D-aspartate receptor function via inhibition of Src tyrosine kinase activity. *Journal of Biological Chemistry, 278*, 23823–23829.

Tovar, K. R., & Westbrook, G. L. (2002). Mobile NMDA receptors at hippocampal synapses. *Neuron, 34*, 255–264.

Vagts, A. J., He, D. Y., Yaka, R., & Ron, D. (2003). Cellular adaptation to chronic ethanol results in altered compartmentalization and function of the scaffolding protein RACK1. *Alcoholism-Clinical and Experimental Research, 27*, 1599–1605.

Vinod, K. Y., & Hungund, B. L. (2005). Endocannabinoid lipids and mediated system: Implications for alcoholism and neuropsychiatric disorders. *Life Science, 77*(14), 1569–1583.

Vissel, B., Krupp, J. J., Heinemann, S. F., & Westbrook, G. L. (2001). A use-dependent tyrosine dephosphorylation of NMDA receptors is independent of ion flux. *Nature of Neuroscience, 4*, 587–596.

Vitolo, O. V., Sant'Angelo, A., Costanzo, V., Battaglia, F., Arancio, O., & Shelanski, M. (2002). Amyloid beta-peptide inhibition of the PKA/CREB pathway and long-term potentiation: Reversibility by drugs that enhance cAMP signaling. *Proceedings of National Academy of Science of USA, 99*, 13217–13221.

Walton, T. G. (1981). Smoking and alcoholism: A brief report. *American Journal of Psychiatry, 11*, 139–140.

Wenthold, R. J., Prybylowski, K., Standley, S., Sans, N., & Petralia, R. S. (2003). Trafficking of NMDA receptors. *Annual Review of Pharmacology and Toxicology, 43*, 335–358.

Williams, J. M., Guevremont, D., Kennard, J. T., Mason-Parker, S. E., Tate, W. P., & Abraham, W. C. (2003). Long-term regulation of N-methyl-D-aspartate receptor subunits and associated synaptic proteins following hippocampal synaptic plasticity. *Neuroscience, 118*, 1003–1013.

Winkler, A., Mahal, B., Kiianmaa, K., Zieglgansberger, W., & Spanagel, R. (1999). Effects of chronic alcohol consumption on the expression of different NR1 splice variants in the brain of AA and ANA lines of rats. *Brain Research. Molecular Brain Research, 72*, 166–175.

Woodward, J. J. (2000). Ethanol and NMDA receptor signaling. *Critical Review in Neurobiology, 14*, 69–89.

World Health Organization. (2001). *The World Health Report, 2001.* World Health Organization, Geneva, Switzerland.

Yaka, R., He, D. Y., Phamluong, K., & Ron, D. (2003). Pituitary adenylate cyclase-activating polypeptide (PACAP(1-38)) enhances N-methyl-D-aspartate receptor function and brain-derived neurotrophic factor expression via RACK1. *Journal of Biological Chemistry, 278*, 9630–9638.

Yaka, R., Thornton, C., Vagts, A. J., Phamluong, K., Bonci, A., & Ron, D. (2002). NMDA receptor function is regulated by the inhibitory scaffolding protein, RACK1. *Proceedings of the National Academy of Science of USA, 99*, 5710–5715.

Yuste, R., & Bonhoeffer, T. (2001). Morphological changes in dendritic spines associated with long-term synaptic plasticity. *Annual Review of Neuroscience, 24*, 1071–1089.

CHAPTER 7

Pharmacotherapies for the Treatment of Alcohol Dependence: Current and on the Horizon

Tara M. Wright, Alicia M. Baros and Raymond F. Anton
Center for Drug and Alcohol Programs, Department of Psychiatry and
Behavioral Sciences, Medical University of South Carolina,
67 President Street, Charleston, SC 29425, USA

Abstract: Alcohol dependence constitutes a major public health concern. The following chapter discusses pharmacotherapies that are currently approved for treatment of alcohol dependence in the United States, and then describes medications that are under investigation as potential treatment options. Barriers to compliance in the treatment of alcohol dependence are discussed, as well as ways to get around them. Finally, future directions in the field of alcohol dependence research are explored.

Translation of Addictions Science into Practice

EPIDEMIOLOGY

The consequences from alcohol abuse and dependence constitute a major public health issue. Based on combined data from SAMHSA's 2002–2004 National Surveys on Drug Use & Health, 7.6% (18.2 million) persons aged 12 or older met the criteria for alcohol dependence or abuse in the past year (Substance Abuse and Mental Health Services Administration, 2004). In 2000, there were an estimated 63,718 deaths attributable to harmful drinking, accounting for 4% of all deaths among men and 1.5% among women in the United States (Rivara et al., 2004). The price of health care alone resulting from alcohol abuse in this country is more than $26 billion per year (US Department of Health and Human Services, 2000). In addition, alcoholism and resulting medical comorbidities result in more frequent hospitalizations and longer hospitalization stays (Walker et al., 1994). A recent study of veteran ambulatory care patients found that those who screened positive for alcohol-related disorders reported significantly greater limitation in mental health function, longer hospitalizations for medical care in the previous years, and fewer outpatient medical visits in the previous 3 months (Mansell et al., 2006).

Alcohol abuse and dependence are also associated with escalated risk-taking behaviors that can lead to extensive indirect harm. For instance, the 2004 National Survey on Drug Use & Health estimated that 13.5% of persons aged 12 or older drove under the influence of alcohol at least once in the past year (Substance Abuse and Mental Health Services Administration, 2005). In addition to alcohol-related motor vehicle crashes, society is impacted by crime, fire, destruction, and social welfare. The productivity impacts due to alcohol-related illness, premature deaths, and alcohol-related crimes have been estimated to be greater than $134 million per year (US Department of Health and Human Services, 2000).

Given the devastation that alcohol dependence can inflict on the individual, his or her family, and society at large, the need for treatment options for this disease is critical. With the introduction of alcoholism clinical research over the past 20 years or so, significant progress toward rigorous evaluation of both existing therapies and newly developed therapies for use in treating alcohol-related problems has occurred (National Institute on Alcohol Abuse and Alcoholism, 2000). This chapter discusses both current and potential pharmacotherapies that may be used in the treatment of alcohol dependence. We begin with the pharmacological management of alcohol withdrawal and detoxification, and then move on to treatments to help maintain sobriety and avoid relapse. We briefly discuss the rational for their use and then outline studies supporting their efficacy. We cover medications that currently have approval by the United States Food and Drug Administration (FDA), and then discuss those medications that are new on the horizon and still under investigation.

ALCOHOL WITHDRAWAL AND DETOXIFICATION

Alcohol withdrawal typically begins 6–8 h from the last drink, peaks 24–28 h after the last drink, and generally resolves within 7 days (Myrick & Anton, 2004). The spectrum of alcohol withdrawal symptoms is wide and can range from mild to life threatening.

Most severe on the spectrum is *delirium tremens* (DTs), or alcohol-withdrawal delirium. DTs is characterized by agitation and tremulousness, autonomic instability, fevers, auditory and visual hallucinations, and disorientation. DTs usually develop 2–4 days from the person's last drink, and the average duration is less than one week. This condition has been estimated to occur in 5% of patients admitted for alcohol-withdrawal (Mayo-Smith, 1997; Mayo-Smith et al., 2004). It must be considered a medical emergency as the mortality rate can be as high as 20% without prompt and adequate treatment (Thompson, Johnson, & Maddrey, 1975; Victor, 1966).

Seizures are another potentially serious complication of alcohol withdrawal and have been estimated to occur in 5–15% of patients who experience alcohol withdrawal symptoms. Seizures, usually grand mal in type, usually occur in the first 24 h from last drink, but they can occur any time in the first 5 days (Victor, 1990).

Assisting the patient safely through detoxification is the first step in the treatment of alcohol dependence. This may include the treatment of comorbid medical issues, rehydration, and correction of electrolyte abnormalities. This is particularly important as many alcohol dependent patients may be suffering from malnutrition and likely have not sought routine medical attention. Oral multivitamin preparations and folic acid are routinely administered to early abstinent alcoholics. Thiamine supplementation is also routine practice, given its role in preventing Wernicke's encephalopathy. Of crucial importance, thiamine should be provided prior to glucose administration to prevent the precipitation of Wernicke's encephalopathy secondary to depletion of thiamine reserves.

Benzodiazepines have long been considered the standard of care in the treatment of alcohol withdrawal. There is a growing awareness that symptoms of alcohol withdrawal might be postponed by the use of benzodiazepines. They can be administered either via fixed dose and taper or on an as-needed basis.

The Clinical Institute Withdrawal Assessment Scale for Alcohol, Revised (CIWA-Ar) is a brief scale used to rate the severity of alcohol withdrawal as observed by a health care professional and is widely used to monitor and medicate patients going through withdrawal. CIWA-Ar scores of 8 points or fewer correspond to mild withdrawal, scores of 9–15 points correspond to moderate withdrawal, and scores of greater than 15 points correspond to severe withdrawal symptoms and an increased risk of delirium tremens and seizures (Sullivan et al., 1989).

Anticonvulsants are gaining more attention for use in alcohol detoxification. Advantages of anticonvulsants over benzodiazepines in detoxification include their lack of abuse potential, lack of sedation, and lack of increased CNS depression if used concomitantly with alcohol (Malcolm et al., 2001). Previous work has suggested that during a taper of benzodiazepines or shortly after their cessation in the treatment of alcohol withdrawal, seizure risk might be enhanced (Malcolm et al., 2002). Another hypothetical advantage of anticonvulsants include their "anti-kindling" properties (Myrick & Anton, 2004). It is well established in the clinical literature that individuals going through alcohol withdrawal are more likely to experience seizures if they have a prior history of multiple medicated detoxifications (Booth & Blow, 1993; Brown et al., 1988; Letchenberg & Worner, 1991; Moak & Anton, 1996). Pre-clinical research has shown that the severity of alcohol withdrawal increases with subsequent withdrawal episodes (Becker, 1994; Becker & Hale, 1993; Becker & Littleton, 1996). Anticonvulsants may be protective against this process. Our group has been on the forefront of studying the potential use of anticonvulsive agents for outpatient alcohol withdrawal (Malcolm et al., 2002) secondary to their increased safety profile, lack of abuse, and improved post-withdrawal effects compared to benzodiazepines. Valproate and carbamazepine are the best studied, and gabapentin is now also being investigated.

RELAPSE PREVENTION

Once detoxification is successfully completed, the goal of treatment is maintenance of abstinence, including reduction of craving and risk of relapse. This can prove to be a formidable task as it has been estimated that approximately 50% or more of alcohol patients will relapse within 3 months after successful detoxification (Whitworth et al., 1996). In a recent outpatient detoxification study at our Institution (Malcolm et al., 2002), the rate of relapse to any drinking during the first 12 days after detoxification was 65%. Psychosocial interventions have been the cornerstone in helping individuals maintain abstinence, and pharmacotherapy is proving to be a valuable addition to this.

DISULFIRAM

Disulfiram was the first medication approved by the FDA for the treatment of alcohol dependence, and has been in use for over 50 years. It is an alcohol deterrent drug, which interrupts the metabolism of alcohol by irreversibly inhibiting aldehyde dehydrogenase, thereby blocking the breakdown of acetaldehyde to acetate. Acetaldehyde is a toxic byproduct of alcohol metabolism.

Table 1
Disulfiram

Mechanism of action	Proposed effect	Dosing	Special precautions	Common side effects
• Inhibits alcohol dehydrogenase • Blocks alcohol metabolism	• Alcohol deterrent • Consuming alcohol produces a severe adverse reaction	• 250–500 mg daily	• Liver toxicity • Avoid all alcohol containing substances (e.g. perfumes and colognes)	• Hepatitis • Skin eruptions • Drowsiness • Fatigability • Impotence • Headache

When alcohol is consumed in conjunction with disulfiram, the accumulation of acetaldehyde results in facial flushing, nausea and vomiting, headache, and changes in blood pressure. It is expected that the patient's fear of this disulfiram-alcohol reaction serves as a strong reinforcement for abstinence. However, since disulfiram does not work through direct brain mechanisms, it does not have a strong biological effect on craving, which may account for low adherence rates during its use. Table 1 illustrates the highlights in utilizing disulfiram.

Fuller and colleagues published a large placebo-controlled, blinded, one-year, randomized trial of disulfiram, investigating medication adherence and its effect on drinking outcomes (Fuller et al., 1986). Six hundred and five male veterans were randomly assigned to 250 mg of disulfiram, 1 mg of disulfiram, or no disulfiram; all received counseling. They found no significant differences among treatment groups in rate of abstinence or time to first drinking day. It is important to note however that there were a minority of disulfiram adherent patients (20% of 577 who completed the study) so patient non-adherence likely contributed to the negative finding for disulfiram. They did find that among patients who drank and had a complete set of assessment interviews, those in the 250 mg disulfiram group reported significantly fewer drinking days than those in the 1 mg or the no-disulfiram groups. They also found a significant relationship between adherence to drug regimen and complete abstinence in all groups. Fuller and colleagues concluded from their findings that disulfiram may help reduce drinking frequency after relapse, but does not enhance counseling in aiding alcoholic patients to sustain continuous abstinence or delay the resumption of drinking (Fuller et al., 1986). Also, these authors suggested that older, more motivated men seemed to be more compliant and to do better with disulfiram.

Adherence is an obstacle in determining the generalization of disulfiram's effectiveness. Some authors have shown that supervised disulfiram treatment and incentive-driven interventions are associated with better outcomes (decreased alcohol consumption and increased rates of abstinence) (Wright & Moore, 1990).

In a detailed meta-analysis, Berglund and colleagues arrived at the conclusion that evidence for efficacy of disulfiram is lacking overall, but also pointed out that some evidence is available for disulfiram being effective when given under supervision (Berglund et al., 2003).

NALTREXONE

Naltrexone (NTX) is a pure opioid antagonist. While its mechanism of action is not fully understood, its competitive antagonism at the opioid receptor is hypothesized to block the release of dopamine induced by the consumption of alcohol (Benjamin, Grant, & Pohorecky, 1993; Gonzales & Weiss, 1998; Middaugh et al., 2003). By reducing the rewarding effects of alcohol, it is thought to reduce craving to drink and loss of control (Sinclair, 2001). Naltrexone was approved by the US FDA in 1994 for the treatment of alcohol dependence after it was shown to reduce drinking frequency and the likelihood of relapse to heavy drinking (O'Malley et al., 1992; Volpicelli et al., 1992).

Srisurapanont and Jarusuraisin performed a large meta-analysis including 27 randomized controlled trials with naltrexone (Srisurapanont & Jarusuraisin, 2005). They reported that short-term treatment with NTX decreased relapse with a risk ratio (RR) of 0.64, with the number needed to treat (NNT) being 7 (NNT being the number of patients treated to achieve a better outcome over placebo response). To put this into perspective, it is important to note that the NNT for many established medical treatments, such as hypertension treatments to prevent stroke, myocardial infarction or premature death is much higher (Pearce et al., 1998). Srisurapanont and Jarusuraisin also reported that, in comparison to the placebo groups, treatment with naltrexone can lower the risk of treatment withdrawal in alcohol-dependent patients by 28% (NNT = 13) (Srisurapanont & Jarusuraisin, 2005).

The COMBINE study was a federally funded, randomized, controlled trial including 1,383 recently abstinent alcoholics from 11 US academic sites that evaluated the efficacy of naltrexone, acamprosate, or both in comparison to each other and placebo, with health care provider delivered medical management and with or without a specialized alcohol counselor delivered combined behavioral intervention (CBI). The results of this study support the efficacy of naltrexone in that those individuals taking naltrexone plus medical management or naltrexone plus medical management and CBI had higher percent days abstinent than those receiving placebo and medical management only (Anton et al., 2006). In addition, naltrexone also reduced the risk of a heavy drinking day over time (Anton et al., 2006). Nevertheless, not all studies with naltrexone have been positive (Gastpar et al., 2002; Krystal et al., 2001), suggesting there might be subtypes of individuals who might more likely respond to naltrexone.

As naltrexone is believed to be effective through blocking endogenous opioids and thereby diminishing the pleasant effects of alcohol consumption, it may be expected to benefit patients whose disease is mostly characterized by reward craving (Heilig & Egli, 2006). Reward craving is typically associated with early onset, type II individuals. Early work with naltrexone supports the idea that it blocks the euphorogenic effects of alcohol (Volpicelli et al., 1995). King and colleagues investigated the effects of naltrexone on subjective response to alcohol in a double-blind, placebo-controlled trial. They found a differential response to naltrexone, based on paternal history of alcoholism and level of stimulation experienced during alcohol drinking (King et al., 1997). In clinical laboratory studies, non-treatment-seeking alcoholics have shown a reduction in drinking, craving, and alcohol stimulation when pre-treated with naltrexone compared to placebo (Anton et al., 2004; Drobes et al., 2003, 2004; O'Malley et al., 2002).

A functional 118G variant allele of the μ opioid receptor that encodes an amino acid substitution which alters the affinity of the receptor for endogenous ligands has been discovered (Bond et al., 1998). Oslin and colleagues retrospectively examined the association between two specific polymorphisms of the gene encoding the μ opioid receptor and treatment outcomes in alcoholics who were prescribed naltrexone or placebo (Oslin et al., 2003). In this post-hoc study which combines several previously collected datasets, subjects of European descent with one or two copies of the 118G variant allele who were treated with naltrexone had significantly lower rates of relapse and a longer time to return to heavy drinking than those homozygous for this allele (Oslin et al., 2003). These differences were not found among those assigned to placebo. Given potential genetic variabilities in the response to naltrexone, meta-analyses may underestimate the effect size for naltrexone due to heterogeneity of patients (Heilig & Egli, 2006).

Compliance is clearly critical in the success of naltrexone pharmacotherapy (Baros et al., 2006; Pettinati et al., 2000). Psychosocial treatments have been used to increase compliance with the medication (Pettinati et al., 2000; 2005). A long-acting injectable naltrexone has been approved by the FDA and recently became available on the market. Garbutt and colleagues performed a randomized, double-blind, placebo-controlled trial of extended release injectable naltrexone in 624 actively drinking alcohol-dependent adults (Garbutt et al., 2005). Participants received either a monthly intramuscular injection of 380 mg of long-acting naltrexone, or 190 mg of long-acting naltrexone, or a matching volume of placebo combined with 12 sessions of low-intensity psychosocial intervention. They found that compared with placebo, 380 mg of long-acting naltrexone resulted in a 25% decrease in the event rate of heavy drinking days and 190 mg of naltrexone resulted in a 17% decrease. In addition, they found that men more than women and those with lead-in abstinence exhibited greater treatment effects (Garbutt et al., 2005).

Table 2
Naltrexone

Mechanism of action	Proposed effect	Dosing	Special precautions	Common side effects
• Opioid antagonist	• Blocks release of dopamine induced by alcohol consumption	• Oral–50–100 mg daily • Extended Release – 380 mg IM once a month	• Opiate withdrawal in opiate dependent people • Special pain management needed • Elevated liver enzymes possible	• Nausea • Headache • Fatigue

Table 2 outlines major clinical caveats of naltrexone. It is important to consider that naltrexone is an opioid antagonist and can therefore induce withdrawal in an opioid-dependent individual. Also special consideration needs to be taken with pain control, as naltrexone will block the effects of opioid analgesics. In a supervised hospital setting, the antagonist properties of naltrexone can be overridden with increased doses of opioid analgesics.

ACAMPROSATE

Acamprosate was approved by the FDA for the treatment of alcohol dependence in the United States in 2004. While new to the USA, it has been used in Europe for a number of years and therefore has an abundant body of literature supporting its utility. Acamprosate is reported to assist in the maintenance of abstinence and decrease negative symptoms associated with the acute post-withdrawal period in recently detoxified alcohol dependent individuals (Forest Pharmaceuticals Inc., 2005; Wilde & Wagstaff, 1997). The mechanism by which acamprosate helps to maintain abstinence is not yet fully elucidated, but is likely involved in the inhibition of neuronal hyperexcitability mediated by antagonism or modulation of pre- and post-synaptic activity of excitatory amino acids, such as glutamate, particularly via modulation of activity at the NMDA receptor (Scott et al., 2005). Acamprosate is structurally similar to gamma–aminobutyric acid (GABA), the major inhibitory neurotransmitter in the central nervous system, and has been found to be active at the N-methyl-D-aspartate (NMDA) receptor (Knopfel et al., 1987). By functioning to increase GABAergic activity and/or inhibiting glutamatergic activity via modulation of the NMDA receptor, acamprosate may ameliorate alcohol withdrawal symptomotology (Boeijinga et al., 2004; Dahchour & De Witte, 2000).

Over 20 controlled clinical trials performed in Europe and elsewhere support the efficacy and safety of acamprosate. Results of these studies have generally been consistent in supporting its efficacy via significant improvement in the rate of total abstinence and in cumulative abstinence duration with acamprosate versus placebo. Mann, Lehert, and Morgan (2004) performed a large meta-analysis of 17 randomized, placebo-controlled trials of acamprosate, including 4,087 individuals (Mann et al., 2004). They found that continuous abstinence rates at 6 months were significantly higher in the acamprosate treated patients. At 12 months, the overall pooled difference between acamprosate and placebo for continued abstinence was 13.3%. The effect sizes in abstinence rates at 3, 6, and 12 months were 1.33, 1.50, and 1.95, respectively (Mann, Lehert, & Morgan, 2004). Bouza et al. (2004) also performed a large meta-analysis including 13 studies of acamprosate and 19 studies of naltrexone. They also found that acamprosate helped maintain abstinence in alcohol dependent individuals once they had stopped drinking (Bouza et al., 2004).

An industry sponsored study (Mason et al., 2006) as well as the COMBINE study (the large US study mentioned above in our discussion of naltrexone (Anton et al., 2006)), both did not support the efficacy of acamprosate under intent to treat analyses. There has been much speculation as to the reasons for this. In addition to population differences, it is possible that differences in the study design between the American studies and those conducted elsewhere may have accounted for this difference (Kranzler, 2006). In many of the European clinical trials, acamprosate was initiated while the patients were hospitalized for alcohol detoxification and many patients had lengthy hospital stays for rehabilitation. In contrast, the US industry-sponsored study included outpatients who were actively drinking (Mason et al., 2006) while the Combine Study patients were initiated on study drugs as outpatients, after obtaining a minimal 4 days of abstinence (Anton et al., 2006). However, over 50% of participants had more than 4 days of reported abstinence prior to randomization. Moreover, a combined analysis of many studies conducted in Europe did not find predictors of response, including alcohol-withdrawal symptoms or severity of alcohol problems (Verheul et al., 2005). The industry sponsored study in the US, however, found that a high commitment to abstinence and lack of other substance abuse were predictive of better acamprosate response (Mason et al., 2006). Therefore, at present, it is unclear which alcoholics will more likely respond to acamprosate but the weight of the data does suggest that those with a strong commitment to abstinence who take the medication for several weeks while abstaining might have better outcomes (more abstinence) in the long run.

Acamprosate has been found to be generally well tolerated in all of the clinical trials to date. Diarrhea is the most common side effect noted, but headache, dizziness, and pruritis have also been reported to a much lesser degree (Forest Pharmaceuticals Inc., 2005). In a meta-analysis including 10 clinical trials, Bouza

Table 3
Acamprosate

Mechanism of action	Proposed effect	Dosing	Special precautions	Common side effects
• Balances excitatory glutamate and inhibitory GABA neurotransmitter systems	• Maintains abstinence • Decrease symptoms of protracted withdrawal in recently detoxified alcoholics	• 666 mg three times daily	• Contraindicated in severe kidney impairment • Patient's should be abstinent prior to initiating treatment	• Diarrhea • Nausea • Rare pruritis

and colleagues found that those on acamprosate reported significantly more gastrointestinal adverse effects compared to those taking placebo, but there were no statistical differences between the groups in rates of premature withdrawals from treatment due to adverse events (Bouza et al., 2004). Table 3 illustrates major clinical points about acamprosate.

TREATMENT OPTIONS ON THE HORIZON

TOPIRAMATE

Topiramate is an anticonvulsant medication, and can be used as monotherapy for the treatment of partial or mixed seizure disorders in adults. The ability of topiramate to diminish alcohol use may be related to its effects on GABA and glutamate neurotransmitter systems. It is believed to increase GABAergic activity and to modulate glutamate receptors, particularly those of the AMPA type which might lead to suppression of cortico-mesolimbic dopamine activity after alcohol intake, inhibiting midbrain-cortical expression of reward (Ait-Daoud, Malcolm, & Johnson, 2006). Johnson et al. (2003) performed a 12-week, double-blind, placebo-controlled trial of topiramate in 150 alcohol-dependent individuals. Topiramate was titrated upward from 25 mg to a maximum of 300 mg per day. Patients taking topiramate had fewer drinks per drinking day, fewer percent heavy drinking days, and an increase in percent days abstinent in comparison to controls (Johnson et al., 2003). While no serious adverse events were reported in this study, dizziness, paraesthesia, psychomotor slowing, and memory or concentration impairment were more frequently reported in individuals taking topiramate than those taking placebo. In 2004, Johnson and colleagues published results reporting that in comparison to placebo, topiramate improved the odds of overall well-being, increased reported abstinence and not seeking alcohol, improved overall life satisfaction, and reduced harmful drinking consequences (Johnson et al., 2004). A large multi-site study is underway to potentially replicate and extend these initial observations.

ONDANSETRON

It has long been hypothesized that there may be a role for serotonergic agents in the treatment of alcohol dependence for those subtypes of alcoholics who have hallmarks of 5–HT abnormalities. Ondansetron is a 5–HT3 antagonist that is used for the treatment of nausea. Three major studies have suggested that ondansetron may be useful in preventing relapse on alcohol. Sellers et al. (1994) found that a 0.25 mg dosage of ondansetron twice daily (but not 2 mg twice daily) reduced alcohol consumption in mildly alcohol dependent subjects (Sellers et al., 1994). Two other trials separated subjects into early and late onset alcoholism. In a randomized, placebo–controlled trial, Johnson et al. (2000) found that patients with early-onset alcoholism who received ondansetron (1, 4, and 16 µg/kg twice per day) compared with those who were administered placebo, had fewer drinks per day and drinks per drinking day. Ondansetron, 4 µg/kg twice per day, was superior to placebo in increasing the percentage of day's abstinent and total days abstinent per study week. In addition, among patients with early-onset alcoholism, there was a significant difference in the mean log carbohydrate deficient (CDT) ratio between those who received ondansetron (1 and 4 µg/kg twice per day) compared with those who received the placebo (Johnson et al., 2000). Kranzler and colleagues (2003) replicated these results in an open label study (Kranzler et al., 2003). It may be that odansetron reduces alcohol use in early-onset alcoholics by suppressing reward-type craving (Heilig & Egli, 2006). However, more replications and multisite examination needs to be conducted before the medication can be recommended. Also, practitioners must be aware of the doses used in the alcohol studies, which were an order of magnitude lower than the FDA approved and marketed doses for nausea suppression.

BACLOFEN

Baclofen is an agonist at the metabotropic GABA-B receptor that has been used for the treatment of spasticity for many years. It has been shown to decrease voluntary alcohol intake and suppress the expected rebound in alcohol intake after alcohol deprivation in rats bred for alcohol preference (Colombo et al., 2000, 2003).

First, in an open label safety trial, and then in a randomized, placebo-controlled trial of 39 alcohol-dependent patients, Addolorato and colleagues explored the efficacy of baclofen for the treatment of alcohol dependence in humans (Addolorato et al., 2000, 2002). In their placebo-controlled trial, they found that the baclofen group had a higher percentage of subjects totally abstinent from alcohol and a higher number of cumulative abstinence days throughout the study period. A decrease in the obsessive and compulsive components of craving was found in the baclofen group; and alcohol intake was reduced in this group compared to placebo. The authors reported that the use of baclofen was easily manageable and there were no patient dropouts due to adverse events (Addolorato et al., 2002). A larger randomized placebo-controlled trial is now underway in the US.

NEUROLEPTICS

Neuroleptics are also being investigated in the treatment of alcohol dependence since dysfunction in the dopaminergic pathway may play a part in alcohol reward and craving. More specifically, reduced D_2 receptor density has been hypothesized to play a role in alcoholism. Early work has been conducted with haloperidol, clozaril, and olanzapine. Aripiprazole, a partial agonist at D_2 receptors, was recently investigated in a large, placebo-controlled, randomized multi-center trial. The results of this trial are pending.

MEDICATION COMPLIANCE AND ITS IMPACT ON ALCOHOL PHARMACOTHERAPY

Medication compliance is an important issue in the pharmacological treatment of alcohol dependence. Compliance is defined as the extent that a patient's medication-taking behavior conforms to the healthcare providers advice (Haynes, Taylor, & Sackett, 1979). Patients with alcoholism take approximately 50–90% of their prescribed medication (Melnikow & Kiefe, 1994; Morris & Schultz, 1992; Nichol, Venturini, & Sung, 1999), this is referred to as partial-compliance. Partial-compliance is a problem that constitutes a major barrier to the effective treatment of alcohol dependence and, as such, it may negatively impact clinical outcome (Cramer et al., 2003). Partially compliant patients usually exhibit either an erratic pattern or a consistent pattern of medication-taking behavior that is different from what the health care provider prescribed (Adams & Howe, 1993; Cramer & Rosenheck, 1998; Cramer, Scheyer, & Mattson, 1990). Thus partial-compliance prevents the patient from receiving full and/or expected effect of the prescribed treatment.

It is well recognized that the benefits of pharmacotherapies diminish in proportion to the degree of compliance. If the minimum therapeutic dose is not reached, the pharmacologic effect of the drug is frequently lacking. The lack of treatment response in non-compliant patients often results in medication changes that otherwise could have been avoided if the first medication was taken as prescribed.

There are disease specific characteristics that could impact medication compliance in the treatment of alcohol dependence. For example, alcoholics have a tendency to forget to take medication when using alcohol (Kranzler et al., 1996). Additionally, compliance appears to worsen as dosage, frequency, and complexity of instructions increase (Balon, Arfken, & Mufti, 1988). It has previously been reported that alcoholics who were not compliant with naltrexone had a greater percentage of relapses and drinking days during the trial, compared to naltrexone-compliant individuals (O'Brien, Volpicelli, & Volpicelli, 1996). A similar evaluation demonstrated that naltrexone only had an effect in individuals whose compliance rates were high (Oslin et al., 1999). This suggests that if alcoholics comply with pill taking, the effects of naltrexone, or other pharmacotherapy, on alcohol consumption will be markedly enhanced as suggested by others (Oslin et al., 1999; Pettinati et al., 2000; Rohsenow et al., 2000; Volpicelli et al., 1997). Such disparity in the efficacy of pharmacotherapy for the treatment of alcohol dependence emphasizes the critical role of medication compliance.

It is important to understand the factors (e.g., medication side effects and complex drug formulations) that lead to low medication compliance in order to design interventions aimed at effectively enhancing compliance. Enhancement of medication compliance in clinical trials on alcoholism has been shown in trials that include behavioral therapy that focuses on diminishing ambivalence and enhancing compliance (O'Malley & Carroll, 1996). Specifically, Pettinati and colleagues demonstrated improved medication compliance with naltrexone in an alcohol-dependent population when a new therapeutic intervention called "BRENDA" was utilized (Pettinati et al., 2000). This and other health care professional delivered interventions, such as that utilized in the COMBINE Study (Pettinati et al., 2005), emphasize the need for medication compliance and examine barriers to compliance and suggest practical approaches to enhance pill-taking behavior. An important finding in the Combine Trial (Anton et al., 2006) was the utility of medical management in the treatment of alcohol dependence. In this study, medical management was delivered by a licensed health care professional who recommended abstinence, provided education about the medications, and developed a medication adherence plan in collaboration with the patient. The utility of medical management in enhancing treatment outcomes is to a large degree related to its utility in enhancing compliance with pharmacotherapy. As medical management can be carried out in multiple settings, including primary care offices, this has far reaching implications in the successful treatment of alcohol-dependent individuals. Furthermore, in combination with psychosocial support to enhance compliance, the development of longer acting formulations, depot preparations, and formulations to minimize side effects will yield substantially improved compliance as well as treatment outcome. To this effect, the introduction of the long-acting injectable naltrexone is a major step in overcoming the barrier of noncompliance in the treatment of alcohol dependence. More research is needed to parcel out the role of therapy and behavioral interventions to optimize compliance with pharmacotherapy in the treatment of alcohol dependence.

Our understanding of medication compliance in alcohol dependence remains incomplete. At this time, no single factor predicts medication adherence, and the need to identify and examine multiple predictors and their interactions is great. More research in this area is essential in order to design pharmacotherapies and clinical interventions to improve adherence, which in turn may lead to improved outcomes in the treatment of alcohol dependence.

CONCLUSIONS AND FUTURE DIRECTIONS

The ultimate goal of alcoholism treatment is to eliminate or reduce alcohol consumption and alcohol-related problems. A considerable amount of attention is focused on the development of pharmacotherapies for the treatment of alcohol dependence. The use of FDA-approved pharmacotherapies in the rehabilitation of alcohol-dependent individuals is increasing due to advances in the development of medications for the treatment of alcohol dependence. However, the lack of clear guidelines for the use of these medications, either alone or in combination with psychosocial treatments, substantially limits the clinical utility of pharmacotherapy for the treatment of alcohol dependence.

Another limitation is the co-morbidity of alcohol dependence and mental illness. Currently there are no conventional pharmacotherapies for the treatment of co-morbid alcoholism and mental illness. The majority of clinical trials testing potential pharmacotherapies for alcohol dependence have excluded individuals manifesting co-morbid psychiatric disorders. However, the National Comorbidity Survey (Kessler et al., 1996) reported that 29% of individuals were alcohol dependent and 12% of individuals manifesting alcohol dependence had co-morbid mood disorders. While 37% and 29%, respectively, presented with concurrent anxiety disorder. These rates are much higher than the rates of mood disorders and anxiety disorders in non-alcohol-dependent individuals (Kessler et al., 1994). It is clear that research-investigating pharmacotherapies for dually diagnosed individuals may have a positive clinical impact in the treatment of alcohol dependence.

While gender differences in regard to pharmacotherapy for alcoholism were not a specific focus in this chapter, this issue is quickly becoming a topic of concern following two recent publications suggesting naltrexone is not as effective in women as in men (Garbutt et al., 2005; Hernandez-Avila et al., 2006). Specifically, Garbutt et al. (2005) examined the efficacy and tolerability of long-acting injectable naltrexone for alcohol dependence, finding the positive treatment effects among men taking naltrexone versus placebo was highly significant, whereas the treatment effect was not significant in women. Similarly, Hernandez–Avila et al. (2006) reported that only men showed a greater reduction in drinks per day following daily oral naltrexone.

Neither study controlled for family history of alcoholism, compliance and side effects in assessing gender effects. These are important variables since research has indicated that there may be different patterns for each of these between women and men. For instance, the heritability of alcoholism is different in women compared to men (Hill & Smith, 1991; Kendler et al., 1992). This might be a salient factor to consider in differential gender treatment response since family history of alcoholism has been reported to be a predictor of naltrexone response (Monterosso et al., 2001; Rubio et al., 2005). In addition, lack of compliance (Pettinati et al., 2000; Rohsenow et al., 2000), and to some degree side effects of naltrexone, have been reported to be negative predictors of response (Mark et al., 2003; Rohsenow et al., 2000). It is important to note that the Garbutt (2005) and Hernandez–Aviala (2006) articles are not consistent with the findings of the predominantly male sample of hazardous drinkers in the Davidson and colleagues study, which reported no gender effects on outcome (Davidson et al., 2004). Therefore, it is still controversial as to whether naltrexone works as well in women as in men. These findings open the door to questions pertaining to whether gender and/or family history of alcoholism predicts treatment outcome in other alcoholism pharmacotherapies.

New pharmacotherapies are being investigated (i.e., topiramate, ondansetron, baclofen, and aripiprazole, to name a few) for their utility in the treatment of alcohol dependence either alone or in combination with the current FDA approved medications (i.e., disulfiram, naltrexone, and acamprosate). It is clear that more investigations and clinical guidelines are needed to distinguish those groups of individuals who may benefit from the use of specific medications or combinations of different treatments. Bearing in mind the pharmacodynamics of alcohol as well the complexity of alcohol dependence, the combined use of pharmacotherapies may be the best approach in the treatment of alcohol dependence.

Our understanding of alcoholism, including predisposing factors, sequala of long-term use and means of relapse, is growing. With this, so is our understanding of potential treatment options. As potential treatment options continue to rise on the horizon, our ability to provide individualized, effective treatment also increases. The need for collaboration between basic science and clinical work is of utmost importance. As we explore new and novel medications in the treatment of alcohol dependence, testing these medications in animal models will allow us to compare pre-clinical and clinical responses in order to identify potential markers which may impact efficacy (Heilig & Egli, 2006).

As we advance in our understanding in the underlying neural mechanisms which both predispose to and result from alcohol dependence, our ability to target specific pharmacotherapies based on individual characteristics will allow us much greater power to fight this debilitating disease.

REFERENCES

Adams, S. G., Jr., & Howe, J. T. (1993). Predicting medication compliance in a psychotic population. *Journal of Nervous and Mental Disease, 181*(9), 558–560.

Addolorato, G., Caputo, F., Capristo, E., Colombo, G., Gessa, G. L., & Gasbarrini, G. (2000). Ability of baclofen in reducing alcohol craving and intake: II–Preliminary clinical evidence. *Alcoholism, Clinical Experimental Research, 24*(1), 67–71.

Addolorato, G., Caputo, F., Capristo, E., Domenicali, M., Bernardi, M., Janiri, L., Agabio, R., Colombo, G., Gessa, G. L., & Gasbarrini, G. (2002). Baclofen efficacy in reducing alcohol craving and intake: A preliminary double-blind randomized controlled study. *Alcohol and Alcoholism, 37*(5), 504–508.

Ait-Daoud, N., Malcolm, R. J., Jr., & Johnson, B. A. (2006). An overview of medications for the treatment of alcohol withdrawal and alcohol dependence with an emphasis on the use of older and newer anticonvulsants. *Addictive Behaviors, 31*(9), 1628–1649.

Anton, R. F., Drobes, D. J., Voronin, K., Durazo-Avizu, R., & Moak, D. (2004). Naltrexone effects on alcohol consumption in a clinical laboratory paradigm: Temporal effects of drinking. *Psychopharmacology (Berl), 173*(1–2), 32–40.

Anton, R. F., O'Malley, S. S., Ciraulo, D. A., Cisler, R. A., Couper, D., Donovan, D. M., Gastfriend, D. R., Hosking, J. D., Johnson, B. A., LoCastro, J. S., Longabaugh, R., Mason, B. J., Mattson, M. E., Miller, W. R., Pettinati, H. M., Randall, C. L., Swift, R., Weiss, R. D., Williams, L. D., & Zweben, A. (2006). Combined pharmacotherapies and behavioral interventions for alcohol dependence: The COMBINE study: A randomized controlled trial. *The Journal of the American Medical Association, 295*(17), 2003–2017.

Balon, R., Arfken, C. L., & Mufti, R. (1988). Patients' preferences about medication dosing regimens. *Psychiatric Services, 49*, 1095.

Baros, A. M., Latham, P. K., Moak, D. H., Voronin, K., & Anton, R. F. (in press, 2007). What role does measuring medication compliance play in evaluating naltrexone efficacy? *Alcoholism, Clinical and Experimental Research.*

Becker, H. C. (1994). Positive relationship between the number of prior ethanol withdrawal episodes and the severity of subsequent withdrawal seizures. *Psychopharmacology (Berl), 116*(1), 26–32.

Becker, H. C., & Hale, R. L. (1993). Repeated episodes of ethanol withdrawal potentiate the severity of subsequent withdrawal seizures: An animal model of alcohol withdrawal "kindling". *Alcoholism, Clinical and Experimental Research, 17*(1), 94–98.

Becker, H. C., & Littleton, J. M. (1996). The alcohol withdrawal "kindling" phenomenon: Clinical and experimental findings. *Alcoholism, Clinical and Experimental Research, 20*, 121A–124A.

Benjamin, D., Grant, E. R., & Pohorecky, L. A. (1993). Naltrexone reverses ethanol-induced dopamine release in the nucleus accumbens in awake, freely moving rats. *Brain Research, 621*(1), 137–140.

Berglund, M., Thelander, S., Salaspuro, M., Franck, J., Andreasson, S., & Ojehagen, A. (2003). Treatment of alcohol abuse: An evidence-based review. *Alcoholism, Clinical and Experimental Research, 27*(10), 1645–1656.

Boeijinga, P. H., Parot, P., Soufflet, L., Landron, F., Danel, T., Gendre, I., Muzet, M., Demazieres, A., & Luthringer, R. (2004). Pharmacodynamic effects of acamprosate on markers of cerebral function in alcohol-dependent subjects administered as pretreatment and during alcohol abstinence. *Neuropsychobiology, 50*(1), 71–77.

Bond, C., LaForge, K. S., Tian, M., Melia, D., Zhang, S., Borg, L., Gong, J., Schluger, J., Strong, J. A., Leal, S. M., Tischfield, J. A., Kreek, M. J., & Yu, L. (1998). Single-nucleotide polymorphism in the human mu opioid receptor gene alters beta-endorphin binding and activity: Possible implications for opiate addiction. *Proceedings of the National Academy of Sciences of the United States of America, 95*(16), 9608–9613.

Booth, B. M., & Blow, F. C. (1993). The kindling hypothesis: Further evidence from a U.S. national study of alcoholic men. *Alcohol and Alcoholism, 28*(5), 593–598.

Bouza, C., Angeles, M., Munoz, A., & Amate, J. M. (2004). Efficacy and safety of naltrexone and acamprosate in the treatment of alcohol dependence: A systematic review. *Addiction, 99*(7), 811–828.

Brown, M. E., Anton, R. F., Malcolm, R., & Ballenger, J. C. (1988). Alcohol detoxification and withdrawal seizures: Clinical support for a kindling hypothesis. *Biological Psychiatry, 23*(5), 507–514.

Colombo, G., Agabio, R., Carai, M. A., Lobina, C., Pani, M., Reali, R., Addolorato, G., & Gessa, G. L. (2000). Ability of baclofen in reducing alcohol intake and withdrawal severity: I–Preclinical evidence. *Alcoholism, Clinical and Experimental Research, 24*(1), 58–66.

Colombo, G., Serra, S., Brunetti, G., Vacca, G., Carai, M. A., & Gessa, G. L. (2003). Suppression by baclofen of alcohol deprivation effect in Sardinian alcohol-preferring (sP) rats. *Drug and Alcohol Dependence, 70*(1), 105–108.

Cramer, J. A., & Rosenheck, R. (1998). Compliance with medication regimens for mental and physical disorders. *Psychiatric Services, 49*(2), 196–201.

Cramer, J., Rosenheck, R., Kirk, G., Krol, W., Krystal, J., & Group, V. A. N. S. (2003). Medication compliance feedback and monitoring in a clinical trial: Predictors and outcomes. *Value in Health, 6*(5), 566–573.

Cramer, J. A., Scheyer, R. D., & Mattson, R. H. (1990). Compliance declines between clinic visits. *Archives of Internal Medicine, 150*(7), 1509–1510.

Dahchour, A., & De Witte, P. (2000). Ethanol and amino acids in the central nervous system: Assessment of the pharmacological actions of acamprosate. *Progress in Neurobiology, 60*(4), 343–362.

Davidson, D., Saha, C., Scifres, S., Fyffe, J., O'Connor, S., & Selzer, C. (2004). Naltrexone and brief counseling to reduce heavy drinking in hazardous drinkers. *Addictive Behaviors, 29*(6), 1253–1258.

Drobes, D. J., Anton, R. F., Thomas, S. E., & Voronin, K. (2003). A clinical laboratory paradigm for evaluating medication effects on alcohol consumption: Naltrexone and nalmefene. *Neuropsychopharmacology, 28*(4), 755–764.

Drobes, D. J., Anton, R. F., Thomas, S. E., & Voronin, K. (2004). Effects of naltrexone and nalmefene on subjective response to alcohol among non-treatment-seeking alcoholics and social drinkers. *Alcoholism, Clinical and Experimental Research, 28*(9), 1362–1370.

Forest Pharmaceuticals Inc. (2005). CAMPRAL (acamprosate calcium) delayed-release tablets prescribing information [online]. Retrieved June 20, 2006, from http:/www.campral.com.

Fuller, R. K., Branchey, L., Brightwell, D. R., Derman, R. M., Emrick, C. D., Iber, F. L., James, K. E., Lacoursiere, R. B., Lee, K. K., & Lowenstam, I. (1986). Disulfiram treatment of alcoholism. A Veterans Administration cooperative study. *The Journal of the American Medical Association, 256*(11), 1449–1455.

Garbutt, J. C., Kranzler, H. R., O'Malley, S. S., Gastfriend, D. R., Pettinati, H. M., Silverman, B. L., Loewy, J. W., & Ehrich, E. W. (2005). Efficacy and tolerability of long-acting injectable naltrexone for alcohol dependence: A randomized controlled trial. *The Journal of the American Medical Association, 293*(13), 1617–1625.

Gastpar, M., Bonnet, U., Boning, J., Mann, K., Schmidt, L. G., Soyka, M., Wetterling, T., Kielstein, V., Labriola, D., & Croop, R. (2002). Lack of efficacy of naltrexone in the prevention of alcohol relapse: Results from a German multicenter study. *Journal of Clinical Psychopharmacology, 22*(6), 592–598.

Gonzales, R. A., & Weiss, F. (1998). Suppression of ethanol-reinforced behavior by naltrexone is associated with attenuation of the ethanol-induced increase in dialysate dopamine levels in the nucleus accumbens. *Journal of Neuroscience, 18*(24), 10663–10671.

Haynes, R. B., Taylor, D. W., & Sackett, D. L. (1979). *Compliance in Health Care.* Baltimore: Johns Hopkins University Press.

Heilig, M., & Egli, M. (2006). Pharmacological treatment of alcohol dependence: Target symptoms and target mechanisms. *Pharmacology and Therapeutics, 111*(3), 855–876.

Hernandez-Avila, C. A., Song, C., Kuo, L., Tennen, H., Armeli, S., & Kranzler, H. R. (2006). Targeted versus daily naltrexone: Secondary analysis of effects on average daily drinking. *Alcoholism, Clinical and Experimental Research, 30*(5), 860–865.

Hill, S. Y., & Smith, T. R. (1991). Evidence for genetic mediation of alcoholism in women. *Journal of Substance Abuse Treatment, 3*(2), 159–174.

Johnson, B. A., Ait-Daoud, N., Akhtar, F. Z., & Ma, J. Z. (2004). Oral topiramate reduces the consequences of drinking and improves the quality of life of alcohol-dependent individuals: A randomized controlled trial. *Archives of General Psychiatry, 61*(9), 905–912.

Johnson, B. A., Ait-Daoud, N., Bowden, C. L., DiClemente, C. C., Roache, J. D., Lawson, K., Javors, M. A., & Ma, J. Z. (2003). Oral topiramate for treatment of alcohol dependence: A randomised controlled trial. *Lancet, 361*(9370), 1677–1685.

Johnson, B. A., Roache, J. D., Javors, M. A., DiClemente, C. C., Cloninger, C. R., Prihoda, T. J., Bordnick, P. S., Ait-Daoud, N., & Hensler, J. (2000). Ondansetron for reduction of drinking among biologically predisposed alcoholic patients: A randomized controlled trial. *The Journal of the American Medical Association, 284*(8), 963–971.

Kendler, K. S., Heath, A. C., Neale, M. C., Kessler, R. C., & Eaves, L. J. (1992). A population-based twin study of alcoholism in women. *The Journal of the American Medical Association, 268*(14), 1877–1882.

Kessler, R. C., McGonagle, K. A., Zhao, S., Nelson, C. B., Hughes, M., Eshleman, S., Wittchen, H. U., & Kendler, K. S. (1994). Lifetime and 12-month prevalence of DSM-III-R psychiatric disorders in the United States. Results from the National Comorbidity Survey. *Archives of General Psychiatry, 51*(1), 8–19.

Kessler, R. C., Nelson, C. B., McGonagle, K. A., Liu, J., Swartz, M., & Blazer, D. G. (1996). Comorbidity of DSM-III-R major depressive disorder in the general population: Results from the US National Comorbidity Survey [see comment]. *British Journal of Psychiatry – Supplementum,* (30), 17–30.

King, A. C., Volpicelli, J. R., Frazer, A., & O'Brien, C. P. (1997). Effect of naltrexone on subjective alcohol response in subjects at high and low risk for future alcohol dependence. *Psychopharmacology (Berl), 129*(1), 15–22.

Knopfel, T., Zeise, M. L., Cuenod, M., & Zieglgansberger, W. (1987). L-homocysteic acid but not L-glutamate is an endogenous N-methyl-D-aspartic acid receptor preferring agonist in rat neocortical neurons in vitro. *Neuroscience Letters, 81*(1–2), 188–192.

Kranzler, H. R. (2006). Evidence-based treatments for alcohol dependence: New results and new questions. *The Journal of the American Medical Association, 295*(17), 2075–2076.

Kranzler, H. R., Escobar, R., Lee, D.-K., & Meza, E. (1996). Elevated rates of early discontinuation from pharmacotherapy trials in alcoholics and drug abusers. *Alcoholism, Clinical and Experimental Research, 20*, 16–20.

Kranzler, H. R., Pierucci-Lagha, A., Feinn, R., & Hernandez-Avila, C. (2003). Effects of ondansetron in early- versus late-onset alcoholics: A prospective, open-label study. *Alcoholism, Clinical and Experimental Research, 27*(7), 1150–1155.

Krystal, J. H., Cramer, J. A., Krol, W. F., Kirk, G. F., & Rosenheck, R. A. (2001). Naltrexone in the treatment of alcohol dependence. *New England Journal of Medicine*, *345*(24), 1734–1739.

Lechtenberg, R., & Worner, T. M. (1991). Relative kindling effect of detoxification and non-detoxification admissions in alcoholics. *Alcohol and Alcoholism*, *26*(2), 221–225.

Malcolm, R., Myrick, H., Brady, K. T., & Ballenger, J. C. (2001). Update on anticonvulsants for the treatment of alcohol withdrawal. *The American Journal of Addictions*, *10*(Suppl), 16–23.

Malcolm, R., Myrick, H., Roberts, J., Wang, W., Anton, R. F., & Ballenger, J. C. (2002). The effects of carbamazepine and lorazepam on single versus multiple previous alcohol withdrawals in an outpatient randomized trial. *Journal of General Internal Medicine*, *17*(5), 349–355.

Mann, K., Lehert, P., & Morgan, M. Y. (2004). The efficacy of acamprosate in the maintenance of abstinence in alcohol-dependent individuals: Results of a meta-analysis. *Alcoholism, Clinical and Experimental Research*, *28*(1), 51–63.

Mansell, D., Penk, W., Hankin, C. S., Lee, A., Spiro, A., 3rd, Skinner, K. M., Hsieh, J., & Kazis, L. E. (2006). The illness burden of alcohol-related disorders among VA patients: The veterans health study. *Journal of Ambulatory Care Management*, *29*(1), 61–70.

Mark, T. L., Kranzler, H. R., Poole, V. H., Hagen, C. A., McLeod, C., & Crosse, S. (2003). Barriers to the use of medications to treat alcoholism. *American Journal of Addiction*, *12*(4), 281–294.

Mason, B. J., Goodman, A. M., Chabac, S., & Lehert, P. (2006). Effect of oral acamprosate on abstinence in patients with alcohol dependence in a double-blind, placebo-controlled trial: The role of patient motivation. *Journal of Psychiatric Research*, *40*(5), 383–393.

Mayo-Smith, M. F. (1997). Pharmacological management of alcohol withdrawal. A meta-analysis and evidence-based practice guideline. American Society of Addiction Medicine Working Group on Pharmacological Management of Alcohol Withdrawal. *The Journal of the American Medical Association*, *278*(2), 144–151.

Mayo-Smith, M. F., Beecher, L. H., Fischer, T. L., Gorelick, D. A., Guillaume, J. L., Hill, A., Jara, G., Kasser, C., & Melbourne, J. (2004). Management of alcohol withdrawal delirium. An evidence-based practice guideline. *Archives of Internal Medicine*, *164*(13), 1405–1412.

Melnikow, J., & Kiefe, C. (1994). Patient compliance and medical research: Issues in methodology. *Journal of General Internal Medicine*, *9*(2), 96–105.

Middaugh, L. D., Szumlinski, K. K., Van Patten, Y., Marlowe, A. L., & Kalivas, P. W. (2003). Chronic ethanol consumption by C57BL/6 mice promotes tolerance to its interoceptive cues and increases extracellular dopamine, an effect blocked by naltrexone. *Alcoholism, Clinical and Experimental Research*, *27*(12), 1892–1900.

Moak, D. H., & Anton, R. F. (1996). Alcohol-related seizures and the kindling effect of repeated detoxifications: The influence of cocaine. *Alcohol and Alcoholism*, *31*(2), 135–143.

Monterosso, J. R., Flannery, B. A., Pettinati, H. M., Oslin, D. W., Rukstalis, M., O'Brien, C. P., & Volpicelli, J. R. (2001). Predicting treatment response to naltrexone: The influence of craving and family history. *American Journal of Addiction*, *10*(3), 258–268.

Morris, S., & Schultz, R. M. (1992). Patient compliance – an overview. *Journal of Clinical Pharmacology and Therapeutics*, *17*, 283–295.

Myrick, H., & Anton, R. (2004). Recent advances in the pharmacotherapy of alcoholism. *Current Psychiatry Reports*, *6*(5), 332–338.

National Institute on Alcohol Abuse and Alcoholism. (2000). New advances in alcoholism treatment. *Alcohol Alerts*, *49*. Retrived from http://pubs.niaaa.nih.gov/publications/aa49.htm

Nichol, M. B., Venturini, F., & Sung, J. C. (1999). A critical evaluation of the methodology of the literature on medication compliance. *Annals of Pharmacotherapy*, *33*(5), 531–540.

O'Brien, C. P., Volpicelli, L. A., & Volpicelli, J. R. (1996). Naltrexone in the treatment of alcoholism: A clinical review. *Alcohol*, *13*, 35–39.

O'Malley, S. S., & Carroll, K. M. (1996). Psychotherapeutic considerations in pharmacological trials. *Alcoholism, Clinical and Experimental Research*, *20*(7 Suppl), 17A–22A.

O'Malley, S. S., Jaffe, A. J., Chang, G., Schottenfeld, R. S., Meyer, R. E., & Rounsaville, B. (1992). Naltrexone and coping skills therapy for alcohol dependence. A controlled study. *Archives of General Psychiatry, 49*(11), 881–887.

O'Malley, S. S., Krishnan-Sarin, S., Farren, C., Sinha, R., & Kreek, M. J. (2002). Naltrexone decreases craving and alcohol self-administration in alcohol-dependent subjects and activates the hypothalamo–pituitary–adrenocortical axis. *Psychopharmacology (Berl), 160*(1), 19–29.

Oslin, D. W., Berrettini, W., Kranzler, H. R., Pettinati, H., Gelernter, J., Volpicelli, J. R., O'Brien, C. P. (2003). A functional polymorphism of the mu-opioid receptor gene is associated with naltrexone response in alcohol-dependent patients. *Neuropsychopharmacology, 28*(8), 1546–1552.

Oslin, D. W., Pettinati, H. M., Volpicelli, J. R., Wolf, A. L., Kampman, K. M., & O'Brien, C. P. (1999). The effects of naltrexone on alcohol and cocaine use in dually addicted patients. *Journal of Substance Abuse Treatment, 16*(2), 163–167.

Pearce, K. A., Furberg, C. D., Psaty, B. M., & Kirk, J. (1998). Cost-minimization and the number needed to treat in uncomplicated hypertension. *American Journal of Hypertension, 11*(5), 618–629.

Pettinati, H. M., Volpicelli, J. R., Pierce, J. D., Jr., & O'Brien, C. P. (2000). Improving naltrexone response: An intervention for medical practitioners to enhance medication compliance in alcohol dependent patients. *Journal of Addictive Diseases, 19*(1), 71–83.

Pettinati, H. M., Weiss, R. D., Dundon, W., Miller, W. R., Donovan, D., Ernst, D. B., & Rounsaville, B. J. (2005). A structured approach to medical management: A psychosocial intervention to support pharmacotherapy in the treatment of alcohol dependence. *Journal of Studies on Alcohol Supplement, 15*, 170–178.

Rivara, F. P., Garrison, M. M., Ebel, B., McCarty, C. A., & Christakis, D. A. (2004). Mortality attributable to harmful drinking in the United States, 2000. *Journal of Studies on Alcohol, 65*(4), 530–536.

Rohsenow, D. J., Colby, S. M., Monti, P. M., Swift, R. M., Martin, R. A., Mueller, T. I., Gordon, A., & Eaton, C. A. (2000). Predictors of compliance with naltrexone among alcoholics. *Alcoholism, Clinical and Experimental Research, 24*(10), 1542–1549.

Rubio, G., Ponce, G., Rodriguez-Jimenez, R., Jimenez-Arriero, M. A., Hoenicka, J., & Palomo, T. (2005). Clinical predictors of response to naltrexone in alcoholic patients: Who benefits most from treatment with naltrexone? *Alcohol and Alcoholism, 40*(3), 227–233.

Scott, L. J., Figgitt, D. P., Keam, S. J., & Waugh, J. (2005). Acamprosate: A review of its use in the maintenance of abstinence in patients with alcohol dependence. *CNS Drugs, 19*(5), 445–464.

Sellers, E. M., Toneatto, T., Romach, M. K., Somer, G. R., Sobell, L. C., & Sobell, M. B. (1994). Clinical efficacy of the 5-HT3 antagonist ondansetron in alcohol abuse and dependence. *Alcoholism, Clinical and Experimental Research, 18*(4), 879–885.

Sinclair, J. D. (2001). Evidence about the use of naltrexone and for different ways of using it in the treatment of alcoholism. *Alcohol and Alcoholism, 36*(1), 2–10.

Srisurapanont, M., & Jarusuraisin, N. (2005). Opioid antagonists for alcohol dependence. *Cochrane Database of Systematic Reviews, 1*, CD001867.

Substance Abuse and Mental Health Services Administration. (2004). The NSDUH Report: Alcohol Dependence or Abuse: 2002, 2003, and 2004. Retrieved July 07, 2006, from http://www.oas.samhsa.gov/2k6/AlcDepend/AlcDepend.htm

Substance Abuse and Mental Health Services Administration. (2005). *Overview of findings from the 2004 national survey on drug use and health* (No. NSDUH Series H-24, DHHS Publication SMA 04-3963).

Sullivan, J. T., Sykora, K., Schneiderman, J., Naranjo, C. A., & Sellers, E. M. (1989). Assessment of alcohol withdrawal: The revised clinical institute withdrawal assessment for alcohol scale (CIWA-Ar). *British Journal of Addiction, 84*(11), 1353–1357.

Thompson, W. L., Johnson, A. D., & Maddrey, W. L. (1975). Diazepam and paraldehyde for treatment of severe delirium tremens. A controlled trial. *Annals of Internal Medicine, 82*(2), 175–180.

US Department of Health and Human Services. (2000). Tenth Special Report to Congress on Alcohol and Health. Bethesda, MD: U.S. Department of Health and Human Services, Public Health Service, National Institutes of Health, National Institute on Alcohol Abuse and Alcoholism.

Verheul, R., Lehert, P., Geerlings, P. J., Koeter, M. W., & van den Brink, W. (2005). Predictors of acamprosate efficacy: Results from a pooled analysis of seven European trials including 1485 alcohol-dependent patients. *Psychopharmacology (Berl)*, *178*(2–3), 167–173.

Victor, M. (1966). Treatment of the neurologic complications of alcoholism. *Modern Treatment*, *3*(3), 491–501.

Victor, M. (1990). *Alcohol Withdrawal Seizures: An Overview*. New York, NY: Davis.

Volpicelli, J. R., Alterman, A. I., Hayashida, M., & O'Brien, C. P. (1992). Naltrexone in the treatment of alcohol dependence. *Archives of General Psychiatry*, *49*(11), 876–880.

Volpicelli, J. R., Rhines, K. C., Rhines, J. S., Volpicelli, L. A., Alterman, A. I., & O'Brien, C. P. (1997). Naltrexone and alcohol dependence. Role of subject compliance. *Archives of General Psychiatry*, *54*(8), 737–742.

Volpicelli, J. R., Watson, N. T., King, A. C., Sherman, C. E., & O'Brien, C. P. (1995). Effect of naltrexone on alcohol "high" in alcoholics. *American Journal of Psychiatry*, *152*(4), 613–615.

Walker, R. D., Howard, M. O., Lambert, M. D., & Suchinsky, R. (1994). Psychiatric and medical comorbidities of veterans with substance use disorders. *Hospital Community Psychiatry*, *45*(3), 232–237.

Whitworth, A. B., Fischer, F., Lesch, O. M., Nimmerrichter, A., Oberbauer, H., Platz, T., Potgieter, A., Walter, H., & Fleischhacker, W. W. (1996). Comparison of acamprosate and placebo in long-term treatment of alcohol dependence. *Lancet*, *347*(9013), 1438–1442.

Wilde, M. I., & Wagstaff, A. J. (1997). Acamprosate. A review of its pharmacology and clinical potential in the management of alcohol dependence after detoxification. *Drugs*, *53*(6), 1038–1053.

Wright, C., & Moore, R. D. (1990). Disulfiram treatment of alcoholism. *American Journal of Medicine*, *88*(6), 647–655.

CHAPTER 8

Agonist Treatment for Stimulant Abuse and Dependence

David Herin and John Grabowski
Substance Abuse Research Center, Department of Psychiatry and Behavioral
Sciences, University of Texas Health Science Center, 1300 Moursund St,
Houston, TX 77030, USA

Abstract: Waves of stimulant abuse over the last century have presented difficult clinical
and social problems. In the last several decades, extensive preclinical and clinical research
has examined basic mechanisms as well as pharmacotherapy and behavioral therapy to treat
stimulant dependence. Though most medications have proven ineffective, mounting
evidence supports use of agonist-like treatments. The approach and conceptualization
parallel the most efficacious pharmacotherapies for opioid and nicotine dependence.
Preclinical and clinical evidence for agonist-like pharmacotherapy for stimulant dependence
are presented. Additionally, the role of each monoamine system as an agonist substitution
pharmacotherapy target is discussed.

RELEVANT SCIENCE, INTRODUCTION AND BACKGROUND

Medications enhancing wakefulness, benefiting performance, or focusing attention are important in the psycho-pharmacotherapeutic armamentarium for treatment of many disorders including attention-deficit hyperactivity disorder (ADHD) and narcolepsy (Prince, 2006; Banerjee, Vitiello, & Grunstein, 2004; Weiss & Laties, 1962). Amphetamine analogs and methylphenidate have long been utilized for these indications, with broad biologic action (notably dopaminergic but modulating other systems) and well-delineated mechanisms. Several other less effective sympathomimetic agents have also been utilized. For example, cocaine derived from chewed coca leaves or brewed tea has long been used for quasi-therapeutic properties in countries where the plant is indigenous. More recent pharmaceutical agents, such as modafinil, reportedly altering glutamatergic and adrenergic function with minimal 'direct' dopaminergic action, have demonstrated efficacy for narcolepsy and possible utility in other conditions treated with 'stimulant' medications while having lower abuse potential than stimulants (see reviews, Jasinski & Kovacevic-Ristanovic, 2000; Myrick et al., 2004).

There is little evidence that abuse stems from well-conceived therapeutic regimens and patients incurring benefit (e.g. narcoleptics) from stimulants may take less prescribed medication than optimal (Rogers et al., 1997). However, abuse and dependence of potent stimulants may emerge in non-therapeutic contexts, particularly when self-administered by injection, smoking/inhalation, or insufflation, with devastating economic, social, and personal consequences for individuals and families. Since cycles of stimulant-type drug abuse have occurred over the past 150 years, the attraction of some effects is clear, and future episodes can be expected (e.g. Musto, 1992, 1998).

Waves of stimulant abuse over the last 30 years in the US and elsewhere have presented difficult clinical, scientific, and social problems (World Health Organization, 2004). In the last decade MDMA use emerged with some commonalities but distinct features. Whereas amphetamine and cocaine abuse are chronic or in extended binges, MDMA is used in relatively constrained circumstances (e.g. raves) albeit with sometimes deadly consequences; interestingly, MDMA use is now diminishing (CEWG, 2006). Overall, clinical consequences of acute overdose, abuse or dependence on stimulants remain consistent, with variation in risk due to drug, route of administration, duration of action and effects.

Since the 1980s, substantial preclinical and clinical research sought to delineate the mechanisms underlying effective treatments and examine candidate medications. Some plausible development directions were slowed by policy and clinical concerns. Given the historical record of consecutive eras of stimulant abuse, development of pharmacotherapies should be rational, persistent, and viewed as evolutionary. This requires systematic application of rigorous clinical and preclinical science based on thoughtful conceptualizations of the problems and therapeutic options.

One strand of stimulant dependence research pursued in recent decades by Kleber and colleagues examined tricyclic antidepressants, notably desipramine (Gawin & Kleber, 1984). While later rigorous clinical trials dimmed optimism, Carroll et al. (1998) demonstrated specific combinations of tricyclics and behavior therapy produce benefit in certain patient groups. Selective serotonin reuptake inhibitor (SSRI) 'anti-depressants' were also examined, with mixed results, but positive results were typically associated with intensive behavioral therapy. Schmitz et al. (1998) has posited that rather than treating 'depression' the SSRIs are likely having effects on specific behavioral elements, perhaps enhanced sensitivity to environmental contingencies and circumstances, resulting in enhanced response to behavioral intervention.

In addition to antidepressant pharmacotherapies, other agents have been investigated for stimulant dependence treatment. During recent decades, much research implicated the dopamine (DA) system in stimulant dependence, leading to numerous clinical trials utilizing DA ligands, with mixed results (see Gorelick, Gardner, & Xi, 2004 for review). Other theoretical frames suggested utility of anti-seizure medications, e.g. carbamazepine, albeit with little apparent benefit (Halikas et al., 1997). Emphasis was also placed on 'antagonist' medications such as haloperi-dol and flupenthixol. While antagonists may be of some value in specific instances, a deterrent to seeking full cocaine or amphetamine antagonists resides in common and serious side effects and adverse events. Higgins et al. (1993), George et al. (2000) and more recently Carroll et al. (2004) reported that disulfiram may have benefit in cocaine-dependent patients without concurrent alcohol dependence. Given that many individuals use alcohol prior to, during, or following cocaine use, the ability of disulfiram to decrease cocaine use requires further clarification. A definitive evaluation would require cocaine-dependent individuals without concurrent alcohol use, and would thus be difficult to accomplish.

A different, but logical alternative emerged based on success in treatment of opioid or nicotine abuse/dependence. This proposal was that administration of a stable, long acting, potent stimulant could stabilize biology and behavior with-out undue risk or further disturbance to already perturbed biological and behav-ioral systems. Inherent was the assumption of a carefully monitored dosing regimen. That stated, it should be clear that as with opioids, the full range of pharmacotherapy options should be explored and available for the diversity of clinical situations and individuals.

As discussed in the final section of this chapter (Speculation), much work is needed to understand essential mechanisms to promote a rational pharmacotherapy with maximum benefit and minimal risk for cocaine dependence. Laboratory behav-ioral dissection of cocaine action indicate that medications directed at one or another specific receptor action can produce favorable responses such as reduced cocaine intake on some but not all components of a possible dose range and differentially affect other behavior such as food intake (e.g. Barrett et al., 2004). The scope of the development effort is clearly represented in a long series of papers related to the 40–50 medications for which the National Institute on Drug Abuse has supported development research (Montoya, 2004). The most common conclusion of these clinical trials is that – gabapentin, calcium channel blockade, fluoxetine, nefazadone, olanzapine, coenzyme Q10/L-carnitine, celecoxib, paroxetine, pentoxifylline, rilu-zole, pramipexole, venlafaxine, methylphenidate – " – use is not supported for the treatment of cocaine abuse and dependence" (e.g. Reid et al., 2005). Still, the National Institute on Drug Abuse (NIDA) while investigating a numerous agents for cocaine dependence at its collaborating CREST sites, determined that cabergoline, reserpine, and tiagabine may have benefit under certain circumstances and that further studies should be conducted (Leiderman et al., 2005).

Scientists and clinicians have encouraged a conceptual refinement that differ-entiates candidate medications based on behavioral features of patients. Thus, it has been proposed that some medications might be particularly useful in 'relapse prevention' (i.e. when patients have achieved abstinence) by blocking stimulant effects while others may be more appropriate for reduction in active drug users. The three agents mentioned above, and the antiparksonian agent L-dopa/carbidopa, may be useful when combined with supportive efforts such as cognitive behavior therapy (CBT) or contingency management (CM) procedures. As in the opioid dependence field, reduction or elimination in active users will likely be best achieved using an agonist-like approach, e.g. with amphetamines, GBR12909, or perhaps special sustained-release preparations of cocaine itself.

IMMEDIATE IMPLICATIONS FOR PREVENTION, ASSESSMENT OR TREATMENT DEVELOPMENTS

BEHAVIORAL TREATMENTS ALONE AND AS PHARMACOTHERAPY PLATFORMS

In an initial letter and later full report, Higgins et al. (1991, 1993) described a behavioral therapy containing supportive elements that produced clear efficacy in cocaine dependence treatment. Ultimately, Higgins and other investigators delineated the essential treatment elements (contingent vouchers or money for abstinence was critical), and this strategy has been refined over the years. Distinctively different in some features, but potentially incorporating CM elements, CBT has been thoroughly studied and been reported by Carroll (see review, 2000) and others to be a valuable platform for behavioral change that may also enhance pharmacotherapy. Indeed, Schmitz et al. (1998) and others have demonstrated the benefit of combined behavior therapy and pharmacotherapy for cocaine dependence relative to either component alone. Although these two behavioral therapies have shown promise, there are some caveats to their efficacy. Individuals exhibiting cognitive impairment from current or recent heavy cocaine use may be less amenable to all behavioral interventions, particularly cognitive approaches, but more amenable to simple and direct CM. In many cases, particularly with 'first treatment episodes,' the optimal treatment may be behavioral therapy plus medication. Behavior therapy is necessarily the only evidence-based option for those who will not accept pharmacotherapy, though at times behavior therapy will also be rejected for therapy forms with no evidence of efficacy.

Pharmacotherapy for Stimulant Abuse and Dependence

Pharmacotherapy development for stimulant dependence has been briefly summarized above and the extensive literature reflects the foibles and evolution of the search for efficacious medications. Our view, certainly not without critics supporting other therapeutic options, is that the most promising results are those found in examining agonist agents as a first-line pharmacotherapy, particularly for those actively using stimulants. Here we use the term agonist broadly, best characterized as 'agonist-like'; and expanding the concept with a key feature that behavioral effects, not simply patterns of receptor action, must be considered. From other 'agonist' therapies and basic science, we can apply the following 'rules' for optimal agents. First, comparatively slow onset of action is preferred to avoid the euphoric 'burst' associated with rapid onset. This can be accomplished by oral administration and special preparation forms. Second, relatively long duration of action is preferable, accomplished with special (sustained-release) preparations administered orally, with transdermal patches, or depot injection. These preparations result in relatively stable levels through the day, resulting in less frequent medication 'offset' that may produce subjective discomfort or 'craving.' Additionally, sustained-release preparations result in fewer difficulties with patient adherence or compliance. Ideally, the agent could be administered even less frequently than once per day, as is levo-alpha-acetylmethadol (LAAM) for opioid dependence.

Four converging lines of evidence, one preclinical and three clinical, support an agonist approach to pharmacotherapy of stimulant dependence as one component of the armamentarium (Grabowski et al., 2004b). Preclinical research by Negus and colleagues (e.g. Negus & Mello, 2003) used constant low dose infusions of D-amphetamine that produced striking reductions in cocaine intake. Less clear is whether chronic stable levels of currently available agents (e.g. methylphenidate or amphetamine analogs) are feasible in humans. However, medication development may provide options assuring continuous 'coverage' without side effects that deter medication taking.

Three distinctive lines of clinical activity have provided evidence that stimulant dependence can be ameliorated with stimulant administration. In the course

of standard treatment, UK clinicians have administered immediate release
D–amphetamine (e.g. Merrill & Tetlow, 1998; Charnaud & Griffiths, 1998). Retrospective chart reviews and other methods have supported that benefit can result with
diminution in amphetamine abuse and a range of correlated antisocial and aberrant
behaviors. Randomized studies in community treatment settings by Shearer and colleagues in Australia suggested dextroamphetamine sulfate immediate-release can
reduce use of cocaine (Shearer et al., 2003) or amphetamine (Shearer et al., 2001).
Finally, reports from rigorous, double-blind placebo-controlled trials in the US have
indicated that sustained-release dextroamphetamine preparations diminish cocaine-
taking. Further, this was demonstrated in patients with single-diagnosis cocaine
dependence (Grabowski et al., 2001) and those with dual cocaine/heroin dependence (Grabowski et al., 2004a).

A review (Grabowski et al., 2004b) and accumulating data support
psychostimulants as agonist treatments for drug dependence. Some stimulant
agents, e.g. dextro-amphetamine and methylphenidate, are available as sustained-
release oral preparations, and transdermal patches are available in some cases. Both
preparations have slower onset and longer duration of action. Although
methylphenidate is ineffective in the treatment of cocaine dependence (Grabowski
et al., 1997), dextro-amphetamine sustained-release is efficacious at about 60 mg/day
(~1 mg/kg), in line with dosing in the preclinical literature (Negus & Mello,
2003). Most of the studies demonstrating some efficacy with escalating doses
approached or surpassed 60 mg. Grabowski et al. (2001, 2004a) found that a period
of 60 mg sustained-release dextro-amphetamine was well-tolerated and produced
greater diminution in cocaine use than a 30 mg dose. As with all medications the
regimen must be individualized. The US studies had rigorous electrocardiogram
(EKG) criteria and repeated testing without serious adverse events. The UK
(Merrill & Tetlow, 1998; Charnaud & Griffiths, 1998) and Australian (Shearer
et al., 2001, 2003) studies were less well-controlled in this regard but resulted in
few problems. The commonalities across the evaluations were striking.

An additional promising compound with 'stimulant-like' properties is
modafinil. This novel wakefulness-promoting agent is approved for narcolepsy
treatment and alleviation of shift work deficits, plus modafinil enhances mood,
energy, and concentration; these qualities suggest the potential of modafinil as an
agonist-like treatment for stimulant dependence. The mechanism of action of
modafinil is unknown but may involve enhancement of dopaminergic (Ferraro
et al., 1996), glutamatergic (Ferraro et al., 1997), or adrenergic (Lin et al., 1992)
function. Preclinical studies have demonstrated subtle stimulant-like discriminative
stimulus and activity-enhancing properties, making modafinil a suitable agonist-like
candidate (Gold & Balster, 1996; Edgar & Seidel, 1997; Deroche-Gamonet et al.,
2002). Modafinil has limited reinforcing effectiveness as determined by self-
administration and then only at high doses (Gold & Balster, 1996), which may explain
its inability to inhibit cocaine-taking by animals (Deroche-Gamonet et al., 2002).

The mechanistic differences between modafinil and cocaine or amphetamine suggest that modafinil will not compete with these compounds for binding to monoamine transporters.

Two case reports suggested safety and effectiveness of modafinil in stimulant abusers (Malcolm et al., 2002; Camacho & Stein, 2002), and initial human laboratory studies indicated low abuse potential compared to cocaine and absence of cocaine-like subjective effects, although both drugs did elicit increases in heart rate and blood pressure (Rush et al., 2002a, 2002b). Malcolm and Devane (2003) reported modafinil blunted subjective feelings of high otherwise induced by cocaine infusions. No adverse events or interactions were found in interaction studies with cocaine (Dackis et al., 2003) or d-amphetamine (Hellriegel et al., 2002). Dackis and O'Brien (2003) in an open trial, and double-blind trial (Dackis et al., 2005), reported reductions in cocaine use. Despite some equivocal reports, most studies support modafinil as an agonist-like treatment for stimulant dependence. Clinical trials examining combinations of D-amphetamine and modafinil are ongoing along with further trials of modafinil alone to identify optimal dosing regimens.

Another novel pharmacologic strategy currently being examined for cocaine dependence utilizes disulfiram, an agent long used for alcohol dependence treatment. Disulfiram decreases alcohol consumption via inhibition of the enzyme aldehyde dehydrogenase, resulting in accumulation of acetaldehyde and aversive consequences (Hald, Jacobsen, & Larsen, 1948; Towell et al., 1983; Wright & Moore, 1990). The mechanism for disulfiram to treat cocaine dependence is uncertain but this agent may enhance dopaminergic function via inhibition of dopamine beta hydroxylase (DBH), an enzyme which converts DA to NE. Thus, disulfiram enhances DA and decreases NE levels (Goldstein & Nakajima, 1967), which may enhance the aversive qualities of cocaine (Hameedi et al., 1995; McCance-Katz et al., 1998a, 1998b). The few preclinical experiments of stimulant–disulfiram interaction (Maj & Przegalinski, 1967; Maj, Przegalinski, & Wielosz, 1968) suggest disulfiram may attenuate rewarding effects of cocaine or amphetamine.

Initial clinical studies indicated disulfiram decreased cocaine use in dual cocaine/alcohol dependence (Carroll et al., 1998, 2000) and two additional studies suggest decreased cocaine use (George et al., 2000; Petrakis et al., 2000) in concurrent cocaine/opioid users. Carroll et al. (2004) reported decreased cocaine use in single dependence (cocaine only) subjects, and further trials and interaction studies are ongoing.

The promising medications proposed here, while available by prescription, have not been explicitly approved by the FDA for treatment of stimulant dependence. That stated, some clinicians do cautiously administer dextro-amphetamine for cocaine or amphetamine abuse and in treatment of dual diagnosis patients with ADHD. Methylphenidate has been examined in individuals with comorbid cocaine dependence plus ADHD, and these data suggest some utility in this population, but interestingly the benefit of methylphenidate is less evident, even for ADHD in this group (Levin et al., 1998; Levin et al., 2006). Given a history of cocaine abuse/dependence, some have hypothesized that dextro-amphetamine preparations might be more effective in these patients.

Overall, the population requiring treatment for stimulant dependence can be roughly divided as those potentially benefiting from behavioral therapy alone, medication alone, or a combination. It appears that among the second and third, a well-designed agonist regimen may be beneficial. In treatment of other dual diagnosis patients, treatment of depression, or bipolar disorder, or other disorders, may or may not alter stimulant abuse/dependence. Still, there are tantalizing reports that concurrent treatment with multiple medications may be an effective alternative. For example, Carnwath, Garvey, and Holland (2002) reported enhanced efficacy of antipsychotics in schizophrenics and diminished D-amphetamine abuse in 7 of 8 schizophrenics with a stable D-amphetamine dose regimen. There is certainly a need for specific rigorous research in this domain and in development of novel medications or medication combinations.

Finally, no medication is risk free. There has long been resistance to use of agonist treatment for heroin such as methadone, and there are risks inherent in agonist therapy for stimulant dependence. The 'safest' of medications may produce less effective response while untreated or under-treated substance abuse/dependence has clear and substantial risk. Still, given public and clinician concerns about D-amphetamine or other potent agonist treatments for stimulant dependence (and absence to date of FDA approval for SUD alone), clinicians are faced with promising data but an uncertain prescribing environment. As discussed in the next section, new medications or medication combinations with higher efficacy and lower risk may be developed and used effectively, whether or not the agonist perspective gains social or policy acceptance.

SPECULATION ON FUTURE DIRECTIONS FOR TRANSLATIONAL DEVELOPMENTS

Although there are no approved medications for stimulant dependence, advances have been made, as shown by the efficacy of amphetamine (Grabowski et al., 2001; Shearer et al., 2001; Shearer et al., 2003; Grabowski et al., 2004a). However, alternatives must be further investigated to provide an armamentarium of pharmacotherapeutic options for stimulant dependence.

An ideal agonist substitution therapy, by definition, should have some neurochemical and subjective effects in common with the psychostimulant, with minimal abuse liability. Psychostimulants such as cocaine (Bradberry et al., 1993; Reith, Li, & Yan, 1997) and amphetamines (Segal & Kuczenski,

1997; Kankaanpaa et al., 1998) enhance extracellular concentrations of dopamine, serotonin (5-HT), and norepinephrine (NE), thus these neurotransmitter systems are a logical target for replacement therapies. While there is little consensus for targeting single vs. multiple systems, the DA system is of particular interest since it has long been implicated in the reinforcing effects of psychostimulants (Koob, 1992). This is supported by trials with D-amphetamine, though amphetamine has several other significant actions. Double-blind placebo-controlled clinical trials utilizing more selective dopaminergic ligands have produced largely negative results (see Gorelick et al., 2004 for review), suggesting that dopaminergic stimulation may not be sufficient for the treatment of stimulant dependence and a broad mechanism of action may be required.

The complexity, integrity, and interaction of CNS systems dictates that 5-HT and NE systems are important but the benefit of direct modulation to alter stimulant self-administration/taking is less clear. Some studies suggest a contribution of these neurotransmitter systems to subjective effects of psychostimulants (Walsh & Cunningham, 1997; Rothman et al., 2001), although double-blind placebo-controlled clinical trials targeting either 5-HT (Covi et al., 1995; Grabowski et al., 1995) or NE (Gawin et al., 1989; Kosten et al., 1992) systems have produced mixed results. Collectively, these data suggest that the subjective experience elicited by psychostimulants involves contributions from each of the monoaminergic systems, supporting the use of pharmacotherapeutic agents with a broad mechanism of action. Here, we highlight evidence supporting the validity of the DA, 5-HT, and NE systems as targets for agonist substitution therapy and propose that the ideal therapeutic agent should broadly target each of the monoamine systems in tandem.

Each monoamine system is extremely diverse in terms of receptor subtypes and reuptake transporters, and a full discussion of these aspects of monoamine pharmacology is beyond the scope of this chapter. Thus, we confine the discussion to ligands modulating monoamine transporter function, specifically reuptake blockers and transporter substrates, and in turn, this characterizes the agents available or likely to be developed in the field. Reuptake blockers bind to monoamine transporters and *inhibit monoamine reuptake*, thereby increasing concentrations of DA, 5-HT, or NE in the synapse (Rothman et al., 2000). Examples of reuptake inhibitors include GBR 12909, fluoxetine, and atomoxetine, which target transporters for dopamine (DAT), 5-HT (SERT), and NE (NET), respectively, and cocaine which blocks each of the monoamine transporters (Rothman et al., 2001; Bymaster et al., 2002). In contrast, transporter substrates are transported into the nerve terminal where they act via a carrier-mediated exchange mechanism to *reverse* the transporter, resulting in enhanced *release* of monoamines (Rothman et al., 2000). Some examples of transporter substrates include the DA/NE releaser amphetamine and the 5-HT releaser fenfluramine (Rothman et al., 2001). Although mechanistically different, both reuptake inhibitors and substrates (releasers) elevate extracellular monoamine concentrations.

DA System as Target for Agonist Substitution Therapy

Acutely, cocaine and the amphetamines prominently enhance extracellular DA levels by blockade, or reversal, of the DAT, respectively (Koe, 1976; Rothman et al., 2001) and many preclinical studies have demonstrated the DA system involvement in stimulant behavior. For example, a role for DA was shown with the drug discrimination assay, a behavioral paradigm that models the subjective effects of drugs in humans (Schuster & Johanson, 1988). In this paradigm, DA agonists substitute for cocaine, suggesting that they generate a similar internal cue as the psychostimulant (Cunningham & Callahan, 1991; Kleven, Anthony, & Woolverton, 1990; Callahan, Appel, & Cunningham, 1991). In keeping with this observation, the dopaminergic system plays an integral role in psychostimulant reinforcement, as lesion of the mesoaccumbens DA circuit attenuated cocaine (Caine & Koob, 1994) or amphetamine (Lyness, Friedle, & Moore, 1979) self-administration. The enhancement of DAergic function elicited by acute psychostimulant administration contributes to their characteristic subjective qualities in humans, as there exists a positive correlation between the euphoric effects of amphetamine in humans and the magnitude of extracellular DA release elicited by the drug (Drevets et al., 2001; but see Rothman et al., 2001). These data strongly indicate a role for enhanced DA transmission in the appetitive effects of psychostimulants and suggest targeting of the DA system in agonist substitution therapy.

Several structurally diverse compounds have thus been developed with selectivity for the DAT over the SERT and NET including GBR-like compounds, tropanes, and methylphenidate analogs. Recent stimulant dependence research has focused on the 1,4-dialkyl-piperazine GBR compounds, especially GBR 12909. GBR 12909 has greater selectivity for the DAT ($K_i = 4.3$ nM) vs. the SERT ($K_i = 73.2$ nM) or NET ($K_i = 79.2$ nM; Rothman et al., 2001) and microdialysis data indicate that this reuptake inhibitor enhances extracellular DA in the nucleus accumbens, a brain region critical for drug reward and reinforcement (Baumann et al., 1994; Delfs, Schreiber, & Kelley, 1990). Preclinical studies indicate that GBR 12909 is self-administered, demonstrating that this compound serves as a reinforcer (Howell & Byrd, 1991). Interaction studies indicated that GBR 12909 inhibited binding of cocaine to the DAT and attenuated the ability of cocaine or amphetamine to elevate extracellular levels of DA, supporting the ability of this ligand to block the neurochemical effects of psychostimulants (Rothman et al., 1989; Rothman et al., 1991; Baumann et al., 1994). In keeping with these observations, GBR 12909 pretreatment reduced cocaine reinforcement to a greater extent than food self-administration, suggesting that this effect is more selective for drug reinforcement (Glowa et al., 1997). These promising preclinical data led to several clinical trials utilizing GBR 12909, however, testing was discontinued after several subjects developed a QTc prolongation in their electrocardiogram (Vocci & Ling, 2005). Although this side effect profile precludes further investigation of GBR 12909, these data suggest the DAT is a promising target for treatment of psychostimulant dependence.

The tropanes are a group of cocaine analogs also being pursued as stimulant dependence treatments, with 2β-propanoyl-3β-(4-tolyl)-tropane (PTT) generating particular interest. PTT has the greatest affinity for the DAT ($K_i = 3.61$ nM), and lesser affinity for the SERT ($K_i = 174$ nM) and NET ($K_i = 51.8$ nM; Lile et al., 2003). This compound is resistant to hydrolysis by esterases, resulting in a greater duration of action than cocaine (Sizemore et al., 2004). PTT dose-dependently enhanced extracellular dopamine levels in the nucleus accumbens (Hemby et al., 1995), and evoked hyperactivity (Porrino et al., 1994; Hemby et al., 1995), a behavioral effect suggestive of reward (Delfs et al., 1990). However, in the self-administration paradigm PTT functioned as a weak reinforcer, suggesting that it may possess minimal abuse liability (Nader et al., 1997; Lile et al., 2002). Other data indicated that PTT reduced cocaine self-administration, albeit at doses that also reduce food self-administration, suggesting a nonspecific effect of this compound to block reinforcement (Lile et al., 2004). Further investigations with PTT or related compounds will elucidate their potential for treatment of stimulant dependence.

Methylphenidate analogs are an additional group of compounds currently in development. Methylphenidate has shown limited utility in the treatment of stimulant dependence (Grabowski et al., 1997; Schubiner et al., 2002; but see Tiihonen et al., 2007), however, several analogs have a much greater selectivity for the DAT. Initial preclinical drug discrimination studies demonstrated that several analogs substituted for cocaine, suggesting that they generate a similar internal cue as cocaine (Schweri et al., 2002). However, the combination of cocaine and some analogs enhanced cocaine discrimination, suggesting that these ligands potentiate cocaine effects (Schweri et al., 2002). Further research is necessary to determine the potential of these ligands.

5-HT SYSTEM AS TARGET FOR AGONIST SUBSTITUTION THERAPY

As noted, the importance of the 5-HT system as a target for agonist substitution therapy is less clear. Although cocaine (Bradberry et al., 1993) and amphetamines (Kankaanpaa et al., 1998) enhance extracellular 5-HT, preclinical studies are inconsistent regarding the role of 5-HT transmission in psychostimulant behavior (see Walsh & Cunningham, 1997 for review; Bubar et al., 2003). For example, mixed results were reported for 5-HT reuptake inhibitors to alter cocaine drug discrimination or self-administration (Carroll et al., 1990; Cunningham & Callahan, 1991; Peltier & Schenk, 1993; Spealman, 1993; Walsh and Cunningham, 1997). Early human studies suggested utility of 5-HT reuptake inhibitors for cocaine dependence treatment (Walsh et al., 1994), although double-blind placebo-controlled trials produced mixed results

(Covi et al, 1995; Grabowski et al., 1995; Batki et al., 1996). Interestingly, one double-blind study indicated that the 5-HT releaser fenfluramine decreased spontaneous craving in cocaine-dependent individuals (Buydens-Branchey et al., 1998). Future investigations will better determine the potential of the 5-HT system for stimulant dependence treatment, although some clinical data do support this possibility.

One candidate 5-HT reuptake inhibitor that shows promise is citalopram. Despite the largely negative clinical data investigating 5-HT reuptake inhibitors as therapies for drug dependence, racemic citalopram has been shown to decrease cocaine use, while increasing treatment retention, when combined with behavior therapy in outpatient clinical trials (Moeller et al., in press). The mechanistic difference between citalopram and other 5-HT reuptake inhibitors is unknown, but could be due to a direct action of citalopram at specific 5-HT receptor subtypes (Moeller et al., in press).

NE System as Target for Agonist Substitution Therapy

The contribution of the NE system in elicitation of the acute effects of psychostimulants has been little investigated, however, there is support for this system as a target for agonist therapies. Acute psychostimulant administration enhances extracellular NE via actions at the NET (Reith et al., 1997; Segal & Kuczenski, 1997), but preclinical studies have produced mixed results regarding the role of NE in the discriminative stimulus and reinforcing properties of psychostimulants (Kleven et al., 1990; Spealman, 1995; Wee et al., 2006). However, several studies suggest that psychostimulant-evoked increases in extracellular NE may contribute to their characteristic subjective effects in humans. For example, the sympathomimetic and subjective effects of amphetamines exhibit a similar time course, suggesting a possible relation between enhanced NE transmission and these subjective effects (Martin et al., 1971; Heishman & Henningfeld, 1991; Rothman et al., 2001). Additionally, the subjective effects evoked following acute administration of amphetamine derivatives are correlated with their potency at releasing NE (Rothman et al., 2001), further suggesting a possible NEergic contribution. Although further investigation of this relationship is necessary, these studies support the NE system as a target for agonist substitution therapy.

One NE ligand currently under investigation as an agonist-like therapy is atomoxetine, a NET reuptake inhibitor used for the treatment of ADHD, with the greatest affinity for the NET ($K_i = 5$ nM), and lesser affinity for the SERT ($K_i = 77$ nM) and DAT ($K_i = 1451$ nM; Bymaster et al., 2002). Preclinical drug discrimination studies have produced mixed results, as atomoxetine fully substituted for cocaine in rodents (Terry, Witkin, & Katz, 1994), although atomoxetine did not substitute for cocaine (Kleven et al., 1990) or methamphetamine (Tidey & Bergman,

1998) in primates. Additionally, atomoxetine is not self-administered, suggesting minimal abuse liability (Gasior et al., 2005). Several clinical studies are currently investigating the efficacy of atomoxetine to treat drug dependence.

RATIONALE FOR COMPOUNDS WITH MIXED DA/5-HT/NE ACTIVITY

We recommend and the data suggest that the ideal agonist substitution therapy, particularly to attenuate active drug use, should target the DA, 5-HT, and NE systems, as this broad-based strategy has several advantages. First, this broad mechanism of action is more likely to mimic the subjective effects of stimulants as opposed to modulation of a single transmitter system. By definition, agonist therapies should evoke tempered behavioral and biological effects akin to the abused drug, with decreased abuse liability. As discussed earlier, this can be accomplished using special preparations and well-delineated regimens. Since the DA, NE, and 5-HT systems are thought to each play a role in the generation of the subjective effects of psychostimulants, an ideal agonist substitution therapy should target each of these transmitter systems.

An additional advantage is that a broad mechanism of action may alleviate some adverse psychological and behavioral effects reported following chronic psychostimulant abuse. Chronic psychostimulant administration results in reduced or hypofunction of the DA and 5-HT systems and alterations in NE transmission (Rothman et al., 2002; McDougle et al., 1994). These perturbations of monoaminergic transmission have been suggested to mediate unfavorable consequences including anhedonia, anxiety, motor and cognitive deficits, depression, obsessional thoughts, decreased impulse control, and drug craving (McDougle et al., 1994; Buydens-Branchey et al., 1998; Rothman et al., 2002; Kelley et al., 2005). Return to, or repeated, use of the abused drug transiently reverses this condition. Recent reports suggest that broad-based enhancement of monoamine transmission may alleviate these deficits (McDougle et al., 1994; Buydens-Branchey et al., 1998; Rothman et al., 2002; Kelley et al., 2005), thus supporting the use of agonist substitution therapies with this mixed action.

Furthermore, agonist therapies that block monoamine reuptake are likely to attenuate the neurochemical effects of psychostimulants should drug use be reinitiated. The ability of psychostimulants to enhance extracellular monoamine concentrations requires binding of the abused drug to monoamine transporters; these transporters are also targeted by monoamine reuptake inhibitors. In vitro studies indicated that pretreatment with the DA reuptake inhibitor GBR 12909 or NE reuptake inhibitor desipramine attenuated the ability of methamphetamine to release DA, or NE, respectively, presumably because these ligands inhibited the ability of methamphetamine to bind to monoamine transporters (Rothman et al., 2000).

Additionally, the mixed DA/5-HT/NE reuptake inhibitor indatraline antago-
nized monoamine release elicited by methamphetamine (Rothman et al., 2000),
providing further support for the utility of monoamine reuptake inhibitors to
block the neurochemical effects of psychostimulants. Thus, an agonist replacement
therapy which blocks each of the monoamine transporters would decrease the
neurochemical effects of the stimulant, resulting in attenuation of the acute subjective effects attributed to the drug. In support of this, Collins and colleagues
(2006) reported decreased responsiveness to cocaine in patients pretreated with
methylphenidate.

The potential utility of mixed agonists is supported by preclinical studies
where the combination of the DA/NE releaser phentermine and 5-HT releaser
fenfluramine reduced cocaine self-administration without effect on food reinforcement (Glowa et al., 1997). Additionally, an open-label clinical study indicated
that phentermine plus fenfluramine alleviated some withdrawal symptoms in
cocaine addicts (Kampman et al., 2000). Unfortunately, this pharmacotherapy is
no longer available, as fenfluramine was linked to heart valve abnormalities, thus
removed from the market, but these data warrant further investigation of mixed
DA/5-HT/NE compounds as agonist treatments for stimulant dependence.

One intriguing prospect for an agonist therapy with a broad mechanism of
action is cocaine itself. This is supported by preclinical data where injection with
low doses of cocaine decreased subsequent cocaine self-administration without
alteration in food responding (Glowa & Fantegrossi, 1997). The reported high
'abuse liability' of cocaine (and other drugs) is related to rapidity of onset and short
duration following intranasal or intravenous administration (Mendelson et al., 1999;
Abreu et al., 2001), however, limited clinical data suggest further investigation of
oral cocaine administration. The oral route of cocaine delivery is attractive for its
slower onset and longer duration of action, thus attenuating abuse liability. Limited
clinical data indicate that oral cocaine is safe when administered humans, as it does
not result in toxicity, and has been reported to decrease drug craving and relapse
(Llosa, 1994a, 1994b, 1996; Walsh et al., 2000; Llosa & Llosa, 2005). Additionally,
an interaction study indicated that oral cocaine administration attenuated subjective
and physiological responses elicited by IV cocaine challenge (Walsh et al., 2000).

Use of an oral cocaine preparation as an agonist substitution therapy is
limited by many theoretical and practical difficulties, for example, crushing of
standard capsules and IV or intranasal administration of the content. However,
recent advances in drug delivery technology may permit the development of an
oral formulation of cocaine that is inactive unless taken by the intended route.
The pharmaceutical industry has recently developed carrier molecules that can be
coupled to drugs of abuse such as the amphetamines and opiates (Jasinski &
Krishnan, 2006). This technology renders the drug inactive unless subjected to
the enzymatic environment of the gastrointestinal tract, thus preventing drug use
via other routes of administration. The development of an oral formulation of

cocaine with this technology would likely be a useful pharmacotherapy in the armamentarium.

One promising molecule currently in preclinical testing is PAL-287. This non-amphetamine compound acts at monoamine transporters to evoke monoamine release, and microdialysis studies indicate that PAL-287 enhances basal extracellular levels of both DA and 5-HT (Rothman et al., 2005). Behavioral studies using the self-administration paradigm indicated that PAL-287 is not an effective reinforcer, suggesting little abuse liability. Combination studies indicated that chronic pretreatment with PAL-287 decreased self-administration of cocaine or food, with greater attenuation of cocaine self-administration (Rothman et al., 2005). These data suggest potential utility for PAL-287 or related compounds as agonist therapies, but more research is necessary.

To date, no medication has proven uniquely effective for the treatment of psychostimulant dependence. Research investigating potential agonist substitution therapies has generally utilized ligands that target single transmitter systems or receptor subtypes with limited success. As the DA, 5-HT, and NE systems each contribute to the subjective experience elicited by psychostimulants, we propose that future studies should utilize ligands with a mixed action to enhance DA, 5-HT, and NE transmission.

The foregoing discussion addressed the strategy of administering medications with broad actions not dissimilar from the abused agent, using preparation forms that reduce subjective effects and abuse liability. In part, this approach addresses previously noted distinctions between active users, a surrogate for severity, and those individuals who have some period of abstinence and for whom the goal is diminishing probability of return to use, or 'relapse prevention.' It is possible that relatively selective agents for DA, 5-HT, or NE, that is 'single target' candidates, may have utility in such circumstances. Thus, the gamut of pharmacotherapy possibilities should be explored.

With a full range of agonist-like agents, a stepped medication approach could be utilized based on treatment entry severity and resultant attenuation of drug use, followed by sequential progress through less potent or more selective agents, with the overall consequence of gradual return to relative biologic and behavioral stability (as suggested by Goldstein (2001) for opioid dependence). Related is the possibility of medication combinations, for example, D-amphetamine and modafinil at lower doses thus diminishing any risk associated with either drug.

Finally, several factors will contribute to future advances in this field. Obviously, one advance will be the identification of efficacious medications and clearly defining optimal regimens. Adherence/compliance are problematic in treatment of many diseases including substance use disorders, and agonist approaches are advantageous as they provide a level of positive reinforcement not characteristic of other medications. Also, it is essential that advances in preparation form technology be applied to minimize risk and enhance safety. And finally, beyond medications, the optimal combined therapeutic regimens (behavioral and pharmacologic) must be delineated where necessary.

REFERENCES

Abreu, M. E., Bigelow, G. E., Fleisher, L., & Walsh, S. L. (2001). Effect of intravenous injection speed on responses to cocaine and hydromorphone in humans. *Psychopharmacology (Berl)*, *154*(1), 76–84.

Banerjee, D., Vitiello, M. V., & Grunstein, R. R. (2004). Pharmacotherapy for excessive daytime sleepiness. *Sleep Medicine Reviews*, *8*(5), 339–354.

Barrett, A. C., Miller, J. R., Dohrmann, J. M., & Caine, S. B. (2004). Effects of dopamine indirect agonists and selective D1-like and D2-like agonists and antagonists on cocaine self-administration and food maintained responding in rats. *Neuropharmacology*, *47*(Suppl 1), 256–273.

Batki, S. L., Washburn, A. M., Delucchi, K., & Jones, R. T. (1996). A controlled trial of fluoxetine in crack cocaine dependence. *Drug and Alcohol Dependence*, *41*(2), 137–142.

Baumann, M. H., Char, G. U., De Costa, B. R., Rice, K. C., & Rothman, R. B. (1994). GBR12909 attenuates cocaine-induced activation of mesolimbic dopamine neurons in the rat. *The Journal of Pharmacology and Experimental Therapeutics*, *271*(3), 1216–1222.

Bradberry, C. W., Nobiletti, J. B., Elsworth, J. D., Murphy, B., Jatlow, P., & Roth, R. H. (1993). Cocaine and cocaethylene: Microdialysis comparison of brain drug levels and effects on dopamine and serotonin. *Journal of Neurochemistry*, *60*(4), 1429–1435.

Bubar, M. J., McMahon, L. R., De Deurwaerdere, P., Spampinato, U., & Cunningham, K. A. (2003). Selective serotonin reuptake inhibitors enhance cocaine-induced locomotor activity and dopamine release in the nucleus accumbens. *Neuropharmacology*, *44*(3), 342–353.

Buydens-Branchey, L., Branchey, M., Hudson, J., Rothman, M., Fergeson, P., & McKernin, C. (1998). Effect of fenfluramine challenge on cocaine craving in addicted male users. *American Journal on Addictions*, *7*(2), 142–155.

Bymaster, F. P., Katner, J. S., Nelson, D. L., Hemrick-Luecke, S. K., Threlkeld, P. G., Heiligenstein, J. H., Morin, S. M., Gehlert, D. R., & Perry, K. W. (2002). Atomoxetine increases extracellular levels of norepinephrine and dopamine in prefrontal cortex of rat: A potential mechanism for efficacy in attention deficit/hyperactivity disorder. *Neuropsychopharmacology*, *27*(5), 699–711.

Caine, S. B., & Koob, G. F. (1994). Effects of mesolimbic dopamine depletion on responding maintained by cocaine and food. *Journal of the Experimental Analysis of Behavior*, *61*(2), 213–221.

Callahan, P. M., Appel, J. B., & Cunningham, K. A. (1991). Dopamine D1 and D2 mediation of the discriminative stimulus properties of D-amphetamine and cocaine. *Psychopharmacology (Berl)*, *103*(1), 50–55.

Camacho, A., & Stein, M. B. (2002). Modafinil for social phobia and amphetamine dependence. *American Journal of Psychiatry*, *159*(11), 1947–1948.

Carnwath, T., Garvey, T., & Holland, M. (2002). The prescription of dexamphetamine to patients with schizophrenia and amphetamine dependence. *Journal of Psychopharmacology*, *16*(4), 373–377.

Carroll, K. M. (2000). Implications of recent research for program quality in cocaine dependence treatment. *Substance Use Misuse*, *35*(12–14), 2011–2030.

Carroll, K. M., Fenton, L. R., Ball, S. A., Nich, C., Frankforter, T. L., Shi, J., & Rounsaville, B. J. (2004). Efficacy of disulfiram and cognitive behavior therapy in cocaine-dependent outpatients: A randomized placebo-controlled trial. *Archives of General Psychiatry*, *61*(3), 264–272.

Carroll, K. M., Nich, C., Ball, S. A., McCance, E., & Rounsavile, B. J. (1998). Treatment of cocaine and alcohol dependence with psychotherapy and disulfiram. *Addiction*, *93*(5), 713–727.

Carroll, K. M., Nich, C., Sifry, R. L., Nuro, K. F., Frankforter, T. L., Ball, S. A., Fenton, L. & Rounsaville, B. J. (2000). A general system for evaluating therapist adherence and competence in psychotherapy research in the addictions. *Drug and Alcohol Dependence, 57*(3), 225–238.

Carroll, M. E., Lac, S. T., Asencio, M., & Kragh, R. (1990). Fluoxetine reduces intravenous cocaine self-administration in rats. *Pharmacology Biochemistry, and Behavior, 35*(1), 237–244.

Charnaud, B., & Griffiths, V. (1998). Levels of intravenous drug misuse among clients prescribed oral dexamphetamine or oral methadone: A comparison. *Drug and Alcohol Dependence, 52*(1), 79–84.

Collins, S. L., Levin, F. R., Foltin, R. W., Kleber, H. D., & Evans, S. M. (2006). Response to cocaine, alone and in combination with methylphenidate, in cocaine abusers with ADHD. *Drug and Alcohol Dependence, 82*(2), 158–167.

Community Epidemiology Workgroup, advance report. (2006). *National Institute on Drug Abuse,* USHDDS/NIH. 45 pp.

Covi, L., Hess, J. M., Kreiter, N. A., & Haertzen, C. A. (1995). Effects of combined fluoxetine and counseling in the outpatient treatment of cocaine abusers. *American Journal of Drug and Alcohol Abuse, 21*(3), 327–344.

Cunningham, K. A., & Callahan, P. M. (1991). Monoamine reuptake inhibitors enhance the discriminative state induced by cocaine in the rat. *Psychopharmacology (Berl), 104*(2), 177–180.

Dackis, C., & O'Brien, C. (2003). Glutamatergic agents for cocaine dependence. *Annals of New York Academy of Sciences, 1003,* 328–345.

Dackis, C. A., Kampman, K. M., Lynch, K. G., Pettinati, H. M., & O'Brien, C. P. (2005). A double-blind, placebo-controlled trial of modafinil for cocaine dependence. *Neuropsychopharmacology, 30*(1), 205–211.

Dackis, C. A., Lynch, K. G., Yu, E., Samaha, F. F., Kampman, K. M., Cornish, J. W., Rowan, A., Poole, S., White, L., & O'Brien, C. P. (2003). Modafinil and cocaine: A double-blind, placebo-controlled drug interaction study. *Drug and Alcohol Dependence, 70*(1), 29–37.

Delfs, J. M., Schreiber, L., & Kelley, A. E. (1990). Microinjection of cocaine into the nucleus accumbens elicits locomotor activation in the rat. *Journal of Neuroscience, 10*(1), 303–310.

Deroche-Gamonet, V., Darnaudery, M., Bruins-Slot, L., Piat, F., Le Moal, M., & Piazza, P. V. (2002). Study of the addictive potential of modafinil in naive and cocaine-experienced rats. *Psychopharmacology (Berl), 161*(4), 387–395.

Drevets, W. C., Gautier, C., Price, J. C., Kupfer, D. J., Kinahan, P. E., Grace, A. A., Price, J. L., & Mathis, C. A. (2001). Amphetamine-induced dopamine release in human ventral striatum correlates with euphoria. *Biological of Psychiatry, 49*(2), 81–96.

Edgar, D. M., & Seidel, W. F. (1997). Modafinil induces wakefulness without intensifying motor activity or subsequent rebound hypersomnolence in the rat. *The Journal of Pharmacology and Experimental Therapeutics, 283*(2), 757–769.

Ferraro, L., Antonelli, T., O'Connor, W. T., Tanganelli, S., Rambert, F., & Fuxe, K. (1997). The antinarcoleptic drug modafinil increases glutamate release in thalamic areas and hippocampus. *Neuroreport, 8*(13), 2883–2887.

Ferraro, L., Tanganelli, S., O'Connor, W. T., Antonelli, T., Rambert, F., & Fuxe, K. (1996). The vigilance promoting drug modafinil increases dopamine release in the rat nucleus accumbens via the involvement of a local GABAergic mechanism. *European Journal of Pharmacology, 306*(1–3), 33–39.

Gasior, M., Bergman, J., Kallman, M. J., & Paronis, C. A. (2005). Evaluation of the reinforcing effects of monoamine reuptake inhibitors under a concurrent schedule of food and i.v. drug delivery in rhesus monkeys. *Neuropsychopharmacology, 30*(4), 758–764.

Gawin, F. H., & Kleber, H. D. (1984). Cocaine abuse treatment. Open pilot trial with desipramine and lithium carbonate. *Archives of General Psychiatry, 41*(9), 903–909.

Gawin, F. H., Kleber, H. D., Byck, R., Rounsaville, B. J., Kosten, T. R., Jatlow, P. I., & Morgan, C. (1989). Desipramine facilitation of initial cocaine abstinence. *Archives of General Psychiatry, 46*(2), 117–121.

George, T. P., Chawarski, M. C., Pakes, J., Carroll, K. M., Kosten, T. R., & Schottenfeld, R. S. (2000). Disulfiram versus placebo for cocaine dependence in buprenorphine-maintained subjects: A preliminary trial. *Biological Psychiatry*, *47*(12), 1080–1086.

Glowa, J. R., & Fantegrossi, W. E. (1997). Effects of dopaminergic drugs on food- and cocaine-maintained responding. IV: Continuous cocaine infusions. *Drug and Alcohol Dependence*, *45*(1–2), 71–79.

Glowa, J. R., Rice, K. C., Matecka, D., & Rothman, R. B. (1997). Phentermine/fenfluramine decreases cocaine self-administration in rhesus monkeys. *Neuroreport*, *8*(6), 1347–1351.

Glowa, J. R., Wojnicki, F. H. E., Matecka, D., Bacher, J. D., Mansbach, R. S., Balster, R. L., & Rice, K. C. (1995). Effects of dopamine reuptake inhibitors on food- and cocaine-maintained responding: I. Dependence on unit dose of cocaine. *Experimental and Clinical Psychopharmacology*, *3*(3), 219–231.

Gold, L. H., & Balster, R. L. (1996). Evaluation of the cocaine-like discriminative stimulus effects and reinforcing effects of modafinil. *Psychopharmacology (Berl)*, *126*(4), 286–292.

Goldstein, A. (2001). *Addiction: From Biology to Drug Policy* (2nd ed.). New York: Oxford University Press.

Goldstein, M., & Nakajima, K. (1967). The effect of disulfiram on catecholamine levels in the brain. *The Journal of Pharmacology Experimental Therapeutics*, *157*(1), 96–102.

Gorelick, D. A., Gardner, E. L., & Xi, Z. X. (2004). Agents in development for the management of cocaine abuse. *Drugs*, *64*(14), 1547–1573.

Grabowski, J., Rhoades, H., Elk, R., Schmitz, J., Davis, C., Creson, D., & Kirby, K. (1995). Fluoxetine is ineffective for treatment of cocaine dependence or concurrent opiate and cocaine dependence: Two placebo-controlled double-blind trials. *Journal of Clinical Psychopharmacology*, *15*(3), 163–174.

Grabowski, J., Rhoades, H., Schmitz, J., Stotts, A., Daruzska, L. A., Creson, D., & Moeller, F. G. (2001). Dextroamphetamine for cocaine-dependence treatment: A double-blind randomized clinical trial. *Journal of Clinical Psychopharmacology*, *21*(5), 522–526.

Grabowski, J., Rhoades, H., Stotts, A., Cowan, K., Kopecky, C., Dougherty, A., Moeller, F. G., Hassan, S., & Schmitz, J. (2004a). Agonist-like or antagonist-like treatment for cocaine dependence with methadone for heroin dependence: Two double-blind randomized clinical trials. *Neuropsychopharmacology*, *29*(5), 969–981.

Grabowski, J., Roache, J. D., Schmitz, J. M., Rhoades, H., Creson, D., & Korszun, A. (1997). Replacement medication for cocaine dependence: Methylphenidate. *Journal of Clinical Psychopharmacology*, *17*(6), 485–488.

Grabowski, J., Shearer, J., Merrill, J., & Negus, S. S. (2004b). Agonist-like, replacement pharmacotherapy for stimulant abuse and dependence. *Addiction Behaviour*, *29*(7), 1439–1464.

Hald, J., Jacobsen, E., & Larsen, V. (1948). The sensitizing effect of tetra-ethylthiuram (Antabuse) to ethyl alcohol. *Acta Pharmacology and Toxicology*, *4*, 285–296.

Halikas, J. A., Crosby, R. D., Pearson, V. L., & Graves, N. M. (1997). A randomized double-blind study of carbamazepine in the treatment of cocaine abuse. *Clinical Pharmacology and Therapeutics*, *62*(1), 89–105.

Hameedi, F. A., Rosen, M. I., McCance-Katz, E. F., McMahon, T. J., Price, L. H., Jatlow, P. I., Woods, S. W., & Kosten, T. R. (1995). Behavioral, physiological, and pharmacological interaction of cocaine and disulfiram in humans. *Biology of Psychiatry*, *37*(8), 560–563.

Heishman, S. J., & Henningfield, J. E. (1991). Discriminative stimulus effects of D-amphetamine, methylphenidate, and diazepam in humans. *Psychopharmacology (Berl)*, *103*(4), 436–442.

Hellriegel, E. T., Arora, S., Nelson, M., & Robertson, P., Jr. (2002). Steady-state pharmacokinetics and tolerability of modafinil administered alone or in combination with dextroamphetamine in healthy volunteers. *Journal of Clinical Pharmacology*, *42*(4), 450–460.

Hemby, S. E., Co, C., Reboussin, D., Davies, H. M., Dworkin, S. I., & Smith, J. E. (1995). Comparison of a novel tropane analog of cocaine, 2 beta-propanoyl-3 beta-(4-tolyl) tropane with cocaine HCl in rats: Nucleus accumbens extracellular dopamine concentration and motor activity. *The Journal of Pharmacology and Experimental Therapeutics*, *273*(2), 656–666.

Higgins, S. T., Budney, A. J., Bickel, W. K., Hughes, J. R., & Foerg, F. (1993a). Disulfiram therapy in patients abusing cocaine and alcohol. *American Journal of Psychiatry, 150*(4), 675–676.

Higgins, S. T., Budney, A. J., Bickel, W. K., Hughes, J. R., Foerg, F., & Badger, G. (1993b). Achieving cocaine abstinence with a behavioral approach. *American Journal of Psychiatry, 150*(5), 763–769.

Higgins, S. T., Delaney, D. D., Budney, A. J., Bickel, W. K., Hughes, J. R., Foerg, F., & Fenwick, J. W. (1991). A behavioral approach to achieving initial cocaine abstinence. *American Journal of Psychiatry, 148*(9), 1218–1224.

Howell, L. L., & Byrd, L. D. (1991). Characterization of the effects of cocaine and GBR 12909, a dopamine uptake inhibitor, on behavior in the squirrel monkey. *The Journal of Pharmacology and Experimental Therapeutics, 258*(1), 178–185.

Jasinski, D. R., & Kovacevic-Ristanovic, R. (2000). Evaluation of the abuse liability of modafinil and other drugs for excessive daytime sleepiness associated with narcolepsy. *Clinical Neuropharmacology, 23*(3), 149–156.

Jasinski, D. R., & Krishnan, S. (2006). Abuse liability of intravenous L-lysine-d-amphetamine(NRP104). College on Problems of Drug Dependence Annual Meeting, Scottsdale, AZ.

Kampman, K. M., Rukstalis, M., Pettinati, H., Muller, E., Acosta, T., Gariti, P., Ehrman, R., & O'Brien, C. P. (2000). The combination of phentermine and fenfluramine reduced cocaine withdrawal symptoms in an open trial. *Journal of Substance Abuse Treatment, 19*(1), 77–79.

Kankaanpaa, A., Meririnne, E., Lillsunde, P., & Seppala, T. (1998). The acute effects of amphetamine derivatives on extracellular serotonin and dopamine levels in rat nucleus accumbens. *Pharmacology Biochemistry, Behavior, 59*(4), 1003–1009.

Kelley, B. J., Yeager, K. R., Pepper, T. H., & Beversdorf, D. Q. (2005). Cognitive impairment in acute cocaine withdrawal. *Cognitive and Behavioral Neurology, 18*(2), 108–112.

Kleven, M. S., Anthony, E. W., & Woolverton, W. L. (1990). Pharmacological characterization of the discriminative stimulus effects of cocaine in rhesus monkeys. *The Journal of Pharmacology and Experimental Therapeutics, 254*(1), 312–317.

Koe, B. K. (1976). Molecular geometry of inhibitors of the uptake of catecholamines and serotonin in synaptosomal preparations of rat brain. *The Journal of Pharmacology and Experimental Therapeutics, 199*(3), 649–661.

Koob, G. F. (1992). Neural mechanisms of drug reinforcement. *Annals of New York Academy of Sciences, 654*, 171–191.

Kosten, T. R., Morgan, C. M., Falcione, J., & Schottenfeld, R. S. (1992). Pharmacotherapy for cocaine-abusing methadone-maintained patients using amantadine or desipramine. *Archives of General Psychiatry, 49*(11), 894–898.

Leiderman, D. B., Shoptaw, S., Montgomery, A., Bloch, D. A., Elkashef, A., LoCastro, J., & Vocci, F. (2005). Cocaine Rapid Efficacy Screening Trial (CREST): A paradigm for the controlled evaluation of candidate medications for cocaine dependence. *Addiction, 100*(Suppl 1), 1–11.

Levin, F. R., Evans, S. M., Brooks, D. J., & Garawi, F. (2006). Treatment of cocaine dependent treatment seekers with adult ADHD: Double-blind comparison of methylphenidate and placebo. *Drug and Alcohol Dependence, 87*, 20–29.

Levin, F. R., Evans, S. M., McDowell, D. M., & Kleber, H. D. (1998). Methylphenidate treatment for cocaine abusers with adult attention-deficit/hyperactivity disorder: A pilot study. *Journal of Clinical Psychiatry, 59*(6), 300–305.

Lile, J. A., Morgan, D., Birmingham, A. M., Davies, H. M., & Nader, M. A. (2004). Effects of the dopamine reuptake inhibitor PTT on reinstatement and on food- and cocaine-maintained responding in rhesus monkeys. *Psychopharmacology (Berl), 174*(2), 246–253.

Lile, J. A., Morgan, D., Birmingham, A. M., Wang, Z., Woolverton, W. L., Davies, H. M., & Nader, M. A. (2002). The reinforcing efficacy of the dopamine reuptake inhibitor 2beta-propanoyl-3beta-(4-tolyl)-tropane (PTT) as measured by a progressive-ratio schedule and a choice procedure in rhesus monkeys. *The Journal of Pharmacology and Experimental Therapeutics*, *303*(2), 640–648.

Lile, J. A., Wang, Z., Woolverton, W. L., France, J. E., Gregg, T. C., Davies, H. M., & Nader, M. A. (2003). The reinforcing efficacy of psychostimulants in rhesus monkeys: The role of pharmacokinetics and pharmacodynamics. *The Journal of Pharmacology and Experimental Therapeutics*, *307*(1), 356–366.

Lin, J. S., Roussel, B., Akaoka, H., Fort, P., Debilly, G., & Jouvet, M. (1992). Role of catecholamines in the modafinil and amphetamine induced wakefulness, a comparative pharmacological study in the cat. *Brain Research*, *591*(2), 319–326.

Llosa, T. (1994a). The standard low dose of oral cocaine: Used for treatment of cocaine dependence. *Substance Abuse*, *15*(4), 215–220.

Llosa, T. (1994b). Double-blind trials with oral cocaine as coca tablets (CTA) used for cocaine dependence treatment. *NIDA Research Monographs*, *153*, 302.

Llosa, T. (1996). Cocalization: The standard low dose of oral cocaine used as substitution therapy in cocaine dependence. *NIDA Research Monograph*, *174*, 186.

Llosa, T., & Llosa, L. (2005). Oral cocaine as an agonist therapy in cocaine dependence. Presented at the College on Problems of Drug Dependence: Abstracts of the Sixty-seventh Annual Scientific Meeting, Orlando, FL.

Lyness, W. H., Friedle, N. M., & Moore, K. E. (1979). Destruction of dopaminergic nerve terminals in nucleus accumbens: Effect on D-amphetamine self-administration. *Pharmacology, Biochemistry, and Behavior*, *11*(5), 553–556.

Maj, J., & Przegalinski, E. (1967). Disulfiram and some effects of amphetamine in mice and rats. *The Journal of Pharmacy and Pharmacology*, *19*(5), 341–342.

Maj, J., Przegalinski, E., & Wielosz, M. (1968). Disulfiram and the drug-induced effects on motility. *The Journal of Pharmacy and Pharmacology*, *20*(3), 247–248.

Malcolm, R., Book, S. W., Moak, D., DeVane, L., & Czepowicz, V. (2002). Clinical applications of modafinil in stimulant abusers: Low abuse potential. *American Journal on Addictions*, *11*(3), 247–249.

Malcolm, R., & Devane, J. (2003). Modafinil dampens multiple aspects of intravenous cocaine high. Paper presented at the College on Problems of Drug Dependence: Abstracts of the Sixty-fifth Annual Scientific Meeting, Bal Harbour, FL.

Martin, W. R., Sloan, J. W., Sapira, J. D., & Jasinski, D. R. (1971). Physiologic, subjective, and behavioral effects of amphetamine, methamphetamine, ephedrine, phenmetrazine, and methylphenidate in man. *Clinical Pharmacology and Therapeutics*, *12*, 245–258.

McCance-Katz, E. F., Kosten, T. R., & Jatlow, P. (1998a). Chronic disulfiram treatment effects on intranasal cocaine administration: Initial results. *Biological Psychiatry*, *43*(7), 540–543.

McCance-Katz, E. F., Kosten, T. R., & Jatlow, P. (1998b). Disulfiram effects on acute cocaine administration. *Drug and Alcohol Dependence*, *52*(1), 27–39.

McDougle, C. J., Black, J. E., Malison, R. T., Zimmermann, R. C., Kosten, T. R., Heninger, G. R., & Price, L. H. (1994). Noradrenergic dysregulation during discontinuation of cocaine use in addicts. *Archives of General Psychiatry*, *51*(9), 713–719.

Mendelson, J. H., Mello, N. K., Sholar, M. B., Siegel, A. J., Kaufman, M. J., Levin, J. M., Renshaw, P. F., & Cohen, B. M. (1999). Cocaine pharmacokinetics in men and in women during the follicular and luteal phases of the menstrual cycle. *Neuropsychopharmacology*, *21*(2), 294–303.

Merrill, J., & Tetlow, V. A. (1998). Prescribing for amphetamine users: Evaluation of a dexamphetamine substitution programme. Paper presented at the Beyond Oral Methadone: Expanded Pharmacotherapies for the Treatment of Drug Dependence, New York.

Moeller, F. G., Schmitz, J. M., Steinberg, J. L., Green, C. M., Reist, C., Lai, L. Y., Swann, A. C., & Grabowski, J. (in press). Citalopram combined with behavioral therapy reduces cocaine use: A double-blind, placebo controlled trial. *American Journal of Drug and Alcohol Abuse*.

Montoya, I. D. (2004). NIDA Medication Development Program. Bethesda MD. Presentation at the annual meeting of NIDA Medication Development Centers investigators. Washington, DC.

Musto, D. F. (1992). Cocaine's history, especially the American experience. *Ciba Foundation Symposium*, *166*, 7–14; discussion 14–19.

Musto, D. F. (1998). International traffic in coca through the early 20th century. *Drug and Alcohol Dependence*, *49*(2), 145–156.

Myrick, H., Malcolm, R., Taylor, B., & LaRowe, S. (2004). Modafinil: Preclinical, clinical, and post-marketing surveillance – a review of abuse liability issues. *Annals of Clinical Psychiatry*, *16*(2), 101–109.

Nader, M. A., Grant, K. A., Davies, H. M., Mach, R. H., & Childers, S. R. (1997). The reinforcing and discriminative stimulus effects of the novel cocaine analog 2beta-propanoyl-3beta-(4-tolyl)-tropane in rhesus monkeys. *Journal of Pharmacology and Experimental Therapeutics*, *280*(2), 541–550.

Negus, S. S., & Mello, N. K. (2003). Effects of chronic D-amphetamine treatment on cocaine- and food-maintained responding under a progressive-ratio schedule in rhesus monkeys. *Psychopharmacology (Berl)*, *167*(3), 324–332.

Peltier, R., & Schenk, S. (1993). Effects of serotonergic manipulations on cocaine self-administration in rats. *Psychopharmacology (Berl)*, *110*(4), 390–394.

Petrakis, I. L., Carroll, K. M., Nich, C., Gordon, L. T., McCance-Katz, E. F., Frankforter, T., & Rounsarille, B. J. (2000). Disulfiram treatment for cocaine dependence in methadone-maintained opioid addicts. *Addiction*, *95*(2), 219–228.

Porrino, L. J., Migliarese, K., Davies, H. M., Saikali, E., & Childers, S. R. (1994). Behavioral effects of the novel tropane analog, 2 beta-propanoyl-3 beta-(4-toluyl)-tropane (PTT). *Life Sciences*, *54*(26), PL511–PL517.

Prince, J. B. (2006). Pharmacotherapy of attention-deficit hyperactivity disorder in children and adolescents: Update on new stimulant preparations, atomoxetine, and novel treatments. *Child and Adolescent Psychiatric Clinics of North America*, *15*(1), 13–50.

Reid, M. S., Casadonte, P., Baker, S., Sanfilipo, M., Braunstein, D., Hitzemann, R., Montgomery, A., Majewska, D., Robinson, J., & Rotrosen, J. (2005). A placebo-controlled screening trial of olanzapine, valproate, and coenzyme Q10/L-carnitine for the treatment of cocaine dependence. *Addiction*, *100*(Suppl 1), 43–57.

Reith, M. E., Li, M. Y., & Yan, Q. S. (1997). Extracellular dopamine, norepinephrine, and serotonin in the ventral tegmental area and nucleus accumbens of freely moving rats during intracerebral dialysis following systemic administration of cocaine and other uptake blockers. *Psychopharmacology (Berl)*, *134*(3), 309–317.

Rogers, A. E., Aldrich, M. S., Berrios, A. M., & Rosenberg, R. S. (1997). Compliance with stimulant medications in patients with narcolepsy. *Sleep*, *20*(1), 28–33.

Rothman, R. B., Baumann, M. H., Dersch, C. M., Romero, D. V., Rice, K. C., Carroll, F. I., & Partilla, J. S. (2001). Amphetamine-type central nervous system stimulants release norepinephrine more potently than they release dopamine and serotonin. *Synapse*, *39*(1), 32–41.

Rothman, R. B., Blough, B. E., & Baumann, M. H. (2002). Appetite suppressants as agonist substitution therapies for stimulant dependence. *Annals of New York Academy of Sciences*, *965*, 109–126.

Rothman, R. B., Blough, B. E., Woolverton, W. L., Anderson, K. G., Negus, S. S., Mello, N. K., Roth, B. L., & Baumann, M. H. (2005). Development of a rationally designed, low abuse potential, biogenic amine releaser that suppresses cocaine self-administration. *The Journal of Pharmacology and Experimental Therapeutics*, *313*(3), 1361–1369.

Rothman, R. B., Mele, A., Reid, A. A., Akunne, H., Greig, N., Thurkauf, A., Rice, K. C., & Pert, A. (1989). Tight binding dopamine reuptake inhibitors as cocaine antagonists. A strategy for drug development. *FEBS Letters*, *257*(2), 341–344.

Rothman, R. B., Mele, A., Reid, A. A., Akunne, H. C., Greig, N., Thurkauf, A., de Costa, B. R., Rice, K. C., & Pert, A. (1991). GBR12909 antagonizes the ability of cocaine to elevate extracellular levels of dopamine. *Pharmacology, Biochemistry, and Behavior*, *40*(2), 387–397.

Rothman, R. B., Partilla, J. S., Dersch, C. M., Carroll, F. I., Rice, K. C., & Baumann, M. H. (2000). Methamphetamine dependence: Medication development efforts based on the dual deficit model of stimulant addiction. *Annals of New York Academy of Sciences, 914*, 71–81.

Rush, C. R., Kelly, T. H., Hays, L. R., Baker, R. W., & Wooten, A. F. (2002a). Acute behavioral and physiological effects of modafinil in drug abusers. *Behavioral Pharmacology, 13*(2), 105–115.

Rush, C. R., Kelly, T. H., Hays, L. R., & Wooten, A. F. (2002b). Discriminative-stimulus effects of modafinil in cocaine-trained humans. *Drug and Alcohol Dependence, 67*(3), 311–322.

Schmitz, J. M., Rhoades, H. M., Elk, R., Creson, D., Hussein, I., & Grabowski, J. (1998). Medication take-home doses and contingency management. *Experimental and Clinical Psychopharmacology, 6*(2), 162–168.

Schubiner, H., Saules, K. K., Arfken, C. L., Johanson, C. E., Schuster, C. R., Lockhart, N., Edwards, A., Donlin, J., & Pihlgren, E. (2002). Double-blind placebo-controlled trial of methylphenidate in the treatment of adult ADHD patients with comorbid cocaine dependence. *Experimental and Clinical Psychopharmacology, 10*(3), 286–294.

Schuster, C. R., & Johanson, C. E. (1988). Relationship between the discriminative stimulus properties and subjective effects of drugs. *Psychopharmacology Series, 4*, 161–175.

Schweri, M. M., Deutsch, H. M., Massey, A. T., & Holtzman, S. G. (2002). Biochemical and behavioral characterization of novel methylphenidate analogs. *The Journal of Pharmacology and Experimental Therapeutics, 301*(2), 527–535.

Segal, D. S., & Kuczenski, R. (1997). An escalating dose "binge" model of amphetamine psychosis: Behavioral and neurochemical characteristics. *Journal of Neuroscience, 17*(7), 2551–2566.

Shearer, J., Wodak, A., Mattick, R. P., Van Beek, I., Lewis, J., Hall, W., & Dolan, K. (2001). Pilot randomized controlled study of dexamphetamine substitution for amphetamine dependence. *Addiction, 96*(9), 1289–1296.

Shearer, J., Wodak, A., van Beek, I., Mattick, R. P., & Lewis, J. (2003). Pilot randomized double blind placebo-controlled study of dexamphetamine for cocaine dependence. *Addiction, 98*(8), 1137–1141.

Sizemore, G. M., Davies, H. M., Martin, T. J., & Smith, J. E. (2004). Effects of 2beta-propanoyl-3beta-(4-tolyl)-tropane (PTT) on the self-administration of cocaine, heroin, and cocaine/heroin combinations in rats. *Drug and Alcohol Dependence, 73*(3), 259–265.

Spealman, R. D. (1993). Modification of behavioral effects of cocaine by selective serotonin and dopamine uptake inhibitors in squirrel monkeys. *Psychopharmacology (Berl), 112*(1), 93–99.

Spealman, R. D. (1995). Noradrenergic involvement in the discriminative stimulus effects of cocaine in squirrel monkeys. *The Journal of Pharmacology and Experimental Therapeutics, 275*(1), 53–62.

Terry, P., Witkin, J. M., & Katz, J. L. (1994). Pharmacological characterization of the novel discriminative stimulus effects of a low dose of cocaine. *The Journal of Pharmacology and Experimental Therapeutics, 270*(3), 1041–1048.

Tiihonen, J., Kuoppasalmi, K., Fohr J., Tuomola, P., Kuikanmaki, O., Vorma, H., Sokero, P., Haukka, J., & Meririnne, E. (2007). A comparison of aripiprazole, methylphenidate, and placebo for amphetamine dependence. *American Journal of Psychiatry, 164*(1), 160–162.

Tidey, J. W., & Bergman, J. (1998). Drug discrimination in methamphetamine-trained monkeys: Agonist and antagonist effects of dopaminergic drugs. *The Journal of Pharmacology and Experimental Therapeutics, 285*(3), 1163–1174.

Towell, J. F., 3rd, Cho, J. K., Roh, B. L., & Wang, R. I. (1983). Disulfiram and erythrocyte aldehyde dehydrogenase inhibition. *Clinical Pharmacology and Therapeutics, 33*(4), 517–521.

Vocci, F., & Ling, W. (2005). Medications development: Successes and challenges. *Pharmacology and Therapeutics, 108*(1), 94–108.

Walsh, S. L., & Cunningham, K. A. (1997). Serotonergic mechanisms involved in the discriminative stimulus, reinforcing and subjective effects of cocaine. *Psychopharmacology (Berl), 130*(1), 41–58.

Walsh, S. L., Haberny, K. A., & Bigelow, G. E. (2000). Modulation of intravenous cocaine effects by chronic oral cocaine in humans. *Psychopharmacology (Berl)*, *150*(4), 361–373.

Walsh, S. L., Preston, K. L., Sullivan, J. T., Fromme, R., & Bigelow, G. E. (1994). Fluoxetine alters the effects of intravenous cocaine in humans. *Journal of Clinical Psychopharmacology*, *14*(6), 396–407.

Wee, S., Wang, Z., He, R., Zhou, J., Kozikowski, A. P., & Woolverton, W. L. (2006). Role of the increased noradrenergic neurotransmission in drug self-administration. *Drug and Alcohol Dependence*, *82*(2), 151–157.

Weiss, B., & Laties, V. G. (1962). Enhancement of human performance by caffeine and the amphetamines. *Pharmacological Reviews*, *14*, 1–36.

Wright, C., & Moore, R. D. (1990). Disulfiram treatment of alcoholism. *The American Journal of Medicine*, *88*(6), 647–655.

World Health Organization. (2004). *Neuroscience of Psychoactive Substance Use and Dependence*. Geneva: WHO.

CHAPTER 9

Topiramate-Induced Neuromodulation of Cortico-Mesolimbic Dopamine: Implications for the Treatment of Nicotine and Alcohol Dependence

Bankole A. Johnson

Department of Psychiatry and Neurobehavioral Sciences, University of Virginia, Charlottesville, VA, USA

Nicotine and Alcohol Dependence:
    The Problem of Comorbidity
        Epidemiology
        Neurochemistry
Topiramate: A Promising New Vista
        General Mechanisms of Action
        Pharmacokinetics
        Safety and Tolerability
        Mechanisms of Action in the Treatment
            of Nicotine and Alcohol Dependence
The Clinical Experience
Conclusions
References

Abstract: Nicotine dependence and alcohol dependence contribute profoundly to morbidity and mortality and often occur as comorbid disorders. The reinforcing effects of nicotine and alcohol are mediated by similar mechanisms that enhance dopaminergic activity, and their neurochemical interactions add to their independent effects. A pharmacological approach to treating both disorders contemporaneously is needed. Topiramate, in a clinical trial, has demonstrated efficacy at treating nicotine and alcohol dependence, presumably due to its ability to modulate cortico-mesolimbic dopamine function. Other mechanisms might also play a role in this effect. Further study is warranted and ongoing.

NICOTINE AND ALCOHOL DEPENDENCE: THE PROBLEM OF COMORBIDITY

Nicotine dependence and alcohol dependence, combined, result in more preventable incidences of morbidity and mortality than any other disease in the United States (Miller & Gold, 1998; Mokdad et al., 2004). The two disorders have a high likelihood of comorbidity, which can be attributed to five factors: (1) their high independent prevalence rates in the general population; (2) the linkage of smoking and drinking behaviors within similar social environments; (3) significant neurochemical pharmacodynamic interactions between nicotine and alcohol that might result in a greater dependence on both substances (Littleton & Little, 2002); (4) pharmacokinetic factors related to the absorption, distribution, and metabolism of the two substances that might cause individuals to administer them in such a way that the effects of one modulate those of the other (Blomqvist et al., 2002; Seaton & Vesell, 1993); and (5) recent genetic evidence indicating that an earlier onset of smoking correlates with a higher likelihood of problem drinking, and that fetal exposure to alcohol could increase susceptibility to smoking behavior (Lê, 2002; Prendergast et al., 2002). Despite the evidence for significant biological and neurochemical overlap between nicotine and alcohol dependence delineated in factors 3–5 above, clinical trials have rarely explored the potential for a common pharmacological approach aimed at treating the two disorders at the same time.

EPIDEMIOLOGY

Prior studies have suggested a strong relationship between smoking behavior and alcohol dependence. With sample sizes between 80 and 1,142, outpatient and inpatient surveys of participants receiving treatment for alcohol dependence revealed an 82–90% smoking rate among women and an 86–97% rate among men (Burling & Ziff, 1988; Dreher & Fraser, 1967; Kozlowski, Jelinek, & Pope, 1986; Walton, 1972). In a study of 325 outpatients attending an alcohol clinic who met DSM-III-R criteria for both disorders, 92% were dependent on nicotine (Batel et al., 1995); there was also a positive correlation between the amounts of alcohol consumed and tobacco smoked and between the severity ratings of the two disorders. Smoking cessation rate estimates among previously treated alcohol-dependent individuals have been reported mainly in retrospective surveys of varying quality and sample size, none of which provided the same degree of verification or standardized definitions of abstinence seen in more traditional smoking cessation literature (e.g., Benowitz, 1983; Ossip-Klein et al., 1986). A large (N = 2,115) epidemiological survey addressing this question noted that current heavy drinkers made the fewest attempts to stop smoking and had the least success, whereas alcohol abstainers quit smoking most often (Zimmerman et al., 1990). In a non-randomized case control study of alcohol-dependent individuals who received no formal treatment for nicotine dependence, DiFranza and Guerrera (1990) reported smoking cessation rates of 7% in the alcoholics and 49% in the non-alcoholic controls. A 4-year follow-up study by Bobo et al. (1986, 1987) revealed a smoking cessation rate of 19% after inpatient treatment for alcohol abuse. Only 62% of the smokers, compared with 92% of those who had stopped smoking, reported sustained abstinence from alcohol. Relapse to cigarette smoking occurred in conjunction with alcohol drinking 37% of the time, and latency to cessation after alcohol treatment did not predict abstinence from smoking. Importantly, spontaneous smoking cessation is rare among alcohol-dependent individuals, and up to 75% of those who are dually dependent require simultaneous treatment for both nicotine and alcohol dependence (Ellingstad et al., 1999).

Miller, Hedrick, and Taylor (1983) demonstrated that alcohol-dependent individuals who quit smoking continued to control their drinking post-treatment – a finding that has been confirmed by Kozlowski et al. (1989). Also, Burling, Marshall, and Seidner (1991) observed that patients were more likely to remain in an alcohol treatment program if they were being treated for both nicotine and alcohol dependence rather than just the latter. Studies also have examined the correlation between drinking behavior and smoking cessation using experimental or quasi-experimental approaches. Hughes (1993) and Murray et al. (1995) conducted retrospective analyses of alcohol consumption among study participants attempting smoking cessation. Hughes (1993) found a 7% smoking cessation rate among smokers with a positive history of alcohol abuse who were given nicotine gum, whereas those with no such history had a 19% cessation rate after treatment with the gum. In a study of 2,649 smokers with small airway disease who were treated with nicotine gum and behavior therapy, Murray et al. (1995) found no correlation between drinking volume at baseline and smoking cessation; however, binge drinking was significantly and negatively related to outcome. Although study participants were not assessed for DSM-III-R criteria for alcohol abuse, overall cessation rates were quite high (>40%), which was expected since these patients were unusually motivated to quit smoking because of their small airway disease.

In a study by Hurt et al. (1994) that directly assessed the treatment of nicotine and drug/alcohol dependence, 100 participants in an inpatient drug and alcohol abuse treatment program were given either drug treatment alone or drug treatment plus concurrent smoking cessation treatment that included 10 behavioral group therapy sessions for nicotine dependence, nicotine gum (which only 11% actually used), and personal feedback letters and telephone follow-up following discharge. These two conditions were carried out in sequential samples, each with 50 patients. At the 1-year follow-up, a 12% smoking abstinence rate was seen in the smoking cessation treatment group versus 0% in the group who had received drug treatment alone. The two groups were similar in their relapse from primary drug abstinence, which ranged from 31.4% to 34%. The results of this study are encouraging, despite the fact that non-random group assignment was utilized, because they suggest that behavioral group intervention for nicotine dependence can have a modest but long-term impact on smoking cessation rates among participants in a drug and alcohol treatment program. One-year abstinence rates were slightly more than double those seen for spontaneous quitters in the general population (4.3–5.5%) (Centers for Disease Control and Prevention, 1994; Cohen et al., 1989) but were well below what are usually observed in studies combining an intensive behavioral intervention with transdermal nicotine replacement (Cinciripini, 1995; Fiore et al., 1994) in non-substance-abusing populations.

Given the prevalence of comorbid nicotine dependence and alcohol dependence, due to the fact that heavy drinking can lead one to smoke and that smoking cessation increases the likelihood of abstinence from drinking, contemporaneous treatment for dual dependence might hold the most hope for success.

NEUROCHEMISTRY

Nicotine and alcohol have important neurochemical interactions that enhance their reinforcing effects and, consequently, the abuse liability of their combination. The reinforcing effects of both substances are mediated via cortico-mesolimbic dopamine (CMDA) pathways (Hemby, 2003; Hemby, Johnson, & Dworkin, 1997; Wise & Bozarth, 1987). Although alcohol exerts its reinforcing effects principally through the disinhibition of the inhibitory effects of γ-amino-butyric acid-A (GABA$_A$) neurons in the ventral tegmental area (VTA) (Johnson, 2004a), it might also excite VTA neurons through nicotinic acetylcholine receptors (Blomqvist et al., 1997, 2002), thereby stimulating dopaminergic activity. As shown in animal studies, chronic nicotine intake can spur an increase in alcohol consumption. For example, chronic nicotine intake up-regulates nicotinic acetylcholine receptors (Collins, 1990; Ksir et al., 1985), therefore increasing CMDA system sensitization to alcohol. The implication in humans would be that smoking might enhance the pleasurable effects of alcohol consumption. Patch clamp study results have helped us arrive at a better understanding of the neurochemical interactions between nicotine and alcohol. The acetylcholine receptor can generate an α-bungarotoxin-sensitive current and an α-bungarotoxin-insensitive current, which originate from the α7-type and α4β2-type subunits, respectively (Albuquerque et al., 1997; Changeux et al., 1998). Alcohol augments the activity of the α4β2-type subunit at physiologically relevant doses and can offset the ability of nicotine to desensitize this subunit, thereby facilitating the recovery of cholinergic currents from nicotine-associated desensitization, which in turn has the effect of promoting smoking behavior (Narahashi et al., 2001). Others, however, have proposed that the primary site of alcohol–nicotine interactions might not be the α4β2-type subunit (Lê et al., 2000), although the nicotinic acetylcholine receptor was nonetheless implicated by evidence that mecamylamine, a non–competitive nicotinic acetyl-choline receptor antagonist, inhibits alcohol consumption (Lê et al., 2000; Smith et al., 1999).

Regardless of the precise molecular pharmacological explanation for the nicotine–alcohol interaction, the nicotinic acetylcholine receptor appears to be heavily involved. The combination of nicotine and alcohol enhances their respective independent impact on reinforcement mechanisms (Tizabi et al., 2002). Hence, an important neuropharmacological approach toward contemporaneous treatment of comorbid nicotine and alcohol dependence would be to develop a compound that profoundly modulates CMDA function (Johnson, 2004b).

TOPIRAMATE: A PROMISING NEW VISTA

GENERAL MECHANISMS OF ACTION

Topiramate, a novel anticonvulsant that is Food and Drug Administration approved for the treatment of childhood epilepsy, is currently being investigated as a potential pharmacotherapeutic agent for a wide range of neuropsychiatric disorders including nicotine, alcohol, cocaine, and methamphetamine dependence. It is a sulfamate-substituted analog of fructose-1,6-diphosphate with the chemical nomenclature of 2,3:4,5-di-O-isopropylidene-β-D-fructopyranose sulfamate. The topiramate molecule is oxygen rich, which might account for its ability to form various chemical bonds related to its multiple neuropharmacological effects. Topiramate originally was synthesized as a potential treatment for diabetes, probably because it can inhibit the enzyme fructose-1,6-biphosphatase and, therefore, gluconeogenesis (Shank et al., 2000). Since topiramate did not decrease glucose levels in normoglycemic rats, it was assumed that it would not have efficacy in treating diabetes, so this line of research was suspended. Fortunately, however, promising new evidence has come to light suggesting that topiramate might reduce glucose levels in hyperglycemic animals, thereby reviving interest in testing it as an antidiabetic agent. The observation that topiramate and acetazolamide have similar structural characteristics (Resor et al., 1995) led to the testing of topiramate for its possible anticonvulsant effects. Topiramate is a potent and highly efficacious antiepileptic medication (Abou-Khalil, 2000; Bialer et al., 1999; Czuczwar & Patsalos, 2001; Montouris, Biton, & Rosenfeld, 2000; Reddy, 2002; White, 2003; Zupanc, 2003) that has strong neuroprotective properties (Angehagen et al., 2003; Edmonds et al., 2001; Khan et al., 2003; Koh & Jensen, 2001; Niebauer & Gruenthal, 1999; Qian & Noebels, 2003).

For its six important mechanisms of action, topiramate: (1) increases inhibitory $GABA_A$-mediated currents at non-benzodiazepine sites on the $GABA_A$ receptor (White et al., 1997, 2000); (2) antagonizes α-amino-3-hydroxy-5-methylisoxazole-4-propionic acid (AMPA) and kainate glutamate receptors (Gibbs et al., 2000; Gryder & Rogawski, 2003; Skradski & White, 2000); (3) inhibits L-type calcium channels and calcium-dependent second messenger systems (Zhang et al., 2000); (4) limits activity-dependent depolarization and excitability of voltage-dependent sodium channels (Taverna et al., 1999); (5) activates potassium conductance (Herrero et al., 2002); and (6) is a weak inhibitor of carbonic anhydrase isoenzymes CA-II and CA-IV (Dodgson, Shank, & Maryanoff, 2000), which are found in neuronal and peripheral tissues. The inhibition of carbonic anhydrase isoenzymes in renal tubules diminishes hydrogen ion secretion and increases secretion of Na^+, K^+, HCO_3^-, and water, consequently enhancing the likelihood of acidosis and renal stone formation (Shank et al., 2000; White et al., 2000).

PHARMACOKINETICS

Topiramate's absolute bioavailability is excellent and is not significantly affected by food, as 81–95% of the ingested compound is absorbed into the bloodstream (Johnson & Johnson Pharmaceutical Research & Development, 2005). Furthermore, its kinetic profile is linear across a wide range of pharmacologically relevant doses (Garnett, 2000; Perucca & Bialer, 1996; Shank et al., 2000). The time to reach maximum concentration of topiramate is approximately 2 h; steady-state concentration is reached in about 4 days, and the elimination half-life typically ranges from 21 to 23 h. Topiramate exists mainly in the free form while in the bloodstream; i.e., only 15% is bound to plasma proteins. For the most part, topiramate is excreted unchanged by the kidneys; less than 20% of the ingested compound is metabolized to inactive constituents. Topiramate dosing is based upon the balance between adverse event profile and clinical response, with no established therapeutic range.

Topiramate can be given safely in combination with other medications since it has only a few interactions with other psychotropic drugs. When it is combined with valproate, an anticonvulsant, plasma topiramate levels decrease by 17%, while topiramate reduces the concentration of valproate by approximately 11% (Rosenfeld et al., 1997b). When it is given with the anticonvulsants carbamazepine or phenytoin, which both tend to enhance hepatic enzyme activity, topiramate levels can be reduced to about 40% of the ingested dose in the case of carbamazepine (Sachdeo et al., 1996) and 50% in the case of phenytoin (Sachdeo et al., 2002). In other interactions, topiramate can raise plasma metformin levels by approximately 18%, decrease plasma digoxin concentrations by about 12% (Garnett, 2000), and reduce plasma lithium by approximately 12%

(Doose et al., 1999). Topiramate dosages of less than 200 mg/day have no significant effect on the plasma concentrations of oral contraceptive drugs (Doose et al., 2003), whereas dosages of 200–800 mg cause dose-related decreases in the estrogenic component of these drugs but do not affect the progestin moiety (Rosenfeld et al., 1997a). These effects, however, are relatively less than those observed with enzyme-inducing anticonvulsants.

SAFETY AND TOLERABILITY

Neuropsychiatric research has shown that topiramate's adverse event profile is relatively benign, and most of the reported symptoms have been classified as mild to moderate (Johnson & Johnson Pharmaceutical Research & Development, 2005). Transient paresthesia is the most common adverse event. Cognitive impairment is perhaps the most bothersome adverse event, but careful observation of those affected has typically revealed just minor word-finding difficulties and a decrease in concentration and attention, which tend to subside within a few days. Word-naming difficulties and paresthesia can usually be avoided or minimized with the use of a slow dose titration schedule; however, between 10% and 15% of topiramate recipients report some cognitive difficulty regardless of the dose titration schedule (Biton et al., 2001).

Several acute but rare adverse events have been reported with topiramate. As of January 2005, the reported incidence of acute myopia or angle-closure glaucoma was 5.2 per 100,000 patient years of exposure (Johnson & Johnson Pharmaceutical Research & Development, 2005). This syndrome usually presents with the acute onset of ocular pain, visual blurring, or both. Typically, it is accompanied by bilateral ophthalmologic findings such as shallowing of the anterior chamber, conjunctival hyperemia, increased intraocular pressure, and myopia. Topiramate administration should be discontinued if this syndrome presents, and then the symptoms usually resolve after several days (Johnson & Johnson Pharmaceutical Research & Development, 2005). Another potentially serious but rare adverse event related to topiramate is oligohidrosis, i.e., decreased sweating, accompanied by hyperthermia (Ben-Zeev et al., 2003). This syndrome is seen most often in children, especially those who engage in vigorous activity, reside in warm climates, or both. The incidence rate of oligohidrosis in topiramate recipients is significantly less than 1%. Nevertheless, physicians who prescribe topiramate to children, particularly in warm climates, should monitor them for oligohidrosis symptoms (Johnson & Johnson Pharmaceutical Research & Development, 2005).

The fact that topiramate is a weak inhibitor of carbonic anhydrase isoenzymes CA-II and CA-IV can result in renal bicarbonate loss, usually around 4 mEq/L, as well as metabolic acidosis. Such incidents are rare, with only 2.2 serious events

having been reported per 100,000 patient years. Prescribing physicians should consider monitoring bicarbonate levels among topiramate recipients who have potentially exacerbating conditions, including a ketogenic diet, the use of other carbonic
anhydrase-inhibiting drugs, and renal disease. A decrease in topiramate dose or discontinuation of its use results in a rapid normalization of bicarbonate values.

The tendency of topiramate to induce acidosis raises the likelihood of kidney
stone formation (Kuo et al., 2002; Shank et al., 2000). Approximately 1.5% of topiramate recipients are at risk of developing kidney stones. The likelihood can be
diminished by ensuring adequate hydration, especially for those topiramate recipients who reside in warm climates.

Overall, topiramate is safe and well tolerated, and the risk of adverse events
can be decreased by adoption of a slow drug titration schedule (Biton et al., 2001;
Dodson et al., 2003).

MECHANISMS OF ACTION IN THE TREATMENT OF
NICOTINE AND ALCOHOL DEPENDENCE

Topiramate, a sulfamate-substituted fructopyranose derivative, might antagonize the reinforcing effects associated with the abuse liability of both alcohol and
nicotine by modulating CMDA function (Moghaddam & Bolinao, 1994). As
previously conceptualized (Johnson, 2004a), topiramate could, theoretically,
suppress extracellular dopamine release by facilitating the inhibitory effects of the
neurotransmitter, γ-amino-butyric acid (GABA), through a non-benzodiazepine
receptor site in the nucleus accumbens and VTA, while also blocking the excitatory effects of AMPA and kainate glutamate receptors on A10 dopaminergic
neurons at these same sites (Breese, Freedman, & Leonard, 1995; Dodd et al., 2000;
Kohl et al., 1998; Moghaddam & Bolinao, 1994; Skradski & White, 2000; Weiss
& Porrino, 2002; White et al., 2000). Basically, the reinforcing effects of both nicotine and alcohol are mediated through CMDA neuronal activity. Nicotine and
alcohol increase VTA dopamine neuronal function by stimulating nicotinic acetylcholine receptors. Alcohol also has the effect of promoting the enhanced dopaminergic neuronal activity of cortico-mesolimbic neurons by disinhibiting the
inhibitory effects of GABA neurons in the nucleus accumbens and VTA.
Topiramate antagonizes the ability of nicotine and alcohol to increase CMDA
activity by facilitating GABA suppression of VTA and nucleus accumbens neurons
and, as mentioned above, blocking the excitatory effects of AMPA and kainate glutamate receptors at these same receptor sites. These effects could be even more pronounced in the chronic condition than in the acute condition because of the ability
of topiramate to reduce glutaminergic sensitization, thereby normalizing midbrain
dopamine function. Despite the lack of studies measuring midbrain extracellular
dopamine levels after topiramate administration, the extant evidence shows that

topiramate can attenuate nicotine-associated increases in nucleus accumbens dopamine release (Schiffer et al., 2001).

Topiramate might have other effects that serve to decrease nicotine or alcohol consumption either independently or in combination. For example, since topiramate can antagonize L-type calcium channel currents and reduce glutaminergic sensitization, it might make it possible for patients to withdraw from nicotine or alcohol more comfortably. In fact, this potential effect, coupled with topiramate's mild anxiolytic properties, may help reduce the likelihood of protracted withdrawal after nicotine or alcohol use is terminated (Johnson, 2004b).

One additional property of topiramate, its potential effect on body weight, could perhaps enhance its appeal as a pharmacotherapeutic agent for the promotion of abstinence from smoking and drinking. The possibility of weight gain when an individual quits smoking is a major reason why some people (Jeffery et al., 2000; Russ et al., 2001; Weekley, Klesges, & Reylea, 1992), especially women (Glasgow et al., 1999; Meyers et al., 1997; Pirie, Murray, & Luepker, 1991; Pomerleau et al., 2000; Pomerleau, Zucker, & Stewart, 2001), do not quit. Although the mechanism for this effect is not known, female smokers, concerned about weight gain after cessation of smoking, have been shown to be more likely than those without this concern to drop out of – or fail to comply successfully with – treatment for nicotine dependence (Meyers et al., 1997). Granted, there is controversy among researchers regarding the impact of concern about weight gain on smoking cessation attempts, with notable discrepancies and criticisms of methodological approach, as well as suggestions that factors such as self-efficacy could be equally important (Borrelli & Mermelstein, 1998). Nevertheless, topiramate might have utility as a putative therapeutic medication to aid in smoking cessation, even among those who are also alcohol dependent, because there would be no fear of weight gain; in fact, weight loss would be anticipated. Topiramate has been demonstrated to promote weight loss in both women and men (McElroy et al., 2003). Thus, it would be reasonable to expect these anti-weight-gain effects of topiramate to enhance its utility as a smoking cessation agent, even among those with comorbid alcohol dependence.

Taken together, all of these mechanisms of action might lead one to conclude that topiramate shows promise as a novel pharmacotherapy for the treatment of both alcohol and nicotine dependence.

THE CLINICAL EXPERIENCE

The efficacy of topiramate was studied recently in the treatment of alcohol-dependent individuals ($N = 150$) (Johnson et al., 2003) as well as a subgroup ($N = 94$) who were also abusing or dependent upon nicotine (Johnson et al., 2005a). In this 12-week, randomized, double-blind trial, subjects received either topiramate (up to 300 mg/day titrated over 8 weeks) or placebo. To enhance medication compliance, all participants were given weekly brief behavioral compliance enhancement treatment. Brief behavioral compliance enhancement treatment, which occurred in 15–20-min sessions, emphasized that the medication and compliance with taking it are the crucial elements in changing drinking behavior. Participants entered this clinical trial while actively smoking and drinking; no quit date for smoking was set, and there was no mention or expectation that the smokers should quit.

Topiramate was significantly more efficacious than placebo at improving all the self-reported drinking outcomes, alcohol craving (measured using the 4-factor empirically derived subscales (Bohn, Barton, & Barron, 1996) of the obsessive compulsive drinking scale (OCDS) (Moak, Anton, & Latham, 1998)), and the biochemical measure of drinking, the level of serum γ-glutamyl transferase (GGT) (Johnson et al., 2003). By the end of the study, topiramate recipients compared with placebo recipients had reduced their drinks per day by 2.88 (95% CI −4.50 to −1.27) more drinks per day ($p = 0.0006$), reduced their drinks per drinking day by 3.10 (95% CI −4.88 to −1.31) more drinks per drinking day ($p = 0.0009$), reduced their heavy drinking days by 27.6% more heavy drinking days ($p = 0.0003$), increased their days abstinent by 26.2% more days abstinent ($p = 0.0003$), and experienced a 0.07 (95% CI −0.11 to −0.02) greater reduction in serum GGT ratio ($p = 0.0046$). Moreover, topiramate, compared with placebo, also decreased all the craving factors on the OCDS ($p \leq 0.001$ for each) (Johnson et al., 2003).

Among the subgroup of alcohol-dependent individuals who were also abusing or dependent upon nicotine, those treated with topiramate were significantly more likely than placebo recipients to become abstinent from nicotine according to self-report (odds ratio = 4.46; 95% CI 1.08–18.39; $p = 0.04$). These results also were consistent with the finding that topiramate recipients were significantly less likely than placebo recipients to have a "positive" serum cotinine level, and that decreases in alcohol consumption were accompanied by smoking reductions in the topiramate group but not the placebo group. Indeed, based on dichotomized serum cotinine level, those who received topiramate, compared with the placebo group, had 4.97 times the odds of being categorized as non-smokers (95% CI 1.1–23.4; $p = 0.04$) (Johnson et al., 2005a).

Topiramate appears to be a promising medication for the treatment of comorbid nicotine dependence and alcohol dependence. It is significant that in the Johnson et al. (2005a) study, smoking cessation occurred even without any instructions or treatment plan to address this condition directly. When this is considered along with the finding that drinking reductions alone were not sufficient to reduce smoking behavior among placebo recipients, one could speculate that topiramate has independent antismoking effects beyond its ability to promote abstinence from drinking and to decrease harmful drinking behavior (Johnson, 2004b).

CONCLUSIONS

Nicotine and alcohol dependence are commonly occurring disorders that together represent the most significant preventable cause of morbidity and mortality in the United States. Despite some disagreement over which disorder should be treated first when they occur in the same individual, there is mounting evidence that a management strategy for addressing both conditions simultaneously would be ideal.

Neuroscientific advances have shown not only that the reinforcing effects of both nicotine and alcohol are mediated by similar mechanisms causing increased activity in the CMDA system, but that their neurochemical interactions can result in an aggregation of these effects. Despite the important neurobiological overlap between nicotine and alcohol consumption, few researchers have taken advantage of this commonality by devising a pharmacological approach toward treating both disorders. Indeed, given the relatively low additional cost, it would be reasonable to propose that all clinical treatment alcohol studies also measure smoking behavior. This should hasten the discovery of therapeutic medications for the treatment of both disorders. A proof-of-concept study by Johnson et al. (2005a) demonstrated that topiramate is a promising medication for the treatment of both nicotine dependence and alcohol dependence, presumably by its profound ability to modulate CMDA function. Other mechanisms, however, might also contribute to this effect.

It is tempting to speculate about the development path of topiramate for the treatment of alcohol dependence, nicotine dependence, or both. The rational development of topiramate for the treatment of alcohol and nicotine dependence might follow three interrelated paths. First, there is ample evidence that multisite studies are now needed to confirm and extend the initial positive findings. If these subsequent studies continue to show efficacy, they will lay the foundation for topiramate's Food and Drug Administration approval for the alcohol and nicotine dependence indications, either individually or together. Obviously, topiramate's clinical utility for alcohol or nicotine treatment, or both, might be enhanced by its combination with other neuromodulators of CMDA function. Pharmacogenetic approaches that might enhance topiramate's utility also need to be pursued. Such studies are ongoing within our clinical group. Second, there is much to learn about the specific neurobehavioral effects of topiramate on drinking and smoking behavior. A much underutilized avenue for such mechanistic research is the human laboratory, which can form a bridge in the development of medications from the animal setting to clinical trials (Johnson et al., 2005b). Such studies should inform further development approaches with topiramate and determine whether it should be targeted toward the reduction of active use or as a relapse prevention agent, or both. Third, the clinical development of topiramate for treating alcohol or nicotine dependence in our group was based upon hypothesized mechanistic relationships among GABA, glutamate, and dopamine systems. This is unusual in drug discovery, where animal studies typically precede clinical development. My colleagues and I have proposed a bi-directional approach to drug development – that is, not only from animals to humans but also from humans to animals. While the utility of this approach would not, at first, appear obvious, its importance is that it would allow better characterization and quantification of the relationship between basic science and clinical effects of the medication. In this way, it would be possible to develop a "fingerprint" by which to identify other medications with similar therapeutic effects in animals that can be tested in humans (Johnson et al., 2005b). Further, it could accelerate scientific advancement in our knowledge of the underlying neurobiology of addiction to alcohol, nicotine, or both.

In sum, topiramate is a promising medication that needs further development for the treatment of alcohol or nicotine dependence, or both. Clinical effort should be geared toward attempts to treat alcohol and nicotine dependence simultaneously. Further studies, from animals to humans, are needed to improve understanding of topiramate's neurobehavioral effects, to develop new knowledge of key neurobehavioral processes in animals that lead to the development of an efficacious medication in humans, and to provide additional information about its clinical utility.

ACKNOWLEDGMENTS

I thank the National Institute on Alcohol Abuse and Alcoholism for its support through grants AA 10522-08, 12964-02, and 14628-01; the National Institute on Drug Abuse for its support through grant DA 12191-05; the staff at the University of Virginia Center for Addiction Research and Education, and Robert H. Cormier, Jr. for his assistance with manuscript preparation.

REFERENCES

Abou-Khalil, B. (2000). Topiramate in the long-term management of refractory epilepsy. Topiramate YOL Study Group. *Epilepsia, 41*(Suppl. 1), S72–S76.
Albuquerque, E. X., Alkondon, M., Pereira, E. F., Castro, N. G., Schrattenholz, A., Barbosa, C. T., Bonfante-Cabarcas, R., Aracava, Y., Eisenberg, H. M., & Maelicke, A. (1997). Properties of neuronal nicotinic acetylcholine receptors: Pharmacological characterization and modulation of synaptic function. *The Journal of Pharmacology and Experimental Therapeutics, 280*, 1117–1136.
Angehagen, M., Ben-Menachem, E., Ronnback, L., & Hansson, E. (2003). Topiramate protects against glutamate- and kainate-induced neurotoxicity in primary neuronal–astroglial cultures. *Epilepsy Research, 54*, 63–71.
Batel, P., Pessione, F., Maitre, C., & Rueff, B. (1995). Relationship between alcohol and tobacco dependencies among alcoholics who smoke. *Addiction 90*, 977–980.
Benowitz, N. L. (1983). The use of biologic fluid samples in assessing tobacco smoke consumption. *NIDA Research Monograph, 48*, 6–26.

Ben-Zeev, B., Watemberg, N., Augarten, A., Brand, N., Yahav, Y., Efrati, O., Topper, L., & Blatt, I. (2003). Oligohydrosis and hyperthermia: Pilot study of a novel topiramate adverse effect. *Journal of Child Neurology*, *18*, 254–257.

Bialer, M., Johannessen, S. I., Kupferberg, H. J., Levy, R. H., Loiseau, P., & Perucca, E. (1999). Progress report on new antiepileptic drugs: A summary of the fourth Eilat conference (EILAT IV). *Epilepsy Research*, *34*, 1–41.

Biton, V., Edwards, K. R., Montouris, G. D., Sackellares, J. C., Harden, C. L., Kamin, M., & Topiramate TPS-TR Study Group. (2001). Topiramate titration and tolerability. *The Annals of Pharmacotherapy*, *35*, 173–179.

Blomqvist, O., Ericson, M., Engel, J. A., & Soderpalm, B. (1997). Accumbal dopamine overflow after ethanol: Localization of the antagonizing effect of mecamylamine. *European Journal of Pharmacology*, *334*, 149–156.

Blomqvist, O., Hernandez-Avila, C. A., Van Kirk, J., Rose, J. E., & Kranzler, H. R. (2002). Mecamylamine modifies the pharmacokinetics and reinforcing effects of alcohol. *Alcoholism, Clinical and Experimental Research*, *26*, 326–331.

Bobo, J. K., Gilchrist, L. D., Schilling, R. F., 2nd, Noach, B., & Schinke, S. P. (1987). Cigarette smoking cessation attempts by recovering alcoholics. *Addictive Behaviors*, *12*, 209–215.

Bobo, J. K., Schilling, R. F., Gilchrist, L. D., & Schinke, S. P. (1986). The double triumph: Sustained sobriety and successful cigarette smoking cessation. *Journal of Substance Abuse Treatment*, *3*, 21–25.

Bohn, M. J., Barton, B. A., & Barron, K. E. (1996). Psychometric properties and validity of the obsessive-compulsive drinking scale. *Alcoholism, Clinical and Experimental Research*, *20*, 817–823.

Borrelli, B., & Mermelstein, R. (1998). The role of weight concern and self-efficacy in smoking cessation and weight gain among smokers in a clinic-based cessation program. *Addictive Behaviors*, *23*, 609–622.

Breese, C. R., Freedman, R., & Leonard, S. S. (1995). Glutamate receptor subtype expression in human postmortem brain tissue from schizophrenics and alcohol abusers. *Brain Research*, *674*, 82–90.

Burling, T. A., Marshall, G. D., & Seidner, A. L. (1991). Smoking cessation for substance abuse inpatients. *Journal of Substance Abuse*, *3*, 269–276.

Burling, T. A., & Ziff, D. C. (1988). Tobacco smoking: A comparison between alcohol and drug abuse inpatients. *Addictive Behaviors*, *13*, 185–190.

Centers for Disease Control and Prevention. (1994). Cigarette smoking among adults – United States, 1993. *MMWR. Morbidity and Mortality Weekly Report*, *43*, 925–930.

Changeux, J. P., Bertrand, D., Corringer, P. J., Dehaene, S., Edelstein, S., Lena, C., Le Novere, N., Marubio, L., Picciotto, M., & Zoli, M. (1998). Brain nicotinic receptors: Structure and regulation, role in learning and reinforcement. *Brain Research. Brain Research Reviews*, *26*, 198–216.

Cinciripini, P. M. (1995). Current trends in smoking cessation research: Psychological therapy, nicotine replacement and changes in smoking behavior. *Cancer Bulletin*, *47*, 259–263.

Cohen, S., Lichtenstein, E., Prochaska, J. O., Rossi, J. S., Gritz, E. R., Carr, C. R., Orleans, C. T., Schoenbach, V. J., Biener, L., Abrams, D., DiClemente, C., Curry, S., Marlatt, G. A., Cummings, K. M., Emont, S. L., Giovino, G., & Ossip-Klein, D. (1989). Debunking myths about self-quitting. Evidence from 10 prospective studies of persons who attempt to quit smoking by themselves. *American Psychologist*, *44*, 1355–1365.

Collins, A. C. (1990). Interactions of ethanol and nicotine at the receptor level. *Recent Developments in Alcoholism*, *8*, 221–231.

Czuczwar, S. J., & Patsalos, P. N. (2001). The new generation of GABA enhancers: Potential in the treatment of epilepsy. *CNS Drugs*, *15*, 339–350.

DiFranza, J. R., & Guerrera, M. P. (1990). Alcoholism and smoking. *Journal of Studies on Alcohol*, *51*, 130–135.

Dodd, P. R., Beckmann, A. M., Davidson, M. S., & Wilce, P. A. (2000). Glutamate-mediated transmission, alcohol, and alcoholism. *Neurochemistry International*, *37*, 509–533.

Dodgson, S. J., Shank, R. P., & Maryanoff, B. E. (2000). Topiramate as an inhibitor of carbonic anhydrase isoenzymes. *Epilepsia, 41*(Suppl. 1), S35–S39.

Dodson, W. E., Kamin, M., Kraut, L., Olson, W. H., & Wu, S. C. (2003). Topiramate titration to response: Analysis of individualized therapy study (TRAITS). *Annals of Pharmacotherapy, 37*, 615–620.

Doose, D. R., Kohl, K. A., Desai-Krieger, D., Natarajan, J., & van Kammen, D. P. (1999). No significant effect of topiramate on lithium serum concentration. Poster presented at the World Congress of Psychiatry (WPA). Hamburg, Germany, August 6–12, 1999.

Doose, D. R., Wang, S. S., Padmanabhan, M., Schwabe, S., Jacobs, D., & Bialer, M. (2003). Effect of topiramate or carbamazepine on the pharmacokinetics of an oral contraceptive containing norethindrone and ethinyl estradiol in healthy obese and nonobese female subjects. *Epilepsia, 44*, 540–549.

Dreher, K. F., & Fraser, J. G. (1967). Smoking habits of alcoholic out-patients. I. *International Journal of the Addictions, 2*, 259–270.

Edmonds, H. L., Jr., Jiang, Y. D., Zhang, P. Y., & Shank, R. (2001). Topiramate as a neuroprotectant in a rat model of global ischemia-induced neurodegeneration. *Life Sciences, 69*, 2265–2277.

Ellingstad, T. P., Sobell, L. C., Sobell, M. B., Cleland, P. A., & Agrawal, S. (1999). Alcohol abusers who want to quit smoking: Implications for clinical treatment. *Drug and Alcohol Dependence, 54*, 259–265.

Fiore, M. C., Kenford, S. L., Jorenby, D. E., Wetter, D. W., Smith, S. S., & Baker, T. B. (1994). Two studies of the clinical effectiveness of the nicotine patch with different counseling treatments. *Chest, 105*, 524–533.

Garnett, W. R. (2000). Clinical pharmacology of topiramate: A review. *Epilepsia, 41*(Suppl. 1), S61–S65.

Gibbs, J. W., Sombati, S., DeLorenzo, R. J., & Coulter, D. A. (2000). Cellular actions of topiramate: Blockade of kainate-evoked inward currents in cultured hippocampal neurons. *Epilepsia, 41*(Suppl. 1), S10–S16.

Glasgow, R. E., Strycker, L. A., Eakin, E. G., Boles, S. M., & Whitlock, E. P. (1999). Concern about weight gain associated with quitting smoking: Prevalence and association with outcome in a sample of young female smokers. *Journal of Consulting and Clinical Psychology, 67*, 1009–1011.

Gryder, D. S., & Rogawski, M. A. (2003). Selective antagonism of GluR5 kainate-receptor-mediated synaptic currents by topiramate in rat basolateral amygdala neurons. *Journal of Neurosciences, 23*, 7069–7074.

Hemby, S. E. (2003). Neurobiology of alcoholism. In B. A. Johnson, P. Ruiz, & M. Galanter (Eds.), *Handbook of Clinical Alcoholism Treatment* (pp. 10–18). Baltimore, MD: Lippincott Williams & Wilkins.

Hemby, S. E., Johnson, B. A., & Dworkin, S. I. (1997). Neurobiological basis of drug reinforcement. In B. A. Johnson, & J. D. Roache (Eds.), *Drug Addiction and its Treatment: Nexus of Neuroscience and Behavior* (pp. 137–169). Philadelphia, PA: Lippincott-Raven.

Herrero, A. I., Del Olmo, N., Gonzalez-Escalada, J. R., & Solis, J. M. (2002). Two new actions of topiramate: Inhibition of depolarizing GABA(A)-mediated responses and activation of a potassium conductance. *Neuropharmacology, 42*, 210–220.

Hughes, J. R. (1993). Treatment of smoking cessation in smokers with past alcohol/drug problems. *Journal of Substance Abuse Treatment, 10*, 181–187.

Hurt, R. D., Eberman, K. M., Croghan, I. T., Offord, K. P., Davis, L. J., Jr., Morse, R. M., Palmen, M. A., & Bruce, B. K. (1994). Nicotine dependence treatment during inpatient treatment for other addictions: A prospective intervention trial. *Alcoholism, Clinical and Experimental Research, 18*, 867–872.

Jeffery, R. W., Hennrikus, D. J., Lando, H. A., Murray, D. M., & Liu, J. W. (2000). Reconciling conflicting findings regarding postcessation weight concerns and success in smoking cessation. *Health Psychology, 19*, 242–246.

Johnson & Johnson Pharmaceutical Research & Development. (December 2005). *Investigator's Brochure: Topiramate (RWJ-17021-000)* (10th ed.). Raritan, NJ: Ortho-McNeil Pharmaceutical, Inc.

Johnson, B. A. (2004a). Progress in the development of topiramate for treating alcohol dependence: From a hypothesis to a proof-of-concept study. *Alcoholism, Clinical and Experimental Research, 28,* 1137–1144.

Johnson, B. A. (2004b). Topiramate-induced neuromodulation of cortico-mesolimbic dopamine function: A new vista for the treatment of comorbid alcohol and nicotine dependence? *Addictive Behaviors, 29,* 1465–1479.

Johnson, B. A., Ait-Daoud, N., Akhtar, F. Z., & Javors, M. A. (2005a). Use of oral topiramate to promote smoking abstinence among alcohol-dependent smokers: A randomized controlled trial. *Archives of Internal Medicine, 165,* 1600–1605.

Johnson, B. A., Ait-Daoud, N., Bowden, C. L., DiClemente, C. C., Roache, J. D., Lawson, K., Javors, M. A., & Ma, J. Z. (2003). Oral topiramate for treatment of alcohol dependence: A randomised controlled trial. *The Lancet, 361,* 1677–1685.

Johnson, B. A., Mann, K., Willenbring, M. L., Litten, R. Z., Swift, R. M., Lesch, O. M., & Berglund, M. (2005b). Challenges and opportunities for medications development in alcoholism: An international perspective on collaborations between academia and industry. *Alcoholism, Clinical and Experimental Research, 29,* 1528–1540.

Khan, S. H., Wright, S. L., Banigesh, A., Miyashita, H., Todd, K., Hemmings, S. J., Wishart, T., & Shuaib, A. (2003). Antiischemic effects of topiramate in a transient global forebrain ischemia model: A neurochemical, histological, and behavioral evaluation. *Neurochemical Research, 28,* 1235–1239.

Koh, S., & Jensen, F. E. (2001). Topiramate blocks perinatal hypoxia-induced seizures in rat pups. *Annals of Neurology, 50,* 366–372.

Kohl, R. R., Katner, J. S., Chernet, E., & McBride, W. J. (1998). Ethanol and negative feedback regulation of mesolimbic dopamine release in rats. *Psychopharmacology, 139,* 79–85.

Kozlowski, L. T., Jelinek, L. C., & Pope, M. A. (1986). Cigarette smoking among alcohol abusers: A continuing and neglected problem. *Canadian Journal of Public Health, 77,* 205–207.

Kozlowski, L. T., Wilkinson, D. A., Skinner, W., Kent, C., Franklin, T., & Pope, M. (1989). Comparing tobacco cigarette dependence with other drug dependencies. Greater or equal 'difficulty quitting' and 'urges to use,' but less 'pleasure' from cigarettes. *JAMA, 261,* 898–901.

Ksir, C., Hakan, R., Hall, D. P., Jr., & Kellar, K. J. (1985). Exposure to nicotine enhances the behavioral stimulant effect of nicotine and increases binding of [3H]acetylcholine to nicotinic receptors. *Neuropharmacology, 24,* 527–531.

Kuo, R. L., Moran, M. E., Kim, D. H., Abrahams, H. M., White, M. D., & Lingeman, J. E. (2002). Topiramate-induced nephrolithiasis. *Journal of Endourology, 16,* 229–231.

Lê, A. D. (2002). Effects of nicotine on alcohol consumption. *Alcoholism, Clinical and Experimental Research, 26,* 1915–1916.

Lê, A. D., Corrigall, W. A., Harding, S., Watchus, J., Juzytsch, W., & Li, T. K. (2000). Involvement of nicotinic receptors in alcohol self-administration. *Alcoholism, Clinical and Experimental Research, 24,* 155–163.

Littleton, J., & Little, H. (2002). Interactions between alcohol and nicotine dependence: A summary of potential mechanisms and implications for treatment. *Alcoholism, Clinical and Experimental Research, 26,* 1922–1924.

McElroy, S. L., Arnold, L. M., Shapira, N. A., Keck, P. E., Jr., Rosenthal, N. R., Karim, M. R., Kamin, M., & Hudson, J. I. (2003). Topiramate in the treatment of binge eating disorder associated with obesity: A randomized, placebo-controlled trial. *American Journal of Psychiatry, 160,* 255–261.

Meyers, A. W., Klesges, R. C., Winders, S. E., Ward, K. D., Peterson, B. A., & Eck, L. H. (1997). Are weight concerns predictive of smoking cessation? A prospective analysis. *Journal of Consulting and Clinical Psychology, 65,* 448–452.

Miller, N. S., & Gold, M. S. (1998). Comorbid cigarette and alcohol addiction: Epidemiology and treatment. *Journal of Addictive Diseases*, *17*, 55–66.

Miller, W. R., Hedrick, K. E., & Taylor, C. A. (1983). Addictive behaviors and life problems before and after behavioral treatment of problem drinkers. *Addictive Behaviors*, *8*, 403–412.

Moak, D. H., Anton, R. F., & Latham, P. K. (1998). Further validation of the Obsessive-Compulsive Drinking Scale (OCDS): Relationship to alcoholism severity. *The American Journal of Addictions*, *7*, 14–23.

Moghaddam, B., & Bolinao, M. L. (1994). Glutamatergic antagonists attenuate ability of dopamine uptake blockers to increase extracellular levels of dopamine: Implications for tonic influence of glutamate on dopamine release. *Synapse*, *18*, 337–342.

Mokdad, A. H., Marks, J. S., Stroup, D. F., & Gerberding, J. L. (2004). Actual causes of death in the United States, 2000. *JAMA*, *291*, 1238–1245.

Montouris, G. D., Biton, V., & Rosenfeld, W. E. (2000). Nonfocal generalized tonic-clonic seizures: Response during long-term topiramate treatment. Topiramate YTC/YTCE Study Group. *Epilepsia*, *41*(Suppl. 1), S77–S81.

Murray, R. P., Istvan, J. A., Voelker, H. T., Rigdon, M. A., & Wallace, M. D. (1995). Level of involvement with alcohol and success at smoking cessation in the lung health study. *Journal of Studies on Alcohol*, *56*, 74–82.

Narahashi, T., Söderpalm, B., Ericson, M., Olausson, P., Engel, J. A., Zhang, X., Nordberg, A., Marszalec, W., Aistrup, G. L., Schmidt, L. G., Kalouti, U., Smolka, M., & Hedlund, L. (2001). Mechanisms of alcohol–nicotine interactions: Alcoholics versus smokers. *Alcoholism, Clinical and Experimental Research*, *25*(5 Suppl. ISBRA), 152S–156S.

Niebauer, M., & Gruenthal, M. (1999). Topiramate reduces neuronal injury after experimental status epilepticus. *Brain Research*, *837*, 263–269.

Ossip-Klein, D. J., Bigelow, G., Parker, S. R., Curry, S., Hall, S., & Kirkland, S. (1986). Classification and assessment of smoking behavior. *Health Psychology*, *5*(Suppl.), 3–11.

Perucca, E., & Bialer, M. (1996). The clinical pharmacokinetics of the newer antiepileptic drugs. Focus on topiramate, zonisamide and tiagabine. *Clinical Pharmacokinetics*, *31*, 29–46.

Pirie, P. L., Murray, D. M., & Luepker, R. V. (1991). Gender differences in cigarette smoking and quitting in a cohort of young adults. *American Journal of Public Health*, *81*, 324–327.

Pomerleau, C. S., Pomerleau, O. F., Namenek, R. J., & Mehringer, A. M. (2000). Short-term weight gain in abstaining women smokers. *Journal of Substance Abuse Treatment*, *18*, 339–342.

Pomerleau, C. S., Zucker, A. N., & Stewart, A. J. (2001). Characterizing concerns about post-cessation weight gain: Results from a national survey of women smokers. *Nicotine & Tobacco Research*, *3*, 51–60.

Prendergast, M. A., Rogers, D. T., Barron, S., Bardo, M. T., & Littleton, J. M. (2002). Ethanol and nicotine: A pharmacologic balancing act? *Alcoholism, Clinical and Experimental Research*, *26*, 1917–1918.

Qian, J., & Noebels, J. L. (2003). Topiramate alters excitatory synaptic transmission in mouse hippocampus. *Epilepsy Research*, *55*, 225–233.

Reddy, D. S. (2002). Newer GABAergic agents for pharmacotherapy of infantile spasms. *Drugs of Today*, *38*, 657–675.

Resor, S. R., Jr., Resor, L. D., Woodbury, D. M., & Kemp, J. W. (1995). Acetazolamide. In R. H. Levy, R. H. Mattson, & B. S. Meldrum (Eds.), *Antiepileptic Drugs* (pp. 969–985). New York: Raven Press.

Rosenfeld, W. E., Doose, D. R., Walker, S. A., & Nayak, R. K. (1997a). Effect of topiramate on the pharmacokinetics of an oral contraceptive containing norethindrone and ethinyl estradiol in patients with epilepsy. *Epilepsia*, *38*, 317–323.

Rosenfeld, W. E., Liao, S., Kramer, L. D., Anderson, G., Palmer, M., Levy, R. H., & Nayak, R. K. (1997b). Comparison of the steady-state pharmacokinetics of topiramate and valproate in patients with epilepsy during monotherapy and concomitant therapy. *Epilepsia*, *38*, 324–333.

Russ, C. R., Fonseca, V. P., Peterson, A. L., Blackman, L. R., & Robbins, A. S. (2001). Weight gain as a barrier to smoking cessation among military personnel. *American Journal of Health Promotion*, *16*, 79–84.

Sachdeo, R. C., Sachdeo, S. K., Levy, R. H., Streeter, A. J., Bishop, F. E., Kunze, K. L., Mather, G. G., Roskos, L. K., Shen, D. D., Thummel, K. E., Trager, W. F., Curtin, C. R., Doose, D. R., Gisclon, L. G., & Bialer, M. (2002). Topiramate and phenytoin pharmacokinetics during repetitive monotherapy and combination therapy to epileptic patients. *Epilepsia*, *43*, 691–696.

Sachdeo, R. C., Sachdeo, S. K., Walker, S. A., Kramer, L. D., Nayak, R. K., & Doose, D. R. (1996). Steady-state pharmacokinetics of topiramate and carbamazepine in patients with epilepsy during monotherapy and concomitant therapy. *Epilepsia*, *37*, 774–780.

Schiffer, W. K., Gerasimov, M. R., Marsteller, D. A., Geiger, J., Barnett, C., Alexoff, D. L., & Dewey, S. L. (2001). Topiramate selectively attenuates nicotine-induced increases in monoamine release. *Synapse*, *42*, 196–198.

Seaton, M. J., & Vesell, E. S. (1993). Variables affecting nicotine metabolism. *Pharmacology and Therapeutics*, *60*, 461–500.

Shank, R. P., Gardocki, J. F., Streeter, A. J., & Maryanoff, B. E. (2000). An overview of the preclinical aspects of topiramate: Pharmacology, pharmacokinetics, and mechanism of action. *Epilepsia*, *41*(Suppl. 1), S3–S9.

Skradski, S., & White, H. S. (2000). Topiramate blocks kainate-evoked cobalt influx into cultured neurons. *Epilepsia*, *41*(Suppl. 1), S45–S47.

Smith, B. R., Horan, J. T., Gaskin, S., & Amit, Z. (1999). Exposure to nicotine enhances acquisition of ethanol drinking by laboratory rats in a limited access paradigm. *Psychopharmacology*, *142*, 408–412.

Taverna, S., Sancini, G., Mantegazza, M., Franceschetti, S., & Avanzini, G. (1999). Inhibition of transient and persistent Na$^+$ current fractions by the new anticonvulsant topiramate. *The Journal of Pharmacology and Experimental Therapeutics*, *288*, 960–968.

Tizabi, Y., Copeland, R. L., Jr., Louis, V. A., & Taylor, R. E. (2002). Effects of combined systemic alcohol and central nicotine administration into ventral tegmental area on dopamine release in the nucleus accumbens. *Alcoholism, Clinical and Experimental Research*, *26*, 394–399.

Walton, R. G. (1972). Smoking and alcoholism: A brief report. *American Journal of Psychiatry*, *128*, 1455–1456.

Weekley, C. K., 3rd, Klesges, R. C., & Reylea, G. (1992). Smoking as a weight-control strategy and its relationship to smoking status. *Addictive Behaviors*, *17*, 259–271.

Weiss, F., & Porrino, L. J. (2002). Behavioral neurobiology of alcohol addiction: Recent advances and challenges. *Journal of Neuroscience*, *22*, 3332–3337.

White, H. S. (2003). Mechanism of action of newer anticonvulsants. *Journal of Clinical Psychiatry*, *64*(Suppl. 8), 5–8.

White, H. S., Brown, S. D., Woodhead, J. H., Skeen, G. A., & Wolf, H. H. (1997). Topiramate enhances GABA-mediated chloride flux and GABA-evoked chloride currents in murine brain neurons and increases seizure threshold. *Epilepsy Research*, *28*, 167–179.

White, H. S., Brown, S. D., Woodhead, J. H., Skeen, G. A., & Wolf, H. H. (2000). Topiramate modulates GABA-evoked currents in murine cortical neurons by a nonbenzodiazepine mechanism. *Epilepsia*, *41*(Suppl. 1), S17–S20.

Wise, R. A., & Bozarth, M. A. (1987). A psychomotor stimulant theory of addiction. *Psychological Review*, *94*, 469–492.

Zhang, X., Velumian, A. A., Jones, O. T., & Carlen, P. L. (2000). Modulation of high-voltage-activated calcium channels in dentate granule cells by topiramate. *Epilepsia*, *41*(Suppl. 1), S52–S60.

Zimmerman, R. S., Warheit, G. J., Ulbrich, P. M., & Auth, J. B. (1990). The relationship between alcohol use and attempts and success at smoking cessation. *Addictive Behaviors*, *15*, 197–207.

Zupanc, M. L. (2003). Infantile spasms. *Expert Opinion on Pharmacotherapy*, *4*, 2039–2048.

SECTION III
PSYCHOLOGY AND SOCIOLOGY

CHAPTER 10

Advances in the Scientific Study of Craving for Alcohol and Tobacco

James MacKillop and Peter M. Monti
Center for Alcohol and Addiction Studies, Brown University, Providence, RI, USA

Abstract: This chapter reviews contemporary empirical research on craving for alcohol and tobacco toward more fully understanding the phenomenon and its relationship to alcohol and tobacco dependence. The emphasis of the chapter is on progress in understanding the determinants, phenomenology, and neurobiology of craving via human and animal laboratory approaches. Following a review of the state of the science of craving, we focus on short-term research priorities, including determining the differential relevance of different types of craving, translating craving into objective measures of motivation, and characterizing the observed variability in the experience of craving across individuals. We conclude with a discussion of important future directions to clarify the role of craving in alcohol and tobacco dependence. A common theme is the need for transdisciplinary research that leverages advances in a number of disciplines toward a more integrative understanding of craving. The treatment of craving is not discussed in this chapter, but in the following chapter in this volume.

Translation of Addictions Science into Practice

INTRODUCTION

The notion of "craving," or intense urges or desires for a drug, has been associated with addiction since antiquity, but has only become the subject of objective research over the last 50 years (Drummond, 2001). In 1954, the World Health Organization convened an expert panel to describe and clarify the nature of craving (Jellinek et al., 1955), a meeting that has commonly been identified as the provenance of formal research in the area. Over the subsequent decades, conceptions of craving have evolved considerably and an extensive research literature has developed characterizing the nature and relevance of craving in addictive behavior.

Despite this long history of research, the relationship between craving and drug use remains highly contentious (Drummond, 2001; Tiffany, 1995; Tiffany & Conklin, 2000). This is, in part, a result of ambiguity in the empirical literature. When evaluated as a potential precipitant of relapse, a number of studies have reported only a limited association between craving and relapse (Hodgins, el-Guebaly, & Armstrong, 1995; Litman et al., 1983; Lowman, Allen, & Stout, 1996; Miller & Gold, 1994). Similarly, studies examining the correspondence between craving and actual substance use in human laboratory research have reported only modest correlations (for reviews, see Tiffany & Conklin, 2000; Tiffany & Carter, 1998).

The relationship between craving and drug use is further complicated by significant methodological limitations to much of the research. For example, in both clinical and laboratory research, many studies are commonly limited by the only recent development of well-validated measures of craving (Sayette et al., 2000; Tiffany, Carter, & Singleton, 2000). Similarly, in studies of post-treatment relapse, the use of retrospective reports may be limited by the fact that craving may commonly take place in conjunction with other experiences that are more readily available for recall or generally poorly encoded in memory (Sayette et al., 2000; Tiffany et al., 2000). Indeed, motivational states, such as hunger, sexual desire, and drug craving, have been collectively proposed to be highly influential, but largely unavailable in retrospect (Loewenstein, 1996, 2001). Further, one other "motivational state", an individual's interest and/or readiness to change the behavior toward which the craving is directed, has been largely ignored. Thus, measurement error may also have obscured the relationship between craving and drug use.

In recent years many of these issues have been addressed and considerable progress has been made. Rather than "throwing the baby out with the bathwater," contemporary research has substantially clarified the nature of craving, its relevance to drug use, and how it can be addressed in treatment. The goals of this chapter are to survey the vanguard of contemporary research in this area and to stimulate further progress by identifying promising avenues for future research.

The first section of the chapter will focus on advances in understanding craving itself, the second section will identify immediate research priorities in understanding craving, and the third section will identify future directions in the field, providing a transdisciplinary framework and emphasizing the importance of integrating multiple approaches to understand this complex phenomenon. Clinical approaches to craving are not discussed in the current chapter, but are directly addressed in the next chapter in this volume. Of note, because the preponderance of research on craving has taken place in reference to alcohol and tobacco dependence and a discussion of all forms of drug craving is beyond the scope of the chapter, these two drugs will be the principal focus.

ADVANCES IN THE SCIENTIFIC STUDY OF CRAVING

In the past several decades, there have been substantial advances in understanding the determinants, phenomenology, and neurobiology of craving, as well as its connection to actual alcohol and tobacco use. These findings were often spurred by contemporary theories of craving, including classical learning (Ludwig & Wikler, 1974; Siegel, 1988; Stewart, deWit, & Eikleboom, 1984), social learning (Niaura, 2000; Niaura et al., 1988; Rohsenow et al., 1991), cognitive (Tiffany, 1990; Tiffany & Conklin, 2000; Kavanagh, Andrade, & May, 2005), affective (Baker, Morse, & Sherman, 1986; Baker et al., 2004), and behavioral economic (Loewenstein, 1996, 2001) approaches. However, at this point empirical research does not unambiguously support any single theory and there is no theoretical consensus (Drummond, 2001; Tiffany, 1995). Therefore, we will not emphasize any single theory in this chapter, but rather focus on the state of the science of craving as reflected in the empirical literature.

DETERMINANTS OF CRAVING

Early conceptualizations of craving focused on its role as a direct function of actual alcohol or tobacco use, or lack thereof. For example, craving was characterized as a key feature of the alcohol and nicotine withdrawal syndromes (Hughes et al., 1984; Ludwig et al., 1974; Jellinek et al., 1955; Sherman, Morse, & Baker, 1986; Shiffman & Jarvik, 1976; West, 1984). Indeed, nicotine deprivation remains a common method of generating high levels of craving in contemporary laboratory approaches (e.g., Baumann & Sayette, 2006; Sayette et al., 2005). Equally, priming doses of alcohol have been reliably demonstrated to generate increased craving to drink (Cohen et al., 1971; Laberg, 1986; Miranda et al., 2005; O'Malley et al., 2002; Swift et al., 1994; Turkkan, McCaul, & Stitzer, 1989), although these have been less investigated in reference to nicotine.

Beyond withdrawal and priming effects, there is extensive evidence that situational factors associated with alcohol or nicotine use can provoke craving. For example, environmental cues, such as visual, tactile, and olfactory stimuli (e.g., MacKillop & Lisman, 2005, Monti et al., 1987), and even contextual stimuli (e.g., Conklin, 2006), that are associated with alcohol or nicotine have been repeatedly demonstrated to elicit a craving response in laboratory studies (for reviews, see Carter & Tiffany, 1999; Niaura et al., 1988). Similarly, endogenous emotional states have been demonstrated to elicit craving in laboratory paradigms, both in the forms of negative affect inductions (Cooney et al., 1997; Litt et al., 1990; Rubonis et al., 1994; Stasiewicz et al., 1997; Tiffany & Drobes, 1990) and stress inductions (Coffey et al., 2002; Niaura et al., 2002; Saladin et al., 2003).

In sum, both facets of actual use and concomitant situational factors may come to elicit craving for alcohol or nicotine. Importantly, however, the situational factors may continue to elicit potent cravings long after the acute detoxification (e.g., Franken et al., 1999; Grusser et al., 2002). As such, associated environmental cues and affective states are considered to present particularly high risks for relapse both in the short- and long-term (Kavanagh et al., 2005; O'Brien et al., 1992; Niaura et al., 1988).

PHENOMENOLOGY OF CRAVING

Contemporary research has also substantially elaborated what is known about the phenomenology, or expression, of craving. This has emerged both as a result of efforts to enhance the assessment of craving itself and an emphasis on the associated phenomena that accompany subjective craving. In the first case, a number of psychometrically validated measures have been developed for use in laboratory settings (Bohn, Krahn, & Staehler, 1995; Cox, Tiffany, & Christen, 2001; MacKillop, 2006) and for collecting short-term retrospective reports (Anton, Moak, & Latham, 1995; Flannery, Volpicelli, & Pettinati, 1999; Tiffany & Drobes, 1991). These measures are based on the premise that craving is a continuous phenomenon, and can be understood as existing on a continuum of urges or desires for a substance (Kozlowski & Wilkinson, 1987; Kozlowski et al., 1989). As would be expected of a complex experiential phenomenon, these measures suggest that craving is represented by an array of related, but nonetheless diverse, semantic representations of desire for alcohol or tobacco. Interestingly, the development of these measures has also revealed different aspects of craving for nicotine and alcohol. Craving for tobacco appears to be binary, comprising both desire for the positive stimulating effects of nicotine and relief from the aversive effects of withdrawal (Tiffany & Drobes, 1991; Cox et al., 2001), thus reflecting facets of positive and negative reinforcement. In contrast, craving for alcohol appears to be unidimensional, reflecting only the degree of incentive urge or desire for alcohol (Anton et al., 1995; Bohn et al., 1995; Flannery et al., 1999; MacKillop, 2006). These differences appear to

reflect differences in the two drugs' basic pharmacology and psychoactive effects, but may also reflect other factors, such as patterns of use.

Recently, there has been increasing interest in examining not only an individual's desire to drink or smoke, but also concurrently examining desire *not* to drink or smoke. These are considered approach and avoidance inclinations, respectively, and although at first glance they may appear to simply be opposites, three recent studies suggest that such competing motivations coexist in response to alcohol and smoking cues (Curtin et al., 2005; MacKillop, O'Hagen, & Lisman, 2006; Stritzke et al., 2004). Thus, craving can be understood as a complex interplay of both approach and avoidance inclinations, and the topography of an individual's competing inclinations may provide important insights into an individual's motivation to continue drinking or smoking, as has recently been demonstrated with adolescents (Curtin et al., 2005).

Beyond the direct assessment of craving, there is evidence of an array of concomitant effects of craving on the individual. A large number of studies have examined the associations between experiential craving and various indices of psychophysiological functioning. In a meta-analysis of 41 studies examining the effects of environmental cues on craving and somatovisceral responses, Carter and Tiffany (1999) reported large magnitude increases in self-reported craving that were accompanied by a profile of somewhat smaller magnitude increases in sweat gland activity and heart rate, and a decrease in skin temperature, all reflecting increased arousal.

The experience of craving also appears to have important effects on cognition. In laboratory studies, craving has been shown to transiently impair cognitive processing in a number of ways. Craving has been demonstrated to increase reaction time on cognitive tasks (Havermans et al., 2003; Munafò et al., 2003; Sayette & Hufford, 1994; Sayette et al., 1994) and diminish cognitive resource allocation (Cepeda-Benito & Tiffany, 1996; Sayette et al., 2001). Similarly, craving has been demonstrated to degrade language comprehension (Zwann & Truitt, 1998) and distort time perception (Sayette et al., 2005). Finally, craving has been demonstrated to impair working memory performance (Madden & Zwaan, 2001), a cognitive faculty that appears to underlie effective decision-making (Bechara & Martin, 2004).

An interesting facet of the cognitive phenomenology of craving is its relationship to imagery. Recent evidence suggests that imagery across sensory channels is central to the experience of craving (Kavanagh et al., 2005). For example, in a study of the phenomenology of craving for alcohol in a clinical sample, Westerberg (2000) found that the imagined taste of alcohol was significantly associated with overall craving. Moreover, in a recent study by May et al. (2004), visualizations and other forms of sensory imagery were evident in craving across a range of substances. Of particular interest, there has been recent evidence that when imagery associated with craving is disrupted, so too is the superordinate experience of craving (Harvey, Kemps, & Tiggemann, 2005; Pannabokke et al., 2004), suggesting that imagery is a critical component of craving.

In addition to the preceding facets of craving, recent research on craving for tobacco has revealed a potentially meaningful distinction in the daily dynamics of craving (e.g., Sayette et al., 2001; Shiffman et al., 1996, 1997) that may apply to craving for alcohol also. Tobacco dependent individuals appear to both experience increases in overall craving for tobacco following cessation (or enforced abstinence in laboratory paradigms; e.g., Sayette et al., 2001) and also experience acute increases in craving in response to situational factors (Shiffman et al., 1996, 1997), such as environmental cues, social stress, or negative affect. These varying experiences of craving can be distinguished into two forms, the first conceptualized as tonic craving, or the general background level of desire for a substance, and the second as phasic craving, or acute transient fluctuations in craving as a result of environmental or experiential variables. Tonic and phasic craving may play independent and interactive roles in the ongoing substance use (Shiffman et al., 1997), and may also play different roles in post-treatment relapse, as is discussed in detail in the following chapter.

Importantly, in considering all of the preceding dimensions, the research that has emerged in recent years suggests that craving is highly variable from person to person. Across the various laboratory studies, it is evident that only a proportion of the participants react to craving-related manipulations and even among those who do, there is considerable variability (Avants et al., 1995; Monti et al., 1999; Rohsenow et al., 1992; Shiffman et al., 2003). Moreover, in recent studies of craving in the natural environment, considerable variability was evident in overall craving and patterns of craving evident in alcohol (Krahn et al., 2005) and tobacco dependent (Shiffman et al., 1996) individuals. Thus, rather than being categorically present, the degree and pattern of craving varies meaningfully across individuals. Indeed, craving actually appears to be an individual difference variable that could be provisionally termed "craving proneness." These differences appear to be partially related to previous patterns of substance use (Glautier & Drummond, 1994; Monti et al., 1987; Rankin, Stockwell, & Hodgson, 1982), but also may be influenced by inherited genetic variation, as we discuss in the following section. Importantly, such variability in the potency and topography of craving from person to person also suggests that its relevance as a treatment target will vary.

NEUROBIOLOGY OF CRAVING

Perhaps the most meteoric recent advances have come from contemporary research characterizing the neurobiological substrates that underlie craving. Animal models of craving (Markou et al., 1993; Koob, 2000) and human neuroimaging studies (Hommer, 1999; McClernon & Gilbert, 2004) have indicated that experiential craving is not a simple, unitary phenomenon neurobiologically.

Rather, it is subserved by at least three neurotransmitter systems, including the dopamine (Berridge & Robinson, 1998; Heinz et al., 2004, 2005), endogenous opioid (Bencherif et al., 2004; Berridge & Robinson, 1998), and serotonin (Ciccocioppo, 1999) systems. Interestingly, these systems appear to be responsible for dissociable facets of motivation, including the incentive salience of the drug (i.e., "wanting"), the hedonic impact of the drug (i.e., "liking"), and modulation of behavior (i.e., the interface of experiential motivation and the execution of behavior), respectively. Of particular interest, evidence of neuroadaptive changes within the dopamine system has also been used to support a distinction between tonic and phasic craving (Grace, 2000), as characterized in the previous section.

Complementing neurotransmitter-level findings, neuroimaging studies of alcohol and tobacco craving have commonly revealed selective activation of the anterior cingulate, dorsolateral prefrontal cortex, and orbitofrontal cortex from a neuroanatomical standpoint (Brody et al., 2002; George et al., 2001; Grusser et al., 2004; McClernon & Gilbert, 2004; Myrick et al., 2004; Tapert et al., 2003, 2004). In studies of non-disordered individuals, these regions have been implicated in arousal, sustained attention, and evaluation of the motivational value of stimuli (Cabeza & Nyberg, 2000; Critchley et al., 2001; London et al., 2000; Rauch et al., 1994) and suggest coordinated activation of structures that subserve pursuit of a highly appetitive environmental goal.

This research is further advanced by studies indicating that genetic variation responsible for functional differences in the preceding neurotransmitter systems is associated with differences in the expression of craving. A number of studies have demonstrated that a polymorphism of the dopamine D_4 receptor gene, commonly termed DRD4 VNTR because it has a variable number of tandem repeats, has been associated with enhanced expression of craving. Specifically, possession of at least one copy of a long allele (defined as 7 or more repeats) has been associated with increased craving following a priming dose of alcohol (Hutchison et al., 2002b), increased craving in response to alcohol cues (McGeary et al., 2006), and increases the influence of craving on the relative value of alcohol (MacKillop et al., 2005). Similar interactions between the DRD4 VNTR genotype and craving have also been found in laboratory studies of smoking, where possession of a long allele has been associated with increased sensitivity to smoking cues (Hutchison et al., 2002a). In addition, recent studies by Erblich et al. (2004, 2005) have reported that polymorphisms of the DRD2 *TaqIA* and SLC6A3 genes, both associated with functional differences within the dopamine system, are associated with greater cue-elicited craving and stress-elicited craving. Although the influence of genetic variation on craving is far from being definitively characterized, these studies provide compelling evidence that it does play a significant role and may explain the considerable individual differences previously noted. Importantly, rather than operating as a "craving genes" per se, these studies suggest that, under certain environmental conditions, functional polymorphisms of genes responsible for the neurobiological substrates of craving exert important influences on the magnitude and expression of craving.

CRAVING AND ACTUAL ALCOHOL AND TOBACCO CONSUMPTION

As noted at the outset of this chapter, craving has been a controversial topic in addiction research because of previous studies suggesting negligible associations between craving and actual alcohol and tobacco use. However, as the methodological limitations that accompanied such studies have been addressed, the connection between craving and both alcohol and nicotine use has come into sharper relief. This is principally a result of the development of well-validated measures of craving and study designs that minimize retrospective bias. For example, Anton et al. (1995) developed and validated the Obsessive Compulsive Drinking Scale for assessing craving and subsequently found that it was significantly associated with actual alcohol use (Anton, Moak, & Latham, 1996). Similarly, using three validated measures including the OCDS, Flannery and colleagues (Flannery et al., 1999, 2003) found that craving significantly predicted both ongoing alcohol use and relapse following treatment. Relatedly, although not focusing on a new measure per se, Monti et al. (1990) improved the ecological validity of assessment by assessing craving during an alcohol-specific role play test and it predicted subsequent treatment outcome at six-month follow-up.

Improved assessment approaches have also revealed a more clear relationship between craving and alcohol use in laboratory studies. In two recent laboratory studies using the Alcohol Urge Questionnaire (Bohn et al., 1995), craving was significantly associated with actual alcohol use under various conditions. O'Malley et al. (2002) found a high magnitude association ($r = 0.65$) between craving and the number of drinks consumed during an alcohol self-administration period and MacKillop (2006) found a moderate correlation ($r = 0.31$) between craving and ad libitum consumption of masked placebo alcohol (rebottled non-alcoholic beer). In addition, although a recent study by Palfai et al. (2001) used only a single item measure of craving, the investigators conducted a fine-grained analysis of craving in anticipation of access to alcohol and found a high magnitude association ($r = 0.59$) between craving and actual alcohol consumption.

Similarly, when retrospective bias is minimized, there is considerable evidence that craving is robustly associated with post-treatment relapse. For example, in three prospective studies of nicotine craving and relapse including over 2,600 smokers, Killen and Fortmann (1997) found extremely rapid relapse in those reporting high levels of craving. Equally, studies of craving and tobacco use using ecological momentary assessment (EMA), or the near real-time assessment of experiences and behavior in the natural environment using palm-top computers, cell phones, or other forms of portable technology (Stone & Shiffman, 1994), have repeatedly demonstrated significant associations between craving and both post-treatment relapse (Shiffman et al., 1996, 1997) and ongoing smoking (Shiffman et al., 2002). Interestingly, recent EMA studies of smoking have also revealed dynamic interactions between craving and self-efficacy such that at high levels of craving, self-efficacy for abstinence collapses in smokers trying to quit (Gwaltney et al., 2005).

In the case of EMA and alcohol use, a number of studies have supported a positive association between craving and alcohol consumption. In an early study using EMA, Collins, Morsheimer, and Shiffman (1998) found that heavy social drinkers reported that an urge or craving was the basis for drinking 41% of the time, which was among the most common motivations. Subsequently, most directly addressing this question, Litt, Cooney, and Morse (2000) found that the frequency and magnitude of craving in the natural environment were significantly associated with post-treatment alcohol consumption in alcohol-dependent individuals. Further indicating the variability of craving among individuals, Litt et al. (2000) also found that participants tended to either show pronounced fluctuations in craving over the three-week period of assessment, or report stable low levels of craving. Similarly, Krahn et al. (2005) reported four clusters of craving among alcohol dependent individuals using EMA, with one cluster exhibiting both highly variable levels of craving; unfortunately, Krahn et al. (2005) did not directly address the relationship between craving and actual alcohol use.

Taken together, the preceding data suggest that craving is significantly associated with alcohol and tobacco use, and post-treatment relapse. However, the associations reported typically ranged from modest to moderate magnitudes, suggesting that craving is far from the *sine qua non* of alcohol or tobacco use, and the same studies indicating positive associations concurrently reported individuals relapsing in the absence of any craving (e.g., Krahn et al., 2005; Shiffman et al., 1996). Rather, these findings may reflect participant samples with an admixture of individuals for whom craving is a prominent motivational factor and those for whom it plays a limited role. As we discuss in subsequent sections, we regard clarifying the differences between such individuals as key to understanding craving.

SYNTHESIS

The preceding review reflects the scientific advances in the contemporary study of craving. The empirical literature reveals that there are multiple pathways to craving and that it is a multidimensional phenomenon, including facets of experiential desire, physiological arousal, and transient cognitive impairment. Craving is subserved by multiple neurotransmitter systems and neuroanatomical structures that suggest the marshalling of resources toward pursuit of a highly salient goal. Critically, when examined using well-validated measures or designs that minimize retrospective bias, craving appears to be substantially related to ongoing alcohol and tobacco use and to post-treatment relapse. However, given the considerable heterogeneity across individuals in their experience of craving, its role is likely to be variable from person to person. Nonetheless, based on the current empirical literature, we propose that craving is a meaningful part of the alcohol and tobacco dependence syndromes and, by extension, a potentially important treatment target.

RESEARCH PRIORITIES IN THE SCIENTIFIC STUDY OF CRAVING

Despite the considerable advances in the study of craving, there is clearly still much progress that remains to be made. In this section, we will detail what we perceive to be the immediate priorities for improving the scientific understanding of craving. These broadly fall into elucidating the potentially different relevance of different types of craving, further characterizing the effects of craving using novel paradigms, and clarifying the genetic basis for individual differences in craving. Although a clear implication of the preceding review is that craving is a worthy treatment target, we will not discuss clinical approaches here, focusing on that area in the following chapter.

One clear priority in research on craving for alcohol and tobacco is clarifying the relevance of different forms of craving. As we noted above, current studies use a number of different methods to elicit craving, with the implicit assumption that the craving elicited across these methods is fundamentally the same. However, there is recent evidence that the craving state elicited via these different methods may be differentially relevant to substance use. A study by Cooney et al. (1997) found that the reactions to a combination of alcohol cues and a negative affect induction predicted treatment outcome, but not either alone. In addition, Sinha et al. (2006) recently reported that for cocaine-dependent individuals stress-induced craving for cocaine predicted treatment outcome, but cue-elicited craving did not. These provocative findings suggest that craving is not a monolithic experience with a number of different eliciting factors, but that even the types of craving differ from each other and may be differentially relevant to actual substance use. Importantly, separating the effects of negative affect and/or stress inductions from those of substance cues is a challenge, especially when studying individuals for whom these have usually been paired through a long and contextually complex learning history. Nonetheless, we regard this as a priority area for understanding the relationship between craving and relapse.

Although there has been considerable progress in understanding the effects of craving on an individual, we continue to regard this as a critical priority toward understanding the mechanisms by which craving translates into actual alcohol or tobacco use. In particular, an area that has received some attention and has considerable promise is the examination of the effect of craving using objective behavioral indices of motivation. Given that some of the ambiguity in understanding the role of craving may be due to the subjectivity of self-report (Sayette et al., 2000; Tiffany et al., 2000), this ambiguity may be substantially reduced by the use of objective methods developed in behavioral pharmacology and behavioral economics to understand the motivational effects of craving on the individual.

A number of studies have obliquely supported this notion by using operant paradigms or monetary choice tasks to examine the motivational significance of craving and reporting that craving-related manipulations (i.e., enforced abstinence, cue exposure) were associated with increases in operant responding or the relative value of a substance (Epstein et al., 1991; Griffiths, Rush, & Puhala, 1996; Perkins, Grobe, & Fonte, 2004). However, these studies were substantially limited by either not concurrently assessing craving or not reporting the relationship between craving and the objective measure. The prospect of examining the effect of craving on objective measures has been more clearly supported by several studies (Sayette et al., 2001; O'Malley et al., 2002; Perkins et al., 1997; Willner, Hardman, & Eaton, 1995), each suggesting that craving does indeed translate into objective indices of motivation. Importantly, in these studies self-reported craving was not collinear with the objective indices of motivation, suggesting that such behavioral measures may capture meaningful aspects of craving beyond the individual's introspective report. Thus, we regard further attempts to understand craving via behavioral indices of motivation as of high priority to bring the relationship between craving and actual substance use into sharper relief. Moreover, translating craving into more objective behavioral indices also has the advantage of permitting a better interface with experimental research using non-human animals because the paradigms parallel each other. For example, a progressive ratio operant schedule can be used to objectively measure drug motivation in either humans (e.g., Bickel et al., 1999; Murphy & MacKillop, 2006) or non-human animals (e.g., Gallate & MacGregor, 1999; Lynch & Taylor, 2005), as is the case for other types of operant schedules or behavioral choice procedures.

In addition to the preceding areas, perhaps the most pressing priority in the science of craving is understanding the observed variability in individuals' experience of craving. As we reviewed, recent research implicates a substantial genetic contribution to the experience of craving, however, despite being very promising, the current literature on genetic influences on craving remains incipient. To date, studies have typically studied only one or two genetic alleles at a time, using one or two laboratory paradigms for studying craving. Given the complex neurobiology underlying the experience of craving and the multiple neurotransmitter systems involved, such studies can provide an incomplete picture at best. Indeed, in a recent review, Kreek et al. (2005) identified 28 genetic polymorphisms that are implicated in addictive behavior, of which a large number may plausibly influence craving. Therefore, we regard studies that examine an array of relevant polymorphisms to more comprehensively characterize the genetic basis for variability in the elicitation or expression of craving to be of very high priority. This is not to denigrate the research to date that has had more circumscribed goals; such studies have been groundbreaking and have played a critical role in generating compelling preliminary evidence of genetic influences. Rather, we argue that such single gene investigations should be complemented with larger, more comprehensive studies that can simultaneously characterize the roles of an array of genetic variants, and examine multiple forms of craving (e.g., priming-elicited, cue-elicited, stress-elicited) to more thoroughly understand gene-by-environment (G × E) interactions. For example, the existing findings implicating genetic variation in the dopamine system (Erblich et al., 2004, 2005; Hutchison et al., 2002a, 2002b, 2003; MacKillop et al., 2005; McGeary et al., 2006; Shao et al., 2006) serve as a compelling basis for a large-scale study concurrently examining all of the functional polymorphisms of the dopamine system with a full complement of laboratory paradigms. Importantly, such large-scale G × E studies would also permit characterizing both potential additive and interactive relationships among genetic variants, as has been the case in other domains (e.g., Noble et al., 1998; Eisenberg et al., 2007).

FUTURE DIRECTIONS IN THE SCIENTIFIC STUDY OF CRAVING

The preceding research priorities represent what we regard as the important directions for extending the current scientific understand of craving, but they also represent sequential steps forward, not leaps or bounds. In this final section of the chapter, we move away from a proximal scientific agenda to discuss the distal prospects for qualitatively advancing the field. To make such progress, we propose that the study of craving must become fully transdisciplinary to integrate the wealth of empirical data relating to craving.

As was likely apparent in the review of contemporary research on craving in an earlier section of the chapter, the advances in understanding craving have taken place in a number of disciplines of behavioral science, with each making important contributions. Human laboratory research has clarified the eliciting factors and expression of craving; basic laboratory research and cognitive neuroscience have illuminated the biological bases of craving via animal models and neuroimaging strategies, respectively; most recently, behavioral genetic studies have refined the understanding of individual differences in craving. However, in general, there remains insufficient interdisciplinary communication and collaboration to leverage the advances from one area to another to more substantively advance the field (Monti, Rohsenow, & Hutchinson, 2000; Monti et al., 2005). Indeed, transdisciplinary collaborations involving basic and clinical scientists with expertise in a number of different areas are the exceptions, rather than the rule (Monti et al., 2000, 2005).

We propose that there needs to be increasing overlap between the disciplines that have advanced the field thus far, including human laboratory

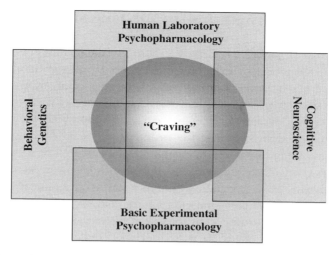

Figure 1 A transdisciplinary approach to the study of craving. Transdisciplinary collaborations leveraging methodologies from multiple disciplines are considered to be critical to make substantive progress on overlapping research agendas and to develop consilience across disciplines.

psychopharmacology, basic behavioral research, cognitive neuroscience, and behavioral genetics, as is illustrated in Figure 1. By developing such collaborations, we believe much more substantial progress could be made beyond the traditional sequential progress within a discipline. As an example, such a transdisciplinary approach might be characterizing the differences in craving individuals with different genetic variants using neuroimaging approaches. Equally, a transdisciplinary approach could improve the consilience between animal models of craving and human laboratory paradigms for studying craving. Such areas will not be addressed following a traditional scientific path. Progress in understanding the nature and relevance of craving will not fall to a single discipline or approach to craving, but rather, it will depend on both advances within multiple disciplines, and, more importantly, advances *across* disciplines.

It is important to note that the lack of transdisciplinary research is not a problem that is specific to research on craving. It reflects a larger problem in behavioral science in general, where the need for increasing research specialization, perceived differences between basic and clinical scientists, poor interdisciplinary communication, and institutional systems that do not encourage collaborative research have created a fragmented scientific community (Daughters et al., 2003; National Advisory Mental Health Council Behavioral Science Workgroup, 2000; Onken & Bootzin, 1998; Zvolensky et al., 2001). In turn, these factors have impeded the effective application of knowledge from basic research to clinical research, making such translational research a high priority across the discipline of behavioral science. Mirroring this larger trend, progress in research on craving will require innovative transdisciplinary collaborations.

SUMMARY AND CONCLUSIONS

In this chapter, we have reviewed advances in the scientific study of craving toward a more comprehensive and integrated understanding of the phenomenon. In doing so, we highlighted the multiple pathways to craving and its multidimensional nature, phenomenologically and neurobiologically. A clear implication of these findings is that, despite considerable variability among individuals, craving is an important motivational factor in the maintenance of alcohol and tobacco use and may play a substantial role in successfully treating alcohol or tobacco dependence. Although the science of craving has unarguably advanced dramatically since the 1950s, it is also clear that there is much progress that remains to be made. Although a number of different individual research areas of high priority can be easily identified, making major steps forward will be more challenging and will depend on the application of a coordinated and integrated transdisciplinary approach to understanding the role of craving in alcohol and tobacco use, and addictive behavior in general.

REFERENCES

Anton, R., Moak, D., & Latham, P. (1995). The Obsessive-Compulsive Drinking Scale: A self-rated instrument for the quantification of thoughts about alcohol and drinking behavior. *Alcoholism: Clinical and Experimental Research, 19*, 92–99.

Anton, R., Moak, D., & Latham, P. K. (1996). The Obsessive-Compulsive Drinking Scale: A new method of assessing outcome in alcoholism treatment studies. *Archives of General Psychiatry, 156*, 225–231.

Avants, S. K., Margolin, A., Kosten, T. R., & Cooney, N. L. (1995). Differences between responders and nonresponders to cocaine cues in the laboratory. *Addictive Behaviors, 20*, 215–224.

Baker, T. B., Morse, E., & Sherman, J. E. (1986). The motivation to use drugs: A psychobiological analysis of urges. In C. Rivers (Ed.). *The Nebraska Symposium on Motivation: Alcohol Use and Abuse*, Vol. 34 (pp. 257–323). Lincoln: University of Nebraska Press.

Baker, T. B., Piper, M. E., McCarthy, D. E., Majeskie, M. R., & Fiore, M. C. (2004). Addiction motivation reformulated: An affective processing model of negative reinforcement. *Psychological Review, 111*, 33–51.

Baumann, S. B., & Sayette, M. A. (2006). Smoking cues in a virtual world provoke craving in cigarette smokers. *Psychology of Addictive Behaviors, 20*, 1–6.

Bechara, A., & Martin, E. M. (2004). Impaired decision making related to working memory deficits in individuals with substance addictions. *Neuropsychology, 18*, 152–162.

Bencherif, B., Wand, G. S., McCaul, M. E., Kim, Y. K., Ilgin, N., Dannals, R. F., & Frost, J. J. (2004). Mu-Opiod receptor binding measured by [^{11}C] Carfentanil Positron Emission Tomography is related to craving and mood in alcohol dependence. *Biological Psychiatry, 55*, 255–262.

Berridge, K. C., & Robinson, T. E. (1998). What is the role of dopamine in reward: Hedonic impact, reward learning, or incentive salience? *Brain Research Review, 28*, 309–369.

Bickel, W. K., & Madden, G. J. (1999). A comparison of measures of relative reinforcing efficacy and behavioral economics: Cigarettes and money in smokers. *Behavioural Pharmacology, 10*, 627–637.

Bohn, M. J., Krahn, D. D., & Staehler, B. B. (1995). Development and initial validation of a measure of drinking urges in abstinent alcoholics. *Alcoholism: Clinical and Experimental Research, 19*, 600–606.

Brody, A. L., Mandelkern, M. A., London, E. D., Childress, A. R., Lee, G. S., Bota, R. G., Ho, M. L., Saxena, S., Baxter, L. R., Jr., Madsen, D., & Jarvik, M. E. (2002). Brain metabolic changes during cigarette craving. *Archives of General Psychiatry, 59*(12), 1162–1172.

Cabeza, R., & Nyberg, L. (2000). Imaging cognition II: An empirical review of 275 PET and fMRI studies. *Journal of Cognitive Neuroscience, 12*(1), 1–47.

Carter, B. L., & Tiffany, S. T. (1999). Meta-analysis of cue reactivity in addiction research. *Addiction, 94*, 327–340.

Cepeda-Benito, A., & Tiffany, S. T. (1996). The use of a dual-task procedure for the assessment of cognitive effort associated with cigarette craving. *Psychopharmacology, 127*, 155–163.

Ciccocioppo, R. (1999). The role of serotonin in craving: From basic research to human studies. *Alcohol and Alcoholism, 34*(2), 244–253.

Coffey, S. F., Saladin, M., Drobes, D. J., Brady, K. T., Dansky, B. S., & Kilpatrick, D. G. (2002). Trauma and substance cue reactivity in individuals with comorbid posttraumatic stress disorder and cocaine or alcohol dependence. *Drug and Alcohol Dependence, 65*(2), 115–127.

Cohen, M., Liebson, I. A., Faillace, L. A., & Speers, W. (1971). Alcoholism: Controlled drinking and incentives for abstinence. *Psychological Reports, 28*(2), 575–580.

Conklin, C. A. (2006). Environments as cues to smoke: Implications for human extinction-based research and treatment. *Experimental and Clinical Psychopharmacology, 14*(1), 12–19.

Collins, R. L., Morsheimer, E. T., & Shiffman, S. (1998). Ecological momentary assessment in a behavioral drinking moderation training program. *Experimental and Clinical Psychopharmacology, 6*, 306–315.

Cooney, N. L., Litt, M. D., Morse, P. A., & Bauer, L. O. (1997). Alcohol cue reactivity, negative-mood reactivity, and relapse in treated alcoholic men. *Journal of Abnormal Psychology, 106*, 243–250.

Cox, L. S., Tiffany, S. T., & Christen, A. G. (2001). Evaluation of the brief questionnaire of smoking urges (QSU-brief) in laboratory and clinical settings. *Nicotine and Tobacco Research, 3*(1), 7–16.

Critchley, H. D., Mathias, C. J., Dolan, R. J., & Unit, A. (2001). Neural activity in the human brain relating to uncertainty and arousal during anticipation. *Neuron, 29*, 537–545.

Curtin, J. J., Barnett, N. P., Colby, S. M., Rohsenow, D. J., & Monti, P. M. (2005). Cue reactivity in adolescents: Measurement of separate approach and avoidance reactions. *Journal of Studies on Alcohol, 66*(3), 332–343.

Daughters, S. B., Lejuez, C. W., Lesieur, H. R., Strong, D. R., & Zvolensky, M. J. (2003). Towards a better understanding of gambling treatment failure. Implications of translational research. *Clinical Psychology Review, 23*, 573–586.

Drummond, D. C. (2001). Theories of drug craving, ancient and modern. *Addiction, 96*, 33–46.

Eisenberg, D. T. A., MacKillop, J., Modi, M., Beauchemin, J., Dang, D., Lum, J. K., Lisman, S. A., & Wilson, D. S. (2007). Examining impulsivity as an endophenotype using a behavioral approach: A DRD2 TaqI A and DRD4 48-bp VNTR Association study. *Behavioral and Brain Functions, 3*.

Epstein, L. H., Bulik, C. M., Perkins, K. A., Caggiula, A. R., & Rodefer, J. (1991). Behavioral economic analysis of smoking: Money and food as alternatives. *Pharmacology, Biochemistry, and Behavior, 38*, 715–721.

Erblich, J., Lerman, C., Self, D. W., Diaz, G. A., & Bovbjerg, D. H. (2004). Stress-induced cigarette craving: Effects of the DRD2 TaqI RFLP and SLC6A3 VNTR polymorphisms. *Pharmacogenomics Journal, 4*, 102–109.

Erblich, J., Lerman, C., Self, D. W., Diaz, G. A., & Bovbjerg, D. H. (2005). Effects of dopamine D2 receptor (DRD2) and transporter (SLC6A3) polymorphisms on smoking cue-induced cigarette craving among African-American smokers. *Molecular Psychiatry, 10*, 407–414.

Flannery, B. A., Poole, S. A., Gallop, & Volpicelli, J. R. (2003). Alcohol craving predicts drinking during treatment: An analysis of three assessment instruments. *Journal of Studies on Alcohol, 64*, 120–126.

Flannery, B. A., Volpicelli, J. R., & Pettinati, H. M. (1999). Psychometric properties of the Penn Alcohol Craving Scale. *Alcoholism: Clinical and Experimental Research, 23*, 1289–1295.

Franken, H. A., de Haan, C. W., van der Meer, P. M., Haffmans, J., & Hendriks, V. M. (1999). Cue reactivity and effects of cue exposure in abstinent post-treatment drug users. *Journal of Substance Abuse Treatment, 16*, 81–85.

Gallate, J. E., & McGregor, I. S. (1999). The motivation for beer in rats: Effects of ritanserin, naloxone and SR 141716. *Psychopharmacology (Berl), 142*, 302–308.

George, M. S., Anton, R. F., Bloomer, C., Teneback, C., Drobes, D. J., Lorberbaum, J. P., Nahas, Z., & Vincent, D. J. (2001). Activation of prefrontal cortex and anterior thalamus in alcoholic subjects on exposure to alcohol-specific cues. *Archives of General Psychiatry, 58*(4), 345–352.

Glautier, S., & Drummond, D. C. (1994). Alcohol dependence and cue reactivity. *Journal of Studies on Alcohol, 55*, 224–229.

Grace, A. A. (2000). The tonic/phasic model of dopamine system regulation and its implications for understanding alcohol and psychostimulant craving. *Addiction, 95*(Suppl. 2), S119–S128.

Griffiths, R. R., Rush, C. R., & Puhala, K. A. (1996). Validation of the Multiple-Choice Procedure for investigating drug reinforcement in humans. *Experimental and Clinical Psychopharmacology, 4*, 97–106.

Grusser, S. M., Heinz, A., Raabe, A., Wessa, M., Podschus, J., & Flor, H. (2002). Stimulus-induced craving and startle potentiation in abstinent alcoholics and controls. *European Psychiatry, 17*, 188–193.

Grusser, S. M., Wrase, J., Klein, S., Hermann, D., Smolka, M. N., Ruf, M., Weber-Fahr, Flor, H., Mann, K., Braus, D. F., & Heinz, A. (2004). Cue-induced activation of the striatum and medical prefrontal cortex is associated with subsequent relapse in abstinent alcoholics. *Psychopharmacology, 175*(3), 296–302.

Gwaltney, C. J., Shiffman, S., Balabanis, M. H., & Paty, J. A. (2005). Dynamic self-efficacy and out-come expectancies: Predictions of smoking lapse and relapse. *Journal of Abnormal Psychology, 114*, 661–675.

Harvey, K., Kemps, E., & Tiggemann, M. (2005). The nature of imagery processes underlying food cravings. *British Journal of Health Psychology, 10*(1), 49–56.

Havermans, R., Debaere, S. Smulders, F. T. Y., Wiers, R .W., & Jansen, A. T. M. (2003). Effect of cue exposure, urge to smoke, and nicotine deprivation on cognitive performance in smokers. *Psychology of Addictive Behaviors, 17*, 336–339.

Havermans, R. C., Keuker, J., Lataster, T., & Jansen, A. (2005). Contextual control of extinguished conditioned performance in humans. *Learning and Motivation, 36*(1), 1–19.

Heinz, A., Siessmeier, T., Wrase, J., Buchholz, H. G., Grunder, G., Kumakura, Y., Cumming, P., Schreckenberger, M., Smolka, M. N., Rosch, F., Mann, K., & Bartenstein, P. (2005). Correlation of Alcohol craving with Striatal Dopamine Synthesis Capacity and $D_{2/3}$ Receptor Availability: A Combined [^{18}F] DOPA and [^{18}F] DMFP PET Study in Detoxified Alcoholic Patients. *American Journal of Psychiatry, 162*, 1515–1520.

Heinz, A., Siessmeier, T., Wrase, J., Hermann, D., Klein, S., Grusser-Sinoploi, S. M., Flor, H., Braus, D. F., Buchholz, H. G., Grunder, G., Schreckenberger, M., Smolka, M. N., Rosch, F., Mann, K., & Bartenstein, P. (2004). Correlation between Dopamine D_2 receptors in the ventral striatum and cen-tral processing of alcohol cues and craving. *American Journal of Psychiatry, 161*, 1783–1789.

Hodgins, D. C., el-Guebaly, N., & Armstrong, S. (1995). Prospective and retrospective reports of mood states before relapse to substance use. *Journal of Consulting and Clinical Psychology, 63*, 400–407.

Hommer, D. W. (1999). Functional imaging of craving. *Alcohol Research and Health, 23*(3), 187–196.

Hughes, J. R., Hatsukami, D. K., Pickens, R. W., Roy, W., & Svikis, S. S. (1984). Consistency of the tobacco withdrawal syndrome. *Addictive Behaviors, 9*(4), 409–412.

Hutchison, K. E., Lachance, H., Niaura, R., Bryan, A., & Smolen, A. (2002a). The DRD4 VNTR polymorphism influences reactivity to smoking cues. *Journal of Abnormal Psychology, 111*, 134–143.

Hutchison, K. E., McGeary, J. E., Smolen, A., Swift, R. M., & Bryan, A. (2002b). The DRD4 VNTR polymorphism moderates craving after alcohol consumption. *Health Psychology, 21*, 139–146.

Hutchison, K. E., Wooden, A., Swift, R. M., Smolen, A., McGeary, J., Adler, L., & Paris, L. (2003). Olanzapine reduces craving for alcohol: A DRD4 VNTR polymorphism by pharmacotherapy interaction. *Neuropsychopharmacology, 28,* 1882–1888.

Jellinek, E. M., Isbell, H., Lundquist, G., Tiebout, H. M., Duchene, H., Mardones, J., & Macleod, L. D. (1955). The "Craving" for alcohol: A symposium by members of the WHO expert committees on mental health and alcohol. *Journal of Studies on Alcohol, 16,* 34–67.

Kavanagh, D. J., Andrade, J., & May, J. (2005). Imaginary relish and exquisite torture: The elaborated intrusion theory of desire. *Psychological Review, 112*(2), 446–467.

Killen, J. D., & Fortmann, S. P. (1997). Craving is associated with smoking relapse: Findings from three prospective studies. *Experimental and Clinical Psychology, 5*(2), 137–142.

Koob, G. F. (2000). Animal models of craving for ethanol. *Addiction, 95*(Suppl. 2), S73–S81.

Kozlowski, L. T., Mann, R. E., Wilkinson, D. A., & Poulos, C. X. (1989). "Cravings" are ambiguous: Ask about urges or desires. *Addictive Behaviors, 14,* 443–445.

Kozlowski, L. T., & Wilkinson, D. A. (1987). Use and misuse of the concept of craving by alcohol, tobacco, and drug researchers. *British Journal of Addiction, 82,* 31–45.

Krahn, D. D., Bohn, M. J., Henk, H. J., Grossman, J. L., & Gosnell, B. (2005). Patterns of urges during early abstinence in alcohol-dependent subjects. *American Journal on Addictions, 14,* 248–255.

Kreek, M. J., Nielsen, D. A., Butelman, E. R., & LaForge, K. S. (2005). Genetic influences on impulsivity, risk taking, stress responsivity and vulnerability to drug abuse and addiction. *Nature Neuroscience, 8,* 1450–1457.

Laberg, J. C. (1986). Alcohol and expectancy: Subjective, psychophysiological and behavioral responses to alcohol stimuli in severely, moderately and non-dependent drinkers. *British Journal of Addiction, 81*(6), 797–808.

Litt, M. D., Cooney, N. L., Kadden, R. M., & Gaupp, L. (1990). Reactivity to alcohol cues and induced moods in alcoholics. *Addictive Behaviors, 15,* 137–146.

Litt, M. D., Cooney, N. L., Morse, P. (2000). Reactivity to alcohol-related stimuli in the laboratory and in the field: Predictors of craving in treated alcoholics. *Addiction, 95,* 889–900.

Litman, G. K., Stapleton, J., Oppenheim, A. N., Peleg, M., & Jackson, P. (1983). Situations related to alcoholism relapse. *British Journal of Addiction, 78,* 381–389.

Loewenstein, G. (1996). Out of control: Visceral influences on behavior. *Organizational Behavior and Human Decision Processes, 65,* 272–292.

Loewenstein, G. (2001). A visceral account of addiction. In P. Slovic (Ed.). *Smoking: Risk, perception, & policy* (pp. 188–215). Thousand Oaks, CA, US: Sage Publications, Inc.

London, E. D., Ernst, M., Grant, S., Bonson, K., & Weinstein, A. (2000). Orbitofrontal cortex and human drug abuse: Functional imaging. *Cerebral Cortex, 10*(3), 334–342.

Lowman, C., Allen, J., & Stout, R. L. (1996). Replication and extension of Marlatt's taxonomy of relapse precipitants, overview of procedures and results. The Relapse Research Group. *Addiction, 91,* 51–71.

Ludwig, A. M., & Wikler, A. (1974). Craving and relapse to drink. *Quarterly Journal of Studies on Alcohol, 35,* 108–130.

Ludwig, A. M., Wikler, A., & Stark, L. H. (1974). The first drink: Psychobiological aspects of craving. *Archives of General Psychiatry, 30,* 539–547.

Lynch, W. J., & Taylor, J. R. (2005). Persistent changes in motivation to self-administer cocaine following modulation of cyclic AMP-dependent protein kinase A (PKA) activity in the nucleus accumbens. *European Journal of Neuroscience, 22,* 1214–1220.

MacKillop, J. (2006). Factor structure of the Alcohol Urge Questionnaire (AUQ) under neutral conditions and during a cue-elicited urge state. *Alcoholism: Clinical and Experimental Research, 30,* 1315–1321.

MacKillop, J., & Lisman, S. A. (2005). Reactivity to alcohol cues: Isolating the role of perceived availability. *Experimental and Clinical Psychology, 13,* 229–237.

MacKillop, J., Menges, D. P., McGeary, J. E., & Lisman, S. A. (in press). Influences of craving and DRD4 VNTR genotype on the relative value of alcohol: An initial human laboratory study. *Behavioral and Brain Functions*.

MacKillop, J., O'Hagen, S., & Lisman, S. A. (June, 2006). Understanding restrained drinking using an approach-avoidance assessment of reactions to alcohol cues. *Alcoholism: Experimental and Clinical Research*, *30*, 148A (Suppl.).

Madden, C. J., & Zwann, R. A. (2001). The impact of smoking urges on working memory performance. *Experimental and Clinical Psychopharmacology*, *9*(4), 418–424.

Markou, A., Weiss, F., Gold, L. H., Caine, S. B., & Koob, G. F. (1993). Animal models of drug craving. *Psychopharmacology*, *112*, 163–182.

May, J., Andrade, J., Panabokke, N., & Kavanagh, D. (2004). Images of desire: Cognitive models of craving. *Memory*, *12*, 447–461.

McClernon, F. J., & Gilbert, D. G. (2004). Human functional neuroimaging in nicotine and tobacco research: Basics, background, and beyond. *Nicotine and Tobacco Research*, *6*, 941–959.

McGeary, J. E., Monti, P. M., Rohsenow, D. J. Tidey, J., Swift, R., & Miranda, R. (2006). Genetic moderators of naltrexone's effects on alcohol cue reactivity. *Alcoholism: Clinical and Experimental Research*, *30*, 1288–1296.

Miller, N. S., & Gold, M. S. (1994). Dissociation of "conscious desire" (craving) from relapse in alcohol and cocaine dependence. *Annals of Clinical Psychiatry*, *6*, 99–106.

Miranda, R., Jr., Monti, P. M., Swift, R., MacKillop, J., Tidey, J., Gwaltney, C., & Rohsenow, D. (2005, December). Dose-dependent effects of topiramate on alcohol cue reactivity and the subjective effects of drinking: Preliminary data [Abstract]. *Neuropsychopharmacology*, *30*, Supplement 1.

Monti, P. M., Abrams, D. B., Binkoff, J. A., Zwick, W. R., Liepman, M. R., Nirenberg, T. D., & Rohsenow, D. J. (1990). Communication skills training, communication skills training with family and cognitive behavioral mood management training for alcoholics. *Journal of Studies on Alcohol*, *51*, 263–270.

Monti, P. M., Binkoff, J. A., Abrams, D. B., & Zwick, W. R. (1987). Reactivity of alcoholic and nonalcoholics to drinking cues. *Journal of Abnormal Psychology*, *96*, 122–126.

Monti, P. M., Miranda, R., Nixon, K., Sher, K. J., Swartzwelder, H. S., Tapert, S. F., White, A., & Crews, F. T. (2005). Adolescence: Booze, brains and behavior. *Alcoholism: Clinical and Experimental Research*, *29*, 207–220.

Monti, P. M., Rohsenow, D. J., & Hutchinson, K. E. (2000). Toward bridging the gap between biological, psychobiological models of alcohol craving. *Addiction*, *95*, 229S–236S.

Monti, P. M., Rohsenow, D. J., Hutchinson, K. E., Swift, R. M., Mueller, T. I., Colby, S. M., & Kaplan, G. B. (1999). Naltrexone's effect on cue-elicited craving among alcoholics in treatment. *Alcoholism: Clinical and Experimental Research*, *23*(8), 1386–1394.

Munafò, M., Mogg, K., Roberts, S., Bradley, B. P., & Murphy, M. (2003). Selective processing of smoking-related cues in current smokers, ex-smokers and never-smokers on the modified Stroop task. *Journal of Psychopharmacology*, *17*, 310–316.

Murphy, J. G., & MacKillop, J. (2006). Relative reinforcing efficacy of alcohol among college student drinkers. *Experimental and Clinical Psychopharmacology*, *14*, 219–227.

Myrick, H., Anton, R. F., Li, X., Henderson, S., Drobes, D., Voronin, K., & George, M. S. (2004). Differential brain activity in alcoholics and social drinkers to alcohol cues. *Neuropsychopharmacology*, *29*, 393–402.

National Advisory Mental Health Council Behavioral Science Workgroup. (2000). *Translating Behavioral Science into Action*. Bethesda, MD: National Institute of Mental Health (NIMH).

Niaura, R. (2000). Cognitive social learning and related perspectives on drug craving. *Addiction*, *95* (Suppl. 2), S155–S163.

Niaura, R. S, Rohsenow, D. J., Binkoff, J. A., Monti, P. M., Pedraza, M., & Abrams, D. B. (1988). Relevance of cue reactivity to understanding alcohol and smoking relapse. *Journal of Abnormal Psychology*, *97*, 133–152.

Niaura, R., Shadel, W. G., Britt, D. M., & Abrams, D. B. (2002). Response to social stress, urge to smoke, and smoking cessation. *Addictive Behaviors*, *27*(2), 241–250.

Noble, E. P., Ozkaragoz, T. Z., Ritchie, T., Zhang, X., Belin, T. R., & Sparkes, R. S. (1998). D2 and D4 dopamine receptor polymorphisms and personality. *American Journal of Medical Genetics*, *81*, 257–267.

O'Brien, C. P., Childress, A. R., McLellan, A. T., & Ehrman, R. (1992). A learning model of addiction. In C. P. O'Brien, & J. H. Jaffe (Eds.). *Addictive States* (pp. 157–177). New York, NY, US: Raven Press. xii, 291 pp.

O'Malley, S. S., Krishnan, S. S., Farren, C., Sinha, R., & Kreek, M. J. (2002). Naltrexone decreases craving and alcohol self-administration in alcohol-dependent subjects and activates the hypo-thalamo–pituitary–adrenocortial axis. *Psychopharmacology*, *160*(1), 19–29.

Onken, L. S., & Bootzin, R. R. (1998). Behavioral therapy development and psychological science: If a tree falls in the wood and nobody hears it. *Behavior Therapy*, *29*, 539–544.

Palfai, T. P., Monti, P. M., Ostafin, B., & Hutchison, K. (2001). Effects of nicotine deprivation on alcohol-related information processing and drinking behavior. *Journal of Abnormal Psychology*, *109*, 96–105.

Panabokke, N., May, J., Eade, D., Andrade, J., & Kavanagh, D. (2004). Visual imagery tasks suppress craving for cigarettes. Unpublished manuscript, University of Sheffield, Sheffield, England.

Perkins, K. A., Grobe, J., & Fonte, C. (1997). Influence of acute smoking exposure on the subsequent reinforcing value of smoking. *Experimental and Clinical Psychopharmacology*, *5*, 277–285.

Rankin, H., Stockwell, T., & Hodgson, R. (1982). Cues for drinking and degrees of alcohol dependence. *British Journal of Addiction*, *77*(3), 287–296.

Rauch, S. L., Jenike, M. A., Alpert, N. M., Baer, L., Breiter, H. C., Savage, C. R., & Fischman, A. J. (1994). Regional cerebral blood flow measured during symptom provocation in obsessive-compulsive disorder using oxygen 15-labeledd CO_2 and positron emission tomography. *Archives of General Psychiatry*, *51*, 62–70.

Rohsenow, D. J., Monti, P. M., Abrams, D. B., & Rubonis, A. V. (1992). Cue elicited urge to drink and salivation in alcoholics: Relationship to individual differences. *Advances in Behaviour Research and Therapy*, *14*, 195–210.

Rohsenow, D. J., Niaura, R. S., Childress, A. R., Abrams, D. B., & Monti, P. M. (1991). Cue reactivity in addictive behaviors: Theoretical and treatment implications. *The International Journal of the Addictions*, *25*, 957–993.

Rubonis, A. V., Colby, S. M., Monti, P. M., & Rohsenow, D. J. (1994). Alcohol cue reactivity and mood induction in male and female alcoholics. *Journal of Studies on Alcohol*, *55*, 487–494.

Saladin, M. E., Drobes, D. J., Coffey, S. F., Dansky, B. S., Brady, K. T., & Kilpatrick, D. G. (2003). PTSD symptom severity as a predictor of cue-elicited drug craving in victims of violent crime. *Addictive Behaviors*, *28*(9), 1611–1629.

Sayette, M. A., & Hufford, M. R. (1994). Effects of cue exposure and deprivation on cognitive resources in smokers. *Journal of Abnormal Psychology*, *103*, 812–818.

Sayette, M. A., Loewenstein, G., Kirchner, T. R., & Travis, T. (2005). Effects of smoking urge on temporal cognition. *Psychology of Addictive Behaviors*, *19*, 88–93.

Sayette, M. A., Martin, C. S., Wertz, J. M., Shiffman, S., & Perrott, M. A. (2001). A multi-dimensional analysis of cue-elicited craving in heavy smokers and tobacco chippers. *Addiction*, *96*, 1419–1432.

Sayette, M. A., Monti, P. M., Rohsenow, D. J., Gulliver, S. B., Colby, S. M., & Sirota, A. D. (1994). The effects of cue exposure on reaction time in male alcoholics. *Journal of Studies on Alcohol*, *55*, 629–633.

Sayette, M. A., Shiffman, S., Tiffany, S. T., Niaura, R. S., Martin, C. S., & Shadel, W. G. (2000). The measurement of drug craving. *Addiction*, *95*(Suppl. 2), S189–S210.

Shao, C., Li, Y., Jiang, K., Zhang, D., Xu, Y., Lin, L., Wang, Q., Zhao, M., & Jin, L. (2006). Dopamine D4 receptor polymorphism modulates cue-elicited heroin craving in Chinese. *Psychopharmacology (Berl)*, *186*, 185–90.

208   James MacKillop and Peter M. Monti

Sherman, J. E., Morse, E., & Baker, T. B. (1986). Urges/craving to smoke: Preliminary results from withdrawing and continuing smokers. *Advances in Behaviour Research and Therapy*, 8(4), 253–269.

Shiffman, S., Engberg, J., Paty, J. A., Perz, W., Gnys, M., Kassel, J. D., & Hickcox, M. (1997). A day at a time: Predicting smoking lapse from daily urge. *Journal of Abnormal Psychology*, 106, 104–116.

Shiffman, S., Gwaltney, C. J., Balabanis, M. H., Liu, K. S., Paty, J. A., Kassel, J. D., Hickcox, M. M., & Gnys, M. (2002). Immediate antecedents of cigarette smoking: An analysis from ecological momentary assessment. *Journal of Abnormal Psychology*, 111, 531–545.

Shiffman, S. M., & Jarvik, M. E. (1976). Smoking withdrawal symptoms in two weeks of abstinence. *Psychopharmacology*, 50(1), 35–39.

Shiffman, S., Paty, J. A., Gnys, M., Kassel, J. D., & Hickcox, M. (1996). First lapses to smoking: Within-subjects analysis of real time reports. *Journal of Consulting and Clinical Psychology*, 64, 366–379.

Shiffman, S., Shadel, W. G., Niaura, R., Khayrallah, M. A., Jorenby, D. E., Ryan, C. F., & Ferguson, C. L. (2003). Efficacy of acute administration of nicotine gum in relief of cue-provoked cigarette craving. *Psychopharmacology*, 166(4), 345–350.

Siegel, S. (1988). Drug anticipation and drug tolerance. In M. Lader (Ed). *The Psychopharmacology of Addiction* (pp. 73–96). New York, NY, US: Oxford University Press.

Sinha, R., Garcia, M., Paliwal, P., Kreek, M. J., & Rounsaville, B. J. (2006). Stress-induced cocaine craving and hypothalamic-pituitary-adrenal responses are predictive of cocaine relapse outcomes. *Archives of General Psychiatry*, 63, 324–331.

Sinha, R., Talih, M., Malison, R., Cooney, N., Anderson, G. M., & Kreek, M. J. (2003). Hypothalamic-pituitary-adrenal axis and sympatho-adreno-medullary responses during stress-induced and drug cue-induced cocaine craving states. *Psychopharmacology*, 170, 62–72.

Stasiewicz, P. R., Gulliver, S. B., Bradizza, C. M., Rohsenow, D. J., Torris, R., & Monti, P. M. (1997). Exposure to negative emotional cues and alcohol cue reactivity with alcoholics: A preliminary investigation. *Behaviour Research and Therapy*, 35(12), 1143–1149.

Stewart, J., deWit, H., & Eikleboom, R. (1984). Role of unconditioned and conditioned drug effects in the self-administration of opiates and stimulants. *Psychological Review*, 91, 251–268.

Stone, A. A., & Shiffman, S. (1994). Ecological momentary assessment (EMA) in behavioral medicine. *Annals of Behavioral Medicine*, 16(3), 199–202.

Stritzke, W. G., Breiner, M. J., Curtin, J. J., & Lang, A. R. (2004). Assessment of substance cue reactivity: Advances in reliability, specificity, and validity. *Psychology of Addictive Behaviors*, 18, 148–159.

Swift, R. M., Whelihan, W., Kuznetsov, O., Buongiorno, G., & Hsuing, H. (1994). Naltrexone-induced alterations in human ethanol intoxication. *American Journal of Psychiatry*, 151(10), 1463–1467.

Tapert, S. F., Brown, G. G., Baratta, M. V., & Brown, S. A. (2004). fMRI BOLD response to alcohol stimuli in alcohol dependent young women. *Addictive Behaviors*, 29(1), 33–50.

Tapert, S. F., Cheung, E. H., Brown, G. G., Frank, L. R., Paulus, M. P., Schweinsburg, A. D., Meloy, M. J., & Brown, S. A. (2003). Neural response to alcohol stimuli in adolescents with alcohol use disorder. *Archives of General Psychiatry*, 60(7), 727–735.

Tiffany, S. T. (1990). A cognitive model of drug urges and drug-use behavior: Role of automatic and nonautomatic processes. *Psychological Review*, 97, 147–168.

Tiffany, S. T. (1995). Potential functions of classical conditioning in drug addiction. In D. C. Drummond, S. T. Tiffany, S. Glautier, & R. Remington (Eds.). *Cue Exposure: Theory and Practice* (pp. 47–71). Oxford, England: Wiley.

Tiffany, S. T., & Carter, B. L. (1998). Is craving the source of compulsive drug use? *Journal of Psychopharmacology*, 12, 23–30.

Tiffany, S. T., Carter, B. L., & Singleton, E. G. (2000). Challenges in the manipulation, assessment, and interpretation of craving relevant variables. *Addiction*, 95, S177–S187.

Tiffany, S. T., & Conklin, C. A. (2000). A cognitive processing model of alcohol craving and compulsive alcohol use. *Addiction*, *95*(Suppl. 2), S145–S153.

Tiffany, S. T., & Drobes, D. J. (1990). Imagery and smoking urges: The manipulation of affective content. *Addictive Behaviors*, *15*(6), 531–539.

Tiffany, S. T., & Drobes, D. J. (1991). The development and initial validation of a questionnaire on smoking urges. *British Journal of Addiction*, *86*(11), 1467–1476.

Turkkan, J. S., McCaul, M. E., & Stitzer, M. L. (1989). Psychophysiological effects of alcohol-related stimuli: II. Enhancement with alcohol availability. *Alcoholism: Clinical and Experimental Research*, *13*(3), 392–398.

West, R. J. (1984). Psychology and pharmacology in cigarette withdrawal. *Journal of Psychosomatic Research*, *28*(5), 379–386.

Westerberg, V. S. (2000). Constituents of craving in a clinical alcohol sample. *Journal of Substance Abuse*, *12*, 415–423.

Willner, P., Hardman, S., & Eaton, G. (1995). Subjective and behavioral evaluation of cigarette cravings. *Psychopharmacology*, *118*, 171–177.

Wise, R. A. (1988). The neurobiology of craving: Implications for the understanding and treatment of addiction. *Journal of Abnormal-Psychology*, *97*, 118–132.

Zvolensky, M. J., Lejuez, C. W., Stuart, G. L., & Curtin, J. J. (2001). Experimental psychopathology in psychological science. *Review of General Psychology*, *5*, 371–381.

Zwann, R. A., & Truitt, T. P. (1998). Smoking urges affect language processing. *Experimental and Clinical Psychopharmacology*, *6*, 325–330.

CHAPTER 11

Advances in the Treatment of Craving for Alcohol and Tobacco

Peter M. Monti and James MacKillop
Center for Alcohol and Addiction Studies, Brown University,
Providence, RI, USA

Abstract: This chapter critically reviews advances in contemporary science-based approaches to the treatment of craving for alcohol and tobacco. It is intended to be the clinical complement to the preceding chapter in this volume, which focused on the empirical scientific literature on craving. We review cue exposure treatment (CET), naltrexone pharmacotherapy, and nicotine replacement therapy (NRT), and conclude that these are promising but only moderately effective approaches at the present time. Priorities for improving these interventions are described, including reducing the context-dependency of extinction in CET, improving the praxis of naltrexone and NRT, and identifying novel pharmacotherapeutic agents. Finally, we identify directions for the future, including

Translation of Addictions Science into Practice

applications of a novel approach to craving, the elaborated intrusion model, and the need for substantive transdisciplinary collaboration.

INTRODUCTION

Concurrent with the advances in the scientific study of craving reviewed in the preceding chapter, so too have there been substantial advances in the clinical treatment of craving. However, formal treatment for substance use disorders have only become widely available in the last several decades (White, 1998) and a focus on attenuating craving has emerged even more recently still. Thus, it is not surprising that there is no "silver bullet" for treating craving and that the current approaches have mixed indications of efficacy. However, these treatments nonetheless represent promising approaches with the potential to be further enhanced or selectively deployed to individuals who may differentially benefit from them.

Toward making progress in the clinical treatment of craving, in this chapter, we critically review the existing clinical approaches that have been developed. We then identify specific priorities and strategies for potentially improving the existing treatments. Finally, we discuss future directions in the treatment of craving, specifically reviewing a novel approach to craving and its treatment, Kavanagh, Andrade, and May's (2005) elaborated intrusion (EI) model; and emphasizing the need for a more comprehensive transdisciplinary approach to craving as a clinical phenomenon and as a treatment target. Of note, although there are treatments for craving for substances other than alcohol and tobacco, because this chapter is the logical counterpart to the previous chapter and to address the treatment of all forms of craving would be beyond the scope of the chapter, we will only focus on the treatment of craving for alcohol and tobacco.

CONTEMPORARY SCIENCE-BASED CLINICAL APPROACHES TO CRAVING

Treatment for craving can be broadly divided into cognitive–behavioral and pharmacotherapeutic interventions, each with strengths and weaknesses and specific areas where improvement is necessary. These two modalities will be discussed separately in this section.

COGNITIVE–BEHAVIORAL TREATMENT OF CRAVING

Cognitive–behavioral approaches to addictive behavior have inherently incorporated craving as a treatment target because of their heavy emphasis on situational factors and coping with high-risk situations (e.g., Marlatt & Gordon, 1985), which could include acute craving. However, cue exposure treatment (CET) was the first psychotherapeutic approach developed to directly address craving *sui generis*. Akin to the behavioral treatment of anxiety disorders (e.g., Foa & Kozak, 1986), the basic premise of CET was that substance-related cues were incorporated into a clinical session to elicit and directly treat craving. Importantly, two variants of CET emerged as a result of differing theoretical approaches. From a strictly behavioral perspective (Drummond, Cooper, & Glautier, 1990; O'Brien et al., 1990; Powell et al., 1990), craving was elicited via environmental cues and extinguished via prolonged exposure with response prevention (i.e., extinction) toward mitigating the effect of environmental cues following treatment. In contrast, from a social learning perspective (Marlatt, 1990; Monti et al., 1989), CET was considered part of a larger package of coping and social skills training. As such, in-session exposure served not only to extinguish the conditioned associations between the individual and the cues, but also permitted an ecologically valid opportunity to practice skills for coping with craving. Both of these components were intended to bolster the client's self-efficacy for coping with craving.

Initial controlled clinical trials of CET were promising. For example, using the coping skills-focused CET approach, our group (Monti et al., 1993) was the first to report that CET resulted in significantly greater overall abstinence, a higher percentage of abstinent days, and fewer drinks per day relative to a control treatment. Similarly, using a strictly exposure-based CET approach, Drummond and Glautier (1994) found CET resulted in longer latency to relapse to heavy drinking and overall heavy drinking. To date, over 25 studies of CET have been conducted and the approach has been applied in both abstinence-oriented and moderation-oriented treatments, as well as in combination with pharmacotherapeutic approaches (e.g., Monti et al., 2001).

However, evidence for the efficacy of CET has been mixed. Conklin and Tiffany (2002) conducted a meta-analysis on the existing clinical trials of CET, but found that the majority of studies were methodologically weak and not viable for inclusion. Of the nine methodologically rigorous studies, Conklin and Tiffany (2002) reported that their overall treatment effect size was minimal and concluded that CET "failed to prove efficacious in treating addiction" (p. 159). In response, Drummond (2002) has rightly criticized this conclusion, questioning the appropriateness of even conducting a meta-analysis given the heterogeneity of the studies. Differences included the type of substance abuser, clinical setting, length and modality of exposure, number of exposure sessions, and frequently inadequate statistical power (Drummond, 2002). This heterogeneity across studies is further corroborated by Conklin and Tiffany's (2002) own report of a significant Q statistic, indicating a violation of the meta-analytic assumption of homogeneity of effect size across studies.

Table 1
Treatment Effects of Controlled Trials of Cue Exposure Treatment for Alcohol, Tobacco, and Opiate Dependence as Reported by Conklin and Tiffany (2002)

Study	Drug	Effect size	Magnitude	Treatment effect	Modality
Drummond and Glautier (1994)	Alcohol	+0.17 to 0.30	Small	Favorable	Inpatient
Monti et al. (2001)	Alcohol	+0.5420	Medium	Favorable	Inpatient
Sitharthan et al. (1997)	Alcohol	+0.6070	Medium	Favorable	Outpatient
Monti et al. (1993)	Alcohol	+0.7345	Large	Favorable	Inpatient
Raw and Russell (1980)	Tobacco	−0.0251	–	–	Outpatient
Niaura et al. (1999)	Tobacco	−0.2029	Medium	Unfavorable	Outpatient
Corty and McFall (1984)	Tobacco	−0.4500	Medium	Unfavorable	Outpatient
Lowe et al. (1980)	Tobacco	−0.5180	Large	Unfavorable	Outpatient
Dawe et al. (1993)	Heroin	+0.0805	–	–	Inpatient

Notes: Magnitude designations are based on Cohen (1988): small = ~0.20, medium = ~0.5, large = ~0.8. Favorable or unfavorable designations are based on the effect size valence: positive effect sizes reflect favorable CET outcomes and negative effect sizes reflect unfavorable CET outcomes. Effect sizes smaller than 0.10 were considered ambiguously close to zero and were not designated with a magnitude or as being favorable or unfavorable.

More importantly, rather than simply being quantitatively heterogeneous, the outcomes among the nine studies were dramatically different for alcohol and tobacco dependence in ways that were potentially meaningful. As shown in Table 1, while the four studies of CET for tobacco dependence yielded uniformly *negative* effect sizes, the four studies of CET for alcohol dependence yielded uniformly *positive* effect sizes. Thus, the combined eight studies of CET for tobacco and for alcohol functionally canceled each other out. The final study, by Dawe et al. (1993), provided CET for opiate dependence and reported a modest positive effect size. In addition, it is of note that since Conklin and Tiffany (2002) meta-analysis, one controlled trial of CET has reported positive outcomes (Monti et al., 2001) and two others found that its effects were equivalent to active cognitive-behavioral treatments (Dawe et al., 2002; Heather et al., 2000). Most recently, Kavanagh et al. (2006) examined the utility of adding alcohol cue exposures and emotional cue exposures to traditional cognitive-behavioral treatment for drinkers who drank to improve negative affect, but found that dropout rates and treatment effects on alcohol consumption were actually progressively weaker for both forms of exposure over standard treatment.

Taken together, it appears that CET has differing efficacy depending on the substance. In the treatment of nicotine dependence, CET seems to have a negligible impact, and even potentially iatrogenic effects, but when applied to alcohol dependence it appears to be more promising. Such disparate results may be due to a number of factors. One possibility is that smoking has a much wider array of cues than drinking, making extinction as it is currently practiced ineffective for the majority of situations. Also, the majority of CET trials for tobacco dependence were conducted in outpatient settings (see Table 1) and the majority of CET trials for alcohol dependence were inpatient trials, suggesting that the latter may facilitate additive extinction effects. Alternatively, the "protection" offered by the inpatient environment might facilitate the development of alternative coping responses. Clearly, this is an area deserving of further study.

However, independent of these qualifications of Conklin and Tiffany's (2002) meta-analysis, their larger message that the promise of CET has not been realized is valid. Moreover, they cogently reason that evidence from basic research on context-dependent learning may explain CET's unrealized potential. Within the domain of basic research on learning, it is now clear that extinction is not the erasure of learning (unlearning), but is new learning that reflects sophisticated and nuanced relationships between stimuli in the form of context-dependent learning, or differential behavior based on environmental context. For example, in a conditioned fear paradigm where pairings of an aversive stimulus with a neutral stimulus (i.e., conditional stimulus) result in an acquired fear response, if extinction takes place in a different context, when the subject returns to the original learning context, the conditioned fear response returns (Bouton & Bolles, 1979; Bouton & Schwartzentruber, 1989; Harris et al., 2000; Rauhut, Thomas, & Ayres, 2001). Indeed, the originally learned fear association, not the extinction, has been demonstrated to readily transfer to a third context (Bouton & Bolles, 1979; Bouton & Brooks, 1993; Gunther et al., 1998; Harris et al., 2000). Thus, context-dependent learning reflects the acquisition of behavior that takes the form of propositional logic: if context A, then behavior X; if context B, then behavior Y.

The implication of context-dependent learning for CET is clear: extinction-based effects of CET may poorly generalize to an individual's natural environment. An individual may indeed experience successively diminishing craving in response to substance cues in the clinical CET context, but not necessarily beyond that context. Equally, an individual may gain coping skills and greater self-efficacy as cue-elicited craving diminishes within-session, however, such benefits may be in vain if there is little diminution of cue-elicited craving outside of the therapeutic context. Indeed, following CET in its current format, patients may be unprepared for the magnitude of their craving in the real world.

PHARMACOLOGICAL TREATMENT OF CRAVING

The second principal approach to the treatment of alcohol and tobacco craving is the use of pharmacological interventions (Swift, 1999; George & O'Malley, 2004; O'Brien, 2005). On a conceptual level, such approaches may serve as highly useful adjuncts to the array of psychosocial interventions in a number of ways. In addition to the obvious advantage of putatively reducing the probability of lapses or relapse during treatment, attenuated craving via pharmacotherapy may also enhance engagement in treatment. Following treatment, reduced craving may also enhance patients' implementation of newly gained coping skills (e.g., Monti et al., 2002), or foster the natural development of alternative forms of reinforcement that are mutually exclusive from continued alcohol or tobacco use (e.g., Tucker, Vuchinich, & Rippens, 2002). Thus, both within-treatment and post-treatment use of pharmacological interventions to reduce craving may serve to enhance over-all treatment outcome. The most common pharmacological approach for craving for alcohol is naltrexone (ReVia©), whereas the most common approach for craving for nicotine is nicotine replacement therapy (NRT). In the case of craving for alcohol, naltrexone is a μ-opioid receptor antagonist and one of several pharmacological agents with evidence of efficacy in treating alcohol dependence. Although naltrexone's mechanism of action has not been definitively characterized, one of its putative mechanisms is that of reducing craving (Garbutt et al., 1999; O'Brien, 2005; Swift, 1999), based on both clinical and experimental data. A large number of methodologically rigorous clinical trials have favored naltrexone over placebo (for meta-analyses, see Feinn & Kranzler, 2005; Kranzler & Van Kirk, 2001), although across these trials, naltrexone has generally been demonstrated to reduce the number of drinking days and percentage of patients relapsing to heavy drinking rather than increase the overall probability of abstinence (Feinn & Kranzler, 2005; Kranzler & Van Kirk, 2001). Interestingly, a recently reported open-label trial of naltrexone has also shown positive effects with alcohol-dependent adolescents (Deas et al., 2005). Most importantly, however, clients receiving naltrexone have often reported significantly reduced craving for alcohol (e.g., Anton et al., 1999; Kiefer et al., 2003; Monti et al., 2001;[1] O'Malley et al., 1992; Petrakis et al., 2005; Volpicelli et al., 1992), hence the attribution that naltrexone may exert its therapeutic effects via attenuating craving for alcohol (Garbutt et al., 1999; O'Brien, 2005; Swift, 1999), particularly following lapses to drinking (O'Malley et al., 2002).

The second, more definitive, basis for the hypothesis that naltrexone reduces craving for alcohol comes from human laboratory studies. A number of studies

[1]Readers may find this study of particular interest because it was an integration of the CBT and pharmacological strategies for reducing craving for alcohol discussed in this chapter. Monti et al. (2001) used a 2 (NAL vs. placebo) × 2 (coping-based CET vs. education/relaxation control) design and found significant independent treatment effects for active treatment, most notably diminished craving for both active conditions, as well as increased coping-skills in the CET condition. Interestingly, however, no interaction effects were evident. Of note, if pharmacotherapy is combined with CET for the treatment of craving, timing of the treatment components is important as urges should be elicited in the context of CET so that coping skills can be taught in response to them. If a client is already taking a medication that reduces craving this can be problematic (see Monti et al., 2002 for further elaboration).

have examined the effects of acute and chronic doses of naltrexone on reactions to alcohol itself and to alcohol cues, finding an array of effects. In the case of alcohol administrations, a number of studies have found that naltrexone attenuates stimulation, potentiates sedation, and reduces craving following alcohol consumption (Davidson et al., 1999; King et al., 1997; McCaul et al., 2000; Swift et al., 1994). In a recent innovative study, O'Malley et al. (2002) examined the effects of naltrexone relative to placebo in an experimental paradigm that modeled a post-treatment lapse by using a priming dose of alcohol followed by a self-administration period with financial incentives for not drinking. In that study, during the self-administration period, participants who received naltrexone drank significantly less, did so significantly more slowly, and reported significantly lower levels of craving.

In terms of reactivity to alcohol cues, two studies have examined effects of naltrexone on cue-elicited craving, finding similarly positive effects. In an initial report, Monti et al. (1999) found that naltrexone reduced the probability that alcohol-dependent individuals would react at all in response to alcohol cues, although it did not reduce the magnitude of cue-elicited craving for those who did react relative to placebo. Subsequently, Rohsenow et al. (2000) found that acute naltrexone dosing resulted in diminished craving in response to alcohol cues and self-reported attention to the alcohol cues. Although not definitive, these studies support the notion that naltrexone attenuates cue-elicited craving.

It must be noted, however, that the data are not uniformly supportive of naltrexone's efficacy in the treatment of alcohol dependence or its attenuation of craving. A number of recent clinical trials have not favored naltrexone relative to placebo (e.g., Kranzler et al., 2000; Krystal et al., 2001; Oslin et al., 1999), and some trials revealing positive clinical effects of naltrexone have reported no effects on craving (e.g., Volpicelli et al., 1995, 1997). Equally, several laboratory studies have reported non-significant effects of naltrexone on craving relative to placebo (Davidson, Swift, & Fitz, 1996; Doty & deWit, 1995; Doty et al., 1997).

These mixed findings are further complicated by considerable heterogeneity in terms of methodologies of the laboratory studies, including variations in the naltrexone administration (chronic vs. acute), levels of alcohol administered, and samples used (social drinkers, heavy drinkers, or inpatient alcohol-dependent individuals). With respect to this last point, it is important to consider that different groups of individuals will differ on their motivation to use (and likely on their craving) depending upon factors such as whether or not they are trying to abstain, their access to alcohol (Wertz & Sayette, 2001), and the philosophy of the treatment program they may be involved with (Rohsenow, 2004), among other variables. Such factors are equally important to consider for the study of nicotine craving as well. Taken together, the current literature indicates that naltrexone cannot be characterized as categorically diminishing craving for alcohol, but provisionally appears to do so.

It is worthy of discussion that naltrexone is not the only pharmacological agent that has been suggested to attenuate craving for alcohol. Clinically, acamprosate (Campral®) has been shown to reduce relapse to drinking following detoxification (for a review, see Myrick et al., 2004) and has been touted as an "anticraving" agent based on evidence that it reduces motivation for alcohol in infrahuman models (e.g., Czachowski, Legg, & Samson, 2001; Kratzer & Schmidt, 1998; Olive et al., 2002) and reduces self-reported craving in some clinical reports (e.g., Chick et al., 2000; Weinstein et al., 2003). Pharmacologically, acamprosate is structurally similar to γ-aminobutyric acid (GABA), the principal inhibitory neurotransmitter, and appears to augment GABAergic activity and attenuate glutamatergic activity in the mesolimbic system (Cowen et al., 2005; Olive et al., 2002). However, acamprosate's effects on craving have been studied far less than naltrexone and, where comparisons have been made, the evidence supporting naltrexone's anticraving effects is greater than acamprosate (Boothby & Doering, 2005). In addition, the recent results of Project COMBINE (Anton et al., 2006), a large multi-site trial of combined pharmacotherapy and psychotherapy for alcohol dependence, indicated a significant effect on craving by naltrexone, but not acamprosate. This paralleled the clinical outcomes in the study, where naltrexone significantly improved outcome but acamprosate did not. Thus, although there continues to be a need for more definitive human laboratory research to examine acamprosate's anticraving potential, the available data are not strongly supportive.

In the case of reducing craving for tobacco, NRT is a well-established approach for treating dependence and its efficacy generally doubles that of placebo in both post-treatment and long-term outcomes (Anderson et al., 2002; Fiore, Jorenby, & Baker, 1997). The five most common forms of NRT are transdermal (i.e., patch), polacrilex gum, nasal spray, vapor inhaler, and lozenge, without substantially different clinical efficacy (George & O'Malley, 2004; Rigotti, 2002; West & Shiffman, 2001). In contrast to an antagonist pharmacotherapy approach that putatively reduces the desire to use a substance by antagonizing the underlying motivational systems (e.g., naltrexone), NRT uses an agonist approach, substituting the nicotine in tobacco with a different modality. The time-limited replacement of the nicotine that the smoker usually receives from tobacco reduces the nicotine withdrawal syndrome and the associated cravings (Rigotti, 2002; Goldstein, 2003). Over time, the steady-state level of nicotine provided by NRT is successively reduced, gradually reducing the individual's physical dependence on nicotine and eventually weaning the individual away from tobacco. During this period, NRT may concurrently foster behavioral changes, eroding automatized behavioral habits related to smoking and improving coping with high-risk situations.

In considering whether NRT effectively reduces craving for tobacco, it is important to return to a distinction we highlighted in the preceding chapter, that

recent research has revealed two dimensions to smokers' craving following cessation. Specifically, smokers report both generalized, or what could be described as
tonic, craving, and acute responses to situational variables (i.e., seeing other people
smoking, smoking paraphernalia, or experiencing affective distress), or phasic, craving (Shiffman et al., 1996, 1997). Against this backdrop, all forms of NRT have
demonstrated consistent efficacy in reducing tonic craving (Fiore et al., 1997; West
& Shiffman, 2001), but have mixed effectiveness with phasic craving.

In particular, although transdermal NRT is the most commonly used form
of NRT, it has not been demonstrated to be successful at addressing phasic craving. In a recent study, Tiffany, Cox, and Elash (2000) examined the effects of the
nicotine patch on abstinence-elicited (i.e., tonic) and cue-elicited (i.e., phasic)
craving in non-treatment seeking smokers, finding that the patch attenuated
tonic, but not phasic, craving. Subsequently, Waters et al. (2004) replicated and
extended this finding using treatment-seeking smokers and a more potent dose of
nicotine. In that study, transdermal NRT again decreased tonic craving, but had
no effect on phasic craving. Of particular interest, Waters et al. (2004) found that
cue-elicited craving predicted relapse among patients who received the patch.
Although previous studies have found cue-elicited changes in heart rate to predict treatment outcome (Abrams et al., 1988; Niaura et al., 1989a, 1989b), this
was the first study to demonstrate this association. Waters et al. (2004) speculate
that this differential relationship may be a result of NRT protecting smokers from
other sources of relapse and making cue-elicited craving a more important source
of vulnerability.

The inadequacy of transdermal NRT to address phasic changes in craving
may be a function of pharmacokinetics. Transdermal nicotine enters the body relatively slowly, reaching peak plasma concentrations in about four to six hours
(Jarvik & Schneider, 1992; Fant, Owen, & Henningfield, 1999), and its speed of
transmission cannot be acutely increased. In contrast, inhaled tobacco smoke
reaches peak plasma concentration in less than three minutes and can be substantially modulated by the individual's smoking topography (Rose et al., 1999). As
such, it is unsurprising that transdermal NRT is not sensitive to swift phasic
responses to environmental or affective changes.

Supporting this hypothesis, two recent studies suggest that forms of NRT
with swifter routes of administration appear to be effective in acutely tamping
down cravings. Shiffman et al. (2003) examined the effect of nicotine gum on
cue-elicited craving and found that gum did significantly reduce craving among
those who reacted to the tobacco cues with an elevated craving response. Similarly,
in a recent study examining acute responses to transdermal patch and nasal spray
following overnight smoking abstinence, Perkins et al. (2004) found that nicotine
nasal spray resulted in a significant decrease in craving for the positively reinforcing effects of nicotine after its second administration. Although this is clearly an
incipient research area, these studies are generally supportive of the notion that

fast-acting forms of NRT may effectively reduce phasic craving. This is important because these approaches may clinically fit into what has been termed a "rescue" approach (Fagerstrom, Schneider, & Lunell, 1993; Shiffman et al., 2003), in which the client is provided with an immediate means to reduce an intense craving when at risk for lapsing.

Taken together, the use of pharmacological interventions for treating craving for nicotine is better supported than for alcohol craving. All forms of NRT have established efficacy in reducing tonic craving following cessation and the data provisionally support pharmacokinetically swift forms (i.e., gum, nasal spray) as attenuating phasic craving. Significant limitations do remain however. Despite the promise of rescue interventions, such approaches using NRT may nonetheless be too late. In Shiffman et al. (2003), the length of time for differential diminution of craving was 15 min, leaving considerable time for the smoker to weather acute craving and resist smoking. In situations in which craving is high enough and tobacco is readily available, this may be too late. Effective approaches to prevent phasic cravings for nicotine, akin to the apparent diminution of phasic craving for alcohol by naltrexone (e.g., Monti et al., 1999; Rohsenow et al., 2000), do not exist at this point.

PRIORITIES FOR IMPROVING THE CONTEMPORARY TREATMENT OF CRAVING

In this section of the chapter, we discuss research priorities to enhance the existing treatments for craving, both psychosocial and pharmacological. A common emphasis will be leveraging the science base to realize these next steps. In addition, like the preceding chapter, we will underscore the need for transdisciplinary research that bridges genetic, biological, and behavioral science to treat craving, and will provide a framework for doing so.

PRIORITIES FOR IMPROVING CUE EXPOSURE TREATMENT

As pointed out earlier in the chapter and by other investigators as well (e.g., Conklin & Tiffany, 2002), there are multiple concerns with the generalizability of the existing in vivo exposure procedures used in CET. Such concerns have stimulated the development of imagery-based manipulations to elicit urges for both alcohol and nicotine. Virtual reality (VR) approaches have recently emerged and are receiving a great deal of attention in the experimental literature. VR has been broadly defined by Burdea and Coiffet (2003) as a "high-end user-computer interface that involves real-time simulation and interactions through multiple sensorial channels" (p. 3). These approaches have benefited from the anxiety and phobia literature where VR has already proven to enhance treatment (Wiederhold & Wiederhold, 2000, 2005).

VR offers a platform for cue exposure that has several advantages over other cue exposure paradigms. Specifically, VR enables a number of multi-modal systems to be engaged to elicit responding to a variety of stimuli simultaneously, much as is the case in the real world. It is thought to be a safe and flexible paradigm that is designed to maximally simulate real-life settings using visual, auditory, and olfactory stimuli. Importantly, its intensity can be varied and its relationship to risk for relapse more accurately gauged. Recent studies have used VR with adolescent (Woodruff et al., 2001) and adult (Bordnick et al., 2004) smokers, and it has been reported to be superior to static pictures in inducing tobacco cravings (Lee et al., 2003). Further, Kuntze et al. (2001) report the effective elicitation of physiological craving and urges through exposure to a rich VR of drug-related cues for outpatient heroin abusers.

In an innovative VR simulation study containing relevant smoking cues, Baumann and Sayette (2006) have successfully manipulated craving in nicotine-deprived addicted smokers who were not seeking treatment. This study used a computer monitor instead of more expensive head-mounted displays and demonstrated that simulations can be personalized such as by offering specific objects, brands, and tailored scenes that are related to an individual's smoking behavior. These procedures resulted in a quite robust effect that compares favorably to previously reported studies of smoking cue reactivity. An important advantage of Baumann and Sayette's approach is that by eliminating the more elaborate equipment, VR technology becomes less cumbersome and more affordable. Further, their inclusion of 3D simulations that allowed subjects to freely navigate the environments and interact, promoted opportunities for exploration and feedback between the participant and clinician about idiosyncratic stimuli that are perceived as triggers.

Thus, the technology employed in this study appears to be quite user-friendly for therapeutic application. As Baumann and Sayette (2006) conclude, because the vast majority of quit smokers who relapse use none of the coping skills they have mastered in treatment during their crisis (e.g., Brandon et al., 1990), VR could lead to advances by making it easier for clinicians to employ craving induction techniques. In addition, VR may be useful across treatment modalities. Baumann and Sayette (2006) note that "behavior therapists could use VR techniques to help smokers extinguish conditioned responses to drug cues. Alternatively, cognitive therapists might use VR-generated craving induction techniques to help patients manage their urges effectively and enhance self-efficacy so that they will maintain abstinence in future high-risk situations" (p. 5). Finally, rather than simply enhancing the provision of CET, VR technologies have the potential to reduce the context-dependency of extinction (i.e., the extent to which it is specific to the treatment setting). By using an array of cues, including potentially critical dimensions such as people, places, and situations that would be essentially impossible to replicate in the traditional form of CET, VR may permit more generalized extinction to alcohol or tobacco cues and skill at coping with urges beyond the treatment context. While VR research is in its infancy, applications in the area of tobacco craving have shown promise. It has the potential to address the principal criticisms of CET — that its modest treatment effects to date may be a function of inadequate generalization — as well as the potential to improve the ease of providing CET.

A second tack toward enhancing CET may come directly from basic research. Recent studies have revealed methods to suppress the context-dependency of extinction (Brooks & Bouton, 1993; Chelonis et al., 1999; Denniston, Chang, & Miller, 2003; Gunther et al., 1998), which may enhance the generalization of CET. Such methods include multiple context extinction (Gunther et al., 1998), massive extinction (Denniston et al., 2003), and the use of extinction cues (Brooks & Bouton, 1993), or specific stimuli that are paired with the extinction context and can be transferred to subsequent contexts. In each case, these approaches suggest relatively straightforward modifications to the parameters of CET that may substantially enhance its clinical efficacy.

Promisingly, recent innovative studies have ported the concepts of context-dependent learning into human laboratory research (Collins & Brandon, 2002; Conklin, 2006; MacKillop & Lisman, 2005; Havermans et al., 2005). For example, Collins and Brandon (2002) demonstrated that an extinction cue enhanced the generalizability of extinction to alcohol cues in heavy drinkers, suggesting that such an approach may be applicable to clinical implementations of CET. Although there is considerable research necessary to validly translate the basic scientific findings into the human domain and, in turn, into the clinical domain, we nonetheless regard this as a high priority for improving CET.

PRIORITIES FOR OPTIMIZING PHARMACOTHERAPY FOR CRAVING

There are a number of clear research priorities for improving the efficacy of pharmacotherapeutic treatment of craving, ranging from optimizing existing approaches to expanding the armory of agents available. In the previous section of this chapter we reviewed a study that combined naltrexone with CET to treat alcohol craving and consumption (Monti et al., 2001). While not many combined treatments have been tested in this regard, we feel there is much untapped potential in such strategies. Though more complex than stand-alone pharmacotherapy or cognitive-behavioral treatment, crossing combined approaches seems likely to facilitate the development of innovative clinical strategies and elucidation of mechanisms of action (McCaul & Monti, 2003). Indeed, examination of combined approaches using fully balanced designs would also facilitate tests of expectancy effects – that is, the pharmacotherapy placebo effects. Moreover, given the presumption that pharmacological treatments would be used adjunctively with psychosocial interventions, specific testing of combinations of pharmacological and psychosocial approaches is a clear priority. This was the premise of the recent Project COMBINE (Anton et al., 2006), which examined the potential of combining naltrexone and acamprosate with two levels of psychosocial intervention, which revealed a number of promising findings, athough no clear combinatorial effects. Nonetheless, we believe further investigation of pharmacotherapy–psychotherapy combinations is warranted.

A second potential avenue for enhancing the use of naltrexone relates to compliance and variability in drug levels over time. While compliance to daily oral medical regimens is a general problem throughout medicine (McLellan et al., 2000), additional challenges among alcohol treatment clients include client motivation and impaired cognitive function (Rinn et al., 2002). Poor compliance has been problematic in the oral naltrexone treatment literature in both our work (e.g., Monti et al., 2001), as well as in that of others (e.g., Volpicelli et al., 1997; Chick et al., 2000). In addition, oral naltrexone dosing results in somewhat variable levels of plasma naltrexone, which may influence its effects clinically and the applicability of more standardized laboratory studies. Therefore, enhanced compliance and stability of administration are important priorities for improving the pharmacotherapy of alcohol craving.

To address these issues, several clinical investigators (e.g., Garbutt et al., 2005; Kranzler et al., 2004; Johnson et al., 2004) have studied the efficacy and tolerability of long-acting injectable naltrexone for alcohol dependence, which has recently been made available for clinical use. This long-acting formulation has potential to eliminate the issue of daily medication compliance, requiring clients to take the drug only monthly, and it effectively eliminates daily variability in plasma naltrexone levels. Further, a steady blood level of naltrexone would enable more careful study of the hypothesis that oral naltrexone may reduce the desirable effects of alcohol and actually motivate an individual to discontinue medication in preparation for a return to drinking. Alternatively, recent studies have attempted to use targeted naltrexone, or acute dosing in preparation for high-risk situations, and have found positive effects relative to daily dosing and placebo (Hernandez-Avila et al., 2006; Kranzler et al., 2003, 2004). Clearly there are a number of different potential dosing strategies for optimizing naltrexone pharmacotherapy and these may plausibly vary in utility by individual.

Interestingly, differences in administration of nicotine replacement for smoking research raise somewhat similar issues. To be sure, transdermal nicotine offers a much steadier dose of nicotine than other methods such as nicotine gum and nasal spray. However, as pointed out earlier, pharmacokinetically swifter methods may be more effective in attenuating phasic craving responses. The promise of experimenting with different methods of nicotine delivery, and calibrating the appropriate amounts and modalities of nicotine to address both tonic and phasic craving appears to be the next step in enhancing NRT.

For the pharmacological treatment of both alcohol and tobacco craving, there is also considerable promise in novel agents beyond those discussed. For example, the anticonvulsant topiramate (Topamax©) has recently been demonstrated to be efficacious in treating alcohol dependence (Johnson et al., 2003; Rubio et al., 2004) and may exert its effect via attenuation of craving (Johnson et al., 2003; Rubio et al., 2004). Indeed, in our recent work, we found that topiramate notably blunted increases in craving following an alcohol challenge relative to placebo (Miranda et al., 2005). Similarly, the dopamine D_2/D_4 receptor antagonist olanzapine has been found to attenuate cue- and priming-elicited craving for alcohol (Hutchison et al., 2001). Moreover, Hutchison et al. (2004) found that olanzapine attenuated cue-elicited craving in smokers, suggesting it has promise to potentially augment NRT in addressing phasic craving.

Finally, pharmacotherapy for craving among adolescent substance users and abusers is in its infancy for both alcohol and tobacco. While these areas are particularly complex due to pharmacokinetics and developmental issues (e.g., Monti et al., 2005), recent preliminary studies have been promising (Deas et al., 2005; Moolchan et al., 2005) and pharmacotherapy to address craving among alcohol and tobacco dependent youth is clearly a direction for future research. In sum, we believe that optimizing pharmacotherapy for craving will come from both improving the understanding and praxis of current approaches, and identifying novel compounds of potentially even greater efficacy for both adults and adolescents.

FUTURE DIRECTIONS IN THE TREATMENT OF CRAVING

The second section of this chapter focused on ways to improve contemporary science-based approaches to treating craving, which can optimistically be described as being promising at the present time with moderate effects. However, for substantial progress to be made, more than just refinement of the current treatments may be necessary. Therefore, in this final section, we review two future directions in the treatment of craving. First, we discuss an innovative new perspective to the phenomenon of craving and its treatment, the EI model of craving (Kavanagh et al., 2005). Although there is little in the way of data from controlled clinical trials from treatments based on this approach, we feel it nonetheless represents a promising departure from the conventional perspectives on craving and may make important clinical contributions. Second, we return to a theme of the preceding chapter, the need for coordinated transdisciplinary research. Such an approach may permit greater understanding of the pharmaco-genetics of alcohol and tobacco dependence, permitting identification of those individuals who are more prone to experience intense craving, clarification of the biological basis for these differences, and, as a result, determination of which treatments – pharmacological or psychosocial – are best suited for that individual.

THE ELABORATED INTRUSION THEORY AND ITS CLINICAL IMPLICATIONS

A complex cognitive formulation of craving has recently been introduced by Kavanagh et al. (2005) and seeks to explain craving for psychoactive substances as well as for other motivational targets. In its distilled form, the elaborated intrusion (EI) theory of desire distinguishes between the initial *associative processes* that prompt intrusive thoughts about an appetitive target (e.g., alcohol), such as situational variables (e.g., cues, affective states), and those controlled *cognitive elaboration processes* that follow and tend to have stronger affective links. The associative processes are thought to underlie apparently spontaneous thoughts about a target that are likely to arise while one is attending to another task, whereas the elaboration processes involve controlled processes of searching for target-relevant information and retaining it in working memory. Importantly, the elaborative search is proposed to be both internal (thereby increasing the salience of episodic memories and target-related thoughts such as expectancies) and external (thereby increasing the salience of situational cues) (Kavanagh et al., 2005). As an illustration, consider the drinker who, while reading a magazine, notices an advertisement for an alcoholic beverage and thinks "I'd really like a drink." He/she next may then imagine having a drink, how good it tastes, with whom he/she might be drinking with, memories of those "drinking buddies," and other pleasant memories of the positive effects of drinking, etc. Thus, following the initial associative cues that pique the individual's attention and desire, elaborative processes reverberate cognitively and amplify the urge via memorial connections to previous positive experiences.

This formulation is grounded in the basic research that demonstrates that imagery plays a significant role in the expression of craving (e.g., Westerberg, 2000; May et al., 2004) and evidence that cognitive elaboration, resulting from directed search and retention of target-related information, shows interference between desire-related ruminations and concurrent cognitive tasks (Harvey, Kemps, & Tiggemann, 2005; Panabokke et al., 2004). The EI theory's focus on the role of imagery is also consistent with a range of studies including evidence on the efficacy of imagery in eliciting desire and studies of self-reported appetitive imagery during craving states (Erblich & Bovbjerg, 2004; Maude-Griffin & Tiffany, 1996; Payne et al., 1992). Further, the generalizability of the theory is supported by various sources including the fact the experience of desire is qualitatively similar across targets (e.g., food, soft drinks, alcohol, and tobacco; May et al., 2004) and that the corticomesolimbic dopamine pathway seems to be a central neurobiological substrate that is common to both evolutionarily significant rewards (i.e., food, sex) and substance-related rewards (Kelley & Berridge, 2002; Wise, 1988). Thus, the EI theory has been useful in integrating the wide body of evidence on drug craving and, perhaps more importantly, placing it in the larger context of human cognitive–emotional mechanisms of motivation and desire.

Kavanagh et al. (2005) propose that a number of aspects of EI theory can increase the effectiveness of existing psychological treatment for control of craving and its effects. For example, for dysfunctional coping, in vivo demonstration of the ineffectiveness of thought suppression and the promotion of acceptance may be a useful clinical technique. Similarly, based on evidence that tasks that interfere with imagery similarly interfere with craving (Panabokke et al., 2004), Kavanagh et al. suggest that once acceptance has been accomplished, the client should apply competing imagery on other tasks with high working memory load to impede elaboration and thereby enhance functional coping. Unfortunately, Pannabokke et al. fail to discuss the potentially important role motivation to quit smoking might play in their results, simply reporting that approximately half of the participants were trying to "cut down." It seems that greater specificity regarding participants' motivation for changing substance misuse can only further help clarify the important role of mechanisms of action for this line of work, as was emphasized earlier in this chapter. Indeed, for the translation of such theoretical work to the clinical arena this will be essential.

THE TRANSDISCIPLINARY STUDY OF CRAVING: CONNECTING THE DOTS

Although the preceding research priorities for existing treatments and theoretical advances hold great promise, our final point is that the most significant progress to be made in the treatment of craving will come from substantive transdisciplinary efforts. Given that craving appears to vary considerably across individuals and is substantially influenced by genetic variables, it seems myopic to not attempt to connect contemporary research on the genetics of craving to the treatment of craving. Toward more integrative future research, we provide a transdisciplinary framework in Table 2. This approach recognizes the importance of microcosmic questions, such as the functional neurobiological expression of an allele associated with craving, or the relationship between the behavioral expression of craving and treatment response; however, more importantly, it emphasizes the connections *across* levels of analysis for comprehensively understanding the phenomenon of craving and its treatment.

Table 2

A Transdisciplinary Framework for Advancing the Basic Science and Clinical Treatment of Craving

Behavioral genetics →	Neurobiological substrates →	Observable behaviors →	Clinical approaches
Candidate polymorphisms	*Candidate phenotypes*	*Candidate endophenotypes*	*Candidate treatments*
DRD4 VNTR (dopamine D_4 receptor)	Postsynaptic receptor density	Degree/pattern of craving	Cue exposure treatment (e.g., extinction-based/coping-based)
	Postsynaptic receptor function	Effects of craving	
DRD2 *TaqI* A (dopamine D_2 receptor)	Intracellular response	Sensitivity to positive/negative reinforcement	Cognitive therapy (e.g., intrusion-based)
DAT (SLC6A3) (dopamine transporter)	Intranuclear gene expression	Sensitivity to punishment	Agonist pharmacotherapy (e.g., nicotine replacement)
OPRM1 (opioid μ-receptor)	Sensitivity to structural/functional neuroadaptation	Preference for immediate reward	Antagonist pharmacotherapy (e.g., naltrexone)

Notes: Genetic polymorphisms are predicted to translate into functional differences in the neurobiological substrates of craving, which in turn affect the behavioral expression of craving, and result in differential treatment effects. At each level of analysis, candidates are provided based on the current empirical literature, however, these lists are only intended to be illustrative, not exhaustive. Similarly, adjacent terms by column are not necessarily connected.

This approach could be highly useful for individuals with a greater genetic loading, determining potential genotype-by-treatment interactions or indicating the need for more intensive intervention in a stepped-care approach (Monti et al., 2003; Sobell & Sobell, 2000). Equally, however, such an approach would be reciprocally relevant for those who may have relatively little genetic loading, or report relatively little craving (e.g., Krahn et al., 2005). As we have reviewed, the current "one-size fits all" approach is at-best moderately successful, therefore, we argue that the most profitable path ahead is by more fully connecting basic science with clinical science. By systematically doing so, progress can be made in determining not only what treatments are effective, but which treatment is best suited for a given individual.

As illustrative examples, several recent empirical studies have examined the intersection of genetics, craving, and pharmacotherapy effects in well-controlled studies. In the first case, given that members of our extended group (e.g., Hutchinson et al., 2002a, 2002b) have demonstrated that craving is substantially influenced by genetic variables and that naltrexone's effects on drinking outcomes are greater in alcoholics with a family history of alcoholism (e.g., King et al., 1997; Monterosso et al., 2001; Rohsenow et al., submitted; Rubio et al., 2005), we examined the possibility that genetic factors may play a role in variables relevant to relapse in a recent study (McGeary, Monti et al., 2006). Specifically, we examined whether a functional polymorphism within the μ-opioid receptor gene (OPRM1) might influence naltrexone's effects in a sample of 90 heavy drinkers. In this case, participants with the OPRM1 variant associated with greater opioid binding affinity actually exhibited greater cue-elicited craving for alcohol when taking naltrexone relative to placebo. Although the exact relationships between OPRM1 genotype, craving, and naltrexone effects remain far from fully characterized, the data nonetheless suggest important interrelationships between genetic polymorphisms, craving, and pharmacotherapy response.

In a similar vein, Hutchison et al. (2003) examined the effects of olanzapine, a dopamine antagonist, and DRD4 VNTR genotype on craving for alcohol in a laboratory protocol using heavy drinkers. Although studied considerably less than naltrexone, olanzapine has indicated some preliminary promise as an anti-craving agent (e.g., Hutchison et al., 2001), and, in this case, olanzapine reduced craving under neutral conditions for all participants, but selectively attenuated cue-elicited and priming-elicited craving for alcohol in individuals with at least one long DRD4 VNTR allele (Hutchison et al., 2003). Most interestingly, in a recent randomized clinical trial, Hutchison et al. (in press) found that olanzapine differentially attenuated cue-elicited craving for alcohol and improved treatment outcome relative to placebo, but in both cases these effects were only evident in individuals with at least one long DRD4 VNTR variant. These findings complement those from earlier studies that found pharmacotherapy-by-genotype interactions between the DRD2 *TaqIA* polymorphism and pharmacological treatments for alcohol dependence (Lawford et al., 1995) and opiate dependence (Lawford et al., 2000), although those studies did not examine craving.

Akin to these findings in alcohol research, a small number of studies in the area of tobacco dependence have reported similar findings. Several studies have found pharmacogenetic interactions in the treatment of nicotine dependence (Berrettini & Lerman, 2005), and a recent study by Lerman et al. (2003) reported a potential three-way gene-by-craving-by-treatment interaction. Although this is an incipient research area and the mechanistic relationships between the genetic factors, expression of craving, and pharmacotherapy effects require further elucidation, across all of these studies, the results demonstrate the potential for important "downstream" influences of genetics not only for craving, but also for treatment response. Finally, it should be noted that although heretofore unstudied, it is equally possible that gene-by-craving-by-treatment interactions may exist for psychosocial interventions. This is clearly a domain worthy of future study.

SUMMARY AND CONCLUSIONS

In this chapter, we critically reviewed the existing clinical approaches to craving for alcohol and tobacco, concluding that both the cognitive-behavioral and pharmacological approaches are promising, but remain only moderately effective. Toward enhancing treatment for craving, we suggested several avenues for future development, commonly emphasizing the application of scientific advances. In the case of psychotherapeutic approaches, we underscored the importance of contextual factors, and recommend leveraging new technologies and methods from basic behavioral research to enhance treatment effects. For pharmacological approaches, the need for more clearly understanding and optimizing current approaches is evident, as is the need for novel pharmacotherapies. In addition, we believe that the existing treatments will also be complemented by new clinical approaches, such as those derived from the EI model of craving (Kavanagh, Andrade, & May, 2004).

Most significantly, as we and others have argued elsewhere (e.g., Abrams & Clayton, 2001; Monti et al., 2000, 2003, 2004), if our goal is improvement in the efficacy and effectiveness of our treatments, the scientific and clinical enterprises must become fully transdisciplinary. This includes not only progress via scientific collaboration, but also an ongoing conversation between scientists and clinicians. Such dialogues are critical to gain further insight into the complex clinical phenomenon of craving and to disseminate the best treatments available. Although this will not be an easy path, connecting the dots across multiple levels of analysis is a necessary next step, an inescapable conclusion of our work, as well as that of others synthesized in this chapter. Only a transdisciplinary approach will enable us to develop both a fully integrated science of craving and maximally efficacious treatments.

REFERENCES

Abrams, D. B., Monti, P. M., Carey, K. B., Pinto, R. P., & Jacobus, S. I. (1988). Reactivity to smoking cues and relapse: Two studies of discriminant validity. *Behaviour Research and Therapy, 26*, 225–233.

Anderson, J. E., Jorenby, D. E., Scott, W. J., & Fiore, M. C. (2002). Treating tobacco use and dependence: Am evidence-based clinical practice guideline for tobacco. *Chest, 121*, 932–941.

Anton, R., Moak, D., & Latham, P. (1995). The Obsessive-Compulsive Drinking Scale: A self-rated instrument for the quantification of thoughts about alcohol and drinking behavior. *Alcoholism: Clinical and Experimental Research, 19*, 92–99.

Anton, R. F., Moak, D. H., Waid, L. R., Latham, P. K., Malcolm, R. J., & Dias, J. K. (1999). Naltrexone and cognitive behavioral therapy for the treatment of outpatient alcoholics: Results of a placebo-controlled trial. *American Journal of Psychiatry*, Nov, *156*(11), 1758–1764.

Anton, R. F., O'Malley, S. S., Ciraulo, D. A., Cisler, R. A., Couper, D., Donovan, D. M., Gastfriend, D. R., Hosking, J. D., Johnson, B. A., LoCastro, J. S., Longabaugh, R., Mason, B. J., Mattson, M. E., Miller, W. R., Pettinati, H. M., Randall, C. L., Swift, R., Weiss, R. D., Williams, L. D., & Zweben, A. (2006). Combined pharmacotherapies and behavioral interventions for alcohol dependence: The COMBINE study: A randomized controlled trial. *Journal of the American Medical Association, 295*, 17.

Baumann, S. B., & Sayette, M. A. (2006). Smoking cues in a virtual world provoke craving in cigarette smokers. *Psychology of Addictive Behaviors, 20*, 1–6.

Berrettini, W. H., & Lerman, C. E. (2005). Pharmacotherapy and pharmacogenetics of nicotine dependence. *American Journal of Psychiatry, 162*, 1441–1451.

Boothby, L. A., & Doering, P. L. (2005). Acamprosate for the treatment of alcohol dependence. *Clinical Therapeutics, 27*, 695–714.

Bordnick, P. S., Graap, K. M., Copp, H., Brooks, J., Ferrer, M., & Logue, B. (2004). Utilizing virtual reality to standardize nicotine craving research: A pilot study. *Addictive Behaviors, 29*, 1889–1894.

Bouton, M. E., & Bolles, R. C. (1979). Contextual control of extinction of conditioned fear. *Learning and Motivation, 10*, 445–466.

Bouton, M. E., & Brooks, D. C. (1993). Time and context effects on performance in Pavlovian discrimination reversal. *Journal of Experimental Psychology: Animal Behavior Processes, 19*, 165–179.

Bouton, M. E., & Swartzenruber, D. (1989). Slow reacquisition following extinction: Context, retrieval, and encoding mechanisms. *Journal of Experimental Psychology: Animal Behavior Processes, 15*, 43–53.

Brandon, T. H., Tiffany, S. T., Obremski, K. M., & Baker, T. B. (1990). Post cessation cigarette use: The process of relapse. *Addictive Behaviors, 15*, 105–114.

Brooks, D. C., & Bouton, M. E. (1993). A retrieval cue for extinction attenuates response recovery (renewal) caused by a return to the conditioning context. *Journal of Experimental Psychology: Animal Behavior Processes, 20*, 366–379.

Burdea, G. C., & Coiffet, P. (Eds.). (2003). *Virtual Reality Technology* (2nd ed.). Hoboken, NJ: Wiley Interscience.

Chelonis, J. J., Calton, J. L., Hart, J. A., & Schachtman, T. R. (1999). Attenuation of the renewal effect by extinction in multiple contexts. *Learning and Motivation, 30*, 1–14.

Chick, J., Anton, R., Checinski, K., Croop, R., Drummond, D. C., Farmer, R., Labriola, D., Marshall, J., Moncrieff, J., Morgan, M. Y., Peters, T., & Ritson, B. (2000). A multicentre, randomized, double-blind, placebo-controlled trial of naltrexone in the treatment of alcohol dependence or abuse. *Alcohol and Alcoholism, 35*(6), 587–593.

Collins, B. N., & Brandon, T. H. (2002). Effects of extinction context and retrieval cues on reactivity among nonalcoholic drinkers. *Journal of Consulting and Clinical Psychology, 70*, 390–397.

Conklin, C. A. (2006). Environments as cues to smoke: Implications for human extinction-based research and treatment. *Experimental and Clinical Psychopharmacology, 14*(1), 12–19.

Conklin, C. A., & Tiffany, S. T. (2002). Applying extinction research and theory to cue-exposure addiction treatment. *Addiction, 97,* 155–167.

Corty, E., & McFall, R. M. (1984). Response prevention in the treatment of cigarette smoking. *Addictive Behaviors, 9*(4), 405–408.

Cowen, M. S., Adams, C., Kraehenbuehl, T., Vengeliene, V., & Lawrence, A. J. (2005). The acute anti-craving effect of acamprosate in alcohol-preferring rats is associated with modulation of the mesolimbic dopamine system. *Addiction Biology, 10,* 233–242.

Czachowski, C. L., Legg, B. H., & Samson, H. H. (2001). Effects of acamprosate on ethanol-seeking and self-administration in the rat. *Alcoholism: Clinical and Experimental Research, 25,* 344–350.

Davidson, D., Palfai, T., Bird, C., & Swift, R. (1999). Effects of naltrexone on alcohol and self-administration in heavy drinkers. *Alcoholism: Clinical and Experimental Research, 23,* 195–203.

Davidson, D., Swift, R., & Fitz, E. (1996). Naltrexone increases the latency to drink alcohol in social drinkers. *Alcoholism: Clinical and Experimental Research, 20,* 732–739.

Dawe, S., Powell, J. H., Richards, D., Gossop, M., Strang, J., & Gray, J. A. (1993). Does post-withdrawal cue exposure improve outcome in opiate addiction? A controlled trial. *Addiction, 88,* 1233–1245.

Dawe, S., Rees, V. W., Mattick, R., & Sitharthan, T. (2002). Efficacy of moderation-oriented cue exposure for problem drinkers: A randomized controlled trial. *Journal of Consulting and Clinical Psychology, 70,* 1045–1050.

Deas, D., May, K., Randall, C., Johnson, N., & Anton, R. (2005). Naltrexone treatment of adolescent alcoholics: An open-label pilot study. *Journal of Child and Adolescent Psychopharmacology, 15,* 723–728.

Denniston, J. C., Chang, R., & Miller, R. R. (2003). Massive extinction treatment attenuates the renewal effect. *Learning and Motivation, 34,* 68–86.

Doty, P., & de-Wit, H. (1995). Effects of naltrexone pretreatment on the subjective and performance effects of ethanol in social drinkers. *Behavioural Pharmacology, 6,* 386–394.

Doty, P., Kirk, J. M., Cramblett, M. J., & de-Wit, H. (1997). Behavioral responses to ethanol in light and moderate social drinkers following naltrexone pretreatment. *Drug and Alcohol Dependence, 47,* 109–116.

Drummond, D. C. (2002). Is cue exposure cure exposure? *Addiction, 97,* 357–359.

Drummond, D. C., Cooper, T., & Glautier, S. P. (1990). Conditioned learning in alcohol dependence: Implications for cue exposure treatment. *British Journal of Addiction, 85,* 725–743.

Drummond, D. C., & Glautier, S. T. (1994). A controlled trial of cue exposure treatment in alcohol dependence. *Journal of Consulting and Clinical Psychology, 62,* 809–817.

Erblich, J., & Bovbjerg, D. H. (2004). In vivo versus imaginal smoking cue exposures: Is seeing believing? *Experimental and Clinical Psychopharmacology, 12,* 208–215.

Fant, R. V., Owen, L. L., & Henningfield, J. E. (1999). Nicotine replacement therapy. *Primary Care, 26,* 633–652.

Fagerstrom, K., Schneider, N., & Lunell, E. (1993). Effectiveness of nicotine patch and nicotine gum as individual versus combined treatments for tobacco withdrawal symptoms. *Psychopharmacology, 111,* 271–277.

Feinn, R., & Kranzler, H. R. (2005). Does effect size in naltrexone trials for alcohol dependence differ for single-site vs. multi-center studies? *Alcoholism: Clinical and Experimental Research, 29,* 983–988.

Fiore, M. C., Jorenby, D. E., & Baker, T. B. (1997). Smoking cessation: Principles and practice based upon the AHCPR guideline, Agency for Health Care Policy and Research. *Annals of Behavioral Medicine, 19,* 213–219.

Foa, E. B., & Kozak, M. J. (1986). Emotional processing of fear: Exposure to corrective information. *Psychological Bulletin, 99*(1), 20–35.

Garbutt, J. C., Kranzler, H. R., O'Malley, S. S., Gastfriend, D. R., Pettinati, H. M., Silverman, B. L., Loewy, J. W., & Ehrich, E. E., for the Vivitrex Study Group. (2005). Efficacy and tolerability of long-acting injectable naltrexone for alcohol dependence: A randomized controlled trial. *The Journal of the American Medical Association, 293*(13), 1617–1625.

Garbutt, J. C., West, S. L., Carey, T. S., Lohr, K. N., & Crews, F. T. (1999). Pharmacological treatment of alcohol dependence: A review of the evidence. *Journal of the American Medical Association*, *281*(14), 1318–1325.

George, T. P., & O'Malley, S. S. (2004). Current pharmacological treatments for nicotine dependence. *Trends in Pharmacological Sciences*, *25*(1), 42–48.

Goldstein, M. G. (2003). Pharmacotherapy for smoking cessation. In D. B. Abrams, R. Niaura, R. A. Brown, K. M. Emmons, M. G. Goldstein, & P. M. Monti (Eds.), *The Tobacco Dependence Treatment Handbook: A Guide to best practices* (pp. 230–249). New York: Guilford Press.

Gunther, L. M., Denniston, J. C., & Miller, R. R. (1998). Conducting exposure treatment in multiple contexts can prevent relapse. *Behavior Research and Therapy*, *36*, 75–91.

Harris, J. A., Jones, M. L., Bailey, G. K., & Westbrook, G. F. (2000). Contextual control over conditioned responding in an extinction paradigm. *Journal of Experimental Psychology: Animal Behavioral Processes*, *26*, 174–185.

Harvey, K., Kemps, E., & Tiggemann, M. (2005). The nature of imagery processes underlying food cravings. *British Journal of Health Psychology*, *10*(1), 49–56.

Havermans, R. C., Keuker, J., Lataster, T., & Jansen, A. (2005). Contextual control of extinguished conditioned performance in humans. *Learning and Motivation*, *36*(1), 1–19.

Heather, N., Brodie, J., Wale, S., Wilkinson, G., Luce, A., Webb, E., & McCarthy, S. (2000). A randomized controlled trial of moderation-oriented cue exposure. *Journal of Studies on Alcohol*, *61*(4), 561–570.

Hernandez-Avila, C. A., Song, C., Kuo, L., Tennen, H., Armeli, S., Kranzler, H. R. Targeted versus daily naltrexone: Secondary analysis of effects on average daily drinking. *Alcoholism: Clinical and Experimental Research*, *30*, 860–865.

Hutchison, K. E., LaChance, H., Niaura, R., Bryan, A., & Smolen, A. (2002a). The DRD4 VNTR polymorphism influences reactivity to smoking cues. *Journal of Abnormal Psychology*, 2002, 134–143.

Hutchison, K. E., McGeary, J. E., Smolen, A., Swift, R. M., & Bryan, A. (2002b). The DRD4 VNTR polymorphism moderates craving after alcohol consumption. *Health Psychology*, *21*, 139–146.

Hutchison, K. E., Ray, L., Sandman, E., Rutter, M. C., Peters, A., Davidson, D., & Swift, R. (in press). The effect of olanzapine on craving and alcohol consumption. *Neuropsychopharmacology*, *31*, 1310–1317.

Hutchison, K. E., Rutter, M. C., Niaura, R., Swift, R. M., Pickworth, W. B., & Sobik, L. (2004). Olanzapine attenuates cue-elicited craving for tobacco. *Psychopharmacology*, *175*, 407–413.

Hutchison, K. E., Swift, R. M., Rohsenow, D. J., Monti, P. M., Davidson, D., & Almeida, A. (2001). Olanzapine reduces urge to drink after drinking cues and a priming dose of alcohol. *Psychopharmacology*, *155*, 27–34.

Hutchison, K. E., Wooden, A., Swift, R. M., Smolen, A., McGeary, J., Adler, L., & Paris, L. (2003). Olanzapine reduces craving for alcohol: A DRD4 VNTR polymorphism by pharmacotherapy interaction. *Neuropsychopharmacology*, Oct, (10), 882–888.

Jarvik, M., & Schneider, N. (1992). Nicotine. In J. Lowinson, P. Ruiz, & R. Millman (Eds.), *Substance Abuse: A Comprehensive Textbook* (pp. 334–356). Baltimore, MD: Lippincott Williams & Wilkins.

Johnson, B. A., Ait-Daoud, N., Aubin, H. J., van den Brink, W., Guzzetta, R., Loewy, J., Silverman, B., & Ehrich, E. (2004). A pilot evaluation of the safety and tolerability of repeat dose administration of long-acting injectable naltrexone (vivitrex) in patients with alcohol dependence. *Alcoholism: Clinical and Experimental Research*, *28*(9), 1356–1361.

Johnson, B. A., Ait-Daoud, N., Bowden, C. L., DiClemente, C. R., Roache, J. D., Lawson, K., Javors, M. A., & Ma, J. A. (2003). Oral topiramate for treatment of alcohol dependence: A randomized controlled trial. *Lancet*, *361*, 1677–1685.

Kavanagh, D. J., Andrade, J., & May, J. (2004). Beating the urge: Implications of research into substance-related desires. *Addictive Behaviors*, *29*, 1359–1372.

Kavanagh, D. J., Andrade, J., & May, J. (2005). Imaginary relish and exquisite torture: The elaborated intrusion theory of desire. *Psychological Review, 112*(2), 446–467.

Kavanagh, D. J., Sitharthan, G., Young, R. M., Sitharthan, T., Saunders, J. B., Shockley, N., & Giannopoulos, V. (2006). Addition of cue exposure to cognitive-behaviour therapy for alcohol misuse: A randomized trial with dysphoric drinkers. *Addiction,* Aug, *101*(8), 1106–1116.

Kelley, A. E., & Berridge, K. C. (2002). The neuroscience of natural rewards: Relevance to addictive drugs. *Journal of Neuroscience, 22,* 3306–3311.

Kiefer, F., Jahn, H., Tarnaske, T., Helwig, H., Briken, P., Holzback, R., et al. (2003). Comparing and combing naltrexone and acamprosate in relapse prevention of alcoholism: A double-blind, placebo-controlled study. *Archives of General Psychiatry, 60*(1), 92–99.

King, A. C., Volpicelli, J. R., Frazer, A., & O'Brien, C. P. (1997). Effect of naltrexone on subjective alcohol response in subjects at high and low risk for future alcohol dependence. *Psychopharmacology, 129,* 15–22.

Krahn, D. D., Bohn, M. J., Henk, H. J., Grossman, J. L., & Gosnell, B. (2005). Patterns of urges during early abstinence in alcohol-dependent subjects. *American Journal on Addictions, 14,* 248–255.

Kranzler, H. R., & VanKirk, J. (2001). Efficacy of naltrexone and acamprosate for alcoholism treatment: A meta-analysis. *Alcoholism: Clinical and Experimental Research, 25*(9), 1335–1341.

Kranzler, H. R., Wesson, D. R., & Billot, L. (2004). Naltexone depot for treatment of alcohol dependence: A mulitcenter, randomized, placebo-controlled clinical trial. *Alcoholism: Clinical and Experimental Research, 28,* 1051–1059.

Kranzler, H. R., Armeli, S., Feinn, R., & Tennen, H. (2004). Targeted naltrexone treatment moderates the relations between mood and drinking behavior among problem drinkers. *Journal of Consulting and Clinical Psychology, 72,* 317–327.

Kranzler, H. R., Armeli, S., Tennen, H., Blomqvist, O., Oncken, C., Petry, N., Feinn, R. (2003). Targeted naltrexone for early problem drinkers. *Journal of Clinical Psychopharmacology, 23,* 294–304.

Kratzer, U., & Schmidt, W. J. (1998). The anti-craving drug acamprosate inhibits the conditioned place aversion induced by naloxone-precipitated morphine withdrawal in rats. *Neuroscience Letters, 252,* 53–56.

Krystal, J. H., Cramer, J. A., Krol, W. F., Kirk, G. F., & Rosenheck, R. A. (2001). Naltrexone in the treatment of alcohol dependence. *New England Journal of Medicine, 345*(24), 1734–1739.

Kuntze, M. F., Stoermer, R., Mager, R., Roessler, A., Mueller, S. F., & Bullinger, A. H. (2001). Immersive virtual environments in cue exposure. *CyberPsychology and Behavior, 4*(4), 497–501.

Lawford, B. R., Young, R. M., Noble, E. P., Sargent, J., Rowell, J., Shadforth, S., Zhang, X., Ritchie, T. (2000). The D$_2$ dopamine receptor A(1) allele and opioid dependence: Association with heroin use and response to methadone treatment. *American Journal of Medical Genetics, 96,* 592–598.

Lawford, B. R., Young, R. M., Rowell, J. A., Qualichefski, J., Fletcher, B. H., Syndulko, K., Ritchie, T., & Noble, E. P. (1995). Bromocriptine in the treatment of alcoholics with the D$_2$ dopamine receptor A1 allele. *Nature Medicine, 1,* 337–341.

Lee, J., Lim, Y., Graham, S. J., Kim, G., Wiederhold, B. K., Wiederhold, M. D., Kim, I. Y., & Kim, S. I. (2004). Nicotine craving and cue exposure therapy by using virtual environments. *CyberPsychology and Behavior, 7,* 705–713.

Lerman, C., Shields, P. G., Wileyto, E. P., Audrain, J., Hawk, L. H., Jr., Pinto, A., Kucharski, S., Krishnan, S., Niaura, R., & Epstein, L. H. (2003). Effects of dopamine transporter and receptor polymorphisms on smoking cessation in a bupropion clinical trial. *Health Psychology, 22,* 541–548.

Lowe, M. R., Green, L., Kurtz, M. S., Ashenberg, Z. S., & Fisher, E. B., Jr. (1980). Self-initiated, cue extinction and covert sensitization procedures in smoking cessation. *Journal of Behavioral Medicine, 3,* 357–372.

MacKillop, J., & Lisman, S. A. (2005). Improving generalizability of extinction to alcohol cues via exposure in multiple contexts. *Alcoholism: Clinical and Experimental Research, 29*(Suppl.), 152A.

Marlatt, G. A. (1990). Cue exposure and relapse prevention in the treatment of addictive behaviors. *Addictive Behaviors, 15*(4), 395–399.

Marlatt, G. A., & Gordon, J. R. (1985). *Relapse Prevention: Maintenance Strategies in the Treatment of Addictive Behaviors.* New York: Guilford.

Maude-Griffin, P., & Tiffany, S. T. (1996). Production of smoking urges through imagery: The impact of affect and smoking abstinence. *Experimental and Clinical Psychopharmacology, 4,* 198–208.

May, J., Andrade, J., Panabokke, N., & Kavanagh, D. (2004). Images of desire: Cognitive models of craving. *Memory, 12,* 447–461.

McCaul, M. E., & Monti, P. M. (2003). Research priorities for alcoholism treatment. *Recent Developments in Alcoholism, 16,* 405–414.

McCaul, M. E., Wand, G. S., Eissenberg, T., Rohde, C. A., & Cheskin, L. J. (2000). Naltrexone alters subjective and psychomotor responses to alcohol in heavy drinking subjects. *Neuropyschopharmacology, 22*(5), 480–492.

McLellan, A. T., Lewis, D., O'Brien, C. P., & Kleber, H. D. (2000). Drug dependence, a chronic medical illness: Implications for treatment, insurance, and outcomes evaluation. *The Journal of the American Medical Association, 284*(13), 1689–1695.

McGeary, J., Monti, P. M., Rohsenow, D. J., Tidey, J. W., Swift, R. M., & Miranda, R. (2006). Genetic Moderators of naltrexone's effect's on alcohol cue reactivity. *Alcoholism: Clinical and Experimental Research, 30,* 1288–1296.

Miranda, R., Jr., Monti, P. M., Swift, R., MacKillop, J., Tidey, J., Gwaltney, C., & Rohsenow, D. (2005, December). Dose-dependent effects of topiramate on alcohol cue reactivity and the subjective effects of drinking: Preliminary data [Abstract]. *Neuropsychopharmacology, 30*(Suppl. 1), S152.

Moolchan, E. T., Robinson, M. L., Ernst, M., Cadet, J. L., Pickworth, W. B., Heishman, S. J., & Schroeder, J. R. (2005). Safety and efficacy of the nicotine patch and gum for the treatment of adolescent tobacco addiction. *Pediatrics, 115,* 407–414.

Monterosso, J. R., Flannery, B. A., Pettinati, H. M., Oslin, D. W., Rukstalis, M., O'Brien, C. P., & Volpicelli, J. R. (2001). Predicting treatment response to naltrexone: The influence of craving and family history. *American Journal on Addictions, 10,* 258–268.

Monti, P. M., Abrams, D., Kadden, R., & Cooney, N. (1989). *Treating Alcohol Dependence: A Coping Skills Training Guide* (1st ed.). New York: Guilford Press.

Monti, P. M., Kadden, R., Rohsenow, D. J., Cooney, N., & Abrams, D. (2002). *Treating Alcohol Dependence: A Coping Skills Training Guide* (2nd ed.). New York: Guilford Press.

Monti, P. M., Miranda, R., Nixon, K., Sher, K. J., Swartzwelder, H. S., Tapert, S. F., White, A., & Crews, F. T. (2005). Adolescence: Booze, Brains and Behavior. *Alcoholism: Clinical and Experimental Research, 29,* 207–220.

Monti, P. M., Niaura, R., & Abrams, D. B. (2003). Ongoing research and future directions. In D. B. Abrams, R. Niaura, R. A. Brown, K. M. Emmons, M. G. Goldstein, & P. M. Monti (Eds.), *The Tobacco Dependence Treatment Handbook: A Guide to Best Practices.* New York: Guilford.

Monti, P. M., Rohsenow, D. J., & Hutchinson, K. E. (2000). Toward bridging the gap between biological, psychobiological and psychosocial models of alcohol craving. *Addiction, 95,* S229–S236.

Monti, P. M., Rohsenow, D. J., & Hutchinson, K. E., Swift, R. M., Mueller, T. I., Colby, S. M., & Kaplan, G. B. (1999). Naltrexone's effect on cue-elicited craving among alcoholics in treatment. *Alcoholism: Clinical and Experimental Research, 23*(8), 1386–1394.

Monti, P. M., Tidey, J., Czachowski, C. L., Grant, K. A., Rohsenow, D. J., Sayette, M., Maners, N., & Pierre, P. (2004). Building bridges: The transdisciplinary study of craving from the animal lab to the lamppost. *Alcoholism: Clinical and Experimental Research, 28,* 279–287.

Monti, P. M., Rohsenow, D. J., Rubonis, A. V., Niaura, R. S., Sirota, A. D., Colby, S. M., Goddard, P., & Abrams, D. B. (1993). Cue exposure with coping skills treatment for male alcoholics: A preliminary investigation. *Journal of Consulting and Clinical Psychology, 61,* 1011–1019.

Monti, P. M., Rohsenow, D. J., Swift, R. M., Gulliver, S. B., Colby, S. M., Mueller, T. I., Brown, R. A., Gordon, A., Abrams, D. B., Niaura, R. S., & Asher, M. K. (2001). Naltrexone and cue exposure with coping and communication skills training for alcoholics: Treatment process and 1-year outcomes. *Alcoholism: Clinical and Experimental Research, 25*, 1634–1647.

Myrick, H., Anton, R. F., Li, X., Henderson, S., Drobes, D., Voronin, K., & George, M. S. (2004). Differential brain activity in alcoholics and social drinkers to alcohol cues. *Neuropsychopharmacology, 29*, 393–402.

Niaura, R., Abrams, D. B., Demuth, B., Pinto, R., & Monti, P. M. (1989a). Reactivity to smoking-related stimuli and early relapse to smoking. *Addictive Behaviors, 14*(4), 419–428.

Niaura, R., Abrams, D., Monti, P. M., & Pedraza, M. (1989b). Reactivity to high risk situations and smoking cessation outcome. *Journal of Substance Abuse, 1*(4), 393–405.

Niaura, R., Abrams, D. B., Shadel, W. G., Rohsenow, D. J., Monti, P. M., & Sirota, A. D. (1999). Cue exposure treatment for smoking relapse prevention: A controlled clinical trial. *Addiction, 94*(5), 685–695.

O'Brien, C. P. (2005). Anticraving medications for relapse prevention: A possible new class of psychoactive medications. *American Journal of Psychiatry, 162*(8), 1423–1430.

O'Brien, C. P., Childress, A. R., McLellan, A. T., & Ehrman, R. (1990). Integrating systematic cue exposure with standard treatment in recovering drug dependent patients. *Addictive Behaviors, 15*(4), 355–365.

Olive, M. F., Nannini, M. A., Ou, C. J., Koenig, H. N., & Hodge, C. W. (2002). Effects of acute acamprosate and homotaurine on ethanol intake and ethanol-stimulated mesolimbic dopamine release. *European Journal of Pharmacology, 437*, 55–61.

O'Malley, S. S., Jaffe, A. J., Chang, G., & Schottenfeld, R. S. (1992). Naltrexone and coping skills therapy for alcohol dependence: A controlled study. *Archives of General Psychiatry, 49*(11), 881–887.

O'Malley, S. S., Krishnan, S. S., Farren, C., Sinha, R., & Kreek, M. J. (2002). Naltrexone decreases craving and alcohol self-administration in alcohol-dependent subjects and activates the hypothalamo–pituitary–adrenocortial axis. *Psychopharmacology, 160*(1), 19–29.

Oslin, D. W., Pettinati, H. M., Volpicelli, J. R., Wolf, A. L., Kampman, K. M., & O'Brien, C. P. (1999). The effects of naltrexone on alcohol and cocaine use in dually addicted patients. *Journal of Substance Abuse Treatment, 16*(2), 163–167.

Panabokke, N., May, J., Eade, D., Andrade, J., & Kavanagh, D. (2004). Visual imagery tasks suppress craving for cigarettes. Unpublished manuscript, University of Sheffield, Sheffield, England.

Payne, T. J., Rychtarik, R. G., Rappaport, N. B., Smith, P. O., Etscheidt, M., Brown, T. A., & Johnson, C. A. (1992). Reactivity to alcohol-relevant beverage and imaginal cues in alcoholics. *Addictive Behaviors, 17*, 209–217.

Perkins, K. A., Lerman, C., Keenan, J., Fonte, C., & Coddington, S. (2004). Rate of nicotine onset from nicotine replacement therapy and acute responses in smokers. *Nicotine and Tobacco Research, 6*(3), 501–507.

Petrakis, I. L., Poling, J., Levinson, C., Nich, C., Carroll, K., & Rounsaville, B. (2005). Naltrexone and disulfiram in patients with alcohol dependence and comorbid psychiatric disorders. *Biological Psychiatry, 57*(10), 1128–1137.

Powell, J., Gray, J. A., Bradley, B. P., Kasvikis, Y., Strang, J., Barrett, L., & Marks, I. (1990). The effects of exposure to drug-related cues in detoxified opiate addicts: A theoretical review and some new data. *Addictive Behaviors, 15*(4), 339–354.

Raw, M., & Russell, M. (1980). A Rapid smoking, cue exposure and support in the modification of smoking. *Behaviour Research and Therapy, 18*(5), 363–372.

Rauhut, A. S., Thomas, B. L., & Ayres, J. B. (2001). Treatments that weaken Pavlovian conditioned fear and thwart its renewal in rats: Implications for treating human phobias. *Journal of Experimental Psychology: Animal Behavioral Processes, 27*, 99–114.

Rinn, W., Desai, N., Rosenblatt, H., & Gastfriend, D. R. (2002). Addiction denial and cognitive dysfunction: A preliminary investigation. *Journal of Neuropsychiatry and Clinical Neurosciences*, 14, 52–57.

Rigotti, N. A. (2002). Treatment of tobacco use and dependence. *New England Journal of Medicine*, 346(7), 506–512.

Rohsenow, D. J. (2004). What place does naltrexone have in the treatment of alcoholism? *CNS Drug Reviews*, 18(9), 547–560.

Rohsenow, D. J., Miranda, R., McGeary, J. E., & Monti, P. M. (submitted). Family history and antisocial traits, not age of onset, moderate naltrexone's effects on drinking outcomes.

Rohsenow, D. J., Monti, P. M., Hutchison, K. E., Swift, R. M., Colby, S. M., & Kaplan, G. B. (2000). Naltrexone's effects on reactivity to alcohol cues among alcoholic men. *Journal of Abnormal Psychology*, 109(4), 738–742.

Rose, J. E., Behm, F. M., Westman, E. C., & Coleman, R. E. (1999). Arterial nicotine kinetics during cigarette smoking and intravenous nicotine administration: Implications for addiction. *Drug and Alcohol Dependence*, 56, 99–107.

Rubio, G., Ponce, G., Jimenez-Arriero, M. A., Palomo, T., Manzanares, J., & Ferre, F. (2004). Effects of topiramate in the treatment of alcohol dependence. *Pharmacopsychiatry*, 37, 37–40.

Rubio, G., Ponce, G., Rodriguez-Jimenez, R., Jimenez-Arriero, A., Hoenicka, J., & Palomo, T. (2005). Clinical predictors of response to naltrexone in alcoholic patients: Who benefits most from treatment with naltrexone? *Alcohol and Alcoholism*, 40(3), 227–233.

Shiffman, S., Engberg, J., Paty, J. A., Perz, W., Gnys, M., Kassel, J. D., & Hickcox, M. (1997). A day at a time: Predicting smoking lapse from daily urge. *Journal of Abnormal Psychology*, 106, 104–116.

Shiffman, S., Paty, J. A., Gnys, M., Kassel, J. D., & Hickcox, M. (1996). First lapses to smoking: Within-subjects analysis of real time reports. *Journal of Consulting and Clinical Psychology*, 64, 366–379.

Shiffman, S., Shadel, W. G., Niaura, R., Khayrallah, M. A., Jorenby, D. E., Ryan, C. F., & Ferguson, C. L. (2003). Efficacy of acute administration of nicotine gum in relief of cue-provoked cigarette craving. *Psychopharmacology*, 166(4), 345–350.

Sobell, M. B., & Sobell, L. C. (2000). Stepped care as a heuristic approach to the treatment of alcohol problems. *Journal of Consulting and Clinical Psychology*, 68, 573–579.

Swift, R. M. (1999). Drug therapy for alcohol dependence. *The New England Journal of Medicine*, 340, 1482–1489.

Swift, R. M., Whelihan, W., Kuznetsov, O., Buongiorno, G., & Hsuing, H. (1994). Naltrexone-induced alterations in human ethanol intoxication. *American Journal of Psychiatry*, 151(10), 1463–1467.

Tiffany, S. T., Cox, L. S., & Elash, C. A. (2000). Effects of transdermal nicotine patches on abstinence-induced and cue-elicited craving in cigarette smokers. *Journal of Consulting and Clinical Psychology*, 68(2), 233–240.

Tucker, J. A., Vuchinich, R. E., & Rippens, P. D. (2002). Predicting natural resolution of alcohol-related problems: A prospective behavioral economic analysis. *Experimental and Clinical Psychopharmacology*, 10, 248–257.

Volpicelli, J. R., Alterman, A. I., Hayashida, M., & O'Brien, C. P. (1992). Naltrexone in the treatment of alcohol dependence. *Archives of General Psychiatry*, 49(11), 876–880.

Volpicelli, J. R., Rhines, K. C., Rhines, J. S., Volpicelli, L. A., Alterman, A. I., & O'Brien, C. P. (1997). Naltrexone and Alcohol dependence: Role of subject compliance. *Archives of General Psychiatry*, 54, 737–742.

Volpicelli, J. R., Watson, N. T., King, A. C., Sherman, C. E., & O'Brien, C. P. (1995). Effect of naltrexone on alcohol "high" in alcoholics. *American Journal of Psychiatry*, 152(4), 613–615.

Waters, A. J., Shiffman, S., Sayette, M. A., Paty, J. A., Gwaltney, C. J., & Balabanis, M. H. (2004). Cue-provoked craving and nicotine replacement therapy in smoking cessation. *Journal of Consulting and Clinical Psychology, 72*(6), 1136–1143.

Weinstein, A., Feldtkeller, B., Feeney, A., Lingford-Hughes, A., & Nutt, D. (2003). A pilot study on the effects of treatment with acamprosate on craving for alcohol in alcohol-dependent patients. *Addiction Biology, 8*, 229–232.

Wertz, J. A., & Sayette, M. A. (2001). A review of the effects of drug abuse opportunity on self-reported urge. *Experimental and Clinical Psychopharmacology, 9*, 3–13.

West, R. J., & Shiffman, S. (2001). Effect of oral nicotine dosing forms on cigarette withdrawal symptoms and craving: A systematic review. *Psychopharmacology, 155*(2), 115–122.

Westerberg, V. S. (2000). Constituents of craving in a clinical alcohol sample. *Journal of Substance Abuse, 12*, 415–423.

White, W. L. (1998). *Slaying the Dragon: The History of Addiction Treatment and Recovery in America.* Bloomington, IL: Chestnut Health Systems.

Wiederhold, B. K., & Wiederhold, M. D. (2000). Lessons learned from 600 virtual reality sessions. *Cyberpsychology & Behavior, 3*, 393–400.

Wiederhold, B. K., & Wiederhold, M. D. (2005). *Virtual Reality Therapy for Anxiety Disorders: Advances in Evaluation and Treatment.* Washington, DC: American Psychological Association.

Wise, R. A. (1988). The neurobiology of craving: Implications for the understanding and treatment of addiction. *Journal of Abnormal Psychology, 97*, 118–132.

Woodruff, S. I., Edwards, C. C., Conway, T. L., & Elliott, S. P. (2001). Pilot test of an internet virtual world chat room for rural teen smokers. *Journal of Adolescent Health, 29*, 239–243.

CHAPTER 12

Cognitive, Affective and Motivational Effects of Smoking

Jane Powell[1] and Lynne Dawkins[2]

[1]Department of Psychology, Goldsmiths, University of London, New Cross, London SE14 6NW, UK
[2]School of Psychology, University of East London, London E15 4LZ, UK

Abstract: Contemporary neurobiological models of smoking dependence have highlighted the effects of nicotine on mesocorticolimbic brain reward circuitry, which is implicated in appetitive motivation, craving, attentional bias, and executive cognitive processes. Pre-existing or smoking-induced disturbances of functioning in this circuitry may contribute to vulnerability to smoking dependence and to difficulties in cessation. The chapter reviews a growing body of empirical research into whether and how individual differences at genetic, personality, affective, and cognitive levels relate to the development of dependence and/or influence the effects of pharmacological and psychological interventions. Important issues for further research are highlighted.

The last four decades have seen a revolution in societal and individual attitudes to smoking. Increasing awareness of the health risks it poses and of its apparent addictive properties mean that the weight of public opinion is now anti-smoking. Bans on smoking in public places, once unthinkable, are becoming the rule rather than the exception; its former aura of sophistication has been largely replaced by connotations of personal weakness. In tandem with this hardening of attitude, smoking has become medicalized; smokers are seen as in need of help, and there has been an explosion of research interest in the brain pathologies or deficits that underlie the apparently compulsive use of nicotine in the face of overwhelming objective reasons not to do so.

This chapter seeks firstly to consider the evidence that chronic smoking may be maintained through the production and/or alleviation of deficits and abnormalities in brain function. Contemporary neurobiological models of addiction have developed through the application of increasingly sophisticated investigative technologies including neuroimaging, behavioral and molecular genetics, and rigorous cognitive and behavioral studies with animals and humans. Individually, but particularly in combination, these different streams of evidence have the potential to enhance our understanding of brain-behavior relationships and to define intervention strategies which not only focused on particular aspects of dysfunction but also might be more effectively targeted according to the characteristics of the individual smoker. While the goal of tailoring treatments to people is by no means new, the prospects for doing so have never been more promising.

NICOTINE PHARMACOLOGY AND MECHANISMS OF ACTION

Nicotine is one of over 4,000 compounds released when tobacco is burned, and the one which appears to be the primary driver of smoking behavior. Smoking is an extremely effective way of delivering nicotine to the brain, being rapidly absorbed from the lungs into the blood and reaching the brain in about seven seconds (Ashton & Stepney, 1982). It then acts on cortical nicotinic acetylcholine receptors via sub cortical neurotransmitter projection systems: cholinergic axons from the pontine nuclei and basal forebrain, and noradrenergic axons from the locus coeruleus (Royal College of Physicians, 2000). These actions are thought to account for the putative increased arousal, enhanced concentration, and stimulant-like profile of brain EEG activation associated with smoking (e.g. Newhouse, Potter, & Singh, 2004). It also has effects on the serotonin, gamma–amino–butyric acid (GABA), and glutamate systems (Seth et al., 2002), but most attention has focused on its action on the dopaminergic 'reward' system implicated in addiction more generally. Nicotinic receptors are principally located on cell bodies of dopaminergic neurons of the mesocorticolimbic pathway which projects from the ventral tegmental area (VTA), through nucleus accumbens (N.Acc.) and thence to anterior cingulate (AC) and prefrontal cortex (PFC). In animals, nicotine administration elevates extracellular N.Acc. and VTA dopamine (DA) levels by directly stimulating dopaminergic burst cell firing (Calabresi, Lacey, & North, 1989). Human neuroimaging studies generally corroborate these findings; Stein et al. (1998), for example, using fMRI, reported a dose-dependent increase in N.Acc., amygdala, AC, and frontal lobe activity with intravenous nicotine. It is to the release of DA in N.Acc. that nicotine's rewarding properties are widely attributed, and it seems plausible that it might also produce effects on cognitive functioning through the efferent projections to PFC and AC, which are involved in "executive" functions including attention, working memory (WM), and response inhibition.

Evidence from neuroimaging studies in other addictions suggests that although drug ingestion produces acute DA-enhancing effects even after chronic use, endogenous DA activity is abnormally low in addicts (see review by Volkow et al., 2004) and they also show abnormalities in the structure and function of PFC and AC (e.g., London et al., 2000). In smokers, Dagher et al. (2001) reported reduced DA D1 receptor binding in the N.Acc. compared with non-smokers. During acute abstinence (e.g., at the start of a quit attempt), when the individual is no longer benefiting from the DA-enhancing effects of nicotine, these abnormalities are theoretically likely to manifest in decreased reactivity to rewards and impaired response inhibition/executive functioning (see e.g., Powell et al., 2004, for more detailed discussion).

COGNITIVE CORRELATES OF SMOKING AND ABSTINENCE FROM SMOKING

Smokers commonly believe that nicotine improves their alertness and cognitive functioning, and intuitively it seems likely that such benefits might motivate continued smoking. While it is clear that they do perform better on tests of vigilance and sustained attention after smoking than when acutely abstinent, much of the research suggests that this reflects a reversal of impairments associated with abstinence rather than a more general enhancement which would also accrue to non-smokers (Heishman, Taylor, & Henningfield, 1994). For instance, Spilich, June and Renner (1992) found that although active smokers outperformed deprived smokers, non-smokers performed better still. Others have similarly found that abstinence from smoking results in attentional deficits and that administration of nicotine restores performance to baseline (smoking) levels both in animals (e.g., Shoaib & Bizarro, 2004) and in humans (e.g., Kleykamp et al., 2005). However, this is not universally the case: a few studies *have* reported nicotine-enhancement of vigilance/sustained attention in rodents (Young et al., 2004) and in non-smokers or non-deprived smokers (e.g., Foulds et al., 1996). The benefits in non-smokers may be apparent primarily when baseline levels of function are impaired for other reasons. Thus, nicotine has recently been found to enhance performance in non-smokers with attentional deficits (Poltavski & Petros, 2006; Bekker et al., 2005).

Given the actions of nicotine on dopaminergic projections to PFC and AC, and the evidence of reduced endogenous DA activity in abstinent smokers, it follows that nicotine administration should improve, and deprivation impair, other aspects of executive functioning including decision-making, inhibitory control, and WM. A number of studies have found smokers to be less rational than non-smokers, for instance favoring small, immediate monetary rewards over larger, delayed rewards (Mitchell, 1999); while Field et al. (2006) reported that acute abstinence increased impulsive choices for both cigarette and monetary rewards in a delay-discounting task. In relation to inhibitory control, we (Powell, Dawkins, & Davis, 2002a; Powell et al., 2004) found acutely abstinent smokers to make more oculomotor response inhibition errors than either satiated or non-smokers; moreover, consistent with the view put forward by Jentsch and Taylor (1999) that such deficits would contribute to impulsive substance use during cessation attempts, we found smokers performing poorly on this task during abstinence to be at elevated risk of early relapse (ms in prep). Elsewhere, nicotine administration has been found to improve response inhibition in individuals with ADHD (Potter & Newhouse, 2003).

The evidence for impairment of WM during nicotine abstinence, or its enhancement by nicotine, is less clear. In one study (Al-Adawi & Powell, 1997), but not a subsequent one (Powell et al., 2002a), we found poorer reversed digit span in abstinent than in satiated smokers. Jacobsen et al. (2005) found that adolescent smokers showed impaired WM which was further disrupted by smoking cessation; and Mendrek et al. (2006) have recently found abstinence-induced impairments on the n-back task, which, interestingly, were not reversed by smoking a single cigarette. However, in some studies nicotine has been shown to impair WM performance, possibly indicating a curvilinear relationship between the effects of nicotine and task difficulty. Thus, Park et al. (2000) reported smokers to perform better on a spatial WM task during abstinence. Intriguingly, Ernst et al. (2001) found equivalent WM in abstaining and ex-smokers, but different patterns of concurrent brain activation indicative of different information-processing strategies. In non-smokers, there have been reports of nicotine-enhancement of WM (e.g. Heishman & Henningfield, 2000; Kumari et al., 2003) but also contradictory findings (e.g. Kleykamp et al., 2005). There is more consistent evidence that smoking abstinence impairs, and nicotine improves, WM in psychopathologies characterized by executive deficits (e.g. schizophrenia; see Newhouse et al., 2004).

To summarize, then, there is fairly consistent evidence that current smokers obtain benefits from nicotine, relative to their functioning when acutely abstinent, on attention, vigilance, response inhibition and (though here the evidence is more mixed) WM. These effects probably reflect reversal of abstinence-related impairments.

PSYCHOLOGICAL/AFFECTIVE CORRELATES OF SMOKING AND ABSTINENCE FROM SMOKING

The complex neurochemical effects of smoking confer a capacity to affect mood and motivational states through various mechanisms. Perhaps most obviously, smoking cessation is associated with a withdrawal syndrome that includes somatic components (e.g. hunger), affective components (depression, irritability, craving), and cognitive components (e.g. poor concentration). Most quitters report only mild physical symptoms which normally subside within a week (Hughes et al., 1991); yet even when the symptoms are attenuated by nicotine replacement therapy (NRT) such that only 10% of quitters report persistent hunger, and fewer than 5% any other somatic disturbance, West, Hajek, and Belcher (1987) found 50% to report episodes of strong craving during the first week of smoking abstinence, and 35% to continue to do so during the fourth week. Thus, craving is more than a response to the anticipation or experience of physical discomfort, albeit that these factors may contribute.

It is unclear to what extent the dysphoria seen during abstinence is a consequence of nicotine dependence as opposed to the continuance of a state which predated smoking. There is some evidence that smokers experience at least transient mood improvements after smoking, and that dysphoria elevates both craving and risk of relapse (see review by Baker, Brandon, & Chassin, 2004). Psychiatric disorders including depression are associated with elevated rates of smoking (e.g. Leonard et al., 2001), and although a recent meta-analysis by Hitsman et al. (2003) suggested that a history of depression does not consistently reduce the chances of successful quitting, it has also been found that a deterioration in mood during early abstinence is associated with heightened relapse risk (Piasecki, Fiore, & Baker, 1998). However, nicotine is not generally effective as a mood-enhancer; for instance, Baker et al. note that many studies have found that smoking fails to reduce stress-induced negative affect. Thus, although smokers may strongly *believe* that smoking will keep them on an emotional even keel, the evidence that it does so is somewhat tenuous and inconsistent.

A strong candidate explanation for some aspects of the dysphoria associated with nicotine abstinence in smokers lies in the hypofunctioning of reward pathways described previously. If the capacity of this circuitry to mediate cognitive and behavioral responses to normally rewarding stimuli is depleted during abstinence, then the abstainer will be correspondingly less likely to notice rewards in the environment, to experience a consequent interest in, desire for, or positive affective response to them, and to seek them out and experience the satisfaction or pleasure they would normally deliver. This 'anhedonic' state is one aspect of depression. The same pathways have elsewhere been shown to be perturbed by stress (e.g. Weiss & Koob, 2001), and may play a general role in mediating subjective and behavioral responses to stimuli with aversive as well as appetitive motivational significance. Their downregulation, whether through drug abstinence or for other reasons, is therefore likely to manifest in a general dampening of affective reactivity.

There is some support for the proposition that nicotine abstinence is associated with impaired responding to non-drug reinforcers. In the animal laboratory, Caggiula's group has demonstrated that nicotine administration increases the incentive value of non-drug rewards (e.g. Palmatier et al., 2006). A seminal study by Epping-Jordan et al. (1998) showed that across four days of withdrawal from nicotine, rats' brain reward thresholds were significantly elevated: i.e., higher than normal levels of rewarding electro-brain stimulation were required to induce instrumental responding. In humans, we have found smoking abstinence to attenuate attentional bias toward words with pleasurable connotations (using a modified Stroop paradigm; Powell, Tait, & Lessiter, 2002b); with reduced responsiveness to financial incentive in a simple card-sorting task (Powell et al., 2002a, 2004); with reduced anticipation of pleasure from normally enjoyable daily activities (Powell et al., 2002a); and with less 'mood uplift' after watching positively valenced video clips (Dawkins, Acaster, & Powell, 2007). Elsewhere, Martin-Soelch et al. (2003) found that increasing levels of monetary reward for task performance produced a corresponding increase in striatal activation in non-smokers, but not in smokers; there was likewise a lack of normal association between reward magnitude and mood changes in the smokers.

This model further implies that appetitive responses to drug-related cues should similarly be reduced during acute abstinence, but here predictions are complicated by the fact that abstinence is likely to have a simultaneous opposing effect of *increasing* the incentive salience of drug cues because of their association with the prospect of withdrawal relief (e.g. Stewart, de Wit, & Eikelboom, 1984). Thus, abstinent smokers are likely to be cognitively preoccupied with thoughts of and desire for a cigarette to restore their physical or affective equilibrium, counteracting any generalized biological reduction in responsivity to reward cues. It is consequently difficult to make simple predictions concerning the effects of deprivation on attentional bias or cue reactivity. In practice, few if any published studies have found abstinent smokers, relative to those who have just smoked, to show elevated cue reactivity (e.g. Tiffany, Cox, & Elash, 2000; Waters et al., 2004), and in one study by our group (Powell et al., 2002b) they showed reduced cue reactivity. However, these studies are compromised by the fact that baseline levels of craving are invariably higher in abstinence than satiety, and consequently ceiling effects may reduce sensitivity to cue reactivity during abstinence. Investigations of attentional bias toward smoking-related cues, for instance using modified Stroop or dot-probe paradigms, have yielded similarly ambiguous results. Thus, although it is consistently found that smokers but not non-smokers are biased toward smoking-related stimuli (e.g. Ehrman et al., 2002; Bradley et al., 2004), and that the degree of bias correlates with subjective craving (Waters et al., 2003) and anticipated pleasantness of smoking (Field, Mogg, & Bradley, 2004), the effects of abstinence are less clear-cut. Some studies have found acute abstinence to be associated with increased *duration* of attention to smoking-related stimuli, but not with other indices of bias such as the speed with which stimuli capture attention (Field et al., 2004) or interference effects (Mogg & Bradley, 2002); and different indices of bias do not intercorrelate highly (e.g. Waters & Feyerabend, 2000; Mogg & Bradley, 2002).

Notwithstanding the multifactorial nature of these phenomena, they are of demonstrated relevance to smoking cessation. In a prospective study of quitters, attentional bias to smoking cues following a few hours abstinence predicted early relapse (Waters et al., 2003). In a similar study our group has recently found, contrary to theoretical prediction, that *low* cue reactivity during acute abstinence predicted relapse within 7 days (Powell et al., ms in prep); interestingly, this replicates a finding reported by Niaura et al. (1999). One possible explanation is that individuals with high cue reactivity are more aware of their risks and take better precautionary measures. Consistent with the notion that the relationship of cue reactivity to outcome might vary depending on the strategies employed to assist cessation, Waters et al. (2004) found that in smokers given NRT but not in those receiving placebo, high cue reactivity predicted rapid relapse. However, within our study, low cue reactivity was associated with high baseline craving (possibly reflecting a ceiling effect) which itself predicted early relapse. Clearly, the potential role of these cognitive and motivational variables in influencing vulnerability to relapse – individually, in combination, and in interaction with specific cessation strategies – is an important area for further investigation.

The complex pharmacological effects produced by smoking, and conversely by abstinence, must differ depending on biological factors which influence their form, speed, or duration; and subjectively they will be experienced differently depending on the psychological context, as determined by both traits and also more transient states such as anxiety or excitement which are responsive to external factors. It is therefore a priori likely that individuals will differ in susceptibility to dependence, in the effects of abstinence, and in the ease with which they can quit. This variability will manifest at the psychological level as personality traits or subjective motives for smoking, at the physiological level as differences in brain structure or function, and at the genotypic level as polymorphisms which code for different aspects of these physiological characteristics.

Personality traits that have been persistently linked to use of addictive substances, including nicotine, include impulsiveness, thrill-seeking, and novelty-seeking (e.g. Zuckerman & Kuhlman, 2000) and have been conjectured to be indicative of a 'reward deficiency syndrome' arising from hypofunctioning of the dopaminergic brain reward circuitry (Blum et al., 2000); such individuals need to seek exogenous means of boosting activity within this circuitry and thus to experience 'normal' levels of pleasure and drive. Consistent with this assertion, Hutchison, Wood, and Swift (1999) found that non-drug users who were highly novelty seeking or sensation seeking responded strongly to a test dose of amphetamine.

At the molecular level, polymorphisms which code in various ways for activity in neurotransmitter systems relevant to the effects of nicotine have been investigated for associations with smoking initiation, consumption, dependence, and cessation. A meta-analysis of 28 such studies conducted since 1994 (Munafò et al., 2004) found evidence for modest effects of the DRD2 receptor gene on smoking initiation and consumption, of the CYP2A6 (the primary nicotine-metabolizing enzyme) gene on consumption and cessation, and of the 5HTT (serotonin transporter) gene on cessation. Of particular interest in the present context is an experiment by Hutchison et al. (2002), which found that smokers with a particular variant (at least one long allele) of the DRD4 receptor gene showed stronger cue reactivity than other participants, consistent with pre-clinical findings implicating this receptor in incentive sensitization (Svingos, Periasamy, & Pickel, 2000). In our recently completed prospective study of smoking cessation, we have replicated this finding (Powell et al., ms in prep), and additionally found smokers with a long allele of the DRD4 gene to respond strongly to financial incentive during acute abstinence but weakly following nicotine administration; the reverse pattern was shown by smokers with two short alleles. Of particular note, the long allele was associated with a significantly increased risk of early relapse. No other studies have yet reported such an association, and clearly it needs replication; however, it is pertinent that there is some evidence that the DRD4 gene has elsewhere been linked with impulsiveness (e.g. Keltikangas-Jarvinen et al., 2003) and that this in turn has been found to predict rapid relapse to smoking (Doran et al., 2004).

SMOKING CESSATION TREATMENTS: CURRENT STATUS

In a recent survey of smokers, over 70% claimed to want to quit, and 41% reported having attempted to do so in the preceding year; yet only about 5% actually succeed in maintaining abstinence for more than 3 months [Centers for Disease Control and Prevention (CDC), 2002]. This huge gulf between aspiration and achievement provides fertile ground for the development, evaluation, and marketing of interventions to aid cessation, and these should logically be informed by the findings of research into the factors which motivate or maintain smoking.

Assessing the outcome of cessation attempts is complicated, since there is no single commonly agreed criterion. The follow-up point is critical: although relapse rates are highest during the first week, smokers continue to relapse over the following months and even years. Short-term 'lapses' to smoking often, but not invariably, lead to a full resumption of smoking, and only a minority of smokers succeed in sustaining a lower level of smoking either permanently or en route to complete cessation (Hughes, 2000). Thus, while some studies report 'continuous' or 'prolonged' abstinence rates in which even a single lapse counts as a failure, others use 'point prevalence' abstinence, which typically refers to abstinence for the previous seven days (verifiable through biochemical markers). Rates of self-reported abstinence typically exceed those that are objectively verified, for instance through salivary continine. Hughes et al. (2003) and Piasecki (2006) provide detailed critiques of these issues. The following brief overview of treatment outcomes focuses primarily on point prevalence abstinence several months post-cessation, since this appears to be reasonably predictive of long-term success and has been widely used.

The preceding section identified a number of psychological and cognitive correlates of smoking and abstinence, some of these are potential obstacles to quitting. Thus, withdrawal symptoms, craving, lack of drive, anhedonia, and dysphoria are likely to be accentuated during acute abstinence and to be experienced as states of discomfort or deficiency which the individual believes can be alleviated by smoking. On the other hand, cue reactivity and attentional bias toward smoking-related stimuli appear to characterize current smokers or recent quitters irrespective of abstinence status, and indeed may contribute to maintaining a near-constant state of appetitive drive to smoke. Cognitive impairments, particularly of decision-making and response inhibition, which appear to characterize abstinence and to be largely remediated by nicotine ingestion, may make it yet more difficult for would-be quitters to resist the urge to smoke.

Interventions range from those which focus on specific deficits or abnormalities to broad spectrum approaches including counseling and environmental controls (bans, taxation, health warnings). Figure 1 shows how a number of fairly well-researched treatments might, theoretically, affect the vulnerability factors identified here.

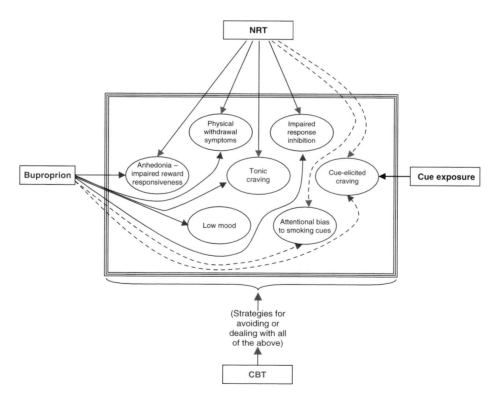

Figure 1 Theoretical impact of pharmacological and psychological interventions on cognitive and affective obstacles to smoking cessation. Key: Solid line indicates treatment is theoretically predicted to reduce the obstacle; Dashed line indicates that treatment may theoretically exacerbate the obstacle.

NRT maintains smokers' neurochemical systems more or less in balance as they attempt to quit smoking; the premise is that this will hold withdrawal symptoms and craving at bay while the habitual behavior patterns of cigarette smoking are broken. The temporal characteristics of NRT differ from smoking, which produces rapid peaks followed by gradual decay over the following few hours, and vary between different delivery systems: e.g., transdermal patches are slow-acting but produce a more or less steady state, while gum and lozenges can be taken *ad libitum* either instead of or as supplements to patches to give a more rapid effect (e.g. Blondal et al., 1999). The consequent differences in subjective experience compared with smoking may partially explain why the efficacy of NRT, though well-established, is modest: a recent overview by Piasecki (2006) of a large number of randomized controlled trials (RCTs) providing NRT with some medical supervision or support indicated that although the medium-term (5+ months) point prevalence abstinence rate is approximately double that achieved without assistance, in absolute terms it nevertheless remains rather low at between 20% and 30%. Success rates appear to be markedly lower when smokers buy NRT over the counter and use it without any supervision or monitoring.

Furthermore, NRT probably does not reduce either the surges in craving triggered when the smoker encounters cues or situations signaling cigarette availability, or his/her attentional bias toward such stimuli. Indeed, if, as has been argued here, nicotine activates brain reward pathways, it may – however delivered – actually augment these response tendencies. This, then, would place another theoretical limitation on the overall efficacy of NRT and would imply a need for adjunctive treatments focusing on either prevention of, or strategies to cope with, these risk factors. The other potentially important relapse precipitant not directly addressed by NRT is low mood (depression and/or anxiety); there is little evidence, despite its apparent role in triggering relapse, that nicotine actually improves mood more than transiently.

Short-term antidepressant treatments, particularly bupropion – which boosts both dopaminergic and noradrenergic activity – but also nortriptyline, have been consistently shown in systematic reviews (Hughes et al., 2003; Tonstad & Johnston, 2004) to aid smoking cessation. Bupropion's effect across groups of smokers who do *not* suffer from major depression has been found to be at least as high as that of NRT, with two recent large (Ns over 700) RCTs reporting point prevalence abstinence at six months of between 35% and 33%, respectively (Jorenby et al., 1999; Tonnesen et al., 2003). Elsewhere, it has been found to have a similarly large effect in smokers with and without a history of major depression (Hayford et al., 1999). Empirically, as well as improving mood even in non-clinically depressed individuals (Ahluwalia et al., 2002), it appears to attenuate withdrawal symptoms to a similar level as NRT (Jorenby et al., 1999), and also to reduce the urge to smoke (e.g. Tonnessen et al., 2003). Theoretically, given its dopaminergic actions, it would be expected to substitute for nicotine in improving reward responsiveness and ameliorating the cognitive deficits (including of inhibitory control) associated with the prefrontal projections of the reward circuitry; however, these effects are as yet untested. By the same token, it might, like NRT, also be predicted to increase cue reactivity and attentional bias toward smoking-related cues. Interestingly, however, Brody et al. (2004) found that after four weeks of bupropion treatment, smokers substantially reduced their consumption and showed lower levels of both baseline craving and cue reactivity than current smokers. The clinical implications of this are potentially important, given that NRT does not seem to produce a similar benefit, but these results require replication.

Bupropion has the apparent advantage over NRT that it additionally targets low mood. On the other hand, NRT should produce effects more similar to those obtained through smoking in terms of its broader profile of neurochemical effects and theoretically therefore might prove superior in enabling smokers to reduce their dependency on cigarettes. There is no medical contraindication to their concomitant use, which might in principle protect against more risks than either independently, but only one-blinded trial to date has evaluated them comparatively. Jorenby et al. (1999) compared 8–9 weeks of treatment with bupropion and NRT, separately and combined, against placebo, and found the combination to be slightly but nonsignificantly superior to bupropion alone (39% vs. 35% point prevalence abstinence at six months). Bupropion outperformed NRT and placebo (35% vs. 21% vs. 19%), but the relatively low abstinence rate for participants on NRT alone conflicts with the usual finding that NRT doubles success rate relative to placebo. While there is no obvious explanation for the discrepancy, this would have made it difficult to find any additive or synergistic effects of the two treatments.

Cue exposure focuses specifically on reducing the surge in craving that smokers experience when faced with cues signaling cigarette availability. Based on learning theory models which incorporate both classical conditioning and instrumental learning processes (the elicitation of reflexive conditioned reactions to smoking cues on the one hand, and smoking to achieve positive effects or relief of aversive states on the other), it entails repeatedly exposing the smoker to smoking cues and waiting for affective and physiological responses first to rise and then to subside. The aim is to achieve habituation, and ultimately extinction, of these responses such that smoking-related stimuli lose their ability to trigger craving when the smoker attempts abstinence. A critical assumption is that weakening of responses to stimuli presented in the therapeutic context will generalize to a larger range of more complex cues in the real world, but unfortunately there is increasing evidence that this is not the case. For instance, Thewissen et al. (2006) were able to extinguish smokers' cue-elicited responses through exposure in one setting; these responses were reinstated when the same cues were presented in the acquisition context. Similarly, a number of studies of cue exposure in both smoking (e.g. Carter & Tiffany, 2001) and other addictions (e.g. Powell, 1995) have observed that the form and strength of the cue-elicited response varies greatly depending on the participant's perception of drug availability. Thus, extinction of responses in a treatment situation where the smoker has little or no expectation of actually using is quite unlikely to generalize to real-life 'high risk' situations where there are fewer deterrents and indeed possibly even social encouragement to smoke. Given these factors, and also the equivocal findings regarding the relationship between cue reactivity and relapse, it is hardly surprising that the one RCT of cue exposure in smokers (Niaura et al., 1999) found it to deliver no incremental benefit when added to cognitive-behavior therapy and NRT.

Finally, more broad-spectrum psychosocial interventions include various forms of *counseling, psychotherapy, or cognitive-behavioral therapy* (CBT). These address different combinations of risk factors through the provision of information and/or assistance with identifying potential problems and then with developing the skills to prevent or cope with them. The most clearly articulated of these approaches within the addiction field is Relapse Prevention (Marlatt & Gordon, 1985); grounded in social learning theory, this provides a structured framework for helping individual smokers to recognize their own profile of risks and vulnerabilities, to anticipate high risk situations, and to plan and rehearse cognitive and behavioral responses accordingly. The implementation of such approaches varies enormously between different smokers, therapists, and settings; in addition, programs differ in terms of many structural factors including number/duration of sessions, format (e.g. group vs. individual), balance of content, by whom it is delivered, and route (e.g. face to face, internet, written information). Meta-analyses of counseling/problem-solving interventions, discussed by Piasecki (2006), reveal that the likelihood of smokers being abstinent five months or more after the start of their quit attempt can be more than doubled relative to unaided efforts with some form of counseling which involves four or more contacts (odds ratio 1.9); success rates improve further with more than eight contacts, and with total amount of contact time. It proves harder to isolate the effects of different components of treatments, because studies tend to specify content fairly vaguely and/or because few of the existing RCTs compare identical programs. However, inclusion of a focus on social support, training in problem-solving, and the use of aversive smoking techniques all appear to be associated with better outcomes. In a systematic review of the efficacy of relapse prevention approaches, Hajek et al. (2005) similarly note that heterogeneity and low power limit the ability of studies to show clear effects of treatment; based on the weak data available, they were unable to find any convincing evidence that training in specific relapse-relevant skills did indeed reduce relapse. Elsewhere, however, individual studies suggest that specific components of treatment may increase success rates for subgroups of smokers to whose vulnerabilities they are directly relevant: e.g., Brown et al. (2001) reported that although adding CBT for depression to a more general smoking cessation package did not improve outcomes in depressed smokers across the board, it *was* associated with greater success in quitting for a subgroup with a longer history of depression. While findings which are based on post hoc sub-analyses clearly need to be replicated in studies designed and adequately powered to detect risk factor-treatment relationships, they do highlight the importance of future treatment studies evaluating the impact of particular psychosocial interventions on relevant process variables. If targeted and well-specified training methods could be shown, for example, to improve response inhibition (and smoking cessation) in smokers who show deficits of inhibitory control, or to enhance appetitive drives as well as abstinence rates in anhedonic individuals, the stage would be set for tailoring individually appropriate combinations of psychological techniques in a more accurate and effective way than is currently possible.

PRIORITIES FOR TRANSLATIONAL RESEARCH

To date evaluation of both drug and psychosocial interventions has been largely focused on their impact in relatively undifferentiated groups of smokers. Recent advances in understanding the psychological factors associated with smoking and abstinence suggest that specific cognitive or motivational mechanisms should mediate treatment effects, yet these variables have rarely been assessed in the context of treatment studies; if they were, then treatments could potentially be made more effective through refining or elaborating the active ingredients to produce stronger effects on the critical mechanisms, through combining treatments with effects on different proximal risk factors, or through targeting well-specified treatments at individuals showing the relevant risk factors. Although some of the larger drug studies have explored whether treatment effects are moderated by demographic or clinical factors such as gender, psychiatric status, or addiction severity, very few have stratified their samples according to individual differences variables which are theoretically likely to interact with the particular drug in influencing cessation. Such variables would include, on the one hand, stable characteristics such as genotype which may be indicative of particular physiological and psychological vulnerabilities, and, on the other, direct measures of the cognitive or affective processes (such as response inhibition, reward responsiveness or attentional bias) which researchers believe both to put the individual at risk of relapse to smoking and to be targeted by the intervention.

A small number of pharmacogenetic studies have begun to demonstrate the potential of this type of research for focusing smoking cessation treatments (see Munafò et al., 2005, for a detailed review of the existing literature and a helpful consideration of methodological issues). For instance, Yudkin et al. (2004) found, in 755 smokers participating in a placebo-controlled trial, that the nicotine patch more than tripled the abstinence rate at the end of the first week of treatment for smokers with both the DRD2 A1 allele, which putatively codes for striatal D2 receptor availability, and the DBH A allele, which may affect levels of endogenous DA. The treatment was less beneficial, relative to placebo, for participants with other genotypes (odds ratio 1.4). The effect remained significant at 12 weeks. Lerman et al. (2002, 2003) have similarly explored whether the effectiveness of bupropion might be moderated by polymorphisms of genes coding either for efficiency of metabolizing the drug (CYP2B6) or for DA function (DRD2 and DAT1). In a sample of over 400 smokers, relapse risk was found to be influenced by CYP2B6 and by a DRD2 × DAT1 interaction; and a complex CYP2B6 × gender × buproprion interaction suggested that bupropion attenuated the effects of this genotype in women.

Given the great number of equally plausible candidate genes potentially involved in modulating the dopaminergic or other effects of different drug treatments, pharmacogenetic studies tend to be hypothesis-generating and to test multiple polymorphisms. The sample sizes required to detect even modest genetic effects with adequate statistical power are consequently in the order of thousands (Cardon et al., 2000) and therefore often either impractical or unaffordable. A complementary approach, and one which is increasingly well-informed by the kind of correlational and experimental research reviewed here, is to conduct hypothesis-driven evaluations of different therapeutic approaches which stratify smokers with respect to a much smaller number of relapse-relevant and measurable process variables such as craving, response inhibition, etc. which the treatment is designed to target. The extent to which these variables are themselves determined by genetic, constitutional, and environmental influences, either individually or in combination, can be investigated in parallel within large enough studies. To illustrate, the evidence that impairments of response inhibition and high craving during acute abstinence predict early relapse suggests that interventions should be designed to target these variables, and that treatment evaluations should (a) measure the extent to which they are changed by the treatment; (b) determine statistically whether any impact on outcome is mediated through them; and (c) explore whether subgroups of smokers showing more pronounced disturbances in these variables at baseline show preferential benefit from the treatment.

Sufficiently detailed information about the mechanisms of action of different treatments in terms of their impact on cognitive and behavioral processes mediating outcome could accelerate the design of synergistic treatment combinations which between them address the profile of deficits shown by particular subgroups of smokers. Relatedly, further research is needed to clarify the persistence and reversibility of some of the risk factors apparent during early abstinence; thus, while the time course of somatic withdrawal symptoms has been well-described, it is not yet clear whether some of the other cognitive and affective abnormalities are transient or permanent (either as antecedents or consequences of chronic smoking). This is crucial to the design of cost-effective intervention strategies, since deficits which show spontaneous recovery may require only short-term management rather than intensive intervention, whereas the reverse is the case for those which represent long-term or permanent vulnerabilities.

REFERENCES

Ahluwalia, J. S., Harris, K. J., Catley, D., Okuyemi, K. S., & Mayo, M. S. (2002). Sustained release bupropion for smoking cessation in African Americans: A randomised controlled trial. *JAMA*, *288*, 468–474.

Al-Adawi, S., & Powell, J. H. (1997). The influence of smoking on reward responsiveness and cognitive functions: A natural experiment. *Addiction*, *92*, 1757–1766.

Ashton, H., & Stepney, R. (1982). The importance of nicotine. In H. Ashton, & R. Stepney (Eds.). *Smoking: Psychology and Pharmacology* (pp. 18–41). London: Tavistock Publications Ltd.

Baker, T. B., Brandon, T. H., & Chassin, L. (2004). Motivational influences on cigarette smoking. *Annual Review of Psychology*, *55*, 463–491.

Bekker, E. M., Bocker, K. B., Van Hunsel, F., van den Berg, M. C., & Kenemans, J. L. (2005). Acute effects of nicotine on attention and response inhibition. *Pharmacology, Biochemistry and Behavior*, *82*, 539–548.

Blondal, T., Gudmundsson, L. J., Olafsdottir, I., Gustavsson, G., & Westin, A. (1999). Nicotine nasal spray with nicotine patch for smoking cessation: Randomised trial with six year follow up. *British Medical Journal*, *318*, 285–288.

Blum, K., Braverman, E. R., Holder, J. M., Lubar, J. F., Monastra, V. J., Miller, D., Lubar, J. O., Chen, T. J. H., & Comings, D. E. (2000). Reward deficiency syndrome: A biogenetic model for the diagnosis and treatment of impulsive, addictive and compulsive behaviours. *Journal of Psychoactive Drugs*, *32*, U3–+.

Bradley, B., Field, M., Mogg, K., & De Houwer, J. (2004). Attentional and evaluative biases for smoking cues in nicotine dependence: Component processes of biases in visual orienting. *Behavioural Pharmacology*, *15*, 29–36.

Brody, A. L., Mandelkarn, M. A., Lee, G., Smith, E., Sadeghi, M., Saxena, S., Jarvik, M. E., & London, E. D. (2004). Attenuation of cue-induced cigarette craving and anterior cingulate cortex activation in bupropion-treated smokers: A preliminary study. *Psychiatry Research*, *132*, 183–184.

Brown, R. A., Kahler, C. W., Niaura, R., Abrams, D. B., Sales, S. D., Ramsey, S. E., Goldstein, M. G., Burgess, E. S., & Miller, I. W. (2001). Cognitive-behavioral treatment for depression in smoking cessation. *Journal of Consulting and Clinical Psychology*, *69*, 471–480.

Calabresi, P., Lacey, M. G., & North, R. A. (1989). Nicotinic excitation of rat ventral tegmental neurones in vitro studies by intracellular recording. *British Journal of Pharmacology*, *98*, 135–140.

Cardon, L. R., Idury, R. M., Harris, T. J., Witte, J. S., & Elston, R. C. (2000). Testing drug response in the presence of genetic information: Sampling issues for clinical trials. *Pharmacogenetics*, *10*, 503–510.

Carter, B. L., & Tiffany, S. T. (2001). The cue-availability paradigm: The effects of cigarette availability on cue reactivity in smokers. *Experimental Clinical Psychopharmacology*, *9*, 183–190.

Centers for Disease Control and Prevention (CDC). (2002). Cigarette smoking among adults–United States, 2000. Morbidity and Mortality Weekly Report, *51*, 642–645.

Dagher, A., Bleicher, C., Aston, J. A. D., Gunn, R. D., Clarke, P. B. S., & Cummings, P. (2001). Reduced dopamine D1 receptor binding in the ventral striatum of cigarette smokers. *Synapse*, *42*, 48–53.

Dawkins, L., Acaster, S., & Powell, J. H. (2007). The effects of smoking and abstinence on experience of happiness and sadness in response to positively valenced, negatively valenced, and neutral film clips. *Addictive Behaviors*, *32*(2), 425–431.

Doran, N., Spring, B., McChargue, D., Pergadia, M., & Richmond, M. (2004). Impulsivity and smoking relapse. *Nicotine and Tobacco Research*, *6*, 641–647.

Ehrman, R. N., Robbins, S. J., Bromwell, M. A., Lankford, M. E., Monterosso, J. R., & O'Brien, C. P. (2002). Comparing attentional bias to smoking cues in current smokers, former smokers, and non-smokers using a dot-probe task. *Drug and Alcohol Dependence*, *67*, 185–191.

Epping-Jordan, M. P., Watkins, S. S., Koob, G. F., & Markou, A. (1998). Dramatic decreases in brain reward function during nicotine withdrawal. *Nature, 393*, 76–79.

Ernst, M., Matochik, J. A., Heishman, S. J., Van Horn, J. D., Jons, P. H., Henningfield, J. E., & London, E. D. (2001). Effect of nicotine on brain activation during performance of a working memory task. *Proceedings of the National Academy of Science, 98*, 4728–4733.

Field, M., Mogg, K., & Bradley, B. P. (2004). Eye movements to smoking-related cues: Effects of nicotine deprivation. *Psychopharmacology, 173*, 116–123.

Field, M., Santarcangelo, M., Sumnall, H., Goudie, A., & Cole, J. (2006). Delay discounting and the behavioral economics of cigarette purchases in smokers: The effects of nicotine deprivation. *Psychopharmacology, 186*, 255–263.

Foulds, J., Stapleton, J., Swettenham, J., Bell, N., McSorley, K., & Russell, M. A. H. (1996). Cognitive performance effects of subcutaneous nicotine in smokers and never-smokers. *Psychopharmacology, 127*, 31–38.

Hajek, P., Stead, L. F., West, R., & Jarvis, M. (2005). Relapse prevention interventions for smoking cessation. *Cochrane Database System Review, 25*, CD0.

Hayford, K. E., Patten, C. A., Rummans, T. A., Schroeder, D. A., Offord, K. P., Croghan, I. T., Glover, E. D., Sachs, D. P., & Hurt, R. D. (1999). Efficacy of bupropion for smoking cessation in smokers with a former history of major depression or alcoholism. *British Journal of Psychiatry, 174*, 173–178.

Heishman, S. J., Taylor, R. C., & Henningfield, J. E. (1994). Nicotine and smoking: A review of effects on human performance. *Experimental and Clinical Psychopharmacology, 2*, 345–395.

Heishman, S. J., & Henningfield, J. E. (2000). Tolerance to repeated nicotine administration on performance, subjective, and physiological responses in nonsmokers. *Psychopharmacology, 152*, 321–333.

Hitsman, B., Borrelli, B., McChargue, D. E., Spring, B., & Niaura, R. (2003). History of depression and smoking cessation outcome: A meta-analysis. *Journal of Consulting and Clinical Psychology, 71*, 657–663.

Hughes, J. R., Gust, S. W., Skoog, K., Keenan, R. M., & Fenwick, J. W. (1991). Symptoms of tobacco withdrawal: A replication and extension. *Archives of General Psychiatry, 48*(1), 52–59.

Hughes, J. R. (2000). Reduced smoking: An introduction and review of the evidence. *Addiction, 95*(Suppl.) S3–S7.

Hughes, J. R., Keely, J. P., Niaura, R. S., Ossip-Klein, D. J., Richmond, R. L., & Swan, G. E. (2003). Measures of abstinence in clinical trials: Issues and recommendations. *Nicotine and Tobacco Research, 5*, 13–25.

Hutchison, K. E., Wood, M. E., & Swift, R. (1999). Personality factors moderate subjective and psychophysiological responses to d-amphetamine in humans. *Experimental and Clinical Psychopharmacology, 7*, 493–501.

Hutchison, K. E., LaChance, H., Niaura, R., Bryan, A., & Smolen, A. (2002). The DRD4 VNTR polymorphism influences reactivity to smoking cues. *Journal of Abnormal Psychology, 111*, 134–143.

Jacobsen, L. K., Krystal, J. H., Mencl, W. E., Westerveld, M., Frost, S. J., & Pugh, K. R. (2005). Effects of smoking and smoking abstinence on cognition in adolescent tobacco smokers. *Biological Psychiatry, 57*, 56–66.

Jentsch, J. D., & Taylor, J. R. (1999). Impulsivity resulting from frontostriatal dysfunction in drug abuse: Implications for the control of behavior by reward-related stimuli. *Psychopharmacology, 146*, 373–390.

Jorenby, D. E., Leischow, S. J., Nides, M. A., Rennard, S. I., Johnston, J. A., Hughes, A. R., Smith, S. S., Muramoto, M. L., Daughton, D. M., Doan, K., Fiore, M. C., & Baker, T. B. (1999). A controlled trial of sustained-release bupripion, a nicotine patch, or both for smoking cessation. *New England Journal of Medicine, 340*, 685–691.

Keltikangas-Jarvinen, L., Elovainio, M., Kivimaki, M., Lichtermann, D., Ekelund, J., & Peltonen, L. (2003). Association between the type 4 dopamine receptor gene polymorphism and novelty seeking. *Psychosomatic Medicine, 65*, 471–476.

Kleykamp, B. A., Jennings, J. M., Blank, M. D., & Eissenberg, T. (2005). The effects of nicotine on attention and working memory in never smokers. *Psychology of Addictive Behaviors, 19*, 433–438.

Kumari, V., Gray, J. A., Ffytche, D. H., Mitterschiffthaler, M. T., Das, M., Zachariah, E., Vythelingum, G. N., Williams, S. C., Simmons, A., & Sharma, T. (2003). Cognitive effects of nicotine in humans: An fMRI study. *Neuroimage, 19*, 1002–1013.

Leonard, S., Adler, L. E., Benhammou, K., Berger, R., Breese, C. R., Drebing, C., Gault, J., Lee, M. J., Logel, J., Olincy, A., Ross, R. G., Stevens, K., Sullivan, B., Vianzon, R., Virnich, D. E., Waldo, M., Walton, K., & Freedman, R. (2001). Smoking and mental illness. *Pharmacology, Biochemistry and Behavior, 70*, 561–570.

Lerman, C., Shields, P. G., Wileyto, E. P., Audrain, J., Pinto, A., Hawk, L., Krishnan, S., Niaura, R., & Epstein, L. (2002). Pharmacogenetic investigation of smoking cessation treatment. *Pharmacogenetics, 12*, 627–634.

Lerman, C., Shields, P. G., Wileyto, E. P., Audrain, J., Pinto, A., Kusharski, S., Krishnan, S., Niaura, R., & Epstein, L. (2003). Effects of dopamine transporter and receptor polymorphisms on smoking cessation in a burprioion clinical trial. *Health psychology, 22*, 541–548.

London, E. D., Ernst, M., Grant, S., Bonson, K., & Weinstein, A. (2000). Orbitofrontal cortex and human drug abuse: Functional imaging. *Cerebral Cortex, 10*, 334–342.

Marlatt, G. A., & Gordon, J. R. (1985). *Relapse Prevention: Maintenance strategies in the treatment of addictive behaviors.* New York: Guilford Press.

Martin-Soelch, C., Missimer, J., Leenders, K. L., & Schultz, W. (2003). Neural activity related to the processing of increasing monetary reward in smokers and nonsmokers. *European Journal of Neuroscience, 18*, 680–688.

Mendrek, A., Monterosso, J., Simon, S. L., Jarvik, M., Brody, A., Olmstead, R., Domier, C. P., Cohen, M. S., Ernst, M., & London, E. D. (2006). Working memory in cigarette smokers: Comparison to non-smokers and effects of abstinence. *Addictive Behaviours, 5*, 833–844.

Mitchell, S. H. (1999). Measures of impulsivity in cigarette smokers and non-smokers. *Psychopharmacology, 146*, 455–464.

Mogg, K., & Bradley, B. P. (2002). Selective processing of smoking-related cues in smokers: Manipulation of deprivation level and comparison of three measures of processing bias. *Psychopharmacology, 16*, 385–392.

Munafò, M. R., Clark, T. G., Johnstone, E. C., Murphy, M. F. G., & Walton, R. (2004). The genetic basis for smoking behaviour: A systematic review and meta-analysis. *Nicotine and Tobacco Research, 6*, 583–597.

Munafò, M. R., Shields, A. E., Berrettini, W. H., Patterson, F., & Lerman, C. (2005). Pharmacogenetics and nicotine addiction treatment. *Pharmacogenomics, 6*, 211–223.

Newhouse, P. A., Potter, A., & Singh, A. (2004). Effects of nicotinic stimulation on cognitive performance. *Current Opinion in Pharmacology, 4*, 36–46.

Niaura, R., Abrams, D. B., Shadel, W. G., Rohsenow, D. J., Monti, P. M., & Sirota, A. D. (1999). Cue exposure treatment for smoking relapse prevention: A controlled clinical trial. *Addiction, 94*, 685–695.

Palmatier, M. I., Evans-Martin, F. F., Hoffman, A., Caggiula, A. R., Chaudhri, N., Donny, E. C., Liu, X., Booth, S., Gharib, M., Craven, L., & Sved, A. F. (2006). Dissociating the primary rein-forcing and reinforcement-enhancing effects of nicotine using a rat self-administration paradigm with concurrently available drug and environmental reinforcers. *Psychopharmacology, 184*(3–4), 391–400.

Park, S., Knopcik, C., McGurk, S., & Meltzer, H. (2000). Nicotine impairs spatial working memory while leaving spatial attention intact. *Neuropsychopharmacology, 22*(2), 200–209.

Piasecki, T. M., Fiore, M. C., & Baker, T. B. (1998). Profiles in discouragement: Two studies of variability in the time course of smoking withdrawal symptoms. *Journal of Abnormal Psychology*, *107*, 238–251.

Piasecki, T. M. (2006). Relapse to smoking. *Clinical Psychology Review*, *26*, 196–215.

Poltavski, D. V., & Petros, T. (2006). Effects of transdermal nicotine on attention in adult non-smokers with and without attentional deficits. *Physiology and Behavior*, *30*, 614–624.

Potter, A. S., & Newhouse, P. A. (2003). The effects of acute nicotine administration on behavioural inhibition in adolescents with attention-deficit/hyperactivity disorder (ADHD). *Biological Psychiatry*, *53*, 83S.

Powell, J. H. (1995). Conditioned responses to drug-related stimuli: Is context crucial? *Addiction*, *90*, 1089–1095.

Powell, J. H., Tait, S., & Lessiter, J. (2002b). Cigarette smoking and attention to pleasure and threat words in the Stroop paradigm. *Addiction*, *97*, 1163–1170.

Powell, J. H., Dawkins, L., & Davis, R. (2002a). Smoking, reward responsivenss, and response inhibition: Tests of an incentive motivational model. *Biological Psychiatry*, *51*, 151–163.

Powell, J. H., Pickering, A. D., Dawkins, L., West, R., & Powell, J. F. (2004). Cognitive and psychological correlates of smoking abstinence and predictors of successful cessation. *Addictive Behaviours*, *29*, 1407–1426.

Royal College of Physicians, Tobacco Advisory Group. (2000). *Nicotine Addiction in Britain*. London: Royal College of Physicians.

Seth, P., Cheeta, S., Tucci, S., & File, S. E. (2002). Nicotinic-serotonergic interactions in brain and behaviour. *Pharmacology, biochemistry and behaviour*, *71*, 795–805.

Shoaib, M., & Bizarro, L. (2004). Deficits in a sustained attention task following nicotine withdrawal in rats. *Psychopharmacology*, *178*, 211–222.

Spilich, G. J., June, L., & Renner, J. (1992). Cigarette smoking and cognitive performance. *British Journal of Addiction*, *87*, 1313–1326.

Stein, E. A., Pankiewicz, M. D., Harsch, H. H., Cho, J. K., Fuller, S. A., Hoffman, R. G., Hawkins, M., Rao, S. M., Bandettini, P. A., & Bloom, A. S. (1998). Nicotine-induced limbic cortical activation in the human brain: A functional MRI study. *American Journal of Psychiatry*, *155*, 1009–1015.

Stewart, J., de Wit, H., & Eikelboom, R. (1984). Role of unconditioned and conditioned drug effects in the self-administration of opiates and stimulants. *Psychological Reviews*, *91*, 251–268.

Svingos, A. L., Periasamy, S., & Pickel, V. M. (2000). Presynaptic dopamine D(4) receptor localization in the rat nucleus accumbens shell. *Synapse*, *36*, 222–232.

Thewissen, R., Snijders, S. J., Havermans, R. C., van den Hout, M., & Jansen, A. (2006). Renewal of cue-elicited urge to smoke: Implications for cue exposure treatment. *Behavior Research and Therapy*, *44*, 1441–1449.

Tiffany, S. T., Cox, L. S., & Elash, C. A. (2000). Effects of transdermal nicotine patches on abstinence-induced and cue-elicited craving in cigarette smokers. *Journal of Consulting and Clinical Psychology*, *68*, 233–240.

Tonnesen, P., Tonstad, S., Hjalmarson, A., Lebargy, F., Van Spiegel, P. I., Hider, A., Sweet, R., & Townsend, J. (2003). A multicentre, randomized, double-blind, placebo-controlled, 1-year study of bupropion SR for smoking cessation. *Journal of International Medicine*, *254*, 184–192.

Tonstad, S., & Johnston, J. A. (2004). Does bupropion have advantages over other medical therapies in the cessation of smoking? *Expert Opinion in Pharmacotherapy*, *5*, 727–734.

Volkow, N. D., Fowler, J. S., Wang, G.- J., & Swanson, J. M. (2004a). Dopamine in drug abuse and addiction: Results from imaging studies and treatment implications. *Molecular Psychiatry*, *9*, 557–569.

Waters, A. J., Shiffman, S., Bradley, B. P., & Mogg, K. (2003). Attentional shifts to smoking cues in smokers. *Addiction*, *98*, 1409–1417.

Waters, A. J., Shiffman, S., Sayette, M. A., Paty, J. A., Gwaltney, C. J., & Balabanis, M. H. (2004). Cue-provoked craving and nicotine replacement therapy in smoking cessation. *Journal of Consulting and Clinical Psychology*, *72*, 1136–1143.

Weiss, F., & Koob, G. F. (2001). Drug addiction: Functional neurotoxicity of the brain reward systems. *Neurotoxicity Research, 3*, 145–156.

West, R. J., Hajek, P., & Belcher, M. (1987). Time course of cigarette withdrawal symptoms during four weeks of treatment with nicotine chewing gum. *Addictive Behaviours, 12*, 199–203.

Young, J. W., Finlayson, K., Spratt, C., Marston, H. M., Crawford, N., Kelly, J. S., & Sharkey, J. (2004). Nicotine improves sustained attention in mice: Evidence for involvement of the alpha7 nicotinic acetylcholine receptor. *Neuropsychopharmacology, 29*, 891–900.

Yudkin, P. L., Munafò, M. R., Hey, K., Roberts, S. J., Welch, S. J., Johnstone, E. C., Murphy, M. F. G., Griffiths S.-E., & Walton, R. T. (2004). Effectiveness of nicotine patches in relation to genotype in women versus men: Randomised controlled trial. *British Medical Journal, 328*, 989–990.

Zuckerman, M., & Kuhlman, D. M. (2000). Personality and risk-taking: Common biosocial factors. *Journal of Personality, 68*, 999–1029.

CHAPTER 13

Therapeutic Outcome Research and Dissemination of Empirically Based Treatment for Alcohol Use Disorders

Paula Wilbourne and Ken Weingardt

Center for Health Care Evaluation, VA Palo Alto Health Care System, Stanford University School of Medicine, Menlo Park, CA 94025, USA

Abstract: Effective, empirically based treatments for alcohol use disorders include brief interventions, motivational interviewing, cognitive-behavioral interventions, and relationship focused therapies. Routine clinical practice does not typically reflect the principles and practices suggested by these treatments. This disparity may be explained on the reliance of researchers on passive dissemination strategies for making research findings available to treatment providers. The importance of macro-strategies promoted at a national level and micro-strategies targeting individual provider behavior for achieve sustained adoption of empirically based treatment are reviewed. Conclusions highlight the importance of collaborative, multi-systemic mechanisms supporting the development, the exploration and the dissemination of effective treatments for alcohol use disorders.

BRIEF HISTORY OF PROBLEM

Human civilization has a long history of grappling with the problems caused by alcohol misuse and has made many attempts to ameliorate the pain and suffering caused by addiction. References to the problems caused by alcohol and prohibitions on the use of it can be seen throughout our history. The scientific exploration of treatments for alcohol problems has a much shorter history, with published clinical trials dating back to the 1950s. Given the long-standing role of alcohol problems in our history and the relatively recent development of a scientific basis for their treatment, it is perhaps not surprising that development of expertise in substance abuse treatment is challenged by gaps in the knowledge gained from clinical practice, research and public policy. These gaps among research, practice and policy grow from the unique perspectives and constraints experienced by professionals working in each of these contexts. Practitioners delivering treatment often find that information from treatment research is inaccessible, takes too long to reach them and to fails to address relevant questions. Researchers often complain that practitioners do not bother to adopt the effective clinical innovations that are developed in clinical trials.

This chapter describes the empirically supported treatments (EST) for alcohol problems and the evidence for effective strategies for dissemination of these treatments. It describes the disparity between routine clinical practice and the strategies that have earned empirical support and outlines the possible causes for this disparity. Finally, models for understanding change in clinical practice behaviors in the field of substance abuse treatment are presented.

TREATMENTS THAT WORK

A large body of empirical research has identified treatments that demonstrate efficacy in the treatment of alcohol problems. These treatments tend to be well-specified, using clear theoretical models. Effective treatments emphasize an individual's ability (self-efficacy) to stop or reduce drinking. Some therapies do this through teaching self-management skills. Other approaches encourage the person to utilize his or her own existing resources. Among EST, there is an emphasis on the client's motivation for change, whether through enhancing the client's intrinsic motivation, specific behavioral contracting, or the rearrangement of social contingencies to favor change. Attention to an individual's social context and support system is also prominent among several of the most supported approaches. These effective interventions are often contrasted to the treatments that are most commonly used in clinical practice. Commonly used, less effective interventions include educational lectures and films, confrontational approaches and insight oriented psychotherapy (Miller & Wilbourne, 2002). Specific empirically supported approaches are described below.

BRIEF THERAPIES

Brief interventions and motivational interventions described in this category are typically designed for delivery in one to four sessions. Interventions such as these are unlikely to teach new skills or alter personality, but they may tip the balance in favor of change and set change processes in motion. Therapies of this type have strong empirical support for their effectiveness.

MOTIVATIONAL INTERVENTIONS

These empirically supported interventions are designed to enhance a person's motivation for change. This approach relies on a client-centered, directive counseling style designed to resolve ambivalence and facilitate change. These interventions are guided by the principles of motivational interviewing which include empathizing with the client's perspective, developing discrepancies between the client's substance use and the client's desired outcomes, rolling with the client's resistance to change, highlighting the client's autonomy and supporting the client's self-efficacy about making change (Miller & Rollnick, 2002). Empirically supported motivational interventions often involve decisional balance exercises and personalized feedback of assessment results (Burke et al., 2004). Typically, they rely on activating or enhancing the client's existing resources for change. The immediate goals of motivational interventions include empathizing with the client's perspective, resolution of the client's ambivalence about change, and reinforcing the client's statements about change. Motivational interviews have been shown to be effective as a pre-treatment for more extensive interventions and as stand-alone interventions. They have strong support in diverse populations (Hettema, Miller, & Steele, 2004).

BRIEF INTERVENTIONS

These brief treatments occur in a single session and may involve providing clients with advice to change. For this review, they are distinguished from motivational interventions. Common elements of empirically supported brief interventions can be summarized by the acronym of "FRAMES": *f*eedback of assessment results, *r*esponsibility, *a*dvice, *m*enu of options, *e*mpathy, *s*elf-efficacy (Miller & Sanchez, 1993). These interventions have consistently performed better than no intervention and better than standard care (Bien, Miller, & Tonigan, 1993; Moyer et al., 2002a). Studies often find no difference between these interventions and more extensive interventions. While these interventions have strong evidence in individuals with mild to moderate drinking problems (the largest portion of the population with alcohol problems), they remain untested in individuals with more severe problems. These interventions may be most appropriate for use in a stepped-care model when working with individuals with more severe alcohol problems (Breslin et al., 1997; Sobell & Sobell, 2000). At present, clients who have positive life contexts and do not have severe skills deficits appear to be the best candidates for brief interventions.

COGNITIVE BEHAVIORAL APPROACHES

Therapies in this category include the community reinforcement approach, coping skills training and behavioral-marital therapy, all of which use elements of cognitive behavioral therapy to address alcohol problems. Most of the treatments in this category work to improve the quality of the clients' social relationships. The efficacy of treatments in this category points to the importance of addressing the social environment, primary support relationships and the contingencies that influence drinking or sobriety. These treatments may be more effective when delivered in the context of a comprehensive treatment program and when working with individuals with less severe alcohol dependence (Longabaugh & Morgenstern, 1999).

COMMUNITY REINFORCEMENT APPROACH (CRA)

This is a broad-spectrum intervention that promotes change in a person's social environment to make sobriety become more reinforcing than continued substance use. This approach employs familial, social-recreational and vocational rewards to assist in the recovery process. CRA emphasizes the development of skills to assist in employment, relationships and recreation. This approach uses functional analyses to identify triggers for substance use and strategies to replace substance use with safer alternative, enjoyable activities. Disulfiram (Antabuse), a medication that induces extreme nausea when alcohol is consumed, is an optional component of the CRA approach. Typically, disulfiram administration is moni-tored and reinforced by a spouse or family member.

This approach has also demonstrated effectiveness when working with concerned significant others to enhance their ability to motivate individuals with substance use problems to seek treatment. Family members are encouraged to avoid "enabling behaviors" and to allow the problem substance user to experience the negative consequences of continued substance use. Reviews of the treatment literature indicate that CRA is more effective than standard care, especially when it includes abstinence based incentives, disulfiram monitoring and social reinforce-ment for pill taking (Higgins, Alessi, & Danton, 2002; Miller et al., 2001; Smith, Meyers, & Delaney, 1998; Smith, Meyers, & Miller, 2001).

BEHAVIORALLY ORIENTED COUPLES AND FAMILY THERAPY

These interventions are designed to reduce drinking and promote sobriety by working with a patient's important relationships. These approaches often begin with a thorough assessment of the identified patient's drinking behavior and the marital relationship. Interventions include behavioral contracts, Antabuse contracts, increasing caring behaviors, communication skills training and plans for recreational activities. The effectiveness of these interventions is supported by substantial research evidence (O'Farrell et al., 1993; O'Farrell, Choquette, & Cutter, 1998; O'Farrell & Fals-Stewart, 2001; Stanton & Shadish, 1997).

COPING SKILLS TRAINING

Skills in these treatments may focus specifically on skills for avoiding alcohol use or issues in other life domains. Among this class of interventions, problem solving skills generally focus on more effectively life management events. Social skills training prepares clients to better navigate relationships with others by training clients in communication skills, assertiveness or drink refusal techniques. Relapse prevention teaches clients cognitive-behavioral skills for the management of drink-ing problems and coping with high-risk situations to minimizing the likelihood of a return to patterns of problematic drinking.

MECHANISMS OF CHANGE

In the past several years there has been growing interest and research into the mechanisms of change that underlie EST. One method for identifying possible mechanisms of treatment is by examining the theoretical basis for effective treat-ments. The interventions described above including motivational interventions, brief interventions, cognitive-behavioral behavioral approaches and therapies focusing on the social environment suggest processes such as increases in self-efficacy, changes in social norms and empathy as possible mechanisms for change (Finney, Wilbourne, & Moos, in press).

Other approaches to understanding the mechanisms of change have utilized elements of statistical analysis and project design to better understand the active ingredients of treatment for alcohol problems. Project MATCH made specific predictions about the types of patients that might benefit from particular treatments. For example, motivational interviewing was predicted to be more effective for patients who were less motivated. However, this hypothesis and most of the theorized matching hypotheses were not supported (Longabaugh et al., 2005). Other studies have failed to find a robust mediation treatment effects and treatment outcome by constructs such as motivation or skill improvement (Dunn, DeRoo, & Rivara, 2001; Morgenstern & Longabaugh, 2000). The elusive nature of matching effects and mediational models may be explained by the fact that treatments may not be as distinct as the theoretical models that define them would lead us to believe. For example, empathy, skill improvement or improved social networks may be a part of many treatments, not just treatments that specifically target these as therapeutic elements. Alternately, treatment may impact elements of a client's experience that have not yet been explored or well defined in empirical investigation.

DISSEMINATION/IMPLEMENTATION

The majority of the evidence-based approaches described have yet to find their way into the clinical practice of community-based treatment providers (Lamb, Greenlick, & McCarty, 1998). The lag between the development of innovative treatments and their adoption into routine practice is not unique to substance abuse treatment. Evidence-based medicine, with its emphasis on the implementation of clinical practice guidelines, has evolved largely in response to a similar gap between current research knowledge and health care as it is routinely delivered in primary care and hospital settings (Grol, 1997, 2001; Grol & Grimshaw, 1999). The mental health professions have also acknowledged a significant gap between research and practice, and have responded with efforts to disseminate empirically supported treatments (EST; Chambless & Ollendick, 2001) and more recently, to promote the evidence-based practice of psychology (EBPP; APA Presidential Task Force, 2006).

In substance abuse treatment, as in medicine and mental health, this disconnection between research and practice has largely been attributed to researchers' over reliance on passive dissemination strategies. Traditional efforts to close the gap have focused on dissemination of information through conferences, journal articles, and reports or brochures (Backer, David, & Soucy, 1995). Although these dissemination-focused activities are valuable, they usually fall far short of producing the significant individual and organizational changes that could result from the large-scale adoption of treatment innovations.

Research has consistently demonstrated that passive dissemination strategies, such as reading about a new treatment approach or attending a continuing education workshop about it, are not sufficient to engender competence in delivering that intervention (Miller et al., 2006). In a review of workshops that provided continuing education for physicians and allied health professionals, Oxman et al. (1995) found that information-only strategies are usually insufficient to produce changes in clinical behavior. Similarly, the literature on the dissemination and implementation of clinical practice guidelines has consistently found that passive educational strategies such as the ubiquitous one or two-day training workshop are generally ineffective at promoting sustained adoption of new clinical practices (Grol, 1999).

THE MACRO LEVEL: EFFORTS TO PROMOTE EVIDENCE-BASED PRACTICES AMONG COMMUNITY COUNSELORS

Over the past two decades, agencies of the U.S. Federal Government have embraced this reality and promoted several ambitious programs and initiatives that employ active, participative strategies to engage providers in implementing evidence-based practices. Given the magnitude of the research–practice gap, and the many fundamental differences between substance abuse researchers and practitioners that serve to perpetuate it (Kalb & Propper, 1976; Sorenson & Midkiff, 2002; Miller et al., 2006), it is not surprising that these efforts have not always been met with complete success. In the section below, we briefly outline several of these ongoing initiatives, with a view toward better understanding the lessons learned from large-scale efforts to implement research-based knowledge in the real world of clinical practice.

One of the earliest large-scale initiatives to disseminate effective, research-based interventions and service protocols to substance abuse treatment and prevention practitioners was NIDA's Technology Transfer Program, established in 1989. Here, the term technology does not refer to electronics or software, but is used more broadly to refer to our current state of knowledge of how to combine resources to produce desired products, to solve problems or to fulfill needs (e.g. deliver evidence-based substance abuse treatment services throughout the nation). From this perspective, efforts to narrow the research-practice gap are framed as efforts to facilitate the transfer of technologies developed in treatment outcomes studies from researchers to community treatment providers. The concept underlying technology transfer approaches is that improvement in drug abuse treatment and prevention practices involves a human process, which, if successful, leads to individual and organizational change. The extensive literature on technology transfer, dating back to the 1960s (see Backer, 1991) reveals that the human dynamics of change must be addressed not only on the individual level, but at the community, organizational and systemic levels as well.

The six key strategies for successful technology transfer efforts (Backer, David, & Soucy, 1995) clearly reflect a deep appreciation of this human process: (1) there needs to be *direct, personal contact* between those who will be adopting the innovation and its developers or others with knowledge about the intervention, (2) a well-developed *strategic plan* for how an innovation will be adopted in a new setting, including attention to possible implementation problems and how they will be addressed, (3) *outside consultation* on the change process to provide conceptual and practical assistance in designing the change effort, (4) *user-oriented information* about the innovation that has been translated into language that potential users can readily understand, (5) *individual and organizational championship* by opinion leaders and community leaders, and (6) *involvement of potential users* who will have to live with the results of the innovation need to be involved in planning for innovation adoption.

Technology transfer activities and products developed by the NIDA technology transfer program include interactive, practitioner-oriented national conferences, a videotape series designed to raise awareness of clinical application of NIDA-sponsored research findings including relapse prevention and dual diagnosis, and "technology transfer packages" that include sets of materials to describe an intervention protocol for an EST approach, as well as materials addressing administrative and other common implementation issues, and clinical reports on selected topics presented in practical format and language to encourage adoption of intervention strategies.

During the 1990s, responsibility for the U.S. federal government's efforts to transfer substance abuse treatment technology from research to practice became increasingly concentrated in the Substance Abuse Mental Health Services Administration (SAMHSA) which is located within the U.S. Department of Health and Human Services (DHHS). In October of 1992, SAMSHA created the *Center for Substance Abuse Treatment* (CSAT; http://csat.samhsa.gov/), with a congressional mandate to expand the availability of effective treatment and recovery services for alcohol and drug problems.

Several CSAT initiatives and programs are focused squarely on promoting the adoption of evidence-based research practices among community treatment providers. For example, *the Addiction Technology Transfer Center* (ATTC) Network (http://www.nattc.org) was created in 1993 with a mandate to upgrade the skills of existing practitioners and other health professionals and to disseminate the latest science to the treatment community. Through its network of 14 regional centers, the ATTC produces a variety of products and services designed to transmit the latest knowledge, skills and attitudes of professional addiction treatment practice. One such resource, "*The Change Book*" (ATTC, 2000) is a step-by-step handbook which includes principles, steps, strategies and activities designed to guide readers through the 10 key steps of technology transfer, concluding with a detailed, educational workbook to put the principles into practice. The results of a recent study by McCarty et al. (2004) suggest that the procedures outlined in *The Change Book* can be effective in promoting evidence-based practices among rural practitioners interested in learning how to use buprenorphine for office-based management of opiate dependence.

A second CSAT initiative focused on narrowing the research-practice gap is the *Practice Improvement Collaboratives* program (PIC; http://csat.samhsa.gov/pic/) which was initiated in 1999 to promote implementation of evidence-based practices for the treatment of alcohol and drug dependence through partnerships of practitioners, investigators, policy makers and consumers. More specifically, the mission of the PIC is to (1) develop and sustain community involvement in, and commitment to, practice improvement in the delivery of substance abuse treatment services, (2) improve the quality of substance abuse treatment through the adoption of evidence-based practices in community-based organizations (CBOs), and (3) identify successful methods and models for implementing evidence-based practices in CBOs. A recent review of the implementation experiences within 11 PICs (Cotter et al., 2005) found that successful development consistently required environmental adaptation, construction of formal organizational structures and processes, recruitment and retention of membership, and implementation of activities that fostered the improvement of the PICs.

A third CSAT initiative to promote evidence-based practices among community treatment providers is referred to as *The Knowledge Application Program* (KAP; http://kap.samhsa.gov/general). The KAP strives to take knowledge about best treatment practices in substance abuse treatment and package and promote it in a way that ensures that its application in the field is widespread. This is accomplished through a strategic program in which KAP staff produces, markets, and distributes publications and products designed to be responsive to its diverse audience of substance abuse treatment providers. KAP products include the *Treatment Improvement Protocol Series* (TIPs) which are the result of a systematic process bringing together clinicians, researchers, program managers, policymakers and non-federal experts to reach a consensus on various state-of-the-art treatment practices. In an effort to further facilitate implementation of the best practices captured in each TIP, the KAP has also developed a series of pocket-sized quick reference guides which present the TIP information in a format designed to facilitate quick access to relevant information.

Finally, the National Institute on Drug Abuse (NIDA) has developed the *Clinical Trials Network* (CTN; http://www.nida.nih.gov/CTN/index.htm) as a mechanism for treatment researchers, and community-based service providers to cooperatively develop, validate, refine and deliver new treatment options to patients in community-level clinical practice. The objectives of the CTN are to conduct studies of behavioral, pharmacological, and integrated behavioral and pharmacological treatment interventions of therapeutic effect in rigorous, multi-site clinical trials to determine effectiveness across a broad range of community-based treatment settings and diversified patient populations; and to insure the transfer of research results to physicians, clinicians, providers and patients. The scientists and programs in the CTN have collaborated to select and design studies testing the efficacy of evidence-based treatment methods when delivered by the staff of a real-world community treatment program (Miller et al., 2006). The initial results of one such collaborative study (Carroll et al., 2002) have shown that training the intake staff of community treatment centers in motivational interviewing techniques can significantly improve rates of treatment engagement.

THE MICRO-LEVEL: CLINICAL TRAINING AS A NECESSARY, BUT INSUFFICIENT INGREDIENT FOR SUSTAINED CLINICAL ADOPTION

The various technology transfer initiatives just described place significant and appropriate emphasis on the organizational changes required to achieve sustained adoption of evidence-based practices. However, they also acknowledge that such changes require that individual practitioners receive adequate training in order to competently conduct evidence-based treatment interventions. In fact, one might argue that the effective and efficient training of front line practitioners is one of the most critical mechanisms for promoting the adoption of evidence-based practices. In the section that follows, we review the empirical literature on the role of clinical training in narrowing the research-practice gap in substance abuse treatment, and address the various theoretical, practical and technical issues surrounding these efforts.

Several authors have applied Everett Roger's (1995) Diffusion of innovation framework to understanding the adoption of evidence-based treatment practices by community treatment providers (Stirman et al.; Miller et al., 2006). According to Rogers, diffusion of information theory describes a process by which an individual such as a practicing clinician, passes from (1) *knowledge*—first knowledge of an innovation, such as awareness of Coping Skills Training or Motivational Interviewing, to (2) *persuasion*—forming an attitude about it, either favorable or unfavorable, to (3) *decision*—a decision to adopt or reject the innovation, to (4) *implementation*—which involves actually putting an innovation to use, for example using MI in one's daily clinical practice, and finally to (5) *confirmation*—which occurs when an individual seeks reinforcement of a decision that has already been made.

Clinical training, whether it is delivered via a traditional face-to-face workshop, or via various technology-based delivery mechanisms (Weingardt, 2004), is critically important at the initial knowledge stage of the diffusion process. It is in this first stage that trainees obtain the required preparatory knowledge via reading, verbal instruction or observing competent practice by others (Miller et al., 2006). The basic "how-to" knowledge required to implement a new evidence-based treatment practice can actually be quite complex, and includes: how to identify clients for whom the treatment is appropriate, how to structure the therapy, how to correctly utilize various clinical techniques and strategies, and how to deal with clients who are not responding to treatment. This preparatory knowledge is critical for practice change, for as Rogers (1995) points out, if an adequate level of knowledge (particularly the nuts-and-bolts or "how-to" knowledge) is not obtained prior to the trial and adoption of an innovation, rejection and discontinuance are likely to result.

Given the central role that clinical training plays in our efforts to implement evidence-based practices, what do we know about the efficacy and effectiveness of clinical training programs for substance abuse treatment providers? In the section that follows, we review the empirical literature in this area with an emphasis on the strengths and limitations of clinical training as a mechanism for facilitating the adoption of research-based psychosocial treatment approaches.

THE EFFICACY AND EFFECTIVENESS OF CLINICAL TRAINING

In the training and development literature, evaluation is typically conceptualized in the context of a model that was originally proposed by Donald Kirkpatrick in the late 1950s (Kirkpatrick, 1959a, 1959b, 1960a, 1960b). To this day, the simplicity and commonsense appeal of this Kirkpatrick model has insured its continued popularity among professionals in training and human performance improvement. According to this model, *Level 1* evaluation measures learners' reactions to the material. *Level 2* measures the degree to which new learning has taken place. *Level 3* measures the extent to which learners are able to transfer newly acquired knowledge and skills into on-the-job performance, and *Level 4* measures the impact that these performance improvements have on the bottom line (in our case, client-level and system-level outcomes).

If we apply Kirkpatrick's model to the literature on clinical training in substance abuse treatment, we find many examples of studies demonstrating the effectiveness of clinical training on Levels 1 and 2. Level 1 evaluations are the ubiquitous paper-and-pencil forms that must be completed at the conclusion of continuing education workshops. Such forms typically ask participants to rate the comfort of the meeting facility, their satisfaction with the instructor, and the degree to which they feel that the training activity met its stated objectives. Training professionals often refer to these forms as "smile sheets," as participants almost always evaluate their experiences very favorably on these measures. One would expect substance abuse counselors to exhibit similar ceiling effects on their ratings of satisfaction with the training sessions they attend.

Level 2 evaluations go beyond measuring learner satisfaction to objectively measure *knowledge transfer*. Knowledge transfer refers to objectively measured improvements in test scores that occur as the result of the training. Level 2 evaluations are often reported in the literature as randomized controlled trials comparing the difference between pre- and post-test scores (e.g. Weingardt, Villafranca & Levin, in press).

Level 3 evaluations measure the extent to which learners are able to transfer newly acquired knowledge and skills into on-the-job performance. Level 3 evaluations look beyond the question of whether counselors can demonstrate that they have acquired new knowledge about an evidence-based practice, to the all-important question of whether counselors are able to competently apply that new practice in the context of their clinical work. This is a critical distinction. Although recent research has documented clear improvements in pre- and post-training test scores for counselors receiving training, and significant improvements in the trainees' perceptions of their own competence at implementing a new treatment approach, these data appear to be largely unrelated to their actual proficiency in delivering the treatment (Carroll et al., 2002; Miller et al., 2004).

In studies evaluating the efficacy of substance abuse treatment, Level 3 evaluations involve the generation of objective ratings of trainees' competence in delivering the target treatment approach. Such ratings are frequently obtained by asking trainees to self-select an audiotape of a session from normal practice as a demonstration of acquired skillfulness in a new method (Miller et al., 2004). These audiotapes are then reviewed by independent coders who use a behaviorally anchored, objective rating scale to quantify the degree to which the trainee adhered to the target approach. Examples of such adherence scales include the Yale Adherence Competence Scale (YACS; Carroll et al., 2000) and the Motivational Interviewing Treatment Integrity scale (MITI; Moyers et al., 2002b). Other Level 3 evaluation strategies include asking trainees to demonstrate their skills by responding to written case scenarios (Miller, Hedrick, & Orlofsky, 1991), case material presented via video or interactive technologies (Weingardt, 2004), or to an actor who has been trained to simulate a patient who presents with substance use disorder (Ockene et al., 1997).

In their recent review of this literature, Miller et al. (2006) conclude that two-day workshop training can produce small measurable changes in clinical practice that can be demonstrated on demand via the various techniques described above, but not enough to make a difference to patients. This brings us to Level 4 of Kirkpatrick's model and the proverbial "bottom line": do all of these efforts to implement evidence-based practices actually improve client outcomes? Although the research has clearly demonstrated that counselors who follow evidence-based practices can significantly improve client outcomes in the context of carefully controlled efficacy studies, it seems unlikely that training alone will be sufficient to promote the sustained adoption that would be required for large-scale improvement of client outcomes.

TRAINING ALONE IS INSUFFICIENT TO PROMOTE SUSTAINED CHANGE IN CLINICAL PRACTICE

We contend that an instructionally sound training intervention is perhaps best understood as a necessary, but insufficient condition for sustained, measurable improvements in clinical practice (Level 3) and client outcomes (Level 4). A training intervention, whether it is a two-day workshop, or an online continuing education course, cannot address psychological reactance and/or rational objections that individual practitioners may have about evidence-based, manual-driven practice (Addis & Krasnow, 2000). Nor can training alone address the many intrapersonal, interpersonal, organizational and systemic barriers that can prevent changes in clinical practice (Goldman et al., 2001; Pincus et al., 2001). Using the framework developed by evidence-based medicine researchers (e.g. Grol, 1997, 2001; Grol & Grimshaw, 1999), training in evidence-based practices for substance abuse treatment can best be classified as an educational approach to changing clinical practice. Because the educational approach relies heavily upon the intrinsic motivation of professionals to acquire new knowledge, skills and abilities, dissemination efforts that rely exclusively on this narrow approach are unlikely to be unsuccessful (Weingardt, 2004).

Interventions designed to change clinical practice are most likely to be successful when they combine multiple approaches (Grol, 2001; Shaneyfelt, 2001). Table 1 summarizes the various approaches that one might employ in an effort to facilitate the adoption of evidence-based practices for substance abuse treatment. The first three approaches outlined, including the educational, epidemiological, and marketing approaches, all attempt to change clinical practice by influencing the internal cognitive and affective processes of the individual practitioner. As such, they alone cannot address the systemic barriers to change that exist at the patient, practice, health plan and consumer levels (Pincus et al., 2001).

By focusing on influences that are external to the individual clinician, a second broad category of interventions focused on factors external to the clinician can serve as powerful complements to training. To be maximally effective, training for substance abuse treatment providers should be embedded in a larger intervention focused on external, systemic influences. For example, a clinician who has completed a training workshop or web-based training course could subsequently receive a visit from an expert consultant who could answer questions and provide on site supervision ("academic detailing," a social interaction approach cf. Mittman, Tonesk, & Jacobson, 1992). Research has demonstrated that it can be very helpful

Table 1
Approaches to Changing Clinical Practice (Reprinted from Weingardt, 2004; adapted from Grol, 1997, 2001; Grol & Grimshaw, 1999, with permission from Blackwell Publishing Ltd.)

Approach	Focus	Example
Approaches that focus on factors *internal* to the clinician		
1. Educational	Intrinsic motivation of professionals	Complete Workshop, Course, WBT
2. Epidemiological	Rational information seeking and decision making	Follow clinical practice guidelines
3. Marketing	Attractive product adapted to needs of target audience	Receive brochure, promotional materials, watch Public Service Announcement
Approaches that focus on factors *external* to the clinician		
4. Behavioral	Reinforcing desired performance	Receive award or monetary bonus for desired behavior
5. Social Interaction	Social influence of significant peers/role models	Convince local opinion leader(s) to support change in practice
6. Organizational	Creating structural and organizational conditions to improve care	Form Total Quality Improvement (TQI) team
7. Coercive	Control and Pressure, external motivation	Receive reprimand, fine, or sanction for failure to perform desired behavior

for both skill acquisition and sustained adoption to have a proficient expert in the new intervention onsite and readily available to line staff to provide ongoing coaching and supervision (Miller et al., 2006).

It would appear that opportunities for supervised practice, feedback and coaching are critical for sustained adoption of evidence-based practice in substance abuse treatment. Unfortunately, the substance abuse treatment system is notoriously resource-constrained, and treatment centers typically lack the funding that would be required to support such efforts. As McLellan and colleagues have clearly documented, substance abuse treatment programs are characterized by unstable organizational and administrative structures (McLellan & Meyers, 2004), and a disturbingly high level of turnover at all levels, from line staff to executive directors, with more than half having been in their jobs for less than a year (McLellan, Carise, & Kleber, 2003).

CONCLUSION

Thus, from our micro-level analysis, focusing on variables internal to the clinician, we come full circle to the macro-level and resume our discussion of external influences on practice. Clinical training can indeed provide the individual counselor with the "how-to," nuts-and-bolts, preparatory knowledge required to implement an evidence-based practice (Level 2–new learning). However, regular, ongoing clinical consultation and supervision is required in order for the counselor to competently use that practice with his or her regular clientele (Level 3–on-the-job performance). Lack of adequate funding means that the resources required for such efforts must necessarily come from sources outside the individual treatment center, and brings us back to the macro-level. Sustained adoption of clinical practice change requires considerable attention to the many systemic, organizational and behavioral factors that shape the context within which counselors do their work. Counselors working in a treatment center are more than group of individual practitioners. They ply their craft in a complex field of forces which invariably includes politics, personal relationships and culturally defined norms of professional behavior.

It would seem that the treatment outcome research community is beginning to embrace the reality that NIDA and SAMHSA have acknowledged for almost 20 years: improvement in substance abuse treatment practices involves a human process, which, if successful, leads to change at not only the individual level but also the community, organizational and systemic levels. Ongoing efforts by the NIDA Clinical Trials Network and SAMHSA's Addiction Technology Transfer Centers (ATTCH) and Practice Improvement Collaborative (PIC) have made important progress toward overcoming the many challenges inherent in disseminating evidence-based practices among community substance abuse treatment providers. Furthermore, there is a growing interest in the active ingredients that mediate effective treatments and the generalizability of EBT to the typical clinical settings in which these treatments are likely to be delivered (Longabaugh et al., 2005). Increased collaboration and communication between NIH-funded treatment outcome researchers and the staff of the various SAMHSA programs and initiatives has the potential to accelerate this process.

REFERENCES

Addiction Technology Transfer Centers. (2000). The change book: A blueprint for technology transfer. Kansas City, MO: ATTC National Office.

Addis, M. E., & Krasnow, A. D. (2000). A national survey of practicing psychologists attitudes towards psychotherapy treatment manuals. *Journal of Consulting and Clinical Psychology*, 68, 331–339.

APA Presidential Task Force. (2006). Evidence-based practice in psychology. *American Psychologist*, 61(4), 271–285.

Backer, T. E. (1991). *Drug Abuse Technology Transfer*. DHHS Publication No. (ADM) 91-1764, Rockville, MD: National Institute on Drug Abuse.

Backer, T. E., David, S. L., & Soucy, G. (Eds.). (1995). *Reviewing the Behavioral Science Knowledge Base on Technology Transfer*. NIH Publication No. 95-4035. Rockville, MD: National Institute on Drug Abuse, National Institutes of Health, Public Health Service.

Bien, T. H., Miller, W. R., & Tonigan, J. S. (1993). Brief interventions for alcohol problems: A review. *Addiction*, 88, 315–336.

Breslin, F. C., Sobell, M. B., Sobell, L. C., Buchan, G., & Cunningham, J. A. (1997). Toward a stepped care approach to treating problem drinkers: The predictive utility of within-treatment variables and therapist prognostic ratings. *Addiction, 92*(11), 1479–1489.

Burke, B. L., Dunn, C. W., Atkins, D., & Phelps, J. S. (2004). The emerging evidence base for motivational interviewing: A meta-analytic & Qualitative Inquiry. *Journal of Cognitive Psychotherapy, 18*(4), 309–322.

Carroll, K. M., Farentinos, C., Ball, S. A., Crits-Cristoph, P., Libby, B., Morgenstern, J., Obert, J. O., Polcin, D., & Woody, G. E. (2002). MET meets the real world: Design issues and clinical strategies in the Clinical Trials Network. *Journal of Substance Abuse Treatment, 23*, 73–80.

Carroll, K. M., Nich, C., Sifry, R., Frankforter, T., Nuro, K. F., Ball, S. A., Fenton, L., & Rounsaville, B. J. (2000). A general system for evaluating therapist adherence and competence in psychotherapy research in the addictions. *Drug and Alcohol Dependence, 57*, 225–238.

Chambless, D. L., & Ollendick, T. H. (2001). Empirically-supported psychological interventions: Controversies and evidence. *Annual Review of Psychology, 52*, 685–716.

Cotter, F., Bowler, S., Mulkern, V., & McCarty, D. (2005). Practice improvement collaboratives: An overview. In E. Edmundson, & D. McCarty (Eds.). *Implementing Evidence-Based Practices for Treatment of Alcohol and Drug Disorders.* New York: Haworth Press.

Dunn, C., DeRoo, L., & Rivara, F. P. (2001). The use of brief interventions adapted from motivational interviewing across behavioral domains: A systematic review. *Addition, 96*(12), 1725–1742.

Goldman, H. H., Ganju, V., Drake, R. E., Gorman, P., Hogan, M., Hyde, P. S., & Morgan, O. (2001). Policy implications for implementing evidence-based practices. *Psychiatric Services, 52*(12), 1591–1597.

Grol, R. (1997). Beliefs and evidence in changing clinical practice. *British Medical Journal, 315*, 418–421.

Grol, R. (2001). Improving the quality of medical care: Building bridges among professional pride, payer profit and patient satisfaction. *Journal of the American Medical Association, 286*(2), 2578–2601.

Grol, R., & Grimshaw, J. (1999). Evidence-based implementation of evidence-based medicine. *The Joint Commission Journal on Quality Improvement, 25*(10), 503–513.

Hettema, J. E., Miller, W. R., & Steele, J. M. (2004). A meta-analysis of motivational interviewing techniques in the treatment of alcohol use disorders. *Alcoholism, Clinical and Experimental Research, 28*, 74A.

Higgins, S. T., Alessi, S. M., & Dantona, R. L. (2002). Voucher-based incentives: A substance abuse treatment innovation. *Addictive Behaviors, 27*, 887–910.

Kalb, M., & Propper, M. S. (1976). The future of alcohology: Craft or science? *American Journal of Psychiatry, 133*, 641–645.

Kirkpatrick, D. L. (1959a). Techniques for evaluating training programs. *Journal of American Society for Training & Development, 13*(11), 3–9.

Kirkpatrick, D. L. (1959b). Techniques for evaluating training programs: Part 2–Learning. *Journal of American Society for Training & Development, 13*(12), 21–26.

Kirkpatrick, D. L. (1960a). Techniques for evaluating training programs: Part 3–Behavior. *Journal of American Society for Training & Development, 14*(1), 13–18.

Kirkpatrick, D. L. (1960b). Techniques for evaluating training programs: Part 4–Results. *Journal of American Society for Training & Development, 14*(2), 28–32.

Lamb, S., Greenlick, M. R., & McCarty, D. (Eds.). (1998). *Bridging the Gap between Practice and Research: Forging Partnerships with Community-Based Drug and Alcohol Treatment.* Institute of Medicine. Washington, DC: National Academy Press.

Longabaugh, R., Donovan, D. M., Karno, M. P., McCrady, B. S., Morgenstern, J., & Tonigan, J. S. (2005). Active ingredients: How and why evidence-based alcohol behavioral treatment interventions work. *Alcoholism: Clinical and Experimental Research, 29*, 235–246.

Longabaugh, R., & Morgenstern, J. (1999). Cognitive-behavioral therapy for alcohol dependence. *Alcohol Health and Research World, 23*(2), 78–85.

McCarty, D., Rieckmann, T., Green, C., Gallon, S., & Knudsen, J. (2004). Training rural practitioners to use buprenorphine: Using the Change Book to facilitate technology transfer. *Journal of Substance Abuse Treatment, 26*, 203–208.

McLellan, A. T., Carise, D., & Kleber, H. D. (2003). Can the national addiction treatment infrastructure support the public's demand for quality care? *Journal of Substance Abuse Treatment, 25,* 117–121.

McLellan, A. T., & Meyers, K. (2004). Contemporary addiction treatment: A review of systems problems for adults and adolescents. *Biological Psychiatry, 56,* 764–770.

Miller, W. R., Hedrick, K. E., & Orlofsky, D. R. (1991). The helpful responses questionnaire: A procedure for measuring therapeutic empathy. *Journal of Clinical Psychology, 47*(3), 444–448.

Miller, W. R., Meyers, R. J., Tonigan, J. S., & Grant, K. A. (2001). Community reinforcement and traditional approaches: Findings of a controlled trial. In R. J. Meyers, & W. R. Miller (Eds.). *A Community Reinforcement Approach to Addiction Treatment* (pp. 79–103). New York: Cambridge University Press.

Miller, W. R., & Rollnick, S. (2002). Motivational interviewing: Preparing people for change. New York: Guilford Press.

Miller, W. R., & Sanchez, V. C. (1993). Motivating young adults for treatment and lifestyle change. In G. Howard (Ed.). *Issues in Alcohol Use and Misuse by Young Adults.* Notre Dame, IN: University of Notre Dame Press.

Miller, W. R., Sorenson, J. L., Selzer, J. A., & Brigham, G. S. (2006). Disseminating evidence-based practices in substance abuse treatment: A review with suggestions. *Journal of Substance Abuse Treatment, 31,* 25–39.

Miller, W. R., & Wilbourne, P. L. (2002). Mesa Grande: A methodological analysis of clinical trials of treatments for alcohol use disorders. *Addiction, 97*(3), 265–277.

Miller, W. R., Yahne, E. E., Moyers, T. B., Martinez, J., & Pirritano, M. (2004). A randomized trial of methods to help clinicians learn motivational interviewing. *Journal of Consulting and Clinical Psychology, 72*(6), 1050–1062.

Mittman, B. S., Tonesk, X., & Jacobson, P. D. (1992). Implementing clinical practice guidelines: Social influence strategies and practitioner behavior change. *Quality Review Bulletin,* Dec, 413–422.

Morgenstern, J., & Longabaugh, R. (2000). Cognitive behavioral treatment for alcohol dependence: A review of evidence for its hypothesized mechanisms of action. *Addiction, 95*(10), 1475–1490.

Moyer, A., Finney, J. W., Swearingen, C. E., & Vergun, P. (2002a). Brief interventions for alcohol problems: A meta-analytic review of controlled investigations in treatment-seeking and non-treatment-seeking populations. *Addiction,* 97(3), 279–292.

Moyers, T. B., Martin, T., Manuel, J. K., & Miller, W. R. (2002b). *The Motivational Interviewing Treatment Integrity (MITI) Code: Version 2.0.* Albuquerque, NM: University of New Mexico Center on Alcoholism, Substance Abuse and Addictions (CASAA).

Ockene, I. E., Adams, A., Hurley, T. G., Wheeler, E. V., & Hebert, J. R. (1999). Brief physician and nurse practitioner delivered counseling for high-risk drinkers: Does it work? *Archives of Internal Medicine, 159*(18), 2198–2205.

O'Farrell, T. J., Choquette, K. A., & Cutter, H. S. G. (1998). Couples relapse prevention sessions after Behavioral Marital Therapy for male alcoholics: Outcomes during the three years after starting treatment. *Journal of Studies on Alcohol, 59,* 357–370.

O'Farrell, T. J., Choquette, K. A., Cutter, H. S. G., Brown, E. D., & McCourt, W. F. (1993). Behavioral Marital Therapy with and without additional couples relapse prevention sessions for alcoholics and their wives. *Journal of Studies on Alcohol, 54,* 652–666.

O'Farrell, T. J., & Fals-Stewart, W. (2001). Family-involved alcoholism treatment: An update. In M. Galanter (Ed.). *Recent Developments in Alcoholism, Volume 15: Services Research in the Era of Managed Care* (pp. 329–356). New York: Plenum Press.

Oxman, A. D., Thomson, M. A., Davis, D. A., & Haynes, R. B. (1995). No magic bullets: A systematic review of 102 trials of interventions to improve professional practice. *Canadian Medical Association Journal, 152,* 1423–1431.

Pincus, H. A., Pechura, C. M., Elinson, L., & Pettit, A. R. (2001). Depression in primary care: Linking clinical and systems strategies. *General Hospital Psychiatry, 23,* 311–318.

Rogers, E. M. (1995). *Diffusion of Innovations* (4th ed.). New York: Free Press.

Sass, H., Soyka, M., Mann, K., & Zieglgänsberger, W. (1996). Relapse prevention by acamprosate: Results from a placebo-controlled study on alcohol dependence. *Archives of General Psychiatry, 53,* 673–680.

Shaneyfelt, T. M. (2001). Building bridges to quality, Editorial. *Journal of the American Medical Association, 286*(20), 2600–2601.

Smith, J. E., Meyers, R. J., & Delaney, H. D. (1998). The community reinforcement approach with homeless alcohol-dependent individuals. *Journal of Consulting and Clinical Psychology, 66,* 541–548.

Smith, J. E., Meyers, R. J., & Miller, W. R. (2001). The community reinforcement approach to the treatment of substance use disorders. *American Journal of Addiction, 10*(Suppl.), 51–59.

Sobell, M. B., & Sobell, L. C. (2000). *Stepped care as a heuristic approach to the treatment of alcohol problems. Journal of Consulting and Clinical Psychology, 68*(4), 573–579.

Sorenson, J. L., & Midkiff, E. E. (2002). Bridging the gap between research and drug abuse treatment. *Journal of Psychoactive Drugs, 32,* 379–382.

Stanton, M. D., & Shadish, W. R. (1997). Outcome, attrition, and family-couples treatment for drug abuse: A meta-analysis and review of the controlled, comparative studies. *Psychological Bulletin, 122*(2), 170–191.

Stirman, S. W., DeRubeis, R. J., Crits-Christoph, P., & Brody, P. E. (2003). Are samples in randomized controlled trials of psychotherapy representative of community outpatients? A new methodology and initial findings. *Journal of Consulting and Clinical Psychology, 71*(6), 963–972.

Weingardt, K. R. (2004). The role of instructional design and technology in the dissemination of empirically-supported, manual based therapies. *Clinical Psychology: Science & Practice, 11*(3), 313–341.

Weingardt, K. R., Villafrana, S. W., & Levin, C. (2006). Technology based training in cognitive behavioral therapy for substance abuse counselors. *Substance Abuse, 27*(3), 19–24.

CHAPTER 14

Implications of Research on Comorbidity for the Nature and Management of Substance Misuse

Kim T. Mueser,[1] David J. Kavanagh[2] and Mary F. Brunette[1]
[1]Department of Psychiatry, Dartmouth Medical School,
New Hampshire-Dartmouth Psychiatric Research Center, Concord, NH, USA
[2]School of Medicine, University of Queensland, Herston, Australia

Abstract: There is still debate over explanations for increased rates of substance use disorders (SUD) in people with severe mental illnesses (SMI) compared with the general population. This chapter finds some supportive evidence for both common factor models and for mutual influences between SUD and SMI. A review of randomized controlled trials on interventions for comorbid SUD/SMI concludes that there is support for integrated treatment across disorders and inclusion of motivational intervention. However, outcomes remain relatively modest and inconsistent. Both prevention and treatment could benefit from further application of research on explanatory models, and better understanding of processes underlying natural recovery.

People with severe mental illnesses (SMI) such as schizophrenia or bipolar disorder are at increased risk for comorbid substance use disorders (SUD) compared to the general population (Kavanagh et al., 2004a; Regier et al., 1990; Teeson et al., 2000). Comorbid SUDs are associated with a wide range of negative outcomes in this population, such as increased rates of relapse and rehospitalization, homelessness, legal problems, violence, treatment non-compliance, HIV infection, and family stress (Drake & Brunette, 1998). Research is actively investigating the causes of the increased comorbidity of SUD in persons with SMI and the implications for treatment.

In this chapter we provide a critical evaluation of different models concerning the etiology of the high rate of SUD in patients with SMI. We focus on theories addressing SUD in schizophrenia (and related diagnoses of schizoaffective and schizophreniform disorders) and bipolar disorder for several reasons. Both schizophrenia and bipolar disorder have a relatively low prevalence in the general population, are characterized by psychotic symptoms, and have a more severe course with greater disability than major depression or anxiety disorders (Goodwin & Jamison, 1990; Keith, Regier, & Rae, 1991). In addition, there is a broad consensus that these disorders are "biological" diseases, in the sense that their etiologies are minimally affected by social factors, and some researchers argue that genetic susceptibility to schizophrenia, schizoaffective disorder and bipolar disorder are due to at least some common or overlapping chromosomal regions (Craddock, O'Donovan, & Owen, 2006; Craddock & Owen, 2005). Finally, the prevalence of SUD in schizophrenia and bipolar disorder is higher than in anxiety and depressive disorders (Regier et al., 1990). These similarities between schizophrenia and bipolar disorder suggest that the same models of SUD comorbidity may apply to each disorder.

Before discussing specific models of comorbidity, we consider whether the high rate of SUD in patients with SMI could be due to sampling bias. Almost all the data on the prevalence of SUD are drawn from clinical samples of patients in treatment, including most of data from the Epidemiologic Catchment Area study (Regier et al., 1990). According to *Berkson's fallacy* (Berkson, 1949), estimates of comorbidity are inflated when samples are obtained from treatment settings, as opposed to the general population, because either disorder increases the likelihood that individuals will receive treatment. In addition, most studies have involved hospitalized patients, further increasing estimates of comorbidity (Galanter, Castaneda, & Ferman, 1988). As a result, most estimates of comorbidity are probably inflated by sampling bias, although it is unlikely that this factor is sufficient to explain the high rates that are observed.

MODELS OF COMORBIDITY

Many explanations have been proposed for the increased risk of SUD in patients with SMI. We organize our review according to four general models of increased comorbidity (Blanchard et al., 2000; Kushner & Mueser, 1993): common factor models, secondary substance use disorder models, secondary psychiatric disorder models, and bidirectional models. According to *common factor models*, high rates of comorbidity are the result of risk factors (such as genetic loading) that are shared across both substance use and SMI disorders. *Secondary substance use disorder models* propose that SMI increases patients' chances of developing SUD. *Secondary psychiatric disorder models* propose the opposite, that substance use precipitates SMI in individuals who would otherwise not develop these disorders. *Bidirectional models* hypothesize that either disorder can increase vulnerability to the other disorder. We contend that different models may account for comorbidity in different groups of patients, and that more than one model may apply for a given individual over time, or in relation to different substances.

COMMON FACTOR MODELS

Common factor models posit that high rates of comorbidity are the result of shared vulnerabilities to both disorders. To the extent that specific factors can independently increase the risk of developing both disorders, increased comorbidity can be explained. Two risk factors have been studied: genetics and antisocial personality disorder. Other factors have been identified but less thoroughly evaluated as reasons for increased rates of comorbidity, including socioeconomic status and cognitive impairment.

GENETIC FACTORS

Family history and twin studies provide strong evidence that genetic factors contribute to the development of schizophrenia, bipolar disorder, and SUD, although single, common genetic causes of these disorders are unknown. The question is whether genetic vulnerability to one disorder also increases risk for another disorder. Research shows that clients with comorbid disorders are more likely to have relatives with SUD than are similar patients with only SMI (Gershon et al., 1988; Noordsy et al., 1994; Tsuang, Simpson, & Kronfol, 1982). These findings suggest that genetic vulnerability for SUD plays a role in the development of some cases of comorbid SUD in clients with SMI.

However, do such genetic factors account for *increased* comorbidity via susceptibility to both disorders? Research examining the rate of SUD in the relatives of patients with SMI and the rate of SMI in relatives of patients with SUD addresses this question. If shared genetic vulnerability to both SMI and SUD accounts for increased comorbidity, higher rates of the other disorder would be expected in the relatives of persons with one of the disorders. There are at least two possible sources of shared genetic vulnerability in families. First, within individual family members, genetic vulnerability to one disorder could also be associated with increased vulnerability to another disorder, with offspring at increased risk of developing both disorders from the genetic contribution of that individual parent. Second, if family members with one disorder were more likely to mate individuals with the other disorder than would be expected by chance alone (i.e., cross-trait *assortative mating*), the offspring would be at increased risk to developing comorbid disorders, due to the genetic contributions from each parent.

Research provides evidence against a simple genetic model. Several studies indicate that genetic risk to schizophrenia or bipolar disorder is not associated with an increased risk of SUD in relatives, or vice versa (Gershon et al., 1988; Maier et al., 1995; Tsuang et al., 1982). These findings suggest that shared genetic factors do not account for increased rates of comorbid SUD in SMI.

Genetic models of the relationship between co-occurring SMI and SUD are probably more complex. For example, Caspi et al. (2005) reported that a genetic variation in the COMT gene moderated the effect of adolescent cannabis use on the later development of psychotic symptoms or schizophrenia. Adult cannabis use did not have the same effect, highlighting that the effect of substance use on the developing brain may be different and more deleterious than the effect of substances on adult brains. This research also exemplifies that genetic risk for dual disorders may be enacted via gene–environment interactions, whereby substance misuse acts as an environmental stressor on the developing brain.

Genetic susceptibility may occur in a multitude of ways. Another line of preliminary research has examined genetic variations of the dopamine D3 receptor (DRD3) and its moderators. D3 receptors are expressed in the mesocorticolimbic dopaminergic system and are increased in postmortem studies of schizophrenia. The DRD3 receptor is highly expressed in the nucleus accumbens, where reward, including substance-induced reward, is mediated. The DRD3 receptor modulates dopamine movement in this structure when substances are used. Although studies have been mixed, some research has shown that homozygosity in a polymorphism in the DRD3 was associated with co-occurring addiction in schizophrenia (Krebs et al., 1998).

ANTISOCIAL PERSONALITY DISORDER (ASPD)

Another possible common factor that has been the focus of recent research is ASPD. Extensive research has shown that ASPD, and its childhood precursor conduct disorder (CD), are strongly related to SUD (Kessler et al., 1997; Regier et al., 1990). In addition, similar associations have been reported between ASPD and SMI.

Specifically, symptoms of CD in childhood, such as repeated fighting, truancy, and lying, have been found to be predictive of the later development of schizophrenia (Asarnow, 1988; Cannon et al., 1993; Robins, 1966), and to a lesser extent, bipolar disorder (Carlson & Weintraub, 1993; Robins, 1966). Furthermore, increased rates of ASPD have been reported in both schizophrenia and bipolar disorder (Bland, Newman, & Orn, 1987; Hodgins, Toupin, & Côté, 1996; Jackson et al., 1991).

The strong associations between CD, ASPD, and SUD, and the increased prevalence of ASPD in persons with SMI, suggest a role for ASPD as a common factor underlying increased comorbidity. More direct support is provided by evidence that clients with SMI and past CD or ASPD are more likely to have comorbid SUD than similar patients without ASPD (Hodgins, Hiscoke, & Freese, 2002; Hodgins, Tiihonen, & Ross, 2005; Mueser et al., 1999; Swartz et al., 2006). Finally, among persons with co-occurring disorders, the additional diagnosis of CD or ASPD (Mueser et al., 2006; Mueser et al., 1997) is associated with a more severe course of SUD and a stronger family history of SUD, consistent with research on ASPD in persons with primary SUD (Alterman & Cacciola, 1991).

Thus, moderately strong evidence suggests that ASPD is a common factor that may contribute to the increased rate of SUD in a subset of SMI patients. Further work is needed to evaluate the role of temperament and to rule out other common factors related to ASPD that could account for its relationships with SUD and SMI.

Secondary Substance Use Disorder Models

A variety of different models posit that SMI increases clients' vulnerability to developing SUD. These models can be broadly divided into three types: *psychosocial risk factor models*, the *supersensitivity model*, and the *brain reward circuitry dysfunction model*.

Psychosocial Risk Factor Models

Three psychosocial risk factor models are consistent with the theory that SUD is secondary to SMI: (1) self-medication, (2) alleviation of dysphoria, and (3) multiple risk factor models. In this section we briefly review the evidence for each.

The Self-medication Model

Self-medication means that people seek specific substances to alleviate specific psychiatric symptoms (Khantzian, 1997). The underlying assumption is that misused substances are not randomly chosen but are selected by the individual based on their specific effects on symptoms. Although research indicates that people are aware of their initial psychological reactions to substances (Mueser et al., 1995), there is little evidence for substance selection related to specific diagnoses or internal states. Convincing evidence for self-medication might include (a) self-report studies in which clients describe particular substances alleviating specific symptoms, (b) epidemiologic studies showing that clients with particular diagnoses select specific substances, (c) studies showing that specific substances are used in response to specific psychiatric symptoms.

The available evidence does not support any of these relationships. First, self-report studies find that clients with dual disorders report that alcohol and other substances alleviate social problems, insomnia, depression, and other problems across diagnoses (Addington & Duchak, 1997; Carey & Carey, 1995; Laudet et al., 2004), but rarely report that specific substances alleviate specific symptoms (Dixon et al., 1991; Noordsy et al., 1991). Second, studies of clinical epidemiology show that individuals with SMI misuse the same substances as others in society but at higher rates (Cuffel, 1996), substance selection is not related to diagnosis (Mueser, Yarnold, & Bellack, 1992; Mueser et al., 1990; Mueser et al., 2000; Regier et al., 1990), and substance selection is related to availability and market forces (Mueser et al., 1992). Third, the amount or type of substance use is not consistently related to severity, type, or phase of SMI symptoms (Bernadt & Murray, 1986; Brunette et al., 1997; Hamera, Schneider, & Deviney, 1995).

The Alleviation of Dysphoria Model

Alleviation of dysphoria represents a more general model than self-medication that proposes people with SMI are prone to misuse substances in response to distress. In support of this model, research shows that people with SMI often experience dysphoria (Birchwood et al., 1993), and self-reports of clients with co-occurring disorders indicate that the alleviation of unpleasant feelings is a common motive for using substances (Addington & Duchak, 1997; Carey & Carey, 1995; Laudet et al., 2004). Furthermore, there is some evidence that clients with co-occurring disorders have higher levels of dysphoria than those with just SMI (Blanchard et al., 1999; Brunette et al., 1997; Hambrecht & Häfner, 2000).

Multiple Risk Factor Models

Although the research generally supports the model of alleviation of dysphoria, other possible indirect mechanisms involve a variety of risk factors related to SMI, such as social isolation, poor interpersonal skills, poor cognitive skills, school and vocational failure, poverty, lack of adult role responsibilities, lack of structured daily activities, association with substance-using subgroups, and living in neighborhoods with high rates of drug availability (Anthony, 1991; Berman & Noble, 1993; Jones et al., 1994). Little research has addressed multiple risk factor models, but self-reports regarding reasons for use are consistent with the identified factors (Warner et al., 1994). If the cognitive, emotional, interpersonal, vocational, societal, and financial consequences of SMI increase clients' risk for SUD, then this could account for increased comorbidity in a subset of individuals.

The Supersensitivity Model

This model is an elaboration of the stress–vulnerability model for schizo-phrenia (Zubin & Spring, 1977), which proposes that environmental stress interacts with psychobiological vulnerability to precipitate the onset of SMI or to trigger relapses. Because vulnerability is defined in terms of increased biological sensitivity to stress, it may also apply to the effects of alcohol and drugs. This sensitivity may render clients with SMI more likely to experience negative consequences from using relatively small amounts of substances.

A number of avenues of research provide support for this model. First, clients with co-occurring disorders tend to misuse lower quantities of substances than those with primary substance use disorders (Lehman et al., 1994), and are less likely than primary SUD populations to develop physical dependence (Corse, Hirschinger, & Zanis, 1995). Second, in pharmacological "challenge" tests, clients with SMI are highly sensitive to low doses of amphetamine and cannabis that produce minimal responses in controls (D'Souza et al., 2005; Lieberman, Kane, & Alvir, 1987). Third, clients with SMI often report negative clinical effects such as symptom relapses following use of small quantities of alcohol or drugs (Knudsen & Vilmar, 1984; Treffert, 1978). Fourth, Drake, and Wallach (1993) reported that fewer than five percent of clients with SMI were able to sus-tain symptom-free drinking over time without negative consequences, in marked contrast to approximately 50 percent of the general population who drink alco-hol over time without developing a disorder, suggesting increased sensitivity to the effects of alcohol.

Brain Reward Circuitry Dysfunction Model

A number of authors have noted overlap in the neural circuitry putatively involved in both SUD and schizophrenia (Chambers, Krystal, & Self, 2001; Greenet et al., 1999). This has led to a model which incorporates aspects of self-medication, affect regulation, and supersensitivity theories described above. This model theorizes that the biological vulnerability to SUD in clients with schizophrenia is an inherent part of its neurobiology. Psychoactive substances activate dopaminergic mesocorticolimbic tracts involved in reward or incentive salience, and repeated use of drugs including amphetamines increases sensitivity to substance effects (Redish, 2004; Robinson & Berridge, 1993). People with schizophrenia appear to have a dysregulation of this circuit, which results in abnormal dopamine-mediated brain responses to rewarding stimuli (Chambers & Self, 2002; Chau, Roth, & Green, 2004). The hypothesis suggests that people with schizophrenia are particularly likely to use substances because these agents transiently ameliorate problems with functioning of the circuit, briefly increasing their ability to experience feelings of satisfaction and pleasure. Similar reward circuitry dysfunction hypotheses have been put forward to explain the etiology of SUD in other contexts (Blum et al., 2000; Volkow, Fowler, & Wang, 2003). The reward dysfunction argument is consistent with research showing that misused substances can increase dopaminergic activity in reward circuitry in both animals (Wise, 1998) and humans (Boileau et al., 2003; O'Leary et al., 2000), as well as data indicating abnormal reward circuitry responsiveness to drug cues in people with primary SUD (Wexler et al., 2001).

Several areas of research have provided indirect support for the hypothesis in schizophrenia. For example, people with schizophrenia do not show the normal increase in P300 event-related potential amplitude to stimuli associated with monetary reward (Brecher & Begleiter, 1983), have abnormal hedonic and brain activation responses to odors (Crespo-Facorro et al., 2001), and have structural and functional brain abnormalities in their reward circuitry, including frontal lobe subregions, striatum, amygdala, and hippocampus (Shenton et al., 2001). However, as a model of increased risk, this hypothesis has specifically been applied to schizophrenia rather than to bipolar disorder, which has different purported brain circuitry abnormalities. Increased risk for substance misuse in bipolar disorder would presumably involve a different neurobiologic substrate.

SECONDARY PSYCHIATRIC ILLNESS MODELS

The theory that SUD can lead to SMI has been hotly debated since the rise of recreational drug use in the 1960s (Blumenfield & Glickman, 1967; Glass & Bowers, 1970). Most of this debate has centered on the effects of drugs such as stimulants, hallucinogens, and cannabis because of their psychotomimetic effects (Krystal et al., 2005). In contrast, there is a general consensus that alcohol misuse does not cause schizophrenia or bipolar disorder, and some debate as to whether is can mask their onset (Goodwin & Jamison, 1990; Hambrecht & Häfner, 1996). The fact that alcohol misuse is not considered to be a cause of secondary SMI limits the potential significance of secondary psychiatric models, given the high prevalence of alcohol use disorder in SMI.

Models proposing that psychotomimetic drug misuse can lead to long-term psychotic disorders typically build on the catecholamine hypothesis of schizophrenia or affective disorders (Bunney & Davis, 1965), and are supported by basic animal research on drug effects. Of special relevance to these theories are the hypothesized roles of behavioral sensitization and kindling due to psychotomimetic drug effects (Post, Rubinow, & Ballenger, 1984). Animal research has shown that repeated or continuous stimulant administration can lead to increased sensitivity of response, or *behavioral sensitization*. Similarly, increased electrophysiological and behavioral responses can be induced by repeated electrical stimulation or stimulant administration, referred to as *kindling*. Behavioral sensitization and kindling due to substance use have been suggested as mechanisms by which drug misuse may precipitate SMI (Lieberman, Kinon, & Loebel, 1990; Strakowski et al., 1996).

Three types of research have been conducted to evaluate the secondary psychiatric disorder model of increased comorbidity.

PROSPECTIVE FOLLOW-UP STUDIES OF SUBSTANCE USERS

McLellan, Woody, and O'Brien (1979) followed up a cohort of 51 male veterans with at least yearly hospitalizations for drug misuse over a six-year period. Although at initial assessment there were no differences in psychiatric symptoms, by the end of 6 years men had developed psychopathology consistent with the pharmacological effects of their preferred drug: 5 of 11 stimulant mis-users had developed psychosis, and 8 of 14 depressant misusers had developed severe depression. These findings are intriguing, but limited in two ways. First, if substance type predicted psychiatric diagnosis, then different diagnostic groups would tend to misuse different types of substances, which is not the case. There is no consistent association with specific substances in people with SMI (Cuffel, 1996; Mueser et al., 1992; Mueser et al., 2000; Regier et al., 1990). Indeed, poly-substance misuse is more common (Chen et al., 1992; Cuffel, 1996). Second, the findings have not been replicated in more than 25 years since publication.

STUDIES OF LONG-TERM PSYCHOSIS FOLLOWING DRUG MISUSE

Several studies have compared clients who develop long-term SMI following drug misuse with SMI clients without SUD, to determine whether they differ in clinical features, biological parameters, response to treatment, or family history of psychiatric illness. Most of this research has failed to find consistent differences between these groups, although clients with co-occurring SUD tend to have better premorbid functioning and less severe negative symptoms (Arndt et al., 1992; Kirkpatrick et al., 1996; Salyers & Mueser, 2001). Furthermore, there are no con-sistent differences between clients with co-occurring disorders whose SUD devel-oped before versus after the SMI (Tsuang et al., 1982; Vardy & Kay, 1983).

SUBSTANCE MISUSE AS A PRECIPITANT OF SMI IN VULNERABLE PERSONS

Andréasson et al. (1987) reported a large 15-year prospective follow-up study of young men conscripted into the Swedish army. There was a strong association between history of cannabis use at conscription and later diagnosis of schizophrenia, which was reduced when other variables were controlled, but nevertheless remained elevated. No associations were found between other drug use and later development of schizophrenia. Subsequent analyses of the subgroup with schizophrenia indicated that the cannabis users had a more rapid onset of illness characterized by positive symptoms, which the authors interpreted as supporting an etiologically distinct subgroup (Allebeck et al., 1993; Andréasson, Allebeck, & Rydberg, 1989). Since this study, several other population-based studies have demonstrated the predictive relationship between cannabis use and the development of schizophrenia, controlling for possible confounders (Arseneault et al., 2002; Fergusson, Horwood, & Swain-Campbell, 2003; Henquet et al., 2005; van Os et al., 2002). Furthermore, these studies report that the relationship between cannabis use and schizophrenia occurs in a dose-dependent fashion, is stronger for earlier cannabis use, and is not modified by other drug use. On the other hand, if cannabis use induced schizophrenia in people who would not otherwise develop it, one would expect increases in the prevalence of schizophrenia in contexts where cannabis use has increased. A study that examined this in birth cohorts in Australia between 1940 and 1979 failed to find such an association (Degenhardt, Hall, & Lynskey, 2003).

While support for a simple causal role for cannabis use in schizophrenia is inconclusive, evidence is stronger that substance use can precipitate psychiatric disorders in vulnerable individuals. Both clients with schizophrenia that was preceded by SUD and those with only schizophrenia have stronger family histories of schizophrenia than clients with only SUD (Tsuang et al., 1982; Vardy & Kay, 1983). Also, cannabis and other drug misuse is associated with an earlier age of schizophrenia onset (Kavanagh et al., 2004a; Mueser et al., 1990; Salyers & Mueser, 2001; Tsuang et al., 1982). This version of the hypothesis is highly consistent with a stress–vulnerability model of schizophrenia (Zubin & Spring, 1977), in which substance use may trigger the psychotic disorder in people who are vulnerable because of genetic or neurodevelopmental risk, but the model sees the substance abuse as just one of many potential influences.

In bipolar disorder, clients whose alcohol use disorder came first have been found to have a *later* age of onset of bipolar disorder than those whose alcoholism came second (Strakowski et al., 1996). Furthermore, lower familial rates of bipolar disorder have been found in clients whose alcoholism antedated their bipolar disorder (DelBello et al., 1999), as well as fewer affective episodes and a more rapid recovery, compared with clients whose bipolar disorder came first (Winokur et al., 1995). These findings suggest that alcohol misuse may precipitate first episodes of mania in some persons who might not otherwise develop the disorder, or may have developed it at a later age (Strakowski & DelBello, 2000).

BIDIRECTIONAL MODELS

Bidirectional models suggest ongoing interactions between SMI and SUD account for increased rates of comorbidity. For example, SUD could trigger SMI in a biologically vulnerable individual, which is subsequently maintained by continued SUD due to socially learned cognitive factors, such as beliefs, expectancies, and motives for substance use (Graham, 1998). Consistent with this model, there is evidence both that SUD worsens the course of SMI, and that worsening symptoms are related to higher substance use (e.g., Hides et al., 2006). Despite the intuitive appeal of bidirectional models, research has not demonstrated that bidirectional interactions lead to greater comorbidity.

TREATMENT OF CO-OCCURRING DISORDERS

Current treatment approaches to co-occurring SMI and SUD evolved primarily out of practical considerations based on clinical experience and outcomes associated with traditional approaches to these disorders. In this section we provide a brief historical perspective on the treatment of co-occurring disorders, followed by a description of integrated co-occurring disorder treatment models. We then summarize controlled research on integrated treatment for co-occurring disorders.

HISTORICAL PERSPECTIVE

Traditional approaches to the treatment of co-occurring disorders typically involved the provision of different services for SMI and SUD, by different treatment providers working for different systems. This segregation of treatment services resulted in two approaches to providing services: the parallel and sequential treatment models. In the *parallel treatment* model, SUD and SMI services were provided simultaneously, by different clinicians who were supposed to be coordinating their efforts with one-another. In the *sequential treatment* model, intervention first focuses on treating or controlling one disorder, followed by the second disorder.

Both of these traditional treatment approaches were associated with a variety of problems (Polcin, 1992). With the parallel treatment model, common problems included lack of successful access to both types of services (e.g., because of different eligibility criteria, low client motivation or different service locations), lack of coordination between SUD and SMI treatment providers, and inconsistent messages regarding illness and treatment by providers. With the sequential treatment model, the most prominent problem was the inherent difficulty of trying to successfully treat or stabilize one disorder without attending to the other. SMI and SUD usually interact and worsen each other, often rendering it impossible to focus treatment on only one disorder. When the sequential treatment is by different providers, many of the same issues as for parallel treatment apply. Other issues include the potential for loss of engagement once the person is no longer in crisis, and the difficulty for some clients (and perhaps therapists) to appreciate the true extent of inter-relationship between disorders when one is currently stabilized. By the late 1980s, reviews of the treatment efficacy of traditional approaches to co-occurring disorders had noted these and other problems, and the poor clinical outcomes associated with such treatment, suggesting a need to develop more effective treatment approaches for these clients (Ridgely, Goldman, & Willenbring, 1990; Ridgely et al., 1987).

INTEGRATED TREATMENT MODELS

As awareness of the limitations of traditional approaches to co-occurring disorders grew, consensus developed that the integration of SMI and SUD services was a key strategy for resolving problems related to service access and treatment consistency. Integrated treatment is generally defined as treatment for both SMI and SUD that is provided by the same clinician or team of clinicians, in which the clinician or team assumes responsibility for integrating treatment for the disorders. Issues in both disorders are addressed simultaneously, with sensitivity to current personal and clinical priorities, so that the specific content and nature of interventions are tailored to the needs and current abilities of the person.

A wide range of integrated treatment programs for co-occurring disorders has been described (Carey, 1996; Drake et al., 1993; Kavanagh, 1995; Minkoff, 1989; Mueser et al., 2003). Although these programs differ somewhat, some features are shared across most or all of them. First, all the programs are designed to be implemented in the context of comprehensive treatment for SMI. They recognize that clients with co-occurring disorders have multiple needs, including housing, medical care, vocational rehabilitation, social skills, illness self-management, and pharmacological treatment. Second, they focus on enhancing motivation to participate in treatment for SUD. In traditional SUD services, treatment is usually initiated when the substance misuse either leads to significant problems in functioning, or legal problems force the person into treatment. In contrast, many clients with co-occurring disorders are already in treatment for the SMI, but have no established motivation for working on their substance use. Incorporation of motivational enhancement techniques, such as motivational interviewing (Miller & Rollnick, 2002) or contingent reinforcement (Bellack et al., 2006), are strategies for harnessing such motivation.

Third, integrated treatment programs tend to avoid direct, stressful interpersonal confrontation, and utilize instead supportive techniques that focus on reducing the harmful consequences of substance use, rather than employing more confrontational methods and insisting on abstinence as the only goal (as occurs in some SUD treatment services, especially in the US). Poor retention of clients with SMI in services employing more confrontational or rigid approaches, together with greater understanding of stress–vulnerability models of SMI (Zubin & Spring, 1977), have led co-occurring disorder programs to adopt less stressful methods. Fourth, many clients with co-occurring disorders are only tenuously engaged in treatment, or have difficulty remembering and keeping appointments, especially during symptom exacerbations (Miner et al., 1997; Pristach & Smith, 1990).

In contrast to traditional SUD services that depend on clinic appointments, integrated treatment programs usually provide assertive outreach into the community in order to engage and retain these clients in treatment.

RESEARCH ON INTEGRATED TREATMENT

Over the past 15 years, as different models of integrated treatment for co-occurring disorders have been articulated, research on the effects of these programs has grown. Tables 1 and 2 summarize results of a systematic review of trials that have been published to date. The 16 randomized controlled trials that focused solely or primarily on people with psychosis and reported substance use outcomes were included in the tables. These criteria excluded several quasi-experimental studies, studies using within-subjects designs, and ones that focused on program engagement or forensic outcomes only.

Inspection of Table 1 indicates that most studies include a significant proportion of clients with schizophrenia, and a mixture of other SMI diagnoses as well. Study groups varied from young, first-episode participants to people with chronic and disabling disorders. Sample sizes ranged from 25 to 485, with an average of 141, and outcome assessments occurred at time points between 3 months and 5 years post-baseline ($M = 18.7$ months). Types of interventions also varied significantly, including residential (Burnam et al., 1995), individual (Graeber et al., 2003; Herman et al., 1997) or group treatment (Hellerstein, Rosenthal, & Miner, 1995; James et al., 2004), case management for delivering integrated treatment (Drake et al., 1998a), and studies of brief, motivational intervention (Baker et al., 2002a, 2002b; Kavanagh et al., 2004b). Intervention contact time ranged accordingly from a single 30–45-min session to intensive case management over 3 years.

As described in previous reviews of this literature, early research on integrated treatment programs was limited by a number of different factors, including use of insensitive measures of substance misuse in the SMI population, small sample sizes, and high drop-out rates (Drake et al., 1998b). However, over time the methodological rigor of research on integrated dual disorder treatment has steadily improved. Even within the controlled trials summarized in Table 3, improvements can be seen over time. We rated studies one point for each methodological criterion they met (>50% of the eligible sample entering the study, confirmation of diagnosis by standard interview, appropriate randomization procedure, baseline equivalence or statistical control, equivalence of contact time, ≤30% loss from attrition, independent checks on protocol adherence, avoidance of therapist/conditon confound, corroboration of substance use reports by toxicology, blind ratings, and intention to treat analyses). The scores rise from 2.0 in 1993 to an average of 7.4 in 2006. Four studies have a score of 8.0 (Drake et al., 1998a; Baker et al., 2006; Edwards et al., 2006; Essock et al., 2006), and three of those were published in 2006.

Table 1

Sample Characteristics for Randomized Controlled Trials on Comorbidity

Study	Sample description	Other exclusions (except consent issues)	Source	N*	% Male	M Age	Non-Anglo Ethnicity (%)	Single/never married (%)	Completed high school (%)	Unemployed (%)	Independent living (%)	Substances misused (%)	Diagnoses	# Prior psychiatric admissions (range)
Lehman et al. (1993)	US OP SCZ/SA/BP/MD + *lifetime* SUD (54% current SUD)	• <18, >40	Clinician referral	54	74%	31	69% Af	NR	NR	NR	NR	Lifetime: 71% al 62% mj 17% cocaine 13% amph 13% opiates 8% sed 21% hall 10% poly 12% other	DSM-III-R 68% SCZ/SA 23% BP 9% MD	NR
Burnam et al. (1995)	US homeless people SCZ or Major Aff + SUD	• Not homeless or ≥ 2 dependent housing situations in previous 6 months	Agencies serving homeless people	276	84%	37	28% Af 14% other	49%	72%	NR	All homeless (for M = 5 years)	Last month use: 47% mj 53% cocaine 8% amph 9% opiates 24% sed 9% other	45% SCZ 93% Aff	NR
Hellerstein et al. (1995, 2001)	US OP SZ spectrum + SUD	• <18 or >50 years • Not desire for SUD treatment	Screening of IPs in dual diagnosis unit	47	77%	32	43% Af 32% Hisp	NR	(M = 11 years ed)	NR	(8% of N = 63 sample in own apart.)	87% cocaine (40% crack) 77% mj 92% al	RDC: 30% SCZ 70% SA	7.5

	Exclusion criteria	Recruitment	N	% male	Age	Ethnicity		Education			Substance use	Diagnosis	
and Miner et al. (1997)	• Life-threatening illness • ASPD • GAF <30 • MMSE <24 • Needing long-term hospitalization										2% IV use 66% cocaine + al + mj		
Herman et al. (1997, 2000) US IP SMD + SUD	• Unmanageable behavior needing extensive seclusion (est. 10%)	IP screening	485	74%†	33†	77% Af†	63%†	(M = 11 years ed)†	NR	7%†	46% al 10% mj 37% cocaine 4% opiod†	DSM-III-R 28% SCZ 21% organic disorders 29% Aff 26% other†	(33% at 1st IP admission)†
Drake et al. (1998a) US OP SZ/SA/BP + SUD	• Age <18 or >60 • Other medical condition, mental retardation	Clinician referral	223	74%	34	4% Non-Anglo	61%	63% (20% post-high school)	82%	81%	74% al 42% other	DSM-III-R 53% SZ 22% SA 24% BP	NR
Barrowclough et al. (2001) and UK OP SZ/SA + SUD and their carer	• Not in current contact with MH services	Screening of IP admission records	32	92%	31	0%	NR	NR	NR	(50% lived with carer)	Use: 83% al 61% mj 11% cocaine 28% amphet	100% SCZ/SA	4.9

Continued

Table 1 (*Continued*)

Study	Sample description	Other exclusions (except consent issues)	Source	N^*	% Male	M Age	Non-Anglo Ethnicity (%)	Single/ never married (%)	Completed high school (%)	Unemployed (%)	Independent living (%)	Substances misused (%)	Diagnoses	# Prior psychiatric admissions (range)
Haddock et al. (2003)		• <18 or >65 years • <10h/week face-to-face contact with carer • Organic brain disease, clinically sig illness, learning disability										11% heroin		
Baker et al. (2002a, 2002b)	Australian psychiatric IP + SUD (90% sample) or weekly illicit use or risky alcohol use‡	• Not capable of interview • Not local residence in next 12 months	Patients agreeing to interview	160	75%	31	NR	60%	9%	(76% pension/ benefit)	NR	6-months SUD: 54% al (61% including risky) 51% mj (66% including weekly use)	DSM-IV 37% SZ 29% Aff 13% other 19% none	4.3

Study	Setting	Exclusion criteria	Recruitment	N	% male	Age	Ethnicity					Substance use	Diagnosis	
Hulse and Tait (2002, 2003)	Australian IP SMD + alcohol dependence	• <18 or >65 years • High alcohol dependence • Memory problems, organic brain disease • Lived outside area • Insufficient English • Too disturbed or aggressive for interview	Screening	120	54%	32	NR	NR	NR	NR	NR	2% cocaine 22% amph (23% incl. weekly use) 19% opiate 11% sed 13% other 100% al	DSM-IV (from files)	NR
Graeber et al. (2003)	US Vets Affairs IP & OP SCZ + current AUD (last 3 months)	• Active intravenous drug abuse	Screening of medical records	30	97%	44	20% Af 40% Hisp	NR	NR	NR	60%	100% al 40% mj 27% cocaine	DSM-IV 100% SCZ	23.0

Continued

Table 1 (*Continued*)

Study	Sample description	Other exclusions (except consent issues)	Source	N*	% Male	M Age	Non-Anglo Ethnicity (%)	Single/ never married (%)	Completed high school (%)	Unemployed (%)	Independent living (%)	Substances misused (%)	Diagnoses	# Prior psychiatric admissions (range)
James et al. (2004)	Australian OP/IP non-organic psychosis + current SUD	• Insufficient English • Developmental disability • Other current SUD treatment • Previous Gp treatment for SUD or psychosis	Referrals from CMHCs	63	71%	28	NR	NR	NR	NR	NR	NR	57% SCZ	NR
Kavanagh et al. (2004b)	Australian IP psychosis + SUD	• <16 or >35 years • ≥ 3 years since MH diagnosis, >2 previous psychotic episodes • Insufficient English	Screening of IPs	25	60%	23	16% Non-anglo	92%	44%	88%	(31% living away from parents/ partner)	Greatest problem: 40% mj (52% daily use) 28% al 16% amphet 8% inhalant 8% nicotine	48% SCZ	(68% at 1st episode)

Study	Population	Exclusion/Inclusion criteria	Recruitment	N										
Calsyn et al. (2005) and Morse et al. 2006	US homeless people SMD + SUD	• Developmental disability or amnestic disorder • Other current SUD treatment • Current opiates; Currently in ICM program	Screening relevant agencies, psych units, street locations	196 (144–149 with data to 24 months)	80%§	40§	73% Af 2% other§	57%§	58%§	NR	0% (all homeless)	40% al disorder 18% drug disorder 42% both Use: 34% cocaine 19% mj§	48% SCZ 19% SA 11% atypical psychosis 11% BP 9% MD 2% delusional§	NR
Baker et al. (2006)	Australian OP psychosis + risky alcohol use,‡ or ≥ weekly use of mj or amphet	• <15 years • Inadequate spoken English • Organic brain impairment • Not local residence in next 12 months	Referrals: CMHCs (34%), IP units (33%), early psychosis service (28%); media ads (3%); research register (2%)	130 (data on 119 with post and 6-months assessments)	78%	29	(9% born outside Australia)	78%	(M age at leaving school: 16 years; 66% post-school qual.)	(88% on welfare support)	NR	DSM Ab/Dep: 67% al (86% lifetime) 73% mj (89% lifetime) 42% amph (54% lifetime)	ICD-10 62% SCZ 13% SA 9% BP mania 16% other psychosis	1.0 (0–6)

Continued

Table 1 (*Continued*)

Study	Sample description	Other exclusions (except consent issues)	Source	N^*	% Male	M Age	Non-Anglo Ethnicity (%)	Single/ never married (%)	Completed high school (%)	Unemployed (%)	Independent living (%)	Substances misused (%)	Diagnoses	# Prior psychiatric admissions (range)
Bellack et al. (2006)	US OP SMD + cocaine/ heroin/mj dependence	• Not stabilized SMD	CMHCs (59%), Vet Med Center Recruitment/ Sampling NR	175	63%	43	75% Af (others NR)	42%	(M = 11 year education)	NR	NR	69% cocaine 25% opiates 7% mj	38% SCZ/SA 55% Aff	5.3
Edwards et al. (2006)	Australian OP 1st episode DSM-IV psychosis + Mj use in last 4 weeks	• Not adequate English	Screening at admission to early psychosis program or at 10 weeks, 3 or 6 months	47	72%	21¶	NR	83%¶	(15% post-sec)¶	NR	NR	SUD: 2% al 49% mj¶	72% SCZ 11% Aff psychoses 17% other psychosis¶	0
Essock et al. (2006)	US OP psychosis (SCZ, SA, BP, MD) +	• Not high service use in last 2 years (≥ 2 of: psychosis IPs, crisis/	ID by CMs in OP and IP services	198	72%	37	55% Af 14% Hisp 4% other	73%	49%	90%	NR	74% al 81% other	76% SCZ/SA 17% Aff 6% other	NR

SUD (last 6 months)	respite care, ER visits, incarcerations) • Not homeless/ unstably housed • Not poor independent living skills • Pending legal charges, illnesses, developmental disability precluding participation • Not scheduled for discharge if IP

*Number entering trial (after eligibility confirmed and baseline assessments obtained).

[†]These data were on the 427 participants completing the discharge interview, as reported in Herman et al. (1997).

[‡]Risky alcohol use was defined as exceeding maximum levels set by the Australian National Health and Medical Research Council for healthy adults in the general population.

[§]These data are on the 149 participants who had 24-month SU and symptom data, reported in Morse et al. (2006).

[¶]These data are as at 10 weeks, on the full sample of 47 participants.

NR: not reported in paper; NA: not applicable; IP: inpatients; OP: outpatients; SMD: unspecified serious mental disorder/s; SZ: schizophrenia/schizophreniform; SA: schizo affective; BP: bipolar; MD: major depression; Aff: affective disorder; PNOS: psychotic disorder not otherwise specified; Anx: anxiety disorder; ASPD: antisocial personality disorder; SUD: substance use disorder (abuse/dependence); AUD: alcohol use disorder (abuse or dependence); GAF: global Assessment of functioning; MMSE: Mini-Mental State Examination; US: United States; Aus: Australian; CMHC: Community Mental Health Centre; Af: African American; Hisp: Hispanic; al: alcohol; mj: marijuana/cannabis; amph.: amphetamine/methamphetamine/other stimulants; sed: sedatives or tranquillizers; hall: hallucinogens.

Table 2

Results of Randomized Controlled Trials

Study	Design	Contact time	Post-baseline assessment timing[*]	Results (vs. or controlling for Baseline)[†]
Lehman et al. (1993)	TAU (SCM, day rehabilitation, housing if needed) vs. TAS + ICM + Gp	Staffing – TAS 1:25; ICM 1:15 Gp: 5 h/week (Ed, Discussion, S-H, Social activity)	12 months	At 12 months, NS between conditions on psychiatric inpatient days; self-reported alcohol, drug, psychiatric severity; life satisfaction
Burnam et al. (1995)	Control vs. non-residential vs. residential. Non-residential & residential had Ed + S-H + Gp + CM + activities	Residential and non-residential more intensive over 1st 3 months – later involvement self-selected Residential: 24 h program × 3 months, then supported housing Non-residential: 8 h/day, 5 days/week; more intensive CM than Residential	3, 6, 9 months	At 3 months (end of intensive treatment phase): • Residential and Non-residential – > fall in days used alcohol than controls NS between residential and non-residential, except non-residential had more time in independent housing At 6 months: • Residential and non-residential – < fall in drug use severity than controls NS between non-residential and residential at 6, 9 months
Hellerstein et al. (1995, 2001) and Miner et al. (1997)	TAU (parallel treatment by MH, SUD services) vs. Int (supportive Gp + Ed re MH and SUD + S-H)[‡]	$2 \times 1\frac{1}{4}$ h Gp sessions/week for self-selected period	4, 8 months post-discharge	At 4 months, Int had: • > retention in treatment (70% vs. 38%) NS across conditions for addiction or psychiatric severity (overall sample improved) To 8 months, Int had: • > retention NS across conditions for hospitalization days Overall sample improved across conditions on addiction (0–8 months) and psychiatric severity (0–8 months and 4–8 months)

Study	Comparison	Assessment	Results
Herman et al. (1997, 2000)	TAU vs. Int (Ed + R-Ed + S-H + Gp)	Discharge/4 weeks; 2, 6, 10, 14, 18 months post-discharge	At discharge, Int had: • > engagement, > knowledge of SU & 12-step programs (not > MH knowledge) • > motivation to control SU, become emotionally/psychologically healthy, remain sober, attend S-H (not > # MH goals) • > ratings of treatment effectiveness. Admission to 2 months post-discharge – Int had: • > drop in alcohol use 2–18 months – little change in alcohol use; NS interaction with condition
Drake et al. (1998a)	SCM vs. ACT	6, 12, 18, 24, 30, 36 months	At 3 years, ACT allocated patients had • < attrition (4% vs. 14% SCM) • < clinician-rated alcohol problems • > clinician-rated substance abuse recovery • > financial support adequacy Across conditions: Equal improvement on alcohol and drug use, clinician-rated drug problems, community days, total BPRS, life satisfaction Those actually receiving ACT also improved more than SCM on alcohol use
Barrowclough et al. (2001) and Haddock et al. (2003)	TAU vs. TAS + Int (MI + CBT for symptoms + FI)	Post (9 months), 12 months, 18 months SU every 3 months	At 9 months (positive), Int had: • > GAF, < negative symptoms, reduction in days relapsed NS between conditions on: • Proportion with MH relapse ($p < 0.10$), total symptoms, social functioning At 12 months, Int had: • > improvement GAF, post symptoms; < proportion with MH relapse (33% vs. 67%), reduction in days relapsed

Continued

Table 2 (*Continued*)

Study	Design	Contact time	Post-baseline assessment timing[*]	Results (vs. or controlling for Baseline)[†]
				• > increase in total days abstinent from all substances over the 12 months NS between conditions on: • Total symptoms, negative symptoms, days in relapse, social functioning • Total days abstinent from preferred substance over the 12 months • Carer needs ($p < 0.10$) At 18 months, Int had: • > improvement GAF, negative symptoms NS between conditions on: • Total symptoms, positive-symptoms, proportion relapsed; days in relapse ($p < 0.10$), days abstinent, social functioning ($p < 0.10$) • Treatment costs
Baker et al. (2002a, 2002b)	Ad + substance service referral vs. MI	MI: 1 × 30–45 min individual session	3, 6, 12 months	Over 3 months, MI had: • > reduction in polydrug use[§] NS between conditions to 3 months: • To 3 months, % attending substance misuse services (MI 17%; control 17%), # sessions attended (MI 4.5, control 5.8); al, mj use, symptoms (both conditions improved). No change in amphet use. • To 12 months, # substances misused, social functioning, global symptom severity (both improved). No change in criminal activity

Study	Conditions	Dose	Follow-up	Results
Hulse and Tait (2002, 2003)	Inf vs. MI	MI: $1 \times \frac{3}{4}$ h session	6 months, 5 years	At 6 months, MI had: • < al intake, > proportion improved To 5 years: • NS between conditions on time to first alcohol-related hospital event Both conditions had > time to 1st hospital event and 1st MH hospitalization, and < # MH episodes than matched patients who left hospital before recruitment to the study
Graeber et al. (2003)	Ed vs. MI	3×1 h weekly sessions	4, 8, 24 weeks after treatment completion	MI had: • < drinking days over follow-up assessments • > abstinence rates at 8 and 24 week assessments. NS between conditions on peak BAC, weekly drinks
James et al. (2004)	TAU + Ed (SUD) vs. TAU + Gp (Ed, MI, CBT)	Ed: 1 h Int: $6 \times 1\frac{1}{2}$ h weekly Gp	3 months	At 3 months, TAS + Gp had: • > improvement in symptoms, drug abuse (functional impact, severity of dependence; mj, al, poly substance use) • > reduction in medication dose; < rate of hospitalization
Kavanagh et al. (2004b)	TAU vs. TAU + MI	MI: max 3 h total over 6–9 sessions + 4 weekly phone calls (max $\frac{1}{2}$ h total)	6 weeks, 3, 6, 9, 12 months	MI had • < SU problems at 6 and 12 months (NS at 6 months; $p < 0.10$ at 12 months if those who left before IM segment included)
Calsyn et al. (2005) and Morse et al. (2006)	TAU vs. ACT vs. Int ACT	As needed	Continuous to 6, 12, 18, 24 months	To 24 months: • Int ACT = ACT > TAS on days stable housing, satisfaction • ACT > Int ACT = TAS on treatment cost NS between conditions: • Criminal justice measures • SU, symptoms (all improved) • IP and emergency shelter costs • Patient maintenance costs (all increased)

Continued

Table 2 (*Continued*)

Study	Design	Contact time	Post-baseline assessment timing[*]	Results (vs. or controlling for Baseline)[†]
Baker et al. (2006)	TAU vs. TAU + MI + Int CBT	MI + CBT: 10 × 1 h weekly sessions	15 weeks, 6 months, 12 months	At post-treatment, NS between conditions on any measure Across conditions: Improvements to 15 weeks on alcohol, poly-drug use, BPRS negative symptoms, BDI-II depression. NS improvement on mj, amphet Over 6–12 months, Exp group had: • < BDI-II depression at 6 months • Better GAF result over 12 months • NS for condition on substance effects Across conditions to 12 months: • Improved alcohol, poly-drug use, BPRS mania, negative symptoms • NS improvement on mj, amphet
Bellack et al. (2006)	Support + Ed vs. MI + CBT for SUD[¶]	Both: Gps 2 × ? h weekly for 6 months	Weekly over 6 months	Over 6 months, MI + BT had • < dropout from treatment, > # sessions attended • Clean urines – > proportion of tests, > % with 4 and 8-week periods, and multiple 4-week periods On separate group analyses, MI + CBT had significant • decline in 90-day Psych./SU admission rates • decline in arrest rates • improved financial QoL, general life satisfaction and overall QoL • improved daily activity performance Support did not improve on these variables, but only on daily activities was the interaction with condition significant

| Edwards et al. (2006) | TAS[□] + Ed vs. TAS[□] + MI + Ed + Int CBT | 10 × 20–60 min weekly sessions over 3 months + booster phone call after 3 months | ≈ 3, 9 months (post, 6 months follow-up) | At 3 months, both conditions fell equally on % days used mj. NS on proportion using mj in past 4 weeks, severity mj use, symptoms, readiness to change, OP attendance

At 9 months, NS between conditions on any variable. Sample was stable across follow-up on % days used mj |
| Essock et al. (2006) | Int SCM vs. ACT | NR | Each 6 months to 3 years | Linear effects to 3 years:
• SCM had > IP, institutionalization days (only at site with higher rates of institution)
• Similar improvement across conditions on SU, symptoms, general life satisfaction |

*Assessment timing is post-baseline unless otherwise stated.

[†]Unless otherwise stated, all listed results were statistically significant ($p < 0.05$ or better).

[‡]Gp is manualized, but issues and skill foci are modified according to individual needs. Housing, medical, prevocational, family interventions are also offered as needed.

[§]Not significant after Bonferroni adjustment for number of measures.

[¶]The authors refer to the control condition as Supportive Treatment for Addiction Recovery (STAR), and the experimental condition as Behavioral Treatment for Substance Abuse in Severe and Persistent Mental Illness (BTSAS).

[□]TAU in Elkins et al. (2006) involved case management, mobile assessment and treatment, family intervention, group programs and a recovery clinic for early psychosis.

N/R: not reported in paper; NA: Not applicable; NS: Not significant; TAU: Treatment as usual or routine care; Int: Integrated treatment for Comorbidity; ACT: Assertive Community Treatment; CM: Case management (ICM: Intensive; SCM: standard); MI: Motivational interviewing; CBT: Cognitive-behaviour therapy; RI: Relatives/carers intervention; FI: Family intervention (patient and relative/s); Voc: Vocational/supported work program; Inc: Incentives; Gp: Group intervention; S-H: AA or other self-help groups; Ed: Patient education (R–Ed: Relatives/carer education); Inf: Written Information; Ad: Advice; SU: substance use; MH: Mental health; QoL: Quality of Life; GAF: Global Assessment of Functioning.

Table 3
Methodology Indices on Randomized Controlled Trials

Study	Started study* (percentage of eligible)†	Started study (percentage of potential sample)‡	Diagnosis confirmed by structured interview	Randomization	Baseline equivalence (statistical control)	Contact time equivalence reported	Attrition from assessments (percentage of baseline sample)	Protocol adherence	Avoided condition/therapist confound	Corroboration of self-reports	Blind ratings	Intention to treat analyses	Quality Score/11§
Lehman et al. (1993)	NR	NR (54 at baseline)	Yes	Individual	NR	No	NR	NR	No	NR	NR	NR	2
Burnam et al. (1995)	57% (276/484)	25% (/1112 screened)	Yes	Individual within gender and SCZ/Aff	NR	No	3 months: 21% 6 months: 24% 9 months: 30% (42% missed ≥ 1 f/u)	NR	NR	No (except housing status)	No	No	4
Hellerstein et al. (1995, 2001) and Miner et al. (1997)	100% (/47)	NR	Yes	Individual	Yes (drug composite score $p < 0.10$ – controlled)	Yes (CM loads not controlled)	Attrition from treatment: < 2 sessions: 38% 4 months: 47% 8 months: 64%	NR	No	NR	NR	Yes	6

Study												
Herman et al. (1997, 2000)	77% (485/627)	17% of new admissions (/2806)	NR	Individual	Yes	No	At discharge: 15% 18 months: 12%	NR	No	No	NR	No–on 429 (88%) with ≥ 1 f/u assessment	4
Drake et al. (1998a)	94% (223/236)	73% (/306)	Yes	Individual	Differed on BPRS disorgani-zation¶ (uncontrolled)	No	3 years: 9%	Clinician records + indep-endent	No	Urine toxi-cology	Yes	No–on 203 (91%) with f/u data	8
Barrow-clough et al. (2001) and Haddock et al. (2003)	55%	NR	No	Individual, indepen-dent within sex, al/drugs/ drugs + al	Yes	No	To 12 months: 11% pts, 25% carers 18 months: 22% pts	Weekly supervi-sion using audio-taped sessions	No	(Checked clinician ratings vs. self-report)	Yes high inter-rater reliab-ility	Yes	6
Baker et al. (2002a, 2002b)	100% (/160)	95% (/169)¶	Psych: No SUD: Yes	Individual	Yes	No	3 months: 30% 6 months: 27% 12 months: 28% (≥1 lost: 44%)	NR	NR (but multi-ple thera-pists)	Atten-dance meas-ured	NA	Not SU– 112 (70%) to 3 months; 89 (56%) all followup	4.5

Continued

Table 3 (*Continued*)

Study	Started study* (percentage of eligible)†	Started study (percentage of potential sample)‡	Diagnosis confirmed by structured interview	Randomization	Baseline equivalence (statistical control)	Contact time equivalence reported	Attrition from assessments (percentage of baseline sample)	Protocol adherence	Avoided condition/therapist confound	Corroboration of self-reports	Blind ratings	Intention to treat analyses	Quality Score/11§
Hulse and Tait (2002, 2003)	83% (120/144)	NR	No	Individual	• Exp had > proportion risky/harmful drinking (controlled) • < days between initial & index admission (uncontrolled)	No	6 months: 31% (36% for al. intake) 5 years: 2% (record linkage)	Therapist checklist; supervision	No	No	Yes	Yes	4.5
Graeber et al. (2003)	NR	NR	Yes	Yoked	Exp had • > Hisp, < anglo (uncontrolled) ($\frac{1}{2}$ # drinks/week, but NS)	Yes	7% (2/30)	NR	No	No	No	No–on 28 (91%) with f/u data	4
James et al. (2004)	86% (63/73)	76% (/83)	No□	Alternation of allocation only	Yes	No	3 months: 8%	No	No	No	Yes	No	4.5

Study													
Kavanagh et al. (2004b)	61% (25/41)	48% of positive screens (/52)	Yes	Individual, within site	Exp had • < IP duration • > confidence controlling SU • > proportion living with relatives (uncontrolled)	No	6 months: 4% 12 months: 32%	Therapist checklist; supervision	No (MI by different therapist)	No	Yes (at 12 months)	Yes	6
Calsyn et al. (2005) and Morse et al. (2006)	100% (/196)	43% (/454)	Yes	Individual	NR (controlled for several potential confounds)	Not equiv. Int ACT > ACT > TAS. SUD service: Int ACT = ACT > TAS	Crime data: 27% SU, symptoms: 24%	ACT checked against Dartmouth ACT Scale. (some indication of diffusion across conditions)	No	Criminal justice records	NA	No	7
Baker et al. (2006)	100% (/130)**	75% (/173)	Yes	Individual	Yes	No	15 weeks: 7% 6 months: 5% 12 months: 20%	Therapist checklist and supervision	Yes?	No	Yes	Yes	8

Continued

Table 3 (*Continued*)

Study	Started study (percentage of eligible)†	Started study (percentage of potential sample)‡	Diagnosis confirmed by structured interview	Randomization	Baseline equivalence (statistical control)	Contact time equivalence reported	Attrition from assessments (percentage of baseline sample)	Protocol adherence	Avoided condition/ therapist confound	Corroboration of self-reports	Blind ratings	Intention to treat analyses	Quality Score/ 11§
Bellack et al. (2006)	68% (175/257)	60% of consenting patients (/293)	NR	Individual within community/Vets center, controlling sex, psych diagnosis, drug of choice, # SUDs	Yes	Yes for frequency. Duration NR	53% (92/175)	Videotapes independently rated – fidelity high	NR (but multiple therapists)	Urinalyses	NA	No–on 110 (63%) engaged in treatment	5.5
Edwards et al. (2006)	62% (47/76)	Percentage of screened: 24% at 10 weeks (31/130), 11% at 3 months (12/105), 4% at 9 months (4/94)	Yes	Independent, individual	Yes	Yes	4% to 3 months (post) 30% to 9 months (6-month f/u)	Supervision	NR (but multiple therapists)	No	Yes high inter-rater reliability	Yes	8

Essock et al. (2006)	81% (198/ 244)	52% (/382 referrals)	Yes	Individual within site	Clinician rating of progress to SU recovery ACT < SCM. (controlled) Some site differences	No (SCM had higher caseload)	3 years: 10% (27% missed ≥ 1 assessment)	Independent ratings, supervision. High fidelity (less ACT services in community than ideal)	No	Urine screens, alcohol saliva tests. (rated from all data). Service use from information systems	Yes high reliability	No	8

The data now permit the drawing of some tentative conclusions. First, brief interventions tend to have limited effects, especially in the longer term (Baker et al., 2002b; Hulse & Tait, 2002, 2003; Kavanagh et al., 2004b), with one clear exception (Graeber et al., 2003). The findings suggest that the primary role of brief interventions for co-occurring disorders, such as motivational interviewing, is engagement in treatment, rather than reduction of substance misuse. Second, studies comparing integrated treatment delivered on assertive community treatment teams (ACT; Stein & Santos, 1998), with integrated treatment provided by standard case management teams reported little or no additional benefit from the more intensive ACT teams (Calsyn et al., 2005; Morse et al., 2006) (Drake et al., 1998a; Essock et al., 2006). Third, longer-term (e.g., 6–9 month) cognitive-behavioral interventions addressing SUD and SMI tend to have better outcomes, although only two studies fell into this category (Barrowclough et al., 2001; Bellack et al., 2006), but the only long-term follow-up (of the intervention originally published by Barrowclough et al.) suggest that gains decay over time (Haddock et al., 2003), differences between conditions in substance use were not maintained. Fourth, integrated programs tended to have superior outcomes to non-integrated controls, although findings were mixed.

Clearly, the results of controlled trials of integrated treatment for co-occurring disorders raise more questions than they answer. Overall, controlled trials of integrated treatments indicate that substance abuse outcomes tend to be modest and inconsistent. At least some of the variability in findings across studies appears due to the different interventions studied and research methodologies. In fact, no standardized intervention has been examined (much less replicated) across more than one published study. Larger reviews of integrated treatment for dual disorders that include a wider range of study methodologies, such as quasi-experimental designs, suggest stronger support for integrated treatment (Drake et al., 2004), but there is clearly still much work to be done to strengthen the evidence base for this work. We are still at the stage of establishing the basic effectiveness of our treatments. We have yet to identify key effective components in the interventions, apart perhaps from motivational aspects, and factors that reliably predict a positive outcome remain to be identified.

FUTURE DIRECTIONS FOR TRANSLATIONAL RESEARCH

The mixed results from controlled research on integrated treatment for co-occurring disorders strongly point to the need for improved treatment models. While current integrated treatments were developed mainly to overcome treatment access, more effective outcomes may be achieved by considering basic research into mechanisms hypothesized to account for the increased comorbidity between SMI and SUD.

IMPLICATIONS FOR PRIMARY PREVENTION

Among models of comorbidity, a supersensitivity explanation (i.e., increased risk of substance abuse among people with SMI, because of their psychobiological vulnerability) has some of the strongest empirical support. Because about a half of SUDs in people with co-occurring disorders develop after the onset of SMI (Hambrecht & Häfner, 1996; Silver & Abboud, 1994), informing clients with recent-onset psychosis and their families about this increased vulnerability to substance effects could prevent some from developing later SUD. This education can be conceptualized as part of training in illness self-management (Mueser et al., 2006), rather than intervention for co-occurring disorders, since it precedes the onset of SUD.

Prospective studies consistently show that cannabis use, especially in adolescence, predicts the development of schizophrenia (Arseneault et al., 2004). The potential role of cannabis as a precipitant of schizophrenia suggests that drug misuse prevention efforts that target cannabis during the vulnerable period of adolescence could actually prevent the onset of some cases of schizophrenia. Such prevention efforts might be most effective if specifically targeted at individuals at increased risk for schizophrenia, such as first-degree relatives of people with the disorder.

IMPLICATIONS FOR IMPROVING TREATMENT

One reason the outcomes of integrated treatment programs may be so modest is that they fail to sufficiently individualize treatment to address the specific needs of individuals with co-occurring disorders. As previously reviewed, the prevailing wisdom that all excess comorbidity can be explained by a simplistic version of the self-medication hypothesis is clearly incorrect. There is modest evidence linking dysphoria to SUD in persons with SMI. More importantly, all of the studies examining reasons for substance use identify a range of different motives, which can be grouped into the broad categories of coping with symptoms, socialization, recreation/leisure, and something to look forward to (Addington & Duchak, 1997; Carey & Carey, 1995; Dixon et al., 1991; Green et al., 2004; Laudet et al., 2004; Warner et al., 1994).

Although a variety of different reasons for using substances exist, each client's specific motives are unique. Individually tailoring integrated treatment to address the specific motives for using substances could improve the effectiveness and efficiency of intervention by targeting the most pressing needs of clients who are contemplating a sober lifestyle. For example, individually tailored treatment could focus on helping clients develop less destructive ways for getting needs met, such as coping strategies for managing distressing symptoms, improved social skills and alternative socialization outlets, new leisure and recreational activities, or other meaningful activity, such as work, school, or effective parenting (Mueser et al., 2003).

Contingent reinforcement has been shown to be effective in the treatment of primary SUD, at least during the administration of the reinforcement (Higgins, Alessi, & Dantona, 2002; Higgins et al., 1994). There is growing evidence from case control studies suggesting contingent reinforcement may be effective at reducing substance misuse in clients with SMI (Roll, Chermack, & Chudzynski, 2004; Roll et al., 1998; Shaner et al., 1997; Sigmon et al., 2000), and one small randomized controlled trial (Ries et al., 2004). Further randomized trials of this type of intervention are warranted. Critical challenges in such programs are to avoid undermining intrinsic motivation to maintain control over substance use, and ensure that behavioral changes continue to be supported by natural reinforcers after extrinsic reinforcement programs are withdrawn.

An intriguing question is whether part of the problem in current approaches to comorbidity is that they do not adequately address the problems created by altered brain circuitry in schizophrenia. At a simple level, perhaps current interventions are simply not rewarding enough for this population. Greater emphasis on pleasurable alternate activities may help, both in maintaining engagement and altering substance use, provided that they are not so challenging as to provoke symptomatic exacerbation. At a more complex level, the addition of pharmacological or other biological interventions to specifically address the dysfunction may be required. It is even conceivable that a specific psychological intervention may have an impact on this brain circuitry. Changes in other aspects of brain function have been reported following other psychological interventions, such as cognitive remediation for schizophrenia (Wexler et al., 2000; Wykes et al., 2002). However, we anticipate that a combination of biological and psychological interventions will be required to address problems with this circuitry.

Further significant advances in the basic science of addiction in people with SMI may be required before substantial leaps in effectiveness of interventions can be achieved. We still know very little about the processes of natural recovery in comorbid populations, about factors that reliably predict outcome, and differences in craving that people with and without SMI experience. The precise nature of brain dysfunctions underpinning SMIs and related comorbidities also remains to be articulated. Increased knowledge about these issues over the next years will greatly assist the design of more effective intervention.

REFERENCES

Addington, J., & Duchak, V. (1997). Reasons for substance use in schizophrenia. *Acta Psychiatrica Scandinavica, 96*, 329–333.

Allebeck, P., Adamsson, C., Engström, A., & Rydberg, U. (1993). Cannabis and schizophrenia: A longitudinal study of cases treated in Stockholm County. *Acta Psychiatrica Scandinavica, 88*, 21–24.

Alterman, A. I., & Cacciola, J. S. (1991). The antisocial personality disorder diagnosis in substance abusers: Problems and issues. *Journal of Nervous and Mental Disease, 179*, 167–175.

Andréasson, S., Allebeck, P., Engström, A., & Rydberg, U. (1987). Cannabis and schizophrenia: A longitudinal study of Swedish conscripts. *The Lancet, December 26*, 1483–1486.

Andréasson, S., Allebeck, P., & Rydberg, U. (1989). Schizophrenia in users and nonusers of cannabis: A longitudinal study in Stockholm County. *Acta Psychiatrica Scandinavica, 79*, 505–510.

Anthony, J. C. (1991). Epidemiology of drug dependence and illicit drug use. *Current Opinion in Psychiatry, 4*, 435–439.

Arndt, S., Tyrrell, G., Flaum, M., & Andreasen, N. C. (1992). Comorbidity of substance abuse and schizophrenia: The role of pre-morbid adjustment. *Psychological Medicine, 22*, 379–388.

Arseneault, L., Cannon, M., Poulton, R., Murray, R., Caspi, A., & Moffitt, T. E. (2002). Cannabis use in adolescence and risk for adult psychosis: Longitudinal prospective study. *British Medical Journal, 325*, 1212–1213.

Arseneault, L., Cannon, M., Witton, J., & Murray, R. M. (2004). Causal association between cannabis and psychosis: Examination of the evidence. *British Journal of Psychiatry, 184*, 110–117.

Asarnow, J. R. (1988). Children at risk for schizophrenia: Converging lines of evidence. *Schizophrenia Bulletin, 14*, 613–631.

Baker, A., Bucci, S., Lewin, T. J., Kay-Lambkin, F., Constable, P. M., & Carr, V. J. (2006). Cognitive-behavioural therapy for substance use disorders in people with psychotic disorders: Randomised controlled trial. *British Journal of Psychiatry, 188*, 439–448.

Baker, A., Lewin, T., Reichler, H., Clancy, R., Carr, V., Garrett, R., et al. (2002a). Evaluation of a motivational interview for substance use within psychiatric in-patient services. *Addiction, 97*, 1329–1337.

Baker, A., Lewin, T., Reichler, H., Clancy, R., Carr, V., Garrett, R., et al. (2002b). Motivational interviewing among psychiatric in-patients with substance use disorders. *Acta Psychiatrica Scandinavica, 106*, 233–240.

Barrowclough, C., Haddock, G., Tarrier, N., Lewis, S., Moring, J., O'Brien, R., Schofield, N., & McGovern, J. (2001). Randomized controlled trial of motivational interviewing, cognitive behavior therapy, and family intervention for patients with comorbid schizophrenia and substance use disorders. *American Journal of Psychiatry, 158*, 1706–1713.

Bellack, A. S., Bennet, M. E., Gearon, J. S., Brown, C. H., & Yang, Y. (2006). A randomized clinical trial of a new behavioral treatment for drug abuse in people with severe and persistent mental illness. *Archives of General Psychiatry, 63*, 426–432.

Berkson, J. (1949). Limitations of the application of four-fold tables to hospital data. *Biological Bulletin, 2*, 47–53.

Berman, S. M., & Noble, E. P. (1993). Childhood antecedents of substance misuse. *Current Opinion in Psychiatry, 6*, 382–387.

Bernadt, M. W., & Murray, R. M. (1986). Psychiatric disorder, drinking and alcoholism: What are the links? *British Journal of Psychiatry, 148*, 393–400.

Birchwood, M., Mason, R., MacMillian, F., & Healy, J. (1993). Depression, demoralization and control over psychotic illness: A comparison and non-depressed patients with a chronic psychosis. *Psychological Medicine, 23*, 387–395.

Blanchard, J. J., Brown, S. A., Horan, W. P., & Sherwood, A. R. (2000). Substance use disorders in schizophrenia: Review, integration, and a proposed model. *Clinical Psychology Review, 20*, 207–234.

Blanchard, J. J., Squires, D., Henry, T., Horan, W. P., Bogenschutz, M., Lauriello, J., & Bustillo, J. (1999). Examining an affect regulation model of substance abuse in schizophrenia: The role of traits and coping. *Journal of Nervous and Mental Disease, 187*, 72–79.

Bland, R. C., Newman, S. C., & Orn, H. (1987). Schizophrenia: Lifetime comorbidity in a community sample. *Acta Psychiatrica Scandinavica, 75*, 383–391.

Blum, K., Braverman, E. R., Holder, J. M., Lubar, J. F., Monastra, V. J., Miller, D., Lubar, J. O., Chen, T. J., & Comings, D. E. (2000). Reward deficiency syndrome: A biogenetic model for the diagnosis and treatment of impulsive, addictive, and compulsive behaviors. *Journal of Psychoactive Drugs, 32*(Suppl. i–iv), 1–112.

Blumenfield, M., & Glickman, L. (1967). Ten months experience with LSD users admitted to a county psychiatric receiving hospital. *New York State Journal of Medicine, 67*, 1849–1853.

Boileau, I., Assaad, J. M., Pihl, R. O., Benkelfat, C., Leyton, M., Tremblay, R. E., & Dagher, A. (2003). Alcohol promotes dopamine release in the human nucleus accumbens. *Synapse, 49*, 226–231.

Brecher, M., & Begleiter, H. (1983). Event-related brain potentials to high-incentive stimuli in unmedicated schizophrenic patients. *Biological Psychiatry, 18*, 661–674.

Brunette, M. F., Mueser, K. T., Xie, H., & Drake, R. E. (1997). Relationships between symptoms of schizophrenia and substance abuse. *Journal of Nervous and Mental Disease, 185*, 13–20.

Bunney, W. E., Jr., & Davis, J. (1965). Norepinephrine in depressive reactions. *Archives of General Psychiatry, 13*, 483–494.

Burnam, M. A., Morton, S. C., McGlynn, E. A., Peterson, L. P., Stecher, B. M., Hayes, C., & Vaccaro, J. V. (1995). An experimental evaluation of residential and nonresidential treatment for dually diagnosed homeless adults. *Journal of Addictive Diseases, 14*, 111–134.

Calsyn, R. J., Yonker, R. D., Lemming, M. R. m., G. A., & Klinkenberg, W. D. (2005). Impact of assertive community treatment and client characteristics on criminal justice outcomes in dual disorder homeless individuals. *Criminal Behaviour and Mental Health, 15*, 236–248.

Cannon, T. D., Mednick, S. A., Parnas, J., Schulsinger, F., Praestholm, J., & Vestergaard, A. (1993). Developmental brain abnormalities in the offspring of schizophrenic mothers. *Archives of General Psychiatry, 50*, 551–564.

Carey, K. B. (1996). Substance use reduction in the context of outpatient psychiatric treatment: A collaborative, motivational, harm reduction approach. *Community Mental Health Journal, 32*, 291–306.

Carey, K. B., & Carey, M. P. (1995). Reasons for drinking among psychiatric outpatients: Relationship to drinking patterns. *Psychology of Addictive Behaviors, 9*, 251–257.

Carlson, G. A., & Weintraub, S. (1993). Childhood behavior problems and bipolar disorder – relationship or coincidence? *Journal of Affective Disorders, 28*, 143–153.

Caspi, A., Moffitt, T. E., Cannon, M., McClay, J., Murray, R., Harrington, H., Taylor, A., Arseneault, L., Williams, B., Braithwaite, A., Poulton, R., & Craig, I. W. (2005). Moderation of the effect of adolescent-onset cannabis use on adult psychosis by a functional polymorphism in the catechol-O-methyltransferase gene: Longitudinal evidence of a gene X environment interaction. *Biological Psychiatry, 57*, 1117–1127.

Chambers, R. A., Krystal, J. H., & Self, D. W. (2001). A neurobiological basis for substance abuse comorbidity in schizophrenia. *Biological Psychiatry, 50*, 71–83.

Chambers, R. A., & Self, D. W. (2002). Motivational responses to natural and drug rewards in rats with neonatal ventral hippocampal lesions: An animal model of dual diagnosis schizophrenia. *Neuropsychopharmacology, 27*, 889–905.

Chau, D. T., Roth, R. M., & Green, A. I. (2004). The neural circuitry of reward and its relevance to psychiatric disorders. *Current Psychiatry Reports, 6*, 391–399.

Chen, C., Balogh, M., Bathija, J., Howanitz, E., Plutchik, R., & Conte, H. R. (1992). Substance abuse among psychiatric inpatients. *Comprehensive Psychiatry, 33*, 60–64.

Corse, S. J., Hirschinger, N. B., & Zanis, D. (1995). The use of the Addiction Severity Index with people with severe mental illness. *Psychiatric Rehabilitation Journal, 19*, 9–18.

Craddock, N., O'Donovan, M. C., & Owen, M. J. (2006). Genes for schizophrenia and bipolar disorder? Implications for psychiatric nosology. *Schizophrenia Bulletin, 32*, 9–16.

Craddock, N., & Owen, M. J. (2005). The beginning of the end for the Kraepelinian dichotomy. *British Journal of Psychiatry, 186*, 364–366.

Crespo-Facorro, B., Paradiso, S., Andreasen, N. C., O'Leary, D. S., Watkins, G. L., Ponto, L. L., & Hichwa, R. D. (2001). Neural mechanisms of anhedonia in schizophrenia; a PET study of response to unpleasant and pleasant odors. *Journal of the American Medical Association, 286*, 427–435.

Cuffel, B. J. (1996). Comorbid substance use disorder: Prevalence, patterns of use, and course. In R. E. Drake, & K. T. Mueser (Eds.), *Dual Diagnosis of Major Mental Illness and Substance Abuse Volume 2:*

Recent Research and Clinical Implications. New Directions in Mental Health Services (Vol. 70, pp. 93–105). San Francisco: Jossey-Bass.

Degenhardt, L., Hall, W., & Lynskey, M. (2003). Testing hypotheses about the relationship between cannabis use and psychosis. *Drug and Alcohol Dependence, 71,* 37–48.

DelBello, M. P., Strakowski, S. M., Sax, K. W., McElroy, S. L., Keck, P. E. J., West, S. A., & Kmetz, G. F. (1999). Effects of familial rates of affective illness and substance abuse on rates of substance abuse in patients with first-episode mania. *Journal of Affective Disorders, 56,* 55–60.

Dixon, L., Haas, G., Weiden, P. J., Sweeney, J., & Frances, A. J. (1991). Drug abuse in schizophrenic patients: Clinical correlates and reasons for use. *American Journal of Psychiatry, 148,* 224–230.

Drake, R. E., Bartels, S. B., Teague, G. B., Noordsy, D. L., & Clark, R. E. (1993). Treatment of substance abuse in severely mentally ill patients. *Journal of Nervous and Mental Disease, 181,* 606–611.

Drake, R. E., & Brunette, M. F. (1998). Complications of severe mental illness related to alcohol and other drug use disorders. In M. Galanter (Ed.), *Recent Developments in Alcoholism: Consequences of Alcoholism* (Vol. 14, pp. 285–299). New York: Plenum Publishing Company.

Drake, R. E., McHugo, G. J., Clark, R. E., Teague, G. B., Xie, H., Miles, K., & Ackerson, T. H. (1998a). Assertive community treatment for patients with co-occurring severe mental illness and substance use disorder: A clinical trial. *American Journal of Orthopsychiatry, 68,* 201–215.

Drake, R. E., Mercer-McFadden, C., Mueser, K. T., McHugo, G. J., & Bond, G. R. (1998b). Review of integrated mental health and substance abuse treatment for patients with dual disorders. *Schizophrenia Bulletin, 24,* 589–608.

Drake, R. E., Mueser, K. T., Brunette, M. F., & McHugo, G. J. (2004). A review of treatments for clients with severe mental illness and co-occurring substance use disorder. *Psychiatric Rehabilitation Journal, 27,* 360–374.

Drake, R. E., & Wallach, M. A. (1993). Moderate drinking among people with severe mental illness. *Hospital and Community Psychiatry, 44,* 780–782.

D'Souza, D. C., Abi-Saab, W. M., Madonick, S., Forselius-Bielen, K., Doersch, A., Braley, G., Gueorguieva, R., Cooper, T. B., & Krystal, J. H. (2005). Delta-9-tetrahydrocannabinol effects in schizophrenia; Implications for cognition, psychosis, and addiction. *Biological Psychiatry, 57,* 594–608.

Edwards, J., Elkins, K., Hinton, M., Harrigan, S. M., Donovan, K., & Athanasopoulos, O. (2006). Randomized controlled trial of a cannabis-focused intervention for young people with first-episode psychosis. *Acta Psychiatrica Scandinavica, 114,* 109–117.

Essock, S. M., Mueser, K. T., Drake, R. E., Covell, N. H., McHugo, G. J., Frisman, L. K., Kontos, N. J., Jackson, C. T., Townsend, F., & Swain, K. (2006). Comparison of ACT and standard case management for delivering integrated treatment for co-occurring disorders. *Psychiatric Services, 57,* 185–196.

Fergusson, D. M., Horwood, L. J., & Swain-Campbell, N. R. (2003). Cannabis dependence and psychotic symptoms in young people. *Psychological Medicine, 33,* 15–21.

Galanter, M., Castaneda, R., & Ferman, J. (1988). Substance abuse among general psychiatric patients: Place of presentation, diagnosis and treatment. *American Journal of Drug and Alcohol Abuse, 14,* 211–235.

Gershon, E. S., DeLisi, L. E., Hamovit, J., Nurnberger, J. I., Maxwell, M. E., Schreiber, J., Dauphinais, D., Dingman, C. W., & Guroff, J. J. (1988). A controlled family study of chronic psychoses: Schizophrenia and schizoaffective disorder. *Archives of General Psychiatry, 45,* 328–336.

Glass, G. S., & Bowers, M. B. (1970). Chronic psychosis associated with long-term psychotomimetic drug abuse. *Archives of General Psychiatry, 23,* 97–103.

Goodwin, F. K., & Jamison, K. R. (1990). *Manic Depressive Illness.* New York: Oxford University Press.

Graeber, D. A., Moyers, T. B., Griffith, G., Guajardo, E., & Tonigan, S. (2003). A pilot study comparing motivational interviewing and an educational intervention in patients with schizophrenia and alcohol use disorders. *Community Mental Health Journal, 39,* 189–202.

Graham, H. L. (1998). The role of dysfunctional beliefs in individual who experience psychosis and use substances: Implications for cognitive therapy and medication adherence. *Behavioural and Cognitive Psychotherapy*, *26*, 193–207.

Green, A. I., Zimmet, S. V., Strous, R. D., & Schildkraut, J. J. (1999). Clozapine for comorbid substance use disorder and schizophrenia: Do patients with schizophrenia have a reward-deficiency syndrome that can be ameliorated by clozapine? *Harvard Review of Psychiatry*, *6*, 287–296.

Green, B., Kavanagh, D. J., & Young, R. McD. (2004). Reasons for cannabis use in men with and without psychosis. *Drug and Alcohol Review*, *23*, 445–453.

Haddock, G., Barrowclough, C., Tarrier, N., Moring, J., O'Brien, R., Schofield, N., Quinn, J., Palmer, S., Davies, L., Lowens, I., McGovern, J., & Lewis, S. (2003). Cognitive-behavioural therapy and motivational intervention for schizophrenia and substance misuse: 18-month outcomes of a randomised controlled trial. *British Journal of Psychiatry*, *183*, 418–426.

Hambrecht, M., & Häfner, H. (1996). Substance abuse and the onset of schizophrenia. *Biological Psychiatry*, *40*, 1155–1163.

Hambrecht, M., & Häfner, H. (2000). Cannabis, vulnerability, and the onset of schizophrenia: An epidemiological perspective. *Australian and New Zealand Journal of Psychiatry*, *34*, 468–475.

Hamera, E., Schneider, J. K., & Deviney, S. (1995). Alcohol, cannabis, nicotine, and caffeine use and symptom distress in schizophrenia. *Journal of Nervous and Mental Disease*, *183*, 559–565.

Hellerstein, D. J., Rosenthal, R. N., & Miner, C. R. (1995). A prospective study of integrated outpatient treatment for substance-abusing schizophrenic outpatients. *American Journal on Addictions*, *4*, 33–42.

Hellerstein, D. J., Rosenthal, R. N., & Miner, C. R. (2001). Integrating services for schizophrenia and substance abuse. *Psychiatric Quarterly*, *72*, 291–306.

Henquet, C., Krabbendam, L., Spauwen, J., Kaplan, C., Lieb, R., Wittchen, H. U., & van Os, J. (2005). Prospective cohort study of cannabis use, predisposition for psychosis, and psychotic symptoms in young people. *British Medical Journal*, *330*, 11.

Herman, S. E., Boots-Miller, B., Jordan, L., Mowbray, C. T., Brown, W. G., Deiz, N., Bandla, H., Solomon, M., & Green, P. (1997). Immediate outcomes of substance use treatment within a State psychiatric hospital. *Journal of Mental Health Administration*, *24*, 126–138.

Herman, S. E., Frank, K. A., Mowbray, C. T., Ribisl, K. M., Davidson, W. S., BootsMiller, B., et al. (2000). Longitudinal effects of integrated treatment on alcohol use for persons with serious mental illness and substance use disorders. *Journal of Behavioral Health Services & Research*, *27*, 286–302.

Hides, L., Dawe, S., Kavanagh, D. J., & Young, R. McD. (2006). A prospective study of psychotic symptom and cannabis relapse in recent onset psychosis. *British Journal of Psychiatry*, *189*, 137–143.

Higgins, S. T., Alessi, S. M., & Dantona, R. L. (2002). Voucher-based incentives: A substance abuse treatment innovation. *Addictive Behaviors*, *27*, 887–910.

Higgins, S. T., Budney, A. J., Bickel, W. K., Foerg, F. E., Donham, R., & Badger, G. J. (1994). Incentives improve outcome in outpatient behavioral treatment of cocaine dependence. *Archives of General Psychiatry*, *51*, 568–576.

Hodgins, S., Hiscoke, U. L., & Freese, R. (2002). The antecedants of aggressive behavior among men with schizophrenia: A prospective investigation of patients in community treatment. *Behavioral Sciences & The Law*, *21*, 523–546.

Hodgins, S., Tiihonen, J., & Ross, D. (2005). The consequences of conduct disorder for males who develop schizophrenia: Associations with criminality, aggressive behavior, substance use, and psychiatric services. *Schizophrenia Research*, *78*, 323–335.

Hodgins, S., Toupin, J., & Côté, G. (1996). Schizophrenia and antisocial personality disorder: A criminal combination. In L. B. Schlesinger (Ed.), *Explorations in Criminal Psychopathology: Clinical Syndromes with Forensic Implications* (pp. 217–237). Springfield, IL: Charles C. Thomas.

Hulse, G. K., & Tait, R. J. (2002). Six-month outcomes associated with a brief alcohol intervention for adult inpatients with psychiatric disorders. *Drug and Alcohol Review*, *21*, 105–112.

Hulse, G. K., & Tait, R. J. (2003). Five-year outcomes of a brief psychiatric intervention for adult in-patients with psychiatric disorders. *Addiction*, *98*, 1061–1068.

Jackson, H. J., Whiteside, H. L., Bates, G. W., Rudd, R. P., & Edwards, J. (1991). Diagnosing personality disorders in psychiatric inpatients. *Acta Psychiatrica Scandinavica, 83,* 206–213.

James, W., Preston, N. J., Koh, G., Spencer, C., Kisely, S. R., & Castle, D. J. (2004). A group intervention which assists patients with dual diagnosis reduce their drug use: A randomised controlled trial. *Psychological Medicine, 34,* 983–990.

Jones, P., Guth, C., Lewis, S., & Murray, R. (1994). Low intelligence and poor educational achievement precede early onset schizophrenic psychosis. In A. S. David, & J. C. Cutting (Eds.), *The Neuropsychology of Schizophrenia* (pp. 131–144). Brighton, England: Lawrence Erlbaum.

Kavanagh, D. J. (1995). An intervention for substance abuse in schizophrenia. *Behaviour Change, 12,* 20–30.

Kavanagh, D. J., Waghorn, G., Jenner, L., Chant, D. C., Carr, V., Evans, M., Herrman, H., Jablensky, A., & McGrath, J. J. (2004a). Demographic and clinical correlates of comorbid substance use disorders in psychosis: Multivariate analyses from an epidemiological sample. *Schizophrenia Research, 66,* 115–124.

Kavanagh, D. J., Young, R., White, A., Saunders, J. B., Wallis, J., Shocklewy, N., Jenner, L., & Clair, A. (2004b). A brief motivational intervention for substance misuse in recent-onset psychosis. *Drug and Alcohol Review, 23,* 151–155.

Keith, S. J., Regier, D. A., & Rae, D. S. (1991). Schizophrenic disorders. In L. N. Robins, & D. A. Regier (Eds.), *Psychiatric Disorders in America: The Epidemiologic Catchment Area Study* (pp. 33–52). New York: Free Press.

Kessler, R. C., Crum, R. M., Warner, L. A., Nelson, C. B., Schulenberg, J., & Anthony, J. C. (1997). Lifetime co-occurrence of DSM-III-R alcohol abuse and dependence with other psychiatric disorders in the National Comorbidity Survey. *Archives of General Psychiatry, 54,* 313–321.

Khantzian, E. J. (1997). The self-medication hypothesis of substance use disorders: A reconsideration and recent applications. *Harvard Review of Psychiatry, 4,* 231–244.

Kirkpatrick, B., Amador, X. F., Flaum, M., Yale, S. A., Gorman, J. M., Carpenter, W. T., Jr., Tohen, M., & McGlashan, T. (1996). The deficit syndrome in the DSM-IV field trial: I. Alcohol an other drug abuse. *Schizophrenia Research, 20,* 69–77.

Knudsen, P., & Vilmar, T. (1984). Cannabis and neuroleptic agents in schizophrenia. *Acta Psychiatrica Scandinavica, 69,* 162–174.

Krebs, M. O., Sautel, F., Bourdel, M. C., Sokoloff, P., Schwartz, J. C., Olie, J. P., Loo, H., & Poirier, M. F. (1998). Dopamine D3 receptor gene variants and substance abuse in schizophrenia. *Molecular Psychiatry, 3,* 337–341.

Krystal, J. H., Perry, E. B., Gueorguieva, R., Belger, A., Madonick, S. H., Abi-Dargham, A., Cooper, T. B., Macdougall, L., Abi-Saab, W., & D'Souza, D. C. (2005). Comparative and interactive human psychopharmacologic effects of ketamine and amphetamine. *Archives of General Psychiatry, 62,* 985–995.

Kushner, M. G., & Mueser, K. T. (1993). Psychiatric co-morbidity with alcohol use disorders. *Eighth Special Report to the U.S. Congress on Alcohol and Health* (Vol. NIH Pub. No. 94-3699, pp. 37–59). Rockville, MD: U.S. Department of Health and Human Services.

Laudet, A. B., Magura, S., Vogel, H. S., & Knight, E. L. (2004). Perceived reasons for substance misuse among persons with a psychiatric disorder. *American Journal of Orthopsychiatry, 74,* 365–375.

Lehman, A. F., Herron, J. D., Schwartz, R. P., & Myers, C. P. (1993). Rehabilitation for adults with severe mental illness and substance use disorders: A clinical trial. *The Journal of Nervous and Mental Disease, 181,* 86–90.

Lehman, A. F., Myers, C. P., Corty, E., & Thompson, J. W. (1994). Prevalence and patterns of "dual diagnosis" among psychiatric inpatients. *Comprehensive Psychiatry, 35,* 106–112.

Lieberman, J. A., Kane, J. M., & Alvir, J. (1987). Provocative tests with psychostimulant drugs in schizophrenia. *Psychopharmacology, 91,* 415–433.

Lieberman, J. A., Kinon, B. J., & Loebel, A. D. (1990). Dopaminergic mechanisms in idiopathic and drug-induced psychoses. *Schizophrenia Bulletin, 16,* 97–110.

Maier, W., Lichtermann, D., Minges, J., Delmo, C., & Heun, R. (1995). The relationship between bipolar disorder and alcoholism: A controlled family study. *Psychological Medicine, 25*, 787–796.

McLellan, T. A., Woody, G. E., & O'Brien, C. P. (1979). Development of psychiatric illness in drug abusers: Possible role of drug preference. *New England Journal of Medicine, 301*(24), 1310–1314.

Miller, W. R., & Rollnick, S. (Eds.). (2002). *Motivational Interviewing: Preparing People for Change* (2nd ed.). New York: Guilford Press.

Miner, C. R., Rosenthal, R. N., Hellerstein, D. J., & Muenz, L. R. (1997). Prediction of compliance with outpatient referral in patients with schizophrenia and psychoactive substance use disorders. *Archives of General Psychiatry, 54*, 706–712.

Minkoff, K. (1989). An integrated treatment model for dual diagnosis of psychosis and addiction. *Hospital and Community Psychiatry, 40*, 1031–1036.

Morse, G. A., Calsyn, R. J., Klinkenberg, W. D., Helminiak, T. W., Wolff, N., Drake, R. E., Yonker, R. D., Lama, G., Lemming, M. R., McCudden, S. (2006). Treating homeless clients with severe mental illness and substance use disorders: Costs and outcomes. *Community Mental Health Journal, 42*, 377–404.

Mueser, K. T., Crocker, A. G., Frisman, L. B., Drake, R. E., Covell, N. H., & Essock, S. M. (2006). Conduct disorder and antisocial personality disorder in persons with severe psychiatric and substance use disorders. *Schizophrenia Bulletin, 32*, 626–636.

Mueser, K. T., Drake, R. E., Ackerson, T. H., Alterman, A. I., Miles, K. M., & Noordsy, D. L. (1997). Antisocial personality disorder, conduct disorder, and substance abuse in schizophrenia. *Journal of Abnormal Psychology, 106*, 473–477.

Mueser, K. T., Meyer, P. S., Penn, D. L., Clancy, R., Clancy, D. M., & Salyers, M. P. (2006). The Illness Management and Recovery program: Rationale, development, and preliminary findings. *Schizophrenia Bulletin, 32*(Suppl. 1), S32–S43.

Mueser, K. T., Nishith, P., Tracy, J. I., DeGirolamo, J., & Molinaro, M. (1995). Expectations and motives for substance use in schizophrenia. *Schizophrenia Bulletin, 21*, 367–378.

Mueser, K. T., Noordsy, D. L., Drake, R. E., & Fox, L. (2003). *Integrated Treatment for Dual Disorders: A Guide to Effective Practice.* New York: Guilford Press.

Mueser, K. T., Rosenberg, S. D., Drake, R. E., Miles, K. M., Wolford, G., Vidaver, R., & Carrieri, K. (1999). Conduct disorder, antisocial personality disorder, and substance use disorders in schizophrenia and major affective disorders. *Journal of Studies on Alcohol, 60*, 278–284.

Mueser, K. T., Yarnold, P. R., & Bellack, A. S. (1992). Diagnostic and demographic correlates of substance abuse in schizophrenia and major affective disorder. *Acta Psychiatrica Scandinavica, 85*, 48–55.

Mueser, K. T., Yarnold, P. R., Levinson, D. F., Singh, H., Bellack, A. S., Kee, K., Morrison, R. L., & Yadalam, K. G. (1990). Prevalence of substance abuse in schizophrenia: Demographic and clinical correlates. *Schizophrenia Bulletin, 16*, 31–56.

Mueser, K. T., Yarnold, P. R., Rosenberg, S. D., Swett, C., Miles, K. M., & Hill, D. (2000). Substance use disorder in hospitalized severely mentally ill psychiatric patients: Prevalence, correlates, and subgroups. *Schizophrenia Bulletin, 26*, 179–192.

Noordsy, D. L., Drake, R. E., Biesanz, J. C., & McHugo, G. J. (1994). Family history of alcoholism in schizophrenia. *Journal of Nervous and Mental Disease, 186*, 651–655.

Noordsy, D. L., Drake, R. E., Teague, G. B., Osher, F. C., Hurlbut, S. C., Beaudett, M. S., & Paskus, T. S. (1991). Subjective experiences related to alcohol abuse among schizophrenics. *Journal of Nervous and Mental Disease, 179*, 410–414.

O'Leary, D. S., Block, R. I., Flaum, M., Schultz, S. K., Boles Ponto, L. L., Watkins, G. L., Hurtig, R. R., Andreasen, N. C., & Hichwa, R. D. (2000). Acute marijuana effects of rCBF and cognition; a PET study. *Neuroreport, 11*, 3835–3841.

Polcin, D. L. (1992). Issues in the treatment of dual diagnosis clients who have chronic mental illness. *Professional Psychology: Research and Practice, 23*, 30–37.

Post, R. M., Rubinow, D. R., & Ballenger, J. C. (1984). Conditioning, sensitization, and kindling: Implications for the course of affective illness. In R. M. Post, & J. C. Ballenger (Eds.), *The Neurobiology of Mood Disorders* (pp. 432–466). Baltimore, MD: Williams & Wilkins.

Pristach, C. A., & Smith, C. M. (1990). Medication compliance and substance abuse among schizophrenic patients. *Hospital and Community Medicine, 41*(12), 1345–1348.

Redish, A. D. (2004). Addiction as a computational process gone awry. *Science, 306*, 1944–1947.

Regier, D. A., Farmer, M. E., Rae, D. S., Locke, B. Z., Keith, S. J., Judd, L. L., & Goodwin, F. K. (1990). Comorbidity of mental disorders with alcohol and other drug abuse: Results from the Epidemiologic Catchment Area (ECA) study. *Journal of the American Medical Association, 264*, 2511–2518.

Ridgely, M. S., Goldman, H. H., & Willenbring, M. (1990). Barriers to the care of persons with dual diagnoses: Organizational and financing issues. *Schizophrenia Bulletin, 16*, 123–132.

Ridgely, M. S., Osher, F. C., Goldman, H. H., & Talbott, J. A. (1987). *Executive Summary: Chronic Mentally Ill Young Adults with Substance Abuse Problems: A Review of Research, Treatment, and Training Issues*. Baltimore: Mental Health Services Research Center, University of Maryland School of Medicine.

Ries, R. K., Dyck, D. G., Short, R., Srebnik, D., Fisher, A., & Comtois, K. A. (2004). Outcomes of managing disability benefits among patients with substance dependence and severe mental illness. *Psychiatric Services, 55*, 445–447.

Robins, L. N. (1966). *Deviant Children Grown Up*. Huntington, NY: Robert E. Krieger Publishing Company.

Robinson, T. E., & Berridge, K. C. (1993). The neural basis of craving: An incentive-sensitization theory of addiction. *Brain Research Reviews, 18*, 247–291.

Roll, J. M., Chermack, S. T., & Chudzynski, J. E. (2004). Investigating the use of contingency management in the treatment of cocaine abuse among individuals with schizophrenia: A feasibility study. *Psychiatry Research, 125*, 61–64.

Roll, J. M., Higgins, S. T., Steingard, S., & McGinley, M. (1998). Use of monetary reinforcement to reduce the cigarette smoking of persons with schizophrenia: A feasibility study. *Experimental and Clinical Psychopharmacology, 6*, 142–161.

Salyers, M. P., & Mueser, K. T. (2001). Social functioning, psychopathology, and medication side effects in relation to substance use and abuse in schizophrenia. *Schizophrenia Research, 48*, 109–123.

Shaner, A., Roberts, L. J., Eckman, T. A., Tucker, D. E., Tsuang, J. W., Wilkins, J. N., & Mintz, J. (1997). Monetary reinforcement of abstinence from cocaine among mentally ill patients with cocaine dependence. *Psychiatric Services, 48*, 807–810.

Shenton, M. E., Dickey, C. C., Frumin, M., & McCarley, R. W. (2001). A review of MRI findings in schizophrenia. *Schizophrenia Research, 49*, 1–52.

Sigmon, S. C., Steingard, S., Badger, G. J., Anthony, S. L., & Higgins, S. T. (2000). Contingent reinforcement of marijuana abstinence among individuals with serious mental illness: A feasibility study. *Experimental and Clinical Psychopharmacology, 8*, 509–517.

Silver, H., & Abboud, E. (1994). Drug abuse in schizophrenia: Comparison of patients who began drug abuse before their first admission with those who began abusing drugs after their first admission. *Schizophrenia Research, 13*, 57–63.

Stein, L. I., & Santos, A. B. (1998). *Assertive Community Treatment of Persons with Severe Mental Illness*. New York: Norton.

Strakowski, S. M., & DelBello, M. P. (2000). The co-occurrence of bipolar and substance use disorders. *Clinical Psychology Review, 20*, 191–206.

Strakowski, S. M., McElroy, S. L., Keck, P. E. J., & West, S. A. (1996). The effects of antecedent substance abuse on the development of first-episode mania. *Journal of Psychiatric Research, 30*, 59–68.

Swartz, M. S., Wagner, H. R., Swanson, J. W., Stroup, T. S., McEvoy, J. P., Canive, J. M., Miller, D. D., Reimherr, F., McGee, M., Khan, A. R. V., Roesenheck, R. A., & Lieberman, J. A. (2006). Substance use in persons with schizophrenia Baseline prevalence and correlates from the NIMH CATIE study. *The Journal of Nervous and Mental Disease, 194*(3), 164–172.

Teeson, M., Hall, W., Lynskey, M., & Degenhardt, L. (2000). Alcohol and drug use disorders in Australia: Implications of the National Survey of Mental Health and Well being. *Australian and New Zealand Journal of Psychiatry, 34*, 206–213.

Treffert, D. A. (1978). Marijuana use in schizophrenia: A clear hazard. *American Journal of Psychiatry, 135*, 1213–1215.

Tsuang, M. T., Simpson, J. C., & Kronfol, Z. (1982). Subtypes of drug abuse with psychosis. *Archives of General Psychiatry, 39*, 141–147.

van Os, J., Bak, M., Hanssen, M., Vijl, R. V., de Graaf, R., & Verdoux, H. (2002). Cannabis use and psychosis: A longitudinal population-based study. *American Journal of Epidemiology, 156*, 319–327.

Vardy, M. M., & Kay, S. R. (1983). LSD psychosis or LSD-induced schizophrenia? A multimethod inquiry. *Archives of General Psychiatry, 40*, 877–883.

Volkow, N. D., Fowler, J. S., & Wang, G. J. (2003). The addicted human brain: Insights from imaging studies. *Journal of Clinical Investigation, 111*, 1444–1451.

Warner, R., Taylor, D., Wright, J., Sloat, A., Springett, G., Amold, S., & Weinberg, H. (1994). Substance use among the mentally ill: Prevalence, reasons for use and effects on illness. *American Journal of Orthopsychiatry, 64*, 30–39.

Wexler, B. E., Anderson, M., Fulbright, R. K., & Gore, J. C. (2000). Preliminary evidence of improved verbal working memory performance and normalization of task-related frontal lobe activation in schizophrenia following cognitive exercises. *American Journal of Psychiatry, 157*, 1694–1697.

Wexler, B. E., Gottschalk, C. H., Fulbright, R. K., Prohovnik, I., Lacadie, C. M., Rounsaville, B. J., & Gore, J. C. (2001). Functional magnetic resonance imaging of cocaine craving. *American Journal of Psychiatry, 158*, 85–96.

Winokur, G., Coryell, W., Akiskal, H. S., Maser, J. D., Keller, M. B., Endicott, J., & Mueller, T. (1995). Alcoholism in manic-depressive (bipolar) illness: Familial illness, course of illness, and the primary-secondary distinction. *American Journal of Psychiatry, 152*, 365–372.

Wise, R. A. (1998). Drug-activation of brain reward pathways. *Drug and Alcohol Dependence, 51*, 13–22.

Wykes, T., Brammer, M., Mellers, J., Bray, P., Reeder, C., Williams, C., & Corner, J. (2002). Effects on the brain of a psychological treatment: Cognitive remediation therapy. *British Journal of Psychiatry, 181*, 144–152.

Zubin, J., & Spring, B. (1977). Vulnerability: A new view of schizophrenia. *Journal of Abnormal Psychology, 86*, 103–126.

CHAPTER 15

The Role of Impulsive Personality Traits in the Initiation, Development, and Treatment of Substance Misuse Problems

Sharon Dawe[1], Natalie J. Loxton[1], Matthew J. Gullo[1], Petra K. Staiger[2], Nicolas Kambouropoulos[2], Laura Perdon[1] and Andrew Wood[1]
[1]Griffith University, Brisbane, Queensland, Australia
[2]Deakin University, Burwood, Victoria, Australia

Abstract: It is clear that an impulsive temperament plays a role in the initiation of substance use, and is implicated in the development of substance misuse. However, the broad trait of impulsivity is more accurately thought of as two related dimensions reflecting an

321

increased sensitivity to reward and a separate trait related to impulsive decision-making. In this chapter, we discuss how treatments could take account of such traits. We consider the way in which universal and targeted approaches to substance misuse prevention could incorporate findings from the personality literature. We then consider how personality may influence the development of problem substance use, the neural changes that are a consequence of chronic use and the associated treatment implications.

THE ROLE OF IMPULSIVE PERSONALITY TRAITS IN THE INITIATION, DEVELOPMENT, AND TREATMENT OF SUBSTANCE MISUSE PROBLEMS

The role played by personality in the initiation of substance use and the development of substance misuse has received growing attention in recent years. One trait that has been consistently identified as a factor in all of the above has been broadly termed "impulsivity" and typically refers to the tendency to engage in behavior that involves rashness, a lack of foresight or planning, or a behavior that occurs without reflection or careful deliberation. The relationship between measures of impulsivity and substance misuse has been widely studied and despite a variety of samples and measures, a consistent relationship has been found in cross-sectional studies (Baker & Yardley, 2002; Cloninger, Sigvardsson, & Bohman, 1988; Johnson, Turner, & Iwata, 2003; Jorm et al., 1999; McGue et al., 2001; Shillington & Clapp, 2002; Simons & Carey, 2002; Soloff, Lynch, & Moss, 2000) and prospective studies measuring substance use from early adolescence (Howard, Kivlahan, & Walker, 1997; Masse & Tremblay, 1997; Tarter et al., 2004).

However, while there are robust findings linking an impulsive temperament with substance abuse, a number of research groups have argued that impulsivity is not a homogenous construct, but rather consists of at least two related dimensions (e.g., Dawe & Loxton, 2004; de Wit & Richards, 2004; Miller, Joseph, & Tudway, 2004; Moeller et al., 2001; Quilty & Oakman, 2004; Reynolds et al., 2006). Previously, we have suggested that the first of these dimensions, "Reward Drive", relates to the motivating factors that are most instrumental in the decision to use substances, and influence the continued use of substances. The second dimension, "Rash Impulsiveness", implicated in drug use, is the decreased ability to cease drug-taking behavior once an approach response has commenced, despite future negative consequences of that behavior (Dawe, Gullo, & Loxton, 2004; Dawe & Loxton, 2004).

We have argued that there is individual variability in both of these dimensions. Some people are strongly motivated by cues associated with reward (high Reward Drive), while others are less reward sensitive. Likewise, some people may find greater difficulty inhibiting behavior once they have begun the process of acting to achieve reward (high Rash Impulsiveness) compared with others. This results in a diminished capacity to consider the future consequences of current actions – including whether or not to use substances. It is proposed that Reward Drive and Rash Impulsiveness (in combination with other environmental and family factors) are influential in determining which individuals develop substance use problems, and contribute to the development of chronic substance misuse (Claridge & Davis, 2003; Jentsch & Taylor, 1999). In this chapter, we will provide a review of the two facets of impulsivity, adding more recent evidence to support the model, discuss how these personality dimensions may (i) influence the initiation of substance use, (ii) contribute to the development of substance misuse problems, and (iii) could be addressed in preventative efforts and the treatment of substance dependence.

THE DIMENSIONS OF IMPULSIVITY

There is now widespread agreement that impulsivity is at least a two-dimensional construct broadly reflecting approach tendencies/reward sensitivity and cognitive disinhibition/impulsivity. Reward Drive draws from Gray's model of personality (Gray, 1970, 1987; Gray & McNaughton, 2000), in which the Behavioral Approach System (BAS) is a primary dimension underlying individual variation in sensitivity to reward. Rash Impulsiveness is associated with disinhibition and is more closely linked with cognitive functioning; it reflects a tendency to act without deliberation and giving in to, rather than resisting urges (Helmers, Young, & Pihl, 1995; Lane et al., 2003). Evidence supporting these two dimensions comes from factor analytic studies and a number of laboratory studies with clinical and non-clinical groups. For instance, studies have repeatedly found that a two-factor solution best represents the relationships between a range of self-report measures of impulsivity (Dawe & Loxton, 2004). These include studies of measures relating to broad constructs of Reward Drive (e.g., BAS Reward Responsiveness and BAS Drive scales,[1] Sensitivity to reward[2] scale) and Rash Impulsivity (e.g., Impulsivity scale,[3] Barrett Impulsiveness scale,[4] Sensation Seeking (SS) Scale[5]).

Likewise, studies using behavioral measures have also shown support for multiple dimensions of impulsivity (Franken & Muris, 2006b; Reynolds et al., 2006; Smillie, Jackson, & Dalgleish, 2006; Smillie, Pickering, & Jackson, 2006). For example, participants who perform better on rewarded behavioral tasks (e.g., earn points/money for fast card sorting, pressing a computer key) tend to also score

---

[1]From the BIS/BAS scales (Carver & White, 1994).
[2]From the sensitivity to punishment and sensitivity to reward questionnaire (Torrubia et al., 2001).
[3]From Eysenck Personality Scales (Eysenck & Eysenck, 1991).
[4]Patton, Stanford, and Barratt (1995).
[5]Zuckerman (1994).

higher on self-report measures of Reward Drive, but not Rash Impulsivity (Kambouropoulos & Staiger, 2004; Smillie & Jackson, 2006). On the other hand, individuals high in Rash Impulsiveness have greater difficulty inhibiting previously rewarded responses (e.g., cannot stop pressing a computer key) when making the response results in loss of points/money. Poor performance on such tasks is not associated with Reward Drive (Marsh et al., 2002; Swann et al., 2002; Vigil-Colet & Codorniu, 2004). Thus, there is growing evidence supporting at least two distinct impulsivity dimensions.

CURRENT MODELS OF IMPULSIVITY AND SUBSTANCE MISUSE

As impulsivity has been so strongly linked with substance misuse it is not surprising that the etiological role played by "impulsivity" has been considered. Verheul and colleagues (Verheul, 2001; Verheul, Van den Brink, & Geerlings, 1999) propose three different causal pathways in the development of personality pathology and subsequent substance abuse. Notably, Verheul (2001) proposes (1) a "reward sensitivity" pathway, which is associated with histrionic and narcissistic personality disorders, and subsequent addiction; and (2) a "behavioral disinhibition" pathway, which is implicated in the development of antisocial and impulsive traits, and in turn link to rule violation and other deviant behaviors, including substance abuse. A third, "stress reduction", pathway is proposed to be associated with anxiety disorders and the use of substances to alleviate negative affect. Verheul also proposes that dysfunction in specific neuro-chemical structures are the biological substrates involved in each of these pathways.

Likewise, de Wit and Richards (2004) propose two motivational processes involved in the initiation, maintenance, and relapse of drug abuse. In particular, this model highlights the importance of factors that both facilitate and inhibit substance misuse. Consistent with our model, it was proposed that these processes are directly related to individual levels of reward sensitivity and behavioral disinhibition (i.e., Rash Impulsivity). Specifically, de Wit and Richards suggest that high levels of reward reactivity and disinhibition combine to promote the development and maintenance of substance use. That is, a heightened sensitivity to the rewarding aspects of substance use, together with insensitivity to short- and long-term negative consequences, results in increased behavioral approach toward drugs of abuse. Like Verheul (1999), de Wit and Richards also draw on evidence from neuroscience research in addiction.

A biologically based, two-dimensional model of substance misuse has also been proposed by our group (Dawe et al., 2004; Dawe & Loxton, 2004). Specifically, we have argued that an individual with heightened Reward Drive should be attracted to drugs and may experience greater pleasure/reward following drug use. The second dimension, Rash Impulsiveness, refers to the tendency to continue with such approach behavior (e.g., drug use), regardless of risk or consideration for future consequences. We suggest that this second dimension may be related to response disinhibition, or the inability to inhibit prepotent approach tendencies. While the extent to which poor inhibitory control predates the use of substances is unclear, there is strong evidence that this is exacerbated with chronic substance abuse (Jentsch & Taylor, 1999).

It is now evident that impulsivity is not a homogenous construct but is more accurately conceptualized as at least a two-dimensional model consisting of reward-driven processes, and an inability to inhibit drug use despite negative consequences. In the following section, we discuss the evidence supporting the role of these two constructs, referred to in our model as Reward Drive and Rash Impulsiveness, in substance abuse.

EVIDENCE SUPPORTING THE ASSOCIATION BETWEEN REWARD DRIVE AND SUBSTANCE USE

It has been proposed that the underlying neural pathways involved in the BAS, and therefore Reward Drive, share similarities with the pathways involved in the reinforcing effects of drugs of abuse (Fowles, 2001). It is now well established that drugs of abuse (and associated cues, such as drug paraphernalia) activate the release of dopamine in the mesolimbic dopaminergic circuits (Childress et al., 1999; Di Chiara, Acquas, & Carboni, 1992). These circuits are commonly referred to as the "reward pathways" with release of dopamine associated with positive affect and motivated approach behavior (Ashby, Isen, & Turken, 1999).[6] Naturally occurring rewards, such as food, are also known as activating dopamine in these regions (Schultz, 1998). This is an adaptive response, promoting species survival by imbuing food, water, and sexual activity with rewarding properties. Reward-sensitive individuals are proposed to be more sensitive to dopamine activation in these regions and to have a greater positive response to reward cues (e.g., experience increased positive affect, pay greater attention). Research in the neuroscience and the behavioral genetics fields is currently focusing on the relationship between self-report reward sensitivity and dopamine activation (e.g., Beaver et al., 2006; Reuter et al., 2005).

---

[6]It should be noted that the mesocorticolimbic dopamine pathways have recently been proposed as responding to stimulus *salience* rather than to reward per se (e.g., salient punishing stimuli have also been found to activate dopamine release; Franken, Booij, & van den Brink, 2005; Hyman, 2005). The issue of Reward Drive and stimulus salience is addressed further when we discuss Robinson and Berridge's (2001, 2003) Incentive Salience Theory.

Correlational studies looking at self-report measures and substance use have found that high Reward Drive is associated with increased level of hazardous drinking in community samples of adults, high school, and college students (Franken & Muris, 2006a; Jorm et al., 1999; Knyazev, 2004; Knyazev et al., 2004; Loxton & Dawe, 2001, in press; O'Connor & Colder, 2005). Further, Reward Drive is higher in clinical groups with substance use disorders compared to controls (Franken, Muris, & Georgieva, 2006; Johnson et al., 2003). Laboratory studies have also supported a relationship between individual differences in Reward Drive and a bias to notice and respond to drug cues. For example, when exposed to cues that are associated with alcohol and drug use, such as a glass of wine or injecting equipment, individuals with heightened Reward Drive are more likely to take notice and attend to such cues (Colder & O'Connor, 2002), show greater physiological arousal (Glautier, Bankart, & Williams, 2000), and report greater cravings and urge to drink (Franken, 2002). Exposure to drug and alcohol cues have also been found to increase general approach behavior in reward-sensitive individuals. For example, following exposure to alcohol cues (sight, smell, and taste of beer), social drinkers who were also high on Reward Drive sorted cards faster when rewarded by money than low Reward Drive social drinkers. It was argued that reward pathways activated by one type of reward (a consideration of the enjoyment of an alcoholic drink) influenced behavior in other reward-driven domains (Kambouropoulos & Staiger, 2001).

In sum, those who (mis)use alcohol and other drugs typically score higher on measures of Reward Drive than those who do not. Heightened Reward Drive is associated with a tendency to notice and respond favorably to drug and alcohol cues. In turn, exposure to drug and alcohol cues appears to further activate Reward Drive. Thus, those with an innate hypersensitivity to reward may be more likely to experiment with, and find greater reinforcement, from drugs of abuse. However, heightened Reward Drive may not only be an inherent predisposition, but may also be a consequence of neural adaptation occurring with chronic substance use. We discuss both these issues further below.

EVIDENCE SUPPORTING THE ASSOCIATION BETWEEN RASH IMPULSIVENESS AND SUBSTANCE USE

Rash Impulsivity also clearly plays a role in substance use. Scores on measures of Rash Impulsiveness in middle childhood have been found to predict experimentation with alcohol and other drugs in later adolescence and early adulthood (Bates & Labouvie, 1995; Lynskey, Fergusson, & Horwood, 1998; McGue et al., 2001; Tarter et al., 2003). Further, heavy drinkers perform more poorly on tasks that require the inhibition of a previously rewarded response (e.g., pressing a computer key) than controls (Colder & O'Connor, 2002; LeMarquand et al., 1999). Similarly, using a gambling task, alcohol-abusing individuals tend to make choices that result in short-term gains, but long-term losses (Bechara & Damasio, 2002; Bechara et al., 2001; Bechara, Dolan, & Hindes, 2002; Bjork et al., 2004). Such findings suggest a decreased ability to "put on the brakes" when in an approach (i.e., winning) mode.

At this point the precise biological substrates underlying Rash Impulsiveness are unknown, although it is possible that impairment in prefrontal functioning, particularly in the orbitofrontal region, occurs (Dawe et al., 2004). For example, Berlin, Rolls, and Kischka (2004) found traumatic brain injury patients with damage to the orbitofrontal region of the prefrontal cortex scored higher on self-report measures of Rash Impulsiveness, and were more impulsive on a range of behavioral tasks, than patients with lesions to other areas of the prefrontal cortex, and normal controls. These findings have been added to by recent neuro-imaging studies in which deficits in the functioning of the prefrontal cortex of heroin users (Lee et al., 2005) and cocaine users (Moeller et al., 2004) have been observed.

Given the extent of evidence from many different research paradigms that substance misuse is associated with personality traits broadly termed impulsivity, it seems reasonable to consider the clinical implications for the addiction field. In the following section, we discuss the role of Reward Drive and Rash Impulsiveness in the (i) initiation of substance use and how this may influence prevention programs, (ii) how impulsive traits may alter during the course of chronic use, and (iii) the treatment implications associated with such changes.

THE ROLE OF REWARD DRIVE AND RASH IMPULSIVENESS IN THE INITIATION OF SUBSTANCE USE

There is wide spread use of substances in Australian adolescents, with 45% of 14–19 year olds drinking alcohol, and almost 11% of young people reporting that they drink more than 7 standard drinks on any one drinking occasion. Further, approximately 28% report that they have used an illicit substance in the last 12 months, with 25% reporting that they have used cannabis (Australian Institute of Health and Welfare, 2002). Such rates of substance use are of concern although when one takes into account that adolescence is a developmental stage characterized by heightened impulsivity (Trimpop, Kerr, & Kirkcaldy, 1999; Vaidya et al., 2004; Zuckerman, 1994), it is not surprising that substance use is one of many risky behaviors that young people engage in.

"Risk taking" per se may in fact be adaptive. Adolescence is marked by a transition from a relative dependence on parents and family, to a greater reliance on peer relationships and independence. This requires exposure to a range of novel, and at times, risky situations (Shedler & Block, 1990). Risk taking during adolescence is found across all races and cultures, and has been observed throughout history (Steinberg, 2004). Indeed, similar behavioral tendencies have been found to characterize the adolescent period in animals (Adriani, Chiarotti, & Laviola, 1998; Darmani, Shaddy, & Gerdes, 1996). It is reasonable to conclude that increased exploration and risk-taking behavior is part of normal adolescent development. Further, that this serves an adaptive function in helping the adolescent to develop independence, and facilitates the adoption of adult roles (Spear, 2000).

What is important is the nature and type of risk that young people engage in, and it appears that while substance use may be attractive at this developmental stage, it is also problematic for many other reasons, not the least the potential impact that such use has on neurodevelopment. There are significant changes in the motivational neural substrates purported to underlie Reward Drive that occurs during adolescence. A change in dopamine functioning has been associated with heightened levels of approach behavior and a preference for more intensely rewarding stimuli during adolescence (Bjork et al., 2004; Haycock et al., 2003; Philpot & Kirstein, 2004). There are also marked changes in the inhibitory functions associated with the prefrontal cortex during adolescence – functions that have been linked to the behavioral tendencies that align with Rash Impulsiveness (see Bjork et al., 2004; Haycock et al., 2003; Philpot & Kirstein, 2004). The prefrontal cortex matures gradually, with improved functioning accompanying the onset of synaptic pruning in late childhood (probably around age 10–12 years). However, although functioning improves during adolescence, development continues into early adulthood, and according to some estimates, maturation is not completed until sometime in the third decade of life (Huttenlocher & Dabholkar, 1997). Thus, the heightened level of risk taking that is characteristic of adolescence (including substance use and misuse), may be related to temporary increases in Reward Drive, within the setting of an immature inhibitory system. Moreover, the use of substances may further impair development of critical executive functioning associated with prefrontal development in the adolescent brain.

Therefore, while some risk taking is adaptive during adolescence, misusing substances such as alcohol is not. How then should intervention programs discourage a novel and rewarding behavior such as substance use in young people? Further, are those young people most at risk, (i.e., the more Rash Impulsive and/or the more Reward-Driven), the least likely to be discouraged by messages about long-term negative consequences?

IMPLICATIONS FOR THE PREVENTION AND TREATMENT OF ADOLESCENT SUBSTANCE USE

There have been many attempts to prevent the use of substances in adolescents. These include universal approaches from large-scale media campaigns, to programs delivered to young people within classroom settings. Such universal interventions aim to discourage substance use by providing information about the many adverse consequences associated with such use. Despite many public health efforts (e.g., media campaigns) to influence adolescent substance use, these have, by and large, been unsuccessful (Flynn et al., 2006; Straub et al., 2003). Similarly, while education-based programs delivered as part of classroom curricula generally result in better-informed recipients, they have had little impact on actual substance use (Foxcroft et al., 2003; Lilja et al., 2003).

Given the failure of most universal programs, it seems reasonable to step back and reconsider the focus and content of these approaches. It could be argued that typical approaches, which emphasize the harm associated with substance use as the major deterrent, have little impact on the young people most at risk. For example, campaigns that provide messages that argue for abstinence, with the implication that recreational use inevitably leads to addiction, may have little impact on those most likely to drink alcohol and smoke cannabis: reward-sensitive young people who are highly sociable and who are most likely to use substances with peers (Dawe & Loxton, 2004; Knyazev, 2004). Should prevention efforts, then, take into account personality and the accompanying motivational factors when developing programs? It seems unlikely that highly reward-driven young people will simply decide not to use substances after being told of the dangers associated with use. Could a range of exciting, stimulating and pro-social alternatives be offered – either in addition to or instead of, the current curricula on the dangers of substance use? Recent innovative approaches that have been tailored to personality and motivational factors hold promise. For instance, Conrod and colleagues (Stewart et al., 2005) developed an indicated prevention program where adolescents were matched to interventions based on their scores on a range of personality measures, including SS. Consistent with previous research, high SS adolescents were more likely to binge drink at baseline. However, they were more responsive to a two-session intervention that specifically attempted to modify positive expectations of alcohol use. The high SS group had a significant reduction in binge drinking episodes at 4-month follow up.

So, how can treatment models for those young people with established substance misuse problems be informed by the current discussion? There are many risk factors associated with the development of substance use problems in adolescents, not the least of which is family environment, school achievement, and peer associations (Graves et al., 2005). Focusing on one particular risk factor, such as personality, to the exclusion of all others would not be a sensible way forward.

Nonetheless, it is reasonable to propose that treatment programs need to incorpo-rate an understanding of the potential influence of Reward Drive and Rash Impulsivity in young people with a substance misuse problem. It may be reason-able to propose that any treatment should include a component in which young people are given the opportunity to experience alternative rewarding and novel activities that involve the fun and excitement of thrill seeking (e.g., sky diving, rock climbing; D'Silva et al., 2001); particularly as participation in sports and other extra-curricular activities reduces the likelihood of substance use in adolescence (e.g., Harrison & Narayan, 2003). It is relevant to note the tentative findings from adventure-based therapy (sometimes called wilderness therapy). This has been reported to be highly successful in reducing behavior problems in youth "at risk" (Rosol, 2000). These programs involve adolescents engaging in challenging and sometimes risky tasks (e.g., white water rafting) with their peers. It is likely that a large proportion of these "at risk" youth also have a history of substance abuse. Unfortunately, few studies have examined the efficacy and effectiveness of these programs and none in the area of adolescent substance abuse treatment.

THE IMPACT OF CHRONIC SUBSTANCE USE ON DIMENSIONS OF IMPULSIVITY

There is now considerable evidence that there are changes to the "hard wiring" of the brain following long-term substance use, and that these changes relate to both Reward Drive and to Rash Impulsiveness (Franken, 2003; Jentsch & Taylor, 1999; Robinson & Berridge, 2000). As discussed above, the "reward circuits" of the mesocorticolimbic dopamine regions of the brain have been asso-ciated with the reinforcing effects of drug and alcohol consumption (Koob & Nestler, 1997; Wise & Bozarth, 1987). These same regions are also involved in the prediction of potential reward in the environment and have been proposed to underlie a tendency to focus attention on those aspects of the environment which have previously been found rewarding (Franken et al., 2005). For example, long-term drug and alcohol users are more likely to notice cues in their environment associated with drug use, such as photographs of alcohol or syringes, than non-drug users (Bruce & Jones, 2004; McCusker, 2001). The tendency to attend to substance use cues in particular, is proposed to be exacerbated in long-term drug users due to neural changes in the reward circuits (Robinson & Berridge, 2003).

The Incentive Salience Theory proposed by Robinson and Berridge (2003) argues that drug use alters the mesolimbic dopaminergic circuits and consequently, the motivational quality of cues associated with drug use. Specifically, chronic drug users become sensitized to drug-related cues; i.e., the cues themselves take on highly salient, "attention grabbing" properties. Subsequently, exposure to these cues elicits a strong desire to use drugs (i.e., incentive motivation). This desire to use drugs following exposure to cues previously associated with drug use is referred to as "wanting" drugs. This is distinguished from the hedonic pleasure associated with the experience of using drugs; the term "liking" has been widely used in this context. Neurologically, the opioid system, rather than the dopamine "reward" system is believed to underlie drug "liking" (Robinson & Berridge, 2003). There is growing evidence for the distinction between wanting and liking drugs. Pecina, Berridge, and Parker (1997) found that mice with elevated dopamine levels (due to dopamine transporter gene mutation) learnt faster on a rewarded task than control mice; a finding interpreted as indicating greater wanting. However, mutant mice showed less positive hedonic reactions (indexed by facial and body reactions, i.e., reduced liking) compared to control mice.

A series of laboratory studies with heavy and light drinkers has also demonstrated dissociation between wanting alcohol and liking alcohol (Hobbs, Remington, & Glautier, 2005). In one of their experiments, a priming dose of alcohol was associated with an increase in "wanting", measured by actual consumption, but no change in "liking", as measured by subjective rating. In another experiment, "liking" was altered after the addition of an unpleasant taste but "wanting" alcohol, did not diminish in heavy drinkers. Furthermore, when pooling the data across all three of their experiments, these researchers found only a small association between measures of "liking" and "wanting".

Thus, it is proposed that reward-sensitive individuals may have a more reactive dopaminergic response to reward cues that influences the incentive salience of the reward, as well as the motivational processes involved in drug wanting (i.e., persons high in Reward Drive will "want" the drug more, and be more likely to experience drug craving). With chronic use, sensitization results in heightened incentive motivation following exposure to drug and alcohol-related cues. This resulting increase in wanting may not be a conscious process (Robinson & Berridge, 2001). It is also possible that there may be variability in the experience of drug "liking" with chronic use. However, to date there have not been any well-controlled investigations of this in humans.

The problem of increased attention to drug cues in problem substance users is further compounded by recent findings that chronic drug use alters not only the reward circuits of the brain, but also areas involved in learning, memory, and more importantly, impulse control (i.e., the prefrontal cortex, Jentsch & Taylor, 1999). For instance, neuropsychological evidence is accumulating to suggest that chronic drug use impairs impulse control to the extent of that seen in patients with prefrontal cortex lesions in the orbitofrontal region (Bechara & Damasio, 2002; Bechara et al., 2001; Bechara et al., 2002; Rogers et al., 1999). As is so often lamented, people with long-term drug or alcohol problems continue to use drugs even when there are serious negative consequences for this use. It is possible that alterations in these brain regions further perpetuate this apparent lessened ability to stop substance use, despite ongoing legal, physical, and social problems

(Jentsch & Taylor, 1999; Lubman, Yucel, & Pantelis, 2004). Further, recent findings indicate that such drug-induced changes to neural reward-detecting and impulse-control systems may be permanent, even following abstinence (e.g., Goldstein & Volkow, 2002; Koob, 2005).

IMPLICATIONS FOR THE TREATMENT OF SUBSTANCE ABUSE AND DEPENDENCE

Thus far we have argued that both Reward Drive and Rash Impulsiveness play a role in the initiation of substance use. Moreover, a heightened sensitivity to cues associated with substance use occurs along with a diminished ability to inhibit approach behavior as chronic drug use progresses. This conceptualization suggests that either one or both of these independent processes (i.e., Reward Drive related incentive salience and/or Rash Impulsive related disinhibition) should be targeted in the treatment of people with longstanding substance misuse problems. In the following section, we will briefly review two current treatment approaches that might address this. Specifically, it is proposed that the work of Linehan and others on Dialectical Behavior Therapy (DBT) (Linehan, 1993; van den Bosch et al., 2002) and more recently mindfulness-based cognitive therapy (Segal, Williams, & Teasdale, 2002; Witkiewitz, Marlatt, & Walker, 2005) may be helpful when considering how psychological treatments could be matched more carefully to concurrent personality traits in people with substance misuse problems.

One treatment model that explicitly addresses impulsive personality traits is DBT (Linehan, 1993), initially developed to treat clients with borderline personality disorders, and more recently, substance abuse disorders (Linehan et al., 1999, 2002; van den Bosch et al., 2002). This model of treatment addresses affect dysregulation and impulsive behavior with one of the core components being mindfulness meditation. Mindfulness has been defined as "paying attention in a particular way: on purpose, in the present moment and non-judgmentally"(Kabat-Zinn, 1994, p. 4). Mindfulness training invites the individual to observe and accept any negative thought as an event that occurs in the mind rather than as an absolute truth. The focus is on recognizing the desire – the prepotent impulse (Jentsch & Taylor, 1999), but to allow for conscious awareness of the impulse without action immediately following.

Mindfulness may be able to equip an individual with skills to become aware of triggers for craving, and provide options that can either prevent or reduce craving (Groves & Farmer, 1994). Learning to notice and accept thoughts about drugs may interrupt an automatic craving response (Robinson & Berridge, 2000; Tiffany, 1990) by allowing for an attentional shift away from the craving response and into a 'here and now' state. A secondary mechanism may also operate by which meditation itself produces an altered state of consciousness that is inherently pleasurable.

This may explain, in part, the self-reported experiences of pleasure reported following meditation (e.g., Kjaer et al., 2002). Highly reward-sensitive individuals are especially sensitive to positive mood states (e.g., Zelenski & Larsen, 1999), and thus may find the 'high' associated with mindfulness meditation particularly appealing.

There is preliminary support for the efficacy of mindfulness-based approaches in the reduction of hazardous levels of substance use. In a very early study, Marlatt and Marques (1977) reported reductions in alcohol use in high-risk drinkers. Later work indicated that meditation impacted on alcohol consumption in heavy drinking college students (Marlatt et al., 1984; Murphy, Pagano, & Marlatt, 1986). Most recently, those who received a meditation-based intervention while in prison, reported less drug use at 3 months compared to those receiving standard care (Witkiewitz et al., 2005). However, in contrast, Alterman and colleagues did not find a treatment benefit when meditation was added to standard care in drug dependent inpatients (Alterman et al., 2004).

Given the studies reviewed above, it may be reasonable to propose that the incorporation of mindfulness-based treatments in some people with substance misuse problems warrants further consideration as part of the "third wave" of cognitive therapy (Hayes, 2004). In particular, it may be valuable for helping the rash-impulsive individual to develop a greater awareness of their current emotional state, to bring into conscious control their pre-potent behavioral tendency and to allow for a more considered response.

CONCLUSION

It is clear that impulsivity plays a central role in drug and alcohol addiction. However, a precise definition of this personality construct has remained elusive. In accordance with the emerging evidence in the personality literature, we propose that there are two fundamental components of impulsivity that are particularly relevant to our understanding of substance misuse. As reviewed above, we propose that a 'Reward Drive' factor is particularly influential in the initiation of substance use as the individual responds to the perceived positive, incentive properties of the drug. We also note a "Rash Impulsivity" factor, which is also characteristic of those who use drugs. However, we have proposed that this factor is more related to continued drug use despite the obvious adverse consequences (i.e., the decreased ability to stop using). There is growing support for models of addiction that incorporate multiple impulsivity dimensions such as Reward Drive and Rash Impulsivity. While research investigating the specific mechanisms linking these two factors with addictive behavior is ongoing, it is hoped that this two-factor conceptualization will provide further directions for the prevention and treatment of substance use problems.

REFERENCES

Adriani, W., Chiarotti, F., & Laviola, G. A. W. (1998). Elevated novelty seeking and peculiar D-amphetamine sensitization in periadolescent mice compared with adult mice. *Behavioral Neuroscience, 112*, 1152–1166.

Alterman, A. I., Koppenhaver, J. M., Mulholland, E., Ladden, L. J., & Baime, M. J. (2004). Pilot trial of effectiveness of mindfulness meditation for substance abuse patients. *Journal of Substance Abuse, 9*, 259–268.

Ashby, F. G., Isen, A. M., & Turken, A. U. (1999). A neuropsychological theory of positive affect and its influence on cognition. *Psychological Review, 106*, 529–550.

Australian Institute of Health and Welfare. (2002). *2001 National Drug Strategy Household Survey: First results. AIHW cat. no. PHE 35. (Drug Statistics Series No. 9)*. Canberra: Australian Institute of Health and Welfare.

Baker, J. R., & Yardley, J. K. (2002). Moderating effect of gender on the relationship between sensation seeking-impulsivity and substance use in adolescents. *Journal of Child & Adolescent Substance Abuse, 12*, 27–43.

Bates, M. E., & Labouvie, E. W. (1995). Personality-environment constellations and alcohol use: A process-oriented study of intraindividual change during adolescence. *Psychology of Addictive Behaviors, 9*, 23–35.

Beaver, J. D., Lawrence, A. D., Van Ditzhuijzen, J., Davis, M. H., Woods, A., & Calder, A. J. (2006). Individual differences in reward drive predict neural responses to images of food. *Journal of Neuroscience, 26*, 5160–5166.

Bechara, A., & Damasio, H. (2002). Decision-making and addiction (part I): Impaired activation of somatic states in substance dependent individuals when pondering decisions with negative future consequences. *Neuropsychologia, 40*, 1675–1689.

Bechara, A., Dolan, S., Denburg, N., Hindes, A., Anderson, S. W., & Nathan, P. E. (2001). Decision-making deficits, linked to a dysfunctional ventromedial prefrontal cortex, revealed in alcohol and stimulant abusers. *Neuropsychologia, 39*, 376–389.

Bechara, A., Dolan, S., & Hindes, A. (2002). Decision-making and addiction (part II): Myopia for the future or hypersensitivity to reward? *Neuropsychologia, 40*, 1690–1705.

Berlin, H. A., Rolls, E. T., & Kischka, U. (2004). Impulsivity, time perception, emotion and reinforcement sensitivity in patients with orbitofrontal cortex lesions. *Brain, 127*, 1108–1126.

Bjork, J. M., Hommer, D. W., Grant, S. J., & Danube, C. (2004). Impulsivity in abstinent alcohol-dependent patients: Relation to control subjects and type 1/type 2-like traits. *Alcohol, 34*, 133–150.

Bjork, J. M., Knutson, B., Fong, G. W., Caggiano, D. M., Bennett, S. M., & Hommer, D. W. (2004). Incentive-elicited brain activation in adolescents: Similarities and differences from young adults. *The Journal of Neuroscience, 24*, 1783–1802.

Bruce, G., & Jones, B. T. (2004). A pictorial Stroop paradigm reveals an alcohol attentional bias in heavier compared to lighter social drinkers. *Journal of Psychopharmacology, 18*, 527–533.

Carver, C. S., & White, T. L. (1994). Behavioral inhibition, behavioral activation, and affective responses to impending reward and punishment: The BIS/BAS Scales. *Journal of Personality and Social Psychology, 67*, 319–333.

Childress, A. R., Mozley, P. D., McGlgin, W., Fitzgerald, J., Reivich, M., & O'Brien, C. P. (1999). Limbic activation during cue-induced cocaine craving. *American Journal of Psychiatry, 156*, 11–18.

Claridge, G., & Davis, C. (2003). *Personality and Psychological Disorders*. London: Arnold.

Cloninger, C., Sigvardsson, S., & Bohman, M. (1988). Childhood personality predicts alcohol abuse in young adults. *Alcoholism: Clinical & Experimental Research, 12*, 494–505.

Colder, C. R., & O'Connor, R. (2002). Attention biases and disinhibited behavior as predictors of alcohol use and enhancement reasons for drinking. *Psychology of Addictive Behaviors, 16*, 325–332.

Darmani, N. A., Shaddy, J., & Gerdes, C. F. (1996). Differential ontogenesis of three DOI-induced behaviors in mice. *Physiology and Behavior, 60,* 1495–1500.

Dawe, S., Gullo, M. J., & Loxton, N. J. (2004). Reward drive and rash impulsiveness as dimensions of impulsivity: Implications for substance misuse. *Addictive Behaviors, 29,* 1389–1409.

Dawe, S., & Loxton, N. J. (2004). The role of impulsivity in the development of substance use and eating disorders. *Neuroscience and Biobehavioral Reviews, 28,* 343–351.

de Wit, H., & Richards, J. B. (2004). Dual determinants of drug use in humans: Reward and Impulsivity. In R. A. Bevins, & M. T. Bardo (Eds.), *Motivational Factors in the Etiology of Drug Abuse* (pp. 19–55). Lincoln, Nebraska: University of Nebraska Press.

Di Chiara, G., Acquas, E., & Carboni, E. (1992). Drug motivation and abuse – a neurobiological perspective. *Annals of the New York Academy of Sciences, 654,* 207–219.

D'Silva, M. U., Harrington, N. G., Palmgreen, P., Donohew, L., & Lorch, E. P. (2001). Drug use prevention for the high sensation seeker: The role of alternative activities. *Substance Use and Misuse, 36,* 373–385.

Eysenck, H. J., & Eysenck, S. B. G. (1991). *Manual of the Eysenck Personality Scales.* London: Hodder & Stoughton.

Flynn, B. S., Worden, J. K., Bunn, J. Y., Dorwaldt, A. L., Dana, G. S., & Callas, P. W. (2006). Mass media and community interventions to reduce alcohol use by early adolescents. *Journal of Studies on Alcohol, 67,* 66–74.

Fowles, D. C. (2001). *Biological Variables in Psychopathology: A Psychobiological Perspective* (3rd ed.). New York, NY: Kluwer Academic/Plenum Publishers.

Foxcroft, D. R., Ireland, D., Lister-Sharp, D. J., Lowe, G., & Breen, R. (2003). Longer-term primary prevention for alcohol misuse in young people: A systematic review. *Addiction, 98,* 397–411.

Franken, I. H. A. (2002). Behavioral approach system (BAS) sensitivity predicts alcohol craving. *Personality and Individual Differences, 32,* 349–355.

Franken, I. H. A. (2003). Drug craving and addiction: Integrating psychological and neuropsycho-pharmacological approaches. *Progress in Neuro-Psychopharmacology and Biological Psychiatry, 27,* 563–579.

Franken, I. H. A., Booij, J., & van den Brink, W. (2005). The role of dopamine in human addiction: From reward to motivated attention. *European Journal of Pharmacology, 526,* 199–206.

Franken, I. H. A., & Muris, P. (2006a). BIS/BAS personality characteristics and college students' substance use. *Personality and Individual Differences, 40,* 1497–1503.

Franken, I. H. A., & Muris, P. (2006b). Gray's impulsivity dimension: A distinction between Reward Sensitivity versus Rash Impulsiveness. *Personality and Individual Differences, 40,* 1337–1347.

Franken, I. H. A., Muris, P., & Georgieva, I. (2006). Gray's model of personality and addiction. *Addictive Behaviors, 31,* 399–403.

Glautier, S., Bankart, J., & Williams, A. (2000). Flavor conditioning and alcohol: A multilevel model of individual differences. *Biological Psychology, 52,* 17–36.

Goldstein, R. Z., & Volkow, N. D. (2002). Drug addiction and its underlying neurobiological basis: Neuroimaging evidence for the involvement of the frontal cortex. *American Journal of Psychiatry, 159,* 1642–1652.

Graves, K. N., Fernandez, M. E., Shelton, T. L., Frabutt, J. M., & Williford, A. P. (2005). Risk and protective factors associated with alcohol, cigarette, and marijuana use during early adolescence. *Journal of Youth and Adolescence, 34,* 379–387.

Gray, J. A. (1970). The psychophysiological basis of introversion-extraversion. *Behavior Research and Therapy, 8,* 249–266.

Gray, J. A. (1987). The neuropsychology of emotion and personality. In S. M. Stahl, S. D. Iverson, & E. C. Goodman (Eds.), *Cognitive Neurochemistry* (pp. 171–190). Oxford, UK: Oxford University Press.

Gray, J. A., & McNaughton, N. (2000). *The Neuropsychology of Anxiety: An Enquiry into the Functions of the Septo-hippocampal System* (2nd ed.). Oxford: Oxford University Press.

Groves, P., & Farmer, I. (1994). Buddhism and addictions. *Addiction Research, 2,* 183–194.

Harrison, P. A., & Narayan, G. (2003). Differences in behavior, psychological factors, and environmental factors associated with participation in school sports and other activities in adolescence. *Journal of School Health, 73,* 113–120.

Haycock, J. W., Becker, L., Ang, L., Furukawa, Y., Hornykiewicz, O., & Kish, S. J. (2003). Marked disparity between age-related changes in dopamine and other presynaptic dopaminergic markers in human striatum. *Journal of Neurochemistry, 87,* 574–585.

Hayes, S. C. (2004). Acceptance and commitment therapy and the new behavior therapies: Mindfulness, acceptance, and relationship. In S. C. Hayes, V. M. Follette, & M. M. Linehan (Eds.), *Mindfulness and Acceptance: Expanding the Cognitive-behavioral Tradition.* New York: The Guilford Press.

Helmers, K. F., Young, S. E., & Pihl, R. O. (1995). Assessment of measures of impulsivity in healthy male volunteers. *Personality & Individual Differences, 19,* 927–935.

Hobbs, M., Remington, B., & Glautier, S. (2005). Dissociation of wanting and liking for alcohol in humans: A test of the incentive-sensitization theory. *Psychopharmacology, 178,* 493–499.

Howard, M. O., Kivlahan, D., & Walker, R. D. (1997). Cloninger's Tridimensional theory of personality and psychopathology: Applications to substance use disorders. *Journal of Studies on Alcohol, 58,* 48–66.

Huttenlocher, P. R., & Dabholkar, A. S. (1997). Developmental anatomy of prefrontal cortex. In N. A. Krasnegor, G. R. Lyon, & P. S. Goldman-Rakic (Eds.), *Development of the Prefrontal Cortex: Evolution, Neurobiology and Behavior* (pp. 69–83). Baltimore: Paul H. Brookes Publishing Co.

Hyman, S. E. (2005). Addiction: A disease of learning and memory. *American Journal of Psychiatry, 162,* 1414–1422.

Jentsch, J., & Taylor, J. R. (1999). Impulsivity resulting from frontostriatal dysfunction in drug abuse: Implications for the control of behavior by reward-related stimuli. *Psychopharmacology, 146,* 373–390.

Johnson, S. L., Turner, R. J., & Iwata, N. (2003). BIS/BAS levels and psychiatric disorder: An epidemiological study. *Journal of Psychopathology & Behavioral Assessment, 25,* 25–36.

Jorm, A. F., Christensen, H., Henderson, A. S., Jacomb, P. A., Korten, A. E., & Rodgers, B. (1999). Using the BIS/BAS scales to measure behavioral inhibition and behavioral activation: Factor structure, validity and norms in a large community sample. *Personality and Individual Differences, 26,* 49–58.

Kabat-Zinn, J. (1994). *Wherever You go there You are: Mindfulness Meditation in Everyday Life.* New York: Hyperion.

Kambouropoulos, N., & Staiger, P. (2004). Personality and responses to appetitive and aversive stimuli: The joint influence of behavioral approach and behavioral inhibition systems. *Personality and Individual Differences, 37,* 1153–1165.

Kambouropoulos, N., & Staiger, P. K. (2001). The influence of sensitivity to reward on reactivity to alcohol-related cues. *Addiction, 96,* 1175–1185.

Kjaer, T. W., Bertelson, C., Piccini, P., Brooks, D., Alving, J., & Lou, H. C. (2002). Increased dopamine tone during meditation-induced change of consciousness. *Cognitive Brain Research, 13,* 255–259.

Knyazev, G. G. (2004). Behavioral activation as predictor of substance use: Mediating and moderating role of attitudes and social relationships. *Drug and Alcohol Dependence, 75,* 309–321.

Knyazev, G. G., Slobodskaya, H. R., Kharchenko, I. I., & Wilson, G. D. (2004). Personality and substance use in Russian youths: The predictive and moderating role of behavioral activation and gender. *Personality and Individual Differences, 37,* 815–843.

Koob, G. F. (2005). The neurocircuitry of addiction: Implications for treatment. *Clinical Neuroscience Research, 5,* 89–101.

Koob, G. F., & Nestler, E. J. (1997). The neurobiology of drug addiction. *The Journal of Neuropsychiatry and Clinical Neurosciences, 9,* 482–297.

Lane, S. D., Cherek, D. R., Rhoades, H. M., Pietras, C. J., & Tcheremissine, O. V. (2003). Relationships among laboratory and psychometric measures of impulsivity: Implications in substance abuse and dependence. *Addictive Disorders and their Treatment, 2,* 33–40.

Lee, T. M. C., Zhou, W.-h., Luo, X.-j., Yuen, K. S. L., Ruan, X.-z., & Weng, X.-c. (2005). Neural activity associated with cognitive regulation in heroin users: A fMRI study. *Neuroscience Letters*, *382*, 211–216.

LeMarquand, D. G., Benkelkat, C., Pihl, R. O., Palmour, R. M., & Young, S. N. (1999). Behavioral disinhibition induced by tryptophan depletion in non-alcohol young men with multigenerational family histories of paternal alcoholism. *American Journal of Psychiatry*, *156*, 1771–1779.

Lilja, J., Wilhelmsen, B. M., Larsson, S., & Hamilton, D. (2003). Evaluation of drug use prevention programs directed at adolescents. *Substance Use and Misuse*, *38*, 1831–1863.

Linehan, M. M. (1993). *Cognitive-behavioral Treatment of Borderline Personality Disorder*. New York: Guilford Press.

Linehan, M. M., Dimeff, L. A., Reynolds, S. K., Comtois, K. A., Welch, S. S., Heagerty, P., & Kivlahan, D. R. (2002). Dialectical behavior therapy versus comprehensive validation therapy plus 12-step for the treatment of opioid dependent women meeting criteria for borderline personality disorder. *Drug and Alcohol Dependence*, *67*, 13–26.

Linehan, M. M., Schmidt, H., Dimeff, L. A., Craft, J. C., Kanter, J., & Comtois, K. A. (1999). Dialectical behavior therapy for patients with borderline personality disorder and drug dependence. *American Journal of Addiction*, *8*, 279–292.

Loxton, N. J., & Dawe, S. (2001). Alcohol abuse and dysfunctional eating in adolescent girls: The influence of individual differences in sensitivity to reward and punishment. *International Journal of Eating Disorders*, *29*, 455–462.

Loxton, N. J., & Dawe, S. (2006). Reward and punishment sensitivity in dysfunctional eating and hazardous drinking women: Associations with family risk. *Appetite*, *47*, 361–371.

Lubman, K. I., Yucel, M., & Pantelis, C. (2004). Addiction, a condition of compulsive behavior? Neuroimaging and neuropsychological evidence of inhibitory dysregulation. *Addiction*, *99*, 1491–1502.

Lynskey, M. T., Fergusson, D. M., & Horwood, L. J. (1998). The origins of the correlations between tobacco, alcohol, and cannabis use during adolescence. *Journal of Child Psychology and Psychiatry*, *39*, 995–1005.

Marlatt, G. A., & Marques, J. K. (1977). Meditation, self-control, and alcohol use. In R. B. Stuart (Ed.), *Behavioral Self-management: Strategies, Techniques, and Outcomes* (pp. 117–153). New York: Brunner/Mazel.

Marlatt, G. A., Pagano, R. R., Rose, R. M., & Marques, J. K. (1984). Effects of meditation and relaxation training upon alcohol use in male social drinkers. In D. H. Shapiro, & R. N. Walsh (Eds.), *Meditation: Classic and Contemporary Perspectives* (pp. 105–120). New York: Aldine.

Marsh, D. M., Dougherty, D. M., Mathias, C. W., Moeller, F. G., & Hicks, L. R. (2002). Comparisons of women with high and low trait impulsivity using behavioral models of response-disinhibition and reward-choice. *Personality and Individual Differences*, *33*, 1291–1310.

Masse, L. C., & Tremblay, R. E. (1997). Behavior of boys in kindergarten and the onset of substance use during adolescence. *Archives of General Psychiatry*, *54*, 62–68.

McCusker, C. G. (2001). Cognitive biases and addiction: An evolution in theory and method. *Addiction*, *96*, 47–56.

McGue, M., Iacono, W. G., Legrand, L. N., & Elkins, I. (2001). Origins and consequences of age at first drink. I. Associations with substance-use disorders, disinhibitory behavior and psychopathology, and P3 amplitude. *Alcoholism: Clinical and Experimental Research*, *25*, 1156–1165.

Miller, E., Joseph, S., & Tudway, J. (2004). Assessing the component structure of four self-report measures of impulsivity. *Personality and Individual Differences*, *37*, 349–358.

Moeller, F. G., Barratt, E. S., Dougherty, D. M., Schmitz, J. M., & Swann, A. C. (2001). Psychiatric aspects of impulsivity. *American Journal of Psychiatry*, *158*, 1783–1793.

Moeller, F. G., Barratt, E. S., Fischer, C. J., Dougherty, D. M., Reilly, E. L., Mathias, C. W., & Swann, A. C. (2004). P300 event-related potential amplitude and impulsivity in cocaine-dependent subjects. *Neuropsychobiology*, *50*, 167–173.

Murphy, T. S., Pagano, R. R., & Marlatt, G. A. (1986). Lifestyle modification with heavy alcohol drinkers: Effects of aerobic exercise and meditation. *Addictive Behaviors, 11*, 175–186.

O'Connor, R. M., & Colder, C. R. (2005). Predicting alcohol patterns in first-year college students through motivational systems and reasons for drinking. *Psychology of Addictive Behaviors, 19*, 10–20.

Patton, J. H., Stanford, M. S., & Barratt, E. S. (1995). Factor structure of the Barratt impulsiveness scale. *Journal of Clinical Psychology, 51*, 768–774.

Pecina, S., Berridge, K. C., & Parker, L. A. (1997). Pimozide does not shift palatability: Separation of anhedonia from sensorimotor suppression by taste reactivity. *Pharmacology Biochemistry and Behavior, 58*, 801–811.

Philpot, R., & Kirstein, C. (2004). Developmental differences in the accumbal dopaminergic response to repeated ethanol exposure. *Annals of the New York Academy of Sciences, 1021*, 422–426.

Quilty, L. C., & Oakman, J. M. (2004). The assessment of behavioral activation – the relationship between impulsivity and behavioral activation. *Personality and Individual Differences, 37*, 429–442.

Reuter, M., Schmitz, A., Corr, P., & Hennig, J. (2005). Molecular genetics support Gray's personality theory: The interaction of COMT and DRD2 polymorphisms predicts the behavioral approach system. *The International Journal of Neuropsychopharmacology, 8*, 1–12.

Reynolds, B., Ortengren, A., Richards, J. B., & de Wit, H. (2006). Dimensions of impulsive behavior: Personality and behavioral measures. *Personality and Individual Differences, 40*, 305–315.

Robinson, T. E., & Berridge, K. C. (2000). The psychology and neurobiology of addiction: An incentive-sensitization view. *Addiction, 95*, 91–118.

Robinson, T. E., & Berridge, K. C. (2001). Incentive-sensitization and addiction. *Addiction, 96*, 103–114.

Robinson, T. E., & Berridge, K. C. (2003). Addiction. *Annual Review of Psychology, 54*, 25–53.

Rogers, R. D., Everitt, B., Baldacchino, A., Blackshaw, A., Swainson, R., Wynne, K., et al. (1999). Dissociable deficits in the decision-making cognition of chronic amphetamine abusers, opiate abusers, patients with focal damage to prefrontal cortex, and tryptophan-depleted normal volunteers: Evidence for monoaminergic mechanisms. *Neuropsychopharmacology, 20*, 322–339.

Rosol, M. (2000). Wilderness therapy for youth-at-risk. *Parks and Recreation, 35*, 42–50.

Schultz, W. (1998). Predictive reward signals of dopamine neurons. *Journal of Neurophysiology, 80*, 1–27.

Segal, Z., Williams, J. M. G., & Teasdale, J. D. (2002). *Mindfulness-based Cognitive Therapy for Depression: A New Approach to Preventing Relapse.* New York: Guilford Press.

Shedler, J., & Block, J. (1990). Adolescent drug use and psychological health: A longitudinal inquiry. *American Psychologist, 45*, 612–630.

Shillington, A., & Clapp, J. (2002). Beer and bongs: Differential problems experienced by older adolescents using alcohol only compared to combined alcohol and marijuana use. *American Journal of Drug & Alcohol Abuse, 28*, 379–397.

Simons, J. S., & Carey, K. B. (2002). Risk and vulnerability for marijuana use problems: The role of affect dysregulation. *Psychology of Addictive Behaviors, 16*, 72–75.

Smillie, L. D., & Jackson, C. J. (2006). Functional impulsivity and reinforcement sensitivity theory. *Journal of Personality, 74*, 47–83.

Smillie, L. D., Jackson, C. J., & Dalgleish, L. I. (2006). Conceptual distinctions among Carver and White's (1994) BAS scales: A reward-reactivity versus trait impulsivity perspective. *Personality and Individual Differences, 40*, 1039–1050.

Smillie, L. D., Pickering, A. D., & Jackson, C. J. (2006). The new reinforcement sensitivity theory: Implications for personality measurement. *Personality and Social psychology Review, 10*, 320–335.

Soloff, P. H., Lynch, K. G., & Moss, H. B. (2000). Serotonin, impulsivity, and alcohol use disorders in the older adolescent: A psychobiological study. *Alcoholism: Clinical & Experimental Research, 24*, 1609–1619.

Spear, L. (2000). Modeling adolescent development and alcohol use in animals. *Alcohol Research and Health, 24*, 115–123.

Steinberg, L. (2004). Risk-taking in adolescence: What changes and why? *Annals of the New York Academy of Sciences, 1021,* 51–58.

Stewart, S. H., Conrod, P. J., Marlatt, G. A., Comeau, M. N., Thush, C., & Krank, M. (2005). New developments in prevention and early intervention for alcohol abuse in youths. *Alcoholism: Clinical and Experimental Research, 29,* 278–286.

Straub, D. M., Hills, N. K., Thompson, P. J., & Moscicki, A. B. (2003). Effects of pro- and anti-tobacco advertising on nonsmoking adolescents' intentions to smoke. *Journal of Adolescent Health, 32,* 36–43.

Swann, A. C., Bjork, J. M., Moeller, F., & Dougherty, D. M. (2002). Two models of impulsivity: Relationship to personality traits and psychopathology. *Biological Psychiatry, 51,* 988–994.

Tarter, R. E., Kirisci, L., Habeych, M., Reynolds, M., & Vanyukov, M. (2004). Neurobehavior disinhibition in childhood predisposes boys to substance use disorder by young adulthood: Direct and mediated etiologic pathways. *Drug and Alcohol Dependence, 73,* 121–132.

Tarter, R. E., Kirisci, L., Mezzich, A., Cornelius, J. R., Pajer, K., Vanyukov, M., Gardner, W., Blackson, T., & Clark, D. (2003). Neurobehavioral disinhibition in childhood predicts early age at onset of substance use disorder. *American Journal of Psychiatry, 160,* 1078–1085.

Teasdale, J. D., Segal, Z., & Williams, J. M. G. (1995). How does cognitive therapy prevent depressive relapse and why should control (mindfulness) training help? *Behavior Research and Therapy, 33,* 25–39.

Tiffany, S. T. (1990). A cognitive model of drug urges and drug use behavior: Role of automatic and nonautomatic processes. *Psychological Review, 97,* 147–168.

Torrubia, R., Avila, C., Molto, J., & Caseras, X. (2001). The sensitivity to punishment and sensitivity to reward questionnaire (SPSRQ) as a measure of Gray's anxiety and impulsivity dimensions. *Personality and Individual Differences, 31,* 837–862.

Trimpop, R. M., Kerr, J. H., & Kirkcaldy, B. (1999). Comparing personality constructs of risk-taking behavior. *Personality & Individual Differences, 26,* 237–254.

Vaidya, J. G., Grippo, A. J., Johnson, A. K., & Watson, D. W. (2004). A comparative developmental study of impulsivity in rats and humans: The role of reward sensitivity. *Annals of the New York Academy of Sciences, 1021,* 395–398.

van den Bosch, L. M. C., Verheul, R., Schippers, G. M., & ven den Brink, W. (2002). Dialectical behavior therapy of borderline patients with and without substance use problems: Implementation and long-term effects. *Addictive Behaviors, 27,* 911–923.

Verheul, R., Van den Brink, W., & Geerlings, P. (1999). A three pathway psychobiological model of craving for alcohol. *Alcohol and Alcoholism, 34,* 197–222.

Verheul, R. (2001). Co-morbidity of personality disorders in individuals with substance use disorders. *European Psychiatry, 16,* 274–282.

Verheul, R., Van den Brink, W., & Geerlings, P. (1999). A three-pathway psychobiological model of craving for alcohol. *Alcohol and Alcoholism, 34,* 197–222.

Vigil-Colet, A., & Codorniu, M. J. (2004). Aggression and inhibition deficits, the role of functional and dysfunctional impulsivity. *Personality and Individual Differences, 37,* 1431–1440.

Wise, R. A., & Bozarth, M. A. (1987). A psychomotor stimulant theory of addiction. *Psychological Review, 94,* 469–492.

Witkiewitz, K., Marlatt, G. A., & Walker, D. (2005). Mindfulness-based relapse prevention for alcohol and substance use disorders. *Journal of Cognitive Psychotherapy: An International Quarterly, 19,* 211–228.

Zelenski, J. M., & Larsen, R. J. (1999). Susceptibility to affect: A comparison of three personality taxonomies. *Journal of Personality, 67,* 761–791.

Zuckerman, M. (1994). *Behavioral Expressions and Biosocial Bases of Sensation Seeking.* New York: Cambridge University Press.

CHAPTER 16

Translational Research Involving Adolescent Substance Abuse[1]

Jack R. Cornelius and Duncan B. Clark

Department of Psychiatry and Pharmaceutical Sciences, Western Psychiatric Institute and Clinic, University of Pittsburgh School of Medicine, 3811 O'Hara Street, PAARC Suite, Pittsburgh, PA 15213, USA

Introduction
Ten Barriers to Translation of Research Findings Involving Adolescent SUDs
Studies Involving Adolescents

Funding

Personnel, Culture, and Communication Issues

High Cost

Long Wait for Results

Commercialization

Increasing Regulatory Burden

Inadequate Informatics

Translation at a Community Level

Lack of Physician Compliance with Clinical Guidelines

---

[1]This work was presented in part by Dr. Cornelius at two recent conferences: (1) the 37th Annual Medical Scientific conference of the American Society on Addiction Medicine (ASAM), Symposium 5, sponsored by the National Institute of Alcohol Abuse and Alcoholism (NIAAA), entitled "Medications Development for Alcoholism: From the Bench to the Patient;" in San Diego, California, May 4–7, 2006; (2) and at a NIAAA symposium at the 159th Annual Meeting of the American Psychiatric Association entitled "Adolescent Alcohol Use Disorders and Psychiatric Comorbidity, which was part of a NIAAA-sponsored program entitled "Rethinking Alcohol Use Disorders: Science, Diagnosis, Treatment, & Policy," in Toronto Canada, May 20–25, 2006.

Examples of Immediate Implications of Prevention, Assessment, or Treatment Developments Involving Adolescent SUDs, as Shown in Two Federal Center Grants
  The CEDAR Center, an Example of a Prevention Study Performing Translational Research Involving Adolescent SUDs
  The PAARC Center, an Example of a Diagnosis and Treatment Study Performing Translational Research Involving Adolescent SUDs
Future Directions for Translational Research Involving Adolescent SUDs
  Funding
  Establishing the Validity of Substance Use Disorders
  Collaborations
  Etiology
  Developing New Medications
  Predictors of Treatment Response
  Long-term Prospective Studies
  Large-scale Epidemiologic Studies
  Inter-agency Partnering
  Engagement with Practitioners
  Effectiveness Trials and Trials Involving Special Populations
  Medication Non-compliance and Dropout from Treatment
  Combinations of Medications
  Development of New More Effective Psychotherapies
  Redesigning the Health Care System for Adolescents with SUDs
Acknowledgments
References

Abstract: Many research advances have been made over the last 25 years that have the potential for preventing substance use disorder (SUD) and for improving the evaluation and treatment of SUD among adolescents. Despite these advances, currently available prevention strategies have limited effectiveness, and few empirically proven treatments exist for most adolescent SUDs. This chapter provides a critical review of the status of translational research involving adolescents with SUDs, identifies barriers to effective translation of research findings, and then provides two comprehensive examples of translational research involving adolescent SUD. Finally, this chapter outlines directions for future research in this field.

INTRODUCTION

In the last few years, medical scientists and public health policy makers have become increasingly concerned that the scientific discoveries of the last 25 years are failing to be translated efficiently into tangible human benefit (Pober, Neuhauser, & Pober, 2001; Sung et al., 2003). A report from the Institute of Medicine (IOM) concluded that a large gap exists between the health care that we now have and the health care that we could have (Institute of Medicine, 2001). For example, life expectancy in the United States is comparable to Cuba, and is behind that of 22 other countries, despite the fact that far more money per capita is spent on health care and health care research in the United States (Lenfant, 2003). A recent review concluded that the gap between practice and research is especially pronounced in the delivery of treatments for alcohol and other drug use disorders (McCarty, Edmundson, & Hartnett, 2006). Consequently, there is continuing concern in the substance treatment field that the growing body of knowledge of effective treatment is not finding its way into clinical practice, including clinical practice involving adolescent substance use disorders (SUD) (Sterling & Weisner, 2006).

In response to this problem, in 2003, the National Institutes of Health (NIH) embarked on an unprecedented endeavor called the NIH Roadmap for Medical Research, as was described by Dr. Zerhouni, the Director of NIH (Zerhouni, 2003, 2005a, 2005b). The previous Director, Dr. Harold Varmus, had floated ideas for radical reorganization near the time of his departure (Varmus, 2002), but nothing concrete had come of those ideas. The Roadmap described by Dr. Zerhouni called for the re-engineering of the national clinical research enterprise, for the transformation of translational clinical science, and for novel interdisciplinary approaches that would advance science and enhance the health of the nation. This effort was intended to "bridge the gap" between clinical research findings and their application in medical practice (Marwick, 2002). Dr. Zerhouni further stated that "It is the responsibility of those of us involved in today's biomedical research enterprise to translate the remarkable scientific innovations we are witnessing into health gains for the nation" (Zerhouni, 2005a).

Since the publication of the NIH Roadmap in 2003, NIH agencies have taken steps to incorporate the ideas of that Roadmap. For example, the National Institute on Drug Abuse (NIDA) published a Program Announcement (PA-04-109) (http://grants1.nih.gov/grants/guide/pa-files/PA-04-109.html) in 2004 that acknowledged that a great deal of basic science knowledge exists, but that the knowledge has not yet been fully exploited in prevention or treatment strategies involving substance abuse. That PA further acknowledged that many youth continue to experiment with and become addicted to drugs, and that current prevention or treatment options are sometimes ineffective. The PA stated that translating knowledge from the basic sciences into practical advance has become a priority for NIDA. Consequently, the purpose of the PA was to foster research that furthers the translation of existing knowledge into treatment through cross-disciplinary research. Another stated purpose of the PA was to foster collaboration between basic and applied researchers with diverse fields of interest, in an effort to enhance translational research. A number of new funding initiatives and mechanisms were implemented by NIDA and by other NIH agencies such as the National Institute of Mental Health (NIMH) and the National Institute on Alcohol Abuse and Alcoholism (NIAAA), in association with the NIH Roadmap, such as the following:

a. Training for a New Interdisciplinary Research Workforce (T90)

b. NIH Director's Pioneer Award, for high-risk, high-gain studies

c. Interdisciplinary Research Consortium (U54)

d. Institutional Clinical and Translational Science Award (CTSA)

e. Planning Grants for CTSAs

f. Proposals for assays for high-throughput screening in the Molecular Libraries Screening Centers network (MLSCN)

g. Building Translational Research in Integrative Behavioral Science (R24) (Issued jointly by NIMH, NIDA, and NIAAA)

h. Building Translational Research in Integrative Behavioral Science (R01) (Issue jointly by NIMH and NIDA).

Also, a Translationally oriented workgroup has been established at NIDA, and a Child & Adolescent Workgroup also exists. However, to date, no PAs or Requests for Applications (RFAs) have been issued by NIDA or NIAAA that specifically address translational research involving drug and alcohol abuse among adolescents. Thus, at NIDA and NIAAA, it appears that translational research involving substance and alcohol abuse among adolescents lags behind translational initiatives involving adults.

TEN BARRIERS TO TRANSLATION OF RESEARCH FINDINGS INVOLVING ADOLESCENT SUDs

A number of barriers have been identified, which slow the translation of research findings into clinical practice involving adolescent substance use disorders. Ten of these barriers are listed below:

STUDIES INVOLVING ADOLESCENTS

There is a general reluctance to conduct research involving adolescents, particularly medication studies (Vitiello & Jensen, 1997). Consequently, as new initiatives are created to develop medications for the treatment of substance use disorders, such as NIDA's Medications Development Program (Whitten, 2006), little additional funding has been directed to research involving adolescents.

FUNDING

Difficulties have clearly developed in obtaining adequate funding for translational research and other research. The NIH budget doubled between 1997 and 2003 (Zerhouni, 2003), which by coincidence is the year when the NIH Roadmap initiative began to be implemented in a major way. However, since 2003, the NIH budget has been stagnant, or has even slightly decreased. This budget decrease at NIH impedes the ability to fully operationalize Roadmap initiatives, and also limits non-Roadmap NIH funding opportunities. This budget situation is crucial in its impact on biomedical research because NIH supports more biomedical research than any other single entity in the world (Zerhouni, 2005b). Until 20 years ago, clinical income often subsidized research, but managed care, increased efficiency in the management of clinical expenses, and reductions in federal support for teaching hospitals have rendered clinical margins insufficient to support the research mission (Loscalzo, 2006).

Budget cuts at the NIH particularly affect basic sciences funding levels, since most of the NIH budget goes toward basic science research, and since other sources of biomedical research funding, such as pharmaceutical companies, typically focus on treatment research rather than basic sciences research. Consequently, Dr. Zerhouni has acknowledged that the NIH focus on funding of basic science research must continue (Zerhouni, 2005b). Nonetheless, critics have already begun to assert that the Roadmap is not working, and that its initiatives are diverting resources away from basic science research (Marks, 2006).

PERSONNEL, CULTURE, AND COMMUNICATION ISSUES

Most new discoveries are now made by professional researchers who primarily work in laboratories or academic environments rather than clinical environments. In contrast, in the past, clinical discoveries were primarily made by prominent clinicians. This separation of researchers from clinicians has contributed to the gap between research findings and clinical applications of those findings (Gray, 2004). In addition, there are different cultures of basic researchers and clinical researchers (Pober et al., 2001). Basic sciences researchers often do not see applied research as part of their mission, and conversely, clinical researchers often do not see basic sciences research as part of their mission. Consequently, basic science researchers and applied researchers rarely communicate with each other (Pober et al., 2001). Also, there are competing authorship needs for various collaborators participating in multidisciplinary translational research. Furthermore, there is a general lack of researchers who are qualified to translate basic sciences findings into clinically useful practice. For example, Dr. Zerhouni has concluded that clinical research is increasingly less attractive to new investigators, and that clinician–scientists are moving away from patient-oriented research (Zerhouni, 2005a). In addition, it has been noted that fewer physicians are going into research careers partly because of financial disincentives (Awasthi et al., 2005).

HIGH COST

The cost of bringing new treatments (e.g., medications) to market has become very high. The cost of developing a new mediation has been estimated to be approximately 800 million dollars (DiMasi, Hansen, & Grabowski, 2003). However, the consulting firm IMS Health found that the alcoholism-treatment medications naltrexone and disulfiram posted less than 25 million dollars in sales combined in 2004. Also, acamprosate, the latest medication to treat alcohol dependence, which hit the US market in January 2005, recorded only six million dollars in sales through its first six months, according to the drug's marketer, Forest Laboratories Inc (CBS News, 2005). Even physicians who specialize in the treatment of additive disorders are unlikely to prescribe naltrexone and other medications to treat alcohol dependence (McCarty et al., 2006). Consequently, it has been challenging for pharmaceutical companies to create commercially successful new medications to treat alcohol or other substance use disorders, despite the widespread prevalence of these disorders. It may be necessary to forge mutually advantageous partnerships among pharmaceutical companies, governmental agencies, and academic researchers to overcome the many challenges in the development of medications to treat alcohol and other substance use disorders in adolescents and adults (Litten et al., 2005).

LONG WAIT FOR RESULTS

A long time is needed until results of clinical studies are available (Institute of Medicine, 2001). This time period can extend from 10 to 12 years or longer.

COMMERCIALIZATION

There are difficulties and delays in commercialization of clinical findings, because of the need for patents, licenses, and contracts.

Increasing Regulatory Burden

An increasing regulatory burden has developed from entities such as Institutional Review Boards (IRBs), Data Safety Monitoring Boards (DSMBs), malpractice law-suits, and HIPAA federal regulations (Pober et al., 2001; Zerhouni, 2005a).

Inadequate Informatics

There is a lack of adequate information systems that store clinical data dealing with adolescents, as well as other age groups (Zerhouni, 2005a). Also, databases are often incompatible (Institute of Medicine, 2001).

Translation at a Community Level

Taking the results of clinical investigations and translating them into clinical practice at the community level is often one of the biggest challenges (Lenfant, 2003). This process requires going beyond efficacy studies to conduct effectiveness studies and demonstration studies, fostering dissemination, changing organizational policies, and changing practice patterns of individual treatment providers. This process can be especially challenging when dealing with younger populations, such as adolescents, since adolescents are perceived as a vulnerable population who must be protected from new practices, which might conceivably be harmful.

Lack of Physician Compliance with Clinical Guidelines

There is a well-established lack of full compliance by practicing physicians with new empirically proven clinical practice guidelines (Cabana et al., 1999). Consequently, despite widespread dissemination, guidelines often have limited effect on changing physician behavior.

EXAMPLES OF IMMEDIATE IMPLICATIONS OF PREVENTION, ASSESSMENT, OR TREATMENT DEVELOPMENTS INVOLVING ADOLESCENT SUDs, AS SHOWN IN TWO FEDERAL CENTER GRANTs

Two broad examples of translational research involving adolescent substance use disorders are provided immediately below. These examples consist of descriptions of translational work involving adolescent substance use disorders at a NIDA-funded center grant and at a NIAAA-funded center grant. The two broad examples of translational research involve center grants because translational research has been easier to conduct in a center grant setting than in settings involving smaller grants.

THE CEDAR CENTER, AN EXAMPLE OF A PREVENTION STUDY PERFORMING TRANSLATIONAL RESEARCH INVOLVING ADOLESCENT SUDs

The CEDAR study is a prospective longitudinal study of 800 families that is designed to elucidate the etiology of substance use disorders, in order to facilitate prevention of those disorders. It is the only NIDA-funded center study focusing on the etiology of substance use disorders, using a longitudinal study design. This study focuses on determining factors leading to SUD, and identifying the trajectories of various groups of persons with SUD. This currently ongoing center study was first funded in 1989, which was well before the current emphasis on translational research started in 2003. Nonetheless, there are many components of this center that deal with translational research. Subjects in this study are recruited at age 10–12, with follow-up assessments at age 12–14, 16, 19, and annually thereafter until the age of 30. Subjects are designated as being at high risk for substance use disorders (the HAR group) or in the low-risk group (the LAR group) based on whether their fathers had been diagnosed with a substance use disorder. The CEDAR center consists of five cores and four research modules, most of which address translational research issues. For example, the Developmental Psychopathology Module addresses psychopathology among adolescents and their parents as it related to the development of substance use disorders. Similarly, the Neurocognition Module addresses neurocognitive processes contributing to SUD, the Genetics Module addresses genetics contributions to SUD, and the family and social ecology module addresses family and environmental factors influencing the development of SUD.

Over 200 publications have resulted from the CEDAR study since it was first funded, though a full listing of those associated findings is beyond the scope of this chapter. Consequently, only a few of the key findings will be presented here. Factors were identified which are associated with the development of SUD, such as conduct disorder (Clark, Vanyukov, & Cornelius, 2002), neurobehavioral disinhibition (Tarter et al., 2003), a history of physical or sexual trauma (Clark, Lesnick, & Hegedus, 1997; Clark et al., 2003a), gender and psychopathology (Clark et al., 1997), and affiliation with deviant peers (Cornelius et al., in press). A more comprehensive listing of the factors leading to SUD is under development, along with a list of their relative effect sizes in contributing to SUD (Clark et al., 2005). Substance use disorder trajectory classes dealing with age of onset, severity, and course have also been developed (Clark et al., 2006). Family history of psychiatric and drug and alcohol use disorders was shown to play a strong role in the development of these same disorders among their offspring (Clark et al., 2004). This knowledge about etiologic factors and course of illness can then be used in determining the best prevention programs for various populations of adolescents. Longitudinal data from the CEDAR study is also useful in addressing a variety of other clinically relevant questions, such as clarifying service utilization patterns and patterns of unmet need for treatment services among adolescents with SUD (Cornelius et al., 2001).

THE PAARC CENTER, AN EXAMPLE OF A DIAGNOSIS AND TREATMENT STUDY PERFORMING TRANSLATIONAL RESEARCH INVOLVING ADOLESCENT SUDs

The PAARC center grant was the only alcohol research center supported by the NIAAA that focused specifically on alcohol abuse and dependence among adolescents. The PAARC study was a prospective longitudinal study of 515 adolescents with DSM-IV Alcohol Use Disorders (AUDs), including alcohol abuse or dependence, along with comparison groups. PAARC was originally funded in 1990, and continued as a center for the next 11 years before splitting into several related R01 projects, which continue until the present time. PAARC faculty consisted of a broad interdisciplinary group of researchers, as is typical of centers conducting translational research. For example, the PAARC center included faculty from five universities, four different schools at the University of Pittsburgh, and four departments within the school of medicine of the University of Pittsburgh. The PAARC project also trained seven postdoctoral trainees who later became funded faculty members at various universities, which is consistent with the training mission stressed in translational research. The PAARC center consisted of five research projects and three supportive cores. The PAARC study included a baseline assessment and follow-up assessments 1, 3, and 5 years after the baseline assessment, and then again at age 25. One of the PAARC studies focused on diagnosis (taxonomy). Consequently, PAARC was the only center grant concerned with determining whether adult taxonomy for alcohol abuse/dependence is appropriate for adolescents. The center also focused on a variety of other factors associated with adolescent AUDs, such as validation of the instruments to assess adolescent AUDs and related disorders, treatment outcome and treatment utilization, etiology of AUDs (including studies of serotonergic functioning such as fenfluramine challenge as well as fMRI neuroimaging), natural history of AUDs (including precipitants of relapse and influence of AUD on the developmental transitions that characterize adolescence), risky sexual practices of adolescents with AUDs, traumatic experiences, clinical heterogeneity, and suicidal behavior and the relation of suicidal behavior to serotonergic functioning.

Over 150 publications resulted from work at the PAARC center, so a full listing of those findings would be beyond the scope of this chapter. Consequently, only a few of the key findings will be presented. PAARC study investigators have identified limitations of DSM-IV diagnostic criteria for AUD in adolescents (Pollock & Martin, 1999). That study also demonstrated that it was possible and relatively common for adolescents not to meet DSM-IV diagnostic criteria for an AUD despite the fact that they demonstrated two diagnostic criteria for alcohol dependence. Those adolescents were called "diagnostic orphans." PAARC study investigators identified limitations in the assessment of DSM-IV cannabis tolerance as an indicator of dependence in adolescents (Chung et al., 2004b). PAARC study investigators demonstrated that a substantial minority of adolescents with AUDs eventually develop non-problem drinking outcomes (Maisto et al., 2002). These investigators demonstrated that relapse to substance use is very common and very rapid among adolescents completing treatment (Cornelius et al., 2003b), and that the presence of Major Depressive Disorder predicts an earlier relapse to alcohol use among adolescents who have completed treatment (Cornelius et al., 2004b). PAARC investigators have shown that supervisory neglect predicts onset of adolescent alcohol use disorders (Clark, Thatcher, & Maisto, 2005). PAARC investigators demonstrated different alcohol and drug use trajectories in the year following treatment among various sub-populations of adolescents with AUDs (Chung et al., 2004a). These investigators have also shown that adolescents with alcohol and other substance use disorders or depressive disorders have a higher risk of attempting suicide (Kelly, Cornelius, & Clark, 2004). Furthermore, PAARC investigators have performed neuroimaging studies that demonstrated that hippocampal volume is less in adolescents with AUDs (De Bellis et al., 2000), and have shown that smaller prefrontal cortex is associated with early-onset drinking in individuals with comorbid mental disorders (De Bellis et al., 2005). These studies dealing with diagnosis, clinical course, and neuroimaging involving adolescents with AUDs will help to inform the development of the relevant sections of the DSM-V and the ICD-XI, which are currently in development, and will also be of use to clinicians in treating their adolescent patients with AUDs.

PAARC investigators have also published data that suggest abnormalities in the metabolism of the neurotransmitter serotonin in adolescents, as shown by abnormal levels of the serotonin precursor tryptophan. Specifically, these investigators have shown a lower ratio of the serotonin precursor tryptophan to other amino acids in serum (tryptophan ratio) in suicidal adolescents with AUDs compared to non-suicidal adolescents with AUDs (Clark, 2003). PAARC investigators have translated those basic sciences findings concerning serotonin into treatment studies involving the serotonergic (SSRI) medication fluoxetine in comorbid adolescents with major depressive disorder and an alcohol use disorder. Specifically, PAARC investigators conducted acute phase and five-year follow-up pilot studies involving fluoxetine in comorbid adolescents, the results of which suggest that treatment with the serotonin agonist fluoxetine may decrease both the drinking and the depressive symptoms of adolescents with comorbid major depression and an alcohol use disorder (Cornelius, 1997; Cornelius, et al., 2001, 2004a; Cornelius et al., 2005a, 2005b; Cornelius et al., 2006).

The PAARC investigators have also performed multiple studies of treatment utilization among adolescents with substance use disorders. For example, those investigators have demonstrated patterns of sharply increasing treatment utilization of SSRIs and other antidepressant medications among adolescents with substance use disorders (Clark et al., 2003b). It is unclear to what extent the promising findings of the PAARC researchers own treatment studies involving SSRI antidepressants in comorbid adolescents may have contributed to the increases in treatment utilization of SSRI antidepressants among comorbid adolescents. The PAARC investigators have also recently demonstrated that the presence of major depressive disorder acts as a predictor of increased treatment utilization among adolescents with alcohol use disorders (Bukstein et al., 2005).

FUTURE DIRECTIONS FOR TRANSLATIONAL RESEARCH INVOLVING ADOLESCENT SUDs

FUNDING

Funding mechanisms should be developed that address translational research among adolescents with substance and alcohol use disorders. These mechanisms should address all of the major areas of translational adolescent substance and alcohol use disorder research, such as etiology, diagnosis, treatment, and treatment utilization.

ESTABLISHING THE VALIDITY OF SUBSTANCE USE DISORDERS

Studies should be conducted to validate the diagnostic criteria for the upcoming DSM-V in adolescent populations as well as in adult populations. Some diagnostic criteria, such as tolerance and withdrawal, have been shown to differ between adolescents and adults, so studies focusing on adolescent populations are essential to validate future versions of diagnostic interviews (Chung et al., 2004b; Chung & Martin, 2005; Pollock & Martin, 1999). Also, the validity of the distinction between abuse and dependence for alcohol and other substance use disorders has been questioned (Proudfoot, Baillie, & Teesson, 2006). In addition, Ting-Kai Li, the Director of NIAAA, has called for the development of dimensional measure of key elements of alcohol use disorder syndromes, as well as revising the current categorical criteria (Li, 2005).

COLLABORATIONS

Collaborations between basic and applied researchers who deal with adolescent substance and alcohol use disorders are needed. These collaborations would have the effect of fostering basic research that is informed by important clinical questions, and in turn would also direct translational research on clinical questions that are informed by basic science findings. Such collaborations are already increasing. For example, NIAAA has recently developed an Integrative Neuroscience Initiative on Alcoholism (INIA), which extends beyond traditional models of collaboration to capture multlildisciplinary input from the many fields that contribute to alcohol research, including genetics, imaging, molecular biology, and behavior (Li, 2005). That program and similar interdisciplinary collaborative initiatives should be further expanded.

ETIOLOGY

Further research is warranted to clarify the etiology of substance use disorders and related comorbid disorder involving both basic sciences research and clinical research (Li, 2004; Volkow, 2004). Investigations are also warranted to understand the mechanisms underlying the association between substance use disorders and psychiatric disorders such as depressive disorders (Li, 2004; Volkow, 2004).

DEVELOPING NEW MEDICATIONS

Studies are warranted to develop new medications for treating substance use disorders in adolescents and adults. The most currently used treatments in adolescents with substance use disorders have no data supporting or refuting their effectiveness (Wagner et al., 1999). Most potentially helpful medications that reduce substance-related symptoms in laboratory animals have not been tested in humans (Hart, 2005). To date, no medication has been shown to alter cannabis self-administration by humans (Hart, 2005). Indeed, to date there have been no completed trials of any medication to decrease cannabis self-administration (Copeland, 2004). No medications have been approved by the Food and Drug Administration for the treatment of cannabis use disorders or cocaine use disorders. Medications currently used to treat alcohol dependence (naltrexone and acamprosate) have to date demonstrated only limited efficacy (Anton et al., 2006), and these medications have not been tested in adolescents. Also, medications used to treat opioid use disorders, such as methodone and buprenorphine, have not been tested for safety and efficacy in adolescent populations.

However, the number of pharmacotherapy studies for alcohol and substance use disorders has increased considerably in recent years. For example, as recently as 12 years ago, NIAAA was supporting only six clinical pharmacotherapy trials.

However, as of 2005, that number of studies funded by NIAAA had increased to 50 (Litten et al., 2005), though very few of those involved adolescents. Also, many promising compounds are currently being developed and tested, involving a variety of different biochemical mechanisms and receptors. For example, medications to treat substance use disorders are currently under development involving serotonin receptors, opioid receptors, gamma–amino butyric acid receptors, dopamine receptors, glutamate receptors, cannabinoid receptors, and corticotrophin–releasing factor receptors, among others (Litten et al., 2005; Dawes et al., 2005). Treatments which are effective in adults are not necessarily safe and effective in adolescents, so those treatments must be tested in adolescent populations.

PREDICTORS OF TREATMENT RESPONSE

Studies should be conducted that address mechanisms, moderators, and predictors of treatment response, in order to clarify the underlying biochemical mechanisms that determine and modulate the effectiveness of various treatments for adolescent substance and alcohol use disorders. For example, biochemical, genetic, environmental, demographic, and neuroimaging studies are warranted to clarify the mechanism of action of many of the pharmaceutical treatments currently in use, in order to clarify why some people have a good response to those treatments while other do not (Cornelius et al., 2003a; Nilsson et al., 2005; Li, 2005; Wells et al., 2001).

LONG-TERM PROSPECTIVE STUDIES

Long-term prospective studies are warranted to clarify the etiology, course, and validity of adolescent substance and alcohol use disorders. The transition from substance experimentation to abuse and then to dependence often occurs as adolescents make the crucial transition to adulthood (Brown et al., 2001; Chung et al., 2003; Chung et al., 2004a; Cornelius et al., 2005).

LARGE-SCALE EPIDEMIOLOGIC STUDIES

Large-scale national epidemiological studies are warranted to address the most compelling questions raised by promising findings from basic research studies (Li, 2005).

INTER-AGENCY PARTNERING

NIDA and NIAAA could partner with other NIH agencies to address clinical problems that extend beyond the scope of any one agency. For example,

NIDA and NIAAA could partner with NIMH to foster translational research addressing the very common occurrence of adolescents with psychiatric disorders such as major depressive disorder in addition to their drug or alcohol use disorder (Cornelius et al., 2005; Litten et al., 2005).

ENGAGEMENT WITH PRACTITIONERS

The practitioner community must be engaged in order to incorporate medications and other new treatments into the treatment process of adolescents (and adults) with alcohol and other substance use disorders (Litten et al., 2005; Sung et al., 2003).

EFFECTIVENESS TRIALS AND TRIALS INVOLVING SPECIAL POPULATIONS

Effectiveness trials and trials involving special populations are warranted to determine whether treatment effects noted in efficacy trials extend to the general community and to special populations, such as adolescents, suicidal patients, and persons in corrections facilities (Cornelius et al., 2003a, 2004).

MEDICATION NON-COMPLIANCE AND DROPOUT FROM TREATMENT

Studies are needed to clarify the reasons for the high rate of medication non-compliance and the high rate of dropout from treatment among adolescents and adults (Edlund et al., 2002). To date, studies involving adults with substance use disorders have suggested a role for several factors in causing non-compliance with treatment, such as side effects, a perception of lack of efficacy, time and cost of treatment, a reluctance to take medications, medication addiction concerns, the non-medication philosophy of Alcoholics Anonymous (Mark et al., 2003). However, it is unclear to what extend those findings involving adults extend to adolescents with substance use disorders.

COMBINATIONS OF MEDICATIONS

Studies are warranted to evaluate the effectiveness of combinations of medications, such as naltrexone, acamprosate, or disulfiram in combination with fluoxetine in adolescents with comorbid alcohol dependence and major depressive disorder. (Anton et al., 2006; Litten et al., 2005; Salloum et al., 1998).

Development of New More Effective Psychotherapies

To date, studies of various psychotherapies for treatment of adolescent substance use disorders have not clearly identified a superior treatment, optimal dosage, or length or required involvement to maximize treatment outcome (Kaminer, 2002). Psychotherapy studies involving adults have produced similar findings. For example, results from project MATCH, the largest and most expensive alcoholism treatment trial ever conducted, showed essentially no patient–treatment matches, and three very different treatments produced nearly identical outcomes. A secondary analysis of the data showed that a median of only 3% of the drinking outcome at follow-up could be attributed to treatment (Cutler & Fishbain, 2005).

Redesigning the Health Care System for Adolescents with SUDs

A number of researchers have called for the redesign of the health care system, including the health care system for adolescents with substance use disorders, because of a number of problems in the current health care system (Angres et al., 1998; Institute of Medicine, 2001; Miller, Swift, & Gold, 1998; Morrison & Smith, 2000). For example, the attempt by managed care to control costs has provided undesirable disincentives to innovation in treatment through lack of reimbursement for innovative treatments (Angers et al., 1998; Morrison & Smith, 2000). The current health care system has been described as being overly complex, poorly organized, inefficient, and uncoordinated, and has also been criticized for not providing high-quality medical care to all Americans (Institute of Medicine, 2001). Funding for health care for adolescents and children is particularly deficient in the United States, including funding for treatment of substance use disorders in adolescents. For example, per capita government spending on health care for children and adolescents in 2001 was only $258, which was much lower than the $4,360 per capita that government spent on health care for the elderly that same year (Berk et al., 2004).

An ideal treatment system would provide a full range of options that allows a program to be tailored to the needs of the individual (Angres et al., 1998; Bukstein & Cornelius, 2006) and to match the patient to the best treatment (Turner et al., 1999). An ideal treatment system would also integrate the care of substance use disorders with the care for psychiatric and medical disorders (Rorro & Gastfriend, 2001; Unutzer et al., 2006). Finally, an ideal treatment system would provide adequate coverage for children and adolescents, including those with substance use disorders, who are widely perceived as a particularly vulnerable group (Berk et al., 2004; Cunningham & Kirby, 2004).

ACKNOWLEDGMENTS

This work was supported in part by grants from the National Institute on Alcohol Abuse and Alcoholism (NIAAA) (R01 AA013370, R01 AA015173, R01 AA13397, R01 AA014357, K24 AA015320, K02 AA00291, and P50 AA08746); the National Institute on Drug Abuse (NIDA) (R01 DA019142, R01 DA014635, P50 DA05605, Clinical Trials Network); and a grant from the Veterans Administration (MIRECC to VISN 4).

REFERENCES

Angres, D. H., Larson, J. K., Pacione, T., Anderson, C. L., & Costabilo, J. F. (1998). An integrated clinical approach to managed care. *Psychiatric Annals, 28*, 691–696.

Anton, R. F., O'Malley, S. S., Ciraulo, D. A., Cisler, R. A., Couper, D., Donovan, D. M., Gastfriend, M. D., Hosking, J. D., Johnson, B. A., LoCastro, J. S., Longabaugh, R., Mason, B. J., Mattson, M. E., Miller, W. R., Pettinati, H. M., Randall, C. L., Swift, R., Weiss, R. D., Williams, L. D., & Zweben, A. (2006). Combined pharmacotherapies and behavioral interventions for alcohol dependence: The COMBINE study: A randomized controlled trial. *Journal of the American Medical Association, 295*, 2003–2017.

Awasthi, S., Beardmore, J., Clark, J., Hadridge, P., Madani, H., Marusic, A., Purcell, G., Rhoads, M., Slixa-Hahnle, K., Smith, R., Edejer, T. T., Tugwell, P., Underwood, T., Ward, R., on behalf of the International Campaign to Revitalise Academic Medicine. (2005). The future of academic medicine: Five scenarios to 2025. Milbank Memorial Fund, http://www.milbank.org/reports/0507FiveFutures/0507Five Futures.html

Berk, M. L., Schur, C. L, Chang, D. I., Knight, E. K., & Kleinman, L. C. (2004). Americans' views about the adequacy of health care for children and the elderly. *Health Affairs September 14 issue*: W4-446-W4-454.

Brown, S. A., D'Amico, E. J., McCarty, D. M., & Tapert, S. F. (2001). Four-year outcomes from adolescent alcohol and drug treatment. *Journal of Studies on Alcohol, 62*, 381–388.

Bukstein, O. G., & Cornelius, J. (2006). Chapter 12: Psychopharmacology of adolescents with substance use disorders: Using diagnostic-specific treatments. In H. A. Liddle, & C. L. Rowe (Eds.), *Adolescent Substance Abuse: Research and Clinical Advances* (pp. 241–263). Cambridge, England: Cambridge University Press.

Bukstein, O. G., Cornelius, J., Trunzo, A. C., Kelly, T. M., & Wood, D. S. (2005). Clinical predictors of treatment in a population of adolescents with alcohol use disorders. *Addictive Behaviors, 30*, 1663–1673.

Cabana, M. D., Rand, C. S., Powe, N. R., Wu, A. W., Wilson, M. H., Abboud, P. C., Rubin, H. R. (1999). Why don't physicians follow clinical practice guidelines? *Journal of the American Medical Association, 282*, 1458–1465.

CBS News. (2005). Alcoholism drugs gain popularity. http://www/cbsnews.com/stories/2005/09/13/health/main841010_page2.shtml

Chung, T., Maisto, S. A., Cornelius, J. R., & Martin, C. S. (2004a). Adolescents' alcohol and drug use trajectories in the year following treatment. *Journal of Studies on Alcohol, 65*, 105–114, 2004.

Chung, R., & Martin, C. S. (2005). What were they thinking? Adolescents' interpretations of DSM-IV alcohol dependence symptom queries and implications for diagnostic validity. *Drug and Alcohol Dependence, 80*, 191–200.

Chung, T, Martin, C. S., Grelia, C. E., Winters, K. C., Abrantes, A. M., & Brown, S. A. (2004). Course of alcohol problems in treated adolescents. *Alcoholism: Clinical and Experimental Research, 27*, 253–261.

Chung, T., Martin, C. S., Winters, K. C., Cornelius, J. R., & Langenbucker, J. W. (2004b). Limitations in the assessment of DSM-IV cannabis tolerance as an indicator of dependence in adolescents. *Experimental and Clinical Psychopharmacology, 12,* 136–146.

Clark, D. B. (2003). Serum tryptophan ratio and suicidal behavior in adolescents: A prospective study. *Psychiatry Research, 119,* 199–204.

Clark, D. B., Cornelius, J. R., Kirisci, L., & Tarter, R. E. (2005). Childhood risk categories for adolescent substance involvement: A general liability typology. *Drug and Alcohol Dependence, 77,* 13–21.

Clark, D. B., Cornelius, J., Wood, D. S., & Vanyukov, M. (2004). Psychopathology risk transmission in children of parents with substance use disorders. *American Journal of Psychiatry, 161,* 1–7.

Clark, D. B., De Bellis, M. D., Lynch, K. G., Cornelius, J. R., & Martin, C. S. (2003a). Physical and sexual abuse, depression and alcohol use disorders in adolescents: Onsets and outcomes. *Drug and Alcohol Dependence, 69,* 51–60.

Clark, D. B., Jones, B. L, Wood, D. S., & Cornelius, J. R. (2006). Substance use disorder trajectory classes: Diachronic integration of onset age, severity, and course. *Addictive Behaviors, 31,* 995–1009.

Clark, D. B., Lesnick, L., & Hegedus, A. (1997). Trauma and other stressors in adolescent alcohol dependence and abuse. *Journal of the American Academy of Child & Adolescent Psychiatry, 36,* 1744–1751.

Clark, D. B., Pollock, N. A., Bromberger, J. T., Bukstein, O. G., Mezzich, A. C., & Donovan, J. E. (1997). Gender and comorbid psychopathology in adolescents with alcohol sue disorders. *Journal of the American Academy of Child and Adolescent Psychiatry, 36,* 1195–1203.

Clark, D. B., Thatcher, D. L., & Maisto, S. A. (2005). Supervisory neglect and adolescent alcohol use disorders: Effects on AUD onset and treatment outcome. *Addictive Behaviors, 30,* 1737–1750.

Clark, D. B., Vanyukov, M., & Cornelius, J. (2002). Childhood antisocial behavior and adolescent alcohol use disorders. *Alcohol Research and Health, 26,* 109–115.

Clark, D. B., Wood, D. S., Cornelius, J. R., Bukstein, O. G., & Martin, C. S. (2003b). Clinical practices in the pharmacological treatment of comorbid psychopathology in adolescents with alcohol use disorders. *Journal of Substance Abuse Treatment, 25,* 293–295.

Copeland, J. (2004). Developments in the treatment of cannabis use disorder. *Current Opinion in Psychiatry, 17,* 161–168.

Cornelius, J. R., Bukstein, O. G., Birmaher, B., Salloum, I. M., Lynch, K., Pollock, N. K., Gershon, S., & Clark, D. (2001). Fluoxetine in adolescents with major depression and an alcohol use disorder: An open-label trial. *Addictive Behaviors, 26,* 735–739.

Cornelius, J. R., Bukstein, O., Salloum, I., & Clark, D. (2003a). Chapter 20, alcohol and psychiatric comorbidity. In M. Galanter (Ed.), *Recent Developments in Alcoholism, Volume 16, Research on Alcoholism Treatment* (pp. 361–374). New York, NY: Kluwer Academic/Plenum Publishers.

Cornelius, J. R., Bukstein, O. G., Salloum, I. M., Kelly, T. M., Wood, D. S., & Clark, D. B. (2004a). Fluoxetine in depressed AUD adolescents: A one-year follow-up evaluation. *Journal of Child & Adolescent Psychopharmacology, 14,* 33–38.

Cornelius, J. R., Clark, D. B., Bukstein, O. G., Birmaher, B., Kelly, T. M., Salloum, I. M., Walters, M., Matta, J., & Wood, D. S. (2006). Fluoxetine in adolescents with comorbid major depression and an alcohol use disorder: A five-year follow-up study. *Dual Disorders, 2,* 9–23.

Cornelius, J. R., Clark, D. B., Bukstein, O. G., Birmaher, B., Salloum, I. M., & Brown, S. A. (2005a). Acute phase and five-year follow-up study of fluoxetine in adolescents with major depression and a comorbid substance use disorder: A review. *Addictive Behaviors, 30,* 1824–1833.

Cornelius, J. R., Clark, D. B., Bukstein, O. G., Kelly, T. M., Salloum, I. M., Wood, D. S. (2005b). Fluoxetine in adolescents with comorbid major depression and an alcohol use disorder: A 3-year follow-up study. *Addictive Behaviors, 30,* 807–814.

Cornelius, J. R., Clark, D. B., Bukstein, O. G., & Salloum, I. M. (2005). Chapter 16, Treatment of co-occurring alcohol, drug, and psychiatric disorders. In M. Galanter (Ed.), *Recent Developments in Alcoholism, Volume 17, Alcohol Problems in Adolescents and Young Adults* (pp. 349–365). New York, NY: Kluwer Academic/Plenum Publishers.

Cornelius, J. R., Clark, D. B., Reynolds, M., Kirisci, L., & Tarter, R. (2007). Early age of first sexual intercourse and affiliation with deviant peers predict development of SUD: A prospective longitudinal study. *Addictive Behaviors, 32,* 850–854.

Cornelius, J. R., Clark, D. B., Salloum, I. M., Bukstein, O. G., & Kelly, T. M. (2004). Interventions in suicidal alcoholics. *Alcoholism: Clinical and Experimental Research, 28,* 89S–96S.

Cornelius, J. R, Maisto, S. A., Martin, C. S., Bukstein, O. G., Salloum, I. M., Daley, D. C., Wood, D. S., & Clark, D. B. (2004b). Major depression associated with earlier alcohol relapse in treated teens with AUD. *Addictive Behaviors, 29,* 1035–1038.

Cornelius, J. R., Maisto, S. A., Pollock, N. K., Martin, C. S., Salloum, I. M., Lynch, K. G., & Clark, D. B. (2003b). Rapid relapse generally follows treatment for substance use disorders among adolescents. *Addictive Behaviors, 28,* 381–386.

Cornelius, J. R., Pringle, J., Jernigan, J., Kirisci, L., & Clark, D. B. (2001). Correlates of mental health service utilization and unmet need among a sample of male adolescents. *Addictive Behaviors, 26,* 11–19.

Cornelius, J. R., Salloum, I. M., Ehler, J. G., Jarrett, P. J., Cornelius, M. D., Perel, J. M., Thase, M. E., & Black, A. (1997). Fluoxetine in depressed alcoholics: A double-blind, placebo-controlled trial. *Archives of General Psychiatry, 54,* 700–705.

Cunningham, P., & Kirby, J. (2004). Children's health coverage: A quarter-century of change. *Health Affairs, 23,* 27–38.

Cutler, R. B., & Fishbain, D. A. (2005). Are alcoholism treatments effective? The Project MATCH data. *BMC Public Health, 5,* 75.

Dawes, M. A., Johnson, B. A., Ait-Daoud, N., Ma, J. Z., & Cornelius, J. R. (2005). A prospective, open-label trial of ondansetron in adolescents with alcohol dependence. *Addictive Behaviors, 30,* 1077–1085.

De Bellis, M. D., Clark, D. B., Beers, S. R., Soloff, P., Boring, A. M., Hall, J., Kersh, A., & Keshavan, M. S. (2000). Hippocampal volume in adolescent onset alcohol use disorders. *American Journal of Psychiatry, 157,* 737–744.

De Bellis, M. D., Narasimhan, A., Thatcher, D. L., Keshavan, M. S., Soloff, P., & Clark, D. B. (2005). Prefrontal cortex, thalamus, and cerebellar volumes in adolescents and young adults with adolescent-onset alcohol use disorders and comorbid mental disorders. *Alcoholism: Clinical and Experimental Research, 29,* 1590–1600.

DiMasi, J. A., Hansen, R. W., & Grabowski, H. G. (2003). The price of innovation: New estimates of drug development costs. *Journal of Health Economics, 22,* 151–185.

Edlund, M. J., Wang, P. S., Berglund, P. A., Katz, S. J., Lin, E., & Kessler, R. C. (2002). Dropping out of mental health treatment: Patterns and predictors among epidemiological survey respondents in the United States and Ontario. *American Journal of Psychiatry, 159,* 845–851.

Gray, J. D. (2004). Campaign to revitalise academic medicine. *British Medical Journal, 328,* 1377–1378.

Hart, C. L. (2005). Increasing treatment options for cannabis dependence: A review of potential pharmacotherapies. *Drug and Alcohol Dependence, 80,* 147–159.

Institute of Medicine. (2001). *Crossing the Quality Chasm: A New Health System for the 21st Century.* Washington, DC: The National Academies Press.

Kaminer, Y. (2002). Adolescent substance abuse treatment: Evidence-based practice in outpatient services. *Current Psychiatry Reports, 4,* 397–401.

Kelly, T. M., Cornelius, J. R., & Clark, D. B. (2004). Psychiatric disorders and attempted suicide among adolescents with substance use disorders. *Drug and Alcohol Dependence, 73,* 87–97.

Lenfant, C. (2003). Clinical research to clinical practice-Lost in translation? *New England Journal of Medicine, 349,* 868–874.

Li, T. K. (2004). Alcohol use disorders and mood disorders: A National Institute on Alcohol Abuse and Alcoholism perspective. *Journal of Biological Psychiatry, 56,* 718–720.

Li, T. K. (2005). NIAAA director discusses research and the future. *Neuroscience Quarterly, Fall* (2005 issue), 18–21.

Litten, R. Z., Fertig, J., Mattson, M., & Egli, M. (2005). Development of medications for alcohol use disorders: Recent advances and ongoing challenges. *Expert Opinion in Emerging Drugs, 10,* 323–343.

Loscalzo, J. (2006). The NIH budget and the future of biomedical research. *New England Journal of Medicine, 354*, 1665–1667.

Maisto, S. A., Martin, C. S., Pollock, N. K., Cornelius, J. R., Chung, T. A. (2002). Non-problem drinking outcomes in adolescents. *Experimental and Clinical Psychopharmacology, 10*, 324–331.

Mark, T. L., Kranzler, H. R., Poole, V. H., Hagen, C. A., McLeod, C., & Crossse, S. (2003). Barriers to the use of medications to treat alcoholism. *The American Journal on Addictions, 12*, 281–294.

Marks, A. R. (2006). Rescuing the NIH before it is too late. *Journal of Clinical Investigation, 116*, 844.

Marwick, C. (2002). Networks aim to bridge gap between clinical research, medical practice. *Journal of the National Cancer Institute, 94*, 478–479.

McCarty, D., Edmundson, E., & Hartnett, T. (2006). Charting a path between research and practice in alcoholism treatment. *Alcohol Research & Health, 29*, 5–10.

Miller, N. S., Swift, R. M., & Gold, M. S. (1998). Health care economics for integrated addiction treatment in clinical settings. *Psychiatric Annals, 28*, 682–689.

Morrison, I., & Smith, R. (2000). Hamster health care: Time to stop running faster and redesign health care. *British Medical Journal, 321*, 1541–1542.

Nilsson, K. W., Sjoberg, R. L., Damberg, M., Alm, P. O., Ohrvik, J., Leppert, J., Lindstrom, L., & Oreland, L. (2005). Role of the serotonin transporter gene and family function in adolescent alcohol consumption. *Alcoholism: Clinical and Experimental Research, 29*, 564–570.

Pober, J. S., Neuhauser, C. S., & Pober J. M. (2001). Obstacles facing translational research in academic medical centers. *The FASEB Journal, 15*, 2303–2313.

Pollock, N. K., & Martin, C. S. (1999). Diagnostic orphans: Adolescents with alcohol symptomatology who do not qualify for DSM-IV abuse or dependence diagnoses. *American Journal of Psychiatry, 156*, 897–901.

Proudfoot, H., Baillie, A. J., & Teesson, M. (2006). The structure of alcohol dependence in the community. *Drug and Alcohol Dependence, 81*, 21–26.

Rorro, M., & Gastfriend, D. R. (2001). Integrating addiction medicine with psychiatry: Clinical collaboration and resource parity. *Psychiatric Annals, 31*, 641–647.

Salloum, I. M., Cornelius, J. R., Thase, M. E., Daley, D. C., Kirisci, L., & Spotts, C. (1998). Naltrexone utility in depressed alcoholics. *Psychopharmacology Bulletin, 34*, 111–115.

Sterling, S., & Weisner, C. (2006). Translating research findings into practice: Example of treatment services for adolescents in managed care. *Alcohol Research & Health, 29*, 11–18.

Sung, N. S., Crowley, W. F., Genel, M., Salber, P., Sandy, L., Sherwood, L. M., Johnson, S. B., Catanese, V., Tilson, H., Getz, K., Larson, E. L., Scheinberg, D., Recce, E. A., Slavkin, H., Dobs, A., Grebb, J., Martinez, R. A., Korn, A., & Rimoin, D. (2003). Central challenges facing the national clinical research enterprise. *Journal of the American Medical Association, 289*, 1278–1287.

Tarter, R. E., Kirisci, L., Mezzich A., Cornelius, J. R., Pajer, K, Vanyukov, M., Gardner, W., Blackson, T., & Clark, D. (2003). Neurobehavior disinhibition in childhood predicts early age onset substance use disorder. *American Journal of Psychiatry, 160*, 1078–1085.

Turner, W. M., Turner, K. H., Reif, S., Gutowski, W. E., & Gastfriend, D. R. (1999). Feasibility of multlidimensional substance abuse treatment matching: Automating the ASAM patient placement criteria. *Drug and Alcohol Dependence, 55*, 35–43.

Unutzer, J., Schoenbaum, M., Druss, B. G., & Katon, W. J. (2006). Transforming mental health care at the interface with general medicine: Report for the president's commission. *Psychiatric Services, 57*, 37–47.

Varmus, H. (2002). Future of the NIH may lie in restructuring, committee told. *Nature, 418*, 572.

Vitiello, B., & Jensen, P. S. (1997). Medication development and testing in children and adolescents: Current problems, future directions. *Archives of General Psychiatry, 54*, 871–876.

Volkow, N. D. (2004). The reality of comorbidity: Depression and drug abuse. *Biological Psychiatry, 56*, 714–717.

Wagner, E. F., Brown, S. A., Monti, P. M., Myers, M. G., & Waldron, H. B. (1999). Innovations in adolescent substance abuse intervention. *Alcoholism: Clinical and Experimental Research, 23*, 236–249.

Wells, K., Klap, R., Koike, A., & Sherbourne, C. (2001). Ethnic disparities in unmet need for alcoholism, drug abuse, and mental health care. *American Journal of Psychiatry*, *158*, 2027–2032.

Whitten, L. (2006). Medications development division nurtures the creation of new addiction treatments. *NIDA Notes*, *20*, 4–5.

Zerhouni, E. (2003). The NIH roadmap. *Science*, *302*, 63–72.

Zerhouni, E. (2005a). Translational and clinical science-Time for a new vision. *New England Journal of Medicine*, *353*, 1621–1623.

Zerhouni, E. (2005b). US biomedical research: Basic, translational, and clinical sciences. *Journal of the American Medical Association*, *294*, 1352–1358.

SECTION IV
PRACTICE AND POLICY

CHAPTER 17

Dissemination of Evidence-Based Treatment into Substance Abuse Clinical Practice

James L. Sorensen, Jennifer E. Hettema and TeChieh Chen
University of California at San Francisco, San Francisco, CA, USA

Translation of Addictions Science into Practice

Abstract: This chapter discusses the dissemination of evidence-based substance abuse interventions into clinical practice and public policy. There is substantial knowledge about dissemination of evidence-based interventions, but the application to substance abuse is at a rudimentary stage. Several models have been developed for understanding the factors that influence dissemination, and efforts are being made to set dissemination policy despite the relatively thin research base for making these decisions. The field has opportunity to make substantial progress in the coming decade.

INTRODUCTION

Recently there has been increased focus on providing more evidence-based treatment (EBT) in substance abuse clinical practice. The vision of a treatment system based on scientific evidence, may appear to be heaven, hell, or purgatory depending on whether one is a researcher, provider, or policy maker, respectively. Researchers have dreams of a treatment system that is based on empirical data about the effectiveness of interventions in lessening the problems of patients. Treatment providers have nightmares of being forced to use a limited arsenal of techniques that were designed in sterile research laboratories and have little relationship to their skills or needs of their patients. Policy makers face a future of endless torture as the treatment system undergoes, yet another in a series of crises that drain resources from direct service so the system can adapt to changing organizational demands. Although research has been conducted about the effectiveness of substance abuse interventions, little evidence is available regarding how to implement EBT into the field. While researchers, clinicians, and policy makers may differ in proximal goals, we share the common goal of reducing the suffering caused by substance abuse.

This chapter discusses dissemination of EBT into clinical practices that treat people with problems of drug abuse. There is a substantial literature about dissemination to substance abuse clinical practice, but there are few controlled studies. Despite this paucity, existing studies indicate preliminary directions for designing and implementing dissemination efforts. In addition, the need for effective dissemination, coupled with an increasing awareness of the problem, provide an open field for the development of important knowledge about dissemination.

CRITICAL REVIEW OF RESEARCH LITERATURE

Limited research exists that addresses how to disseminate EBT to substance abuse treatment providers and policy makers. Numerous articles have described what amounts to essentially "stories" – people's experiences with knowledge dissemination – but only a few experimental studies have been conducted. Instead, the field is dominated by anecdotes and testimonial evidence about the widening gap between research and treatment, barriers to successful dissemination, and strategies to resolve the situation. In 2004, one of the authors prepared an annotated bibliography addressing recent developments in technology transfer in the area of substance abuse treatment (Sorensen, Lin, & Sera, 2004). The search engines PsycInfo and PubMed, revealed over a hundred articles discussing the topic. Yet, only a minority of articles provided scientific data, and even fewer were controlled trials. If empirical thinking follows concepts introduced in elementary science classes, then we are in the problem recognition and hypothesis generating stage of discovery. It is important to recognize the budding state of dissemination research, take a cautionary approach to the stories that dominate the field today, and contribute to the knowledge base with evidence-based information. We divide the existing literature into five categories: descriptive research, within group research, controlled studies, reviews, and dissemination models.

DESCRIPTIVE RESEARCH

To date, the majority of professional literature devoted to EBT dissemination in substance abuse practice has relied on observational or case study techniques that provide largely qualitative, descriptive data. Such efforts can be viewed as "story telling," as they contribute to our understanding of dissemination for the field, but can only speculate about causal mechanisms of dissemination.

Many descriptive research studies provide strong evidence of a gap between research and practice. One salient example of this phenomenon is the use of Behavioral Couples Therapy (BCT), which is a treatment intervention for sexual partners that attempts to reduce substance use by changing relationship patterns that help sustain use (Fals-Stewart et al., 2004a). This approach has a strong evidence-base for positive outcomes (Epstein & McCrady, 1998). Yet, when Fals-Stewart and Birchler (2001) surveyed 398 outpatient substance abuse treatment programs about their use of BCT they found that fewer than 5% of providers used any form of BCT. Furthermore, Fals-Stewart, Logsdon, and Birchler (2004b) discovered most clinics trained to use BCT quit using it within one year of study completion. Unfortunately, failure to adopt EBT is not limited to family therapy, and many descriptive studies cite similar results. For example, Guydish et al. (2005) found that only one of eight clinics that participated in a study of the Matrix treatment approach to methamphetamine abuse (Rawson et al., 2004) actually adopted the treatment in their practice, despite positive results of the trial.

In addition to failing to adopt EBT, programs often adopt interventions with poor evidence of effectiveness. The DARE (Drug Abuse Resistance Education) program is a classic example. The 1980s witnessed the birth of DARE, a school-based prevention program that includes a drug-prevention curriculum taught by specially trained law enforcement officers. Numerous well-designed studies since 1991 have indicated little positive effect for DARE (see meta-analysis by

West & O'Neal, 2004), but the program flourished to become the country's largest school-based prevention program in terms of federal support (McNeal & Hanson, 1995).

As previous examples illustrate, dissemination of research into clinical practice is suboptimal. Interventions with strong evidence bases are not implemented, and those with little or no evidence are being routinely provided. In addition to noting differences between reported dissemination and learning strategies, researchers have sought to determine what individual therapist characteristics might influence EBT adoption. Knudsen et al. (2005), surveyed nearly 3,000 substance abuse treatment counselors about their knowledge and opinions of buprenorphine, a medication with a strong evidence-base for treating opioid addiction. The authors found that several therapist characteristics were related to knowledge of and positive attitudes toward buprenorphine. Specifically, therapists who were in recovery and had fewer years of experience were less likely to know about the medication's effectiveness, and those who endorsed a 12-step model and had a bachelor's versus a master's degree were more likely to have negative views about effectiveness. Another factor that has been found to influence adoption is therapist attitude toward treatment manuals. Addis, Wade, and Hatgis (1999), gathered early observational evidence suggesting that therapists find research-generated treatment manuals impractical in real-world settings, unable to meet the diverse needs of their clients, not tailored to their backgrounds, inflexible, and damaging to the therapeutic relationship.

WITHIN GROUP RESEARCH

Another method for increasing knowledge regarding EBT dissemination involves the use of within-group designs. *The Change Book: A Blueprint for Technology Transfer* (Addiction Technology Transfer Center Network, 2004) was created as a guide to implementing research into practice. Although the text is based largely on anecdotal evidence, its common-sense, problem-solving approach mirrors program evaluation techniques provides a sequence of steps that can be used to generate and test specific dissemination strategies.

McCarty et al. (2004), tested the effectiveness of dissemination using *The Change Book* as a guide. Via training, these authors sought to increase physician delivery of buprenorphine treatment and improve linkage to substance abuse counseling. Pre-post measures of attitudes toward the drug showed improvements after training. In addition, eight months after training, 10 of 17 physicians had authorization to prescribe buprenorphine; six were treating their clients with the medication. An approach similar in philosophy is the Drug Evaluation Network System, which emphasizes developing a collaborative relationship between researchers and practitioners in implementing meaningful client evaluation systems (Carise, Cornely, & Gurel, 2002; Carise & Gurel, 2003).

CONTROLLED STUDIES

Only a handful of randomized clinical trials have directly tested what techniques lead to dissemination of substance abuse interventions. Sorensen et al. (1988) conducted a study about the effectiveness of dissemination methods for a Job Seeker's Workshop. The Job Seekers' Workshop (Hall et al., 1977; Hall et al., 1981a, 1981b) is a cognitive-behaviorally oriented small-group intervention for patients in substance abuse treatment, which has improved drug users' interviewing skills and likelihood of being employed at follow-ups. Substance abuse treatment programs ($N = 172$) were randomized to receive the following education about the workshop: (a) written materials, (b) on-site one-day training, (c) two-day off-site training conference, or (d) no-information. At a 3-month follow-up, the on-site and off-site trainings had much greater adoption rates.

A more recent study used a randomized clinical trial to test substance abuse dissemination strategies. Drawing on motivation research, Miller et al. (2004) randomized licensed health professionals to one of the five experimental conditions: (a) two-day workshop, (b) workshop plus feedback, (c) workshop plus coaching, (d) workshop plus feedback and coaching, and (e) self-training control that received a manual and videotapes. Feedback was given at each of three follow-ups, and coaching involved up to six 30-minute telephone sessions that included discussion, collaborative problem solving, and role-playing. Results revealed post-training skill increases among all workshop groups. At a four-month follow-up point, the four workshop training conditions showed significantly greater increases in skill compared to the self-instruction condition. Participants who received feedback, coaching, or both were more likely than workshop-only participants to meet proficiency standards at four- and eight-month follow-up points.

REVIEWS

Several reviews have been published about dissemination of EBT in substance abuse clinical practice. The first of these (Backer, 1991) was conducted under contract to National Institute on Drug Abuse (NIDA), with the aim of providing further input to the definition of technology transfer, providing contextual background to the emerging technology transfer program of NIDA, and presenting ideas for future technology transfer. The document moved the field forward by defining terms (for example distinguishing between "dissemination," the process of sending information out to larger audiences, and "diffusion," the spread of information about innovations). It also pointed out several special circumstances in the drug abuse field that affect technology transfer such as fears of legal action, moral values, and societal pressures for "quick fix solutions." These factors can make it more difficult to disseminate treatments when the pressure is to punish rather than treat the drug user.

Subsequently, Backer, David, and Soucy (1995) co-edited a NIDA monograph on technology transfer that brought together scientists from different but related disciplines to provide their perspectives about technology transfer. Backer's volume emphasized that improving drug abuse treatment and prevention involves "a human process" which, if successful, leads to individual and organizational change" (p. 2).

A more recent review, by Miller et al. (2006), provides a comprehensive evaluation of the state of the field and provides suggestions for future directions. The authors highlight that many disconfirmed treatment approaches, such as educational films and lectures, are commonly practiced within substance abuse treatment, despite research indicating that they are ineffective. The authors argue that, while failure to provide treatment that is consistent with current research is not unique to substance abuse, the magnitude of this phenomenon within addiction may be attributable to the development of addiction treatment within a model that is driven by the folk wisdom of compassionate peers. The authors suggest that such clinicians may be more likely to learn through a "craft model," in which they rely more on observation and personal experience than on researchers' dissemination venues, such as academic journals and manuals. Also, the influence of systemic factors, such as resource insufficiencies, is identified as a barrier to adoption. The authors provide practical suggestions for factors that may increase adoption, such as including system level incentives for the practice of EBT, modeling of pharmaceutical marketing techniques, teaching new skills using feedback, supervision, and coaching, conducting research within community clinics, and the creation of blending teams charged with the task of dissemination. Lastly, the authors argue that evidence-based dissemination strategies themselves are needed and highlight measures that may be effective in evaluating such strategies.

DISSEMINATION MODELS FOR SUBSTANCE ABUSE CLINICAL PRACTICE

Scientific inquiry provides utility by generating and testing theories that can then be used to inform practice. Although no comprehensive theories of EBT dissemination in substance abuse have been put forth to date, some general models of dissemination principles have been posited. Some models (Simpson, 2002) view dissemination as a process that occurs in stages, whereas others (Roman & Johnson, 2002; Thomas et al., 2003) shed light on general characteristics that may influence dissemination.

Dwayne Simpson's "process model of program change" (2002) originated in research about substance abuse programs. According to Simpson's model, innovation adoption is a staged process, during which change comes about incrementally. First, *exposure* to innovation occurs, often via training. For this to occur there needs to be adequate readiness for change (i.e., motivation and resources). In a second stage, *adoption*, a decision is made to try an innovation. Motivation and perceived need for change are keys to reaching this stage. Thirdly, in *implementation*, an innovation is tested. Successful implementation occurs with a climate conducive to change (e.g., clarity of goals) and organizational support (e.g., feedback, incentives to reinforce change).

Roman and Johnson (2002), as well as Thomas et al. (2003) created models of dissemination that were also developed in the substance abuse treatment field. Roman and Johnson's model developed with 450 treatment centers in a study of the diffusion of naltrexone (a narcotic antagonist medication) into treatment programs. Their model focuses on organizational characteristics such as structure, leadership, and caseload of a treatment center as variables that influence a program's likelihood of adopting an innovative treatment. Their model is advantageous as it distinguishes several easily identifiable variables that influence innovation diffusion. Thomas et al. (2003) created a model that was also developed in the study of naltrexone. Adoption of an innovation adoption results from an interactive process, which occurs when the following interact: (1) characteristics of clinicians, such as training approach; (2) organizational structure; (3) treatment environment; (4) characteristics of innovation; and (5) patient population.

These models overlap somewhat and reflect similar views of the processes of organizational change. Currently, there has been little research contrasting the utility of the various models, which may be an area for future knowledge development.

IMMEDIATE IMPLICATIONS

Although there is a small research base in the substance abuse area, evidence already available provides several concrete suggestions for EBT dissemination into the field.

ACKNOWLEDGE THE GAP

Descriptive studies clearly identify numerous differences between the research and clinical worlds in the substance abuse area, such as varying levels of education, what is valued in treatment modalities, and preferred methods of learning. Such research has been helpful in providing information about dissemination efforts of researchers and learning techniques of clinicians. One would hope for a high degree of overlap between these respective strategies, but this is not the case. While researchers report that their primary avenue for dissemination is publication in peer-reviewed journals and presentations at professional conferences, clinicians report learning about new interventions from local sources such as colleagues or newsletters and seminars (Arkfen, Agius, & Dickson, 2005).

In considering how to disseminate EBT, innovators should acknowledge these learning style differences. Recognize that most publishing or information-distributing venues are insufficient to translate EBT into practice. Consider taking advantage of experience-based learning systems, provision of incentives, use of change agents, coaching, and obtaining consultation from clinicians.

USE INTERACTIVE DISSEMINATION STRATEGIES

Descriptive studies as well as clinical trials indicate that the influence of dissemination efforts on practice is maximized when conducted in an interactive manner, with ongoing monitoring. Lee and Garvin (2003) criticize most dissemination practices for modeling themselves after one-sided educational monologues. Communication is not a one-way process; one cannot successfully impart change by transferring knowledge to patients as if they were a vessel to fill, and dissemination techniques suffer equally from this unidirectional approach. Dissemination of EBT should be thought of as more information exchange than information provision. Researchers can share information about what treatments are efficacious, but they should also listen and respond to clinicians' perspectives on what information is needed, skepticism regarding the truthfulness and validity of findings, and perceptions of barriers to change. Interactive dissemination allows the dialogue to be personalized, making learning more experiential and increasing the provision of tacit knowledge (Barwick et al., 2005). When information is exchanged through personal, bi-directional interactions, trusting relationships, in which successful information exchange takes place, are more likely to develop. Consistent with motivational research regarding the importance of feedback on behavior, dissemination efforts should not be limited to one-time interactions, but should be spread out across time and incorporate feedback and reinforcement to clinicians and organizations.

DEVELOP EARLY, ONGOING RESEARCH-PRACTICE COLLABORATIONS

In their 2005 report, which found that the Matrix approach was adopted in only one of the eight clinics that were trained to use it, Guydish et al., discussed factors likely to affect adoption. The authors compared randomized clinical trials to spaceships that conduct foreign and invasive procedures at clinics, and then fly away never to be seen again. Indeed, researchers often enter clinics with a pre-formulated research question and plan, mandate strict, inflexible protocols, and then leave along with any resources or staff they may have brought with them. Little consideration is given to staff views of the merit or timeliness of the research question or the influence of the protocol on their therapeutic goals and values.

Allowing clinic staff to have an early influence on the development of research trials will allow projects to be modified to avoid potential barriers to adoption and can increase clinician investment in the projects.

Incorporating clinician input during the research-development phase may provide clinicians with an understanding of research protocol firewalls and allow them the flexibility they desire to be implemented in creation versus application. Early and ongoing clinician involvement may allow for studies to have both high and internal validity and adoption. It is important to acknowledge, however, that collaborative models require mutual respect, and reform-oriented policy makers may prefer to change the system more drastically. The issue of "top-down" dissemination versus a collaborative model deserves much more attention in the research literature on dissemination; which model is superior is an empirical question.

ATTEND TO PRACTICAL BARRIERS

Several dissemination models emphasize how important it is to assess readiness to change and the complexity of interventions when deciding what dissemination strategy to use. One would hope that the focus on dissemination of EBT is constant and as popular as Prochaska and DiClemente's (1992) Stages of Change (SOC) Model, which evolved into the Transtheoretical Model. The model has far-reaching influence and has been applied to a diversity of topics by different perspectives, such as obesity, co-occurring disorders from mental and medical treatment systems, and newspaper coverage of tobacco farming issues. Dissemination models that developed within the field emphasize the complex interaction between practical barriers and dissemination strategies. Barriers include policy emphasis on quick, punishment-oriented solutions to the drug problem, lack of resources to adopt new technologies, staff objections to using a scientific approach, interventions that are incompatible with the existing program (for example, medications are impractical when most programs have no medical staff), and a need to adapt treatments to the special needs of patients. Innovators interested in dissemination need to view these as real barriers, not as "clinical resistance" to a scientific approach.

As Miller et al. (2006) point out in their review, clinicians who learn through a craft model are more apt to learn from observation and personal experience rather than research dissemination outlets, such as academic journals or manuals. Knudsen et al. (2005) discovered that clinicians with a 12-step approach were less receptive to buprenorphine dissemination. This suggests that clinicians' personal backgrounds should be strongly considered when an evidence-based approach is introduced to a clinic; One's background can act as either a barrier or facilitator of diffusion. Also, as suggested by McCarty et al. (2004), allocating one's resources to effectively link up agents of EBTs with existing community treatment programs, is a necessary step in diffusion. In addition, given the heterogeneous substance abuse treatment settings and provider backgrounds, "matching" dissemination efforts to specific populations may well be warranted and deserves the attention of future research.

ATTEND TO POLICY

In addition to disseminating EBT to clinical settings, efforts to increase the adoption of effective programs should be aimed at governmental and other organizing institutions that provide funding, oversight, or training in the treatment of substance abuse. The relationship between research, treatment, and policy is complex, multi-directional, and requires ongoing information exchange to maximize outcome.

Several successful models for bridging the gap between research and policy are available in the state and federal arenas. At the level of the state legislature, the State of Oregon is implementing a policy that requires 75% of state funds for substance abuse treatment to go to EBT by July 2009 (Oregon Department of Human Services, 2005). At the federal level, the publication of an Institute of Medicine report, *Bridging the Gap Between Practice and Research* (Lamb, Greenlick, & McCarty, 1998), spurred the creation of several programs that bring relevant research results to the attention of the field. These programs include the NIDA Clinical Trials Network (Hanson, Leshner, & Tai, 2002), and two programs from the national Center for Substance Abuse Treatment: Practice Improvement Collaboratives (Gleghorn & Cotter, 2003), and Addiction Technology Transfer Centers (http://www.nattc.org/index.html). The field's current status is that little is known empirically about what dissemination strategies will most effectively facilitate the dissemination of EBT to policy makers. Some promising models are described above, but ultimately different techniques must be implemented and scientifically evaluated.

SPECULATION ON FUTURE DIRECTIONS FOR
TRANSLATIONAL DEVELOPMENTS

The scientific field of dissemination and implementation is at an early stage of recognizing problems and generating the principles that might be used to overcome them. The substance abuse field has aspects that make it different from others, including the cost of the problem, conflicting moral versus scientific understandings, disproportionate allocation of resources, and significant differences among researchers, practitioners, and policy makers. We recognize the budding state of dissemination research and encourage colleagues to take a cautionary approach to the stories that dominate the field today. While research indicates that there is indeed a significant gap between research and treatment, few controlled studies are available to suggest causal mechanisms of adoption. In addition, among the studies that have been conducted, lack of consistency in the measurement of independent, dependent, or mediating variables makes generalizations difficult.

Valuable research has been conducted on the dissemination of EBT, and more is needed to gain a comprehensive understanding of the phenomenon so that we may make scientifically grounded recommendations. New and innovative research opportunities are presenting themselves, in areas that can have serious impact on the well being of individuals.

ESTABLISHMENT OF METHODOLOGICAL STANDARDS

A common language and consistent measurement are needed for substance abuse dissemination research. Measurement of dissemination varies widely across the dissemination outcome studies that have been conducted to date. Proximal measures of outcome, such as changes in clinician attitudes and motivation to change are commonly used. Yet, little is known about the relationship between these measures and actual adoption. Additionally, adoption itself is often measured using self-report; few studies use actual treatment integrity measures of outcome. Lastly, despite evidence that rates of adoption tend to diminish across time, few standards regarding follow-up length have been established.

CHANGING TECHNOLOGY

Dissemination studies in the area of substance abuse field have indicated that face-to-face interventions are far more effective than printed materials, videos, and other impersonal approaches. We echo the comment of Backer, David, and Soucy (1995) that effective dissemination is a personal process that can result in organizational improvements. Yet technology is advancing rapidly, so that in-person interventions do not necessarily need to be "face-to-face." Advancements in communications can have drastic impact on EBT dissemination, including interactive use of Internet and video conferencing, dissemination chat rooms, and live-line distance supervision. The attitude that "the world is flat" (Friedman, 2005) implies that technology can make EBT interventions more available than ever before to a range of geographically distant sites. Dissemination research has barely moved into the 21st century, and it is likely that upcoming studies will explore ways to exploit the availability of improved technology.

ECONOMIC STUDIES

While several studies indicate that in-person dissemination is more effective, and continuing feedback elicits longer-lasting results, there is a need to study the cost-effectiveness of dissemination interventions involving different levels of intensity and offered in staged designs. It may be that low-cost dissemination strategies can draw attention to an effective technique, and those who are likely to use the intervention can then participate in more intensive training to promote adoption in their settings. Also, small differences in dissemination efficiency can have large effect sizes in societal savings. Cost-effectiveness studies can make valuable contributions to our knowledge base.

ADOPTION AS AN OUTCOME OF CLINICAL INTERVENTION TRIALS

We suggest that trials of EBT interventions should plan from the beginning to implement their project in such a way that the clinic will be able to adopt the intervention, if it is effective. Activities that facilitate adoption could include training existing clinical staff as "interventionists" (rather than bringing in outside clinicians), offering training conducted by local experts that could be available after the trial (rather than sending staff to distant training), attending to cost and reimbursement issues with the clinic that provides the intervention, and making results available to the clinic as soon as possible. More research is needed to understand research activities that facilitate and hinder adoption of interventions.

TAILORING DISSEMINATION TO RECIPIENTS

Researchers, clinicians, and policy makers in the substance abuse area have commonalities, but effective dissemination strategies need to acknowledge their different needs. In the researcher's ideal system, information regarding EBT would be effectively disseminated from scientists to policy makers, who would use this information to create funding and oversight policies. However, researchers attempt to reach both the groups through publication in peer-reviewed journals, while policy decisions are often influenced by stories and testimony regarding recovery successes and failure. At the National Conference of State Legislators it was suggested that state legislators are not likely to rely on information from academic sources when making decisions (Chandler, 2006). Legislators cited difficulty accessing material and the long lag between problem recognition and scientific results as reasons for not utilizing research results.

INVOLVEMENT OF INTEREST GROUPS AND DISCIPLINES

Unfortunately, the time-consuming and involved nature of clinical research often leaves little time to pursue policy issues. Chandler (2006) summarized factors that have been found to be helpful in influencing public policy, including knowledge about policy processes, providing relevant and timely information, and building strong relationships with interest groups and decision makers. Public interest groups often mediate communication between researchers and policy makers and rely heavily on grassroots organizations, lobbyists, and ethnic associations when making decisions about how to receive research results (Jackson-Elmoore, 2005). These groups are often formed of some combination of concerned citizens, researchers, clinicians, and policy makers that have a vested personal or professional interest in promoting positive policy change in the area of substance abuse.

In addition, professional associations can have important roles. For example, the Association for Medical Education and Research in Substance Abuse (AMERSA) was designed to influence policy at the university training level (Samet, Galanter, & Bridden, 2006). This group of experts seeks to advance substance abuse education by advising national and international organizations regarding state-of-the-art scientific information and education strategies. AMERSA offers standards, strategic plans, and recommendations to inform the federal government and others about faculty development in substance abuse. Currently, there is no association formally devoted to translating addiction science into practice, but this may be a development worthy of consideration in the next decade.

CONCLUSION

Upon reflection, it seems ironic that, as clinical researchers promoting the use of EBT, we neglected to apply scientific evidence tests and standards to our own dissemination efforts. Many strategies we use are inconsistent with the principles of change that compose the EBT that we promote. We would not independently create treatment plans for patients with whom we had not established rapport, tell them what changes to make, monitor these changes for a short period of time, end the relationship, and expect the changes to endure. Nor would we expect our patients to access and search through a large database of difficult-to-interpret treatment plans and expect them to apply the principles to their current circumstance. Clinical researchers would be well suited to use what we already know, based on our work with clients and test those principles as they apply to dissemination. Some of the most salient conclusions of a century of clinical research may prove equally as effective when applied to health professionals. These principles include understanding and respecting the goals and values of the individual, forming a strong working alliance, providing accurate empathy, and being non-judgmental and non-confrontational.

During an interview in the Guydish et al. (2005) study a participant commented:

> There wasn't a whole lot of thought in the beginning of any of our studies about what happens. The presumption has been, 'We'll find truth out there, and we'll publish the truth, and we'll let people know what happened, and something will magically happen, and the truth will be used' (p. 540).

The magical something identified by a qualitative interview participant is diffusion into treatment programs, and for it to successfully take place, more communication needs to occur between researchers, community treatment providers, and policy makers.

Additionally, continual communication must occur, with a conscious effort to see each other's perspective. Researchers, community treatment providers, and policy makers all face external pressure, from pressure to generate positive outcomes to adapting to the ever-changing funding sources, which depend on political climate. To avoid artificial agreement among treatment shareholders, communication needs to occur so that the field does not fall prey to Irving Janis's "groupthink," whereby dissenting opinions are ignored, resulting in false consensus which can result in adverse results (Riggio, 2003). As Carise et al. (2002), made clear in their previously mentioned collaboration story, all shareholders involved in the field have the same goal: To deliver effective substance treatment. However, our language and focus can act as barriers to effective communication and delivery of EBT. Although the focus on translational science is recent, the stories, studies, reviews, models, and policy developments discussed here can facilitate the study and delivery diffusion of evidence-based care.

ACKNOWLEDGMENTS

Supported in part by grants U10DA15815, R01 DA14922, P50DA09253, and T32DA07250 from National Institutes of Health.

REFERENCES

Addiction Technology Transfer Center Network. (2004). *The Change Book: A Blueprint for Technology Transfer* (2nd ed.). Kansas City, MO: ATTC National Office.

Addis, M. E., Wade, W. A., & Hatgis, C. (1999). Barriers to dissemination of evidence-based practices: Addressing practitioners' concerns about manual-based psychotherapies. *Clinical Psychology: Science and Practice, 6*, 430–441.

Arkfen, C. L., Agius, E., & Dickson, M. W. (2005). Clinicians' information sources for new substance abuse treatment. *Addictive Behaviors, 30*, 1592–1596.

Backer, T. E. (1991). *Drug Abuse Technology Transfer*. Rockville, MD: National Institute on Drug Abuse.

Backer, T. E., David, S. L., & Soucy, G. (Eds.). (1995). *Reviewing the Behavioral Science Knowledge Base on Technology Transfer*. (NIDA Research Monograph 155). Rockville, MD: National Institute on Drug Abuse.

Barwick, M. A., Boydell, K. M., Stasiulis, E., Ferguson, H. B., Blase, K., & Fixsen, D. (2005). *Knowledge Transfer and Evidence-based Practice in Children's Mental Health*. Toronto, ON: Children's Mental Health Ontario.

Carise, D., Cornely, W., & Gurel, O. (2002). A successful researcher-practitioner collaboration in substance abuse treatment. *Journal of substance Abuse Treatment, 23*, 157–162.

Carise, D., & Gurel, O. (2003). Integrating assessment technology with treatment – the DENS project. In J. L. Sorensen, R. A. Rawson, J. Guydish, & J. E. Zweben (Eds.), *Drug Abuse Treatment Through Collaboration: Practice and Researcher Partnerships that Work* (pp. 181–195). Washington, DC: American Psychological Association.

Chandler, S. M. (2006). University involvement in public policy deliberation: An example. *Professional Psychology: Research and Practice, 37*, 154–157.

Epstein, E. E., & McCrady, B. S. (1998). Behavioral couples treatment of alcohol and drug use disorders: Current status and innovations *Clinical Psychology Review, Special Issue: Behavioral Couples Therapy, 18*, 689–711.

Fals-Stewart, W., & Birchler, G. R. (2001). A national survey of the use of couples therapy in substance abuse treatment. *Journal of Substance Abuse Treatment, 20*, 277–283.

Fals-Stewart, W., O'Farrell, T. J., Birchler, G. R., Golden, J., & Logsdon, T. (2004a). Behavioral couples therapy for substance abuse: Rationale, methods, and findings. *Science and Practice Perspectives, 2*, 30–43.

Fals-Stewart, W., Logsdon, T., & Birchler, G. R. (2004b). Diffusion of an empirically supported treatment for substance abuse: An organizational autopsy of technology transfer success and failure. *Clinical Psychology: Science and Practice, 11*, 177–182.

Friedman, T. L. (2005). The *World is Flat: A Brief History of the Twenty-first Century*. New York, NY: Farrar, Straus, & Giroux.

Gleghorn, A. A., & Cotter, F. (2003). National and local perspectives on the center for substance abuses treatment practice/research collaborative and practice improvement collaborative initiatives. In J. L. Sorensen, R. A. Rawson, J. Guydish, & J. E. Zweben (Eds.), *Drug Abuse Treatment Through Collaboration: Practice and Research Partnerships that Work* (pp. 213–225). Washington, DC: American Psychological Association.

Guydish, J., Manser, S. T., Jessup, M., Tajima, B., & Sears, C. (2005). Multi-level assessment protocol (MAP) for adoption in multi-site clinical trials. *Journal of Drug Issues, 35*, 529–546.

Hall, S. M., Loeb, P., Coyne, K., & Cooper, J. (1981a). Increasing employment in ex-heroin addicts, I: Criminal justice sample. *Behavioral Therapy, 12*, 443–452.

Hall, S. M., Loeb, P., LeVois, M., & Cooper, J. (1981b). Increasing employment in ex-heroin addicts, II: Methadone maintenance sample. *Behavioral Therapy, 12*, 453–460.

Hall, S. M., Loeb, P., Norton, J., & Yang, R. (1977). Improving vocational placement in drug treatment clients: A pilot study. *Addictive Behaviors, 15*, 438–441.

Hanson, G. R., Leshner, A. I., & Tai, B. (2002). Putting drug abuse research to use in real-life settings. *Journal of Substance Abuse Treatment, 23*(2), 69–70.

Jackson-Elmoore, C. (2005). Informing state policymakers: Opportunities for social workers. *Social Work, 50*, 251–261.

Knudsen, H. K., Ducharme, L. J., Roman, P. M., & Link, T. J. (2005). Buprenorphine diffusion: The attitudes of substance abuse treatment counselors. *Journal of Substance Abuse Treatment, 29*, 95–106.

Lamb, S., Greenlick, M. R., & McCarty, D. (Eds.). (1998). *Bridging the Gap between Practice and Research*. Washington, DC: National Academy Press.

Lee, R. G., & Garvin, T. (2003). Moving from information transfer to information exchange in health and health care. *Social Science and Medicine*, *56*, 449–464.

McCarty, D., Rieckman, T., Green, C., Gallon, S., & Knudsen, J. (2004). Training rural practitioners to use buprenorphine using The Change Book to facilitate technology transfer. *Journal of Substance Abuse Treatment*, *26*(3), 203–208.

McNeal, R. B., & Hanson, W. B. (1995). An examination of strategies for gaining convergent validity in natural experiments: D.A.R.E. as an illustrative case study. *Evaluation Review*, *19*, 131–158.

Miller, W. R., Sorensen, J. L., Selzer, J. A., & Brigham, J. S. (2006). Disseminating evidence-based practices in substance abuse treatment: A review with suggestions. *Journal of Substance Abuse Treatment*, *31*, 25–39.

Miller, W. R., Yahne, C. E., Moyers, T. B., Martinez, J., & Pirritano, M. (2004). A randomized clinical trial of methods to help clinicians learn motivational interviewing. *Journal of Consulting and Clinical Psychology*, *72*(6), 1050–1062.

Oregon Department of Human Services. (2005). *Implementation of Evidence-based Practices (EBP) in Oregon*. Retrieved July 12, 2005 from Oregon Department of Human Services, Office of Mental Health and Addiction Services web site: http://www.oregon.gov/DHS/mentalhealth/ebp//main.shtml

Prochaska, J. O., & DiClemente, C. C. (1992). Stages of change in the modification of problem behaviors. *Progress in Behavior Modification*, *28*, 183–218.

Rawson, R. A., Marinelli-Casey, P., Anglin, M. D., Dickow, A., Frazier, Y., Gallagher, C., Galloway, G., Herrell, J. M., Huber, A., McCann, M. J., Obert, J., Pennell, S., Reiber, C., Vandersloot, D., & Zweben, J. and the Methamphetamine Treatment Project Corporate Authors. (2004). A multi-site comparison of psychosocial approaches for the treatment of methamphetamine dependence. *Addiction*, *99*, 708–717.

Riggio, R. E. (2003). *Introduction to Industrial/Organizational Psychology* (4th ed.). Upper Saddle River, NJ: Prentice-Hall.

Roman, P. M., & Johnson, J. A. (2002). Adoption and implementation of new technologies in substance abuse treatment. *Journal of Substance Abuse Treatment*, *22*(4), 211–218.

Samet, J. H., Galanter, M., & Bridden, C. (2006). Association for medical education and research in substance abuse. *Addiction*, *101*, 10–15.

Simpson, D. D. (2002). A conceptual framework for transferring research to practice. *Journal of Substance Abuse Treatment*, *22*(4), 171–182.

Sorensen, J. L., Hall, S. M., Loeb, P., Allen, T., Glaser, E., & Greenberg, P. D. (1988). Dissemination of a job seekers' workshop to drug treatment programs. *Behavior Therapy*, *19*, 143–155.

Sorensen, J. L., Lin, C. Y., & Sera, R. E. (2004). *Technology Transfer in Drug Abuse Treatment: Annotated Bibliography* (2nd ed.). San Francisco, University of California, San Francisco. Internet resource available at: http://ctndisseminationlibrary.org/PDF/2004_Sorensen_01.pdf. Accessed 7-6-06.

Thomas, C. P., Wallack, S. S., Lee, S., McCarty, D., & Swift, R. (2003). Research to practice: Adoption of naltrexone in alcoholism treatment. *Journal of Substance Abuse Treatment*, *24*(1), 1–11.

West, S. L., & O'Neal, K. L. (2004). Project D.A.R.E. outcome effectiveness revisited. *American Journal of Public Health*, *94*, 1027–1029.

CHAPTER 18

Alcohol Screening and Intervention in Medical and Surgical Settings

Scott H. Stewart[1,2] and Peter M. Miller[1]

[1]Center for Drug and Alcohol Programs, Department of Psychiatry and Behavioral Sciences, Charleston, SC, USA

[2]Division of General Internal Medicine, Department of Medicine, Medical University of South Carolina, Charleston, SC, USA

Abstract: Heavy alcohol consumption and alcohol use disorders cause or exacerbate a number of medical conditions and surgical complications. Valid and reliable self-report and alcohol biomarker measures are available to detect hazardous drinking in medical and surgical settings. Brief intervention strategies have also been developed and tested. However, clinical research alone will not change practice and more research is needed on variables related to the successful dissemination and implementation of screening, intervention and referral. Medical management of alcohol use disorders, including pharmacotherapy, in medical and surgical settings is a fruitful area of future investigations.

CURRENT STATE OF THE SCIENCE

Given the high prevalence and cost of alcohol misuse in direct patient care settings (Reid, Fiellin, & O'Connor, 1999; Cherpitel et al., 2005a; Cherpitel et al., 2005b; Spies et al., 2001), effective detection and management of harmful alcohol use is essential. This chapter will review recent research that impacts detection and treatment, and discuss directions for future research aimed at improving care.

The term "risky drinking" is used to designate detrimental drinking patterns (hazardous drinking and drinking above health–related guidelines) in the absence of an alcohol use disorder. "Alcohol use disorder" refers to alcohol abuse and/or dependence in the DSM–IV classification (American Psychiatric Association, 1994), and harmful drinking and dependence in the ICD classification (World Health Organization, 1992).

REVIEW OF DETECTION RESEARCH

Self-Report Instruments

Self-report instruments that have been developed for detecting alcohol use disorders typically focus on the adverse consequences of heavy drinking. Those that are more accurate in detecting risky drinking emphasize the assessment of consumption. Regardless of which particular instrument is used, positive screens should be followed-up with a more comprehensive assessment of current drinking patterns and indicators of alcohol use disorders.

Screening brevity is essential in medical and surgical settings. Thus, only instruments that can typically be administered in one or two minutes and have been validated in medical and surgical settings are discussed in this chapter (Table 1).

Table 1
Suggested Use of Brief, Self-Report Screening Instruments in Medical and Surgical Settings*

Instrument	Detection	
	Risky drinking	Alcohol use disorders
Heavy-drinking item	√	
AUDIT	√	√
AUDIT-C	√	
FAST[†]	√	√
CAGE		√
CAGE-QF	√	√
Brief-MAST		√
Short-MAST		√
RAPS4		√
RAPS4-QF	√	√

*Instruments for risky drinking detection include items assessing quantity and/or frequency of drinking. Instruments for detecting alcohol use disorders include items assessing alcohol-related problems.
[†]Has only been validated using the AUDIT as a criterion.

The most rudimentary alcohol screen used by medical personnel is a quantity-frequency question, asking if any alcohol has been consumed over the past year and, if so, then how often and, on average, how much. A modification of this approach is currently recommended by the National Institute on Alcohol Abuse and Alcoholism (NIAAA) in primary care medical settings. In this adaptation, patients are asked, "How many times in the past year have you had 5 or more drinks (for men)/4 or more drinks (for women) (U.S. Department of Health and Human Services, 2005). This one question alone has been shown to have useful characteristics for detecting risky drinking (Canagasaby & Vinson, 2005; Bradley et al., 2003; Williams & Vinson, 2001; Gordon et al., 2001). However, use of a single question is likely to have limited specificity, and, thus, may lead to unnecessary interventions.

The Alcohol Use Disorders Identification Test (AUDIT) is a 10-item instrument designed by the World Health Organization (WHO) to detect risky drinking in primary health care settings (Saunders et al., 1993). Total scores range from 0 to 40, with scores of 8 or higher having positive predictive value for risky drinking or alcohol use disorders. Some authorities recommend a graded rather than dichotomous interpretation, with intensity of treatment proportional to the score (Babor et al., 2005). A number of briefer instruments have been developed from the AUDIT, including the AUDIT-C (Bush et al., 1998) and the Fast Alcohol Screening Test (FAST) (Hodgson et al., 2002, 2003). The AUDIT-C includes the first three AUDIT items dealing with alcohol consumption and compares favorably with the parent instrument in medical settings. The FAST uses a stepwise approach that first applies the single third AUDIT item concerning maximum number of drinks on one occasion. If positive, three additional AUDIT items are used to further assess for drinking problems. This approach seems to retain most of the information from the full AUDIT, enhances the expected low specificity of using a heavy drinking item alone, and has the advantage of a short average administration time (most patients will not need the additional 3 items). However, the FAST has only been studied using the AUDIT as a criterion. Research findings on the AUDIT have been thoroughly reviewed in a recent paper by Reinert and Allen (2002).

CAGE (Mayfield, McLeod, & Hall, 1974) is an acronym for four questions: (1) Have you ever tried to *cut-back* the amount you drink? (2) Have you been *annoyed* by people talking about your alcohol use? (3) Have you ever felt *guilty* about your drinking? and (4) Have you ever had a drink in the morning to steady your nerves (*eye-opener*)? A positive response to two or more items suggests an alcohol use disorder. A cut-off of one positive item increases sensitivity and may be more suitable for screening, although at a considerably increased risk of false positive results. The CAGE is probably best suited for use when screening for alcohol abuse and/or dependence. More sensitive instruments are available when screening is intended to identify risky drinking. Alternatively, to address this limitation, using a quantity-frequency question combined with the CAGE (Saitz et al., 2003; Bradley et al., 2001) is suggested.

The 13-item Short Michigan Alcoholism Screening Test (MAST) (Selzer, Vinokur, & Van Rooijen, 1975) and 10-item Brief MAST (Pokorny, Miller, & Kaplan, 1972) are versions of the 25-item MAST (Selzer, 1971). Like the CAGE, the MAST versions focus on adverse consequences of drinking. The Brief-MAST has reasonable specificity for detecting those with self-recognized drinking-related consequences, but may be less sensitive than the AUDIT and versions of the AUDIT for less severe alcohol problems (Hearne, Connolly, & Sheehan, 2002; MacKenzie, Langa, & Brown, 1996). Similar to the CAGE, use of the shorter derivatives of the MAST may be best when detection of alcohol use disorders rather than risky drinking is of interest.

The Rapid Alcohol Problems Screen (RAPS), RAPS4, and RAPS4-QF were largely developed for use in emergency care settings. The RAPS is a 5-item instrument that incorporates items from the AUDIT (guilt and role failure), Brief MAST (losing friends), and TWEAK (Russell et al., 1991) (having blackouts or need for an eye opener) (Cherpitel, 2005b). The RAPS4 omits the item concerning losing friends because of drinking (Cherpitel, 2000). The RAPS4-QF contains two items about consumption patterns, specifically having 5 or more drinks on any occasion in the past year and drinking at least monthly (Cherpitel, 2002). In emergency medical settings, the RAPS4 is a reasonable screen for alcohol use disorders, and the RAPS4-QF incorporates the ability to screen for risky drinking (Cherpitel, 2005).

Biomarkers

Several alcohol biomarkers have potential clinical utility (Table 2) in medical and surgical settings. The optimal biomarker depends on the nature of the clinical question. Specifically, is there interest in acute toxic effects of alcohol, elucidating the possible role of recent or sub-acute ingestion in a clinical problem, or potential effects of frequent, heavy, consumption? Measurement of alcohol itself (i.e. through blood alcohol concentration assessment) is all that is needed for acute ingestion. This subject has been reviewed recently by Swift (2003).

Recent Ingestion

The main limitation of direct ethanol measurement (i.e., blood alcohol concentration) is rapid elimination. Measurement of longer-lived non-oxidative ethanol metabolites can improve insight into alcohol-related disease or injury.

Early work on ethyl glucuronide (EtG) as a marker for recent ingestion has been discussed by Wurst and Metzger (2002). EtG is an ethanol metabolite resulting from the enzymatic conjugation of ethanol with glucuronic acid. EtG is detectable

Table 2
A Selection of Biomarkers for Recent and Chronically Heavy Drinking

Recent ingestion	Window for detection after last drink
Detectable with modest ingestion	
Urinary ethyl glucuronide (EtG)*	Up to 3–4 days
Urinary 5-HTOL/5-HIAA*	Up to 24 h
FAEE's (serum)*	Up to 24 h
Chronically heavy ingestion	
Require weeks of heavy drinking	
Gamma-glutamyltransferase	Normalizes over~1–2 months
Carbohydrate-deficient transferrin	Normalizes over~2–4 weeks
Phosphatidyl ethanol*	Eliminated over~2 weeks
Beta-hexosaminidase*	Normalizes of~2–4 weeks
Sialic acid index of apolipoprotein J*	Normalizes over~2 months

*Require additional validation in medical-surgical settings.

in urine for about 3–4 days following the last alcoholic drink, and has been found to correlate well with other alcohol markers and self-reports of recent consumption and abstinence (Wurst & Metzger, 2002). Additional work suggests that, at an optimal cut-off of 0.145 mg/l determined by ROC analysis, the test has high sensitivity (83.5%) for detecting drinking within the past 4 days, and a modest specificity of 68.3% (Wurst et al., 2004). However, the authors note that there are a number of individuals with positive markers for very recent ingestion (ethanol and/or elevated urinary 5-HTOL/5-HIAA ratio) who report no use within 4 days. This suggests that the specificity of urinary EtG is underestimated by using self-report as a criterion. Urinary EtG was evaluated in a group of healthy, male volunteers who consumed various quantities of alcohol (ranging from 64 to 184 g) over 6 h. Sensitivity of detecting any EtG (> 0.1 mg/l) was 100% up to 39.3 h following drinking cessation, with a sensitivity of 76.5% at 54.3 h (Borucki et al., 2005). Clinically, it will probably be most useful to use a low cut-off, and consider a positive test as indicative of some ethanol ingestion within the past 3–5 days, but additional validation in medical and surgical settings is required prior to routine use.

Other tests for recent ingestion include fatty acid ethyl esters, methanol, and urinary ratio of 5-HTOL/5-HIAA. However, because these markers in blood or urine are only useful for very recent ingestion, hours to perhaps 1 or 2 days post–drinking cessation, they have less potential clinical utility in medical and surgical settings than EtG.

Chronic, Heavy Ingestion

Detection of chronic, heavy alcohol consumption is of most interest in medical and surgical settings. A common marker for this pattern of drinking is gamma glutamyltransferase (GGT), and this enzyme has been thoroughly reviewed by

Whitfield (2001). For detecting chronic, heavy drinking, i.e., 60–80 g or more per day, GGT elevation has a sensitivity of approximately 50%, with an approximate 70% specificity in general clinical populations. GGT values normalize within 1–2 months of abstinence. Specificity is likely to be lower in inpatient settings, where other factors (e.g., anti-convulsive medications, biliary disease) will commonly result in GGT elevation. GGT is positively correlated with body mass index, and may be less sensitive in women compared to men.

Chronic, heavy drinking can decrease the carbohydrate content of transferrin (reviewed by Sillanaukee et al., 2001), rendering carbohydrate-deficient transferrin (CDT), a marker for this pattern of drinking. CDT elevation typically requires an average of 60 g or more of alcohol consumption daily for the past 2 weeks or longer. Elevated levels tend to decrease by 30% or normalize after 2–4 weeks of abstinence or reduced alcohol consumption (Borg, 1993). Some work suggests consumption at even higher levels may be necessary for CDT elevation (Lesch et al., 1996). Reviews (Koch et al., 2004; Allen et al., 2000) illustrate that sensitivity of the CDT assays is not optimal, but specificity is high, ranging from 77% to 100%. In clinical settings, sensitivity is likely somewhere between 40% and 60% (Anton, 2001). Fleming et al. (2004) have reviewed factors other than heavy drinking that influence CDT levels. False negative results are more likely in women, binge drinkers, and those with severe blood loss. This latter factor may be especially relevant when screening trauma or emergency department patients. False positives are more likely with advanced liver disease and certain genetic variants. Of note, GGT and CDT have similar validity for detecting chronic heavy drinking, but are poorly correlated. This has led to evaluations of their combined use, which may increase sensitivity at a minimal loss of specificity (Litten, Allen, & Fertig, 1995; Huseby, Nilssen, & Kanitz, 1997; Allen, Sillanaukee, & Anton, 1999; Sillanaukee & Olsson, 2001). While such combinations appear best for men, GGT alone may be preferable in women (Chen et al., 2003).

A promising marker is phophatidylethanol, formed in the presence of ethanol by phospholipase D. This biomarker tends to be elevated when heavy drinking has occurred for about 2 or more weeks (Varga et al., 1998), and appears to be detectable for up to 2 weeks following cessation of drinking (Hansson et al., 1997). Phosphatidylethanol levels do not appear to increase following a binge-drinking episode, nor with more frequent but moderate consumption.

Conigrave et al. (2003) have reviewed research on traditional laboratory markers, including aspartate transaminase (AST), alanine transaminase (ALT), and mean corpuscular volume (MCV). All of these markers are relatively insensitive, although MCV is somewhat more specific. While not suitable for screening, drinking habits should be thoroughly evaluated as part of the diagnostic assessment for abnormal findings, particularly if the AST/ALT ratio is greater than 2.

Other potential markers for chronic heavy drinking include beta-hexosaminidase (Stowell et al., 1997), sialic acid (Ponnio et al., 1999), and sialic acid index of apolipoprotein J (Ghosh, Hale, & Lakshman, 2001). These markers have clinical potential, but have been understudied relative to other markers such as CDT. Additional validation is required in patient-care settings.

In addition to their use in screening, biomarkers are also clinically useful for monitoring drinking behavior after brief intervention and/or treatment (Miller, 2004). In alcohol-dependent patients, a 30% decrease in either GGT or CDT is indicative of abstinence or a significant reduction in drinking, while a 30% increase might indicate relapse (Anton et al., 2002). Biomarker monitoring with routine feedback to patients about their results has been shown, along with brief intervention, to reduce drinking, sick days lost from work, hospitalizations, and mortality over a 6–8 year period compared to a non-treatment control group (Kristenson, 1987). Further development of biomarkers thus has therapeutic potential as well as diagnostic utility.

REVIEW OF TREATMENT RESEARCH

Risky Drinking

Brief interventions are the standard of care for risky drinking based on a large body of research, summarized in several meta-analyses (Moyer et al., 2002; Poikolanen, 1999; Wilk, Jensen, & Havighurst, 1997; D'Onofrio & Degutis, 2002). Typically, after a positive screening result, a brief counseling intervention is conducted, using a FRAMES approach (Miller & Sanchez, 1994), often accompanied by a discussion of medical concerns and at least one follow-up session. FRAMES is an acronym encompassing *feedback* about drinking behavior and associated problems, an emphasis on personal *responsibility* for change, providing specific *advice* and a *menu* for how to comply with this advice, showing *empathy* for the patient, and enhancing the patient's *self-efficacy*. In primary care settings, brief interventions roughly double the probability of drinking reduction over 6–12 months, and result in an average reduction of about one drink daily relative to controls. Brief interventions may also save health costs (Fleming et al., 2002; Gentilello et al., 2005), decrease injuries (Gentilello et al., 1999), and save lives (Cuijpers, Riper, & Lemmers, 2004).

Despite convincing effectiveness research, screening and brief intervention in medical settings remains the exception rather than the rule (D'Amico et al., 2005; Coffield et al., 2001). In recognition of the fact that randomized controlled effectiveness trials alone will not change practice, researchers have evaluated provider-level factors that limit implementation. Barriers include lack of time, low provider self-efficacy in delivering alcohol treatment, lack of simple guidelines, uncertainty about need to intervene for risky drinking, interruption of normal patient care, confidentiality of the medical record, and reimbursement

(Barry et al., 2004; Schermer et al., 2003; Ferguson, Ries, & Russo, 2003; Beich, Gannik, & Malterud, 2002; McAvoy et al., 2001; Miller et al., 2006a; Rivara et al., 2000; Kaner et al., 1999a).

Additional research has compared methods for dissemination and implementation of screening and brief intervention (McCormick et al., 1999; Hansen et al., 1999; Gomel et al., 1998; Lock et al., 1999). This work has shown that telemarketing or academic detailing (visits to primary medical care providers by trained personnel) results in more implementation than mailing guideline information, and telemarketing seems to be the most cost-effective approach. Following dissemination, practice-based training with telephone support has increased implementation of screening and brief intervention (Kaner et al., 1999b). However, considering the number of generalist physicians originally approached for participation and less than full implementation by participating physicians, the overall utilization and screening rates were low.

Alcohol Use Disorders

Counseling

Treatment of alcohol use disorders remains primarily in addiction and mental health settings or with mutual-help groups (e.g., Alcoholics Anonymous). In screening and brief intervention programs, most experts recommend referral to specialty care for patients suspected of alcohol dependence. However, of importance to medical practitioners, research has shown that relatively brief and simple counseling strategies coupled with naltrexone (i.e., an initial 40–60 min session followed by eight 15–30 min sessions over 16 weeks) can be as effective as more intensive strategies (i.e., 12–20 longer sessions over 16 weeks incorporating motivational interviewing and individualized treatment plans) (Anton et al., 2006; Pettinati et al., 2004). Additional research has demonstrated that treatment of medical patients in typical clinical settings is effective (Kiritze-Topor et al., 2004; O'Malley et al., 2003; Willenbring & Olson, 1999). Despite these encouraging findings, it is unknown if pharmacotherapy with very brief counseling interventions (e.g., 5–15 min with less frequent follow-up) suitable for primary medical settings would be effective.

Pharmacotherapy

Advances in pharmacotherapy (Myrick & Anton, 2004) suggest a potentially greater role for health care providers in the treatment of alcohol use disorders. Several meta-analyses of the effects of naltrexone and acamprosate have been published (Srisurapanont & Jarusuraisin, 2005; Bouza et al., 2004; Streeton & Whelan, 2001; Kranzler & van Kirk, 2001, Garbutt et al., 1999).

These reviews concluded that both medications have significant but small effects, although the efficacy of acamprosate has been challenged by a recent large trial (Anton et al., 2006). Naltrexone may be most efficacious in preventing relapse rather than maintaining abstinence, while acamprosate may be better for maintaining abstinence. Kranzler and van Kirk (2001) point out that these medications, relative to pharmacotherapy for depression, have small effects, and that this may limit widespread use. In addition to naltrexone and acamprosate, strong evidence exists for the efficacy of topiramate in drinking reduction (Johnson et al., 2003), and for ondansetron in early onset alcoholics (Kranzler et al., 2003; Johnson et al., 2000). Currently, researchers are evaluating the relative effects of these and other medications used alone and in combination. Importantly, pharmacotherapy for alcohol use disorders is underutilized, even in addiction treatment settings. Reasons for this appear to be related to physician knowledge, concerns about time needed for management, patient reluctance to take medication, adverse medication effects, price, and small effect sizes (Mark et al., 2003a, 2003b). For naltrexone, clinicians may also be concerned about difficulty in emergency pain management and the potential for narcotic overdosing in acute care as naltrexone is metabolized.

CURRENT IMPLICATIONS FOR DETECTION AND TREATMENT

Many patients with hazardous drinking patterns and severe alcohol use disorders are undetected in medical and surgical settings (Saitz et al., 1997). Research has firmly established that detection can be improved with the use of self-report screening instruments, supplemented with laboratory biomarkers for recent and chronic heavy drinking when needed (Miller et al., 2006b). Screening instruments could be administered by practice staff, reserving physician time for those with positive results. Positive screens should be followed by a more detailed assessment of alcohol involvement as well as potential social consequences and impaired control. Useful diagnostic questions in assessing alcohol use disorders have been disseminated by NIAAA (U.S. Department of Health and Human Services, 2005). If dependence or abuse is suspected then referral to an addiction specialist is appropriate. Referral pathways should be as clear as they would be for referral of traditional medical and surgical disorders, and might be initiated through mental health managed care organizations, public-domain substance abuse services, or web-based services such as the Substance Abuse and Mental Health Service Administration (SAMSHA) website (http://findtreatment.samhsa.gov, accessed 2/15/06), which identifies facilities, contact information, treatment services offered, and insurance accepted.

When providing advice to abstain, health care providers must consider the potential for serious withdrawal, including delirium, seizure, and autonomic instability. Patients with a history of severe withdrawal, current heavy drinking, or unstable medical or psychiatric conditions should be referred to a detoxification facility for treatment. Alternatively, for lower-risk patients, outpatient detoxification regimens are possible, if reliable, short-term, daily follow-up is practical (Blondell, 2005).

In addition to referral, medical care providers should also consider prescribing naltrexone or acamprosate to eligible patients, particularly in regions where pharmacotherapy may not be available in the majority of addiction treatment facilities (McLellan & Meyers, 2004). This provides a greater direct role in treatment relative to specialty referral alone, and must include follow-up similar to any other actively managed chronic condition. The optimal duration of medication treatment is unknown given the brief duration of pharmacotherapy trials (Srisurapanont & Jarusuraisin, 2005), but 3–6 months of treatment with continuing follow-up after cessation of pharmacotherapy is reasonable. If alcohol misuse is limited to risky drinking, brief advice in a FRAMES-like style (Miller & Sanchez, 1994) and accompanied by at least one follow-up visit is indicated. Feasible roles for primary medical care providers in helping patients with a spectrum of drinking problems have been thoroughly reviewed by Fiellin, Reid, and O'Connor (2000), including their important role in relapse prevention (Friedmann, Saitz, & Samet, 1998).

Biomarkers for chronic heavy consumption such as GGT and CDT would be helpful in situations where self-report is unobtainable or when it is considered to be unreliable, but limited sensitivities mean that negative results should be interpreted with caution (Miller, 2004; Miller & Anton, 2004; Miller, Anton, & Dominick, 2005). Application in circumstances where acute alcohol-related risks need to be considered (e.g., risk-stratifying for withdrawal, immunosuppression in some perioperative settings, or in trauma facilities) seems justified (Neumann & Spies, 2003). Use in primary care medical settings however is less straightforward, and the pros and cons of confronting patients with the result of an imperfect test should be considered, particularly if measurement follows suspect self-report. In such circumstances, depending on the acuity of the clinical presentation, spending time in cultivating a trusting relationship with the patient may be preferable. Despite this concern, preliminary evidence suggests that patients are not offended by biomarker utilization (Miller et al., 2006b; Miller, Thomas, & Mallin, 2006c), a finding that should be confirmed in additional patient samples. Biomarkers of recent ingestion have potential clinical applications for monitoring patients in treatment or for investigating potentially alcohol-related disease, but such assays are not yet widely available, nor have they been well validated in direct patient-care settings.

DIRECTIONS FOR FUTURE TRANSLATIONAL RESEARCH

SCREENING AND BRIEF INTERVENTION FOR RISKY DRINKING

Ample research on screening and brief intervention for risky drinking has been conducted in medical and surgical settings (including trauma), and additional validity data for brief self-report instruments and short-term effectiveness data for brief interventions are not required. Rather, there is a pressing need for investigations into translational methods to facilitate the routine implementation of evidence-based detection and treatment methods in healthcare settings. This is basically a health services research and quality improvement issue, as health care systems, providers, and payers would be targeted for intervention rather than patients. Research foci might address overcoming provider-level barriers to care, determining the optimal frequency of screening in typically busy medical practices, and developing systems tools to encourage provider training and screening, which may be unique to specific healthcare systems. While studies in large organizations, such as the Veteran's Administration in the US (Rubenstein et al., 2000; Finney, Willenbring, & Moos, 2000) are informative, research should also focus on methods appropriate for small, community practices.

Unfortunately, as Babor and colleagues have noted (Babor et al., 2004, 2005), research on the process whereby alcohol screening and intervention are adopted in community-based medical settings is scarce. However, Miller et al. (in press-a) and Babor et al. (2005) have begun to pinpoint specific organizational factors and provider and staffing characteristics that are essential to routine implementation in primary care settings. Some of these include making alcohol screening an organizational priority, involvement of the entire practice staff in the process, and increasing provider experience and comfort through practical exposure to the process.

Applied research previously cited on dissemination and implementation also provides a starting point, as does work by Saitz et al. (2003) on providing reminders about screening results, but additional methods are needed to increase utilization. For example, some evidence suggests that the use of electronic medical record templates as well as screening and intervention algorithms may facilitate the process (Miller, 2004; Miller et al., 2006; Miller et al., in press-a).

Since the aim of this research is to systematically change patterns of care in order to provide an educational intervention, investigations should be based on appropriate theory or a guiding framework, such as the Chronic Care Model (Wagner, 1998; Watkins et al., 2003), the PRECEDE model (Green & Kreuter, 1999), or the Practice Partner Research Network's-Translating Research into Practice (PPRNet-TRIP) quality improvement model (Miller et al., in press-a).

All of these provide an empiric or theory-based system for identifying potentially important determinants of care including patient, provider, health-care organization, and societal factors. This will allow a systematic, outcomes-oriented approach in determining and addressing the multi-level factors that will mediate the success of screening and intervention programs.

Other health services research should focus on increasing knowledge about the cost-effectiveness of treatment from the insurer's and society's perspectives. Such work would include measuring the utilities of various alcohol-related states, and expanding the currently limited longer-term outcomes data, specifically reductions in alcohol-related consequences, mortality, and health care costs. This type of research will provide valuable comparisons with other health interventions in competing for limited preventive medicine resources (Yarnall et al., 2003), and will facilitate reimbursement for treatment services.

BIOMARKERS

Similar to screening and brief intervention, there is a need to establish and disseminate optimal methods for the utilization of well-studied chronic heavy drinking markers, notably GGT and CDT. Indeed, Miller et al. (2004) found that primary care physicians have little knowledge of the newer alcohol biomarkers, although most physicians report that their use of biomarkers would increase with additional knowledge about availability, use, and interpretation. Diffusion of bio-markers into medical settings might include dissemination of knowledge on the strengths and limitations of these markers to health care providers, and evaluations of how they can be used as a complement to self-reports. Closely related to this issue are the findings by Miller et al. (2006) and Miller et al. (in press-b) of high patient acceptance of biomarker use by physicians.

Other markers of chronic heavy drinking, such as phosphatidyl ethanol, sialic acid index of apolipoprotein J, and beta-hexosaminidase, have promise, but additional validation studies are needed in patient populations. Validation studies should also include methods for determining optimal combinations of biomark-ers within genders.

In addition to markers for chronic heavy use, clinical studies are also needed on biomarkers of recent ingestion. This includes validation studies in medical and surgical settings, and methods for optimally utilizing these highly relevant markers for improving patient outcomes, similar to use of urinary EtG in impaired profes-sionals (Skipper et al., 2004). For example, pre-operative patients with a history of chronic heavy drinking but negative urinary EtG should be at low risk for peri-operative withdrawal, and patients with acute, alcohol-related disease are likely to have undetectable ethanol, but positive markers for recent and/or chronically heavy ingestion at the time of hospitalization. This may lead to improved care (e.g., avoiding loading doses of phenytoin in patients with alcohol withdrawal seizure, or focusing on other causes of seizure if recent ingestion markers are negative). Ethical issues will also be important with increased use of biomarkers, particularly if results were used to exclude or postpone care in the absence of cor-roborating self-report.

TREATMENT OF ALCOHOL USE DISORDERS

Detection of alcohol use disorders overlaps the detection of risky drinking. One immediate research need resulting from screening for unhealthy alcohol use is increasing the referral of patients with alcohol use disorders, since even this level of involvement in alcoholism treatment is unusual in US primary medical practice (McGlynn et al., 2003). Studies on methods for effectively linking med-ical and surgical providers to specialty care for alcoholism, generalizable to most health care settings, are indicated (D'Amico et al., 2005; Fucito et al., 2003).

Detoxification needs must be considered in managing alcohol-dependent patients. In acute care settings using a symptom-triggered or fixed dose benzo-diazepine regimen for a continuously monitored patient, detoxification is com-mon and safe. However, ambulatory management is complicated by the use of frequently abused benzodiazepines that will enhance the depressive action of alco-hol and possibly increase adverse events. Improved outpatient regimens are needed to lessen the risk of adverse, medication-related consequences, and to minimize the need for short-term daily follow-up. Anticonvulsants (Malcolm et al., 2002) might be a better alternative to benzodiazepines for ambulatory medical settings, but such an approach requires confirmation and more general effectiveness data.

Pharmacotherapy for relapse prevention will likely become an increasingly important treatment method, and a number of investigators recognize the need to integrate pharmacotherapy with relatively brief counseling strategies. This has resulted in the publication of several protocols including BRENDA (Volpicelli et al., 2001), BBCET (Johnson et al., 2003), and Medical Management from Project COMBINE. While these interventions utilize skills typically found in primary care, they are still lengthy for routine application in general medical set-tings. Efficacy research that integrates pharmacotherapy with truly brief counsel-ing (5–15 min) for alcohol dependence is a potentially fruitful research area. Additional work on pharmacotherapy is also needed to assess treatment response in general medical settings and in the less selected populations seen there, to eval-uate optimal treatment duration, and to assess the impact of medication on long-term outcomes such as alcohol-related morbidity, mortality, and healthcare expenditures (Poldrugo et al., 2005). Medically based treatment research should also include evaluations of high-risk indicators (i.e., psychiatric comorbidities, addiction severity, polysubstance abuse, homelessness, etc.) that may indicate the need for immediate specialty referral and collaborative management, as well as factors effecting medication compliance.

As discussed above, for screening and intervention for risky drinking, clinical research alone will not change practice in caring for alcohol-dependent patients. Evidence-based research on the efficacy of alcohol biomarkers, and pharmacotherapy, and brief intervention strategies in medical settings, will need to be followed by applied research designed to evaluate and overcome patient, physician, healthcare system, and insurer barriers to use.

REFERENCES

Allen, J. P., Litten, R. Z., Fertig, J. B., & Sillanaukee, P. (2000). Carbohydrate-deficient transferrin, gamma-glutamyltransferase, and macrocytic volume as biomarkers of alcohol problems in women. *Alcoholism: Clinical and Experimental Research*, *24*(4), 492–496.

Allen, J. P., Sillanaukee, P., & Anton, R. (1999). Contribution of carbohydrate deficient transferrin to gamma glutamyl transpeptidase in evaluating progress of patients in treatment for alcoholism. *Alcoholism: Clinical and Experimental Research*, *23*(1), 115–120.

American Psychiatric Association. (1994). *Diagnostic and Statistical Manual* (4th ed.). Washington, DC: American Psychiatric Association.

Anton, R. F. (2001). Carbohydrate-deficient transferrin for detection and monitoring of sustained heavy drinking. What have we learned? Where do we go from here? *Alcohol*, *25*(3), 185–188.

Anton, R. F., Lieber, C., Tabakoff, B., & CDTect Study Group. (2002). Carbohydrate-deficient transferrin and gamma-glutamyltransferase for the detection and monitoring of alcohol use: Results from a multisite study. *Alcoholism: Clinical and Experimental Research*, *26*(8), 1215–1222.

Anton, R. F. O'Malley, S. S., Ciraulo, D. A., Cisler, R. A., Couper, D., Donovan, D. M., Gastfriend, D. R., Hosking, J. D., Johnson, B. A., LoCastro, J. S., Longabaugh, R., Mason, B. J., Mattson, M. E., Miller, W. R., Pettinati, H. M., Randall, C. L., Swift, R., Weiss, R. D., Williams, L. D., Zweben, A. COMBINE Study Research Group. (2006). Combined pharmacotherapies and behavioral interventions for alcohol dependence: The COMBINE study: A randomized controlled trial. *JAMA*, *295*(17), 2003–2017.

Babor, T. F., Higgins-Biddle, J., Dauser, D., Higgins, P., & Burleson, J. A. (2005). Alcohol screening and brief intervention in primary care settings: Implementation models and predictors. *Journal of Studies on Alcohol*, *66*, 361–368.

Babor, T. F., Higgins-Biddle, J., Higgins, P. S., Gassman, R. A., & Gould, B. E. (2004). Training medical providers to conduct alcohol screening and brief interventions. *Substance Abuse*, *25*, 17–26.

Barry, K. L., Blow, F. C., Willenbring, M. L., McCormick, R., Brockman, L. M., & Visnic, S. (2004). Use of alcohol screening and brief interventions in primary care settings: Implementation and barriers. *Substance Abuse*, *25*(1), 27–36.

Beich, A., Gannik, D., & Malterud, K. (2002). Screening and brief intervention for excessive alcohol use: Qualitative interview study of the experiences of general practitioners. *British Medical Journal*, *325*(7369), 870–874.

Blondell, R. D. (2005). Ambulatory detoxification of patients with alcohol dependence. *American Family Physician*, *71*(3), 495–502.

Borg, S. (1993). Carbohydrate deficient transferrin, CDT TM, a specific marker for regular high alcohol consumption. *Alcologia*, *5*, 117–120.

Boruki, K., Schreiner, R., Dierkes, J., Jachau, K., Krause, D., Westphal, S., Wurst, F. M., Luley, C., & Schmidt-Gayk, H. (2005). Detection of recent ethanol intake with new markers: Comparison of fatty acid ethyl esters in serum and of ethyl glucuronide and the ratio of 5-hydroxytryptophol to 5-hydroxyindole acetic acid in urine. *Alcoholism: Clinical and Experimental Research*, *29*(5), 781–787.

Bouza, C., Angeles, M., Munoz, A., & Amate, J. M. (2004). Efficacy and safety of naltrexone and acamprosate in the treatment of alcohol dependence: A systematic review. *Addiction, 99*(7), 811–828.

Bradley, K. A., Bush, K. R., Epler, A. J., Dobie, D. J., Davis, T. M., Sporleder, J. L., Maynard, C., Burman, M. L., & Kivlahan, D. R. (2003). Two brief alcohol-screening tests from the Alcohol Use Disorders Identification Test (AUDIT): Validation in a female Veterans Affairs patient population. *Archives of Internal Medicine, 163*(7), 821–829.

Bradley, K. A., Kivlahan, D. R., Bush, K. R., McDonell, M. B., & Fihn, S. D. (2001). Variations on the CAGE alcohol screening questionnaire: Strengths and limitations in VA general medical patients. *Alcoholism: Clinical and Experimental Research, 25*(10), 1472–1478.

Bush, K., Kihlavan, D. R., McConell, M. B., Fihn, S. D., & Bradley, K. A. (1998). The AUDIT alcohol consumption questions (AUDIT-C): An effective brief screening test for problem drinking. *Archives of Internal Medicine, 158*, 1789–1795.

Canagasaby, A., & Vinson, D. C. (2005). Screening for hazardous or harmful drinking using one or two quantity-frequency questions. *Alcohol and Alcoholism, 40*(3), 208–213.

Chen, J., Conigrave, K. M., Macaskill, P., Whitfield, J. B., & Irwig, L. (2003). Combining carbohydrate-deficient transferrin and gamma-glutamyltransferase to increase diagnostic accuracy for problem drinking. *Alcohol and Alcoholism, 38*, 574–582.

Cherpitel, C. J. (1995). Screening for alcohol problems in the emergency room: A rapid alcohol problems screen. *Drug and Alcohol Dependence, 40*, 133–137.

Cherpitel, C. J. (2000). A brief screening instrument for problem drinking in the emergency room: The RAPS4. *Journal of Studies on Alcohol, 61*(3), 447–449.

Cherpitel, C. J. (2002). Screening for alcohol problems in the US general population: Comparison of the CAGE, RAPS4, and RAPS4-QF by gender, ethnicity, and service utilization. *Alcoholism: Clinical and Experimental Research, 26*(11), 1686–1691.

Cherpitel, C. J., Ye, Y., & Bond, J. (2005a). Attributable risk of injury associated with alcohol use: Cross-national data from the Emergency Room Collaborative Alcohol Analysis Project. *American Journal of Public Health, 95*(2), 266–272.

Cherpitel, C. J., Ye, Y., Bond, J., Borges, G., Cremonte, M., Marais, S., Poznyak, V., Sovinova, H., Moskalewicz, J., & Swiatkiewicz, G. (2005b). Cross-national performance of the RAPS4/RAPS4-QF for tolerance and heavy drinking: Data from 13 countries. *Journal of Studies on Alcohol, 66*(3), 428–432.

Coffield, A. B., Maciosek, M. V., McGinnis, M., Harris, J. R., Caldwell, B., Teutsch, S. M., Atkins, D., Richland, J. H., & Haddix, A. (2001). Priorities among recommended clinical preventive services. *American Journal of Preventive Medicine, 21*(1), 1–9.

Conigrave, K. M., Davies, P., Haber, P., & Whitfield, J. B. (2003). Traditional markers of excessive alcohol use. *Addiction, 98*(Suppl. 2), 31–43.

Cuijpers, P., Riper, H., & Lemmers, L. (2004). The effects on mortality of brief interventions for problem drinking: A meta-analysis. *Addiction, 99*, 839–845.

D'Amico, E. J., Paddock, S. M., Burnam, A., & Kung, F. Y. (2005). Identification of and guidance for problem drinking by general medical providers: Results from a national survey. *Medical Care, 43*(3), 229–236.

D'Onofrio, G., & Degutis, L. C. (2002). Preventive care in the emergency department: Screening and brief intervention for alcohol problems in the emergency department: A systematic review. *Academic Emergency Medicine, 9*(6), 627–638.

Ferguson, L., Ries, R., & Russo, J. (2003). Barriers to identification and treatment of hazardous drinkers as assessed by urban/rural primary care doctors. *Journal of Addictive Diseases, 22*(2), 79–90.

Fiellin, D. A., Reid, M. C., & O'Connor, P. G. (2000). Outpatient management of patients with alcohol problems. *Annals of Internal Medicine, 133*(10), 815–827.

Finney, J. W., Willenbring, M. L., & Moos, R. H. (2000). Improving the quality of VA care for patients with substance-use disorders: The Quality Enhancement Research Initiative substance abuse module. *Medical Care, 38*(6 Suppl. 1), I-105–I-113.

Fleming, M. F., Anton, R. F., & Spies, C. D. (2004). A review of genetic, biological, pharmacological, and clinical factors that affect carbohydrate-deficient transferrin levels. *Alcoholism: Clinical and Experimental Research, 28*, 1347–1355.

Fleming, M. F., Mundt, M. P., French, M. T., Manwell, L. B., Stauffacher, E. A., & Barry, K. L. (2002). Brief physician advice for problem drinkers: Long-term efficacy and benefit-cost analysis. *Alcoholism: Clinical and Experimental Research, 26*(1), 36–43.

Friedmann, P. D., Saitz, R., & Samet, J. H. (1998). Management of adults recovering from alcohol or other drugs problems: Relapse prevention in primary care. *Journal of the American Medical Association, 279*(15), 1227–1231.

Fucito, L., Gomes, B., Murnion, B., & Haber, P. (2003). General practitioners' diagnostic skills and referral practices in managing patients with drug and alcohol-related health problems: Implications for medical training and education programs. *Drug and Alcohol Review, 22*(4), 417–424.

Garbutt, J. C., West, S. L., Carey, T. S., Lohr, K. N., & Crews, F. T. (1999). Pharmacological treatment of alcohol dependence: A review of the evidence. *Journal of the American Medical Association, 281*(14), 1318–1325.

Gentilello, L. M., Ebel, B. E., Wickizer, T. M., Salkever, D. S., & Rivara, F. P. (2005). Alcohol interventions for trauma patients treated in emergency departments and hospitals: A cost benefit analysis. *Annals of Surgery, 241*(4), 541–550.

Gentilello, L. M., Rivara, F. P., Donovan, D. M., Jurkovich, G. J., Daranciang, E., Dunn, C. W., Villaveces, A., Copass, M., & Ries, R. R. (1999). Alcohol interventions in a trauma center as a means of reducing the risk of injury recurrence. *Annals of Surgery, 230*(4), 473–480.

Ghosh, P., Hale, E. A., & Lakshman, M. R. (2001). Plasma sialic-acid index of apolipoprotein J (SIJ): A new alcohol intake marker. *Alcohol, 25*(3), 173–179.

Gomel, M. K., Wutzke, S. E., Hardcastle, D. M., Lapsley, H., & Reznick, R. B. (1998). Cost effectiveness of strategies to market and train primary health care physicians in brief intervention techniques for hazardous alcohol use. *Social Science and Medicine, 47*(2), 203–211.

Gordon, A. J., Maisto, S. A., McNeil, M., Kraemer, K. L., Conigliaro, R. L., Kelley, M. E., & Conigliaro, J. (2001). Three questions can detect hazardous drinkers. *Journal of Family Practice, 50*(4), 313–320.

Green, L. W., & Kreuter, M. W. (1999). *Health promotion planning: An educational and ecological approach*. Mountain View, CA: Mayfield Publishing Co.

Hansen, L. J., Olivarius, N., Beich, A., & Barfod, S. (1999). Encouraging GP's to undertake screening and brief intervention in order to reduce problem drinking: A randomized controlled trial. *Family Practice, 16*(6), 551–557.

Hansson, P., Caron, M., Johnson, G., Gustavsson, L., & Alling, C. (1997). Blood phophatidylethanol as a marker of alcohol abuse: Levels in alcoholic males during withdrawal. *Alcoholism: Clinical and Experimental Research, 21*(1), 108–110.

Hearne, R., Connolly, A., & Sheehan, J. (2002). Alcohol abuse: Prevalence and detection in a general hospital. *Journal of the Royal Society of Medicine, 95*(2), 84–87.

Hodgson, R., Alwyn, T., John, B., Thom, B., & Smith, A. (2002). The FAST alcohol screening test. *Alcohol and Alcoholism, 37*(1), 61–66.

Hodgson, R. J., John, B., Abbasi, T., Hodgson, R. C., Waller, S., Thom, B., & Newcombe, R. G. (2003). Fast screening for alcohol misuse. *Addictive Behaviors, 28*(8), 1453–1463.

Huseby, N. E., Nilssen, O., & Kanitz, R. D. (1997). Evaluation of two biological markers combine as a parameter of alcohol dependency. *Alcohol and Alcoholism, 32*, 731–737.

Johnson, B. A., Ait-Daoud, N., Bowden, C. L., DiClemente, C. C., Roache, J. D., Lawson, K., Javors, M. A., & Ma, J. Z. (2003). Oral topiramate for treatment of alcohol dependence: A randomized controlled trial. *Lancet, 361*(9370), 1677–1685.

Johnson, B. A., DiClemente, C. C., Ait-Daoud, N., & Stoks, S. M. (2003). Brief behavioral compliance enhancement treatment (BBCET) manual. In B. A. Johnson, P. Ruiz, & M. Galanter (Eds.), *Handbook of Clinical Alcoholism Treatment*. Baltimore, MD: Lipincott Williams and Wilkins.

Johnson, B. A., Roache, J. D., Javors, M. A., DiClemente, C. C., Cloninger, C. R., Prihoda, T. J., Bordnick, P. S., Ait-Daoud, N., & Hensler, J. (2000). Ondansetron for reduction of drinking among biologically predisposed alcoholic patients: A randomized controlled trial. *Journal of the American Medical Assocaition, 284*(8), 963–971.

Kaner, E. F., Haighton, C. A., McAvoy, B. R., Heather, N., & Gilvarry, E. (1999b). A RCT of three training and support strategies to encourage implementation of screening and brief alcohol intervention by general practitioners. *British Journal of General Practice, 49*(446), 699–703.

Kaner, E. F., Heather, N., Mcavoy, B. R., Lock, C. A., & Gilvarry, E. (1999a). Intervention for excessive alcohol consumption in primary health care: Attitudes and practices of English general practitioners. *Alcohol and Alcoholism, 34*(4), 559–566.

Kiritze-Topor, P., Huas, D., Rosenzweig, C., Comte, S., Paille, F., & Lehert, P. (2004). A pragmatic trial of acamprosate in the treatment of alcohol dependence in primary care. *Alcohol and Alcoholism, 39*(6), 520–527.

Koch, H., Meerkerk, G. J., Zaat, J. O., Ham, M. F., Scholten, R. J., & Assendelft, W. J. (2004). Accuracy of carbohydrate-deficient transferrin in the detection of excessive alcohol consumption: A systematic review. *Alcohol and Alcoholism, 39*(2), 75–85.

Kranzler, H. R., Pierucci-Lagha, A., Feinn, R., & Hernandez-Avila, C. (2003). Effects of ondansetron in early versus late onset alcoholics: A prospective, open label study. *Alcoholism: Clinical and Experimental Research, 27*(7), 1150–1155.

Kranzler, H. R., & van Kirk, J. (2001). Efficacy of naltrexone and acamprosate for alcoholism treatment: A meta-analysis. *Alcoholism: Clinical and Experimental Research, 25*(9), 1335–1341.

Kristenson, H. (1987). Methods of intervention to modify drinking patterns in heavy drinkers. *Recent Developments in Alcoholism, 5*, 403–423.

Lesch, O. M., Walter, H., Antal, J., Heggli, D. E., Kovacz, A., Leitner, A., Neumeister, A., Stumpf, I., Sundrehagen, E., & Kasper, S. (1996). Carbohydrate deficient transferrin as a marker of alcohol intake: A study with healthy subjects. *Alcohol and Alcoholism, 31*, 265–271.

Litten, R. Z., Allen, J. P., & Fertig, J. B. (1995). Gamma-glutamyltranspeptidase and carbohydrate deficient transferrin: Alternative measures of excessive alcohol consumption. *Alcoholism: Clinical and Experimental Research, 19*, 1541–1546.

Lock, C. A., Kaner, E. F., Heather, N., McAvoy, B. R., & Gilvarry, E. (1999). A randomized trial of three marketing strategies to disseminate a screening and brief alcohol intervention program to general practitioners. *British Journal of General Practice, 49*(446), 695–698.

MacKenzie, D., Langa, A., & Brown, T. M. (1996). Identifying hazardous or harmful alcohol use in medical admissions: A comparison of AUDIT, CAGE, and brief MAST. *Alcohol and Alcoholism, 31*(6), 591–599.

Malcolm, R., Myrick, H., Roberts, J., Wang, W., Anton, R. F., & Ballenger, J. C. (2002). The effects of carbamazepine and lorazepam on single versus multiple previous alcohol withdrawals in an outpatient randomized trial. *Journal of General Internal Medicine, 17*(5), 349–355.

Mark, T. L., Kranzler, H. R., Poole, V. H., Hagen, C. A., McLeod, C., & Crosse, S. (2003a). Barriers to the use of medications to treat alcoholism. *American Journal on Addictions, 12*(4), 281–294.

Mark, T. L., Kranzler, H. R., Song, X., Bransberger, P., Poole, V. H., & Crosse, S. (2003b). Physicians' opinions about medications to treat alcoholism. *Addiction, 98*(5), 617–626.

Mayfield, D., McLeod, G., & Hall, P. (1974). The CAGE questionnaire: Validation of a new alcoholism screening instrument. *American Journal of Psychiatry, 131*, 1121–1123.

McAvoy, B. R., Donovan, R. J., Jalleh, G., Saunders, J. B., Wutzke, S. E., Lee, N., Kaner, E. F., Heather, N., McCormick, R., Barfod, S., & Gache, P. (2001). General practitioners, prevention and alcohol- a powerful cocktail? Facilitators and inhibitors of practicing preventive medicine in general and early intervention for alcohol in particular: A 12-nation key informant and general practitioner study. *Drugs: Education, Prevention and Policy, 8*(2), 103–117.

McLellan, A. T., & Meyers, K. (2004). Contemporary addiction treatment: A review of systems problems for adults and adolescents. *Biological Psychiatry, 56*(10), 764–770.

McCormick, R., Adams, P., Powell, A., Bunbury, D., Paton-Simpson, G., & McAvoy, B. R. (1999). Encouraging general practitioners to take up screening and early intervention for problem use of alcohol: A marketing trial. *Drug and Alcohol Review*, *18*(2), 171–177.

McGlynn, E. A., Asch, S. M., Adams, J., Keesey, J., Hicks, J., DeCristofaro, A., & Kerr, E. A. (2003). The quality of health care delivered to adults in the United States. *New England Journal of Medicine*, *348*(26), 2635–2645.

Miller, P. M., & Anton, R. F. (2004). Biochemical alcohol screening in primary medical care. *Addictive Behaviors*, *28*(7), 1425–1434.

Miller, P. M., Anton, R. F., & Dominick, C. (2005). Carbohydrate-deficient transferrin test: A tool for detecting alcohol abuse. *Current Psychiatry*, *4*(6), 80–87.

Miller, P. M., Ornstein, S., Nietert, P., & Anton, R. F. (2004). Self-report and biomarker alcohol screenin by primary care physicians: The need to translate research into guidelines and practice. *Alcohol and Alcoholism*, *39*(4), 325–328.

Miller, P. M., Spies, C., Neumann, T., Javors, M. A., Hoyumpa, A. M., Roache, J., Webb, A., Kashi, M., Sharkey, F. E., Anton, R. F., Egan, B. M., Basile, J., Nguyen, S., Fleming, M. F., & Dillie, K. S. (2006a). Alcohol biomarker screening in medical and surgical settings. *Alcoholism: Clinical and Experimental Research*, *30*(2), 185–193.

Miller, P. M., Stockdell, R., Nemeth, L., Feifer, C., Jenkins, R., Nietert, P. J., Wessell, A., Liszka, H., & Ornstein, S. (2006b). Initial steps by nine primary care practices to implement alcohol screening guidelines with hypertensive patients: The AA-TRIP project. *Substance Abuse*, *27*, 61–70.

Miller, P. M., Thomas, S., Mallin, R. (2006c). Patient attitudes toward self-report and biomarker alcohol screening by primary care physicians. *Alcohol and Alcoholism*, *41*, 306–310.

Miller, W. R., & Sanchez, V. C. (1994). Motivating young adults for treatment and lifestyle change. In G. Howard (Ed.), *Issues in Alcohol use and Misuse by Young Adults*. Notre Dame, IN: University of Notre Dame Press.

Moyer, A., Finney, J. W., Swearingen, C. E., & Vergun, P. (2002). Brief interventions for alcohol problems: A meta-analytic review of controlled investigations in treatment-seeking and non-treatment-seeking populations. *Addiction*, *97*, 279–292.

Myrick, H., & Anton, R. (2004). Recent advances in pharmacotherapy of alcoholism. *Current Psychiatry Reports*, *6*(5), 332–338.

Neumann, T., & Spies, C. (2003). Use of biomarkers for alcohol use disorders in clinical practice. *Addiction*, *98*(Suppl. 2), 81–91.

O'Malley, S. S., Rounsaville, B. J., Farren, C., Namkoong, K., Wu, R., Robinson, J., O'Connor, P. G. (2003). Initial and maintenance naltrexone treatment for alcohol dependence using primary care vs. specialty care: A nested sequence of 3 randomized trials. *Archives of Internal Medicine*, *163*(14), 1694–1704.

Pettinati, H. M., Weiss, R. D., Miller, W. R., Donovan, D., Ernst, D. B., & Rounsaville, B. J. (2004). COMBINE Monograph Series, Volume 2. *Medical Management Treatment Manual: A Clinical Research Guide for Medically Trained Clinicians Providing Pharmacotherapy as Part of the Treatment for Alcohol Dependence*. DHHS Publication No. (NIH) 04–5289. Bethesda, MD: NIAAA.

Poikolanen, K. (1999). Effectiveness of brief interventions to reduce alcohol intake in primary health care populations: A meta-analysis. *Preventive Medicine*, *28*, 503–509.

Pokorny, A. D., Miller, B. A., & Kaplan, H. B. (1972). The Brief MAST: A shortened version of the Michigan Alcoholism Screening Test. *American Journal of Psychiatry*, *129*(3), 342–345.

Poldrugo, F., Haeger, D. A., Comte, S., Walburg, J., & Palmer, A. J. (2005). A critical review of pharmacoeconomic studies of acamprosate. *Alcohol and Alcoholism*, *40*(5), 422–430.

Ponnio, M., Alho, H., Heinala, P., Nikkari, S. T., & Sillanaukee, P. (1999). Serum and saliva levels of sialic acid are elevated in alcoholics. *Alcoholism: Clinical and Experimental Research*, *23*(6), 1060–1064.

Project MATCH Research Group. (1993). Project MATCH: Rationale and methods for a multisite clinical trial matching patients to alcoholism treatment. *Alcoholism: Clinical and Experimental Research*, *17*(6), 1130–1145.

Reid, M. C., Fiellin, D. A., & O'Connor, P. G. (1999). Hazardous and harmful alcohol consumption in primary care. *Archives of Internal Medicine, 159*(15), 1681–1689.

Reinert, D. F., & Allen, J. P. (2002). The Alcohol Use Disorders Identification Test (AUDIT): A review of recent research. *Alcoholism: Clinical and Experimental Research, 26*(2), 272–279.

Rivara, F. P., Tollefson, S., Tesh, E., & Gentilello, L. M. (2000). Screening trauma patients for alcohol problems: Are insurance companies barriers? *Journal of Trauma-Injury Infection and Critical Care, 48*(1), 115–118.

Rubenstein, L. V., Mittman, B. S., Yano, E. M., & Mulrow, C. D. (2000). From understanding health care provider behavior to improving health care: The QUERI framework for quality improvement. *Medical Care, 38*(6 Suppl. 1), I-129–I-141.

Russell, M., Czarnecki, D. M., Cowan, R., McPherson, E., & Mudar, P. J. (1991). Measures of maternal alcohol use as predictors of development in early childhood. *Alcoholism: Clinical and Experimental Research, 15*(6), 991–1000.

Saitz, R., Horton, N. J., Sullivan, L. M., Moskowitz, M. A., & Samet, J. H. (2003). Addressing alcohol problems in primary care: A cluster randomized, controlled trial of a systems intervention. *Annals of Internal Medicine, 138*, 372–382.

Saitz, R., Mulvey, K. P., Plough, A., & Samet, J. H. (1997). Physician unawareness of serious substance abuse. *American Journal of Drug and Alcohol Abuse, 23*, 343–354.

Saunders, J. B., Aasland, O. G., Babor, T. F., De la Fuente, J. R., & Grant, M. (1993). Development of the alcohol use disorders identification test (AUDIT): WHO collaborative project on early detection of persons with harmful alcohol consumption. *Addiction, 88*, 791–803.

Schermer, C. R., Gentilello, L. M., Hoyt, D. B., Moore, E. E., Moore, J. B., Rozycki, G. S., & Feliciano, D. V. (2003). National survey of trauma surgeons' use of alcohol screening and brief intervention. *Journal of Trauma-Injury Infection and Critical Care, 55*(5), 849–856.

Selzer, M. L., Vinokur, A., & Van Rooijen, L. J. (1975). A Self-Administered Short Michigan Alcohol Screening Test (SMAST). *Journal of Studies on Alcohol, 36*, 117–126.

Selzer, M. L. (1971). The Michigan Alcoholism Screening Test: The quest for a new diagnostic instrument. *American Journal of Psychiatry, 127*(12), 1653–1658.

Sillanaukee, P., & Olsson, U. (2001). Improved diagnostic classification of alcohol abusers by combining carbohydrate-deficient transferrin and gamma-glutamyltransferase. *Clinical Chemistry, 47*, 681–685.

Sillanaukee, P., Strid, N., Allen, J. P., & Litten, R. Z. (2001). Possible reasons why heavy drinking increases carbohydrate-deficient transferrin. *Alcoholism: Clinical and Experimental Research 1, 25*(1), 34–40.

Skipper, G. E., Wienmann, W., Thierauf, A., Schaefer, P., Wiesbeck, G., Allen, J. P., Miller, M., & Wurst, F. M. (2004). Ethyl glucuronide: A biomarker to identify alcohol use by health professionals recovering from substance use disorders. *Alcohol and Alcoholism, 39*(5), 445–449.

Spies, C., Tonnesen, H., Andreasson, S., Helander, A., & Conigrave, K. (2001). Perioperative morbidity and mortality in chronic alcoholic patients. *Alcoholism: Clinical and Experimental Research, 25*(5 Suppl.), 164S–170S.

Srisurapanont, M., & Jarusuraisin, N. (2005). Opioid antagonists for alcohol dependence. *Cochrane Database of Systematic Reviews, 1*, CD001867

Stowell, L., Stowell, A., Garrett, N., & Robinson, G. (1997). Comparison of serum beta-hexosaminidase isoenzyme B activity with serum carbohydrate-deficient transferrin and other markers of alcohol abuse. *Alcohol and Alcoholism, 32*(6), 703–714.

Streeton, C., & Whelan, G. (2001). Naltrexone, a relapse prevention maintenance treatment of alcohol dependence: A meta-analysis of randomized controlled trials. *Alcohol and Alcoholism, 36*(6), 544–552.

Swift, R. (2003). Direct measurement of alcohol and its metabolites. *Addiction, 98*(Suppl. 2), 73–80.

U.S. Department of Health and Human Services. (2005). *Helping Patients Who Drink Too Much* (NIH Publication No. 05-3769). Rockville, MD.

Varga, A., Hansson, P., Lundqvist, C., & Alling, C. (1998). Phosphatidylethanol in blood as a marker of ethanol consumption in healthy volunteers: Comparison with other markers. *Alcoholism: Clinical and Experimental Research, 22*(8), 1832–1837.

Volpicelli, J., Pettinati, H. M., McLellan, A. T., & O'Brien, C. P. (2001). *Combining Medication and Psychosocial Treatments for Addictions. The BRENDA Approach.* New York, NY: The Guilford Press.

Wagner, E. H. (1998). Chronic disease management: What will it take to improve care for chronic illness? *Effective Clinical Practice, 1*, 2–4.

Watkins, K., Pincus, H. A., Tanielian, T. L., & Lloyd, J. (2003). Using the Chronic Care Model to improve treatment of alcohol use disorders in primary care settings. *Journal of Studies on Alcohol, 64*, 209–218.

Whitfield, J. B. (2001). Gamma glutamyl transferase. *Critical Reviews in Clinical Laboratory Sciences, 38*, 262–355.

Wilk, A. I., Jensen, N. M., & Havighurst, T. C. (1997). Meta-analysis of randomized controlled trials addressing brief interventions in heavy alcohol drinkers. *Journal of General Internal Medicine, 12*, 274–283.

Willenbring, M. L., & Olson, D. H. (1999). A randomized trial of integrated outpatient treatment for medically ill alcoholic men. *Archives of Internal Medicine, 159*(16), 1946–1952.

Williams, R., & Vinson, D. C. (2001). Validation of a single screening question for problem drinking. *Journal of Family Practice, 50*, 307–312.

World Health Organization. (1992). *The ICD-10 Classification of Mental and Behavioral Disorders.* Geneva: World Health Organization.

Wurst, F. M., Alling, C., Aradottir, S., Pragst, F., Allen, J. P., Weinmann, W., Marmillot, P., Ghosh, P., Lakshman, R., Skipper, G. E., Neumann, T., Spies, C., Javors, M., Johnson, B. A., Ait-Daoud, N., Akhtar, F., Roache, J. D., & Litten. R. (2005). Emerging biomarkers: New directions and clinical applications. *Alcoholism: Clinical and Experimental Research, 29*(3), 465–473.

Wurst, F. M., Wiesbeck, G. A., Metzger, J. W., Weinmann, W., & Graf, M. (2004). On sensitivity, specificity, and the influence of various parameters on ethyl glucuronide levels in urine-results from the WHO/ISBRA study. *Alcoholism: Clinical and Experimental Research, 28*(8), 1220–1228.

Wurst, F. M., & Metzger, J. (2002). The ethanol conjugate ethyl glucuronide is a useful marker of recent alcohol consumption. *Alcoholism: Clinical and Experimental Research, 26*(7), 1114–1119.

Yarnall, K. S., Poliak, K. I., Østbye, T., Krause, K. M., & Michener, J. L. (2003). Primary care: Is there enough time for prevention? *American Journal of Public Health, 93*(4), 635–641.

CHAPTER 19

Internet–Based Interventions for Alcohol, Tobacco and Other Substances of Abuse

John A. Cunningham

Centre for Addiction and Mental Health, and University of Toronto, Ontario, Canada M5S 2S1

Abstract: This chapter provides a summary of the state of Internet-based Interventions (IBIs) for substance abuse to-date. First, common elements in IBIs are discussed. Next, a rationale for IBIs is provided. Third, the research conducted to evaluate IBIs for alcohol, tobacco and other substances of abuse is summarized. The chapter concludes with a discussion of what questions still need answering as IBIs are further developed in the next few years.

INTRODUCTION

Interventions for substance abuse have been available for several years on the Internet. Are these Internet-based interventions (IBIs) just interesting toys, of little or no use in the business of treating substance abuse concerns? Or, are IBIs the wave of the future, destined to become the predominant means of providing help to those with substance abuse and other health concerns? The reality will probably end up somewhere between these two extremes, with IBIs becoming one further means, along with existing treatment options, of providing services to those in need. This chapter will address several questions that are key to understanding how and why the science of addictions treatment is being translated into the practice of IBIs. Topics to be covered include: (1) What do IBIs for alcohol, tobacco and other drug concerns look like?; (2) Why bother? Who uses the Internet and why won't they show up in treatment?; (3) What is the evidence that IBIs work?; and (4) Future Directions – What questions need answering and what might IBIs for substance abuse look like in the future? The intent of this chapter is to provide a critical review of current IBIs, discuss their immediate implication for assessment and treatment, and identify gaps in both research and practice that need to be addressed as the science of addictions treatment progresses to the practice of IBIs.

WHAT DO INTERNET-BASED INTERVENTIONS FOR ALCOHOL, TOBACCO AND OTHER DRUG CONCERNS LOOK LIKE?

There are a variety of different websites available that provide help for substance abusers – from those that are purely informational through to fully developed IBIs. In this section an example IBI, the Alcohol Help Center (AHC; located at www.alcoholhelpcenter.net), will be used to illustrate many of the common elements that appear in IBIs and will also be used to highlight some of the different ways in which IBIs can be structured.

ACCESSING THE WEBSITE

One of the first elements to be aware of is that some websites are available free-of-charge (such as the AHC) and others charge a fee for service (e.g., Drinker's Check-up (DCU), Hester, Squires, & Delaney, 2005). Beyond the reality that some IBIs have to charge a fee in order to stay in operation, there are some clear advantages to making some IBIs available at no cost because this removes a potential barrier to access for some groups of potential users. However, it should also be considered that a minimal fee might have the advantage of increasing the perceived worth of the IBI to the user (i.e., "I paid a fee so I'm going to use the site as much as possible in order to get my money's worth").

Almost all IBIs have some sort of home page that describes the website and, depending on the quality of the site, provides information on the developers as well as freely available educational materials about the substance of concern (for more details on the quality control content of good IBIs see, Evers et al., 2005; Walther et al., 2005). Also common, regardless of fee structure or other registration procedures, is some sort of screener test that allows the potential user to evaluate whether their alcohol, tobacco or drug use may be a problem. In the AHC, this screener is called the 'Check Your Drinking' screener and is available for use without any form of registration on the site (Cunningham et al., 2006). In addition to providing a measurement of the severity of participants' drinking concerns using a validated measure (the AUDIT in this case, Babor et al., 1989; Saunders et al., 1993), the Check Your Drinking screener provides a number of other useful feedback elements that have been designed to help participants evaluate their drinking and increase their motivation to change. Primary to this motivational material is normative feedback that compares participants' drinking to that of others of the same age, sex and country of origin (for Canada, USA and the United Kingdom; other countries to be added at a later date; see Figure 1 for an example feedback chart). While personalization of feedback material to make it more relevant to participants might serve to strengthen its motivational content, it should also be noted that such personalization can serve to limit the usefulness of the website for participants from countries for which there is no personalized data available. This same limitation is true for the language in which the website is available (i.e., a

Figure 1   Example personalized feedback generated by the Check Your Drinking screener.

website that is only available in English will not be of much use to people who do not speak English).

After taking the screener test and reviewing the information on the content of the website, the participant is usually asked to register. While registration is not always required (e.g., Moderation Management, Hall & Tidwell, 2003; Humphreys & Klaw, 2001), it does have some advantages. Primarily, registration can allow for some continuity in participants' experience. The website can keep a record of participants' earlier visits and facilitate transition through a programmatic intervention (e.g., by providing a drinking diary such as the one discussed below). Registration might also serve to discourage unhelpful participation on group elements of an IBI's website (e.g., people posting 'spam' on an online support group). The disadvantage of registration is that it may raise concern in potential participants about issues of privacy and anonymity. These concerns are valid and information should be contained on the website about ways to promote privacy (e.g., registering using an e-mail address that does not contain personal identifiers) as well as the privacy policy of the website. Ideally, the website should strike a balance between the advantages of keeping a record of each participant's use of the website and the disadvantages of potentially excluding someone in need because they have concerns about privacy. These issues are discussed in some detail in privacy legislation for health information that is promoted by various national and international organizations ("Health Insurance Portability and Accountability Act of 1996 (United States of America)" Pub L No. 104–191, 1996; "Personal Information Protection and Electronic Documents Act (Canada)". (2000, amended 2004); van Mierlo et al., 2006, May).

INSIDE THE INTERNET-BASED INTERVENTION

Perhaps one of the largest differences in various IBIs is how the website is structured and the choices participants have in how they access information. As an example, can participants pick and choose between the content and decide in what order they choose to use the various tools? Or, is the person restricted to following a particular programmatic route through the materials, more akin to a multi-session face-to-face addictions treatment program (for more details on the strengths and weaknesses of different IBI structures see, Danaher, McKay, & Seeley, 2005)? Beyond the structure of the IBI, there are several common elements from traditional cognitive behavioral treatments for substance abuse that are often included in these online programs. These elements will be discussed briefly using the AHC as an example. The first of these common elements is a diary that participants can use to track their patterns of drinking over the period in which they use the website (see Figure 2 for an example summary output). IBIs for smoking also usually contain such diaries (see Stop Smoking Center, www.stopsmokingcenter.net) and all serve to allow participants to track the patterns of their substance use and

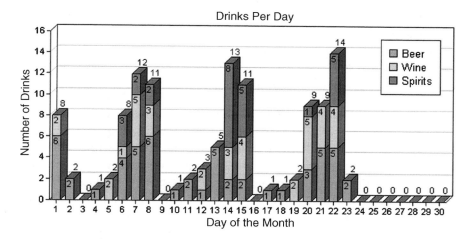

Figure 2 Example drinking diary summary generated by the Alcohol Help Center.

identify times and situations where they have most difficulty in dealing with their substance abuse concerns.

Alongside the diary function, most IBIs also contain a section in which participants write down their goal. In the AHC, participants have the choice of choosing abstinence or moderate drinking goals and advice is provided as to when an abstinence goal may be more appropriate (see Figure 3). Also relevant in such goal setting sections is the ability to change a goal if the person's first choice was problematic (e.g., tried a moderate drinking goal, found that it did not work and then switched to abstinence). The ability to incorporate this type of choice for the participant coincides well with recommendations regarding ways to motivate change among those substance abusers who are ambivalent (e.g., Miller & Page, 1991). Some websites also incorporate the ability for participants to make a public pledge about their goal (for an example, see the Stop Smoking Center).

One of the somewhat surprising features of IBIs is their ability to create a supportive community. This may seem counter-intuitive as IBIs are, by their nature, something that most people will interact with in isolation (i.e., sitting by themselves in front of a computer). However, the anonymity of a computer interaction appears to allow respondents to open up about their concerns and to provide support to one another (Humphreys & Klaw, 2001; Walther et al., 2005). Such support is often clearly much appreciated by people who have felt isolated in their concerns and have turned to an IBI as a way to communicate with others without exposing themselves because of fears about stigma. There is also some indication that some people who are too embarrassed to seek out treatment might first access help online. Then, if they desire more help, the experience of communicating online helps the substance abuser to feel more comfortable seeking out similar support in a face-to-face setting (Cooper, 2004). One concern about support

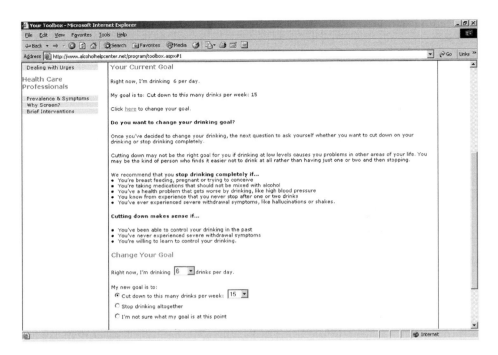

Figure 3   Example goal setting exercise in the Alcohol Help Center.

groups is that this anonymity could also promote the chance that users will become abusive to one-another. However, having a professional moderator available, as well as clear user agreements that specify the nature of allowable communications and the sanctions associated with abusive language, often greatly reduce the frequency of such counter-productive behavior (see Figure 4).

There is also an array of components that can be included in an IBI to promote continued participation and motivate change over time. As an example, the AHC incorporates a function where the person can ask to be sent e-mail messages that incorporate tips to promote change (see Figure 5). The intent of these messages is to keep the participant thinking about their drinking goal and to provide additional support. As another example, the Stop Smoking Center has a downloadable 'quit meter' that provides updates on how long participants have been smoke free, how much money they have saved, and their increase in life-expectancy resulting from quitting smoking. The advantage of an IBI for this type of on-the-go tool is that, once programmed, its upkeep can be inexpensive, providing the opportunity to promote ongoing motivation for change in a cost efficient manner.

Beyond these elements that are common to many IBIs, there are a range of other tools that are available. As examples, the AHC contains exercises that allow the participant to evaluate the costs and benefits of changing and also, to identify ways

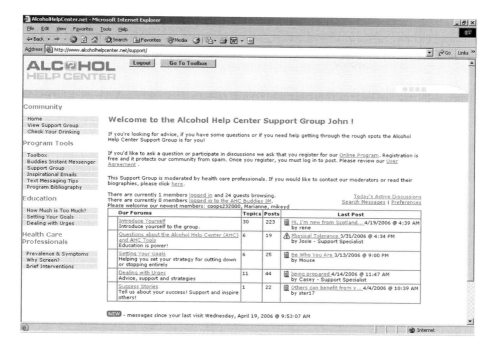

Figure 4   Example support group content in the Alcohol Help Center.

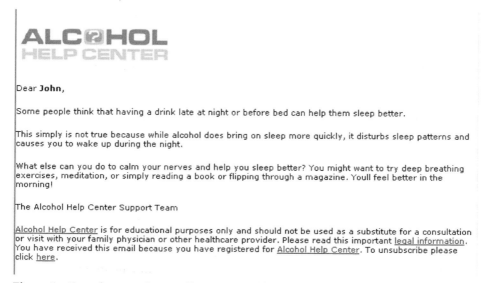

Figure 5   Example supportive e-mail message sent by the Alcohol Help Center.

to deal with urges and cravings to drink. Ideally, the content of an IBI should be evolving over time as new tools that might be helpful to participants are identified and modified to make them usable in an online format.

WHY BOTHER? WHO USES THE INTERNET AND WHY WON'T THEY SHOW UP IN TREATMENT?

One of the enduring facts about treatment for alcohol, tobacco and other substance abuse concerns is that most people will never show up for treatment. Using alcohol as an example, the estimated ratio of treated to untreated problem drinkers ranges from about 1:3–1:14 (Burton & Williamson, 1995; Cunningham & Breslin, 2004; Hasin, 1994; Roizen, Cahalan, & Shanks, 1978; Sobell, Sobell, & Toneatto, 1992). These estimates are usually generated from general population survey data and are derived by first assessing the number of problem drinkers in a population and then asking these problem drinkers if they have ever used any type of treatment for their alcohol concerns, including Alcoholics Anonymous and talking with a family doctor as well as other, more formal, types of treatment. The ratio of treated to untreated varies marginally depending on country of residence but the primary factor explaining different levels of accessing treatment appears to be severity of drinking problems. That is, the more severe the definition of alcohol problems, the more likely it is that people who meet this criterion are to have accessed some type of treatment (Cunningham, 1999). However, the fact remains that, even with people who have severe alcohol problems (such as alcohol dependence), the majority will never have accessed any type of treatment for alcohol concerns. This means that there are large numbers of problem drinkers who are underserved by traditional treatment services. The same pattern of results has also been found for smokers (Hughes, 1999) and other drug users (Cunningham, 2000; Robins, 1980).

Even if there are many people who will never seek treatment, is it worthwhile trying to find other ways to help? Many people with alcohol, tobacco or other drug problems deal with their respective concerns without treatment (Cunningham, 1999, 2000; Hughes, 1999; Robins, 1980). However, while most substance abusers recover without treatment, they can cause themselves (and others) considerable lasting harm before doing so. In addition, many alcohol, tobacco and other drug users say that they are interested in receiving help (Cunningham, 2005; Cunningham et al., 2003; Koski-Jännes & Cunningham, 2001) but are reluctant to seek formal treatment because of embarrassment, fear of stigma and concerns about availability (Cunningham et al., 1993; Grant, 1997; Roizen, 1977; Sobell et al., 1992; Tuchfeld, 1976). These barriers to treatment are precisely the reasons that some people with addictions concerns give for using IBIs (Cooper, 2004; Humphreys & Klaw, 2001). Combined with the fact that substance abusers often voice a desire to deal with their concerns by themselves (Cunningham et al., 1993; Grant, 1997), it would appear that there is a substantial audience for self-help services such as those that are available on the Internet.

One final issue in considering the potential worth of the Internet as a means of providing services for those with substance abuse concerns is accessibility. While estimates of access to the Internet continue to grow, particularly in wealthy countries (current estimates of Internet access in Canada and the USA are 70–75% of the adult population, Internet World Stats, 2005; Ipsos-Reid, 2004), it is possible that these numbers will not hold true for those with addictive behaviors. This is because substance abuse is associated with factors that can marginalize the addicted individual from mainstream society (low socio-economic status, unemployment and concurrent psychiatric disorders, Cunningham et al., 2006a) and such marginalization is associated with less access to the Internet (United States Department of Commerce, 2002). An analysis employing general population data collected in 2002 and 2004 in Ontario, Canada, did find some disparity of Internet access depending on substance abuse status (Cunningham et al., 2006a). Of drinkers, smokers, cocaine and cannabis users, the only substance that was clearly associated with limited Internet access was smoking – pack a day smokers were less likely to have access to the Internet even after controlling for socio-economic status.

There are two things to learn from these analyses (Cunningham et al., 2006a). First, many substance abusers have regular access to the Internet and second, substance abuse exists on a continuum of which the vast majority of substance abusers have mild to moderate rather than severe addictions concerns (Institute of Medicine, 1990a, 1990b). Thus, when we think about substance abusers it is important to remember that the majority has less severe addiction concerns, precisely the type of problems that might benefit from self-help services such as those available on the Internet. Given that one of the primary uses of the Internet is seeking information about health concerns (Ipsos-Reid, 2002) and that substance abusers are willing to give information about their use online (Nicholson, White, & Duncan, 1999), it would seem that it is clearly worthwhile to explore the utility of IBIs for substance abusers.

WHAT IS THE EVIDENCE THAT INTERNET-BASED INTERVENTIONS WORK?

Bessell et al. (2002) summarized research evaluating IBIs for health concerns. They concluded that "there is almost no evidence regarding the effect of consumer Internet use on health outcomes" and that "well-designed controlled studies,… are urgently needed" (p. 34). Recent reviews of Internet sites for alcohol or substance abuse (Copeland & Martin, 2004; Toll et al., 2003; Walters, Wright, & Shegog, 2006) also concluded that there is a need for controlled trials evaluating these online services. However, research evaluating IBIs for some substances of abuse is clearly more advanced than for others, with IBIs for smokers being the most advanced, those for drinkers in the middle, and those for other substances of abuse trailing far behind.

WHAT TYPES OF EVIDENCE EXIST?

Publications reporting on IBIs for substance abuse come in three classes. The first consists of papers that simply describe the existence of a website along with a summary of the number of people who use the site (traffic), and often, some preliminary data of the users' reactions to the website (e.g., Cloud & Peacock, 2001). The second consists of studies that report some type of outcome data of users of the IBI, whether consisting of the changing substance abuse status of respondents who use the website over a period of time (Linke, Brown, & Wallace, 2004) or of respondents who used the IBI and then were re-contacted after several months to ask about their status at follow-up (Cunningham et al., 2006). The final and most stringent evaluation consists of randomized controlled trials (RCT) that compare the outcome of respondents who use the IBI to a comparison group of some type. In the latter, membership in the group who are exposed to the IBI or in the comparison group is decided by random assignment so that the researchers can then make causal statements that any differences observed between the groups are due to the IBI. The few RCTs conducted to-date will be reviewed after a brief discussion of these three classes of evaluation.

While all three classes of studies have value, they vary in the strength of causal statements that can be made based on their findings. The first, descriptions of websites and participant reactions, are useful because they inform the reader of the existence of the website and provide information on traffic to the IBI and whether users' reactions are generally positive or negative. This type of process information helps to identify potential problems with the website. However, it provides no evidence as to whether using the website leads to a reduction in substance use. The second class, studies that include outcome data, are useful because they can provide pilot data that indicates that some substance abusers who used the website reduced their consumption or quit. However, it is important to be aware that it is inappropriate to claim that the website actually caused the reduction in substance use in this type of study. This is because people who access an IBI are most likely those who are already considering quitting. As many people quit different substances of abuse without treatment (Cunningham, 1999, 2000; Hughes, 1999; Robins, 1980), it is quite possible that they would have stopped their substance abuse even without accessing the website. This fact is the reason why RCTs are important because only RCTs are designed to test whether the addition of the IBI (or some other intervention) causes the observed reduction in substance use. Finally, it is important to recognize that RCTs also have their weaknesses, with the primary one often being that the characteristics of people who choose to participate in the randomized trial may be unrepresentative of the people who use websites in real life. Thus, there is often concern about whether the same type of result would be obtained by all users of the website (generalizability). RCTs are sometimes conducted in situations that are quite different from the conditions under which an IBI would normally be accessed. As an example, having participants come into a health care setting and sitting them in front of a computer to receive an IBI is a qualitatively different experience from the participant accessing the intervention from home. For instance, long assessments that the participant might feel compelled to fill out when face-to-face could easily result in participants leaving an Internet site when accessed from home. However, research evaluation is a cumulative activity in which one study is rarely taken as a gold standard of proof. Thus, increased confidence can be given to the effectiveness of an IBI if there are RCTs in different populations, outcome studies without comparison groups but consisting of participants who are using the IBI in real life and even positive process evaluation studies demonstrating that many people use the IBI and report that they found it helpful.

CIGARETTES

There are already a number of recent, high quality reviews of IBIs for smokers available (Etter, 2006a, 2006b; Walters et al., 2006). This information will not be repeated here in interests of saving space. There have also been several RCTs that will be summarized here because they are the only trials that demonstrate that IBIs for smokers are effective.

Etter (2005) reported on a RCT of the efficacy of two Internet computer-tailored smoking cessation programs, one a modification of the other. Subjects, visitors to the Stop-tabac.ch website (a French language website), were randomly assigned to one of the two programs. The original program, based on psychological and addiction theory, had a longer baseline questionnaire and provided more information on health risks and coping strategies. The shorter modified program provided more information on nicotine replacement and nicotine dependence. Both programs provided personalized counseling letters, monthly email reminders, and the opportunity to re-do the assessment questionnaire to obtain another counseling letter. At the 11-week follow-up, the outcome measure was self-reported smoking abstinence in the past seven days. Analysis was done on an intention-to-treat (ITT) basis, i.e., all non-respondents to follow-up were classified as smokers. Of the 11,969 current (74%) and former (26%) smokers who completed the baseline questionnaire, 4,237 (35%) responded to the follow-up question. In the ITT analysis, abstinence rates at follow-up were higher for those in the original program than those in the modified program for both baseline-current and baseline-former smokers.

Strecher et al. (2005) reported on a RCT of the efficacy of two different web-based smoking cessation support programs for nicotine patch users. Subjects who had purchased a particular brand of nicotine patch, connected to a website for free support materials, and met other eligibility criteria were randomly assigned to web-based programs that provided either tailored behavioral smoking cessation materials or non-tailored materials. At 6- and 12-week follow-ups the outcome measures were self-reported 28-day continuous abstinence, and 10-week continuous abstinence, respectively. Each of the three different approaches to the analysis (all that enrolled, $n = 3,971$; all who logged on, $n = 3,501$; all who used the materials, did not use other cessation treatments and responded to follow-up, $n = 1,228$ at 6-weeks and $n = 864$ at 12-weeks) found that subjects in the tailored program had higher continuous abstinence rates at both 6-week and 12-week follow-ups than subjects in the non-tailored program. The subjects in the tailored program also reported higher levels of satisfaction with their program than did subjects in the non-tailored program.

Swartz et al. (2006), reported on a RCT of the short-term efficacy of an automated Internet-based smoking cessation program. Daily smokers who were considering quitting smoking in the next 30 days and who had access to the Internet were recruited through worksites and randomly assigned to the treatment condition or to the wait-list control condition. The treatment was a website program (1-2-3 Smokefree) offering demographically targeted versions (based on user age, sex and ethnicity ascertained at baseline) and designed to approximate the experience of consulting a live smoking cessation counselor. The control group received no intervention until after the follow-up. Of 351 subjects at baseline, 197 completed the 90-day follow-up. Whether based on all subjects (ITT analysis) or just those with follow-up data, the 7-day abstinence rate at 90-day follow-up was greater for the treatment group than for the control group.

Finally, it should be mentioned that there are also special population websites in the tobacco cessation area. An example would be one for pregnant smokers (Selby et al., 2006, February). The rationale for this type of website is that there are groups of smokers who have special needs that would not be of great interest to most smokers but for whom an IBI can be designed that can still serve a useful purpose. The example of pregnant smokers is a good one because of the stigma that is associated with this activity. A website that is designed to help such smokers quit could help to circumvent the stigma that pregnant smokers might feel in talking about smoking in a regular health care setting. However, this type of special population website is still in its infancy so there are no published evaluation data available as of yet.

ALCOHOL

A growing number of pilot studies have reported on participants' initial evaluations of Internet sites providing self-help materials for problem drinkers

(Cloud & Peacock, 2001; Cunningham, Humphreys, & Koski-Jännes, 2000; Lieberman, 2003; Linke et al., 2004; Linke, Harrison, & Wallace, 2005; Saitz et al., 2004; Squires & Hester, 2002, 2004; Westrup et al., 2003). In addition, there have been several good reviews on available Internet sites, both in general population (Toll et al., 2003) and college student samples (Walters, Miller, & Chiauzzi, 2005). However, there have only been two published RCTs to-date and both were conducted in face-to-face settings.

Hester et al. (2005), conducted a waiting-list control randomized trial to evaluate the Drinker's Check-up (DCU) screener. The DCU is a well-validated brief intervention developed by Miller and colleagues (Miller, Sovereign, & Krege, 1988) that has been found to motivate problem drinkers to reduce their consumption by providing personalized feedback in a non-confrontational manner. The DCU was provided to subjects on a computer in the presence of a research assistant. Sixty-one subjects, recruited through media ads and assessed to meet inclusion criteria (which included an AUDIT score of 8 or more, Saunders et al., 1993), were randomly assigned to Immediate or Delayed Treatment. At 4-week follow-up, the Immediate Treatment group reported significantly reduced drinking. The Delayed Treatment group then received the intervention, and a further 4 weeks later they had also reduced their drinking, but not significantly. Drinking for both groups was further reduced at 12-month follow-up, at which point the two groups did not differ.

Kypri et al. (2004), conducted a double-blind evaluation of a brief intervention program that is provided free of charge on the Internet. The intervention, as with the DCU, again comprised of an assessment and personalized feedback package. A total of 104 university students who met inclusion criteria (including an AUDIT score of 8 or more) were randomly assigned to a web-based assessment and feedback intervention (completed in the presence of a research assistant) or to a leaflet-only control group. At 6-week follow-up, the intervention group reported significant reductions in drinking compared to the control group, although by 6-month follow-up the groups did not differ on consumption.

One final randomized trial is nearing completion but again uses an IBI administered in a face-to-face setting (Bischof et al., 2006). Thus, RCTs of the effectiveness of IBIs for problem drinking, delivered and evaluated when they are administered on the Internet, are very much needed.

OTHER DRUG USE

There is almost no literature available on IBIs for other substances of abuse. One study (Jordan, 2005) did report on the usage statistics of a web-based portal for connecting drug users to health care professionals. Another pilot study by Villafranca et al. (2005) described the use of a website that provided personalized feedback for alcohol, tobacco and cannabis. Finally, there is a report on the use of online support groups for different substance abuse concerns (Hall & Tidwell, 2003).

However, there are no outcome studies available to-date. This lack of research points to a gap in the development and evaluation of IBIs for substance abuse that will no doubt be filled in the near future.

FUTURE DIRECTIONS – WHAT QUESTIONS NEED ANSWERING AND WHAT MIGHT IBIs FOR SUBSTANCE ABUSE LOOK LIKE IN THE FUTURE?

It is difficult to know what IBIs will look like five years from now. With the speed of technology development, the options for the type and design (or "look and feel") of IBIs can only increase. However, more important than the exact design of IBIs are considerations of the issues that need to be addressed for IBIs to mature. How these questions are answered will heavily influence the nature of future IBIs.

What is greatly needed, particularly outside the smoking arena, is the development of a stronger research base. While several trials are underway, there is almost no existing research that evaluates whether brief interventions are effective when delivered over the Internet. This question is very important because it is not safe to assume that, just because an intervention works in a face-to-face setting, it will also work when delivered over the Internet. On the Internet, more than anywhere else, the participant is able to turn the off-switch at any time so that issues such as usability, length of screening assessment, and other as yet unanticipated factors could strongly influence the effectiveness of an IBI. This ability for the participant to discontinue contact also makes conducting research on IBIs challenging as issues of "lost" participants can greatly impair the validity of any research findings (Eysenbach, 2005).

One of the advantages of a more developed research base will be the potential for quality control. There is a huge amount of information available on the Internet and, without a strong research base, there is the possibility that IBIs can do as much harm as good. With the development of high quality IBIs in which participants are informed who the developers are and what has been done to demonstrate the IBI's effectiveness, the potential participant will at least have the option of 'shopping' for a tool with a good track record.

In what other ways might IBIs evolve over the next several years? One important issue is the integration of IBIs with existing health care services. IBIs contain tools that could be very useful to clinicians in specialized health care settings. As an example, personalized feedback summaries (such as those provided by some online screeners) and access to self-help tools have been found to motivate change in problem drinkers, whether they return for treatment or not (Cunningham et al., 2001). In general health care settings, where there is an opportunity to address substance abuse concerns but often little time to meet these demands, the option of employing an IBI might promote the accessibility of treatment for substance abuse (Kypri & McAnally, 2005; Linke et al., 2005). The IBIs also contain possibilities for customization, allowing modifications of tools for special populations (e.g., adding tools for mood management to a smoking cessation IBI, Munoz et al., 2006). In addition, the flexibility of IBIs might allow traditionally underserved patients in health care settings (e.g., those concerned about stigma; individuals with limited access to treatment services) to gain access to help for their substance abuse concerns (Cunningham et al., 2006a; Postel, de Jong, & de Haan, 2005). Finally, with the growing awareness that many individuals suffer from multiple substance abuse concerns and the fact that concurrent mental health disorders are a pressing issue, IBIs may provide one fruitful option for the provision of care for complex addictions and mental health concerns (Cunningham, Selby, & van Mierlo, 2006; Farvolden et al., 2003). Whatever their format, in the next few years IBIs will help to expand the diversity of treatment options available for those seeking help for substance abuse concerns.

ACKNOWLEDGMENTS AND CONFLICT-OF-INTEREST STATEMENT

I would like to thank Joanne Cordingley for her assistance in the writing of this chapter. Dr. Cunningham has acted as a paid consultant to Van Mierlo Communications Consulting Inc. Toronto, ON, Canada, the owner of the Alcohol Help Center (AHC) software.

REFERENCES

Babor, T. F., De La Fuente, M. F., Saunders, J. B., & Grant, M. (1989). *AUDIT - The Alcohol use Disorders Identification Test: Guidelines for use in Primary Health Care*. Geneva, Switzerland: World Health Organization.

Bessell, T. L., McDonald, S., Siagy, C. A., Anderson, J. N., Hiller, J. E., & Sansom, L. N. (2002). Do Internet interventions for consumers cause more harm than good? A systematic review. *Health Expectations, 5*, 28–37.

Bischof, G., Reinhardt, S., Grothues, J., John, U., & Rumpf, H. J. (2006). The Expert Test and Report on Alcohol (ExTRA): Development and evaluation of a computerized software program for problem drinkers. In D. R. Baye (Ed.), *New Research on Alcoholism*. New York, NY: Nova Publishers.

Burton, T. L., & Williamson, D. L. (1995). Harmful effects of drinking and the use and perceived effectiveness of treatment. *Journal of Studies on Alcohol, 56*, 611–615.

Cloud, R. N., & Peacock, P. L. (2001). Internet screening and interventions for problem drinking: Results from the www.carebetter.com pilot study. *Alcoholism Treatment Quarterly, 19*, 23–44.

Cooper, G. (2004). Exploring and understanding online assistance for problem gamblers: The pathways disclosure model. *Community: International Journal of Mental Health and Addiction, 1*, 32–38.

Copeland, J., & Martin, G. (2004). Web-based interventions for substance use disorders: A qualitative review. *Journal of Substance Abuse Treatment, 26*(2), 109–116.

Cunningham, J. (2005). Is level of interest among cannabis users in self-help materials and other services aimed at reducing problem use? *Addiction*, *100*(4), 561–562.

Cunningham, J. A. (1999). Resolving alcohol-related problems with and without treatment: The effects of different problem criteria. *Journal of Studies on Alcohol*, *60*, 463–466.

Cunningham, J. A. (2000). Remissions from drug dependence: Is treatment a prerequisite? *Drug and Alcohol Dependence*, *59*, 211–213.

Cunningham, J. A., & Breslin, F. C. (2004). Only one in three people with alcohol abuse or dependence ever seek treatment. *Addictive Behaviors*, *29*(1), 221–223.

Cunningham, J. A., Ferrence, R., Cohen, J., & Adlaf, E. M. (2003). Interest in self-help materials among a general population sample of smokers. *Addictive Behaviors*, *28*(4), 811–816.

Cunningham, J. A., Humphreys, K., & Koski-Jännes, A. (2000). Providing personalized assessment feedback for problem drinking on the Internet: A pilot project. *Journal of Studies on Alcohol*, *61*, 794–798.

Cunningham, J. A., Humpheys, K., Kypri, K., & van Mierlo, T. (2006). Formative evaluation and three-month follow-up of an online personalized assessment feedback intervention for problem drinkers. *Journal of Medical Internet Research*, *8*(2), e5.

Cunningham, J. A., Sdao-Jarvie, K., Koski-Jännes, A., & Breslin, F. C. (2001). Motivating change at assessment for alcohol treatment. *Journal of Substance Abuse Treatment*, *20*, 301–304.

Cunningham, J. A., Selby, P., Kypri, K., & Humpheys, K. (2006a). Access to the Internet among drinkers, smokers and illicit drug users: Is it a barrier to the provision of interventions on the World Wide Web? *Medical Informatics and the Internet in Medicine*, *31*, 53–58.

Cunningham, J. A., Selby, P., & van Mierlo, T. (2006). Integrated online services for smokers and drinkers? Use of the Check Your Drinking assessment screener by participants of the Stop Smoking Center. *Nicotine and Tobacco Research*, *8*(Suppl. 1), S21–S25.

Cunningham, J. A., Sobell, L. C., Sobell, M. B., Agrawal, S., & Toneatto, T. (1993). Barriers to treatment: Why alcohol and drug abusers delay or never seek treatment. *Addictive Behaviors*, *18*, 347–353.

Danaher, B. G., McKay, H. G., & Seeley, J. R. (2005). The information architecture of behavior change websites. *Journal of Medical Internet Research*, *7*(2), e12.

Etter, J. F. (2005). Comparing the efficacy of two Internet-based, computer-tailored smoking cessation programs: A randomized trial. *Journal of Medical Internet Research*, *7*(1), e2.

Etter, J. F. (2006a). Internet-based smoking cessation programs. *International Journal of Medical Informatics*, *75*(1), 110–116.

Etter, J. F. (2006b). The internet and the industrial revolution in smoking cessation counselling. *Drug and Alcohol Review*, *25*(1), 79–84.

Evers, K. E., Cummins, C. O., Prochaska, J. O., & Prochaska, J. M. (2005). Online health behavior and disease management programs: Are we ready for them? Are they ready for us? *Journal of Medical Internet Research*, *7*(3), e27.

Eysenbach, G. (2005). The law of attrition. *Journal of Medical Internet Research*, *7*(1), e11.

Farvolden, P., McBride, C., Bagby, R. M., & Ravitz, P. (2003). A Web-based screening instrument for depression and anxiety disorders in primary care. *Journal of Medical Internet Research*, *5*(3), e23.

Grant, B. F. (1997). Barriers to alcoholism treatment: Reasons for not seeking treatment in a general population sample. *Journal of Studies on Alcohol*, *58*, 365–371.

Hall, M. J., & Tidwell, W. C. (2003). Internet recovery for substance abuse and alcoholism: An exploratory study of service users. *Journal of Substance Abuse Treatment*, *24*(2), 161–167.

Hasin, D. S. (1994). Treatment/self-help for alcohol-related problems: Relationship to social pressure and alcohol dependence. *Journal of Studies on Alcohol*, *55*(6), 660–666.

Health Insurance Portablility and Accountability Act of 1996 (United States of America) Pub L No. 104–191. (1996). Retrieved July 21, 2004, from http://www.hhs.gov/ocr/hipaa

Hester, R. K., Squires, D. D., & Delaney, H. D. (2005). The Drinker's Check-up: 12-month outcomes of a controlled clinical trial of a stand-alone software program for problem drinkers. *Journal of Substance Abuse Treatment*, *28*(2), 159–169.

Hughes, J. R. (1999). Four beliefs that may impede progress in the treatment of smoking. *Tobacco Control, 8*(3), 323–326.

Humphreys, K., & Klaw, E. (2001). Can targeting nondependent problem drinkers and providing internet-based services expand access to assistance for alcohol problems? A study of the moderation management self-help/mutual aid organization. *Journal of Studies on Alcohol, 62*(4), 528–532.

Institute of Medicine. (1990a). *Broadening the Base of Treatment for Alcohol Problems*. Washington, DC: National Academy Press.

Institute of Medicine. (1990b). *Treating Drug Problems*. Washington, DC: National Academy Press.

Internet World Stats. (2005). Internet World Stats: Usage and Population Statistics. Retrieved 1/18/2005, from http://www.internetworldstats.com/stats2.htm#north

Ipsos-Reid. (2002). Broadband goes mainstream. Retrieved 1/14/2003, from http://www.ipsos-reid.com/media/dsp_displayr.us.cfm?id_to_view=1491

Ipsos-Reid. (2004). The 2004 Little Internet Fact Guide. Retrieved 1/17/2005, from http://www.ipsos.ca/pdf/Ipsos_InternetFactGuide2004.pdf

Jordan, S. (2005). [www.drugcom.de – an Internet based information and counselling project for the prevention of addiction]. *Prax Kinderpsychol Kinderpsychiatr, 54*(9), 742–754.

Koski-Jännes, A., & Cunningham, J. A. (2001). Interest in different forms of self-help in a general population sample of drinkers. *Addictive Behaviors, 26*, 91–99.

Kypri, K., & McAnally, H. M. (2005). Randomized controlled trial of a web-based primary care intervention for multiple health risk behaviors. *Preventive Medicine, 41*(3–4), 761–766.

Kypri, K., Saunders, J. B., Williams, S. M., McGee, R. O., Langley, J. D., Cashell-Smith, M. L. (2004). Web-based screening and brief intervention for hazardous drinking: A double-blind randomized controlled trial. *Addiction, 99*, 1410–1417.

Lieberman, D. Z. (2003). Determinants of satisfaction with an automated alcohol evaluation program. *Cyberpsychology and Behavior, 6*(6), 677–682.

Linke, S., Brown, A., & Wallace, P. (2004). Down your drink: A web-based intervention for people with excessive alcohol consumption. *Alcohol and Alcoholism, 39*(1), 29–32.

Linke, S., Harrison, R., & Wallace, P. (2005). A Web-based intervention used in general practice for people with excessive alcohol consumption. *Journal of Telemedicine and Telecare, 11*(Suppl. 1), 39–41.

Miller, W. R., & Page, A. C. (1991). Warm turkey: Other routes to abstinence. *Journal of Substance Abuse Treatment, 8*, 227–232.

Miller, W. R., Sovereign, R. G., & Krege, B. (1988). Motivational interviewing with problem drinkers: II. The Drinker's Check-up as a preventive intervention. *Behavioural Psychotherapy, 16*, 251–268.

Munoz, R. F., Lenert, L. L., Delucchi, K., Stoddard, J., Perez, J. E., Penilla, C., et al. (2006). Toward evidence-based Internet interventions: A Spanish/English Web site for international smoking cessation trials. *Nicotine and Tobacco Research, 8*(1), 77–87.

Nicholson, T., White, J., & Duncan, D. F. (1999). A survey of adult recreational drug use via the World Wide Web: The DRUGNET study. *Journal of Psychoactive Drugs, 31*, 415–422.

Personal Information Protection and Electronic Documents Act (Canada). (2000, amended 2004). Retrieved July 21, 2004, from http://privcom.gc.ca/legislation/02_06_01_e.asp

Postel, M. G., de Jong, C. A., & de Haan, H. A. (2005). Does e-therapy for problem drinking reach hidden populations? *American Journal of Psychiatry, 162*(12), 2393.

Robins, L. N. (1980). The natural history of drug abuse. Acta Psychiatrica Scandinavica, 62, 7–20.

Roizen, R. (1977). *Barriers to Alcoholism Treatment*. Berkeley, CA: Alcohol Research Group.

Roizen, R., Cahalan, D., & Shanks, P. (1978). Spontaneous remission among untreated problem drinkers. In D. B. Kandel (Ed.), *Longitudinal Research on Drug use: Empirical Findings and Methodological Issues* (pp. 197–221). Washington, DC: Hemisphere.

Saitz, R., Helmuth, E. D., Aromaa, S. E., Guard, A., Belanger, M., & Rosenbloom, D. L. (2004). Web-based screening and brief intervention for the spectrum of alcohol problems. *Preventive Medicine, 39*(5), 969–975.

Saunders, J. B., Aasland, O. G., Babor, T. F., De La Fuente, J. R., & Grant, M. (1993). Development of the Alcohol Use Disorders Identification Test (AUDIT): WHO collaborative project on early detection of persons with harmful alcohol consumption – II. *Addiction, 88*, 791–804.

Selby, P., Dragonetti, R., Brewster, J., & Chow, V. (2006). *PREGNETS (Network for the PREvention of Gestational and Neonatal Exposure to Tobacco Smoke) II: Integrating smoke free interventions into pre-natal nutrition programs.* Paper presented at the Society for Research on Nicotine and Tobacco, Orlando, FL, USA.

Sobell, L. C., Sobell, M. B., & Toneatto, T. (1992). Recovery from alcohol problems without treatment. In N. Heather, W. R. Miller, & J. Greeley (Eds.), *Self-control and the Addictive Behaviors* (pp. 198–242). New York, NY: Maxwell MacMillan.

Squires, D. D., & Hester, R. K. (2002). Development of a computer-based, brief intervention for drinkers: The increasing role for computers in the assessment and treatment of addictive behaviors. *The Behavior Therapist, 25*, 59–65.

Squires, D. D., & Hester, R. K. (2004). Using technical innovations in clinical practice: The Drinker's Check-Up software program. *Journal of Clinical Psychology, 60*(2), 159–169.

Strecher, V. J., Marcus, A., Bishop, K., Fleisher, L., Stengle, W., Levinson, A., et al. (2005). A randomized controlled trial of multiple tailored messages for smoking cessation among callers to the cancer information service. *Journal of Health Communication, 10*(Suppl. 1), 105–118.

Swartz, L. H., Noell, J. W., Schroeder, S. W., & Ary, D. V. (2006). A randomised control study of a fully automated internet based smoking cessation programme. *Tobacco Control, 15*(1), 7–12.

Toll, B. A., Sobell, L. C., D'Arienzo, J., Sobell, M. B., Eickleberry-Goldsmith, L., & Toll, H. J. (2003). What do Internet-based alcohol treatment websites offer? *Cyberpsychology and Behavior, 6*(6), 581–584.

Tuchfeld, B. S. (1976). *Changes in Patterns of Alcohol use Without the Aid of Formal Treatment: An Exploratory Study of Former Problem Drinkers.* Research Triangle Park, NC: Research Triangle Institute.

United States Department of Commerce. (2002). *A Nation Online: How Americans are Expanding their use of the Internet.* Washington, DC: Economics and Statistics Administration, National Telecommunications and Information Administration.

van Mierlo, T., Cunningham, J. A., Farvolden, P., Fournier, R., Pakizeh Rooh, P., Selby, P., et al. (2006). *Determining the Validity of Self-Reported Alcohol Dependence and Treatment Data Collected via the World Wide Web: Legality, Legitimacy and Limitations.* Paper presented at the 32nd Annual Epidemiology Symposium of the Kettle Bruun Society, Maastricht, Netherlands.

Villafranca, S. W., Weingardt, K. R., Humphreys, K., & Cunningham, J. A. (2005). Providing normative feedback on the Internet to stimulate self-evaluation of alcohol, tobacco, and cannabis use. *International Journal of Self-help and Self-care, 3*, 87–101.

Walters, S. T., Miller, E., & Chiauzzi, E. (2005). Wired for wellness: e-Interventions for addressing college drinking. *Journal of Substance Abuse Treatment, 29*(2), 139–145.

Walters, S. T., Wright, J. A., & Shegog, R. (2006). A review of computer and Internet-based interventions for smoking behavior. *Addictive Behaviors, 31*(2), 264–277.

Walther, J. B., Pingree, S., Hawkins, R. P., & Buller, D. B. (2005). Attributes of interactive online health information systems. *Journal of Medical Internet Research, 7*(3), e33.

Westrup, D., Futa, K. T., Whitsell, S. D., Mussman, L., Wanat, S. F., Koopman, C., et al. (2003). Employees' reactions to an interactive website assessing alcohol use and risk for alcohol dependence, stress level and coping. *Journal of Substance Use, 8*, 104–111.

CHAPTER 20

Alcohol Use Among Undergraduate Students: From Brief Interventions to Behavioral Economics

Amber M. Henslee, Jessica G. Irons and Christopher J. Correia
Department of Psychology, Auburn University, Auburn, AL, USA

Abstract: Alcohol use among undergraduate students has been identified as a significant public health problem. This chapter summarizes recent statistics on the prevalence and consequences of undergraduate drinking, and discusses some specific groups that have been identified as high-risk. The literature on the use of brief interventions to reduce the harm associated with alcohol use among undergraduates is summarized. Recent studies using a behavioral economic approach to address undergraduate drinking are also discussed, with the goal of providing a model for how basic and clinical research can be integrated to better inform clinical practice and public policy.

Translation of Addictions Science into Practice

UNDERGRADUATE STUDENT DRINKING: FROM BRIEF INTERVENTIONS TO BEHAVIORAL ECONOMICS

The headlines are hard to ignore. In recent years, several prominent US newspapers have run stories highlighting the dangers associated with undergraduate student drinking (Cada, 2004; Davis & DeBarros, 2006). These stories have drawn national attention to alcohol-related fatalities and provide a human element to some sobering statistics. Each year, approximately 1700 undergraduates at colleges and universities in the United States die as a result of an unintentional alcohol-related injury (Hingson et al., 2005). The rate of alcohol-related fatalities, along with the full spectrum of physical and psychological consequences of alcohol use, has led some to declare that alcohol use is the single most serious public health problem confronting American colleges (Wechsler & Dowdall, 1998; United States Department of Health and Humans Services, 2000).

Alcohol use among undergraduates has been an area of scientific research for several decades (e.g., Straus & Bacon, 1953). The goal of this chapter is to provide an overview of the current scientific literature on alcohol use among undergraduates. We will begin by summarizing some of the most recent statistics on the prevalence and consequences of undergraduate drinking, and discuss some specific groups that have been identified as high-risk. We will then review the literature on the use of brief interventions, and more specifically the Brief Alcohol Screening and Intervention for College Students (BASICS; Dimeff et al., 1999) program, to prevent and treat problematic alcohol use among high-risk undergraduates. We will end the chapter by highlighting some recent studies that have used behavioral economic models to understand and address undergraduate drinking. In preparing this chapter, we made an effort to draw attention to current and emerging trends in the literature. We also hope to provide a model of how laboratory findings can be translated into clinical research and ultimately impact clinical practices.

A quick note on terminology. We use the term "undergraduate" throughout the chapter. An undergraduate is typically a student who has completed secondary school requirements and is now enrolled in a 3 (in the UK) or 4 (in the US) year college or university program and working toward a bachelors degree. Most undergraduates are between 18 and 23 years old.

ALCOHOL USE AMONG UNDERGRADUATE STUDENTS

RATES OF ALCOHOL USE

A number of recent national studies provide data on the prevalence and associated consequences of undergraduate drinking in the United States, including the National College Health Risk Behavior Survey (Centers for Disease Control and Prevention (CDC), 1997), the National Household Survey on Drug Use and Health (NSDUH; Substance Abuse and Mental Health Services Administration, 2005), the Monitoring the Future study (Johnston et al., 2004), the Core Institute study (Presley, Meilman, & Cashin, 1996), and the Harvard College Alcohol Study (CAS; Wechsler et al., 1995; Wechsler et al., 2000b). A comprehensive presentation of the methodology and results of each study is beyond the scope of the current chapter, and interested readers are referred to a recent review by O'Malley and Johnston (2002). A review of studies assessing alcohol use among undergraduates in the United Kingdom is also available (Gill, 2002).

Despite methodological differences, the five US studies have reported similar rates of alcohol use among undergraduates. As an example, we will highlight findings from the Harvard CAS studies. In 1993, Wechsler and his colleagues initiated the Harvard CAS, which was the most nationally representative survey of undergraduate student alcohol use to date (Wechsler et al., 1995). Additional surveys were conducted in 1997, 1999, and 2001. The most recent survey (Wechsler et al., 2002) included data from 10,904 students across 119 nationally representative four-year colleges and universities selected from accredited institutions identified by the American Council on Education. To assess "binge" or "heavy episodic drinking", male students were asked to "Think back over the last two weeks. How many times have you had five or more drinks in a row?" Female students were asked to report the number of times they consumed four or more drinks in a row. Just under 20% of the students identified themselves as non–drinkers, 36% reportedly drank alcohol but did not engage in an episode of binge drinking, and 44% of students participated in binge drinking episodes within the past two weeks. Thus, the majority of US undergraduates identify themselves as drinkers, and close to half report a recent episode of binge or heavy episodic drinking. Recent evidence suggests that rates of binge drinking among undergraduates in the UK also exceed both their same–aged peers in the general UK population and those reported by undergraduates in the US (Gill, 2002). For example, Delk and Meilman (1996) reported that Scottish students were more than US students to report an episode of binge drinking (63% vs. 40%), and more likely to report engaging in three or more episodes of binge drinking over the previous 2 weeks (31% vs. 16%). Finally, reports from a wide range of countries, including Brazil (Stempliuk et al., 2005), Kenya (Odek-Ogunde & Pande-Leak, 1999), Poland (Mellibruna, Nikodemska, & Fronczyk, 2003), and Lebanon (Karam, Maalouf, & Ghandour, 2004) all suggest that undergraduates consume more alcohol than members of the general population and are considered at-risk for a variety of alcohol-related consequences.

CONSEQUENCES OF UNDERGRADUATE STUDENT ALCOHOL USE

Alcohol use, and particularly binge drinking, among undergraduates can lead to a host of alcohol-related consequences. The negative effects of alcohol range from fairly minor problems (e.g., oversleeping and missing class) to alcohol-induced auto fatalities and alcohol poisoning, and alcohol use that leads to a prolonged pattern of negative consequences can result in a diagnosis of alcohol abuse or dependence. The consequences are not limited to the drinker, but instead have the potential to impact everyone in the drinker's environment.

A recent review integrated data from the National Highway Traffic Safety Administration, the CDC, national coroner studies, census and college enrollment data for 18–24-year-olds, the NSDUH, and the Harvard CAS to gain a more comprehensive view of the magnitude of alcohol-related mortality and morbidity among US undergraduates (Hingson et al., 2005). The review concluded that approximately 1700 students died in the past year as the result of an unintentional alcohol-related injury. Approximately 2.8 million students reported driving under the influence of alcohol, and more than 3 million students rode with an intoxicated driver. Finally, more than 500,000 students suffered an injury while drinking.

Students routinely report that alcohol use can adversely affect their academic performance, interpersonal behavior, and overall health. Participants in the Core survey (Presley et al., 1996) reported that the most common negative consequences from heavy drinking include feeling hung-over (64.3%), feeling nauseous or vomiting (55.7%), doing something which was later regretted (39.1%), memory loss (34.4%), and missing class (32.9%). CAS data indicated that among students who drank alcohol during the past 30 days, 27% reportedly experienced blackouts, 22% fell behind in school work, 21% engaged in unplanned sex, and 10% engaged in unprotected sex (Wechsler & Dowdall, 1998). Frequent binger drinkers (47%) are more likely to report experiencing five or more alcohol-related problems than infrequent (14%) or non-binge (3%) drinkers (Wechsler et al., 1994). Similar behavioral and academic consequences have been reported by undergraduate drinkers in the UK (Gill, 2002) and New Zealand (Mcgee & Kypri, 2004).

The development of an alcohol-related disorder is another possible consequence of alcohol consumption. Estimated rates of alcohol abuse and dependence among undergraduates in the US come from a variety of sources, including the 1999 CAS study (Knight et al., 2002) the 2001–2002 National Epidemiological Surveys on Alcohol and Related Conditions (Dawson et al., 2004), and 2001 NSDUH data (Slutske, 2005). The reported prevalence of abuse (5.3–31.6%) and dependence (6.3–20.2%) differ across studies and varies as a function of the diagnostic instrument used, making it difficult to establish a true prevalence rate. Among CAS participants, frequent binge drinkers (defined as 3 or more episodes of binge drinking over the past 2 weeks) were 19 times more likely to meet criteria for alcohol dependence and 13 times more likely to meet criteria for abuse.

The literature also recognized that there are second-hand effects of binge drinking, a concept that is similar to the second-hand effects of cigarette smoke. Wechsler and Dowdall (1998) reported the most frequent second-hand alcohol-related problems were having study time or sleep interrupted (60.6%), having to take care of a drunken student (50.2%), and being insulted or humiliated (28.6%). Regarding more serious consequences, over 600,000 students reported being hit or assaulted by a student who had consumed alcohol, and more than 70,000 students experienced a date rape perpetrated by a student who had consumed alcohol (Hingson et al., 2005). In the UK, 15% of heavy male drinkers reported hurting someone as a result of alcohol use (File, Mabbutt, & Shaffer, 1994).

SPECIAL AT-RISK COLLEGE POPULATIONS

There appear to be subgroups of students who are identified as at-risk for developing abusive patterns of alcohol consumption and experiencing negative consequences. Full accounts of the interpersonal and environmental risk factors can be found in Ham and Hope (2003) and Baer (2002). Some examples of identified at-risk populations include white males, freshmen, student-athletes, and members of "Greek" organizations. These risk groups are presented here and then reconsidered in the section on behavioral economics.

White Males

Gender differences in the drinking practices of college students have been widely reported. For example, according to 2001 CAS data (Wechsler et al., 2002), 49% of males reported episodes of binge drinking, compared to 41% of the females. White students (50%) were also more likely to report binge drinking than students who identified themselves as Hispanic (35%), Black or African American (22%), or Asian (26%). Students with diagnoses of alcohol abuse or dependence are also more likely to be white males (Knight et al., 2002). Alcohol use among white males does appear to be influenced by the campus environment, as white males who attend schools with increased enrollment among minority and female students reported less binge drinking (Wechsler & Kuo, 2003). Finally, it should be noted that studies conducted in the US and the UK suggest that female students are becoming more like their male counterparts in regards to their drinking behavior (Gill, 2002; Ham & Hope, 2003).

Freshmen

In the US, first year undergraduates are referred to as freshman. The majority of freshman enter the university below the legal drinking age of 21. *USA Today* recently presented National Center for Education Statistics data, as analyzed by the American Council on Education, on the consequences of alcohol use among college freshman (Davis & DeBarros, 2006). The report analyzed 620 alcohol-related fatalities that occurred at 4-year colleges and universities since 2000 and found that freshman were over-represented. Although freshmen account for 24% of the undergraduate population, they were involved in 35% of the fatalities. The *USA Today* report reflects trends that have been reported in more traditional scientific sources. As many as 42% of freshmen meet the criteria for binge drinking (Wechsler et al., 2000a), and many freshman drink at levels that exceed the binge drinking threshold (White, Kraus, & Swartzwelder, 2006a). Freshman may also be especially vulnerable to experiencing negative alcohol-related consequences (O'Neill, Parra, & Sher, 2001).

Student–Athletes

Wechsler, Davenport, and Dowdall (1997) used 1993 CAS data to investigate the relationship between alcohol use and participation in athletics. For both males and females, increased involvement and investment in intercollegiate sports was associated with higher rates of binge drinking. More recent CAS data (Nelson & Wechsler, 2001) also indicated that collegiate athletes are more likely to binge drink, drink in order to get drunk, and experience alcohol-related consequences than their non-athlete peers. Other studies have reported an interaction between gender and athletic status, with male athletes reporting higher levels of risky behaviors (e.g., binge drinking and driving while intoxicated) than male non-athletes, and female athletes reporting lower levels of risky behaviors than female non-athletes (Kokotailo et al., 1996). Both US and French studies suggest that student-athletes playing contact-sports are at higher risk than those who play non-contact sports (Nattiv, Puffer, & Green, 1997; Peretti-Watel et al., 2003).

Fraternity and Sorority Members

In the US, a sizable minority of students join specific social clubs called fraternities or sororities. There is a substantial amount of literature that indicates that members of fraternity and sorority organizations (also referred to as "Greeks"), drink alcohol more frequently, consume more alcohol per occasion, and experience more alcohol-related consequences than their non-fraternity and sorority peers (Wechsler et al., 1995, 1996; Cashin, Presley, & Meilman, 1998). Utilizing the CAS 1993 data, Wechsler et al. (1996) reported that fraternity and sorority members who lived in Greek housing reported higher levels of binge drinking and more severe alcohol-related negative consequences than members who did not live in Greek housing and non-Greek students. Data from the Core survey has also documented increased alcohol use among students in Greek organizations, and suggested that alcohol use was positively related to a student's level of involvement in the organization (Cashin et al., 1998). Borsari and Carey (1999) provide a thorough review of the literature on alcohol use among fraternity members.

THE USE OF BRIEF INTERVENTIONS TO REDUCE COLLEGE STUDENT DRINKING

Although some students will decrease their alcohol consumption without any intervention (Baer et al., 2001; Vik, Cellucci, & Ivers, 2003), the prevalence of undergraduate drinking and the resulting negative consequences has spurred research on the development of intervention techniques specific to this population. Undergraduate drinking is typically conceptualized from a harm reduction approach and treatment has centered on brief interventions (e.g., Larimer & Croce, 2002). Brief interventions target individuals with mild to moderate substance-related problems in an attempt to reach individuals who may not seek traditional forms of substance abuse treatment such as hospitalization or 12-Step support groups (Zweben & Fleming, 1999). The primary goal of these interventions is to increase an individual's motivation to change their substance-related behavior. More specifically, brief interventions aim to (a) increase awareness regarding the costs and consequences of substance use, (b) strengthen an individual's beliefs about their ability to change their behavior, (c) utilize helping techniques to support change, (d) encourage individuals to accept responsibility for change, and (e) promote commitment to change (Zweben & Fleming, 1999).

Brief interventions have become a viable alternative to more intensive treatments; they are more effective than no treatment, can be as effective as more intensive treatment, and are more efficient in terms of time and cost (Bien, Miller, & Tonigan, 1993). In a review of brief interventions, Zweben and Fleming (1999) identified 14 studies (of which only 5 were conducted in North America) comparing brief interventions to control interventions among groups of non-dependent drinkers. The studies suggested that brief interventions delivered in primary care settings promoted reductions in drinking across both genders, motivated individuals to pursue specialized alcohol treatment programs, and reduced the utilization of other health care services. More recently, a meta-analysis of 22 studies evaluating brief interventions for excessive drinking reported that the interventions were effective across a range of settings and demographic groups (Vasilaki, Hosier, & Cox, 2006).

BASICS: A Brief Alcohol Screening and Intervention for College Students

The Brief Alcohol Screening and Intervention for College Students program – or BASICS – was developed by researchers at the University of Washington specifically for undergraduates who experience or are at risk for experiencing negative consequences related to alcohol use (Dimeff et al., 1999). The model on which the BASICS program was developed consists of three assumptions. First, many students lack important information and coping skills to drink moderately. Second, certain developmental milestones in a young adult's life contribute to heavy drinking (e.g., separation from parents and assumption of adult privileges). Third, personal factors (e.g., faulty beliefs about alcohol) and environmental factors (e.g., peer pressure, heavy drinking friends, and a mindset of drinking in order to get drunk) inhibit the use of behavioral skills that students possess (Dimeff et al., 1999). In addition to following these three assumptions, the BASICS program utilizes the harm reduction approach. This approach focuses on moderation of alcohol use, not abstinence, and therefore is different from the traditional disease model of alcoholism or the "Just Say No" program, both of which establish abstinence as the primary goal. A harm reduction approach views alcohol–related problems on a continuum and encourages incremental changes toward less risky alcohol use patterns. Finally, BASICS incorporates several elements of motivation interviewing (Miller & Rollnick, 2002), including a supportive rather than a confrontational approach, expressions of empathy, rolling with resistance, developing a discrepancy between the student's perceived and actual self, and supporting self-efficacy for change.

A typical BASICS–style intervention lasts between 2 and 4 sessions with a trained clinician (Dimeff et al., 1999). In a two-session model (e.g., Borsari & Carey, 2000), a participant spends the first session answering interview questions and completing self-report surveys on a wide range of alcohol-related variables. The clinician uses the information collected during the initial session to create a personalized feedback form, and the feedback form is presented during the second session. The feedback form provides students with normative information about how their beliefs about alcohol use, and their drinking practices, compare too actual drinking behavior on campus. Personalized feedback can also includes a review of relevant risk factors (e.g., family history of abuse or dependence) for the development of longer term drinking problems; information about estimated blood alcohol content on a typical or heavy night of alcohol use; discussion of the negative alcohol-related consequences reported during the initial session; a summary of the amount of money and time devoted to alcohol use; and a review of the calories consumed through alcohol and the time required to expend these calories through exercise.

BASICS: EMPIRICAL SUPPORT

In 2002, the National Institute on Alcohol Abuse and Alcoholism released a report on college student drinking (NIAAA, 2002). The BASICS program was specifically mentioned as an intervention strategy that had demonstrated its effectiveness in reducing alcohol. BASICS has in fact enjoyed fairly consistent empirical support. Two early studies which were fundamental to the development of BASICS were conducted at the University of Washington (Baer et al., 1992;

Marlatt et al., 1998). Baer et al. (1992) conducted a longitudinal study to compare at-risk college students across three brief intervention experimental groups: 6–week classroom format, 6–unit self-help correspondence format, and 1–hour individualized feedback and advice format. There was an overall reduction of alcohol use at the end of treatment, with the greatest effects seen within the classroom group, although these effects were not significantly different than those in the individualized group. Thus, the 1–hour session was as effective as the more intensive classroom–based intervention, and changes in alcohol use patterns were maintained throughout a 2–year follow–up period. Marlatt et al. (1998) also conducted a longitudinal study to compare at-risk high school students entering the university to a normative comparison sample. In a randomized controlled trial, at–risk students were assigned either to a brief intervention group or a no treatment control group. A third group of incoming freshmen served as a natural history comparison. Participants in the treatment group, when compared to the control groups, reported drinking less frequently, drinking less alcohol per occasion, and consuming a lower peak quantity of alcohol at the 2–year follow–up. The treatment group also reported a significant decrease in the number of self–reported alcohol–related problems.

The initial studies by Baer et al. (1992) and Marlatt et al. (1998) led to the development and dissemination of a BASICS treatment manual, and recent studies have tested the effectiveness of the manualized protocol. Three studies reported on the use of the BASICS protocol with groups of at-risk students recruited from more general samples of undergraduate drinkers. Borsari and Carey (2000) compared at-risk students in two experimental groups: a brief intervention group and a no treatment control group. Murphy et al. (2001) also evaluated the efficacy of the BASICS model among heavy drinking students. The Murphy study randomly assigned students to one of three experimental conditions: the BASICS condition, an education condition, and an assessment only control group. The results from these two studies suggest that BASICS can lead to short–term reductions in the frequency and quantity of alcohol consumption, and that the intervention appears to be more effective for heavier drinkers. Finally, Baer et al. (2001) utilized the BASICS manual in a longitudinal study of freshmen. The authors randomized incoming freshmen to one of three groups: high–risk prevention, high–risk control, and natural history. The high–risk prevention group received personalized feedback from a clinician during their first year, and mailed personalized feedback during their second year followed by phone contact. Both the prevention and control groups decreased the quantity, frequency, and negative consequences of alcohol use. However, the prevention reported more significant reductions over the course of the four-year study.

Two more recent studies have tested the effectiveness of BASICS when used with students who have been referred or mandated to treatment because of a specific alcohol-related incident or violation of an alcohol-related policy (Borsari & Carey, 2005; White et al., 2006a). Both of the studies suggest that referred students assigned to a BASICS intervention show reductions in alcohol consumption and related negative consequences. However, White and her colleagues (2006b) also reported that simply providing written personalized feedback produced significant reductions in alcohol use, and that the changes were similar to those produced by the BASICS intervention delivered by a trained clinician.

SUMMARY AND FUTURE DIRECTIONS

Research suggests that the BASICS program can be an effective tool for reducing risky drinking, and to a lesser extent alcohol-related negative consequences, among college students. Treatment effect sizes for the BASICS intervention vary between modest (Marlatt et al., 1998) and more robust (Borsari & Carey, 2000) for long-term and immediate follow-up. BASICS appears especially effective for those undergraduates who are heavy drinkers (Borsari & Carey, 2000; Murphy et al., 2001). Reductions in alcohol use patterns have persisted for up to 2 years (Baer et al., 1992; Marlatt et al., 1998) and reductions in related negative consequences have been shown at a 4-year follow-up (Baer et al., 2001). Furthermore, BASICS is as effective as more intense interventions (Baer et al., 1992). Finally, the BASICS program is rated favorably by undergraduates (Marlatt et al., 1998; Borsari & Carey, 2000; Murphy et al., 2001).

Despite the growing research in support of the BASICS program, there are several questions that warrant future research. To date, all of the studies testing the manualized version of BASICS have been conducted in the US. While the student samples utilized in these studies may have been heavy drinkers or exhibited risky alcohol use patterns, there have been only two published studies on the effectiveness of BASICS when used with referred students (Borsari & Carey, 2005; White et al., 2006b). Research suggests that mandated students may engage in more occasions of heavy drinking and report more alcohol-related negative consequences (Barnett et al., 2004). While the literature suggests that heavier drinking students may actually be more responsive to brief interventions, it is still important to confirm that the effects seen with high-risk students generalize to students who are mandated to treatment. Although BASICS was not originally designed to treat students with alcohol dependence, the potential for the program to increase motivation to change and reduce alcohol use in diagnosed students should also be established.

Several studies have attempted to determine the components of BASICS that are most responsible for changes in alcohol use. For example, a number of studies have suggested that normative feedback, delivered with or without a clinician, can lead to changes in behavior (see Walters & Neighbors, 2005, for a review). As noted, a recent study suggested that simply providing written personalized feedback can lead to changes in mandated students similar to those produced by a clinician-guided BASICS-style intervention (White et al., 2006b). This finding is consistent with other recent studies suggesting that personalized feedback delivered via the mail or internet can effectively reduce drinking among undergraduates (e.g., Agostinelli, Brown, & Miller, 1995; Collins, Carey, & Sliwinski, 2002; Murphy et al., 2004; Walters, Bennett, & Miller, 2000). Given the effectiveness of the personalized feedback forms in reducing alcohol use, the potential to use events such as National Alcohol Screening Day (Greenfield et al., 2003) to efficiently deliver personalized feedback to large numbers of undergraduates is very promising (Benson et al., 2004; Henslee et al., in press).

THE BEHAVIORAL ECONOMIC PERSPECTIVE

Undergraduates have a seemingly limitless array of activities to which they could devote their time and energy. In addition to studying and pursuing other academic endeavors, students might also be employed, become involved in a service-based organization, or join an athletic team. Students also have many options when it comes to enjoying their leisure time. Thus, along with going to class, studying, working, and playing video games with friends, alcohol use is one of several activities in which a student may choose to engage. In psychology and the behavioral sciences, a variety of theories have attempted to understand the choices that people make. Behavioral economics refers to a theoretical development that uses economic principles, such as the law of demand, to understand choice behavior and patterns of behavioral allocation (Madden, 2000). A related theoretical development, the behavioral choice perspective, refers to a collection of operant-based research and theory utilized to explain the establishment of preferences among available reinforcers (Vuchinich & Tucker, 1988). The terms behavioral economics and behavioral choice are used somewhat interchangeably, and both rest on the assumption that choice behavior is determined by the reinforcing value of one behavioral option relative to the reinforcing value of all other competing behavioral options.

Vuchinich and Tucker (1983) were among the first to propose behavioral theories of choice as a framework for understanding the environmental context surrounding alcohol use and abuse. These authors described the behavioral choice perspective as a molar account of how organisms allocate their behavior among a set of available activities, with the full set of available activities constituting the surrounding context. Thus, the behavioral choice perspective recognizes that preferences for alcohol arise within a broader environmental context that includes the availability or utilization of other competing reinforcers and their associated environmental constraints. In other words, decisions to use alcohol are the result of an interaction between the reinforcing properties of alcohol, the availability of the alcohol, and the reinforcing value and availability of alternative alcohol-free activities. Analyses emerging from this perspective aim to identify the variables that control the reinforcing value of alcohol relative to the reinforcing value of other available activities (Vuchinich & Tucker, 1988). After reviewing the work of Premack (1965), Herrnstein (1970), and other behavioral choice researchers, Vuchinich and Tucker (1983) proposed the following generalization: If constraints on a particular reinforcer are increased, there is a tendency for its consumption to be reduced and for behavior to be reallocated among the other available reinforcers. When applied to substance use, the generalization suggests that the environmental context surrounding alcohol use can be investigated as a function of two classes of variables: (a) the direct constraints imposed on access to alcohol use, and (b) reinforcers other than alcohol use that are available and the constraints imposed on access to them. The behavioral choice and behavioral economic perspectives have been applied to a wide range of addictive behaviors, including the prediction of cigarette smoking, eating and physical activity, and drug and alcohol abuse (Bickel et al., 1990; DeGrandpre & Bickle, 1996; Epstein et al., 1991a, 1991b; Vuchinich & Tucker, 1983, 1988). The following sections will review research that demonstrates how these perspectives can be applied to alcohol use among undergraduates.

ACCESS TO ALCOHOL

Constraints usually refer to any factor that limits the availability or use of alcohol. Constraints can consist of the price or monetary cost of alcohol, the time and effort required to obtain alcohol, and the potential for negative legal and health consequences. Much has been written about the relationship between the price of alcohol and consumption among the general public (see Osterberg, 2001, for a review of studies conducted in the US and Europe). Availability theory refers to the notion that the level of alcohol-related harm in any society is closely tied to the availability of alcohol (Bruun et al., 1975). Bars and package-shops often surround campuses, which make alcohol readily and conveniently available (Dowdall & Wechsler, 2002). Indeed, rates of binge drinking are higher on campuses with a high density of alcohol outlets (Weitzman et al., 2003). Many businesses target the student population by offering drink specials (i.e., decreased purchase price) and advertising in college publications or on campus bulletin boards, and these practices have also been associated with higher rates of binge drinking (Kuo, Wechsler, Greenberg, & Lee, 2003). The impact of environmental access and constraints can also be seen in fraternity houses (Borsari & Carey, 1999). Within fraternity houses, there are minimal constraints on drinking, residents drink more frequently, intoxication is tolerated, and assistance is given to those who experience negative consequences of alcohol use (e.g., hangovers). All of these factors serve to decrease the price of alcohol consumption for fraternity members. Indeed, a study conducted in Sydney, Australia (Basten, Psychol, & Kavanagh, 1996) found that undergraduate college residents (the closest equivalent to the US fraternity system) reported more alcohol use than non-college residents during the academic term. However, the two groups did not differ in their drinking patterns during a vacation between semesters, suggesting that the availability of alcohol and the local norms played a role in the alcohol consumption of college residents.

Although constraints on access to alcohol can affect all students, access to alcohol may have a particularly strong impact on patterns of alcohol consumption among freshmen and underage drinkers. Harford, Wechsler, and Seibring (2002) reported that freshmen were more likely than upperclassmen to drink at fraternity houses or off-campus locations, and that freshmen were more likely to report heavy drinking when attending these parties. In the US, students under the legal drinking age of 21 were also more likely to report that alcohol could be purchased at low or discounted prices; approximately 58% of underage students reported that they paid less than one dollar for a drink, did not pay anything, or paid one set price (i.e., a cover fee) for all they could drink. In comparison, students aged 21–23 were more likely to report drinking in off-campus bars, and were far less likely to report obtaining alcohol at such low prices (Wechsler, 2000). Thus, constraints such as legal restrictions can influence the setting in which consumption occurs and the per-drink price, and these factors in turn influence how much a student will consume.

Several laboratory studies have been used to model the relationship between price and alcohol consumption. An early study used an experimental laboratory to simulate the effect of "happy hour" on alcohol consumption (Babor et al., 1978). Predictably, both heavy and light drinkers consumed more alcohol when the price of a drink decreased. More recent studies have used laboratory procedures to study factors that influence alcohol consumption among undergraduates. Murphy and MacKillop (2006) used a simulated alcohol purchase task to assess levels of alcohol consumption across a range of prices. The average number of drinks consumed was approximately 7 when the price was $0.25 or less per drink, remained at or above 5 drinks at prices up to $1.50 per drink, then showed a steady linear decrease as prices increased. Students estimated that they would consume less than 1 standard drink at prices higher than $6.00. Not surprisingly, binge drinkers were willing to spend more to consume alcohol. Another series of laboratory studies used a multiple choice procedure to alcohol preference among undergraduates (Correia et al., 2006; Little & Correia, in press). Students were asked to complete a laboratory task during which they made a series discrete choices between various amounts of alcohol that were available for immediate consumption and monetary payments. Participants showed a strong preference for alcohol, and were less likely to chose a monetary payment, as higher doses became available.

These laboratory studies have produced findings that are similar to patterns observed in the natural environment. The procedures allow researchers to control variables, such as access and price, that cannot be easily isolated in the natural environment, and could be used to model the impact a variety of environmental manipulations and public policy initiatives (e.g., price increases, taxes, response requirement, response cost) might have on alcohol consumption. Laboratory procedures could also be used to identity behavioral processes (e.g., strong preference for alcohol despite increased price, impulsive decision making) that place students at risk for abusive patterns of alcohol without relying strictly on self-reports of use patterns and negative consequences (Murphy & MacKillop, 2006). Thus, the behavioral economic perspective and associated laboratory procedures that model the relationship between constraints and consumption can be used to inform the assessment and prevention of problematic alcohol use among undergraduates.

ALTERNATIVE REINFORCERS

One of the clearest implications of the behavioral economics literature is the importance of alternative reinforcers. The behavioral economic perspective suggests that the reinforcing value of any particular behavior depends on the availability of alternative reinforcers. Vuchinich and Tucker (1988, 1996) reviewed numerous operant-based laboratory studies, and concluded that alcohol use may emerge as a highly preferred activity when constraints on access to alcohol are minimal and alternative reinforcers are either sparse, delayed, or difficult to acquire. In one laboratory study, preference for alcohol consumption among male undergraduates was studied as a function of the value and delay of an alternative reinforcer (Vuchinich & Tucker, 1983). Participants could earn points by responding with button presses, and the points could be redeemed for either money or alcohol. All alcohol earned in the study had to be consumed during the experimental session. The investigators manipulated the monetary value of the points (2¢ or 10¢) and the delay before money was received (no delay, 2-week delay, or 8-week delay); the price of alcohol remained the same across conditions. As predicted, participants showed greater preference for alcohol under the low money condition, and participants in both delay conditions preferred alcohol more than participants in the no-delay condition. Similar results have been shown on a multiple choice procedure, with undergraduate drinkers showing a stronger preference for alcohol consumption when an alternative monetary reward was delayed than when the reward was immediately available (Little & Correia, in press).

Similar to laboratory studies modeling the relationship between price and consumption, laboratory studies on the relationship between alcohol consumption and alternative reinforcers are mirrored by findings from more naturalistic research. For example, male and female student-athletes report higher rates of alcohol use during the off-season (Selby, Weinstein, & Burd, 1990), and some have discussed the "void" felt by athletes when they are not playing their sport and the tendency to fill this void with substance use (Tricker, Cook, & McGuire, 1989). From a behavioral economic perspective, participation in athletics would appear to be an alternative reinforcer that competes with and reduces alcohol use during the season, and alcohol use increases as reinforcement related to athletics becomes less available. Studies with more general samples of undergraduates have reported similar relationships: the amount of reinforcement derived from substance-free activities is predictive of the frequency, quantity, and negative consequences of alcohol use (e.g., school work, relationships, employment; Correia, Carey, & Borsari, 2002; Correia et al., 1998); students who engage in frequent binge drinking derive less reinforcement from a variety of substance free activities than lighter-drinking students (Correia et al., 2003); and increases in substance-free activities like exercise can lead to decreases in substance use (Correia, Benson, & Carey, 2005). Ideally, studies from both the laboratory and the natural environment would be used to understand the impact alternative reinforcers have on alcohol use, and how this knowledge can be used to inform prevention and intervention strategies.

A number of behavioral treatment approaches attempt to alter the consequences of an individual's behavior, such that rewards for alternative behaviors begin to outweigh the rewards associated with substance use. For example, contingency management programs have been used to decrease the reinforcing value of substance use by providing tangible reinforcers (e.g., vouchers, monetary payments, prizes) for evidence of drug abstinence. Contingency management programs have been used to decrease the use of a number of substances, including cocaine (Higgins et al., 1991), opioids (Silverman et al., 1996), alcohol (Petry et al., 2000), and cigarettes (Corby et al., 2000). Although contingency management has not been used to address alcohol use among undergraduates, recent studies using incentives to help students reduce cigarette smoking and initiate abstinence (Correia & Benson, 2006; Rooney et al., 2005) suggest that the approach warrants further investigation.

The behavioral economic approach also has the potential to inform our use of BASICS and other brief interventions. Murphy and colleagues (2005) exposed heavy-drinking undergraduates to a brief intervention that included personalized drinking feedback. The feedback forms were based on the BASICS program. Prior to the intervention, students completed a measure of substance-related and substance-free activity reinforcement. Female students who derived a smaller proportion of their reinforcement from substance use showed a greater reduction in alcohol use after the intervention. For both male and female students, decreases in alcohol use were mirrored by increases in the proportion of reinforcement derived from substance-free activities. Interestingly, students who reduced their alcohol use actually reported a decrease in their substance-free social interactions. These findings highlight the important role alcohol plays in the lives of students, and perhaps the need to provide a range of alcohol-free reinforcers that can effectively compete with the social functions of alcohol.

FINAL THOUGHTS ON BRIEF INTERVENTIONS AND BEHAVIORAL ECONOMICS

This chapter began with a review of studies on the prevalence and consequences of alcohol use among undergraduates. Brief interventions, especially the BASICS program, were then presented as a prevention and intervention strategy that has been shown to effectively reduce alcohol use among undergraduates. Finally, the behavioral economic perspective was presented as a theory that has started to influence that way researchers understand and investigate student drinking. From a clinical perspective, the utility of both brief interventions and behavioral economics depends on their usefulness in reducing alcohol consumption and the associated negative consequences. Integrating the two literatures could allow for some interesting research on a wide range of clinically relevant topics.

As previously noted, basic research could be used to model the environmental factors and behavioral processes that underlie the development and maintenance of risky alcohol consumption, to inform assessment, and help predict how students will respond to a range of interventions that target the drinking environment or the individual drinker. For example, Murphy and Vuchinich (2002) suggest that a primary implication of the behavioral economic framework is that clinicians should increase assessment of activities and domains outside of alcohol use, since access to and utilization of potentially reinforcing alternative activities are predictive of alcohol consumption. Alternative reinforcers can be assessed in a variety of ways, including measures of time allocation and social support, as well as reinforcement surveys. Additional knowledge of potentially reinforcing but underutilized sources of alternative reinforcers may also provide clues about activities that could compete with the reinforcement currently derived from alcohol. The brief interventions reviewed in this chapter typically focus on patterns of alcohol consumption and the associated risks and negative consequences. Several authors have suggested that brief interventions could be expanded by incorporating material on how decisions about alcohol consumption are impacted by a variety of goals, life pursuits, and environmental variables (e.g., Cox & Klinger, 2004). The behavioral economic perspective is in an excellent position for conceptualizing and empirically testing how an explicit focus on alternative reinforcers can improve the already impressive findings that brief interventions have produced.

Laboratory procedures could also be used to inform assessment and broaden our understanding of how intervention techniques work and with whom they are most likely to be effective. Murphy and MacKillop's (2006) simulated alcohol purchase task and more general measures of relative reinforcing value (e.g., Bickel, Marsch, & Carroll, 2000) could eventually be used to inform a clinician's understanding of how a client's decision making process regarding alcohol consumption is influenced by a range of environmental factors. In addition, basic research could be conducted to determine if the results of a laboratory procedure can be used to predict responses to a range of intervention techniques typically employed as part of a brief intervention (e.g., normative feedback, decisional balance exercises), and in turn to determine if the intervention techniques have an impact on the behavioral processes that underlie performance on the laboratory procedures. Once again, the behavioral economics seemingly provides an excellent framework integrating laboratory and more traditional clinical research. The continued public health implications of alcohol use among undergraduate students certainly demand that researchers and clinicians explicitly work toward building integrative frameworks.

REFERENCES

Agostinelli, G., Brown, J. M., & Miller, W. R. (1995). Effects of normative feedback on consumption among heavy drinking college students. *Journal of Drug Education*, *25*, 31–40.

Babor, T. F., Mendelson, J. H., Greenberg, I., & Kuehnle, J. (1978). Experimental analysis of the 'Happy Hour': Effects of purchase price on alcohol consumption. *Psychopharmacology*, *58*, 35–41.

Baer, J. S. (2002). Student factors: Understanding individual variation in college drinking. *Journal of Studies on Alcohol*, *14*, 40–53.

Baer, J. S., Kivlahan, D. R., Blume, A. W., McNight, P., & Marlatt, G. A. (2001). Brief intervention for heavy-drinking college students: 4-year follow-up and natural history. *American Journal of Public Health*, *91*, 1310–1316.

Baer, J. S., Marlatt, G. A., Kivlahan, D. R., Fromme, K., Larimer, M. E., & Williams, E. (1992). An experimental test of three methods of alcohol risk reduction with young adults. *Journal of Consulting and Clinical Psychology*, *60*, 974–979.

Barnett, N. P., O'Leary, T., Fromme, K., Borsari, B., Carey, K. B., Corbin, W. R., Colby, S. M., & Monti, P. M. (2004). Brief alcohol interventions with mandated or abjudicated college students. *Alcoholism: Clinical and Experimental Research*, *28*, 966–975.

Basten, C. J., Psychol, M., & Kavanagh, D. J. (1996). Alcohol consumption by undergraduate students. *Substance Use and Misuse*, *31*, 1379–1399.

Benson, T. A., Ambrose, C. A., Mulfinger, A. M. M., & Correia, C. J. (2004). Integrating mailed personalized feedback and alcohol screening events: A feasibility study. *Journal of Drug Education*, *34*, 327–334.

Bickel, W. K., DeGrandpre, R. J., Higgins, S. T., & Hughes, J. R. (1990). Behavioral economics of drug self-administration. I. Functional equivalence of response requirement and drug dose. *Life Science*, *47*, 1501–1510.

Bickel, W. K., Marsch, L. A., & Carroll, M. E. (2000). Deconstructing relative reinforcing efficacy and situating the measures of pharmacological reinforcement with behavioral economics: A theoretical proposal. *Psychopharmacology*, *153*, 44–56.

Bien, T. H., Miller, W. R., & Tonigan, J. S. (1993). Brief interventions for alcohol problems: A review. *Addiction*, *88*, 315–336.

Borsari, B. E., & Carey, K. B. (1999). Understanding fraternity drinking: Five recurring themes in the literature, 1980–1998. *Journal of American College Health*, *48*, 30–37.

Borsari, B., & Carey, K. B. (2000). Effects of a brief motivational intervention with college student drinkers. *Journal of Consulting and Clinical Psychology*, *68*, 728–733.

Borsari, B., & Carey, K. B. (2005). Two brief alcohol interventions for mandated college students. *Psychology of Addictive Behaviors*, *19*, 296–302.

Bruun, K., Edwards, G., Lumio, M., Makela, K., Pan, L., Popham, R., et al. (1975). *Alcohol Control Policies in Public Health Perspective*. The Finnish Foundation for Alcohol Studies, Vol. 25. Helsinki: Forssa.

Cada, C. (2004, November 1). Two alcohol poisoning deaths on Colorado campuses stir change. *The Boston Globe*. Retrieved July 20th, 2006, from http://www.boston.com/news/nation/articles/2004/11/01/two_alcohol_poisoning_deaths_on_colo_campuses_stir_change/

Cashin, J. R., Presley, C. A., & Meilman, P. W. (1998). Alcohol use in the Greek system: Follow the leader? *Journal of Studies on Alcohol*, *59*, 63–71.

Centers for Disease Control and Prevention. (1997). Youth risk behavior surveillance: National college health risk behavior survey. *Surveillance Summaries*, *46*, 1–54. Retrieved March 20, 2006 from http://www.cdc.gov/mmwr/preview/mmwrhtml/00049859.htm

Collins, S. E., Carey, K. B., & Sliwinski, M. J. (2002). Mailed personalized normative feedback as a brief intervention for at-risk college drinkers. *Journal of Studies on Alcohol, 63*, 559–567.

Corby, E. A., Roll, J. M., Ledgerwood, D. M., & Schuster, C. R. (2000). Contingency management interventions for treating the substance abuse of adolescents: A feasibility study. *Experimental and Clinical Psychopharmacology, 8*, 371–376.

Correia, C. J., & Benson, T. A. (2006). The use of contingency management to reduce cigarette smoking among college students. *Experimental and Clinical Psychopharmacology, 14*, 171–179.

Correia, C. J., Benson, T. A., & Carey, K. B. (2005). Decreased substance use following increases in alternative behaviors: A preliminary investigation. *Addictive Behaviors, 30*, 19–27.

Correia, C. J., Carey, K. B., & Borsari, B. (2002). Measuring substance-free and substance-related reinforcement in the natural environment. *Psychology of Addictive Behaviors, 16*, 28–34.

Correia, C. J., Carey, K. B., Simons, J., & Borsari, B. E. (2003). Relationships between binge drinking and substance-free reinforcement in a sample of college students a preliminary investigation. *Addictive Behaviors, 28*, 361–368.

Correia, C. J., Little, C., Benson, T. A., & Henslee, A. M. (June, 2006). Use of a multiple choice procedure to study alcohol use among college students. In J. G. Murphy (Chair) (Ed.), *Translational Research on Alcohol Misuse Using Behavioral Economics*. Symposium conducted at the meeting of the Research Society on Alcoholism, Baltimore, MD.

Correia, C. J., Simons, J., Carey, K. B., & Borsari, B. E. (1998). Predicting drug use: Application of behavioral theories of choice. *Addictive Behaviors, 23*, 705–709.

Cox, W. M., & Klinger, E. (2004). *Handbook of Motivational Counseling: Concepts, Approaches, and Assessment*. West Sussex, England: Wiley.

Davis, R., & DeBarros, A. (2006, January 25). First year in college is the riskiest. *USA Today*, pp. 1A, 2A.

Dawson, D. A., Grant, B. F., Stinson, F. S., & Chou, P. S. (2004). Another look at heavy episodic drinking and alcohol use disorders among college and noncollege youth. *Journal of Studies on Alcohol, 65*, 477–488.

de A. Stempliuk, V., Barrosa, L. P., Andrade, A. G., Nicastri, S., & Malbergier, A. (2005). Comparative study of drug use among undergraduate students at the University of Sao Paulo – Sao Paulo campus in 1996 and 2001. *Revista Brasileira de Psiquiatria, 27*, 185–193.

DeGrandpre, R. J., & Bickel, W. K. (1996). Drug dependence as consumer demand. In L. Green, & J. Kagel (Eds.), *Advances in Behavioral Economics* (Vol. 3, pp. 1–36). Norwood, NJ: Ablex Publishing Corporation.

Delk, E. W., & Meilman, P. W. (1996). Alcohol use among college students in Scotland compared with norms from the United States. *Journal of American College Health, 44*, 274–281.

Dimeff, L. A., Baer, J. S., Kivlahan, D. R., & Marlatt, G. A. (1999). *Brief Alcohol Screening and Interventions for College Students: A Harm Reduction Approach*. New York: The Guilford Press.

Dowdall, G. W., & Wechsler, H. (2002). Studying college alcohol use: Widening the lens, sharpening the focus. *Journal of Studies on Alcohol, 14*, 14–22.

Epstein, L. H., Bulik, C. M., Perkins, K. A., Caggiula, A. R., & Rodefer, J. (1991a). Behavioral economic analysis of smoking: Money and food as alternatives. *Pharmacology Biochemistry and Behavior, 38*, 715–721.

Epstein, L. H., Smith, J. A., Vara, L. S., & Rodefer, J. S. (1991b). Behavioral economic analysis of activity choice in obese children. *Health Psychology, 10*, 311–316.

File, S. E., Mabbutt, P. S., & Shaffer, J. (1994). Alcohol consumption and lifestyle in medical students. *Journal of Psychopharmacology, 8*, 22–26.

Gill, J. S. (2002). Reported levels of alcohol consumption and binge drinking within the UK undergraduate student population over the last 25 years. *Alcohol and Alcoholism, 37*, 109–120.

Greenfield, S. F., Keliher, A., Sugarman, D., Kozloff, R., Reizes, J. M., Kopans, B., & Jacobs, D. (2003). Who comes to voluntary, community-based alcohol screening? Results of the first annual National Alcohol Screening Day, 1999. *American Journal of Psychiatry, 160*, 1677–1683.

Ham, L. S., & Hope, D. A. (2003). College student and problematic drinking: A review of the literature. *Clinical Psychology Review, 23*, 719–759.

Harford, T. C., Wechsler, H., & Seibring, M. (2002). Attendance and alcohol use at parties and bars in college: A national survey of current drinkers. *Journal of Studies on Alcohol, 63*, 726–733.

Henslee, A. M., Irons, J. G., Day, J. M., Butler, L., Benson, T. A., & Correia, C. J. (in press). Using National Alcohol Screening Day to deliver personalized feedback: A pilot study. *Journal of Drug Education.*

Herrnstein, R. J. (1970). On the law of effect. *Journal of the Experimental Analysis of Behavior, 13*, 243–266.

Hingson, R., Heeren, T., Winter, M., & Wechsler, H. (2005). Magnitude of alcohol-related mortality and morbidity among U.S. college students ages 18–24: Changes from 1998 to 2001. *Annual Review of Public Health, 26*, 259–279.

Higgins, S. T., Delaney, D. D., Budney, A. J., Bickel, W. K., Hughes, J. R., Foerg, F., & Fenwick, J. W. (1991). A behavioral approach to achieving initial cocaine abstinence. *American Journal of Psychiatry, 148*, 1218–1124.

Johnston, L. D., O'Malley, P. M., Bachman, J. G., & Schulenberg, J. E. (2004). *Monitoring the Future National Survey Results on Drug Use, 1975–2003. Volume II: College Students and Adults Ages 19–45* (NIH Publication No. 04-5508). Bethesda, MD: National Institute on Drug Abuse.

Karam, E. G., Maalouf, W. E., & Ghandour, L. A. (2004). Alcohol use among university students in Lebanon: Prevalence, trends and covariates. The IDRAC University Substance Use Monitoring Study (1991 and 1999). *Drug and Alcohol Dependence, 76*, 273–286.

Knight, J. R., Wechsler, H., Kuo, M., Seibring, M., Weitzman, E. R., & Schuckit, M. A. (2002). Alcohol abuse and dependence among U.S. college students. *Journal of Studies on Alcohol, 63*, 263–270.

Kokotailo, P. K., Henry, B. C., Koscik, R. E., Fleming, M. F., & Landry, G. L. (1996). Substance use and other health risk behaviors in collegiate athletes. *Clinical Journal of Sports Medicine, 6*, 183–189.

Kuo, M., Wechsler, H., Greenberg, P., & Lee, H. (2003). The marketing of alcohol to college students. *American Journal of Preventative Medicine, 25*(3), 204–211.

Larimer, M. E., & Cronce, J. M. (2002). Identification, prevention and treatment: A review of individual-focused strategies to reduce problematic alcohol consumption by college students. *Journal of Studies on Alcohol, 63*, 148–164.

Little, C., & Correia, C. J. (2006). Use of a multiple choice procedure with college student drinkers. *Psychology of Addictive Behaviors, 20*, 445–454.

Madden, G. J. (2000). A behavioral economics primer. In W. K. Bickel, & R. E. Vuchinich (Eds.), *Reframing Health Behavior Change with Behavioral Economics* (pp. 3–26). Mahwah, NJ: Lawrence Erlbaum Associates.

Marlatt, G. A., Baer, J. S., Kivlahan, D. R., Dimeff, L. A., Larimer, M. E., Quigley, L. A., Somers, J. M., & Williams, E. (1998). Screening and brief interventions for high-risk college student drinkers: Results from a two-year follow-up assessment. *Journal of Consulting and Clinical Psychology, 66*, 604–615.

Mcgee, R., & Kypri, K. (2004). Alcohol-related problems experienced by university students in New Zealand. *Australian and New Zealand Journal of Public Health, 28*, 321–323.

Mellibruna, J., Nikodemska, S., & Fronczyk, K. (2003). Use and abuse of alcohol and other psychoactive substances among Polish university students. *Medycyny Wieku Rozwojowego, 7*, 135–155.

Miller, W. R., & Rollnick, S. (2002). *Motivational Interviewing* (2nd ed.). New York: The Guilford Press.

Murphy, J. G., Benson, T. Vuchinich, R. E., Deskins, M., Eakin, D., Flood, A. M., McDevitt-Murphy, M., & Torrealday, O. (2004). A comparison of personalized feedback for college student drinkers delivered with and without a counseling session. *Journal of Studies on Alcohol, 65*, 200–204.

Murphy, J. G., Correia, C. J., Colby, S. M., & Vuchinich, R. E. (2005). Using behavioral theories of choice to predict drinking outcomes following a brief intervention. *Experimental and Clinical Psychopharmacology, 13*(2), 93–101.

Murphy, J. G., Duchnick, J. J., Vuchinich, R. E., Davison, J. W., Karg, R. S., Olson, M., Smith, A. F., & Coffey, T. T. (2001). Relative efficacy of a brief motivational intervention for college student drinkers. *Psychology of Addictive Behaviors*, *15*, 373–379.

Murphy, J. G., & MacKillop, J. (2006). Relative reinforcing efficacy of alcohol among college student drinkers. *Experimental and Clinical Psychopharmacology*, *14*, 219–227.

Murphy, J. G., & Vuchinich, R. E. (2002). Implications of behavioral theories of choice for substance use assessment. *The Addictions Newsletter*, *9*, 2–6.

National Institute of Alcohol Abuse and Alcoholism. (2002). *A Call to Action: Changing the Culture of Drinking at U.S. Colleges*. Retrieved March 20, 2006 from http://www.collegedrinking prevention.gov/NIAAACollegeMaterials/TaskForce/CallToAction_02.aspx

Nattiv, A., Puffer, J. C., & Green, G. A. (1997). Lifestyles and health risks of collegiate athletes: A multi-center study. *Clinical Journal of Sport Medicine*, *7*, 262–272.

Nelson, T. F., & Wechsler, H. (2001). Alcohol and college athletes. *Medicine and Science in Sports and Exercise*, *33*, 43–47.

Odek-Ogunde, M., & Pande-Leak, D. (1999). Prevalence of substance use among students in a Kenyan University: A preliminary report. *East African Medical Journal*, *76*, 301–306.

O'Malley, P. M., & Johnston, L. D. (2002). Epidemiology of alcohol and other drug use among American college students. *Journal of Studies on Alcohol*, *63*, 23–40.

O'Neill, S. E., Parra, G. R., & Sher, K. J. (2001). Clinical relevance of heavy drinking during the college years: Cross section and prospective perspectives. *Psychology of Addictive Behaviors*, *15*, 350–359.

Osterberg, E. (2001). Effects of price and taxation. In N. Heather, T. J. Peters, & T. Stockwell's (Eds.), *International Handbook of Alcohol Dependence and Problems* (pp. 685–698). New York: Wiley.

Petry, N. M., Martin, B., Cooney, J. L., & Kranzler, H. R. (2000). Give them prizes and they will come: Contingency management for treatment of alcohol dependence. *Journal of Consulting and Clinical Psychology*, *68*, 250–257.

Peretti-Watel, P., Guagliardo, V., Verger, P., Pruvost, J., Mignon, P., & Obadia, Y. (2003). Sporting activity and drug use: Alcohol, cigarette and cannabis use among elite student athletes. *Addiction*, *98*, 1249–1256.

Premack, D. (1965). Reinforcement theory. In D. Levine (Ed.), *Nebraska Symposium on Motivation* (pp. 123–180). Lincoln, NE: University of Nebraska Press.

Presley, C. A., Meilman, P. W., & Cashin, J. R. (1996). *Alcohol and Drugs on American College Campuses: Use, Consequences, and Perceptions of the Campus Environment, Volume IV: 1992–94*. Carbondale, IL: Core Institute.

Rooney, B. L., Silha, P., Gloyd, J., & Kreutz, R. (2005). Quit and Win smoking cessation contest for Wisconsin college students. *Wisconsin Medical Journal*, *104*, 45–49.

Selby, R., Weinstein, H. M., & Bird, T. S. (1990). The health of university athletes: Attitudes, behaviors, and stressors. *Journal of American College Health*, *39*, 11–18.

Silverman, K., Higgins, S. T., Brooner, R. K., Montoya, I. D., Cone, E. J., Schuster, C. R., & Preston, K. L. (1996). Sustained cocaine abstinence in methadone maintenance patients through voucher-based reinforcement therapy. *Archives of General Psychiatry*, *53*(5), 409–415.

Slutske, W. S. (2005). Alcohol use disorders among US college students and their noncollege-attending peers. *Archives of General Psychiatry*, *62*, 321–327.

Straus, R., & Bacon, S. D. (1953). *Drinking in College*. New Haven: Yale University Press.

Substance Abuse and Mental Health Services Administration. (2005). *Results from the 2004 National Survey on Drug Use and Health: National Findings* (Office of Applied Studies, NSDUH Series H-28, DHHS Publication No. SMA 05-4062). Rockville, MD.

Tricker, R., Cook, D. L., & McGuire, R. (1989). Issues related to drug abuse in college athletics: Athletes at risk. *The Sport Psychologist*, *3*, 155–165.

U.S. Department of Health and Human Services. (2000). *Healthy People 2010* (conference edition), *2*, 26–29. Washington, DC: USDHHS.

Vasilaki, E. I., Hosier, S. G., & Cox, W. M. (2006). The efficacy of motivational interviewing as a brief intervention for excessive drinking: A meta-analytic review. *Alcohol and Alcoholism, 41*, 328–335.

Vik, P. W., Cellucci, T., & Ivers, H. (2003). Natural reduction of binge drinking among college students. *Addictive Behaviors, 28*, 643–655.

Vuchinich, R. E., & Tucker, J. A. (1983). Behavioral theories of choice as a framework for studying drinking behavior. *Journal of Abnormal Psychology, 92*, 408–416.

Vuchinich, R. E., & Tucker, J. A. (1988). Contributions from behavioral theories of choice to an analysis of alcohol abuse. *Journal of Abnormal Psychology, 97*(2), 181–195.

Vuchinich, R. E., & Tucker, J. A. (1996). The molar context of alcohol abuse. In L. Green, & J. Kagel (Eds.), *Advances in behavioral economics* (Vol. 3, pp. 133–162). Norwood, NJ: Ablex Publishing Corporation.

Walters, S. T., Bennett, M. E., & Miller, J. H. (2000). Reducing alcohol use in college students: A controlled trial of two brief interventions. *Journal of Drug Education, 30*, 361–372.

Walters, S. T., & Neighbors, C. (2005). Feedback interventions for college alcohol misuse: What, why, and for whom? *Addictive Behaviors, 30*, 1168–1182.

Wechsler, H. (2000). *Binge Drinking on America's College Campuses: Findings from the Harvard School of Public Health College Alcohol Study.* Retrieved March 20, 2006 from http://www.hsph.harvard.edu/cas/Documents/monograph_2000/cas_mono_2000.pdf

Wechsler, H., Davenport, A. E., & Dowdall, G. W. (1997). Binge drinking, tobacco, and illicit drug use and involvement in college athletics: A survey of students at 140 American colleges. *Journal of the American Medical Association, 272*, 1672–1677.

Wechsler, H., Davenport, A. E., Dowdall, G., Moeykens, B., & Castillo, S. (1994). Health and behavioral consequences of binge drinking in college: A national survey of students at 140 campuses. *Journal of American Medical Association, 272*, 1672–1677.

Wechsler, H., & Dowdall, G. W. (1998). Changes in binge drinking and related problems among American college students between 1993 and 1997. *Journal of American College Health, 47*, 57–69.

Wechsler, H., Dowdall, G. W., Davenport, A., & Castillo, S. (1995). Correlates of college student binge drinking. *American Journal of Public Health, 85*, 921–926.

Wechsler, H., & Kuo, M. (2003). Watering down the drinks: The moderating effect of college demographics on alcohol use of high risk groups. *American Journal of Public Health, 93*, 1929–1933.

Wechsler, H., Kuh, G., & Davenport, A. E. (1996). Fraternities, sororities, and binge drinking: Results from a national study of American colleges. *NASPA Journal, 33*, 260–279.

Wechsler, H., Kuo, M., Lee, H., & Dowdall, G. W. (2000a). Environmental correlates of underage alcohol use and related problems of college students. *American Journal of Preventive Medicine, 19*, 24–29.

Wechsler, H., Lee, J. E., Kuo, M., & Lee, H. (2000b). College binge drinking in the 1990s: A continuing problem. Results of the Harvard School of Public Health 1999 College Alcohol Study. *Journal of American College Health, 48*, 199–210.

Wechsler, H., Lee, J. E., Kuo, M., Seibring, M., Nelson, T., & Lee, H. (2002). Trends in college binge drinking during a period of increased prevention efforts: Findings from 4 Harvard School of Public Health College Alcohol Student Surveys: 1993–2001. *Journal of American College Health, 50*, 203–217.

Weitzman, E. R., Folkman, A., Lemieux Folkman, K., & Wechsler, H. (2003). The relationship of alcohol outlet density to heavy and frequent drinking and drinking-related problems among college students at eight universities. *Health and Place, 9*, 1–6.

White, A. M., Kraus, C. L., & Swartwelder, H. S. (2006a). Many college freshman drink at levels far beyond the binge threshold. *Alcoholism: Clinical and Experimental Research, 30*, 1006–1010.

White, H. R., Morgan, T. J., Pugh, L. A., Celinska, K., Labouvie, E. W., & Pandina, R. J. (2006b). Evaluating two brief substance-use interventions for mandated college students. *Journal of Studies on Alcohol, 67*, 309–317.

Zweben, A., & Fleming, M. F. (1999). Brief interventions for alcohol and drug problems. In J. A. Tucker, D. M. Donovan, & G. A. Marlatt (Eds.), *Changing Addictive Behavior: Bridging Clinical and Public Health Strategies*. New York: The Guilford Press.

CHAPTER 21

Ethical and Policy Issues in the Translation of Genetic and Neuroscience Research on Addiction

Adrian Carter[1] and Wayne Hall[2]

[1]Queensland Brain Institute, University of Queensland, St Lucia, QLD 4072, Australia

[2]School of Population Health, University of Queensland, St Lucia, QLD 4072, Australia

Translation of Addictions Science into Practice

Abstract: Neuroscience and genetic research of addiction has the potential to improve the treatment and possibly the prevention of addictive disorders and lead to more humane and effective social policies to deal with persons with these disorders. A balanced appreciation of the value of this research must also consider the possibility that simple-minded policies derived from misrepresentations or misunderstandings of this research may produce unintended harm. In this chapter, we highlight some of the potentially unwelcome uses that may be made of this research with the aim of ensuring that the full benefit of neurobiological research on addiction is realized and potential harms are minimized.

INTRODUCTION

The increasing evidence that many addictive phenomena have a genetic and neurobiological basis promises improvements in societal responses to addiction that raise important ethical and social policy issues. Many addiction researchers argue that identifying the neural correlates of compulsive behavior in addiction will lead to more humane treatment of addiction sufferers, and to increased funding for addiction treatment (Dackis & O'Brien, 2005; Volkow & Li, 2005a). This is a hope that we share but we believe that it needs to be tempered by analyses of possibly unwelcome uses of neuroscience that may flow from overly simplistic community interpretations of research on the neuroscience and genetics of addiction. In this chapter, we highlight some unwelcome uses of this research with the aim of minimizing the likelihood of their occurrence.

Neuroscience and genetic research is opening up the possibility of novel pharmacological treatments and psychotherapeutic strategies that target abnormalities in specific aspects or stages of addictive behavior. But in order to do the research required to realize this promise, it will be necessary to address ethical doubts raised about the capacity of addicted persons to give free and informed consent to participate in studies that involve the administration of drugs of dependence. Researchers and clinicians will also need to consider the ethical implications of prescribing drugs that modify neural pathways that are involved in behaviors that have nothing to do with drug use or addiction.

Neuroscience and genetic research on addiction promises to transform the long running debate between moral and medical models of addiction by providing a detailed causal explanation of addiction in terms of brain processes. It is widely assumed that this will lead to popular support for less punitive ways of dealing with addiction, and increased funding of medical treatments. However, causal models of addiction, if misinterpreted, may lead to the neglect of social policy options for reducing addiction and drug use. Causal accounts of addiction may also be used to justify the coercive use of pharmacotherapies and drug vaccines.

Neuroscientists must also anticipate ethical issues that will arise from the use of pharmacological interventions to enhance or modify behavior in healthy individuals. Advances in genetic testing and neuroimaging that enable us to identify "addicts" or predict future risk of addiction will raise concerns about invasion of privacy, third party use of genetic and neuroimaging data, the powers of courts to coerce defendants to undergo such tests, and consumer protection against the over-interpretation of test results. There is significant public and media interest in the results of addiction research. Neuroscientists and geneticists have a moral obligation and professional interest in minimizing popular misunderstandings of their work, particularly in the media, that may rebound to its detriment.

THEORIES OF ADDICTION: SKEPTICAL VIEWS AND MEDICAL MODELS

The dominant "common sense" view of addiction holds that "addicts" are simply drug users who knowingly and willingly choose to use drugs without regard for the consequences that their actions inevitably bring upon themselves and others. In this skeptical view, "addiction" is an excuse for continuing to use drugs while avoiding responsibility for the consequences (Davies, 1997; Szasz, 1975).

Skeptical views make sense of a number of features of "addictive behavior". Drug use is initially a voluntary choice that only leads to addictive patterns of drug use in a minority of those who use drugs. Among the minority of drug users who do become addicted, most stop using drugs by themselves (Peele, 2004). Skeptical views are also consistent with the everyday experiences of the majority of people who decide to stop using drugs and do so with a minimum of difficulty.

Skeptical views of addiction are less consistent with a number of dependable empirical observations that correlate drug use with addictive behaviors. A significant minority of people who use drugs become addicted to that drug, and the risk of becoming addicted is dependent on the way the drug is consumed and its pharmacological action (Anthony & Helzer, 1991). There is also an identifiable subset of individuals who are more likely to develop an addiction. This includes people who have more contact with drugs or peers who use drugs, who use drugs at an earlier age, who are from socially disadvantaged backgrounds or perform poorly in school, who have a family history of addictive behavior, or suffer from a mental disorder (Hawkins, Catalano, & Miller, 1992). Also, the use of drugs in the face of serious negative health and social consequences, and in the absence of any pleasure derived from consuming the drug would suggest addiction is more than mere willful bad behavior.

The worldwide acceptance of skeptical views of addiction has led to the application of punitive laws to deal with drug users, and a lack of investment in medical research and interventions. Despite the broad acceptance of these policies, these efforts have largely proven ineffective in reducing drug use and addiction, and have often contributed to the social cost of addiction by leading to the imprisonment of many drug users who typically return to drug use and re-offend on release from imprisonment (Gerstein & Harwood, 1990; National Research Council, 2001). The fact that these policies have been largely unsuccessful in reducing drug use or addiction indicates that alternative explanations are required that consider the effect that repeated drug use has on an individual's ability to choose whether or not to use that drug.

NEUROBIOLOGICAL THEORIES OF ADDICTION

Neuroscience and genetic research of addiction has challenged traditional notions of addiction as a voluntary choice. Studies have shown that prolonged drug use results in long-lasting, and possibly irreversible, changes in brain structure and function that undermine voluntary control (Leshner, 1997; Volkow & Li, 2004). Studies of the effects of repeated drug use on brain function, combined with knowledge of how environmental, genetic, and developmental factors can influence vulnerability to addiction, increases our ability to treat and possibly to prevent addictive disorders (Cami & Farre, 2003; Leshner, 1997; National Academy of Sciences, 1996). Neuroscience and genetic research may also change the way in which we think about addiction, and the social policies we adopt to deal with it (Dackis & O'Brien, 2005; Leshner, 1997; Volkow & Li, 2004).

Neurobiological theories of addiction attempt to identify the molecular and cellular mechanisms of how drugs act on the brain in ways that may impair control over drug use. Such a theory of addiction, now in ascendance in the United States, is the "chronic, relapsing brain disease model" (Leshner, 1997). According to the National Institute on Drug Abuse (NIDA), addiction is caused by chronic, self-administration of drugs that produce enduring changes in brain neurotransmitter systems that leave addicts vulnerable to relapse after abstinence has been achieved (Leshner, 1997; Volkow & Li, 2005b). In the same way that cardiovascular disease is a result of abnormal heart tissue, the chronic disease model of addiction holds that addiction is the result of abnormal neural tissue (Volkow & Li, 2004).

Neuroscience research has shown that all drugs of dependence act on key neurotransmitter systems that directly or indirectly produce large and fast increases of dopamine in the limbic brain regions, most notably the nucleus accumbens (NAc) (Koob & Le Moal, 2001). These changes in limbic dopamine levels are thought to mediate the acute reinforcing effects of addictive drugs (Hyman & Malenka, 2001).

Neuroimaging studies of the last 5–10 years have also identified changes in brain regions involved in the cognitive processes of salience, motivation, memory and conditioned learning, and inhibitory control. Studies have shown that chronic drug use actually results in a significant decrease in dopaminergic activity that is involved in the disruption of limbic and prefrontal regions (Volkow & Li, 2005b). Adaptations in limbic regions cause addicted individuals to be less sensitive to the rewarding effects of natural reinforcers (everyday stimuli such as food, work, and relationships), while disruption of prefrontal regions focuses attention on drug use and impairs impulse inhibition and decision-making (Volkow & Fowler, 2000; Volkow, Fowler, & Wang, 2003). These neuroadaptations can persist for months after abstinence (Volkow & Li, 2004).

These results are beginning to produce a neurophysiological picture of how addictive drugs can "hijack" endogenous reward circuits that are essential to survival that make drugs so appealing to the exclusion of all other activities (Dackis & O'Brien, 2005). It also explains why those addicted to drugs continue to take the drug despite tolerance to the pleasurable effects of the drug and in the face of serious aversive consequences.

Evidence from twin and adoption studies suggests that there is a substantial genetic contribution to addiction vulnerability (Ball & Collier, 2002; Goldman, Oroszi, & Ducci, 2005; Hall, 2002a; True et al., 1999), which has been estimated to be between 40% and 60% (Uhl et al., 2004). While promising candidate genes have been identified that may explain this vulnerability (Ball & Collier, 2002; Tyndale, 2003), few of these have been consistently replicated and many of the associations are modest (Tyndale, 2003).

POTENTIAL CONSEQUENCES OF NEUROSCIENCE ADDICTION RESEARCH

In addition to providing more effective methods and pharmacological strategies to treat and even prevent addiction, proponents of neurobiological theories of addiction hope that their work will reduce community skepticism about the "reality" of addiction (Dackis & O'Brien, 2005; Leshner, 1997; Volkow & Li, 2004). They hope that the neurobiological model of addiction as a "chronic, relapsing brain disease" (Leshner, 1997) will supplant the "commonsense" moral view and that the punitive policies it encourages will be replaced by more humane ones, such as reducing stigmatization and providing better access to more effective forms of treatment.

More skeptical social scientists point to a number of potentially less welcome social uses of the "brain disease" model of addiction. The "chronic brain disease" view may be seen as warranting heroic interventions in the brain's function, such as, ultra-rapid opiate detoxification for heroin dependence (Hall, 2000), or the neurosurgical treatment of addiction (Hall, 2006). Moreover, a "brain disease" model of addiction might be used to justify coerced treatment if addicts are seen to be at the mercy of the state of their neurotransmitters (Valenstein, 1998) and hence incapable of acting in their own best interests.

Medical models of addiction may also lead to an underestimation of the value of social policies in reducing drug-related harm. By focusing on addiction as a categorical brain disease and disregarding the dimensional nature of drug use and dependence, we run the risk of ignoring the detrimental effects of drug use in the absence of addiction. For example, identifying those who are genetically vulnerable to alcohol dependence may give some the impression that they can use alcohol with impunity, ignoring the very serious health risks associated with alcohol abuse (Hall & Sannibale, 1996). It can also possibly lead addicts to abdicate responsibility for their behavior (Nelkin & Lindee, 1996; Valenstein, 1998). A deterministic account of addiction is not peculiar to genetics and neuroscience; similarly deterministic arguments could be made for the role of social factors which lead to drug use or make some vulnerable to addiction, such as socio-economic background, or early adolescent exposure to hard core parental drug use. However, neurobiological and neurominaging evidence arguably makes the scientific case for a causal account more compelling and persuasive than appeals to social circumstances. Also, appeals to "faulty genes" provide a more mechanistic account of addiction that may make it appear more real and difficult to resist.

The promise of neuroscience and genetic research for understanding addiction raises major ethical and social issues (Ashcroft, Campbell, & Capps, 2005; Hall, Carter, & Morley, 2003, 2004a). These can be considered under two broad headings: (1) ethical issues that arise from the potential use of technologies developed from neuroscience and genetic research, and (2) the broader social and ethical implications of the understanding of the nature of addiction offered by neuroscience and genetic research, and their impacts on public understanding of and policies toward addiction. In the following sections, we outline the major ethical and social issues that will require more systematic and detailed analysis by neuroscience researchers, ethicists, policy makers, and the broader community.

PRACTICAL APPLICATIONS OF GENETIC AND NEUROSCIENCE RESEARCH

PREDICTIVE GENETIC TESTING

If susceptibility genes are identified for addiction risk then children and adolescents could be genetically tested and those at higher risk provided with preventive behavioral and pharmacological interventions to reduce their likelihood of using drugs (Collins, 1999). There are a number of good reasons why on current information genetic screening for addiction is unlikely to be a good policy (Hall, 2005; Holtzman & Marteau, 2000).

First, when multiple genes predispose to a common disease, individual susceptibility alleles only predict a very modestly *increased risk* of dependence (Hall, Morley, & Lucke, 2004b). Testing multiple genetic variants that were individually weak predictors would improve prediction (Khoury et al., 2004) but the larger the number of genes that are involved in disease susceptibility, the less useful *most* individuals will find information about their genotype (Hall et al., 2004b;

Khoury et al., 2004). This is because as the number of alleles increases, the risk distribution tends to the log normal (Pharoah et al., 2002). This means that the number of individuals with a very high-risk combination of multiple genes is small and the majority of individuals are at "average" genetic risk. It also means that a very large number of individuals need to be screened to identify the few who have a significant risk (Vineis, Schulte, & McMichael, 2001; Yang et al., 2003).

Second, predictive genetic testing may have unintended adverse effects. This would be the case, for example, if testing adolescents for susceptibility to addiction *increased* their preparedness to try drugs, as could happen, for example, if they were prompted to test the accuracy of the genetic predictions (Hall et al., 2002).

Third, screening is only ethically justifiable if there is an effective intervention to prevent the disorder in those who are identified as being at increased risk (Khoury et al., 2003). No such interventions currently exist, although the prospect of preventive vaccination against cocaine and nicotine may raise this possibility in the future (Hall & Carter, 2004).

VACCINES TO TREAT ADDICTION

Researchers are now developing immunotherapies (e.g. vaccines) that treat drug addiction by blocking the psychoactive effects of a drug by either stimulating the immune system to produce antibodies (active immunization) or through the introduction of synthetic monoclonal antibodies into the blood stream (passive immunization) (Harwood & Myers, 2004). These antibodies bind to the target drug, preventing it from acting on receptors in the brain (Nutt & Lingford-Hughes, 2004; Vocci & Chiang, 2001).

Studies have shown that anti-drug vaccines reduce the rush and euphoria associated with the target drug, the amount of drug that reaches the brain, dopamine release in the nucleus accumbens, the rate of clearance across the blood–brain barrier, and the volume of drug distribution, and self administration of the target drug (Hall, 2002b; Kosten & Owens, 2005). Vaccines have a very clear advantage over traditional small molecule agonists and antagonists in that they are long lasting, highly specific, and as they remain primarily in the blood stream, have no apparent central nervous system side effects. These advantages suggest that immunotherapies may be effective in reducing relapse to drug use, a major hurdle in overcoming addiction.

Immunotherapies also raise ethical concerns. Firstly, individuals would have to give fully informed consent. It is likely that immunotherapies would be most often used in situations that are inherently coercive, as treatment will often be the result of encounters with the justice system, such as a condition of release from prison or to avoid incarceration, in pregnant women, or parents involved in the child welfare system. The benefits will need to be balanced against rights of the individual to privacy and liberty (Ashcroft et al., 2005).

Secondly, vaccines may also prove counterproductive if an individual attempts to overcome the antagonistic action of the vaccine by increasing drug dose. Those who ambivalently agree to vaccination may later switch to using other possibly more dangerous drugs, different routes of administration (e.g. intravenous injection), or much higher than usual doses (Murray, 2004). Vaccines may also paradoxically make experimentation with drugs seem less risky, and therefore unwittingly increase drug use. The likelihood of this occurring should not be underestimated given the compulsion and motivation to use drugs, even in the face of certain negative consequences. The use of vaccines under any form of coercion will therefore require careful monitoring by the treating physician.

Thirdly, vaccines will produce long-lasting (possibly life-long) markers that will be detectable in the blood and urine, and may lead to false positive drug tests (Murray, 2004). This raises the issue of confidentiality and discrimination, which could discourage some from seeking immunotreatment.

Fourthly, vaccines do not ameliorate underlying problems that may be associated with compulsive drug use and addiction. Many will be wary of a treatment that prevents them from using drugs to either relieve withdrawal symptoms or to attenuate the symptoms of an undiagnosed mental illness (McGregor & Gallate, 2004), other sub-clinical conditions involving distress, or the effects of a stressful or abusive social situation. This is not to uncritically accept self-medication as an explanation of addiction (Mueser, Drake, & Wallach, 1998); it acknowledges that psychological and social factors may sustain drug use that vaccination alone will not address.

Finally, the use of a vaccine may also block the action of agonists or partial agonists (e.g. methadone and buprenorphine for opioid dependence) eliminating the future use of maintenance therapies. This would be disastrous if an effective and inexpensive treatment was developed. Vaccines may also block the action of medications used in the treatment of other physiological conditions (e.g. opioid analgesics for pain relief) (Ashcroft et al., 2005).

Preventive Vaccination Against Addiction

Given that adolescent drug use is a strong risk factor in developing addiction, some parents will inevitably be prompted to vaccinate their children (Cohen, 1997). As minors, children would not be legally able to consent to vaccination but some have argued that vaccination against nicotine and other drugs is simply another decision that parents should be able to make on behalf of their children (Cohen, 1997). Given that there is a fundamental difference in vaccinations to prevent infection and vaccines to control behavior, this argument is likely to be contested by civil libertarians and others who place a high value on personal autonomy (Hasman & Holm, 2004), as well as adolescents who disagree with their parents' wishes.

There are also major practical obstacles to the preventive vaccination in children. First, the limited period of protection provided by existing vaccines would require booster injections, perhaps every two or three months throughout adolescence (Kosten et al., 2002). Second, the fact that a vaccine could be circumvented by using higher doses of drugs means that vaccination could be counterproductive if adolescents were prompted to test its efficacy. Third, it would be costly to universally vaccinate children with a vaccine of modest preventive efficacy (Hall, 2002b).

Vaccination of "high risk" adolescents seems a more plausible and less expensive option. But the feasibility of even this approach is doubtful given the low predictive validity of genetic screening, the doubtful preventive efficacy of drug vaccines, and the possible adverse effects of vaccination, such as stigmatization of those who screened positive, and discrimination against them by third parties, such as life or health insurance companies (Hall, 2005).

Vaccines may also be problematic if viewed as "magic bullets". They do not deal with the underlying addictive condition (such as craving, loss of control or withdrawal), events that may lead to relapse, or a comorbid mental conditions (Ashcroft et al., 2005). Addiction is a chronic condition and vaccines, like traditional addiction medications, will presumably need to be used in conjunction with behavioral treatments if life-long abstinence is to be achieved (Nutt & Lingford-Hughes, 2004).

RELAPSE PREVENTION AND MAINTENANCE WITH DEPOT MEDICATIONS

Depot medications are sustained-release formulations of current medications for treating addiction, generally antagonists, that block the brain receptors for the target drugs. They involve a slow, timed release of medications to counteract the effects of drugs. Depot medications have an advantage over traditional treatment medications, as they are only required to be taken once a month, as compared to 3–4 times a week for the conventional medical treatments. This has made depot medications an attractive option in preventing relapse. Sustained-release preparations of the antagonists naltrexone for alcohol and opioid dependence (Comer et al., 2002; Kranzler, Modesto-Lowe, & Nuwayser, 1998) and lofexidine for nicotine dependence (Rawson et al., 2000) have been developed.

The ethical considerations for the use of sustained release antagonists are similar to those for immunotherapy (Murray, 2004). As with immunotherapies, the use of depot medications for preventing relapse is most likely to occur in situations where capacity to give free consent is compromised. The advantage of depot medications is that the treatment will not be detectable once the depot medication is used up, posing less of a concern for privacy and discrimination. Depot antagonists also present similar safety concerns regarding changes in patterns of drug use or attempts to overcome their antagonist effects (Murray, 2004).

DIAGNOSTIC AND PREDICTIVE USES OF NEUROIMAGING

Neuroimaging may prove a useful clinical tool in the diagnosis and treatment of addiction in individual subjects, by identifying subtypes of addiction or comorbid mental health issues. The ability to identify the neural correlates of addiction may also have other uses outside the clinic. For example, neuroimaging studies are able to detect dramatic changes in limbic responses to drug-related cues that would identify an individual as drug dependent (Childress et al., 1999). This opens up the possibility for discrimination, and the violation of privacy (Canli & Amin, 2002; Farah & Wolpe, 2004; Illes & Racine, 2005). It may even raise concerns for consent, given that these neuroimaging tests could be applied using images of drug cues presented without the subject's awareness (Whalen et al., 1998).[1] Given the enormous costs associated with addiction, this technology may be used by employers, insurance companies, and courts. Because the changes in the limbic regions that respond to drug-related cues persist well into abstinence, there is the possibility that an individual will be discriminated against despite being drug-free. The fairness of such a discriminatory policy would need to be established.

Future improvements in neuroimaging may, even if imperfectly, disclose facts about a person that they may prefer to keep private (Ross, 2003). Advances in neuroimaging technology are making it possible to obtain personal information about an individual that may predict behavior or identify aspects of personality (Abler, Walter, & Erk, 2005; Canli & Amin, 2002; Farah & Wolpe, 2004; Fischer et al., 2001; Fischer, Wik, Fredrikson, 1997; Singer et al., 2004). The claims of entrepreneurs promoting these technologies to the public (e.g. truth-telling, personality matching, and as tests of marital fidelity) raise the need for consumer protection against the over-interpretation of equivocal test results and bogus claims (Caplan, 2002; Farah, 2002, 2005).

Important ethical issues would be raised if persons were compelled to undergo these tests by courts, insurance companies or employers. During the course of neuroimaging studies, up to 40% of brain scans of research participants show "suspicious" brain anomalies, with between 0.5% and 8% of research brain scans uncovering clinically significant neuropathologies (Illes et al., 2006, 2004a). The emergence of incidental findings from neuroimaging research can lead to discrimination, which makes consent to these studies problematic (Anon, 2005; Illes et al., 2006, 2004b). This issue is amplified if imaging is conducted under coercion.

Neuroscience investigations may also provide information that proves to be predictive of disease risk in the same way as genes for Mendelian disorders like

---

[1]It is possible to mask images by presenting them for intervals that are too short to be perceived consciously so that the viewer is not aware of having viewed the image, yet produces changes in neural activity that are detectable by neuroimaging.

Huntington's disease (Foster, Wolpe, & Caplan, 2003; Greely, 2002). Characteristic patterns of brain activity in childhood and adolescence, for example, may predict increased risks of addiction later in adult life (Volkow et al., 2003). This possibility raises the same ethical issues (e.g. privacy and discrimination) that are raised by testing for alleles that predict an increased risk of serious neurological disease (Greely, 2002).

NEUROENHANCEMENT

Although most psychotropic drugs are intended for therapy, they are increasingly being used for non-medical purposes, such as to improve scores on exams, to achieve a body image that adheres to unrealistic expectations, to enhance sociability, or by adults trying to cope with highly competitive environments (Chatterjee, 2006; Farah et al., 2004; Volkow & Li, 2005b). This pattern reflects an apparent growing trend in the use of drugs to enhance performance in normal wellbeing (Parens, 1998a, 1998b, 2002); to make one "better than well" (Caplan & Elliott, 2004; Elliott, 2003; Hall, 2004).

Some critics have suggested that well-known psychiatric medications, such as the selective serotonin reuptake inhibitors (SSRIs, e.g. Prozac) and methylphenidate (Ritalin), are already being used by those who are not suffering from a mental illness in order to change mood and personality or improve cognition and attention (Fukuyama, 2002). There is already speculation that drugs being developed to treat neuropsychiatric diseases, such as Alzheimer's disease and post-traumatic stress disorder (PTSD), will be used by healthy individuals to enhance memory and cognition (Glannon, 2006; Hall, 2003; Lynch, 2002; Rose, 2002). Several of these drugs, including modafinil, SSRIs, and beta-adrenergic antago-nists have also been implicated in the treatment of addiction (Dackis & O'Brien, 2005; Dackis et al., 2005; Lingford-Hughes & Nutt, 2003; Volkow & Li, 2005b). The possible consequences of this will need to be considered before addiction treatments gain market approval.

There are good reasons to be concerned about the possible harms that indi-viduals who use enhancements might experience. Adverse side effects to thera-peutic drugs are common but these risks are generally outweighed by the relief from the symptoms of disease and disability they offer. However the balance between adverse effects and uncertain benefits of enhancement is less clear in healthy individuals (Chatterjee, 2004; Wolpe, 2002).

The widespread use of enhancement technologies also has broader social implications. Some have argued that pharmacological enhancement may exacer-bate existing social inequities (Farah et al., 2004; Fukuyama, 2002; Parens, 2002) while others see this as more a criticism of existing social hierarchies than a com-pelling objection to enhancement (Caplan, 2002). Private education and healthcare, academic coaching, and cosmetic surgery are all forms of enhancement that are allowed in society. Some have argued that this objection could be overcome by making all forms of enhancement freely available to all at low cost, e.g. publicly subsidizing the use of enhancement technologies (Caplan & Elliott, 2004) although the economic viability of this suggestion is yet to be established.

A second concern is that widespread use of enhancement technologies will raise standards for what is considered "normal" (Farah, 2005; Farah et al., 2004; Parens, 2005). Critics suggest that this form of social coercion would lead to a spiraling of pharmacological use as individuals endeavor to keep up with society (Chatterjee, 2006). This enhancement dilemma would be felt acutely by parents in deciding whether to give their child "every opportunity". Such a trend could increase discrimination against the disabled and those with medical conditions who decline to be enhanced (Parens, 2002). However, proponents of enhancement question whether those who do not want to be enhanced should be able to coercively prevent those who do from being enhanced (Caplan, 2002; Caplan & Elliott, 2004).

EPISTEMIC IMPLICATIONS OF GENETIC AND NEUROSCIENTIFIC KNOWLEDGE

IMPLICATIONS FOR CONDUCTING HUMAN NEUROSCIENCE RESEARCH ON ADDICTION

If taken literally, the "brain disease" model of addiction may undermine the capacity of neuroscientists to undertake research on addiction that involves studies of the effects of drugs of addiction, drug analogues, or drug-related cues (e.g. injecting equipment) on behavior (Hall et al., 2004a). The international ethical consensus is that biomedical research on humans (Brody, 1998; Jonsen, 1998) requires independent ethical review of the risks and benefits of proposed research, free and informed consent from research participants, and protection of privacy and confidentiality of information (Brody, 1998). Research involving persons who are cognitively or physically impaired requires special ethical consideration (Brody, 1998) because such vulnerable persons may not be capable of providing informed consent (National Bioethics Advisory Commission, 1999).

The commonly held view among addiction researchers has been that drug dependent people are able to give free and informed consent so long as they are not intoxicated or suffering acute withdrawal symptoms (Adler, 1995; Gorelick, Pickens, & Benkovsky, 1999). However, this assumption has recently been challenged by some who argue that the behavioral characteristics that define addiction, namely the compulsion to use drugs and the loss of control over drug use, prevents those who are drug dependent from giving *free* and informed consent to participate in research studies that involve the administration of their drug of dependence (Charland, 2002; Cohen, 2002). These arguments could be seen to be given more weight by recent imaging studies of addicted brains, which depict an impaired ability to make decisions (Volkow & Li, 2004). If ethics review committees accept these arguments, the outcome could be that no experimental or clinical research will be undertaken in which drug dependent people receive their drug of dependence.

USE OF COERCED TREATMENT OF ADDICTION

The most obvious benefit of neuroscience and genetic research on addiction is improved treatment of drug dependent persons. However, studies suggesting that addiction is a disease that impairs decision-making ability and the capacity to consent to treatment may be used to justify the use of legally coerced treatment. While this in principle could be used as part of a treatment strategy to "save addicts from themselves", coerced treatment is most often advocated for drug dependent people who have committed a criminal offence.

Legally coerced drug treatment for persons charged with or convicted of an offence to which their drug dependence has contributed is usually provided as an alternative to incarceration under the threat of imprisonment if the person fails to comply with treatment (Hall, 1997; Spooner, Hall, & Mattick, 2001). One of the major justifications for this practice is that treating offenders' drug dependence will reduce the likelihood of their re-offending (Gerstein & Harwood, 1990; Inciardi & McBride, 1991).

A consensus view on drug treatment under coercion prepared for the World Health Organization (WHO) (Porter, Arif, & Curran, 1986) concluded that such treatment was legally and ethically justified only if (1) the rights of the individuals were protected by "due process" (in accordance with human rights principles), and (2) effective and humane treatment was provided. Some argue that any form of treatment is ineffective if compulsory, suggesting that rehabilitation requires internal motivation (Newman, 1974). If treatment under coercion were ineffective (as Newman claims), then there would be no ethical justification for providing it. In the absence of due process, coerced treatment could become de facto imprisonment without judicial oversight.

The uncertain benefits of coerced treatment have led some proponents to argue that offenders should be allowed two "constrained choices" (Fox, 1992). The first choice would be whether they participate in drug treatment or not. If they declined to be treated, they would be dealt with by the criminal justice system in the same way as anyone charged with their offence. The second constrained choice would be given to those who agreed to participate in drug treatment: this would be a choice of the type of treatment they received. Clearly, programs which aim to increase participant involvement and choice in treatment offer a more ethically acceptable form of coerced treatment. Studies have also shown that coerced treatment programs that require some "voluntary interest" by the offender are also more effective than coerced treatments that do not (Gerstein & Harwood, 1990).

If pharmacological treatments are used under legal coercion, their safety, effectiveness, and cost-effectiveness should be rigorously evaluated (National Research Council, 2001). Prescribing drugs that interfere with brain circuits responsible for addictive behaviors may have effects on other aspects of their lives, such as their ability to make decisions (Bechara, 2005), derive pleasure, and form and maintain social bonds (Aragona et al., 2006). These drugs may even diminish an individual's free will or autonomy, even if taken with consent (Caron et al., 2005). We accordingly need to ensure that due process is observed and that effective and humane treatment is provided to drug dependent offenders.

FUTURE DIRECTIONS FOR ADDICTION POLICY

NEUROSCIENCE AND THE MEDIA

Public interest in scientific findings and the political imperative for scientists to justify public funding have increased pressure on scientists to report their research findings in the popular media (Resnik, 1998). Given public interest in neuroscience research and the potential for misunderstandings to rebound to the detriment of the research, neuroscientists and geneticists arguably have a moral responsibility to be proactive in their dealings with the media (Blakemore, 2002). They need to ensure that accurate information is released to the media and that their publications include prominent disclaimers that anticipate and correct predictable misinterpretations of their findings. They need to make it clear that addiction is not a simple Mendelian disorder, i.e. it is not the case that if you have "the gene" then you will become addicted and that you will not if you do not. Given the seductive power of colorful brain images, neuroscientists also should clearly convey the limitations of neuroimaging as an experimental and diagnostic tool (Dumit, 2004).

THE TASKS AHEAD FOR ETHICISTS

A major challenge for addiction policy and ethics will be finding ways to acknowledge the neurobiological contribution to drug use and addiction while recognizing that both are nonetheless affected by individual and social choices. In the best of all possible worlds, addiction neurobiology may allow us to reconsider our social responses to the minority of drug users who become addicted, by reducing their stigmatization and increasing their access to more effective psychological and biological treatments. However, an improved understanding of the neurobiology of addiction will not relieve us of the obligation to try to prevent problem drug use, by reducing susceptibility to its appeal and addressing the social conditions that contribute to personal vulnerability (Spooner & Hall, 2002).

REFERENCES

Abler, B., Walter, H., & Erk, S. (2005). Neural correlates of frustration. *Neuroreport, 16*(7), 669–672.

Adler, M. W. (1995). Human subject issues in drug-abuse research. *Drug and Alcohol Dependence, 37*(2), 167–175.

Anon. (2005). How volunteering for an MRI scan changed my life. *Nature, 434*(3), 17.

Anthony, J. C., & Helzer, J. (1991). Syndromes of drug abuse and dependence. In L. N. Robins, & D. A. Regier (Eds.), *Psychiatric Disorders in America* (pp. 116–154). New York: Academic Press.

Aragona, B. J., Liu, Y., Yu, Y. J., Curtis, J. T., Detwiler, J. M., Insel, T. R., & Wang, Z. X. (2006). Nucleus accumbens dopamine differentially mediates the formation and maintenance of monogamous pair bonds. *Nature Neuroscience, 9*(1), 133–139.

Ashcroft, R. E., Campbell, A. V., & Capps, B. (2005). *Foresight State of the Art Science Review: Ethical Aspects of Developments in Neuroscience and Drug Addiction.* London: Department of Trade and Industry.

Ball, D., & Collier, D. (2002). Substance misuse. In P. McGuffin, M. J. Owen, & I. I. Gottesman (Eds.), *Psychiatric Genetics and Genomics.* Oxford: Oxford University Press.

Bechara, A. (2005). Decision making, impulse control and loss of willpower to resist drugs: A neurocognitive perspective. *Nature Neuroscience, 8*(11), 1458–1463.

Blakemore, C. (2002). From the "Public understanding of science" to scientists' understanding of the public. In S. J. Marcus (Ed.), *Neuroethics: Mapping the Field.* New York: Dana Press.

Brody, B. A. (1998). *The Ethics of Biomedical Research: An International Perspective.* New York: Oxford University Press.

Cami, J., & Farre, M. (2003). Drug addiction. *New England Journal of Medicine, 349*(10), 975–986.

Canli, T., & Amin, Z. (2002). Neuroimaging of emotion and personality: Scientific evidence and ethical considerations. *Brain Cognition, 50*(3), 414–431.

Caplan, A. (2002). No brainer: We can cope with the ethical ramifications of new knowledge of the human brain. In S. Marcu (Ed.), *Neuroethics: Mapping the Field* (pp. 95–131). San Francisco: The Dana Press.

Caplan, A., & Elliott, C. (2004). Is it ethical to use enhancement technologies to make us better than well? *PLoS Medicine, 1*(3), e52.

Caron, L., Karkazis, K., Raffin, T. A., Swan, G., & Koenig, B. A. (2005). Nicotine addiction through a neurogenomic prism: Ethics, public health, and smoking. *Nicotine & Tobacco Research, 7*(2), 181–197.

Charland, L. C. (2002). Cynthia's dilemma: Consenting to heroin prescription. *American Journal of Bioethics, 2*(2), 37–47.

Chatterjee, A. (2004). Neuroethics: Toward broader discussion. *Hastings Center Report, 34*(6), 4; author reply 4–5.

Chatterjee, A. (2006). The promise and predicament of cosmetic neurology. *Journal of Medicine and Ethics, 32*(2), 110–113.

Childress, A. R., Mozley, P. D., McElgin, W., Fitzgerald, J., Reivich, M., & O'Brien, C. P. (1999). Limbic activation during cue-induced cocaine craving. *American Journal of Psychiatry, 156*(1), 11–18.

Cohen, P. J. (1997). Immunization for prevention and treatment of cocaine abuse: Legal and ethical implications. *Drug and Alcohol Dependence, 48*(3), 167–174.

Cohen, P. J. (2002). Untreated addiction imposes an ethical bar to recruiting addicts for non-therapeutic studies of addictive drugs. *Journal of Law Medicine and Ethics*, 30(1), 73–81.

Collins, F. S. (1999). Shattuck lecture – medical and societal consequences of the human genome project. *New England Journal of Medicine*, 341(1), 28–37.

Comer, S. D., Collins, E. D., Kleber, H. D., Nuwayser, E. S., Kerrigan, J. H., & Fischman, M. W. (2002). Depot naltrexone: Long-lasting antagonism of the effects of heroin in humans. *Psychopharmacology*, 159(4), 351–360.

Dackis, C. A., & O'Brien, C. (2005). Neurobiology of addiction: Treatment and public policy ramifications. *Nature Neuroscience*, 8(11), 1431–1436.

Dackis, C. A., Kampman, K. M., Lynch, K. G., Pettinati, H. M., & O'Brien, C. P. (2005). A double-blind, placebo-controlled trial of modafinil for cocaine dependence. *Neuropsychopharmacology*, 30(1), 205–211.

Davies, J. B. (1997). *The Myth of Addiction* (2nd ed.). Amsterdam: Harwood Academic Publishers.

Dumit, J. (2004). *Picturing Personhood: Brain Scans and Biomedical Identity*. Princeton: Princeton University Press.

Elliott, C. (2003). *Better than Well: American Medicine Meets the American Dream*. New York: W.W. Norton.

Farah, M. J. (2002). Emerging ethical issues in neuroscience. *Nature Neuroscience*, 5(11), 1123–1129.

Farah, M. J. (2005). Neuroethics: The practical and the philosophical. *Trends in Cognitive Science*, 9(1), 34–40.

Farah, M. J., Illes, J., Cook-Deegan, R., Gardner, H., Kandel, E., King, P., Parens, E., Sahakian, B., & Wolpe, P. R. (2004). Neurocognitive enhancement: What can we do and what should we do? *Nature Reviews Neuroscience*, 5(5), 421–425.

Farah, M. J., & Wolpe, P. R. (2004). Monitoring and manipulating brain function: New neuroscience technologies and their ethical implications. *Hastings Center Report*, 34(3), 35–45.

Fischer, H., Tillfors, M., Furmark, T., & Fredrikson, M. (2001). Dispositional pessimism and amygdala activity: A PET study in healthy volunteers. *Neuroreport*, 12(8), 1635–1638.

Fischer, H., Wik, G., & Fredrikson, M. (1997). Extraversion, neuroticism and brain function: A PET study of personality. *Personality and Individual Differences*, 23(2), 345–352.

Foster, K. R., Wolpe, P. R., & Caplan, A. L. (2003). Bioethics & the brain. *IEEE Spectrum*, 40(6), 34–39.

Fox, R. G. (1992). The compulsion of voluntary treatment in sentencing. *Criminal Law Journal*, 16, 37–54.

Fukuyama, F. (2002). *Our Posthuman Future: Consequences of the Biotechnology Revolution*. London: Profile Books.

Gerstein, D. R., & Harwood, H. J. (1990). *Treating Drug Problems Volume 1: A Study of Effectiveness and Financing of Public and Private Drug Treatment Systems*. Washington, DC: Institute of Medicine, National Academy Press.

Glannon, W. (2006). Psychopharmacology and memory. *Journal of Medicine and Ethics*, 32(2), 74–78.

Goldman, D., Oroszi, G., & Ducci, F. (2005). The genetics of addictions: Uncovering the genes. *Nature Reviews Genetics*, 6(7), 521–532.

Gorelick, D., Pickens, R. W., & Benkovsky, F. O. (1999). Clinical research in substance abuse: Human subjects issues. In H. A. Pinchus, J. A. Lieberman, & S. Ferris (Eds.), *Ethics in Psychiatric Research: A Resource Manual for Human Subjects Protection*. Washington, DC: American Psychiatric Association.

Greely, H. T. (2002). Neuroethics and ELSI: Some comparisons and considerations. In S. J. Marcus (Ed.), *Neuroethics: Mapping the Field* (pp. 83–94). New York: The Dana Press.

Hall, S. S. (2003). The quest for a smart pill. *Scientific American*, 289(3), 54–57.

Hall, W. (1997). The role of legal coercion in the treatment of offenders with alcohol and heroin problems. *Australian and New Zealand Journal of Criminology*, 30(2), 103–120.

Hall, W. (2000). UROD: An antipodean therapeutic enthusiasm. *Addiction*, 95(12), 1765–1766.

Hall, W. (2002a). Taking Darwin seriously: More than telling "just so" stories. *Addiction*, *97*(4), 472–473.

Hall, W. (2002b). The prospects for immunotherapy in smoking cessation. *Lancet*, *360*(9339), 1089–1091.

Hall, W. (2004). Feeling 'better than well' – can our experiences with psychoactive drugs help us to meet the challenges of novel neuroenhancement methods? *EMBO Reports*, *5*(12), 1105–1109.

Hall, W. (2006). Stereotactic neurosurgical treatment of addiction: Minimizing the chances of another 'great and desperate cure'. *Addiction*, *101*(1), 1–3.

Hall, W., & Carter, L. (2004). Ethical issues in using a cocaine vaccine to treat and prevent cocaine abuse and dependence. *Journal of Medical Ethics*, *30*(4), 337–340.

Hall, W., Carter, L., & Morley, K. I. (2003). Addiction, neuroscience and ethics. *Addiction*, *98*(7), 867–870.

Hall, W., Carter, L., & Morley, K. I. (2004a). Neuroscience research on the addictions: A prospectus for future ethical and policy analysis. *Addictive Behaviors*, *29*(7), 1481–1495.

Hall, W., Madden, P., & Lynskey, M. (2002). The genetics of tobacco use: Methods, findings and policy implications. *Tobacco Control*, *11*(2), 119–124.

Hall, W., & Sannibale, C. (1996). Are there two types of alcoholism? *Lancet*, *348*(9037), 1258.

Hall, W. (2005). Will nicotine genetics and a nicotine vaccine prevent cigarette smoking and smoking-related diseases? *PLoS Medicine*, *2*(9), e266; quiz e351.

Hall, W., Morley, K. L., & Lucke, J. C. (2004b). The prediction of disease risk in genomic medicine: Scientific prospects and implications for public policy and ethics. *EMBO Reports*, *5*, S22–S26.

Harwood, H. J., & Myers, T. G. (2004). *New treatments for addiction: Behavioral, ethical, legal, and social questions*. Washington, DC: National Academies Press.

Hasman, A., & Holm, S. (2004). Nicotine conjugate vaccine: Is there a right to a smoking future? *Journal of Medical Ethics*, *30*(4), 344–345.

Hawkins, J. D., Catalano, R. F., & Miller, J. Y. (1992). Risk and protective factors for alcohol and other drug problems in adolescence and early adulthood: Implications for substance abuse prevention. *Psychological Bulletin*, *112*(1), 64–105.

Holtzman, N. A., & Marteau, T. M. (2000). Will genetics revolutionize medicine? *New England Journal of Medicine*, *343*(2), 141–144.

Hyman, S. E., & Malenka, R. C. (2001). Addiction and the brain: The neurobiology of compulsion and its persistence. *Nature Reviews Neuroscience*, *2*(10), 695–703.

Illes, J., Kirschen, M. P., Edwards, E., Stanford, L. R., Bandettini, P., Cho, M. K., Ford, P. J., Glover, G. H., Kulynych, J., Macklin, R., Michael, D. B., & Wolf, S. M. (2006). Ethics. Incidental findings in brain imaging research. *Science*, *311*(5762), 783–784.

Illes, J., Kirschen, M. P., Karetsky, K., Kelly, M., Saha, A., Desmond, J. E., Raffin, T. A., Glover, G. H., & Atlas, S. W. (2004a). Discovery and disclosure of incidental findings in neuroimaging research. *Journal of Magnetic Resonance Imaging*, *20*(5), 743–747.

Illes, J., & Racine, E. (2005). Imaging or imagining? A neuroethics challenge informed by genetics. *American Journal of Bioethics*, *5*(2), 5–18.

Illes, J., Rosen, A. C., Huang, L., Goldstein, R. A., Raffin, T. A., Swan, G., & Atlas, S. W. (2004b). Ethical consideration of incidental findings on adult brain MRI in research. *Neurology*, *62*(6), 888–890.

Inciardi, J. A., & McBride, D. C. (1991). *Treatment Alternatives to Street Crime: History, Experiences and Issues*. Rockville, MD: National Institute of Drug Abuse.

Jonsen, A. R. (1998). *The Birth of Bioethics*. New York: Oxford University Press.

Khoury, M. J., McCabe, L. L., & McCabe, E. R. B. (2003). Genomic medicine – population screening in the age of genomic medicine. *New England Journal of Medicine*, *348*(1), 50–58.

Khoury, M. J., Yang, Q. H., Gwinn, M., Little, J. L., & Flanders, W. D. (2004). An epidemiologic assessment of genomic profiling for measuring susceptibility to common diseases and targeting interventions. *Genetics in Medicine*, *6*(1), 38–47.

Koob, G. F., & Le Moal, M. (2001). Drug addiction, dysregulation of reward, and allostasis. *Neuropsychopharmacology, 24*(2), 97–129.

Kosten, T. R., & Owens, S. M. (2005). Immunotherapy for the treatment of drug abuse. *Pharmacology and Therapeutics, 108*(1), 76–85.

Kosten, T. R., Rosen, M., Bond, J., Settles, M., St Clair Roberts, J., Shields, J., Jack, L., & Fox, B. (2002). Human therapeutic cocaine vaccine: Safety and immunogenicity. *Vaccine, 20*(7–8), 1196–1204.

Kranzler, H. R., Modesto-Lowe, V., & Nuwayser, E. S. (1998). Sustained-release naltrexone for alcoholism treatment: A preliminary study. *Alcoholism Clinical and Experimental Research, 22*(5), 1074–1079.

Leshner, A. I. (1997). Addiction is a brain disease, and it matters. *Science, 278*(5335), 45–47.

Lingford-Hughes, A., & Nutt, D. (2003). Neurobiology of addiction and implications for treatment. *British Journal of Psychiatry, 182*, 97–100.

Lynch, G. (2002). Memory enhancement: The search for mechanism-based drugs. *Nature Neuroscience, 5*, 1035–1038.

McGregor, I. S., & Gallate, J. E. (2004). Rats on the grog: Novel pharmacotherapies for alcohol craving. *Addictive Behaviors, 29*(7), 1341–1357.

Mueser, K. T., Drake, R. E., & Wallach, M. A. (1998). Dual diagnosis: A review of etiological theories. *Addictive Behaviors, 23*(6), 717–734.

Murray, T. (2004). Ethical issues in immunotherapies or depot medications for substance abuse. In H. J. Harwood, & T. G. Myers (Eds.), *New Treatments for Addiction: Behavioral, Ethical Legal and Social Questions* (pp. 188–212). Washington, DC: National Academies Press.

National Academy of Sciences. (1996). *Pathways of Addiction: Opportunities in Drug Abuse Research.* Washington, DC: National Academies Press.

National Bioethics Advisory Commission. (1999). *Research Involving Persons with Mental Disorders that May Affect Decision-making Capacity.* Rockville, MD: National Bioethics Advisory Commission.

National Research Council. (2001). *Informing America's Policy on Illegal Drugs: What we Don't Know Keeps Hurting us.* Washington, DC: National Academy Press.

Nelkin, D., & Lindee, M. S. (1996). "Genes made me do it": The appeal of biological explanations. *Politics and the Life Sciences, 15*(1), 95–97.

Newman, R. (1974). Involuntary treatment of drug addiction. In P. G. Bourne (Ed.), *Addiction.* New York: Academic Press.

Nutt, D., & Lingford-Hughes, A. (2004). Infecting the brain to stop addiction? *Proceedings of the National Academy of Sciences of the United States of America, USA, 101*(31), 11193–11194.

Parens, E. (1998a). *Enhancing Human Traits: Ethical and Social Implications.* Washington, DC: Georgetown University Press.

Parens, E. (1998b). Is better always good? The enhancement project. *Hastings Center Report, 28*(1), S1–S17.

Parens, E. (2002). How far will the treatment/enhancement distinction get us as we grapple with new ways to shape ourselves? In S. J. Marcus (Ed.), *Neuroethics: Mapping the Field* (pp. 152–158). New York: Dana Press.

Parens, E. (2005). Authenticity and ambivalence: Toward understanding the enhancement debate. *Hastings Center Report, 35*(3), 34–41.

Peele, S. (2004). The surprising truth about addiction. *Psychology Today, 37*(3), 43.

Pharoah, P. D., Antoniou, A., Bobrow, M., Zimmern, R. L., Easton, D. F., & Ponder, B. A. (2002). Polygenic susceptibility to breast cancer and implications for prevention. *Nature Genetics, 31*(1), 33–36.

Porter, L., Arif, A., & Curran, W. J. (1986). *The Law and the Treatment of Drug- and Alcohol-Dependent Persons: A Comparative Study of Existing Legislation.* Geneva: WHO.

Rawson, R. A., McCann, M. J., Hasson, A. J., & Ling, W. (2000). Addiction pharmacotherapy 2000: New options, new challenges. *Journal of Psychoactive Drugs, 32*(4), 371–378.

Resnik, D. B. (1998). *The Ethics of Science: An Introduction*. London: New York: Routledge.

Rose, S. P. R. (2002). Smart drugs: Do they work? Are they ethical? Will they be legal? *Nature Reviews Neuroscience, 3*(12), 975–979.

Ross, P. (2003). Mind readers. *Scientific American, 289*(3), 74–77.

Singer, T., Seymour, B., O'Doherty, J., Kaube, H., Dolan, R. J., & Frith, C. D. (2004). Empathy for pain involves the affective but not sensory components of pain. *Science, 303*(5661), 1157–1162.

Spooner, C., & Hall, W. (2002). Preventing drug misuse by young people: We need to do more than 'just say no'. *Addiction, 97*(5), 478–481.

Spooner, C., Hall, W., & Mattick, R. P. (2001). An overview of diversion strategies for Australian drug-related offenders. *Drug and Alcohol Review, 20*(3), 281–294.

Szasz, T. S. (1975). *Ceremonial Chemistry: The Ritual Persecution of Drugs, Addicts, and Pushers*. London: Routledge.

True, W. R., Xian, H., Scherrer, J. F., Madden, P. A. F., Bucholz, K. K., Heath, A. C., Eisen, S. A., Lyons, M. J., Goldberg, J., & Tsuang, M. (1999). Common genetic vulnerability for nicotine and alcohol dependence in men. *Archives of General Psychiatry, 56*(7), 655–661.

Tyndale, R. F. (2003). Genetics of alcohol and tobacco use in humans. *Annals de Medicine, 35*(2), 94–121.

Uhl, G. R., Li, M. D., Gelertner, J., Berrettini, W., & Pollock, J. (2004). Molecular genetics of addiction vulnerability and treatment responses. *Neuropsychopharmacology, 29*, S26–S26.

Valenstein, E. S. (1998). *Blaming the Brain: The Truth about Drugs and Mental Health*. New York: Free Press.

Vineis, P., Schulte, P., & McMichael, A. J. (2001). Misconceptions about the use of genetic tests in populations. *Lancet, 357*(9257), 709–712.

Vocci, F. J., & Chiang, C. N. (2001). Vaccines against nicotine – how effective are they likely to be in preventing smoking? *CNS Drugs, 15*(7), 505–514.

Volkow, N., & Li, T. K. (2005a). The neuroscience of addiction. *Nature Neuroscience, 8*(11), 1429–1430.

Volkow, N. D., & Fowler, J. S. (2000). Addiction, a disease of compulsion and drive: Involvement of the orbitofrontal cortex. *Cerebral Cortex, 10*(3), 318–325.

Volkow, N. D., Fowler, J. S., & Wang, G. J. (2003). The addicted human brain: Insights from imaging studies. *Journal of Clinical Investigation, 111*(10), 1444–1451.

Volkow, N. D., & Li, T. K. (2004). Drug addiction: The neurobiology of behaviour gone awry. *Nature Reviews Neuroscience, 5*(12), 963–970.

Volkow, N. D., & Li, T. K. (2005b). Drugs and alcohol: Treating and preventing abuse, addiction and their medical consequences. *Pharmacology and Therapeutics, 108*(1), 3–17.

Whalen, P. J., Rauch, S. L., Etcoff, N. L., McInerney, S. C., Lee, M. B., & Jenike, M. A. (1998). Masked presentations of emotional facial expressions modulate amygdala activity without explicit knowledge. *Journal of Neuroscience, 18*(1), 411–418.

Wolpe, P. R. (2002). Treatment, enhancement, and the ethics of neurotherapeutics. *Brain Cognition, 50*(3), 387–395.

Yang, Q., Khoury, M. J., Botto, L., Friedman, J. M., & Flanders, W. D. (2003). Improving the prediction of complex diseases by testing for multiple disease-susceptibility genes. *American Journal of Human Genetics, 72*(3), 636–649.

SECTION V
CONCLUSION

CHAPTER 22

Pathways to Innovation in Addiction Practice

David J. Kavanagh[1] and Peter M. Miller[2]
[1]University of Queensland, Brisbane, Australia
[2]University of South Carolina, Charleston, SC, USA

**Processes of Translation from Basic Science
   to Practice
An Alternate Pathway to Improved Practice
A Way Forward
References**

Abstract: Despite significant advances in basic science, we still face substantial limitations to our ability to address addiction problems in the community. Potential barriers to application occur at all stages of transition from an advance in basic science to its routine application. Many treatment innovations occur by intuitive or accidental changes in clinical practice, with scientific understanding lagging behind. Without that understanding, the meaning of clinical changes can be misunderstood, and other implications missed. Today, efficient translation of good ideas often needs both divergent interpretation of observations, and effective collaboration. We hope this volume will encourage both.

Over the last 25 years, there have been significant advances in effective interventions for addictive disorders (Volkow & Li, 2005). We now have a body of evidence-based procedures for substance use disorders, which produce moderately powerful effects (Carroll & Onken, 2005; Miller & Wilbourne, 2002; Piasecki, 2006). On the other hand, there are considerable challenges that lie before us. Many people are not engaged in treatment, or do not respond to it, and we continue to see high rate of subsequent relapse (Piasecki & Baker, 2001; Shiffman, 1993). Furthermore, the size of additional effects from new treatments is often relatively modest (Bouza et al., 2004). While some preventive programs show promise (Foxcroft et al., 2003; Gates et al., 2006; Velleman, Templeton, & Copello, 2005), research on prevention is littered with failures to obtain positive results (Foxcroft et al., 2003). Even where emerging evidence clearly favors changes in treatment, there is often limited uptake into routine practice (Corry et al., 2004;

Translation of Addictions Science into Practice

Mark, Kranzler, & Song, 2003; Thomas et al., 2003). In fact, most people with addictive problems are still not accessing any professional assistance at all (Gerada, 2005).

These limitations to effectiveness are in the context of continued high rates of substance use (AIHW, 2005; Condon & Smith, 2003; Maxwell, 2003) and related problems (Rehm et al., 2005; SAMHSA, 2004), and an increased knowledge of the neurological harm associated with substance misuse, especially in late adolescence and early adulthood (Volkow & Li, 2005). There is clearly much more that could be done to promote the rapid translation of scientific research into effective practice.

PROCESSES OF TRANSLATION FROM BASIC SCIENCE TO PRACTICE

'Dans les champs de l'observation le hasard ne favorise que les esprits préparés' (In the field of observation, chance favors only the prepared mind; Pasteur, Lecture at the University of Lille, December 7, 1854).

A rational process of discovery and dissemination of a treatment innovation, from discovery of a phenomenon in basic science, to its use and dissemination, is displayed in Figure 1. The steps are of particular relevance to the development of new drugs, but also have application to other developments. The basic scientific advance is initially applied in an analogue environment (e.g. the drug is given to animals) to provide an initial test of the concept (e.g. what the drug has acted on), together with its effects and potential risks. This initial stage is currently being further refined, with the use of functional genomics and proteomics to drive the initial development of potential agents (Holsboer, 2001; Lerner & Beutel, 2002).

It may then be tested in a healthy human population ('Phase I' trial). In development of psychological treatments, a test is conducted in a human population with a disorder analogue (e.g. heavy drinking college students). The intervention is then examined in pilot studies with humans who have the target disorder, to assess short-term effects, risks, and effective doses ('Phase I/II'). Then, large-scale randomized controlled trials are undertaken ('Phase III'). 'Phase IV' trials are undertaken (in the case of pharmacotherapies, after approval and release) to assess effectiveness and risks in large-scale applications.

The process of developing drugs to the point of national drug authority approval typically takes 7–12 years (Fernandez & Huie, 2004), although there has been ongoing pressure from pharmaceutical companies to reduce the actual review

Figure 1 Rational process of development of clinical innovations, from scientific advance to applications in routine practice.

period (Abraham et al., 2002; Deyo, 2004), in order to maximize earnings before patent protection is lost (Fernandez & Huie, 2004). Public protection clearly requires adequate testing across Phases I–III before drug release. Despite ongoing concerns about risks inherent in the current approval processes (Abraham et al., 2002; Deyo, 2004), few drugs have to be subsequently withdrawn for safety reasons (Kleinke, 2002). However, it is difficult to see how significantly more rapid applications than at present could be achieved without substantial compromises on safety.

Is there therefore a problem in translation to practice, and if so, at what stage may it be occurring?

Issues appear to arise at several stages. At the stage of a scientific advance, the implications of discoveries may not be appreciated. The oft-quoted dictum of Pasteur at the start of this section makes this point. One potential error at this stage is that the meaning of the observation may not be appreciated. For example Baumeister (2006), reports that the discovery of the site of pleasurable brain stimulation by Olds and Milner (Olds & Milner, 1954) was preceded by an observation of the same phenomenon in humans by a psychiatric researcher named Robert Heath, who was undertaking studies involving brain stimulation of patients with schizophrenia. However, Heath did not appreciate the significance of his observation until after the publication by Olds and Milner, because he was attempting to test a theory of psychotic phenomena and interpreted his findings in that light. Similarly, the discovery of *Helicobacter* (H.) *pylori* by Warren and Marshall in 1982 (Marshall & Warren, 1984) was apparently preceded by other observations of spiral bacteria in the gut, but the meaning of the discoveries were not appreciated, perhaps because of the prevailing view that such organisms could not survive in a normal stomach (Pincock, 2005).

Part of the problem is that we tend to become 'stuck' in a specific theoretical vision, and attempt its defense in the presence of conflicting results, rather than recognizing empirical refutation (Kuhn, 1962) – hardly in the spirit of hypothetico-deductive reasoning, but understandable in terms of the well established concept of cognitive dissonance (Festinger, 1957). It sometimes takes a radical change in perspective before the implications of an observation are understood (Kuhn, 1962).

Sometimes these implications can only be fully appreciated in the light of knowledge from a very different area. In a set of disorders with such complex neurobiological, psychological and social components as addictive disorders, we may also have been hampered at the basic science stage by traditional divisions between areas of research, which have often involved separate research teams, different target journals, conferences, language and interests. Even when we present at the same conference, we often avoid presentations from areas that are very disparate from our own. The narrow focus of our specific research or practice interest tends to limit both the understanding and valuing of other views. For example, while psychological theories of addiction do not deny the importance of neurobiological factors, they are historically based on models that do not articulate in any detail the relationships between psychological or social factors and specific neurobiology. Conversely, presentations on neurobiological research sometimes display scant acknowledgment of psychological or social research.

For whatever reason, we ignore relevant research from other discipline areas at our peril. Early research on pharmacotherapies to prevent relapse in alcohol dependence was insufficiently informed by existing psychological research on its nature and measurement, and relied on crude retrospective reports over long time periods. While later research with more sophisticated methodology has supported some of the early conclusions, it has refined our understanding of the effects – for example, suggesting that naltrexone may operate partly or primarily through a modification of alcohol effects, which then have an impact on subsequent craving, rather than through a direct and immediate effect on craving (Rohsenow et al., 2000; Volpicelli et al., 1995). 'Blindsight' outside our own area limits the development of creative theory and research that integrates learning across multiple domains, and that may offer a quantum shift in our ability to address addictive problems.

Sometimes the critical barriers to translation are a need for practical assistance from collaboration. When Alexander Fleming returned from vacation in 1928 to find that staphylococci in a discarded Petrie dish were not in an area where a mould was growing, he went on to show that a solution of penicillin inhibited the growth of staphylococci in human blood without affecting leukocytes, and that it did not appear to have toxic effects on animals (Ligon, 2004). However, he was hampered by his inability to produce a stable, concentrated supply (Hare, 1982). It was left to Florey, Chain and Heatley in 1940 to produce larger quantities and undertake key tests of its intravenous administration for systemic infections in rats and then in humans.

There is now a concerted effort to engage in effective collaborations for research into addictions, although no doubt as individuals we remain bound to some extent by preconceptions and by conceptual frameworks created by our training. We may expect that disciplines that are closer in background, language and research focus may find it easier to communicate, as may those whose primary interests are closer together on the basic to applied continuum. It is much harder to form linkages across more separated areas. So, for example, it is hard to see the application of molecular or cellular animal research to cognitive-behavior therapy, but it is much easier to see its application to pharmacotherapy. If there is a potential application across this divide – such as the implications of genetic risks for outcomes from different types of cognitive-behavior therapy – it may take longer than if the discipline areas and the communication are more closely aligned.

Fleming had also encountered a barrier at pre-clinical and pilot testing. He was discouraged by initial observations that penicillin concentrations quickly fell in blood, and believed that it would not be suited to deep-seated infections. While he did do a few studies of its application to surface infections in humans, these had limited success, because the referred conditions were inappropriate (Hare, 1982). He therefore did not pursue clinical studies further.

Serendipity at analogue or pilot stages can also work in more positive ways. A prominent example is the discovery by John Cade of the benefits of lithium for treatment of bipolar disorder (Mitchell, 1999). He had been testing the toxic effects of urea, having noted that the urine of patients with mania was more toxic to animals than was urine from controls. Because uric acid was insoluble in water, he pursued the research by injecting a solution of lithium urate into guinea pigs, and noted that this moderated the toxic effect. He also observed a sedative effect on the animals (now thought due to lithium toxicity), and thought it may be useful in the treatment of his patients. After injecting lithium himself without ill effects, he tested it in a small group of patients, and stumbled upon its mood stabilizing qualities. This rapid application to humans without a more complete understanding of its effects and risks now appears both naïve and dangerous to us. However, the example illustrates another potential block that we often experience in our attempts to develop new therapies – the analogues that we use (e.g. animal models) do not always provide sufficient information on the key problem. For example, there are significant limitations to animal models of craving for alcohol and other drugs (McGregor & Gallate, 2004), since they have to rely on observations of behavior, which in humans are not strongly correlated with the subjective experience of craving (Tiffany, 1990).

At the transition from pilot studies to full randomized controlled trials, a significant challenge that we face is our ability to obtain the substantial funding support that is required for trials of sufficient size and duration to offer a sound test of the procedure. The need for funding makes the progress to application dependent on the policies, procedures and available resources of the funding bodies. Corporate funds (apart from *pro bono* programs) are typically subject to outcomes of a business case concerning the ultimate commercial benefit from the procedure. This case includes non-research factors such as the size of the market, likely competing products, the company's strategic vision and priorities, internal competitors for funds and the size of the funding pool. Products developed by small companies or by external research teams often have difficulty obtaining sufficient support to take a potential product to full testing.

Government funding is also subject to factors apart from the quality of the research idea. Overall priorities for research areas and programs and the size of the funding pool have obvious impact on the number of large grants that can be funded. Fiscal responsibility also dictates that the research team will spend funds wisely and complete the project, so that scores are given not only for the quality of the research idea, but also for an established track record and for feasibility. In a highly competitive funding environment, this tends to skew funding to low-risk ideas (often of limited innovation) and to teams that have had particularly high levels of past success, and away from more creative ideas from rising stars. The peer review system, as sound as it is, also means that ideas that are inconsistent with existing orthodoxy may sometimes find it difficult to receive support. While some funding programs try to correct for these tendencies, it is still the case that progression to a full trial of an idea often requires a happy coincidence of a creative idea, a very persuasive case (in writing, and sometimes through lobbying), and a research team that can easily attract funding. Many potential innovations are inevitably lost or delayed at this point.

Problems can also occur at later stages. Published trials sponsored by pharmaceutical companies rarely report negative results from their own product (Lerner & Beutel, 2002). There has been concern over the potential for the influence of commercial interests on the conduct and interpretation of research, and on suppression of negative results, leading to a push for prior registration of clinical trials. Some sources of bias can be subtle – selected doses, sample selection and statistical analyses may lead to a particular medication appearing to have superior results in comparative trials (Heres et al., 2006). Conversely, there can be difficulty in obtaining publication of contentious ideas – as for example apparently occurred in relation to *H. pylori* and stomach ulcers (Pincock, 2005).

Perhaps the greatest challenges to translation occur in applications to routine practice. Once again, uptake of the *H. pylori* findings provides a good example. As late as 1997, a study of patients 65 years and older who were admitted to California hospitals for peptic ulcer disease found that only 39% were tested for *H. pylori* infection, and less than half who had a positive test result then received antibiotic treatment (Roll, Weng, & Newman, 1997). Awareness of advances is an issue, and as researchers we need to be acutely aware of marketing to practitioners through practice-oriented journals, conferences and workshops. However, as earlier chapters in this volume note, uptake of innovative interventions requires not only awareness and facility in their use, but cues and incentives to apply them routinely (Kavanagh et al., 1993).

Pharmaceutical companies apply sophisticated marketing strategies to facilitate uptake that merit emulation by proponents of other treatment innovations. However, even they sometimes have difficulty obtaining practitioner changes, as is highlighted by the relatively slow uptake of naltrexone for alcohol dependence (Mark et al., 2003; Thomas et al., 2003). Furthermore, the extent of investment in marketing and the primary disorder target are subject to commercial decisions. The cannabis antagonist Rimonabant (SR 141716) may be effective in not only addressing cannabis and other substance abuse, but in the management of obesity. It will be interesting to see which indications for its prescription are marketed more assertively.

AN ALTERNATE PATHWAY TO IMPROVED PRACTICE

'There is nothing so practical as a good theory' (Lewin, 1951, p. 169).

A rational progression from basic science, through efficacy and effectiveness trials to dissemination is not the only way in which new interventions are

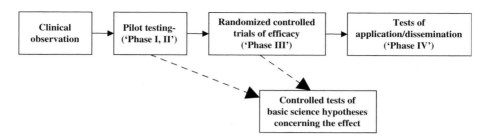

Figure 2 Serendipitous discovery of innovations in practice: Where science lags behind apparent practice advances.

introduced (Figure 2). Sometimes, a perceived improvement in practice is developed within clinical work – an inspired solution to a clinical problem, an unexpected side effect, an observation of unusual responses to accepted treatment, or a method derived from religious or cultural beliefs. In the case of sildenafil citrate (Viagra™), observations that an anti-allergy compound had vasodilative effects led to tests of sildenafil for angina and hypertension. Unexpected effects on erectile dysfunction were obtained with trial participants, leading to later marketing emphasizing these effects. However, this represents only a small departure from the rational process depicted in Figure 1.

On occasions, the development of scientific understanding occurs only after piloting or controlled trials (Figure 2). For example, the use of doxepin for smoking cessation was suggested by the observation that withdrawal includes some symptoms that are similar to those seen in depression (Edwards et al., 1989). A detailed understanding of the effect of nicotine on both serotonin and other neurotransmitters is still proceeding (Rossi et al., 2005).

Clinical psychology saw this phenomenon relatively recently in the rise of 'Eye Movement Desensitization-Reprocessing' for traumas and other conditions (Shapiro, 1989). The treatment reportedly arose from a chance observation by its proponent that a reduction in her emotional reaction to a train of thought was correlated with lateral eye movements. A series of pilot cases and randomized controlled trials followed. The speed of dissemination at early stages of testing and the apparent absence of a sound foundation in psychological science drew substantial criticism (Lohr et al., 1992). Subsequently, it emerged that eye movements were not essential to the procedures, which probably have about the same effectiveness (Bradley et al., 2005) and mode of effect, as the well-established phenomena of habituation and cognitive reframing (Kavanagh & Ryan, 1996). However, the clinical work spawned laboratory studies, which established that eye movements could reduce the vividness and emotional response to emotional imagery without affecting habitation, and demonstrated that it did this by both competing for working memory processing and by introducing conflicting perceptual information (Kavanagh et al., 2001). This work then suggested ways in which eye movements could benefit other therapies, including management of substance-related craving (Kavanagh, Andrade, & May, 2004).

Historically, commonly used interventions for addiction have been heavily influenced by approaches that have their roots in intuition, ideology, or spiritual or even religious beliefs rather than in advances in basic science. Some (as in alcoholic anonymous, AA) incorporate strategies that now also have a strong empirical basis (e.g. public commitment, social support, cues and incentives, etc.). There is substantial evidence supporting the effectiveness of AA for those who regularly attend (Vaillant, 2005), although it does not always fare well in treatment comparisons (Miller & Wilbourne, 2002; cf. Babor & Del Boca, 2002). Regardless of later findings, the origin of the philosophy and procedures of AA was not empirical research, and there have not subsequently been substantial modifications to them on the basis of subsequent research.

A more recent example of this process of innovation is ongoing research on the application of meditation mindfulness to addiction (Breslin, Zack, & McKain, 2002; Kavanagh et al., 2004). Meditation mindfulness has its origin in Buddhist traditions rather than Western science, although aspects have been described in relation to cognitive science (Teasdale, 1999). A version combining meditation mindfulness with cognitive therapy has been effectively used in randomized controlled trials on depression (Ma & Teasdale, 2004), and work on potential components of the procedures has begun (Baer et al., 2006). We await the publication of trials of its application to addiction, and of further work on the science that may underpin its utility.

While serendipity will always have a place in the development of new treatments, approaches to practical problems need not rely on traditional practices, accident or intuition. The psychology pioneer Kurt Lewin, quoted at the start of this section, addressed applied issues with the approach of a scientist, using the observations to derive hypotheses that may have much wider application. The development and testing of the scientific questions is a vital step when the application appears to have outpaced the science. There is much that we can learn from apparent innovations in practice (Rothman, 2004). Even when the treatment has been developed via the rational pathway depicted in Figure 1, subsequent study can uncover important new information about the treatment's mode of action, which may have implications for future innovation. Ongoing study of the mechanism of acamprosate effects (Cowen et al., 2005) is a case in point.

A WAY FORWARD

Returning to our question above – is translation a problem in addiction research and practice? – our answer is yes, although the true extent of the problem is difficult to gauge, since at the early stages, the existence of a previous barrier only emerges when it is bridged. What then should be done?

Establishment of centers or institutes to solve key questions in addictive disorders has potential for more lasting impact, especially where they cross traditional discipline boundaries and link basic to applied areas. However, after establishment of any research unit, there is a tendency both to increase collaboration within it, and to reduce collaboration outside it (because of co-location, development of common interests, and promotion of financial viability for the unit). Care needs to be taken in establishing these centers, that they retain flexibility in focus and composition and continue to promote innovative external collaborations, lest we develop new boundaries that will inhibit future innovation.

Other strategies involve more time-limited collaborations. In an effort to address transition from basic science to applications, the Addictions 2004 conference and related special issue of *Addictive Behaviors* focused on this topic. As discussed in the Preface, the current volume grew from that special issue, and some of the same researchers have contributed to both. We believe that a partial solution involves efforts like these, where researchers at various stages on the translational continuum, and with very different research interests, join together to consider issues of application in their field.

No doubt some of the speculation in the current volume will turn out to be as inaccurate as many other forecasts of the future. Our hope, however, is that some at least will later be seen as prescient. Perhaps more importantly, we hope that this volume will encourage readers to think even more divergently than at present, about the meaning of their research findings, and the potential for innovative collaboration and application.

REFERENCES

Abraham, J., Bardelay, D., Kopp, C., Kleinke, J. D., & Bennion, E. (2002). Education and debate: Making regulation responsive to commercial interests: Streamlining drug industry watchdogs. *British Medical Journal, 325,* 1164–1169.

AIHW. (2005). *2004 National Drug Strategy Household Survey: First Results. AIHW cat no. PHE 57.* Canberra: Australian Institute of Health and Welfare.

Babor, T. F., & Del Boca, F. K. (2002). *Treatment Matching in Alcoholism.* Cambridge: Cambridge University Press.

Baer, R. A., Smith, G. T., Hopkins, J., Krietemeyer, J., & Toney, L. (2006). Using self-report assessment methods to explore facets of mindfulness. *Assessment, 13,* 27–45.

Baumeister, A. A. (2006). Serendipity and the Cerebral Localization of Pleasure. *Journal of the History of the Neurosciences, 15,* 92–98.

Bouza, C., Angeles, M., Munoz, A., & Amate, J. (2004). Efficacy and safety of naltrexone and acamprosate in the treatment of alcohol dependence: A systematic review. *Addiction, 99,* 811–828.

Bradley, R., Greene, J., Russ, E., Dutra, L., & Westen, D. (2005). A multidimensional meta-analysis of psychotherapy for PTSD. *American Journal of Psychiatry, 162,* 214–227.

Breslin, F. C., Zack, M., & McKain, S. (2002). An information-processing analysis of mindfulness: Implications for relapse prevention in the treatment of substance abuse. *Clinical Psychology: Science and Practice, 9,* 275–299.

Carroll, K. E., & Onken, L. S. (2005). Behavioral therapies for drug abuse. *The American Journal of Psychiatry, 162*, 1452–1460.

Condon, J., & Smith, N. (2003). *Prevalence of Drug Use: Key Findings from the 2002/2003 British Crime Survey* (Vol. 229). London: Home Office Findings.

Corry, J., Sanderson, K., Issakidis, C., Andrews, G., & Lapsley, H. (2004). Evidence-based care for alcohol use disorders is affordable. *Journal of Studies on Alcohol, 65*, 521–529.

Cowen, M. S., Adams, C., Kraehenbuehl, T., Vengeliene, V., & Lawrence, A. J. (2005). The acute anti-craving effect of acamprosate in alcohol-preferring rats is associated with modulation of the mesolimbic dopamine system. *Addiction Biology, 10*, 233–242.

Deyo, R. A. (2004). Gaps, tensions, and conflicts in the FDA approval process: Implications for clinical practice. *Journal of the American Board of Family Practice, 17*, 142–149.

Edwards, N. B., Murphy, J. K., Downs, A. D., Ackerman, B. J., & Rosenthal, T. L. (1989). Doxepin as an adjunct to smoking cessation: A double-blind study. *The American Journal of Psychiatry, 146*, 373–376.

Fernandez, D. S., & Huie, J. T. (2004). Balancing US patent and FDA approval processes: Strategically optimizing market exclusivity. *Drug Discovery Today, 9*, 509–512.

Festinger, L. (1957). *A Theory of Cognitive Dissonance*. Oxford, England: Row, Peterson.

Foxcroft, D. R., Ireland, D., Lister-Sharp, D. J., Lowe, G., & Breen, R. (2003). Longer-term primary prevention for alcohol misuse in young people: A systematic review. *Addiction, 98*, 397–411.

Gates, S., McCambridge, J., Smith, L. A., & Foxcroft, D. R. (2006). Interventions for prevention of drug use by young people delivered in non-school settings. *Cochrane Database of Systematic Reviews, 1*, CD005030.

Gerada, C. (2005). Drug misuse: A review of treatments. *Clinical Medicine, 5*, 69–73.

Hare, R. (1982). New light on the history of penicillin. *Medical History, 26*, 1–24.

Heres, S., Davis, J., Maino, K., Jetzinger, E., Kissling, W., & Leucht, S. (2006). Why olanzapine beats risperidone, risperidone beats quetiapine, and quetiapine beats olanzapine. An exploratory analysis of head-to-head comparison studies of second-generation antipsychotics. *The American Journal of Psychiatry, 163*, 185–194.

Holsboer, F. (2001). Prospects for antidepressant drug discovery. *Biological Psychology, 57*, 47–65.

Kavanagh, D. J., Andrade, J., & May, J. (2004). Beating the urge: Implications of research into substance-related desires. *Addictive Behaviors, 29*, 1357–1370.

Kavanagh, D. J., Freese, S., Andrade, J., & May, J. (2001). Effects of visuospatial tasks on habituation to emotive memories. *British Journal of Clinical Psychology, 40*, 267–280.

Kavanagh, D. J., Piatkowska, O., Clark, D., O'Halloran, P., Manicavasagar, V., Rosen, A., & Tennant, C. (1993). Application of a cognitive-behavioural family intervention for schizophrenia in multi-disciplinary settings: What can the matter be? *Australian Psychologist, 28*, 181–188.

Kavanagh, D. J., & Ryan, C. (1996). Eye movement desensitization and re-processing (EMDR): Pseudoscientific fad or unique and significant advance in treatment? *Bulletin of the Australian Psychological Society, 18*, 14–17.

Kleinke, J. D. (2002). Commentary: Much ado about a good thing. *British Medical Journal, 325*, 1168.

Kuhn, T. S. (1962). Historical structure of scientific discovery. *Science, 136*, 760–764.

Lerner, C. G., & Beutel, B. A. (2002). Antibacterial drug discovery in the post-genomics era. *Current Drug Targets-Infectious Disorders, 2*, 109–119.

Lewin, K. (1951). *Field Theory in Social Science: Selected Theoretical Papers*. New York: Harper & Row.

Ligon, B. L. (2004). Penicillin: Its discovery and early development. *Seminars in Paediatric Infectious Diseases, 15*, 52–57.

Lohr, J. M., Kleinknecht, R. A., Conley, A. T., Dal Cerro, S., Schmidt, J., & Sonntag, M. E. (1992). A methodological critique of the current status of eye movement desensitization (EMD). *Journal of Behavior Therapy and Experimental Psychiatry, 23*, 159–167.

Ma, S. H., & Teasdale, J. D. (2004). Mindfulness-based cognitive therapy for depression: Replication and exploration of differential relapse prevention effects. *Journal of Consulting & Clinical Psychology*, *72*, 31–40.

Mark, T. L., Kranzler, H. R., & Song, X. (2003). Understanding US addiction physicians' low rate of naltrexone prescription. *Drug and Alcohol Dependence*, *71*, 219–228.

Marshall, B. J., & Warren, J. R. (1984). Unidentified curved bacilli in the stomach of patients with gastritis and peptic ulceration. *Lancet*, *8390*, 1311–1315.

Maxwell, J. C. (2003). Update: Comparison of drug use in Australia and the United States as seen in the 2001 National Household Surveys. *Drug and Alcohol Review*, *22*, 347–357.

McGregor, I. S., & Gallate, J. E. (2004). Rats on the grog: Novel pharmacotherapies for alcohol craving. *Addictive Behaviors*, *29*, 1341–1357.

Miller, W. R., & Wilbourne, P. L. (2002). Mesa Grande: A methodological analysis of clinical trials for alcohol use disorders. *Addiction*, *97*, 265–277.

Mitchell, P. B. (1999). On the 50th anniversary of John Cade's discovery of the anti-manic effect of lithium. *Australian and New Zealand Journal of Psychiatry*, *33*, 623–628.

Olds, J., & Milner, P. (1954). Positive reinforcement produced by electrical stimulation of septal area and other regions of rat brain. *Journal of Comparative and Physiological Psychology*, *47*, 419–427.

Piasecki, T. M. (2006). Relapse to smoking. *Clinical Psychology Review*, *26*, 196–215.

Piasecki, T. M., & Baker, T. B. (2001). Any further progress in smoking cessation treatment? *Nicotine and Tobacco Research*, *3*, 311–323.

Pincock, S. (2005). Nobel Prize winners Robin Warren and Barry Marshall. *Lancet*, *366*, 1429.

Rehm, J., Room, R., van den Brink, W., & Kraus, L. (2005). Problematic drug use and drug use disorders in EU countries and Norway: An overview of the epidemiology. *European Neuropsychopharmacology*, *15*, 389–397.

Rohsenow, D. J., Monti, P. M., Hutchison, K. E., Swift, R. M., Colby, S. M., & Kaplan, G. B. (2000). Naltrexone's effects on reactivity to alcohol cues among alcoholic men. *Journal of Abnormal Psychology*, *109*, 738–742.

Roll, J., Weng, A., & Newman, J. (1997). Diagnosis and treatment of *Helicobacter pylori* infection among California medicare patients. *Archives of Internal Medicine*, *157*, 994–998.

Rossi, S., Singer, S., Shearman, E., Sershen, H., & Lajtha, A. (2005). The effects of cholinergic and dopaminergic antagonists on nicotine-induced cerebral neurotransmitter changes. *Neurochemical Research*, *30*, 541–558.

Rothman, A. J. (2004). Is there nothing more practical than a good theory? Why innovations and advances in health behavior change will arise if interventions are used to test and refine theory. *International Journal of Behavioral Nutrition and Physical Activity*, *1*, 11.

SAMHSA. (2004). *Results from the 2003 National Survey on Drug Use and Health (NSDUH Series H-25)*. Rockville, MD: Office of Applied Studies, Substance Abuse and Mental Health Services Administration.

Shapiro, F. (1989). Eye movement desensitization: A new treatment for post-traumatic stress disorder. *Journal of Behavior Therapy and Experimental Psychiatry*, *20*, 211–217.

Shiffman, S. (1993). Smoking cessation treatment: Any progress? *Journal of Consulting and Clinical Psychology*, *61*, 718–722.

Teasdale, J. D. (1999). Emotional processing, three modes of mind and the prevention of relapse in depression. *Behaviour Research and Therapy*, *37*(Suppl. 1), S53–S77.

Thomas, C. P., Wallack, S. S., Lee, S., McCarty, D., & Smith, R. (2003). Research to practice: Adoption of naltrexone in alcoholism treatment. *Journal of Substance Abuse Treatment*, *24*, 1–11.

Tiffany, S. T. (1990). A cognitive model of drug urges and drug-use behavior: Role of automatic and nonautomatic processes. *Psychological Review*, *97*, 147–168.

Vaillant, G. E. (2005). Alcoholics Anonymous: Cult or cure? *Australian and New Zealand Journal of Psychiatry*, *39*, 431–436.

Velleman, R. D., Templeton, L. J., & Copello, A. G. (2005). The role of the family in preventing and intervening with substance use and misuse: A comprehensive review of family interventions, with a focus on young people. *Drug and Alcohol Review*, *24*, 93–109.

Volkow, N. D., & Li, T. (2005). Drugs and alcohol: Treating and preventing abuse, addiction and their medical consequences. *Pharmacology and Therapeutics*, *108*, 3–17.

Volpicelli, J. R., Watson, N. T., King, A. C., Sherman, C. E., & O'Brien, C. P. (1995). Effect of naltrexone on alcohol 'high' in alcoholics. *American Journal of Psychiatry*, *152*, 613–615.

SUBJECT INDEX

A

Abstinence duration
  acamprosate pharmacotherapy for alcohol
    addiction, 131–132
  nicotine pharmacology, 241–242
  psychological/affective correlates,
    smoking/abstinence from smoking,
    242–246
  smoking cessation treatments, 247–251

Acamprosate
  alcoholism treatment, 16–17, 104, 130–132
  alcohol use disorders, 386–387
  cerebral excitability reduction with, 71–72
  cravings therapy with, 218–220
  medical settings-based alcohol addiction
    detection and treatment, 387–388
  multiple ethanol withdrawals and, 64–65
  withdrawal management with, 74–75

Accessibility issues
  alcohol use reduction in undergraduate
    students, 428–433
  internet-based intervention strategies,
    400–402

Acetaldehyde, alcoholism metabolism,
  disulfiram pharmacotherapy, 126–128

Acidosis, topiramate pharmacokinetics, 176

Acute pain
  future research on management of, 52
  in opioid-dependent patients, 47–48

Addiction (generally). *See also* addiction to
  specific substances, e.g. Alcohol addiction
  acute pain management with, 47–48
  adaptation and hyperadaptation, 49–50
  antisocial personality disorder comorbidity
    with, 24–26
  assessment, treatment and prevention of
    hyperalgesia and, 48–49
  in chronic pain patients, 45–48
  clinical care research, 32–34
  endocannabinoid system and, 93
  ethics and policy issues
    coerced treatment issues, 451–452
    current research issues, 440–441

    human neuroscience research, 450–451
    media coverage issues, 452–453
    neurobiological theories, 442–443
    neuroenhancement issues, 449–450
    neuroimaging diagnosis and prediction,
      448–449
    neuroscience addiction research, 443–444
    policy-making issues, 452–453
    predictive genetics testing, 444–445
    preventive vaccination research, 446–447
    relapse prevention and depot medication
      maintenance, 447
    skeptical views and medical models,
      441–444
    vaccine research, 445–446
  genetic vulnerabilities, 26–28
  hyperalgesia and aetiology of, 45–48
  innovative research on
    clinical practice improvements, 466–468
    overview of, 461–462
    translational from science to practice,
      462–466
  molecular genetics, 29–30
  opioid use and, 39–53
  to prescription opioids, increases in, 46–47
  psychopathology and genetics of, 30–32

Addiction Technology Transfer Center (ATTC)
  Network, alcohol addiction therapies,
  266–268, 273

Adenylyl cyclase, cannabinoid receptor
  inhibition, 88–89

ADH1C loci, alcohol abuse and, 9–10

Adolescent patients
  cravings pharmacotherapy in, 224
  ethical issues in addiction research, vaccine
    therapies and, 446–447
  impulsive personality traits and substance
    abuse in, 322–323
    chronic abuse and, 330–332
    future research issues, 333
    rash impulsiveness and, 326–328
    reward drive and, 325–328
    treatment implications, 329–330, 332–333